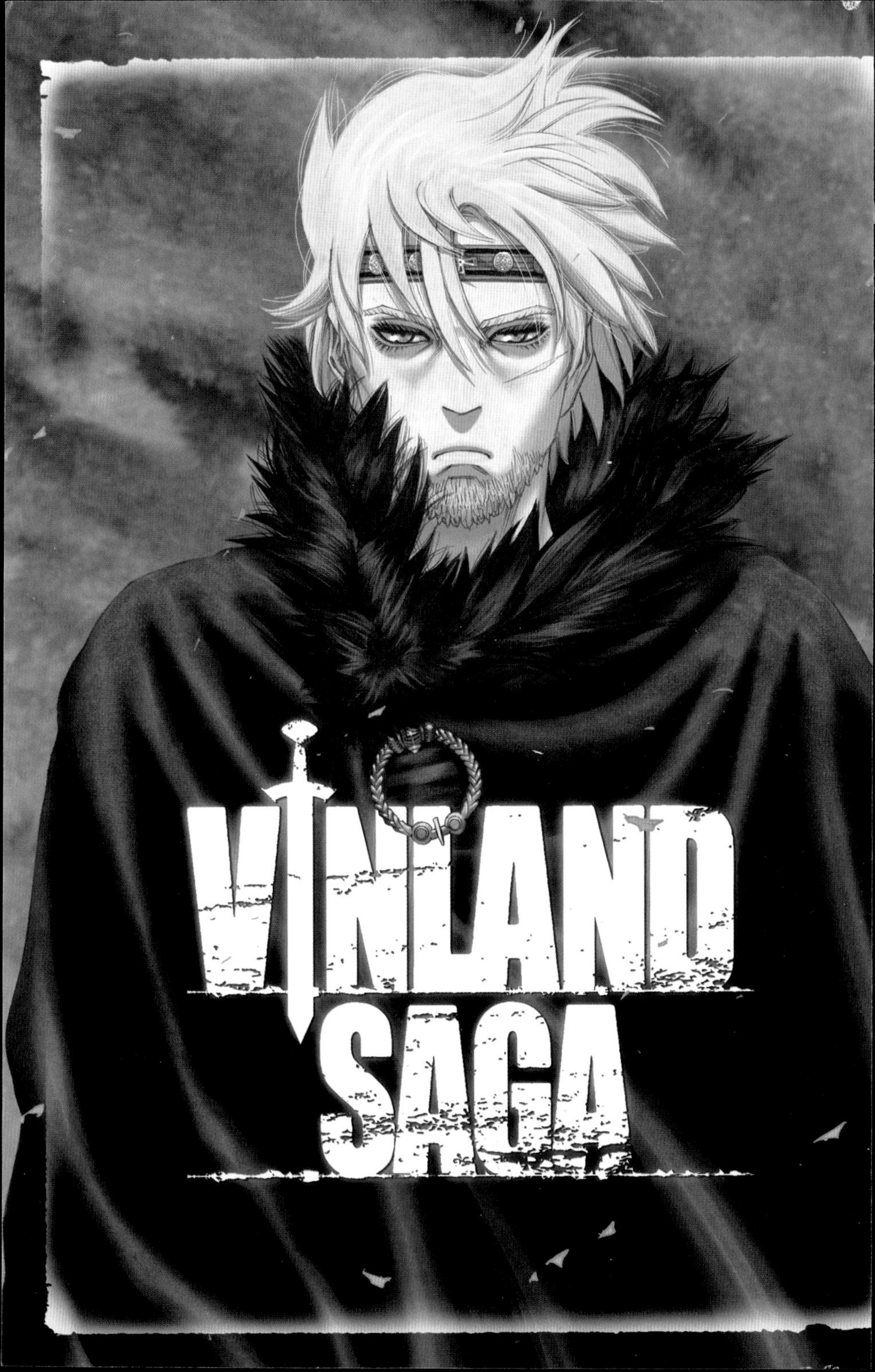
VINLAND
SAGA

TABLE OF CONTENTS

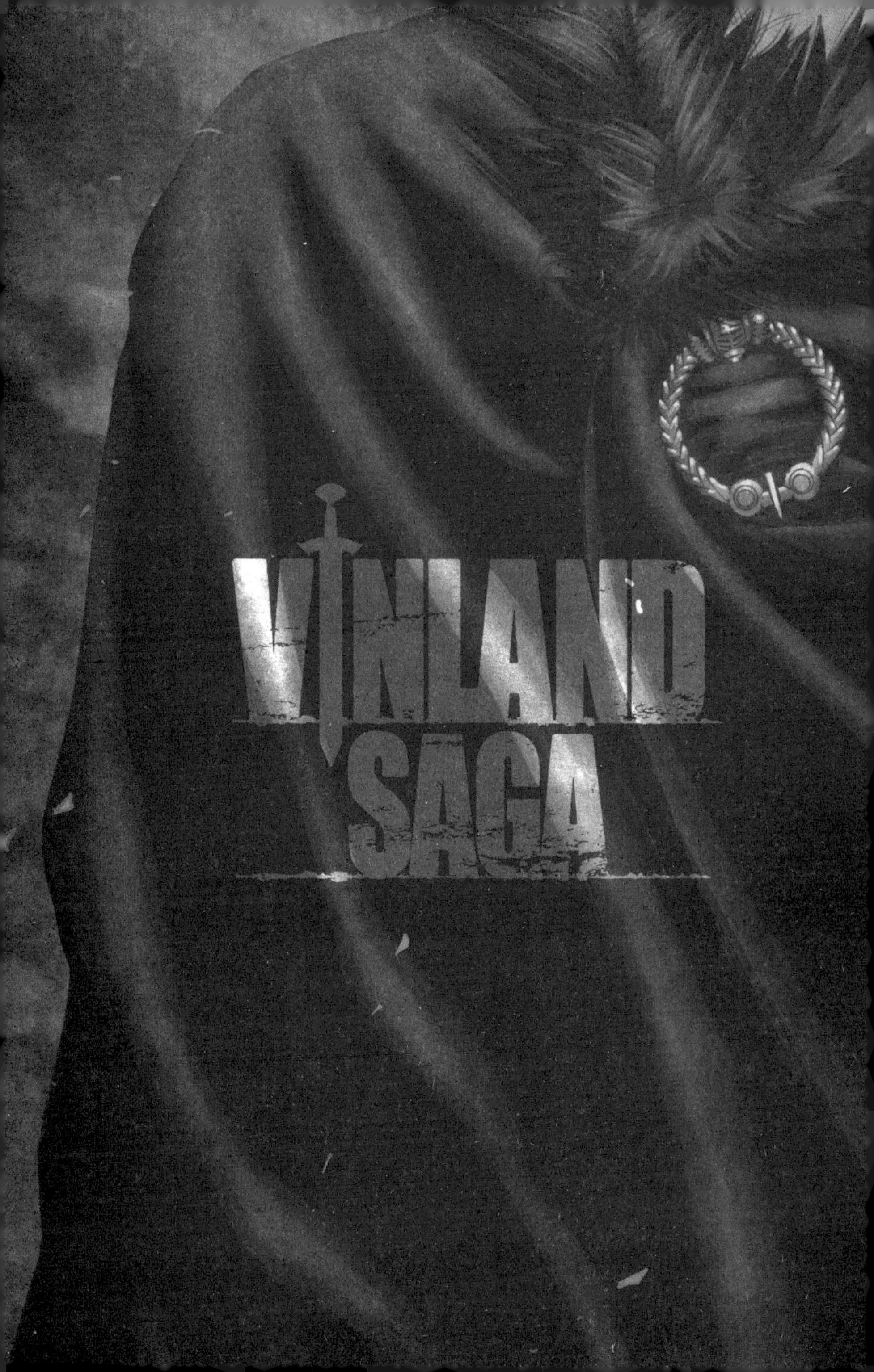
VINLAND
SAGA

THE STORY SO FAR

IN ELEVENTH-CENTURY SCANDINAVIA, A MAN NAMED THORS WAS THE GREATEST AND MOST FEARED WARRIOR ALIVE, KNOWN AS "THE TROLL OF JOM."

WHEN HE GREW WEARY OF FIGHTING, HE ABANDONED HIS WARRIOR'S CALLING AND TOOK HIS WIFE AND DAUGHTER INTO HIDING IN ICELAND.

ONCE THEY HAD ESTABLISHED THEMSELVES THERE, THORS MADE A LIVING CULTIVATING THE LAND AND FATHERED A SON.

THE BOY'S NAME WAS THORFINN, AND HE GREW INTO A HEALTHY SIX-YEAR-OLD UNDER THE GUIDANCE OF THORS AND HIS FAMILY.

BUT THE JOMSVIKINGS, THORS'S FORMER BAND, LEARNED OF HIS WHEREABOUTS AND CAME TO DRAFT HIM INTO THE WAR BETWEEN DENMARK AND ENGLAND.

WHEN THORS WAS ALREADY UNDERWAY, HE DISCOVERED THAT THORFINN HAD SNUCK ABOARD THE SHIP OUT OF CURIOSITY AND DESIRE TO BE A WARRIOR.

BEFORE THEY COULD FINISH THEIR VOYAGE, THORS WAS ATTACKED BY ASKELADD'S BAND OF VIKINGS, AND HE GAVE HIS LIFE PROTECTING HIS SON.

BEFORE THORFINN COULD LEARN WHY THORS HAD GIVEN UP THE SWORD FOR GOOD, HE LOST HIS FATHER...

AFTER THAT, THORFINN JOINED ASKELADD'S BAND FOR THE SOLE PURPOSE OF EVENTUALLY AVENGING HIS FATHER'S MURDER. HE PARTICIPATED IN MANY BATTLES AND DEVELOPED INTO A FEARSOME FIGHTER.

IN THE MIDST OF THE WAR WITH ENGLAND, ASKELADD SUCCEEDED IN FREEING THE CAPTIVE CANUTE, SECOND PRINCE OF DENMARK, AND LAUNCHED A PLOY TO CAPTURE THE THRONE. BUT AFTER KILLING KING SWEYN OF DENMARK, ASKELADD PERISHED BEFORE THORFINN'S EYES.

WITHOUT A PURPOSE IN LIFE, THE EMPTY THORFINN FELL FROM WARRIOR TO SLAVE, AND EVENTUALLY WOUND UP LIVING ON AN ENORMOUS FARM OWNED BY A MAN NAMED KETIL.

THERE, HE MET A WHOLE NEW HOST OF PEOPLE: HIS FELLOW SLAVE, EINAR; THE OLD MASTER SVERKEL, WHO HOPES TO DIE OUT IN THE FIELDS; KETIL'S SLAVE AND LOVER ARNHEID; AND "SNAKE," THE HEAD OF THE FARM'S BODYGUARDS.

IN HIS NEW LIFE WITH THEM, THORFINN GRADUALLY BEGAN TO UNDERSTAND SOMETHING OF THE "TRUE WARRIOR'S LIFE" THAT HIS FATHER THORS SOUGHT.

WHAT DO WORKERS GAIN
FROM THEIR TOIL? I HAVE SEEN
THE BURDEN GOD HAS LAID
ON THE HUMAN RACE. HE HAS
MADE EVERYTHING BEAUTIFUL
IN ITS TIME. HE HAS ALSO
SET ETERNITY IN THE HUMAN
HEART; YET NO ONE CAN
FATHOM WHAT GOD HAS DONE
FROM BEGINNING TO END.

(ECCLESIASTES 3:9-11)

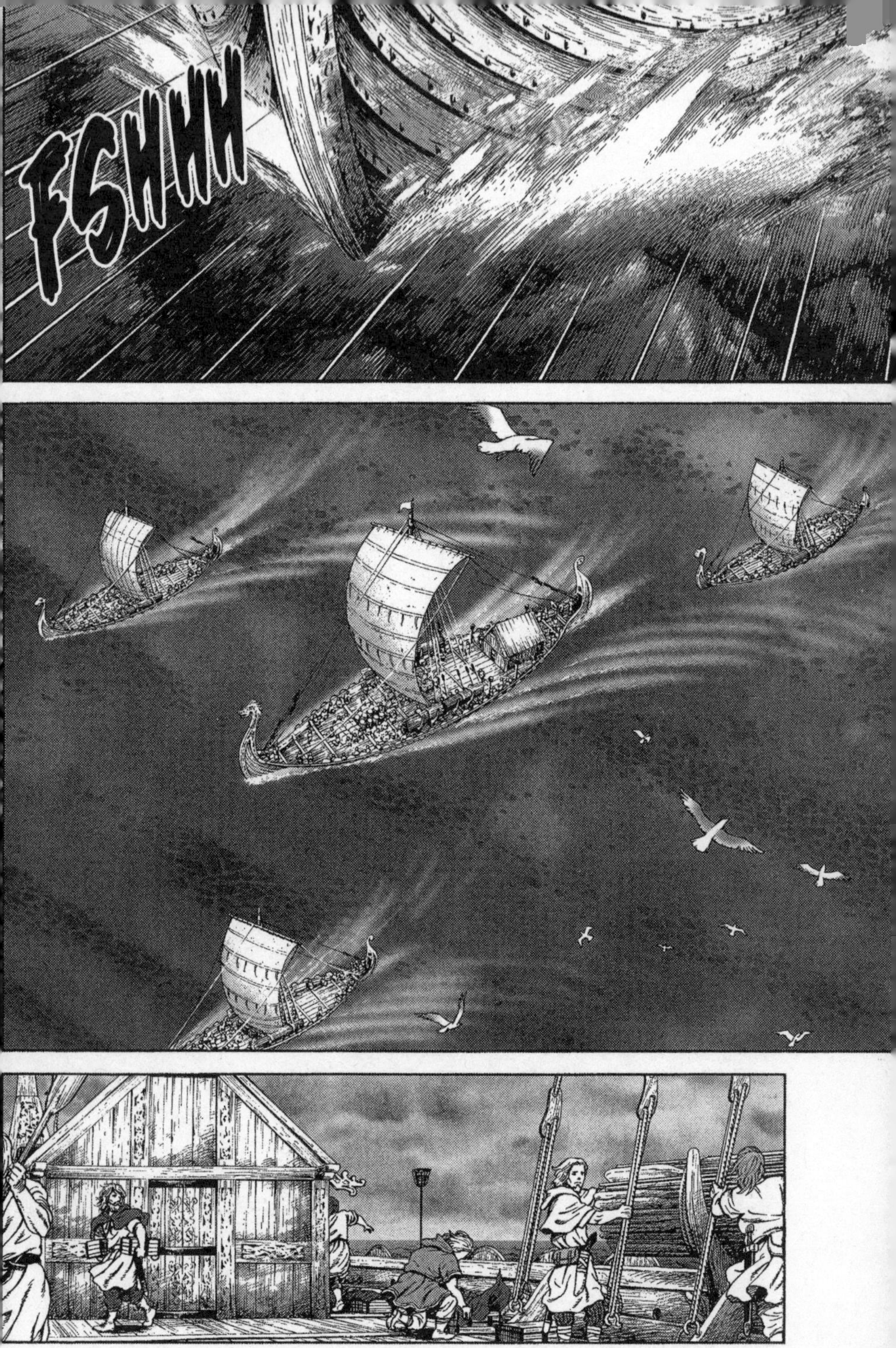
FSHHH

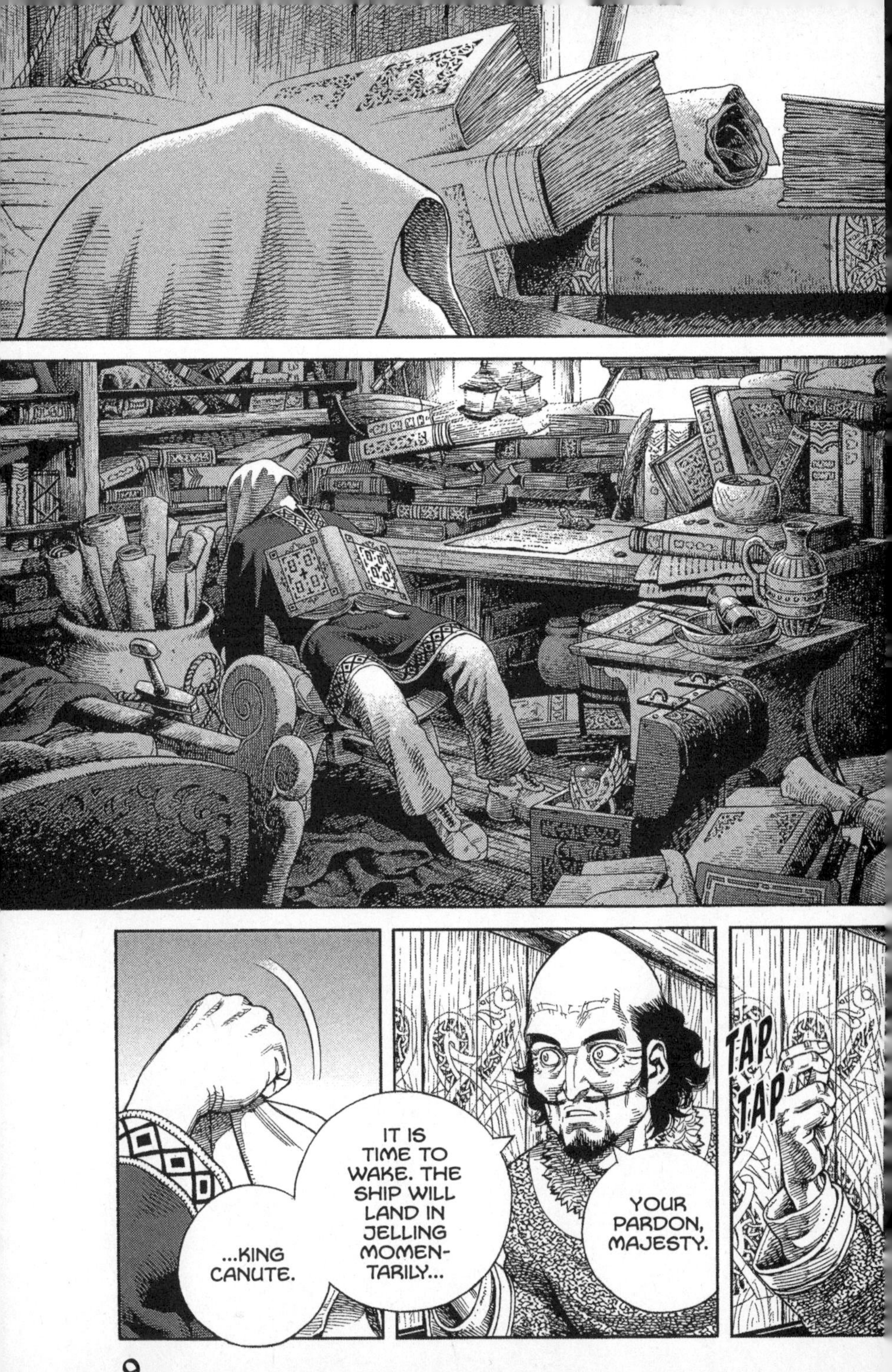
TAP TAP
YOUR PARDON, MAJESTY.
IT IS TIME TO WAKE. THE SHIP WILL LAND IN JELLING MOMENTARILY...
...KING CANUTE.

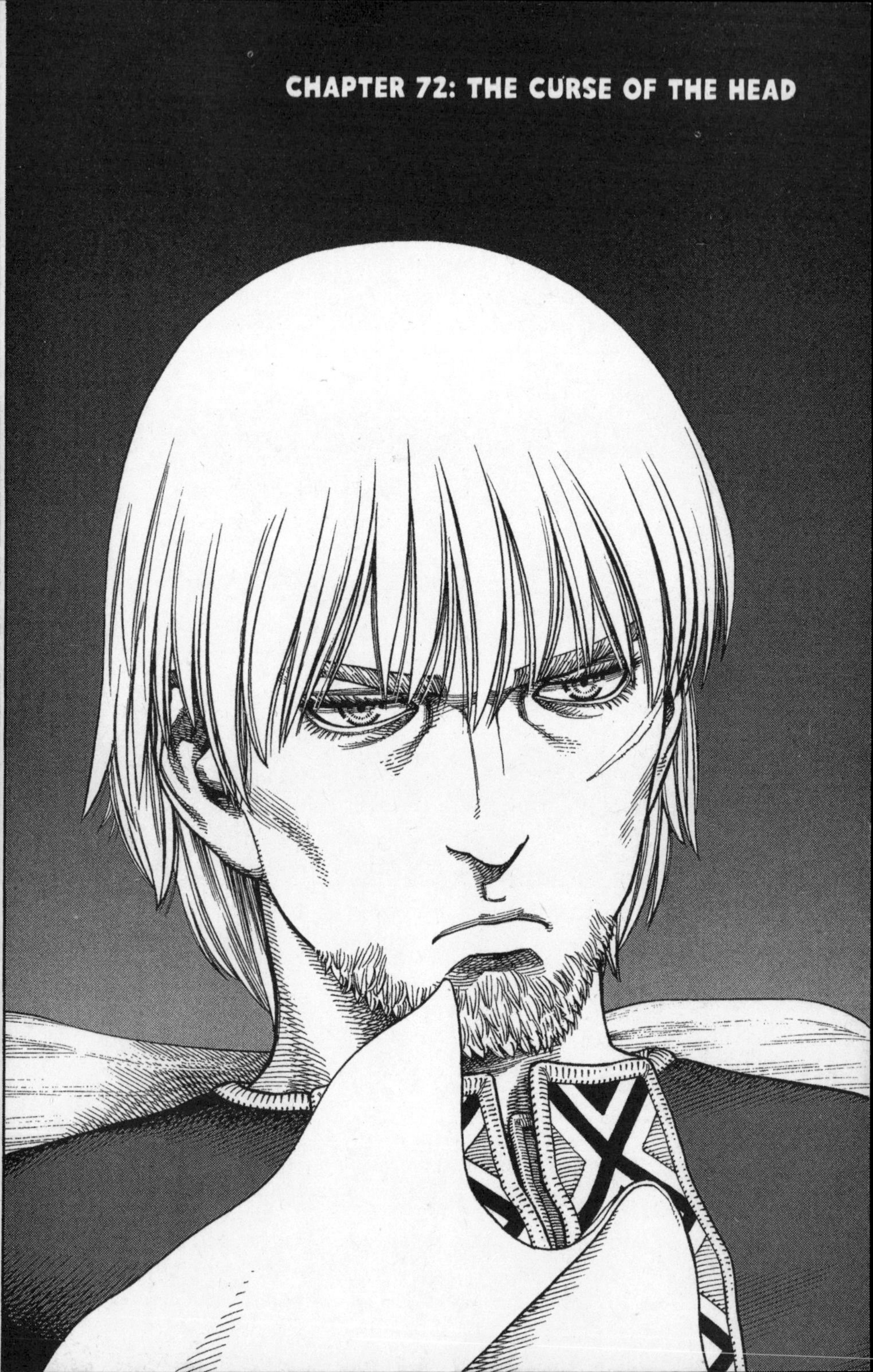
CHAPTER 72: THE CURSE OF THE HEAD

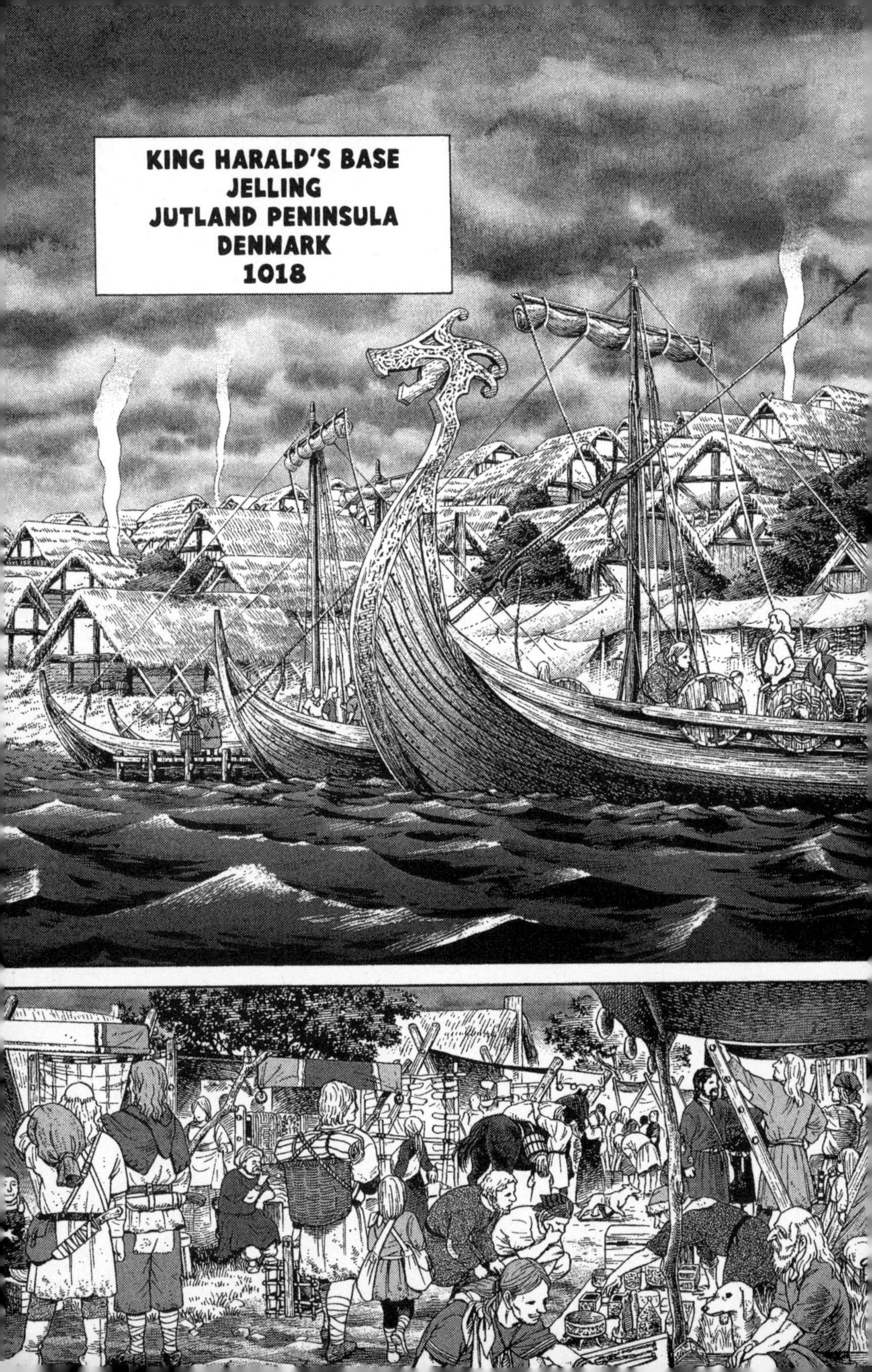
KING HARALD'S BASE
JELLING
JUTLAND PENINSULA
DENMARK
1018

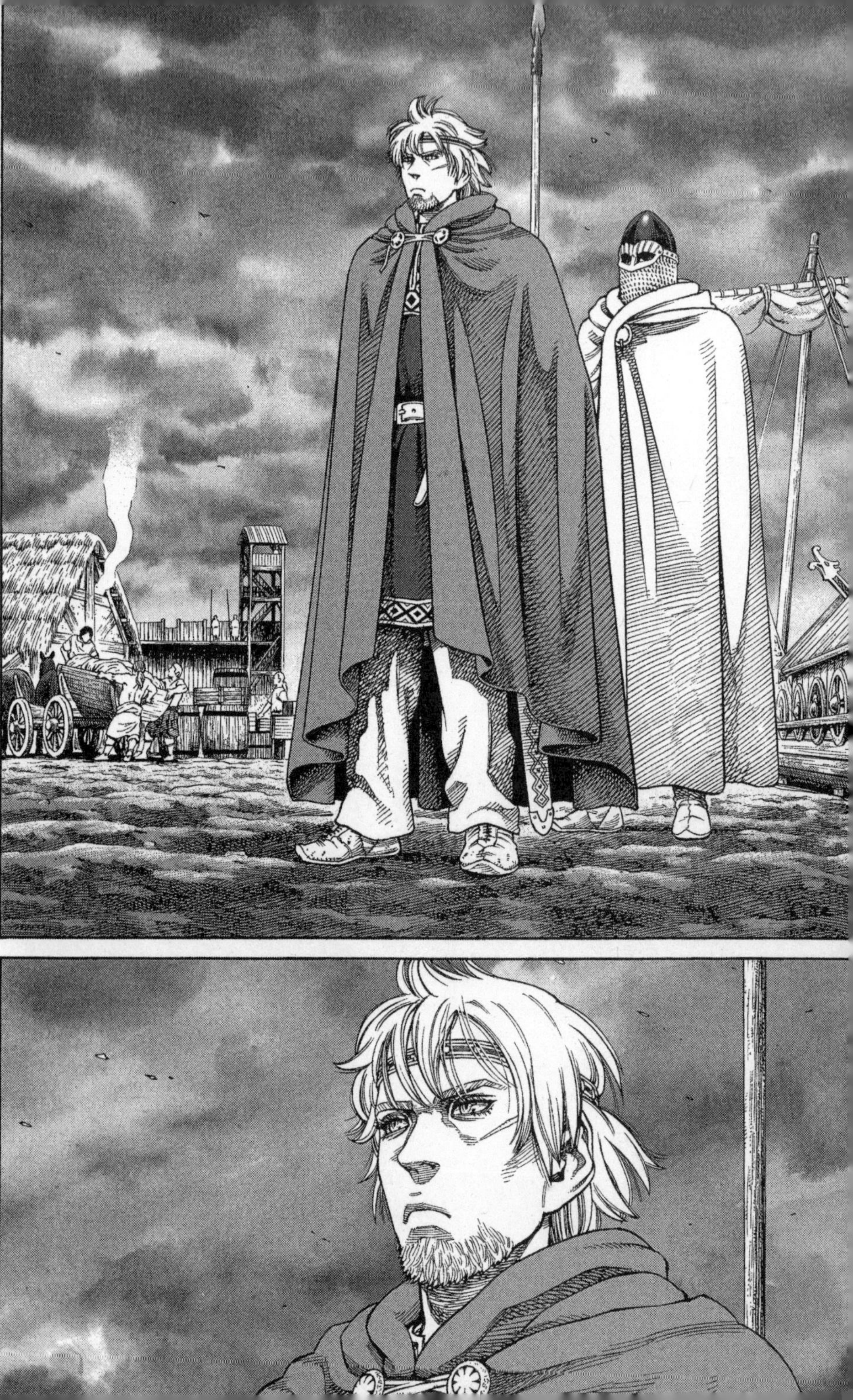

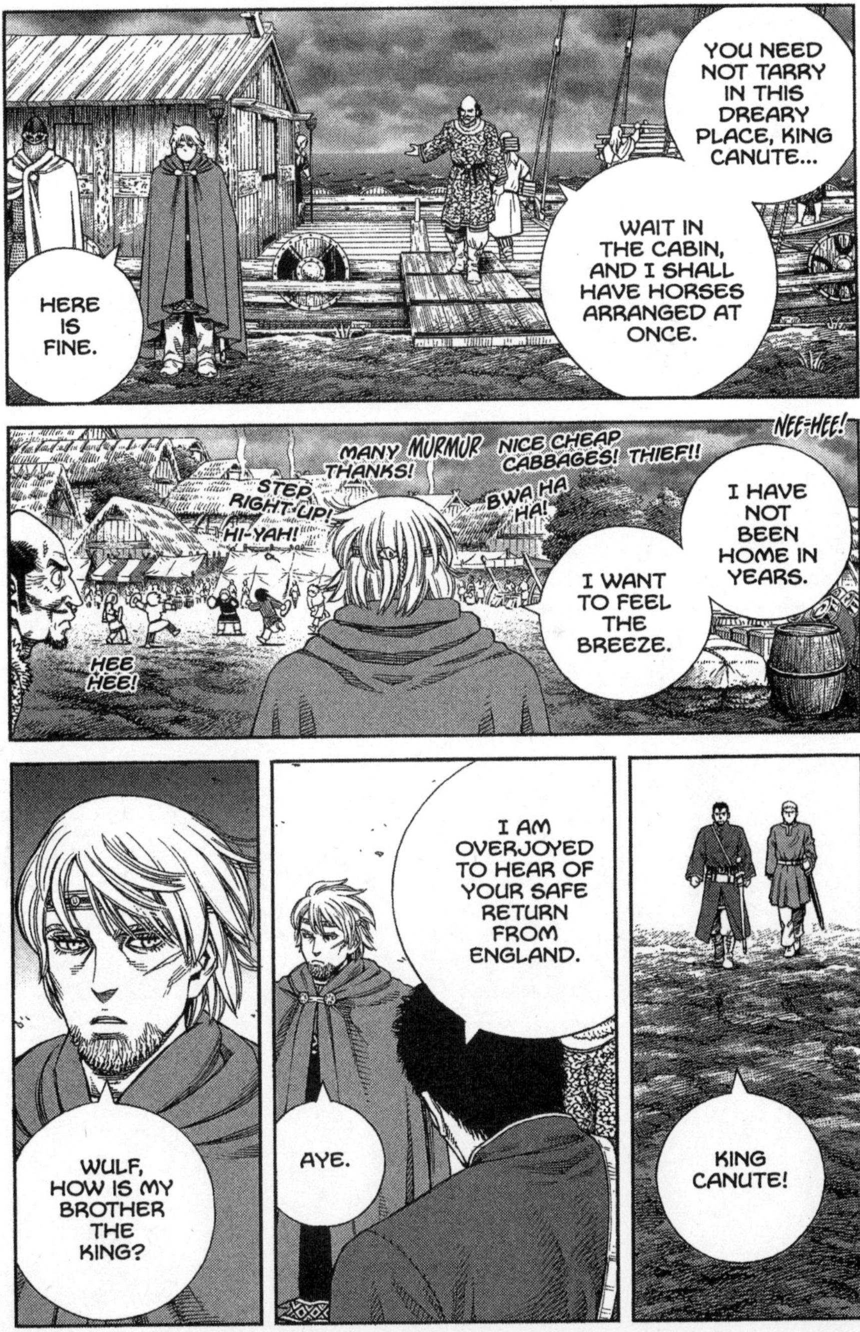

YOU NEED NOT TARRY IN THIS DREARY PLACE, KING CANUTE...
WAIT IN THE CABIN, AND I SHALL HAVE HORSES ARRANGED AT ONCE.
HERE IS FINE.
NEE=HEE!
THIEF!!
NICE CHEAP CABBAGES!
MURMUR
MANY THANKS!
BWA HA HA!
STEP RIGHT UP!
HI-YAH!
I HAVE NOT BEEN HOME IN YEARS.
I WANT TO FEEL THE BREEZE.
HEE HEE!
KING CANUTE!
I AM OVERJOYED TO HEAR OF YOUR SAFE RETURN FROM ENGLAND.
AYE.
WULF, HOW IS MY BROTHER THE KING?

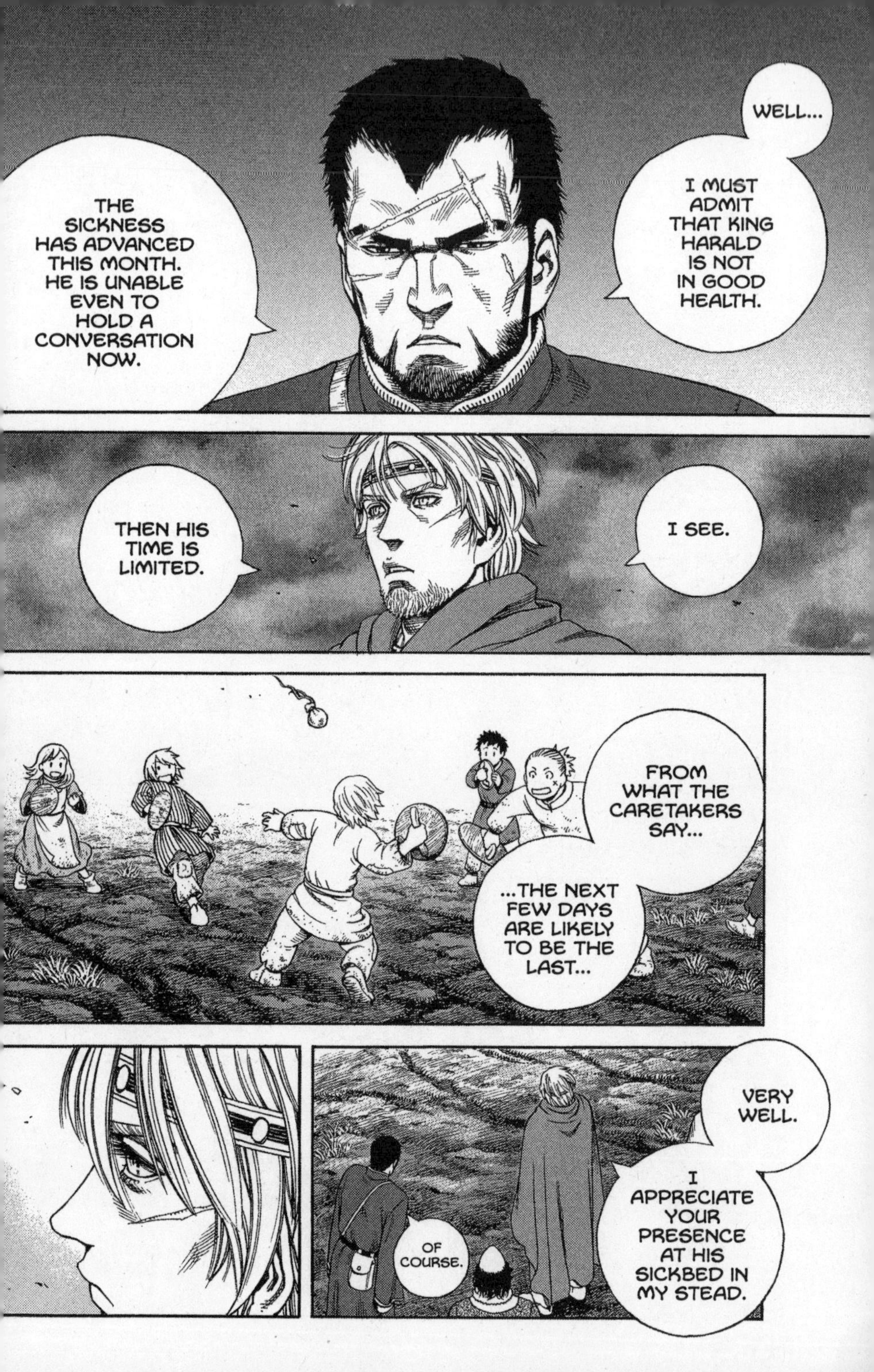
WELL...
I MUST ADMIT THAT KING HARALD IS NOT IN GOOD HEALTH.
THE SICKNESS HAS ADVANCED THIS MONTH. HE IS UNABLE EVEN TO HOLD A CONVERSATION NOW.
I SEE.
THEN HIS TIME IS LIMITED.
FROM WHAT THE CARETAKERS SAY...
...THE NEXT FEW DAYS ARE LIKELY TO BE THE LAST...
VERY WELL.
I APPRECIATE YOUR PRESENCE AT HIS SICKBED IN MY STEAD.
OF COURSE.

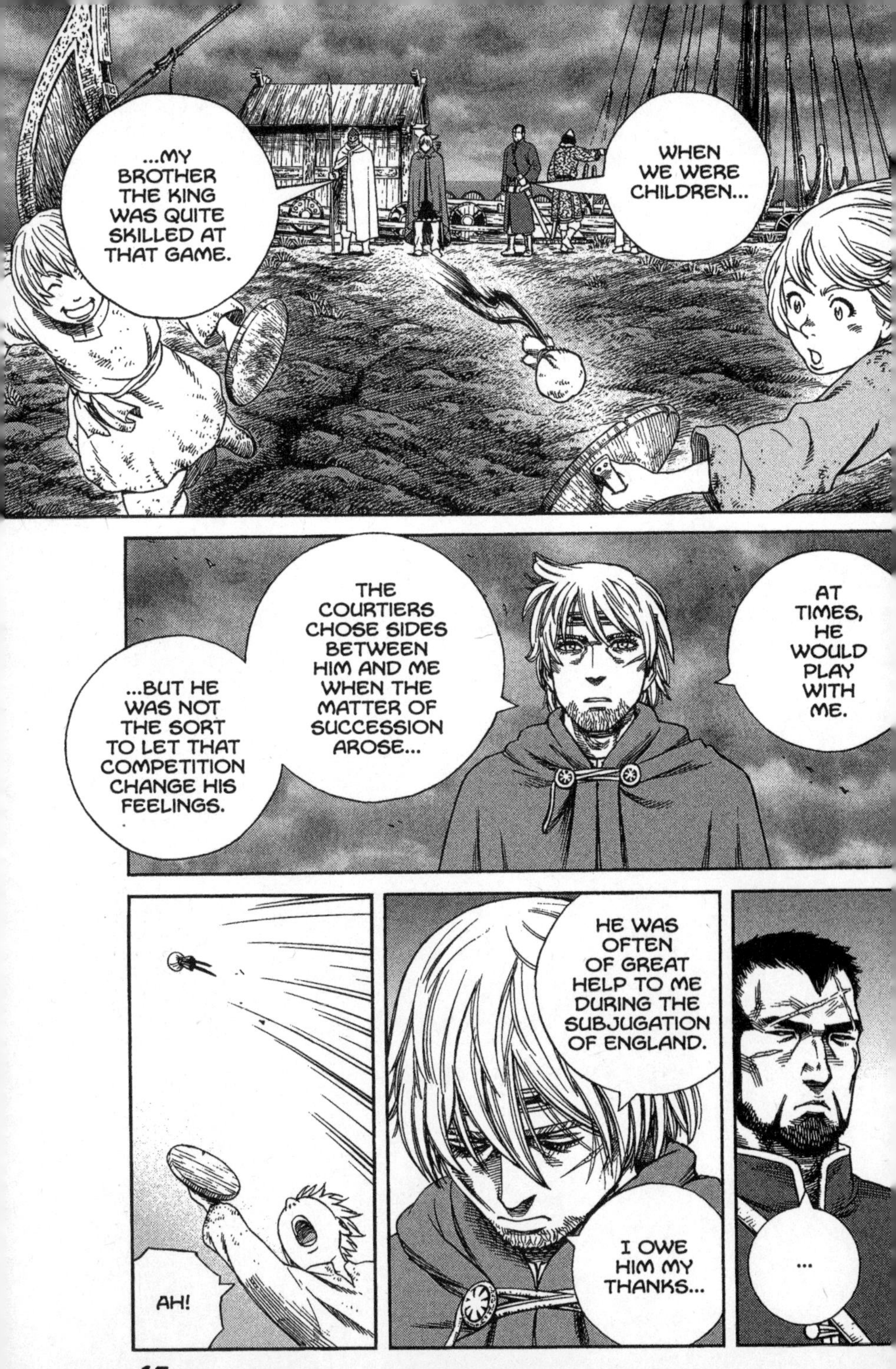
WHEN WE WERE CHILDREN...
...MY BROTHER THE KING WAS QUITE SKILLED AT THAT GAME.
AT TIMES, HE WOULD PLAY WITH ME.
THE COURTIERS CHOSE SIDES BETWEEN HIM AND ME WHEN THE MATTER OF SUCCESSION AROSE...
...BUT HE WAS NOT THE SORT TO LET THAT COMPETITION CHANGE HIS FEELINGS.
...
HE WAS OFTEN OF GREAT HELP TO ME DURING THE SUBJUGATION OF ENGLAND.
I OWE HIM MY THANKS...
AH!

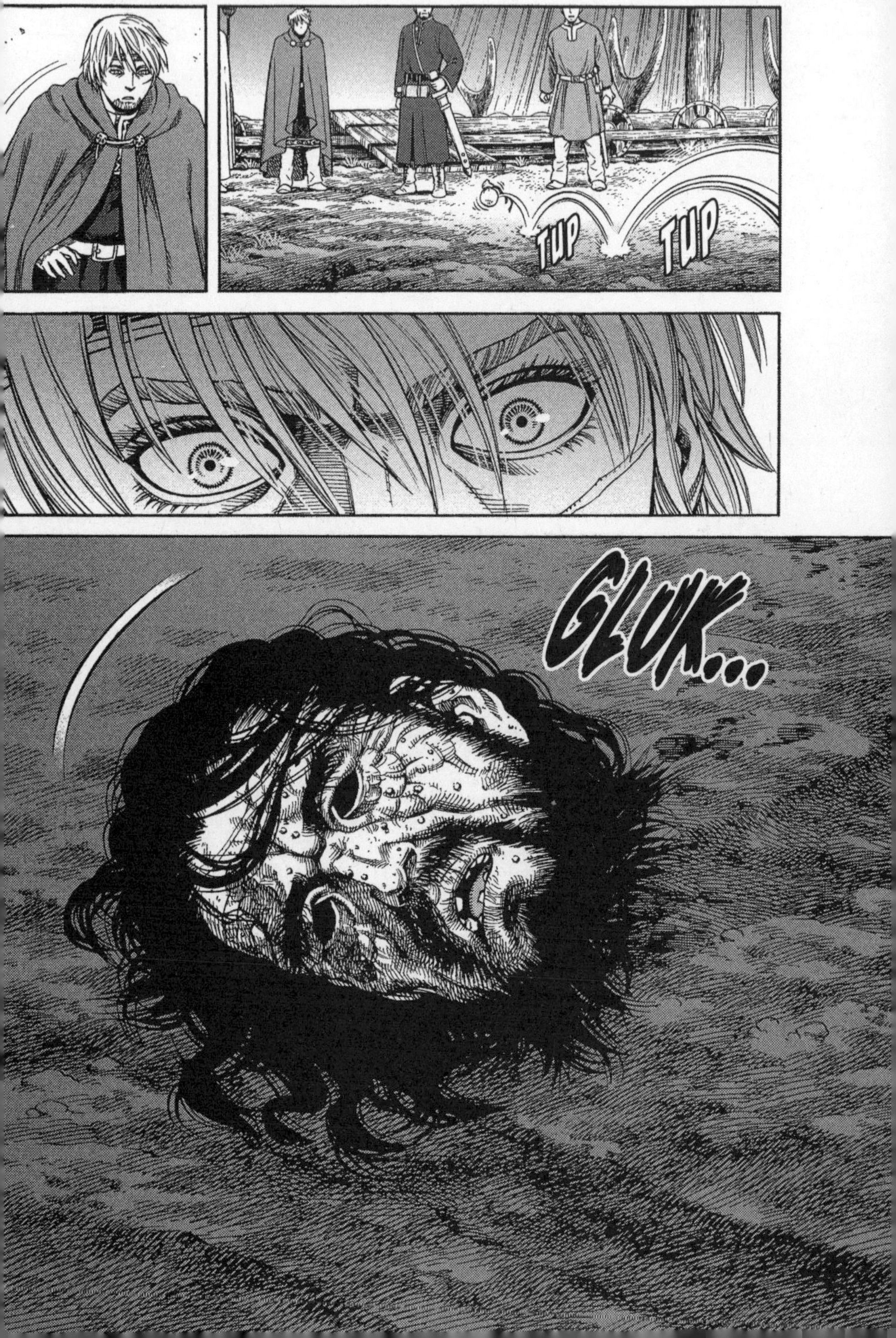
TUP
TUP
GLUK...

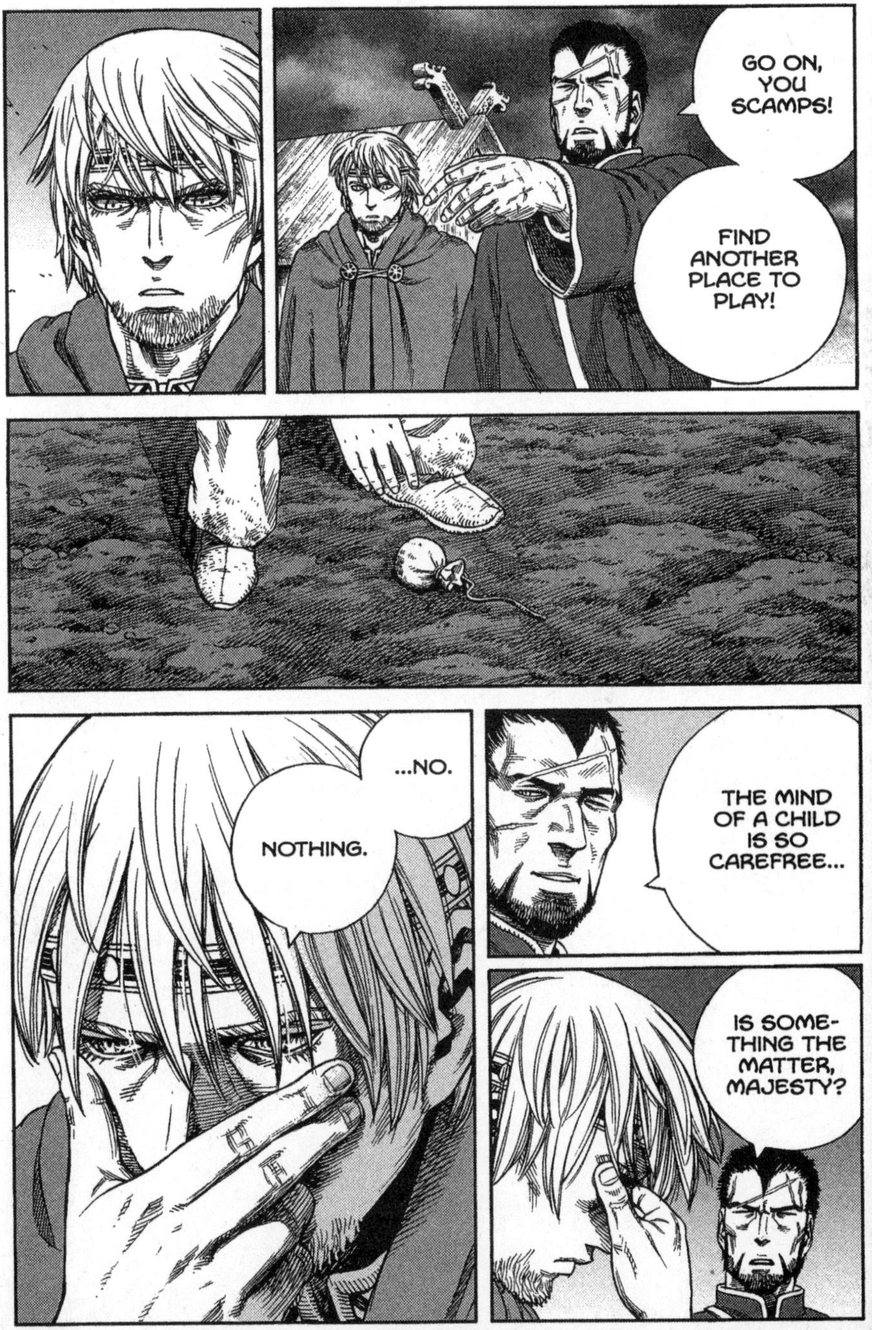
GO ON, YOU SCAMPS!
FIND ANOTHER PLACE TO PLAY!
THE MIND OF A CHILD IS SO CAREFREE...
IS SOMETHING THE MATTER, MAJESTY?
...NO.
NOTHING.

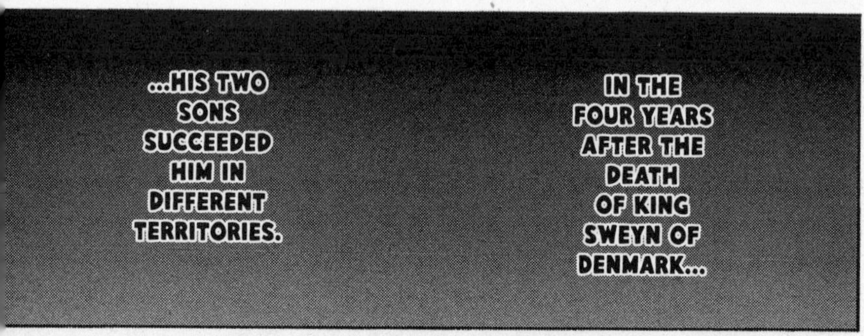
IN THE FOUR YEARS AFTER THE DEATH OF KING SWEYN OF DENMARK...
...HIS TWO SONS SUCCEEDED HIM IN DIFFERENT TERRITORIES.

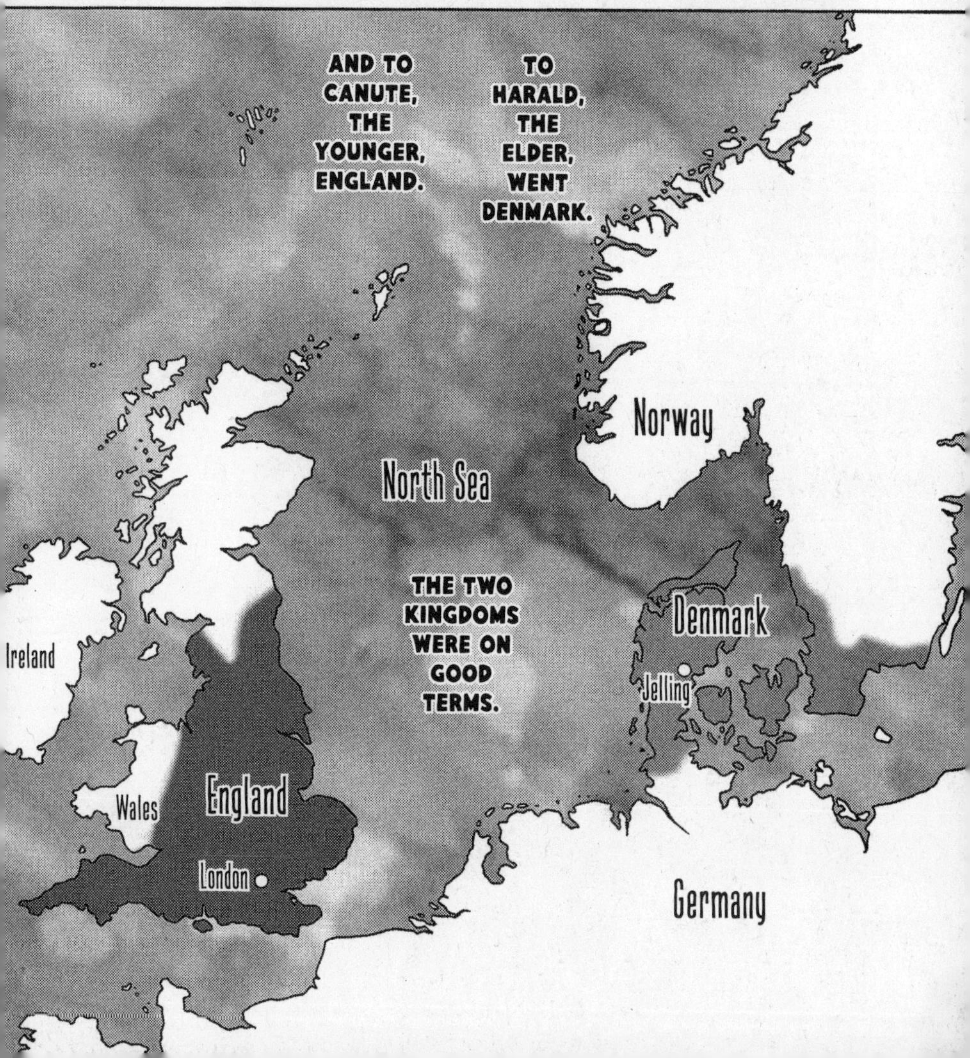
TO HARALD, THE ELDER, WENT DENMARK.
AND TO CANUTE, THE YOUNGER, ENGLAND.
Norway
North Sea
Denmark
Jelling
THE TWO KINGDOMS WERE ON GOOD TERMS.
Ireland
England
Wales
London
Germany

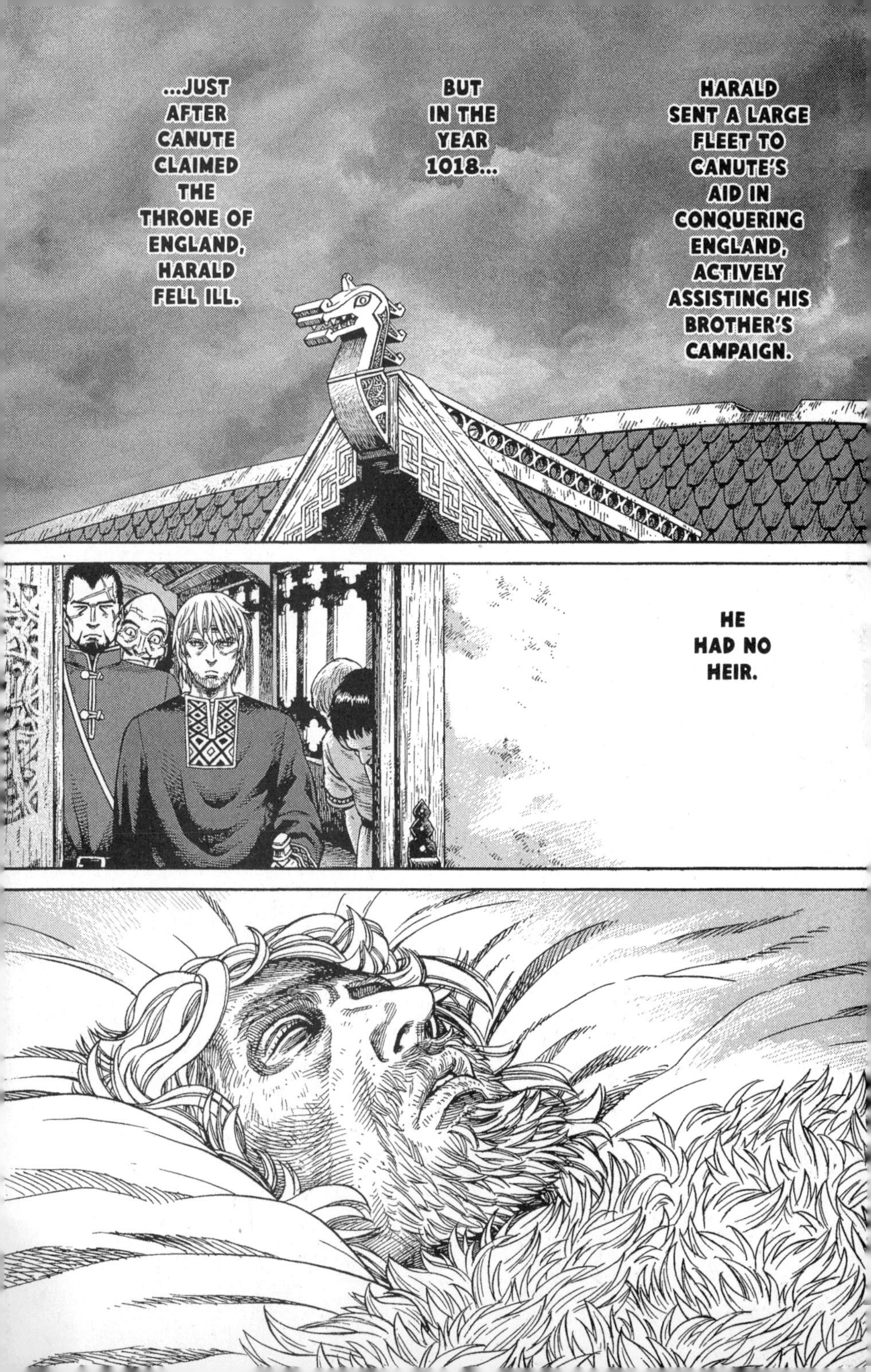
HARALD SENT A LARGE FLEET TO CANUTE'S AID IN CONQUERING ENGLAND, ACTIVELY ASSISTING HIS BROTHER'S CAMPAIGN.
BUT IN THE YEAR 1018...
...JUST AFTER CANUTE CLAIMED THE THRONE OF ENGLAND, HARALD FELL ILL.
HE HAD NO HEIR.

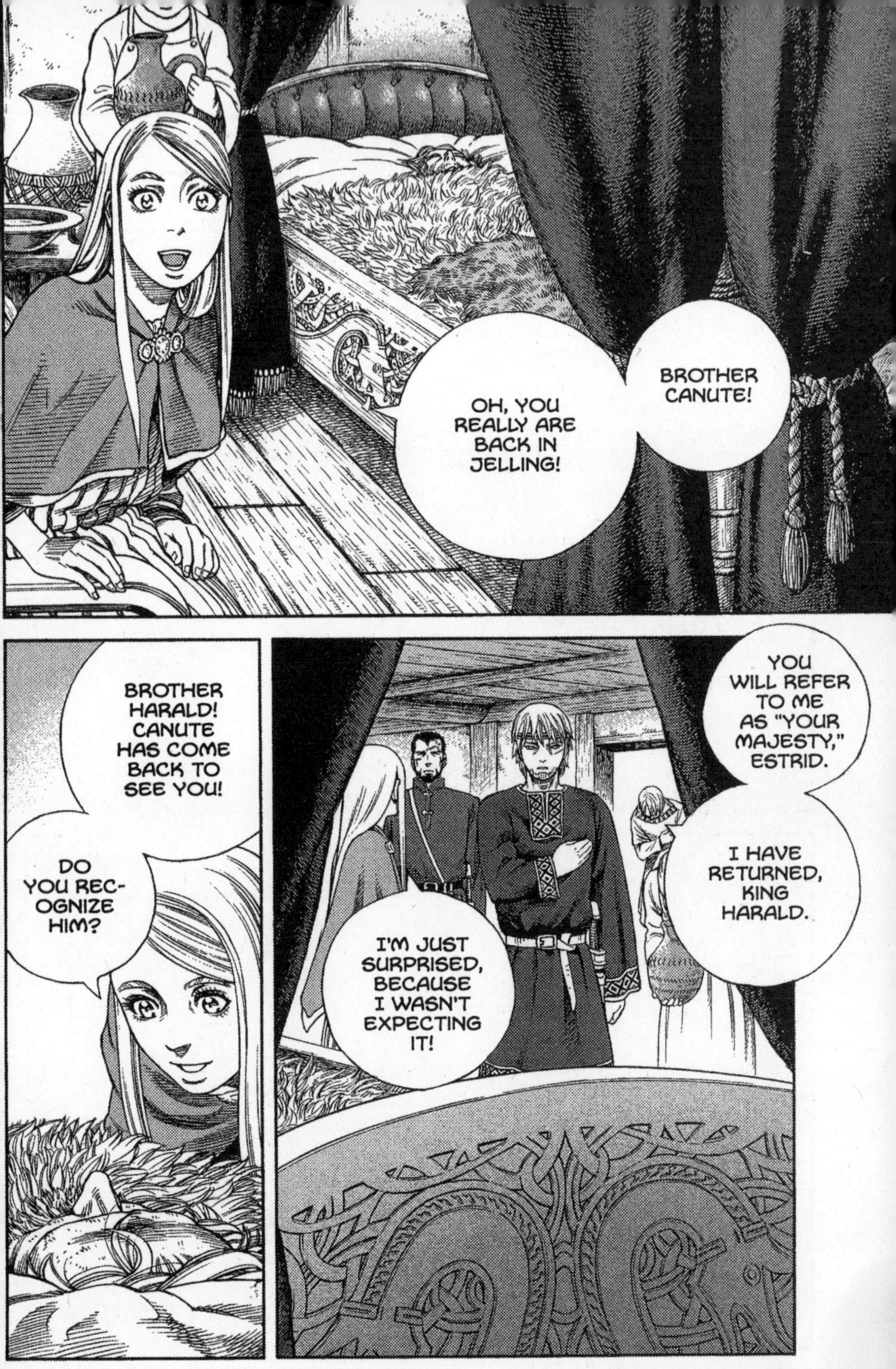
BROTHER CANUTE!
OH, YOU REALLY ARE BACK IN JELLING!
YOU WILL REFER TO ME AS "YOUR MAJESTY," ESTRID.
I HAVE RETURNED, KING HARALD.
I'M JUST SURPRISED, BECAUSE I WASN'T EXPECTING IT!
BROTHER HARALD! CANUTE HAS COME BACK TO SEE YOU!
DO YOU RECOGNIZE HIM?

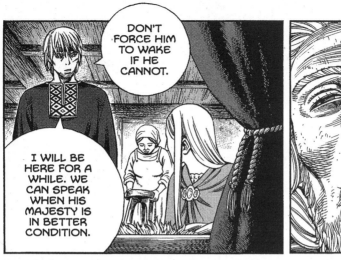

DON'T FORCE HIM TO WAKE IF HE CANNOT.

I WILL BE HERE FOR A WHILE. WE CAN SPEAK WHEN HIS MAJESTY IS IN BETTER CONDITION.

...UTE...

CAN...

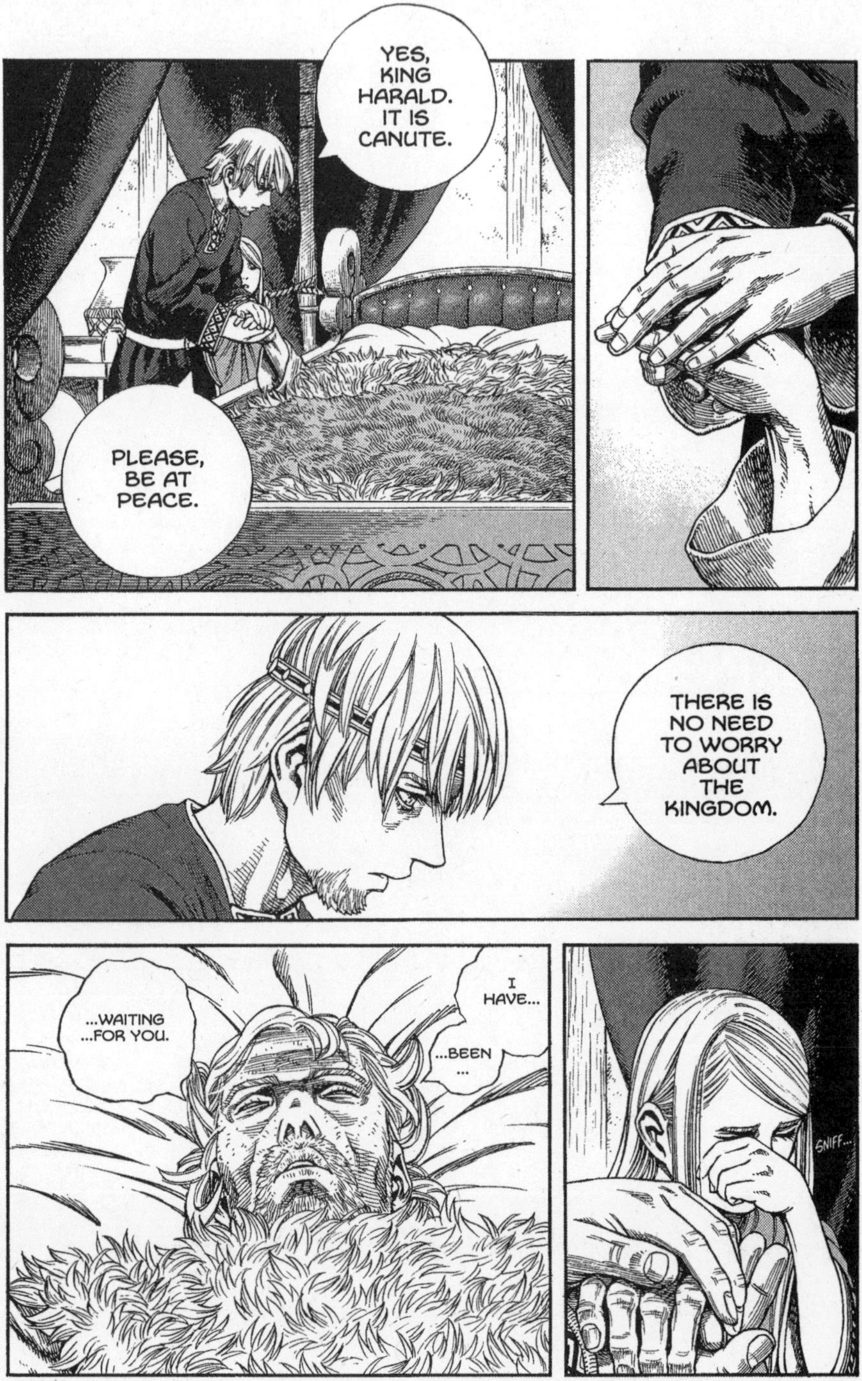
YES, KING HARALD. IT IS CANUTE.
PLEASE, BE AT PEACE.
THERE IS NO NEED TO WORRY ABOUT THE KINGDOM.
SNIFF...
I HAVE...
...BEEN ...
...WAITING ...FOR YOU.

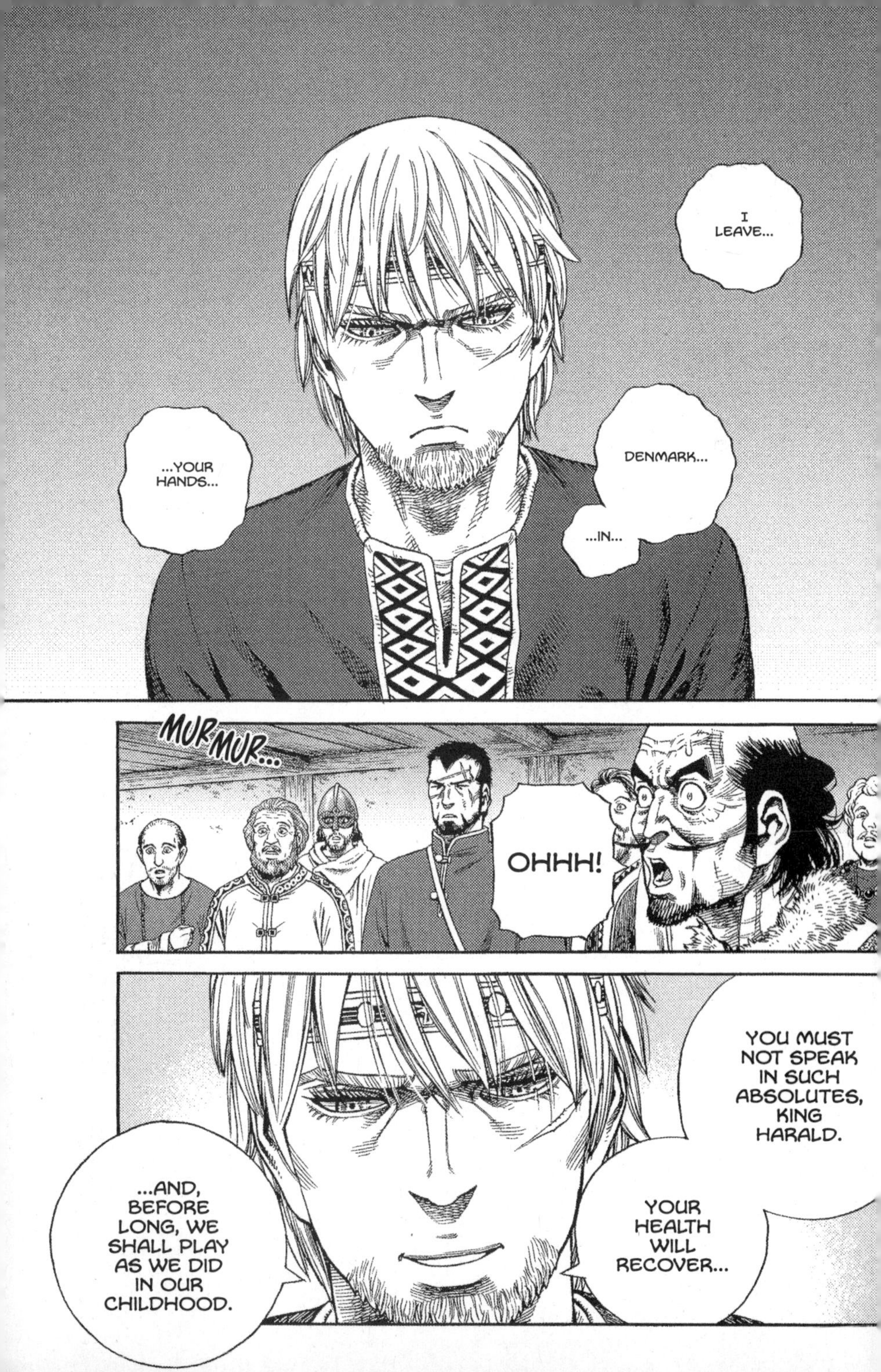
I LEAVE...
DENMARK...
...IN...
...YOUR HANDS...
OHHH!
MUR MUR...
YOU MUST NOT SPEAK IN SUCH ABSOLUTES, KING HARALD.
YOUR HEALTH WILL RECOVER...
...AND, BEFORE LONG, WE SHALL PLAY AS WE DID IN OUR CHILDHOOD.

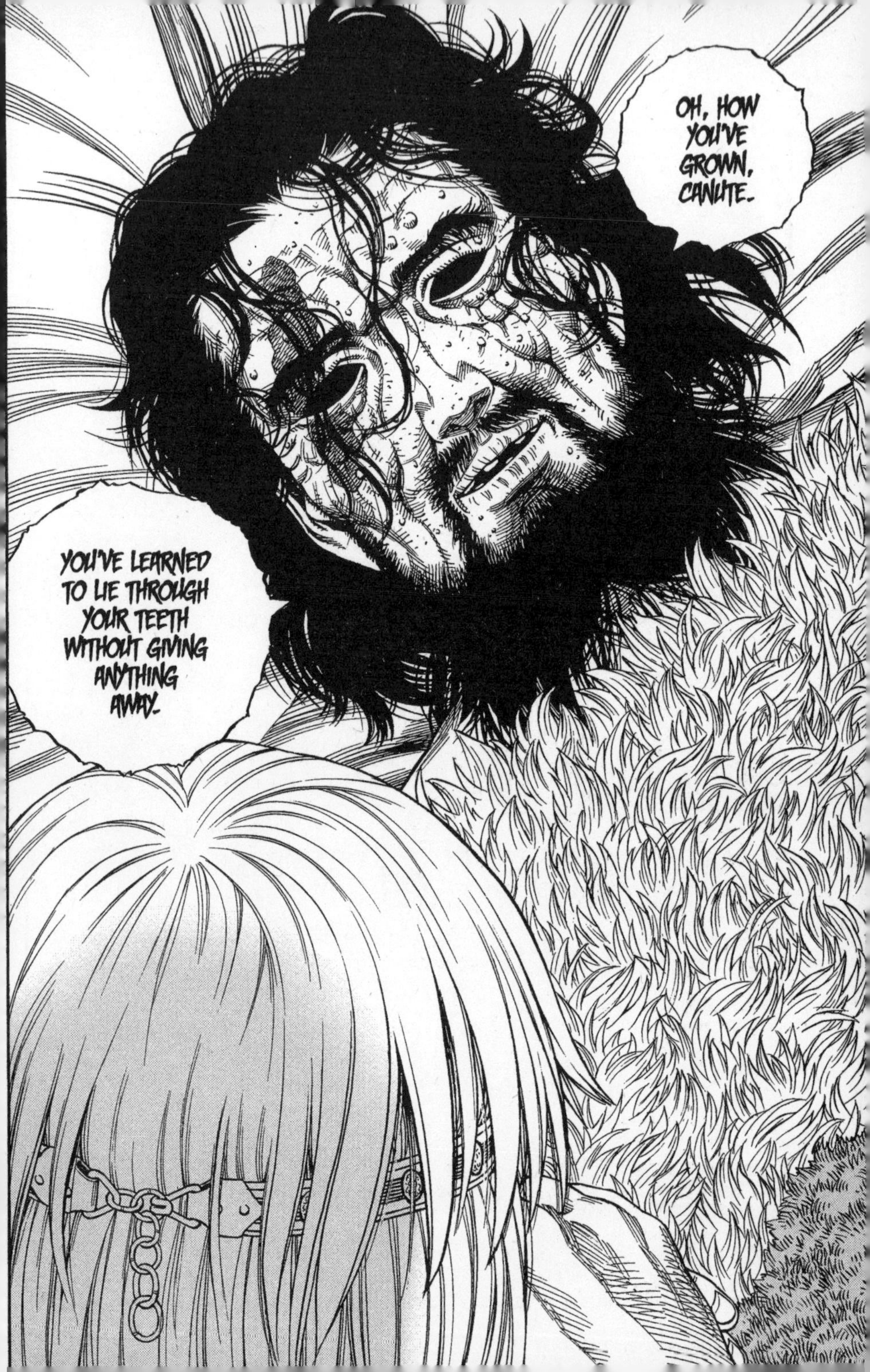
OH, HOW YOU'VE GROWN, CANUTE.
YOU'VE LEARNED TO LIE THROUGH YOUR TEETH WITHOUT GIVING ANYTHING AWAY.

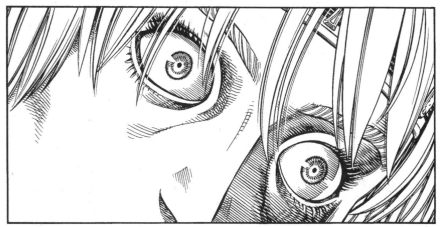

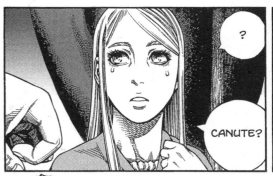

?
CANUTE?
WHAT A PIOUS FARCE. OFFERING PLATITUDES TO THE MAN YOU POISONED AS HE LIES ON HIS DEATHBED.
AND WHAT DO YOU STAND TO GAIN FROM THIS?

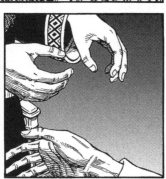

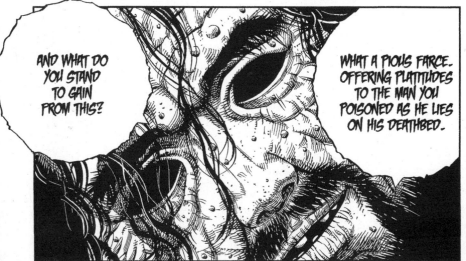

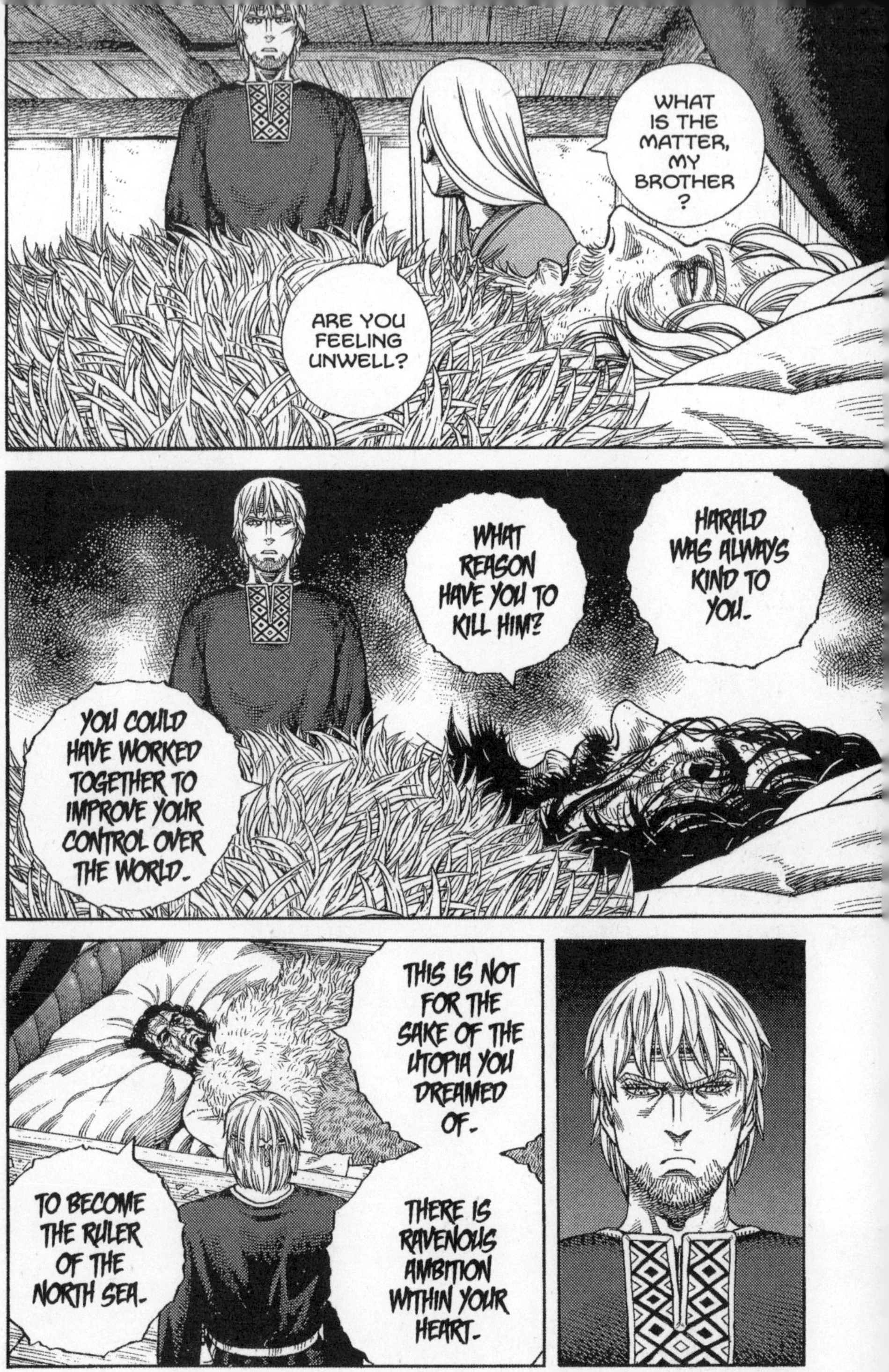
WHAT IS THE MATTER, MY BROTHER?
ARE YOU FEELING UNWELL?
HARALD WAS ALWAYS KIND TO YOU.
WHAT REASON HAVE YOU TO KILL HIM?
YOU COULD HAVE WORKED TOGETHER TO IMPROVE YOUR CONTROL OVER THE WORLD.
THIS IS NOT FOR THE SAKE OF THE UTOPIA YOU DREAMED OF.
THERE IS RAVENOUS AMBITION WITHIN YOUR HEART.
TO BECOME THE RULER OF THE NORTH SEA.

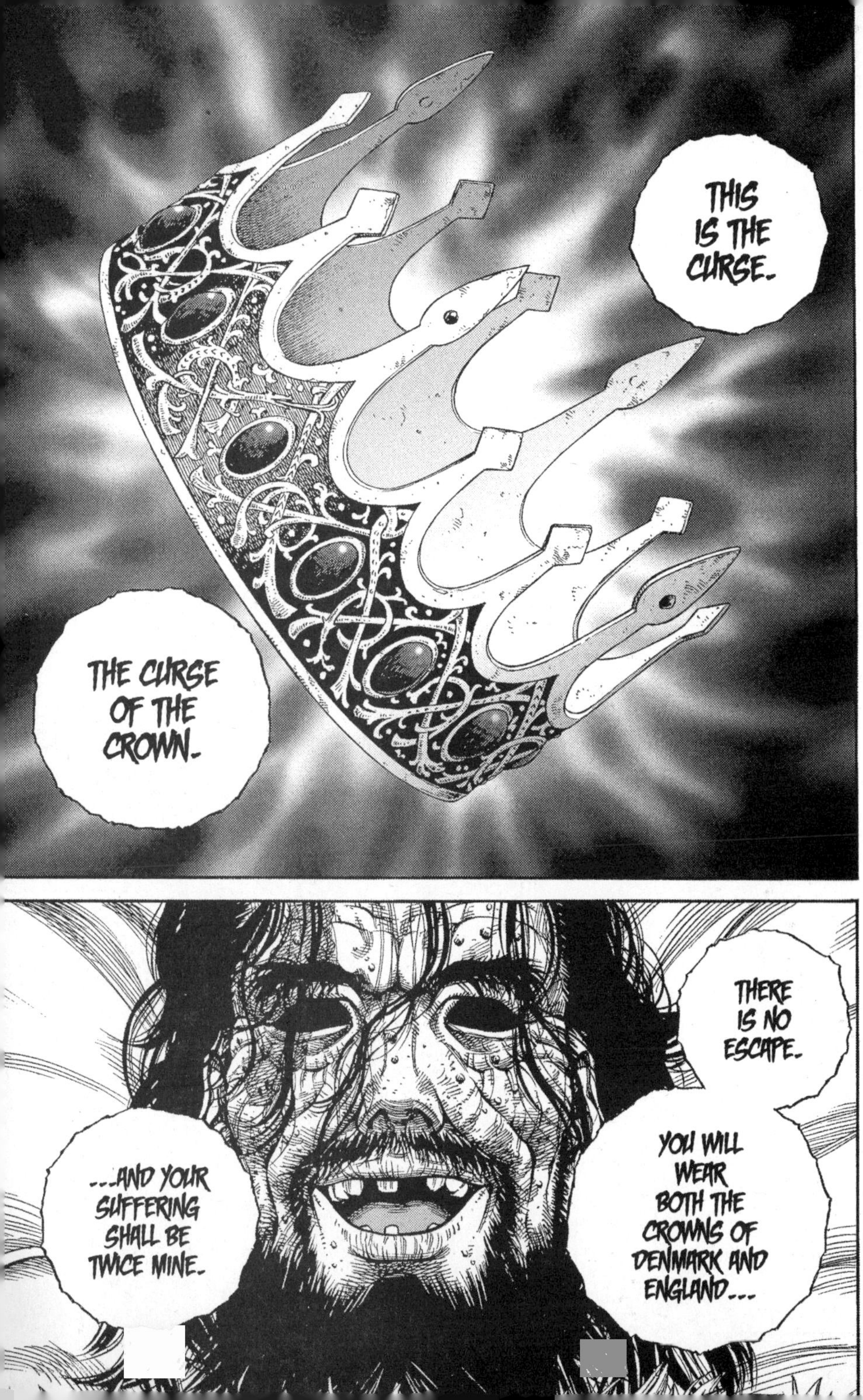
THIS IS THE CURSE.
THE CURSE OF THE CROWN.
THERE IS NO ESCAPE.
YOU WILL WEAR BOTH THE CROWNS OF DENMARK AND ENGLAND...
...AND YOUR SUFFERING SHALL BE TWICE MINE.

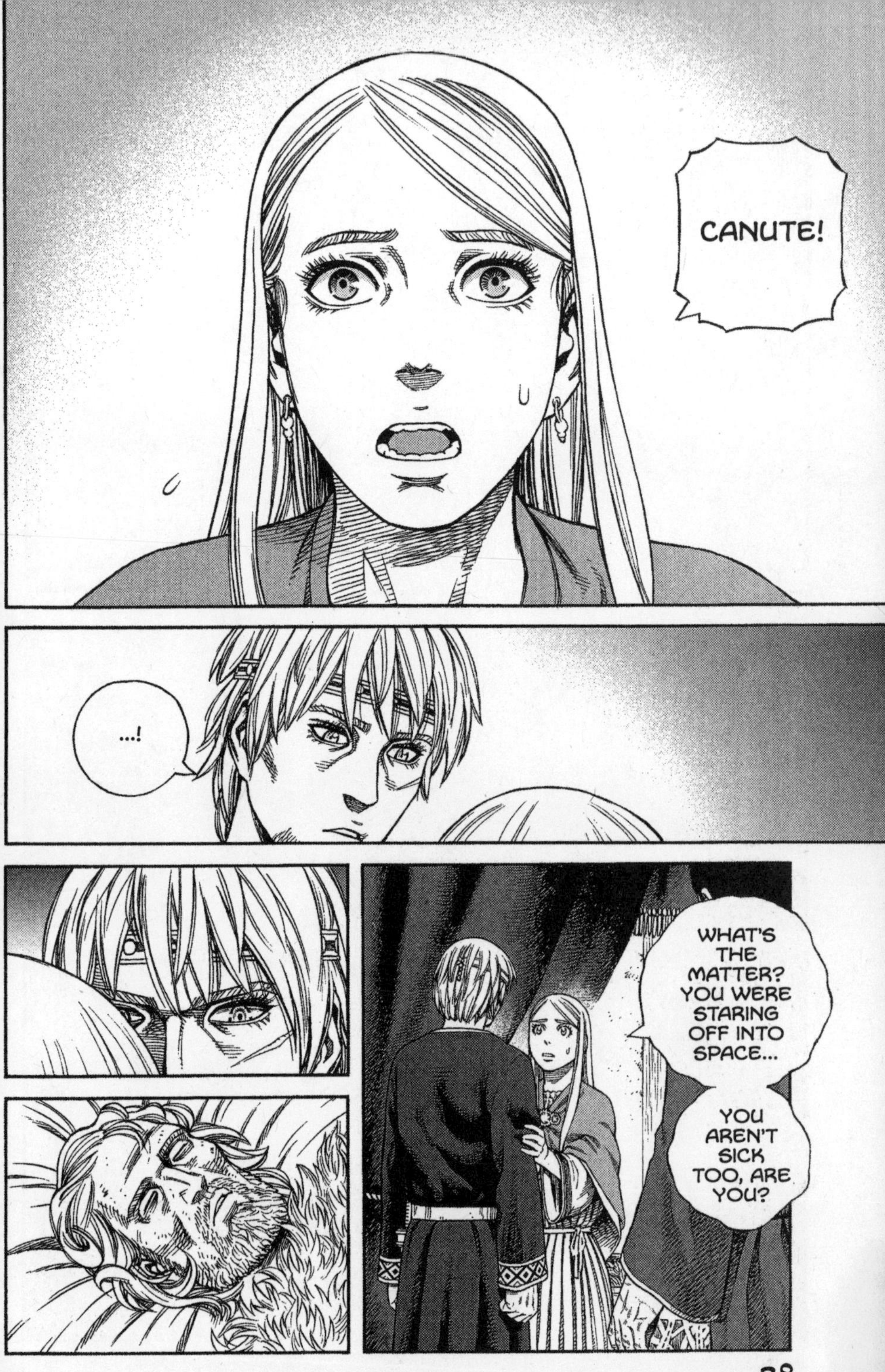
CANUTE!
...!
WHAT'S THE MATTER? YOU WERE STARING OFF INTO SPACE...
YOU AREN'T SICK TOO, ARE YOU?

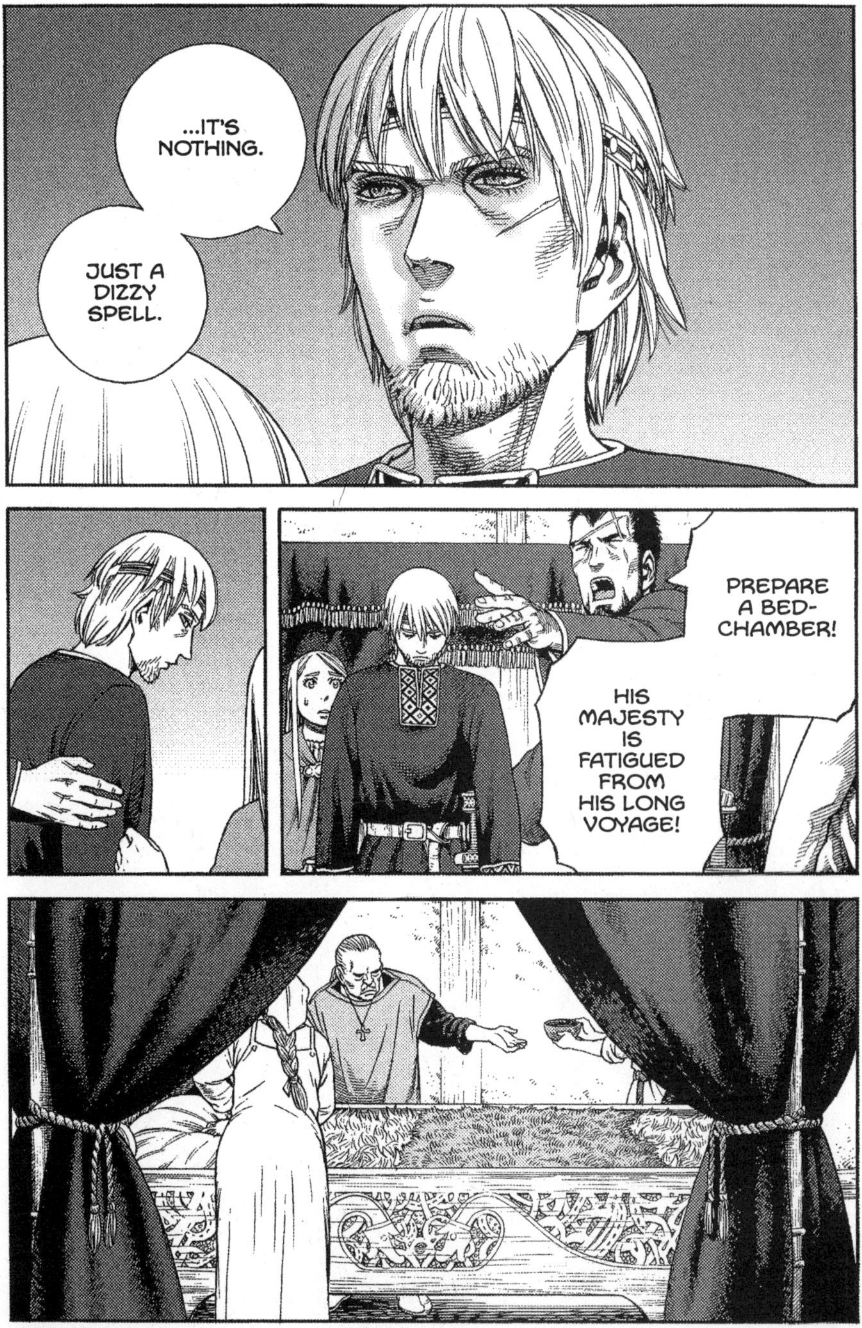
...IT'S NOTHING.
JUST A DIZZY SPELL.
PREPARE A BED-CHAMBER!
HIS MAJESTY IS FATIGUED FROM HIS LONG VOYAGE!

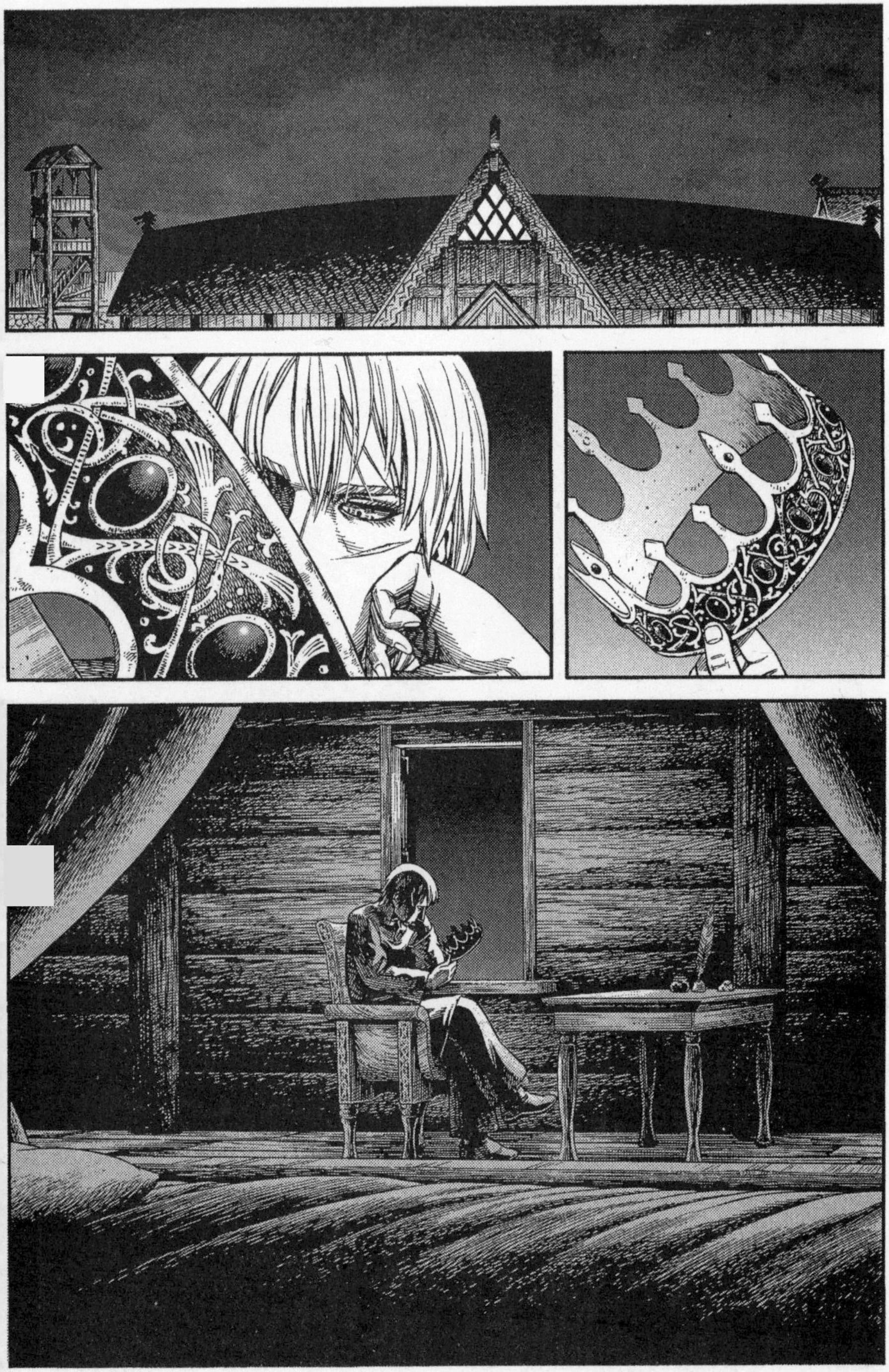

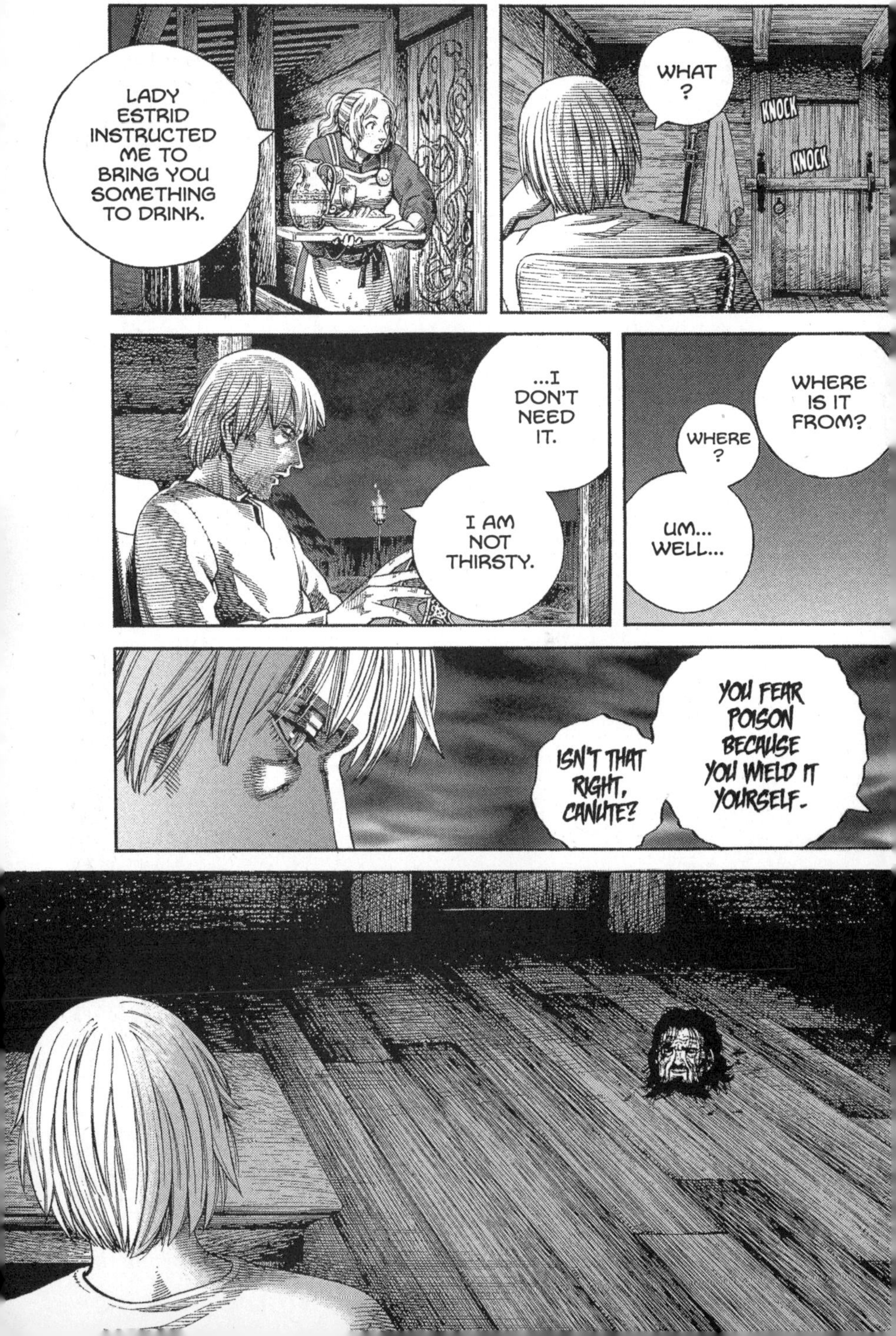
KNOCK
KNOCK
WHAT?
LADY ESTRID INSTRUCTED ME TO BRING YOU SOMETHING TO DRINK.
WHERE IS IT FROM?
WHERE?
UM... WELL...
...I DON'T NEED IT.
I AM NOT THIRSTY.
YOU FEAR POISON BECAUSE YOU WIELD IT YOURSELF.
ISN'T THAT RIGHT, CANUTE?

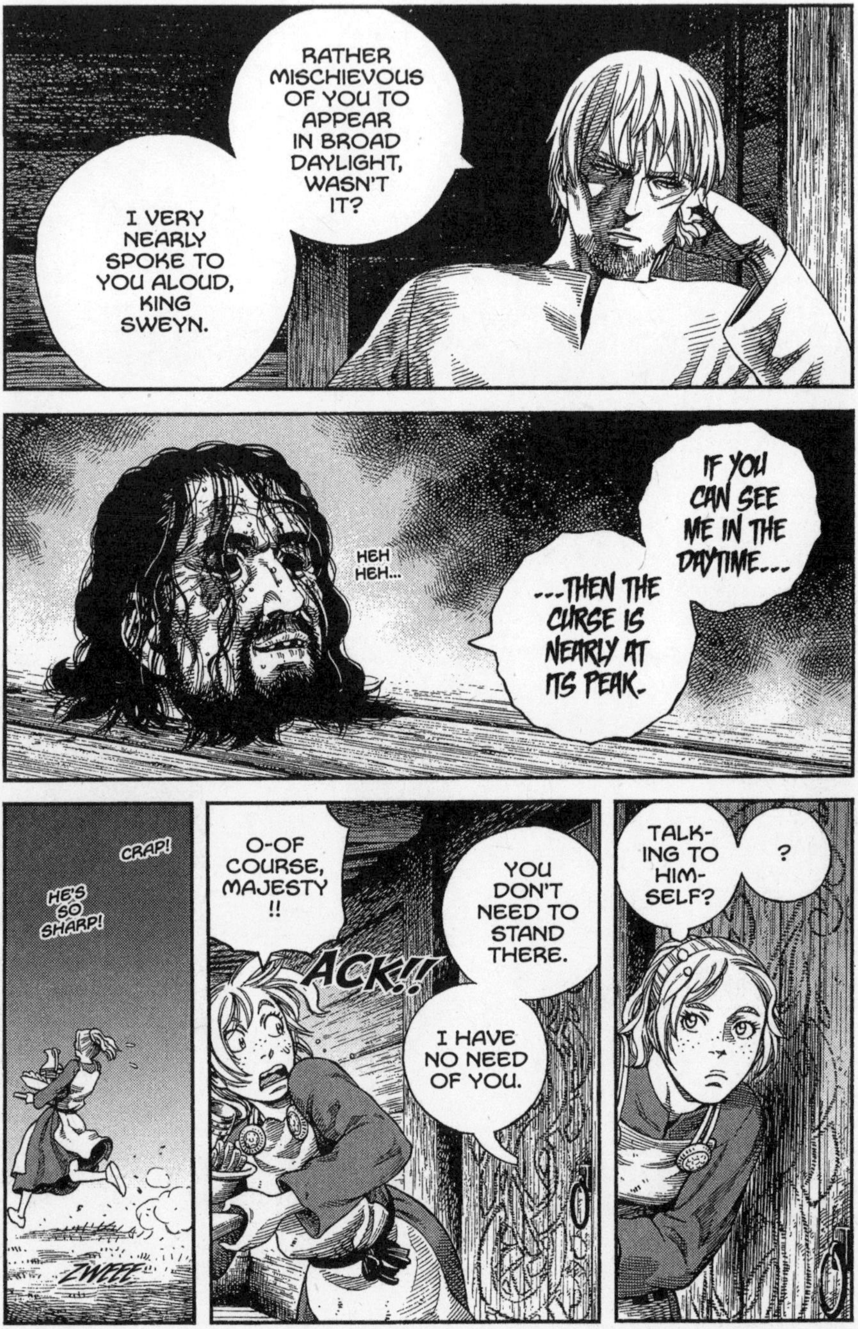
RATHER MISCHIEVOUS OF YOU TO APPEAR IN BROAD DAYLIGHT, WASN'T IT?
I VERY NEARLY SPOKE TO YOU ALOUD, KING SWEYN.
IF YOU CAN SEE ME IN THE DAYTIME...
...THEN THE CURSE IS NEARLY AT ITS PEAK.
HEH HEH...
?
TALK-ING TO HIM-SELF?
YOU DON'T NEED TO STAND THERE.
I HAVE NO NEED OF YOU.
ACK!!
O-OF COURSE, MAJESTY !!
CRAP!
HE'S SO SHARP!
ZWEEE

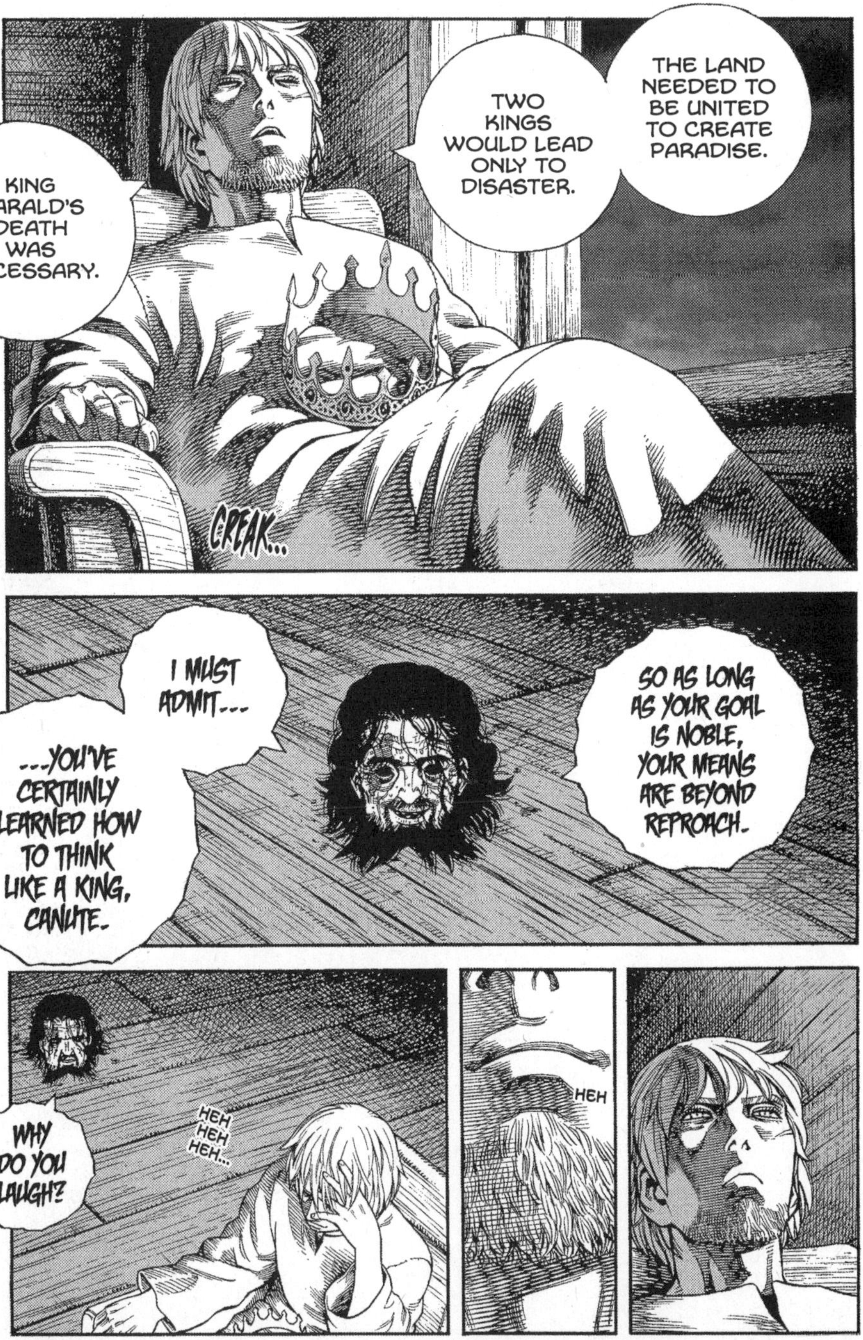
THE LAND NEEDED TO BE UNITED TO CREATE PARADISE.
TWO KINGS WOULD LEAD ONLY TO DISASTER.
KING HARALD'S DEATH WAS NECESSARY.
CREAK...
SO AS LONG AS YOUR GOAL IS NOBLE, YOUR MEANS ARE BEYOND REPROACH.
I MUST ADMIT...
...YOU'VE CERTAINLY LEARNED HOW TO THINK LIKE A KING, CANUTE.
HEH
HEH HEH HEH...
WHY DO YOU LAUGH?

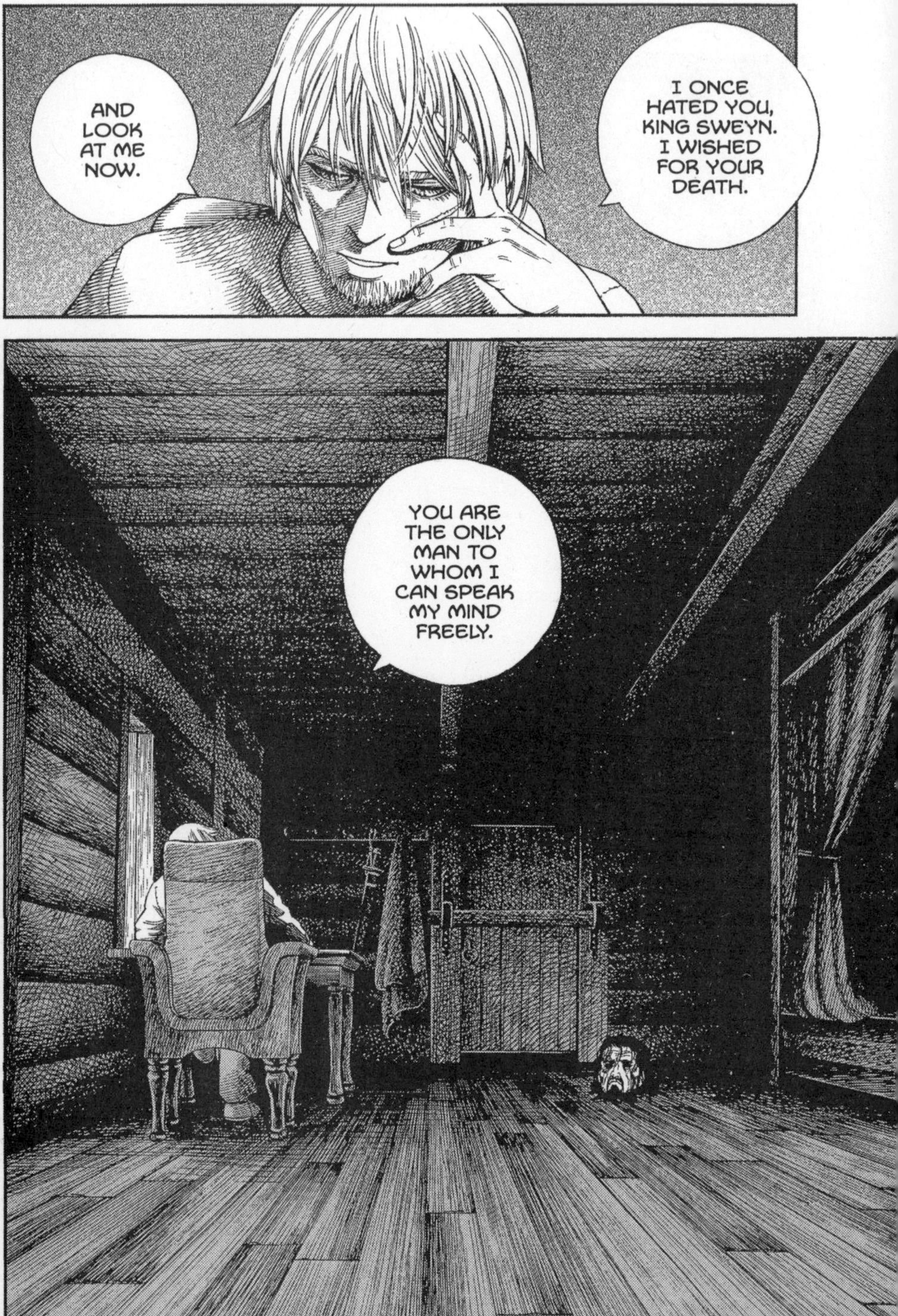
I ONCE HATED YOU, KING SWEYN. I WISHED FOR YOUR DEATH.
AND LOOK AT ME NOW.
YOU ARE THE ONLY MAN TO WHOM I CAN SPEAK MY MIND FREELY.

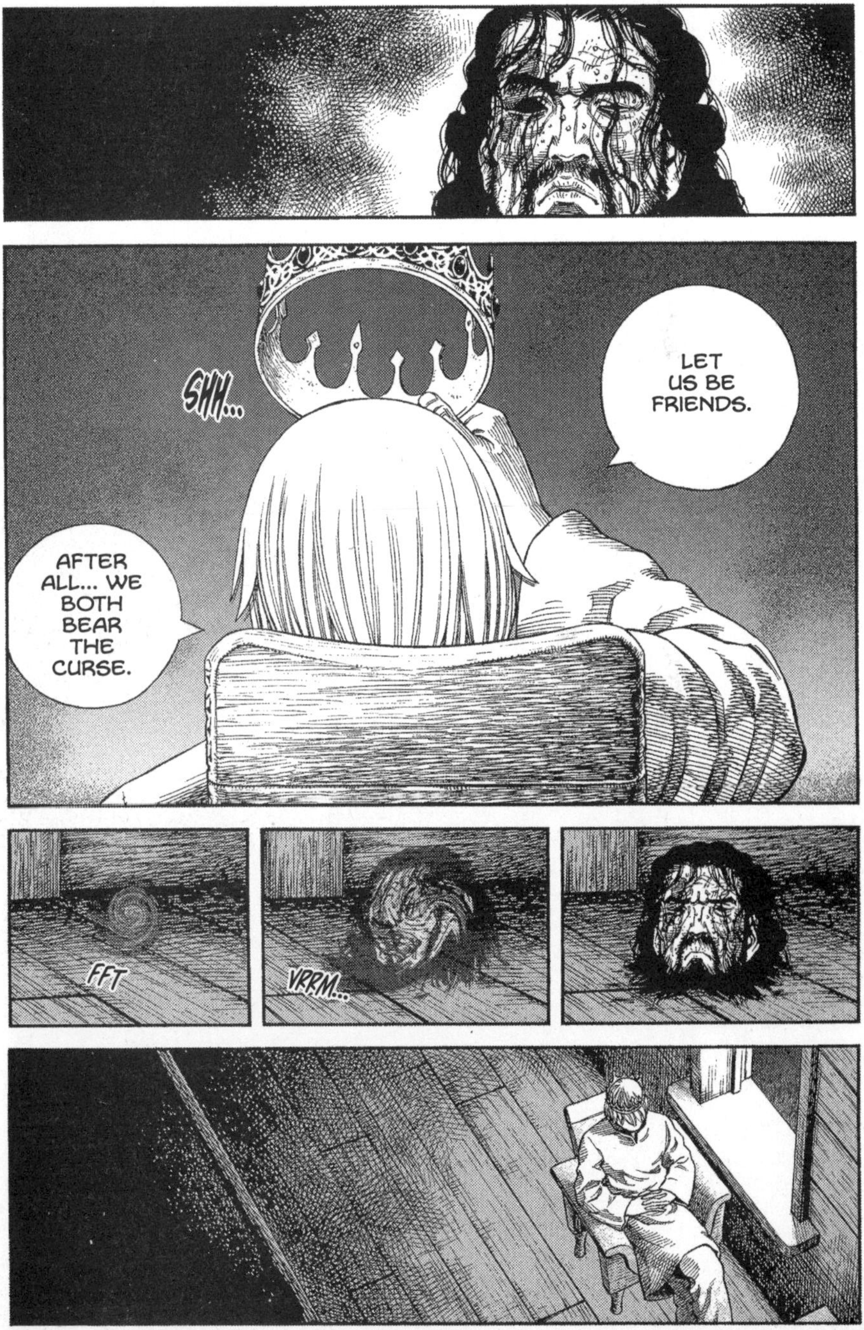
LET US BE FRIENDS.
SHH...
AFTER ALL... WE BOTH BEAR THE CURSE.
VRRM...
FFT

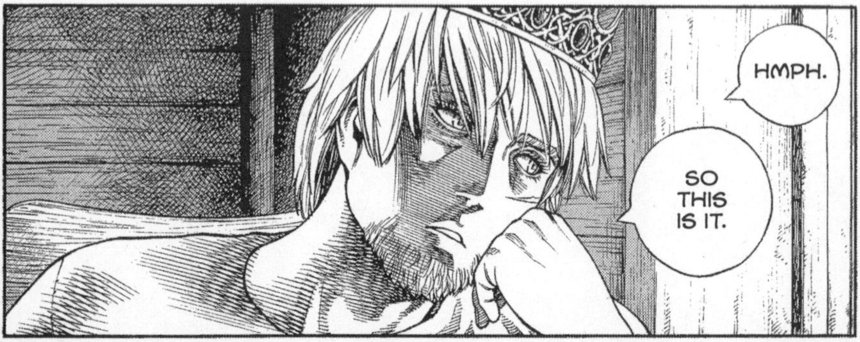
HMPH.
SO THIS IS IT.
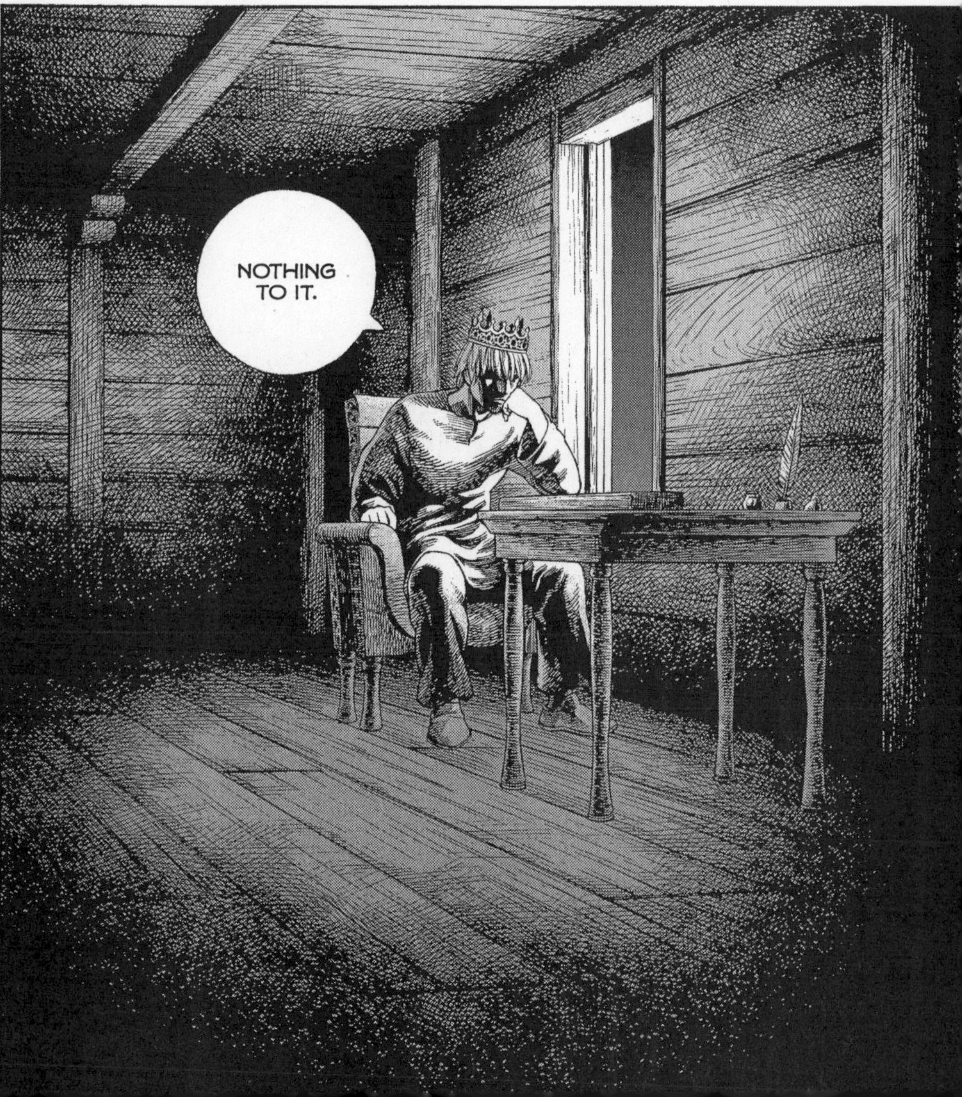
NOTHING TO IT.

CHAPTER 73: WHEN YOU'RE FREE

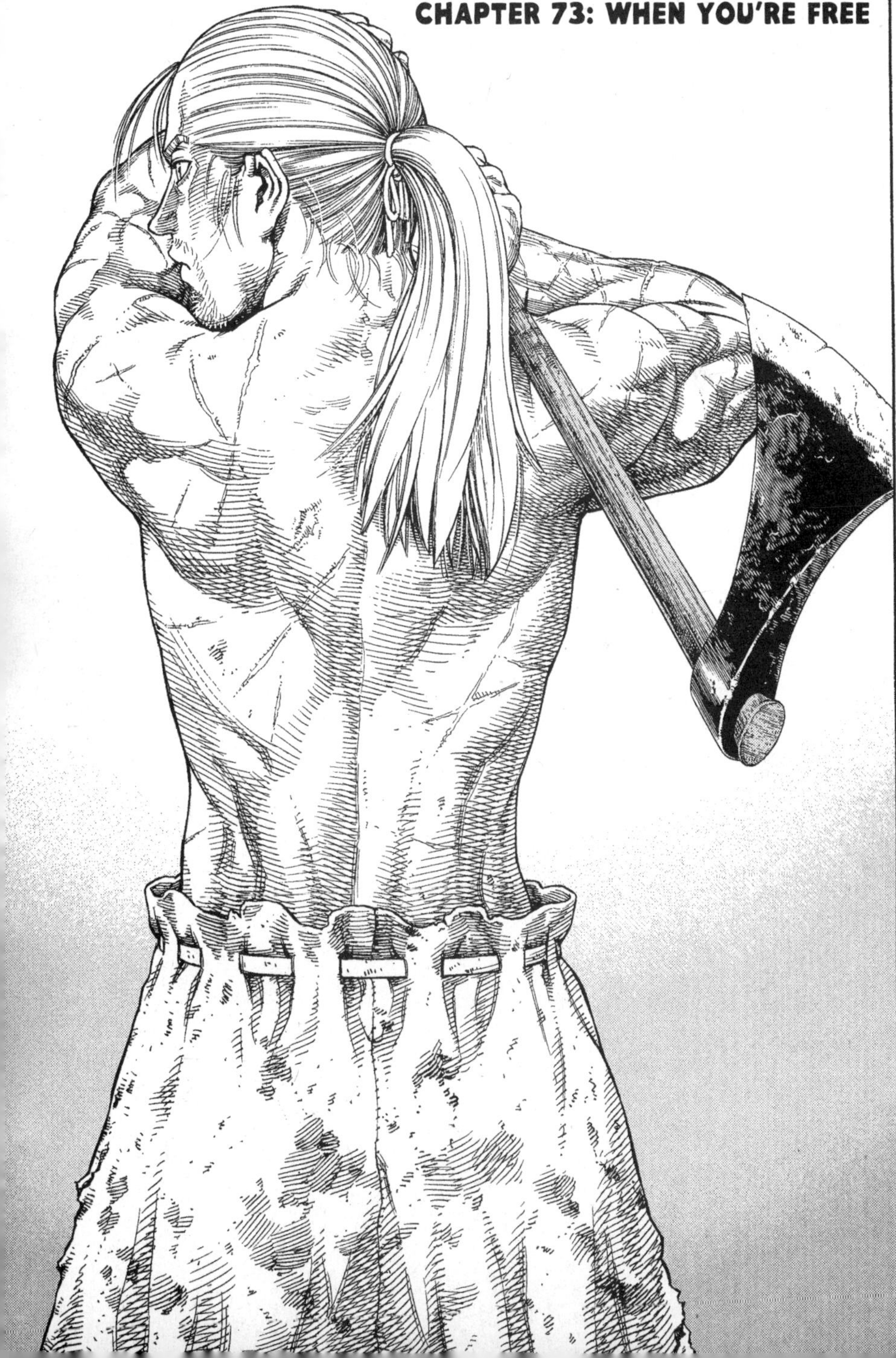

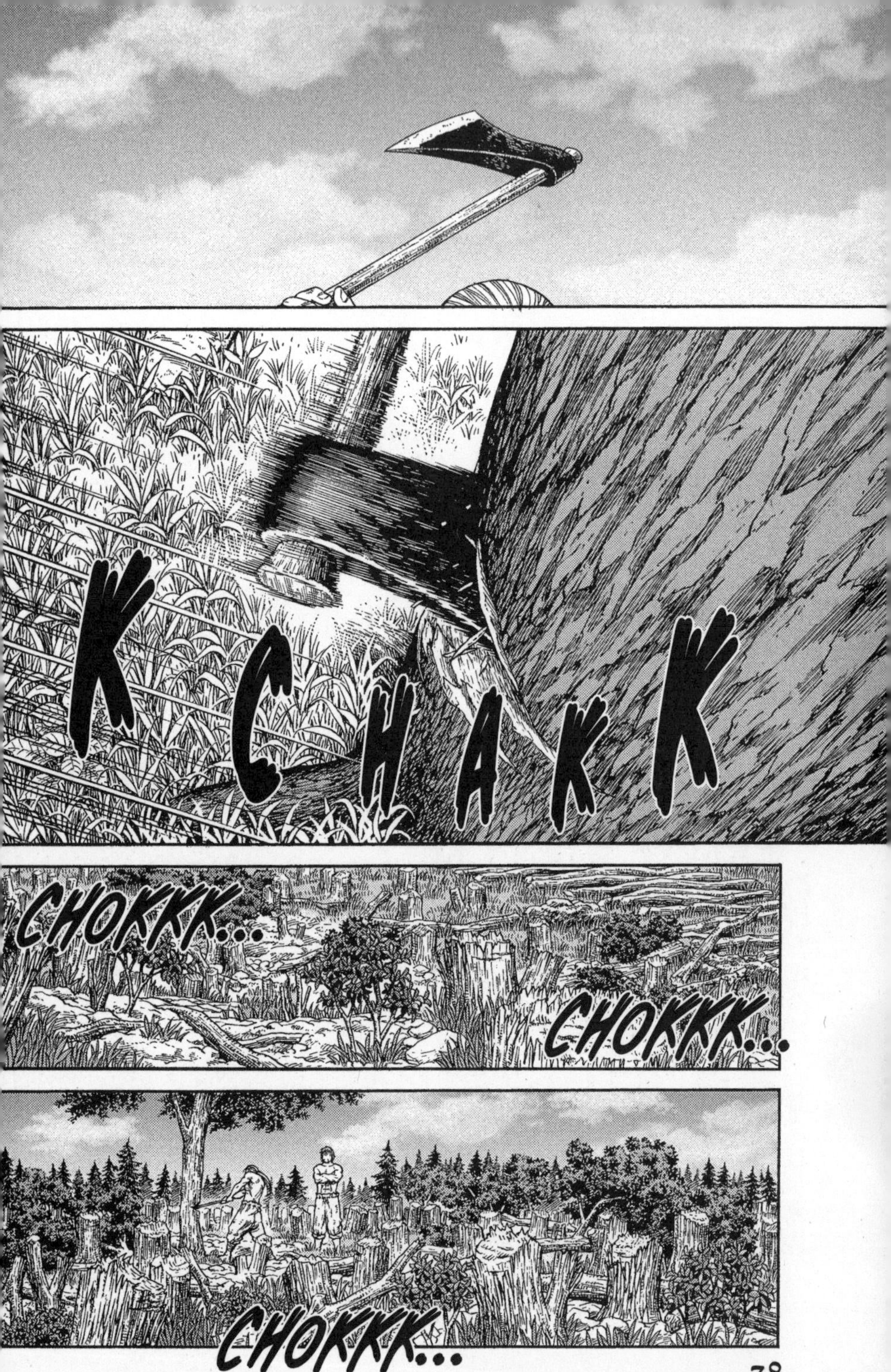
KCHAKK
CHOKKK...
CHOKKK...
CHOKKK...

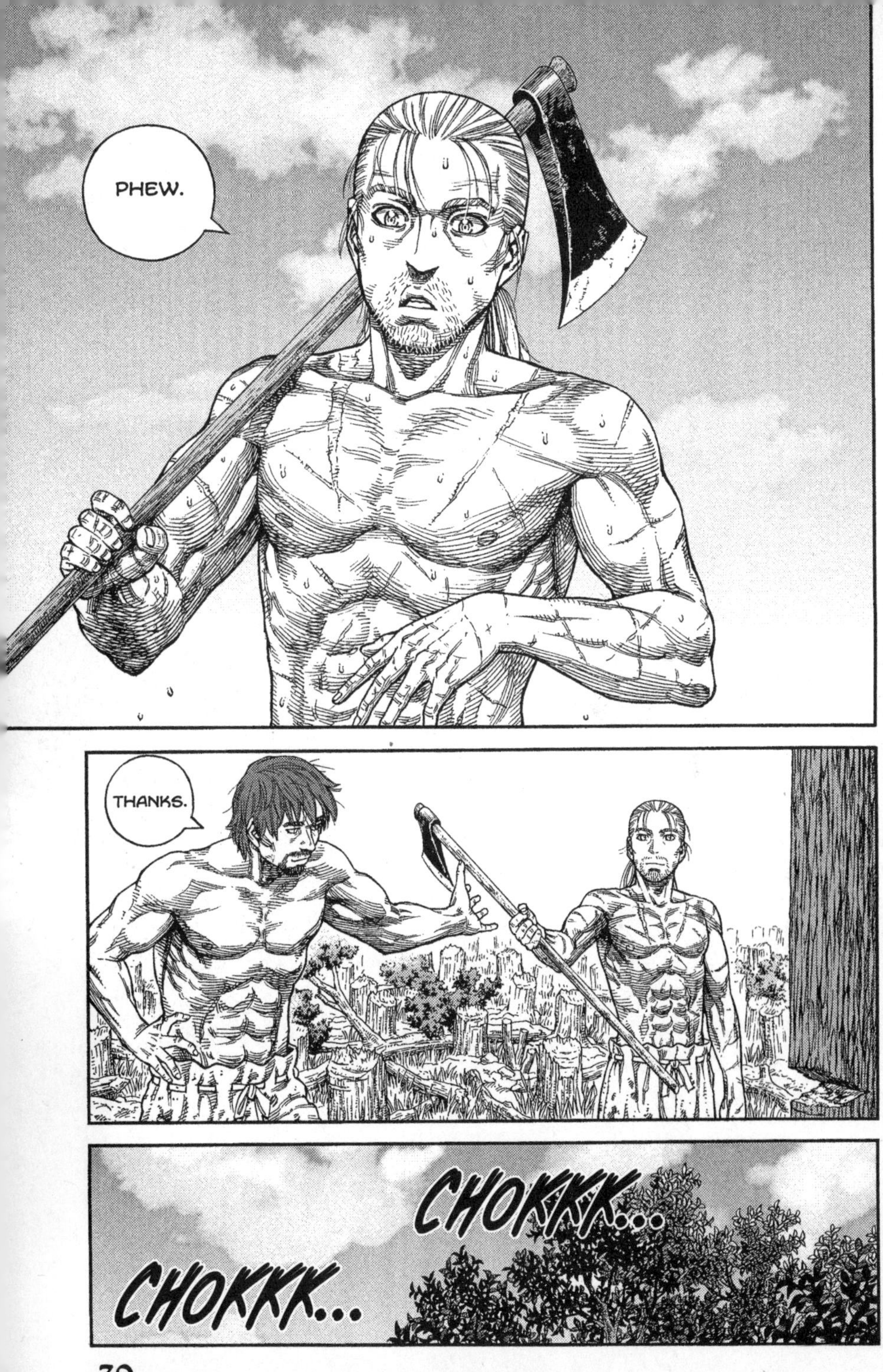
PHEW.
THANKS.
CHOKKK...
CHOKKK...

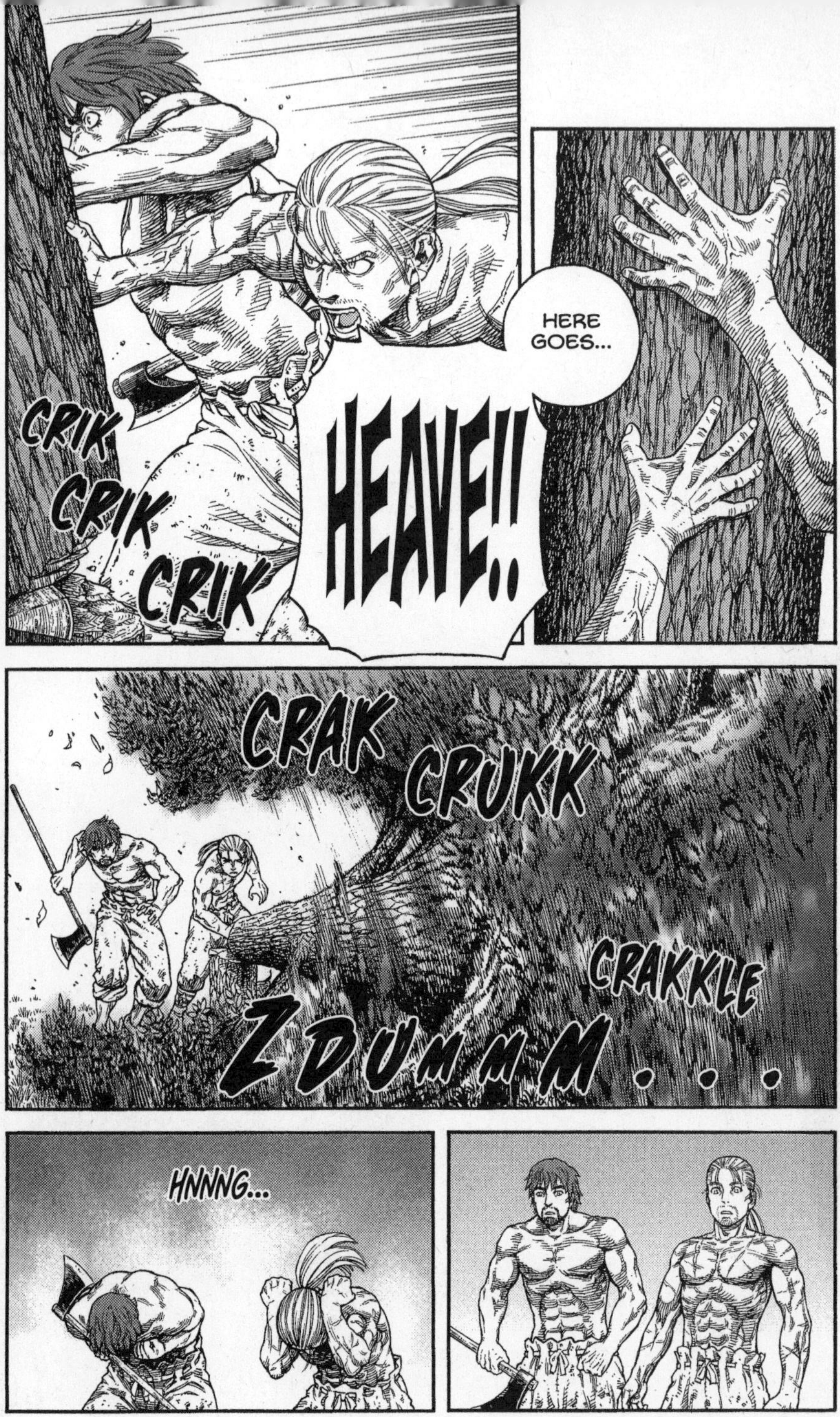
HERE GOES...
HEAVE!!
CRIK
CRIK
CRIK
CRAK
CRUKK
CRAKKLE
ZDUMMM . . .
HNNNG...

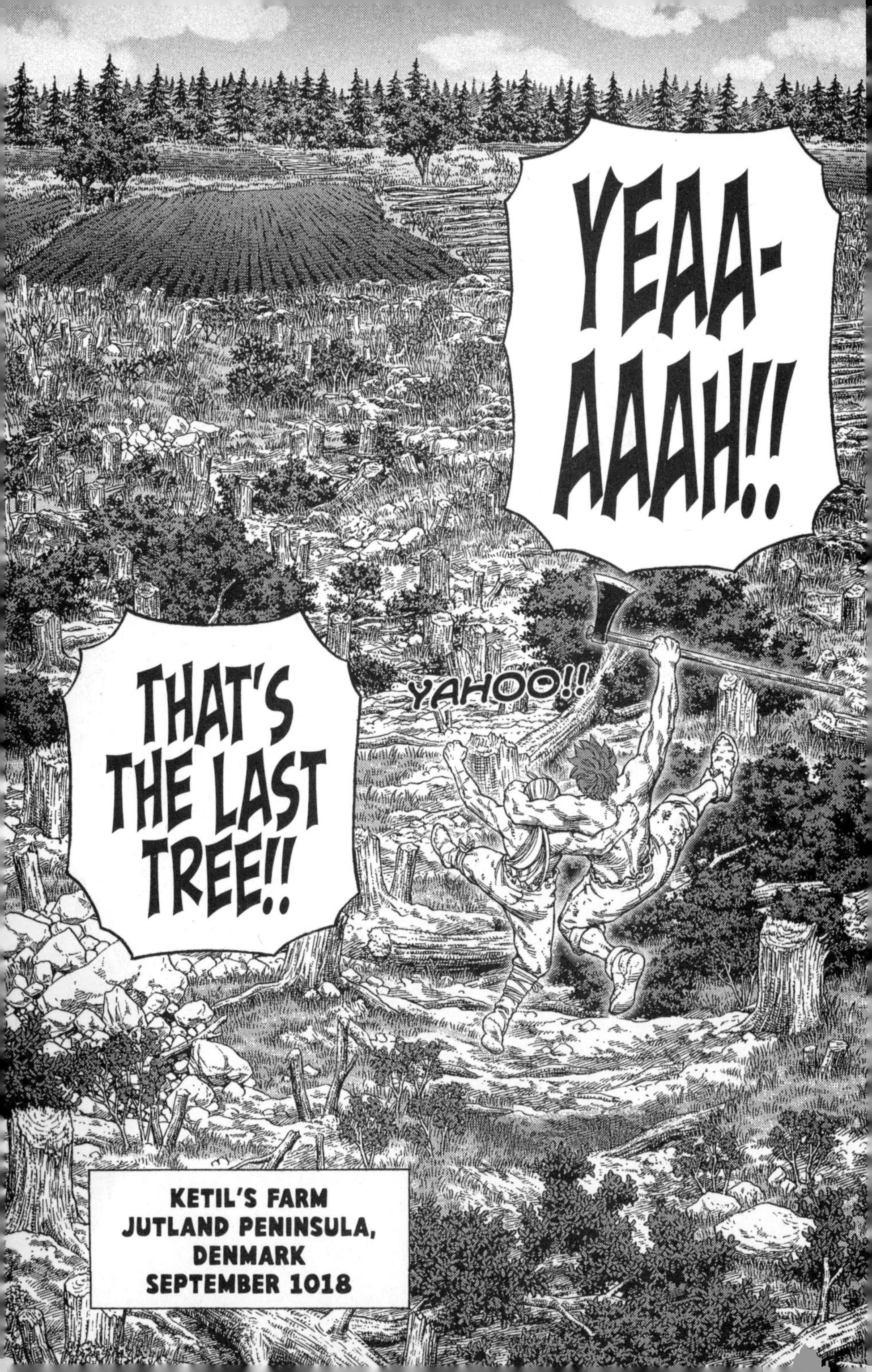
YEAA-AAAH!!
THAT'S THE LAST TREE!!
YAHOO!!
KETIL'S FARM
JUTLAND PENINSULA,
DENMARK
SEPTEMBER 1018

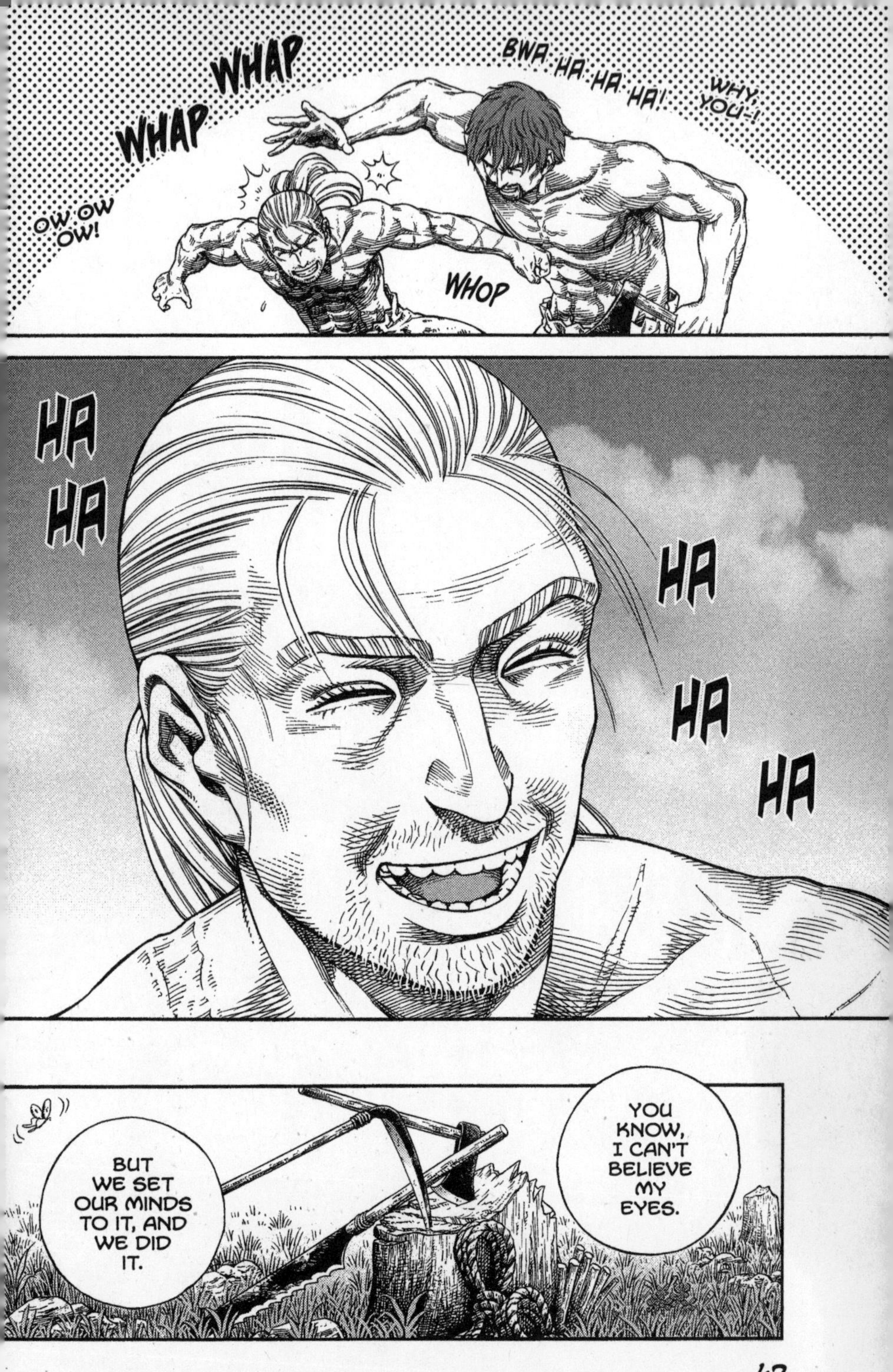
WHY, YOU-!
BWA HA HA HA!
WHAP WHAP
OW OW OW!
WHOP
HA HA HA
HA HA
YOU KNOW, I CAN'T BELIEVE MY EYES.
BUT WE SET OUR MINDS TO IT, AND WE DID IT.

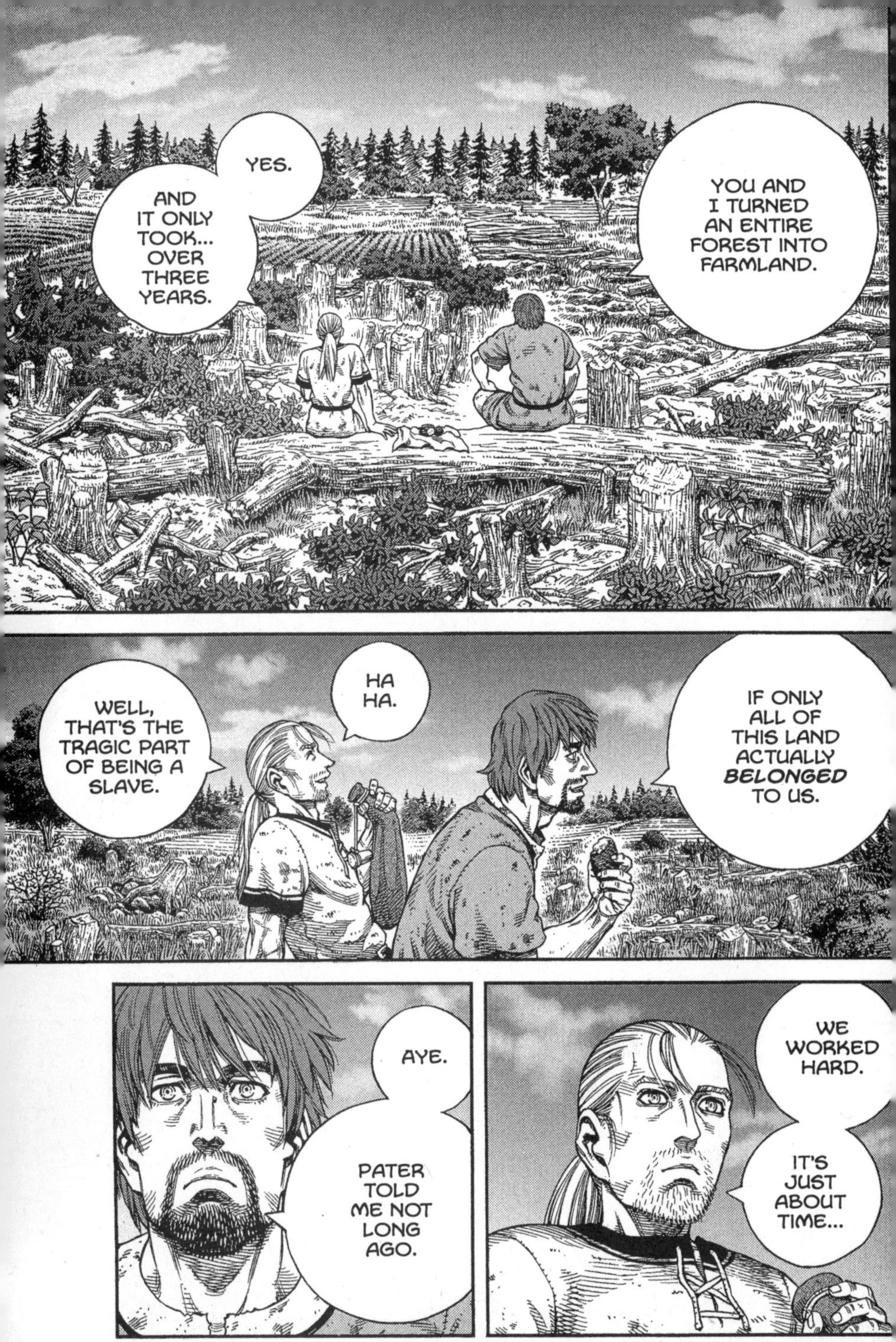
YOU AND I TURNED AN ENTIRE FOREST INTO FARMLAND.
YES.
AND IT ONLY TOOK... OVER THREE YEARS.
IF ONLY ALL OF THIS LAND ACTUALLY *BELONGED* TO US.
HA HA.
WELL, THAT'S THE TRAGIC PART OF BEING A SLAVE.
WE WORKED HARD.
IT'S JUST ABOUT TIME...
AYE.
PATER TOLD ME NOT LONG AGO.

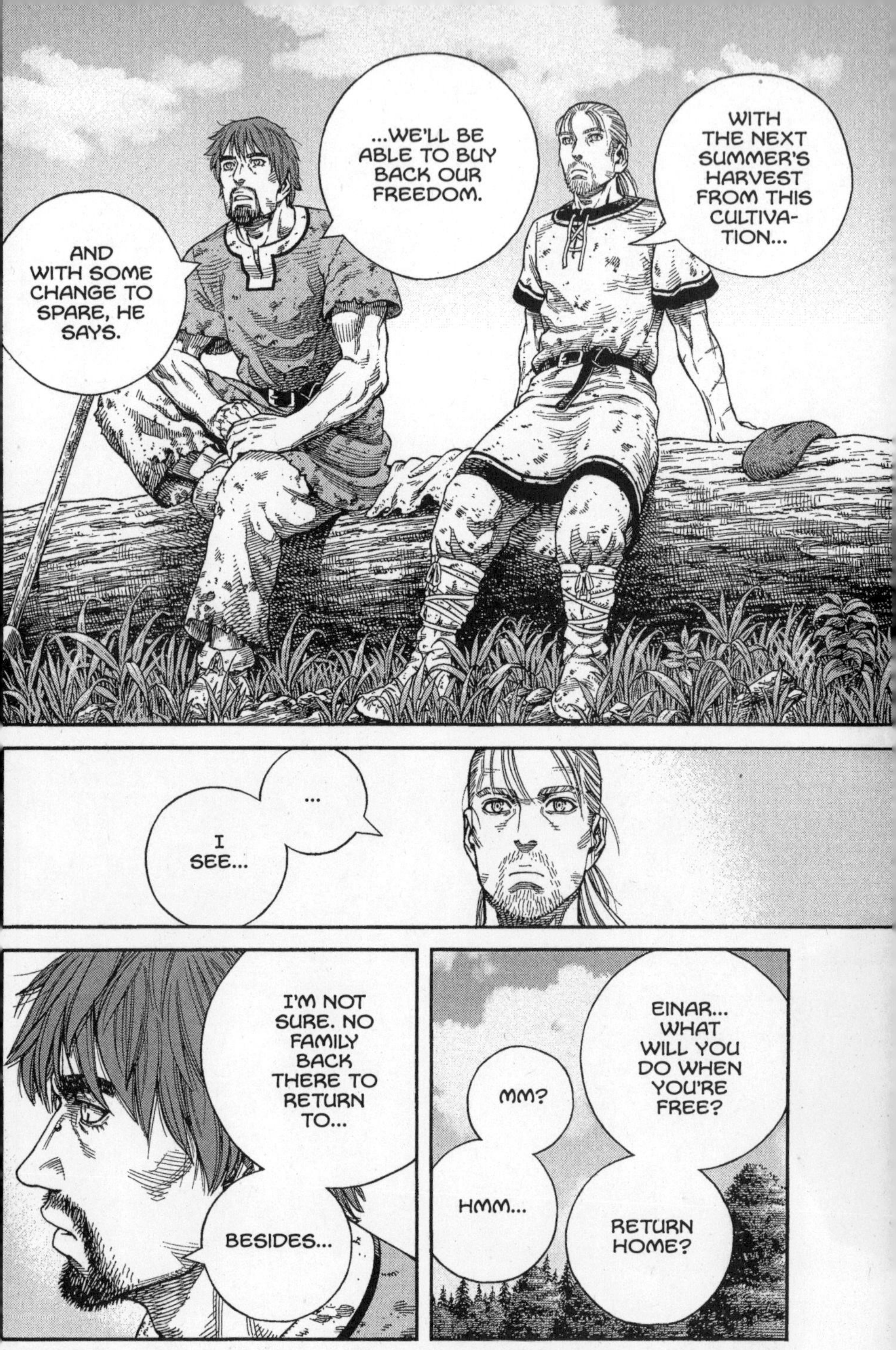
WITH THE NEXT SUMMER'S HARVEST FROM THIS CULTIVATION...
...WE'LL BE ABLE TO BUY BACK OUR FREEDOM.
AND WITH SOME CHANGE TO SPARE, HE SAYS.
...
I SEE...
EINAR... WHAT WILL YOU DO WHEN YOU'RE FREE?
MM?
RETURN HOME?
HMM...
I'M NOT SURE. NO FAMILY BACK THERE TO RETURN TO...
BESIDES...

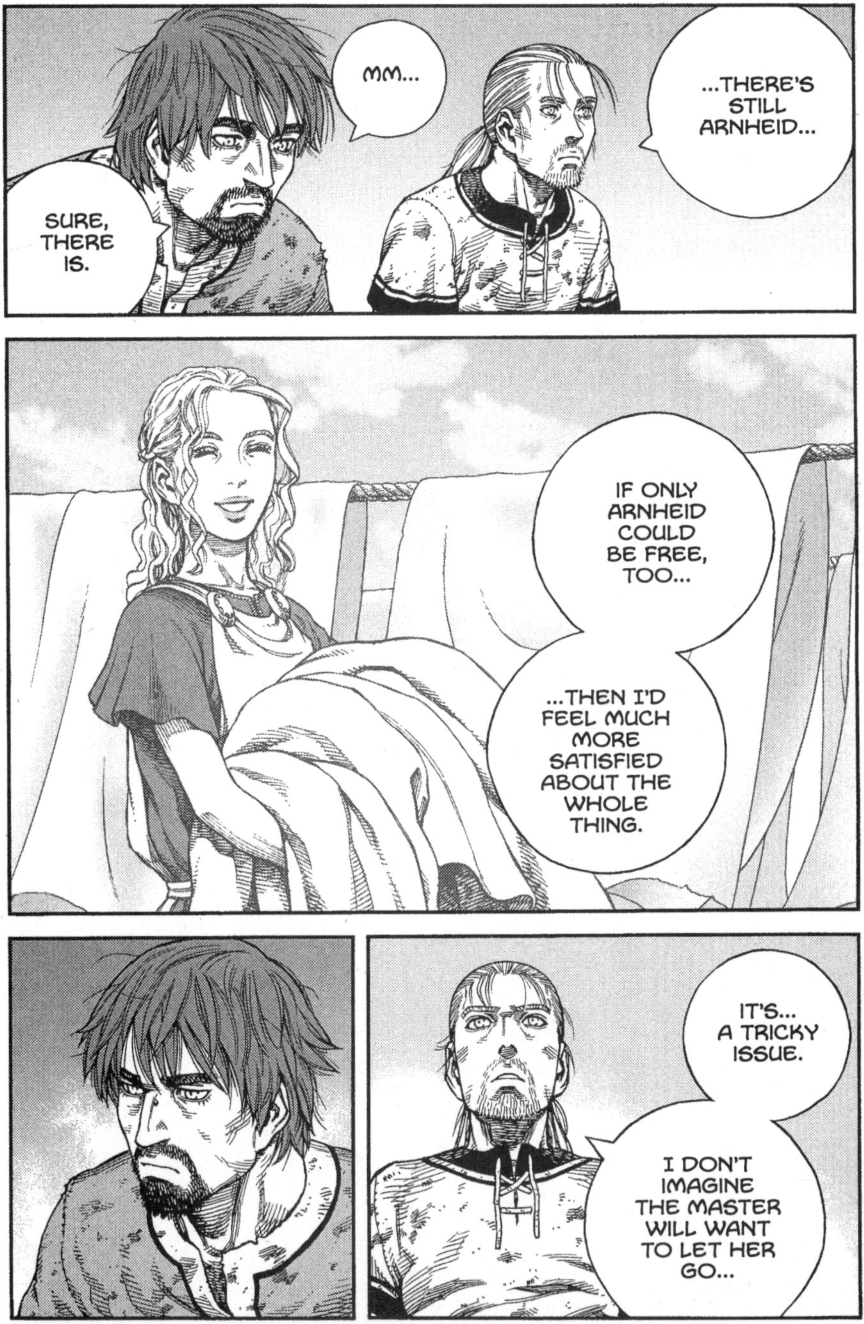
...THERE'S STILL ARNHEID...
MM...
SURE, THERE IS.
IF ONLY ARNHEID COULD BE FREE, TOO...
...THEN I'D FEEL MUCH MORE SATISFIED ABOUT THE WHOLE THING.
IT'S... A TRICKY ISSUE.
I DON'T IMAGINE THE MASTER WILL WANT TO LET HER GO...

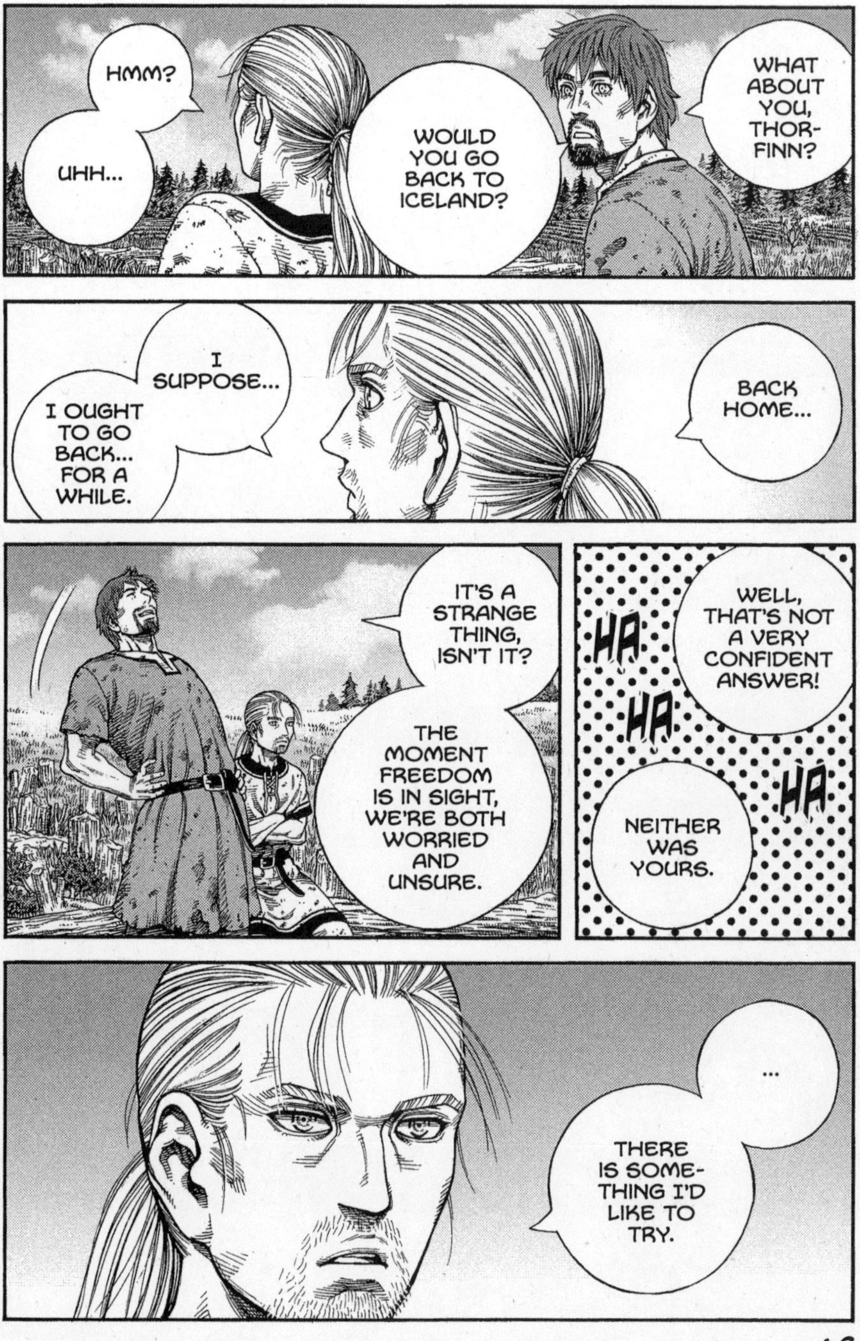
WHAT ABOUT YOU, THORFINN?
WOULD YOU GO BACK TO ICELAND?
HMM?
UHH...
BACK HOME...
I SUPPOSE...
I OUGHT TO GO BACK... FOR A WHILE.
WELL, THAT'S NOT A VERY CONFIDENT ANSWER!
HA HA HA
NEITHER WAS YOURS.
IT'S A STRANGE THING, ISN'T IT?
THE MOMENT FREEDOM IS IN SIGHT, WE'RE BOTH WORRIED AND UNSURE.
...
THERE IS SOMETHING I'D LIKE TO TRY.

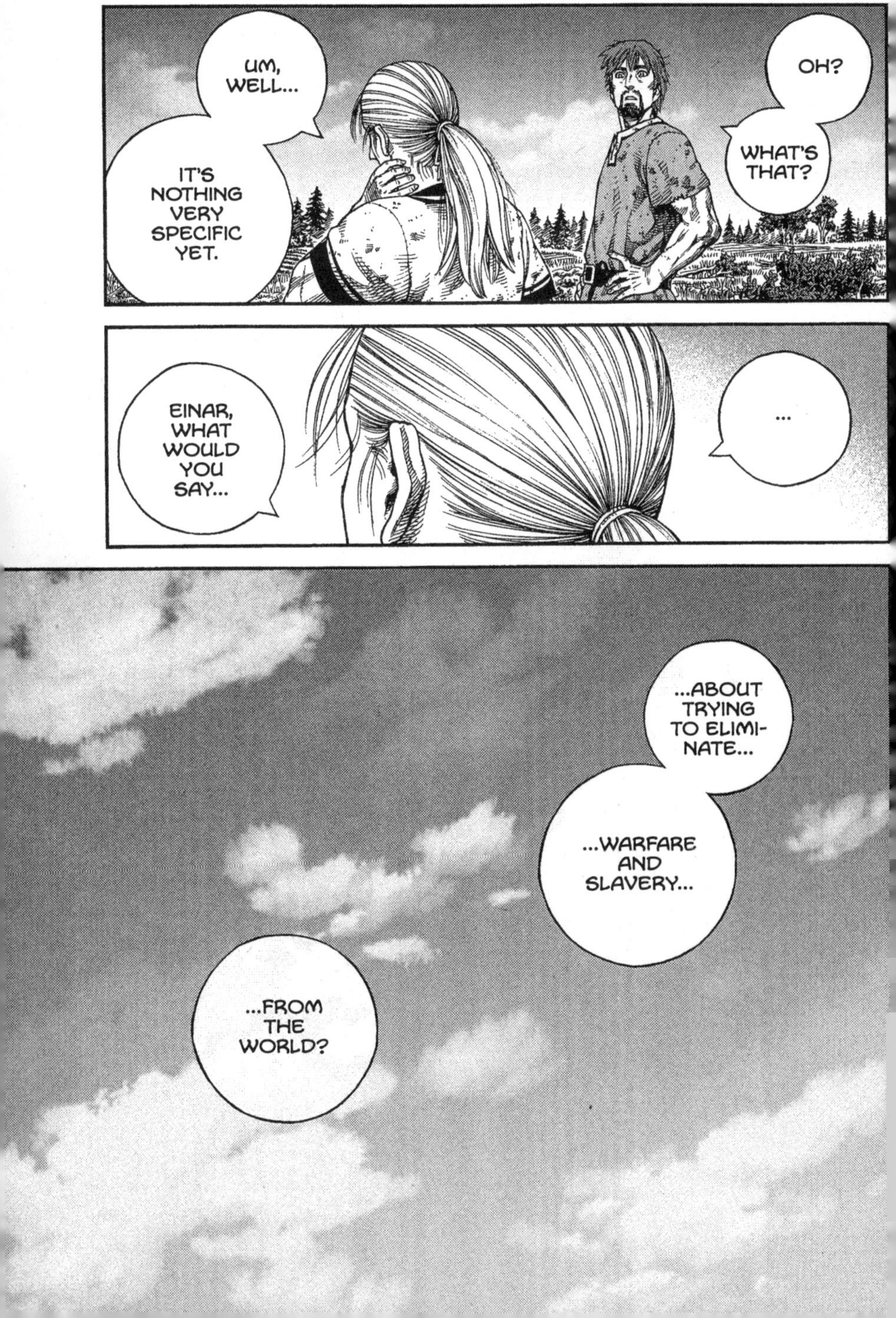
OH?
WHAT'S THAT?
UM, WELL...
IT'S NOTHING VERY SPECIFIC YET.
...
EINAR, WHAT WOULD YOU SAY...
...ABOUT TRYING TO ELIMI-NATE...
...WARFARE AND SLAVERY...
...FROM THE WORLD?

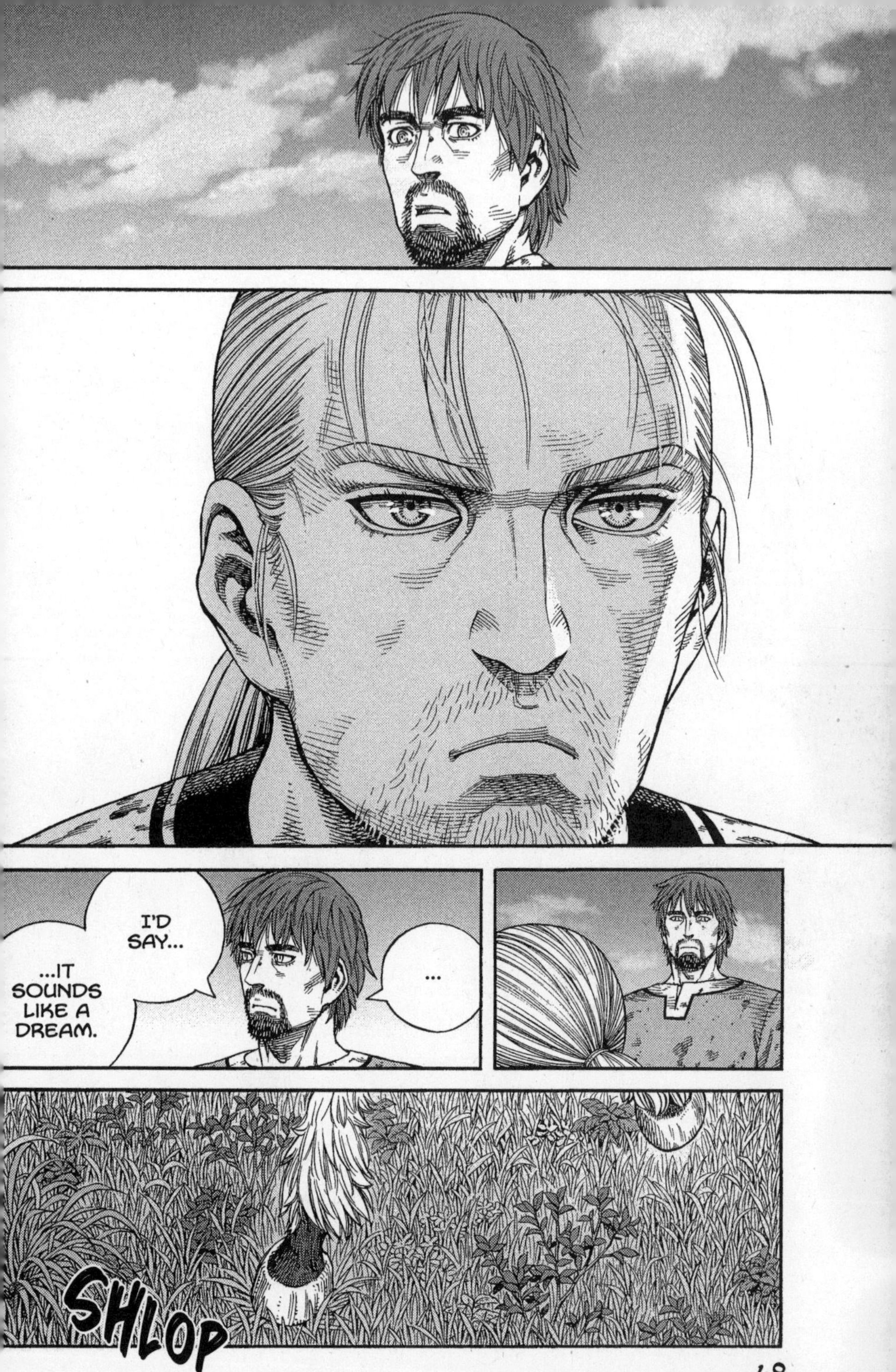

...
I'D SAY...
...IT SOUNDS LIKE A DREAM.
SHLOP

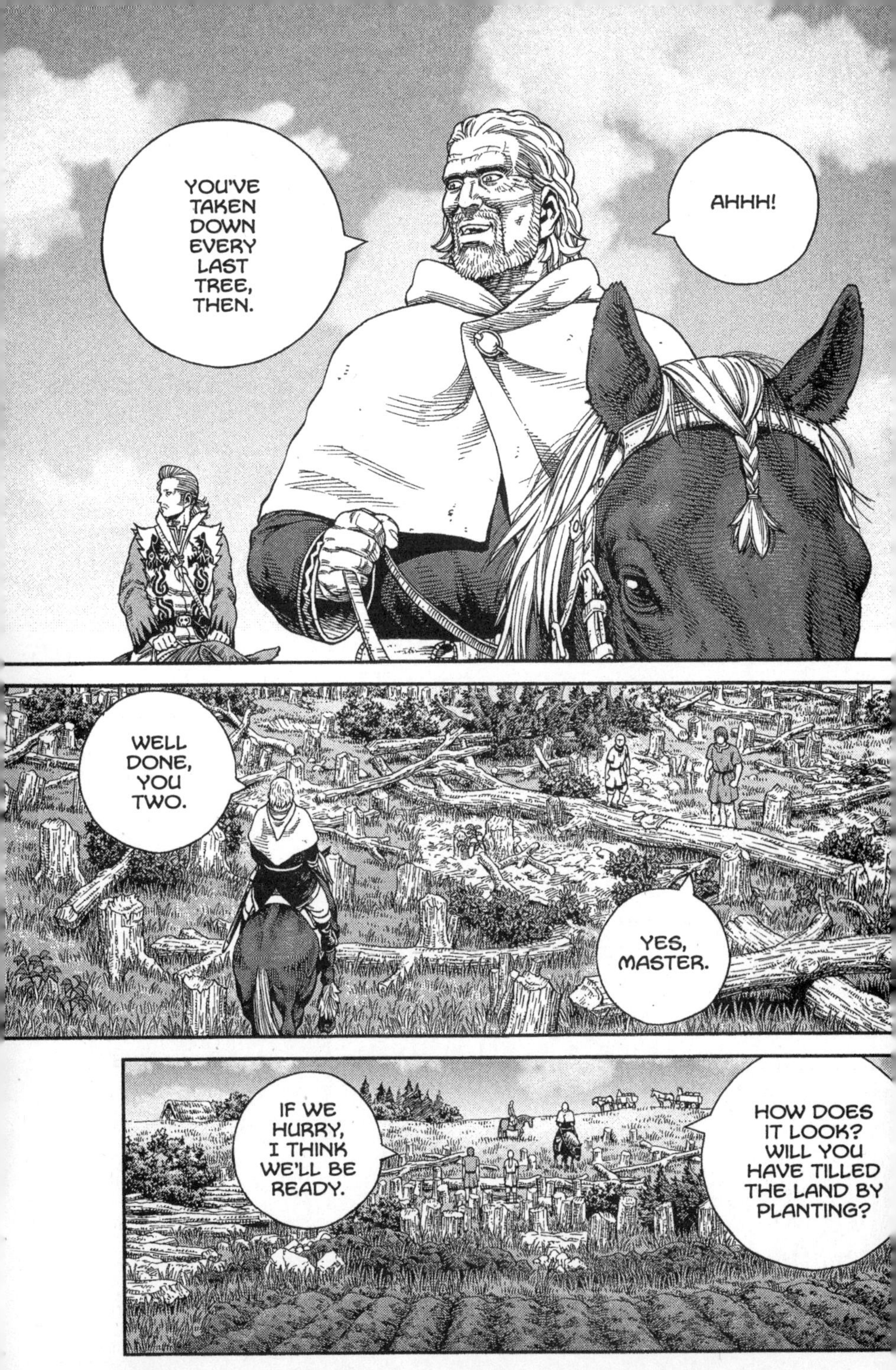
AHHH!
YOU'VE TAKEN DOWN EVERY LAST TREE, THEN.
WELL DONE, YOU TWO.
YES, MASTER.
HOW DOES IT LOOK? WILL YOU HAVE TILLED THE LAND BY PLANTING?
IF WE HURRY, I THINK WE'LL BE READY.

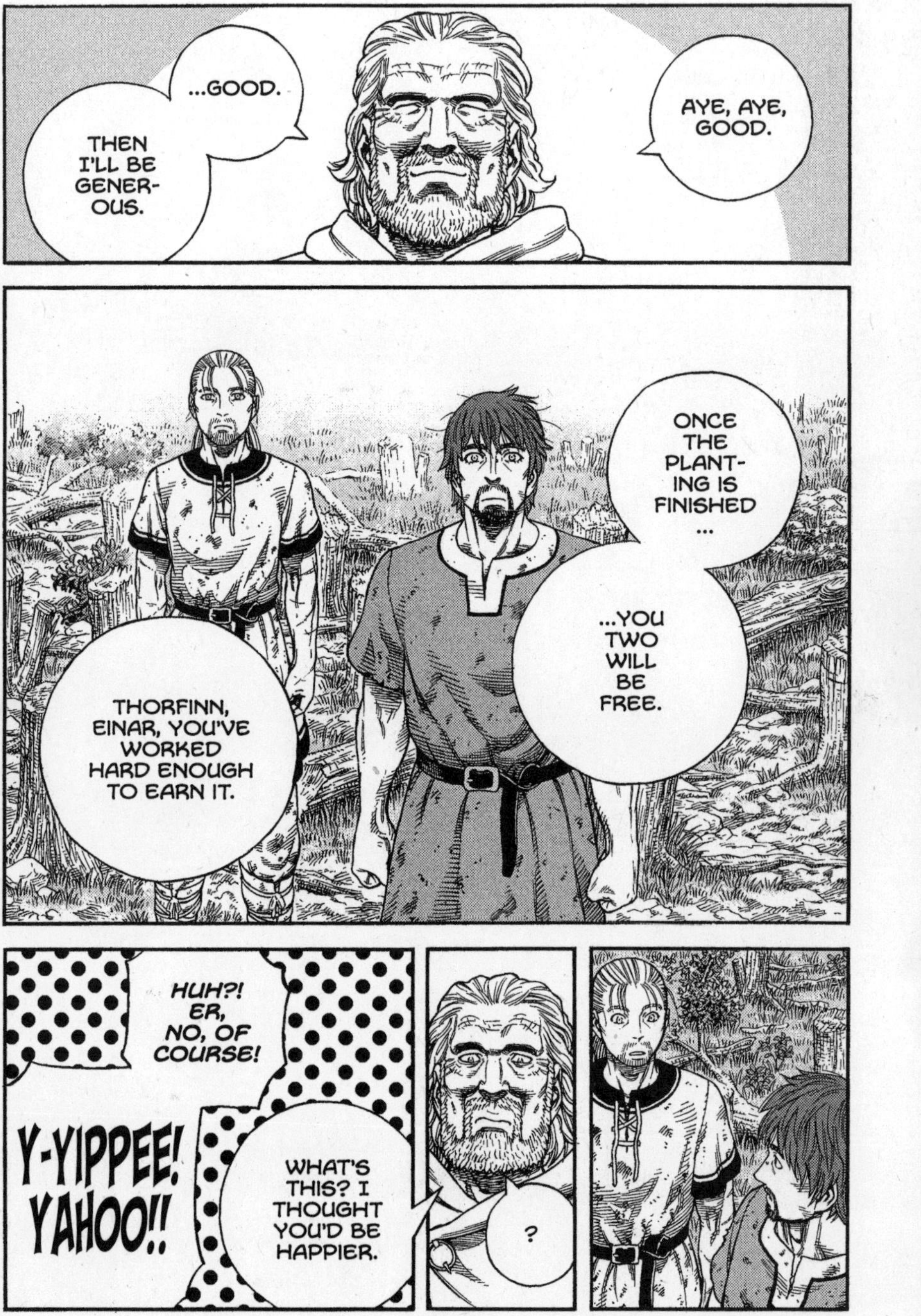
AYE, AYE, GOOD.
...GOOD.
THEN I'LL BE GENER-OUS.
ONCE THE PLANT-ING IS FINISHED ...
...YOU TWO WILL BE FREE.
THORFINN, EINAR, YOU'VE WORKED HARD ENOUGH TO EARN IT.
?
WHAT'S THIS? I THOUGHT YOU'D BE HAPPIER.
HUH?! ER, NO, OF COURSE!
Y-YIPPEE! YAHOO!!

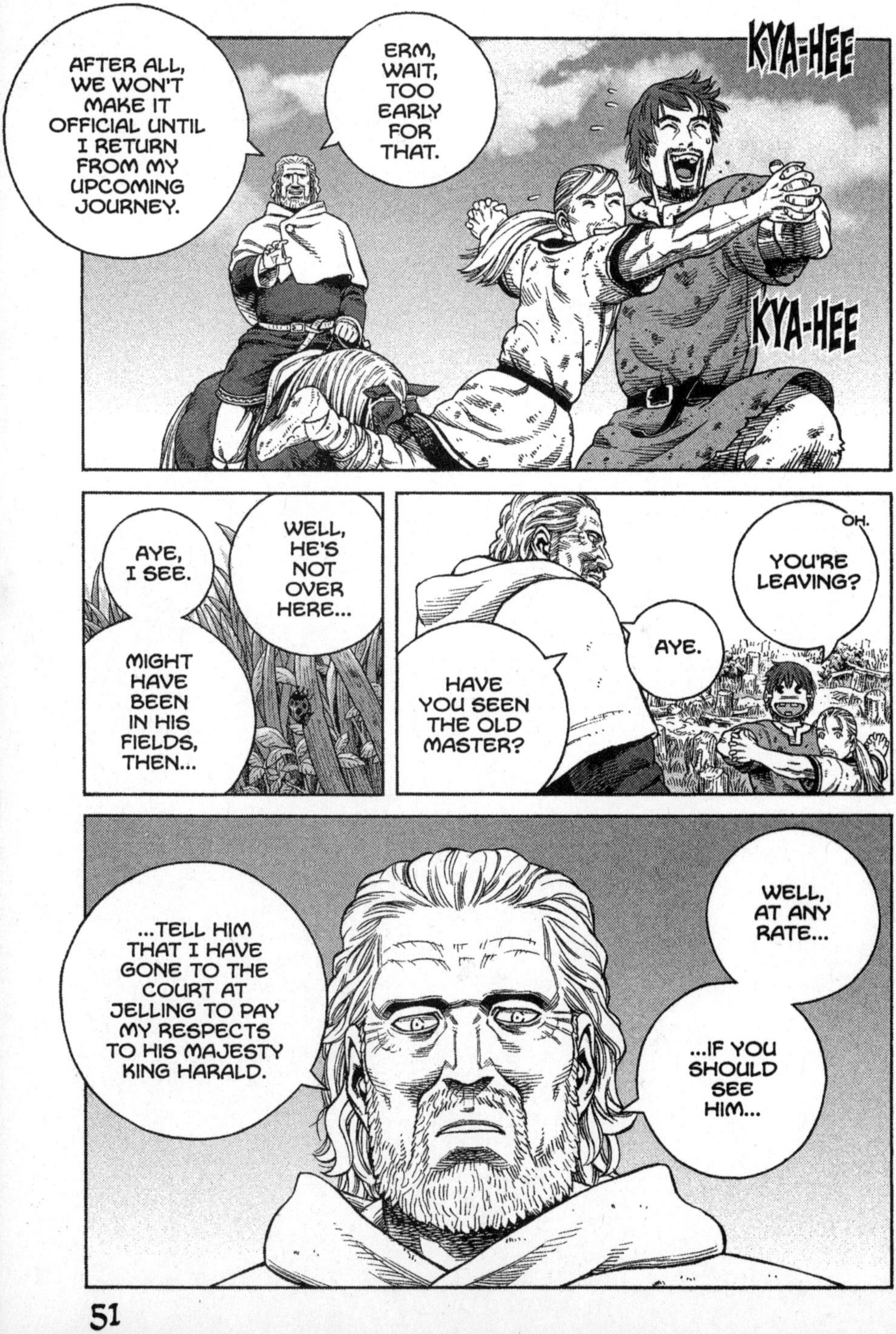
KYA-HEE
ERM, WAIT, TOO EARLY FOR THAT.
AFTER ALL, WE WON'T MAKE IT OFFICIAL UNTIL I RETURN FROM MY UPCOMING JOURNEY.
KYA-HEE
OH.
YOU'RE LEAVING?
AYE.
HAVE YOU SEEN THE OLD MASTER?
WELL, HE'S NOT OVER HERE...
AYE, I SEE.
MIGHT HAVE BEEN IN HIS FIELDS, THEN...
WELL, AT ANY RATE...
...IF YOU SHOULD SEE HIM...
...TELL HIM THAT I HAVE GONE TO THE COURT AT JELLING TO PAY MY RESPECTS TO HIS MAJESTY KING HARALD.

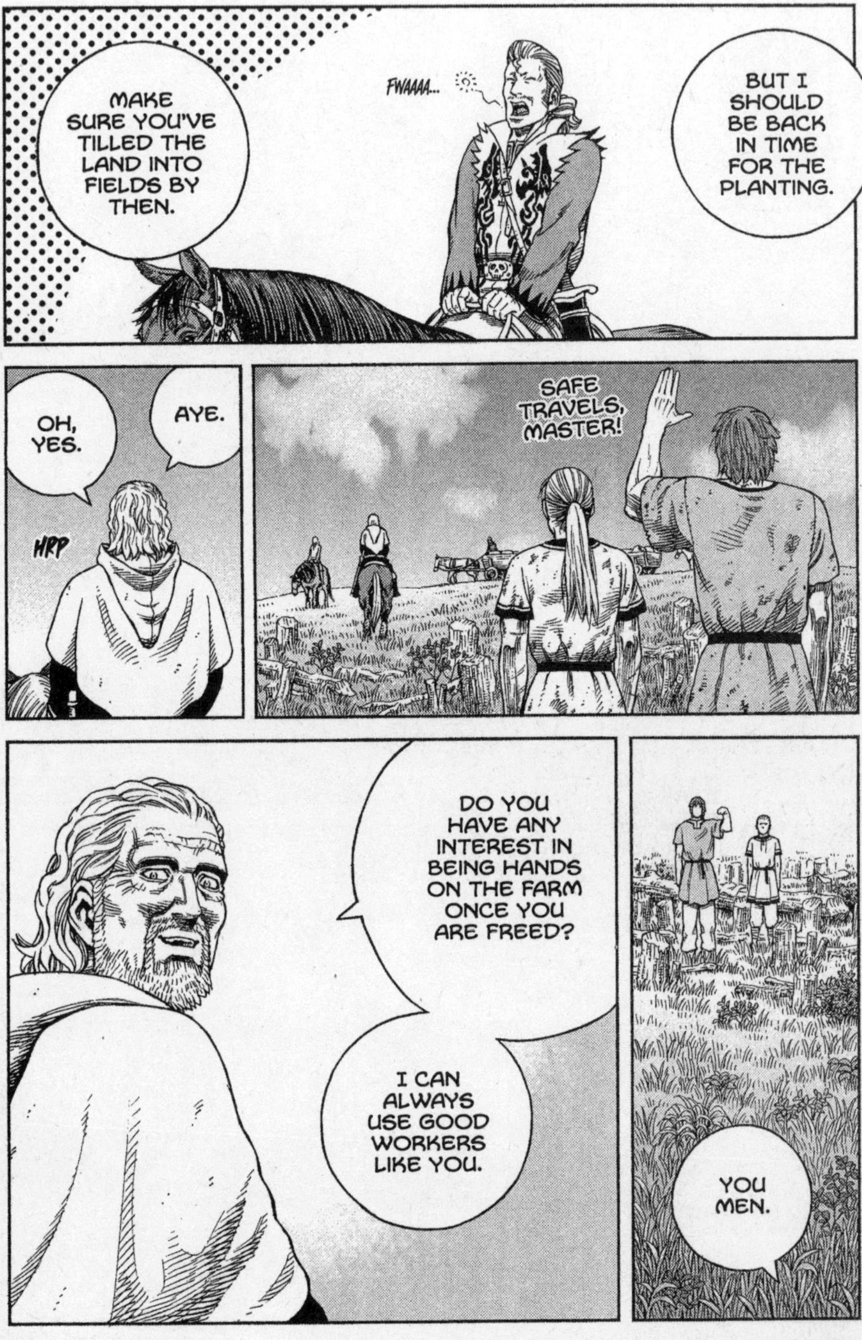
BUT I SHOULD BE BACK IN TIME FOR THE PLANTING.
FWAAAA...
MAKE SURE YOU'VE TILLED THE LAND INTO FIELDS BY THEN.
SAFE TRAVELS, MASTER!
AYE.
OH, YES.
HRP
YOU MEN.
DO YOU HAVE ANY INTEREST IN BEING HANDS ON THE FARM ONCE YOU ARE FREED?
I CAN ALWAYS USE GOOD WORKERS LIKE YOU.

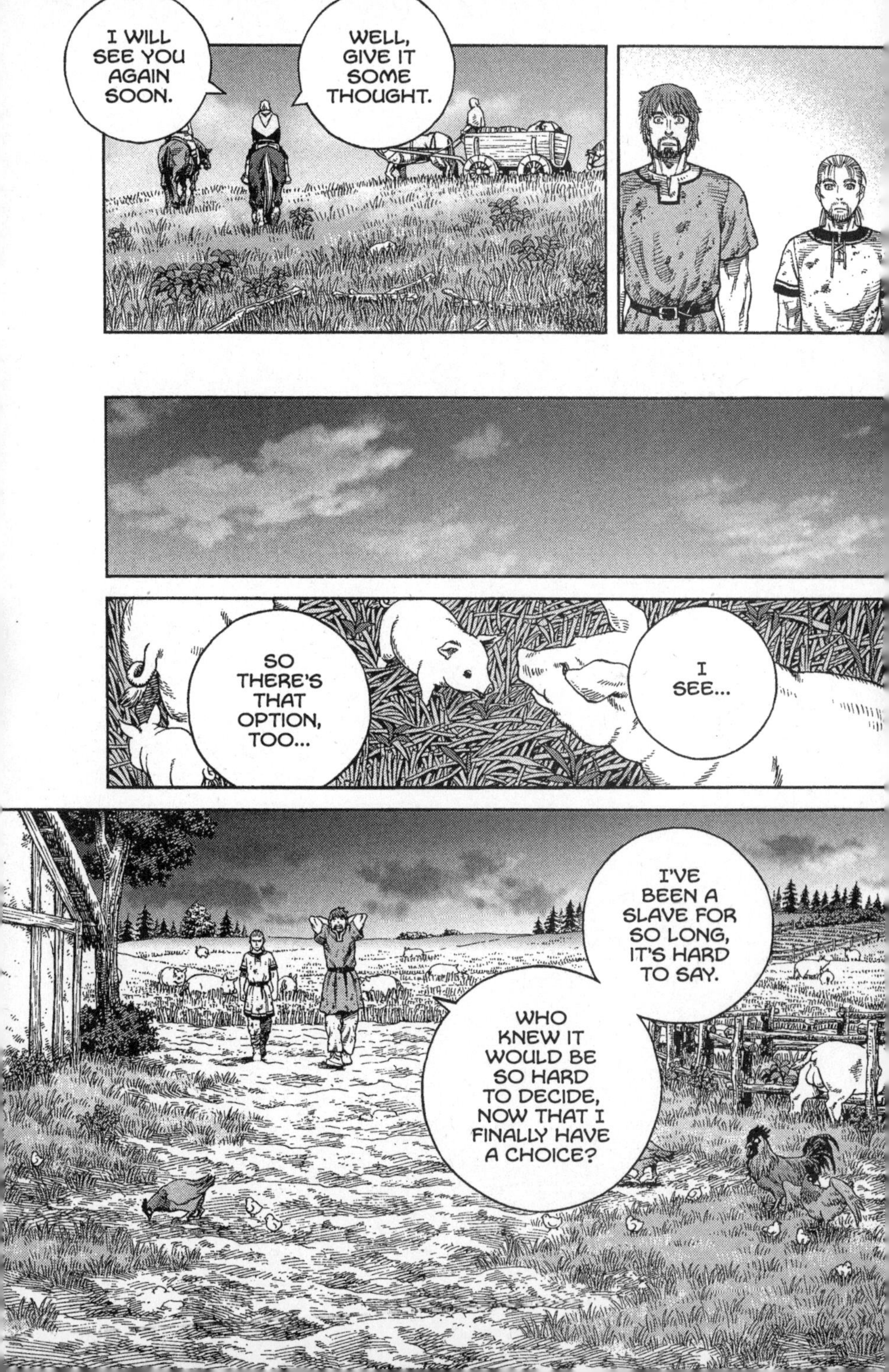
WELL, GIVE IT SOME THOUGHT.
I WILL SEE YOU AGAIN SOON.
I SEE...
SO THERE'S THAT OPTION, TOO...
I'VE BEEN A SLAVE FOR SO LONG, IT'S HARD TO SAY.
WHO KNEW IT WOULD BE SO HARD TO DECIDE, NOW THAT I FINALLY HAVE A CHOICE?

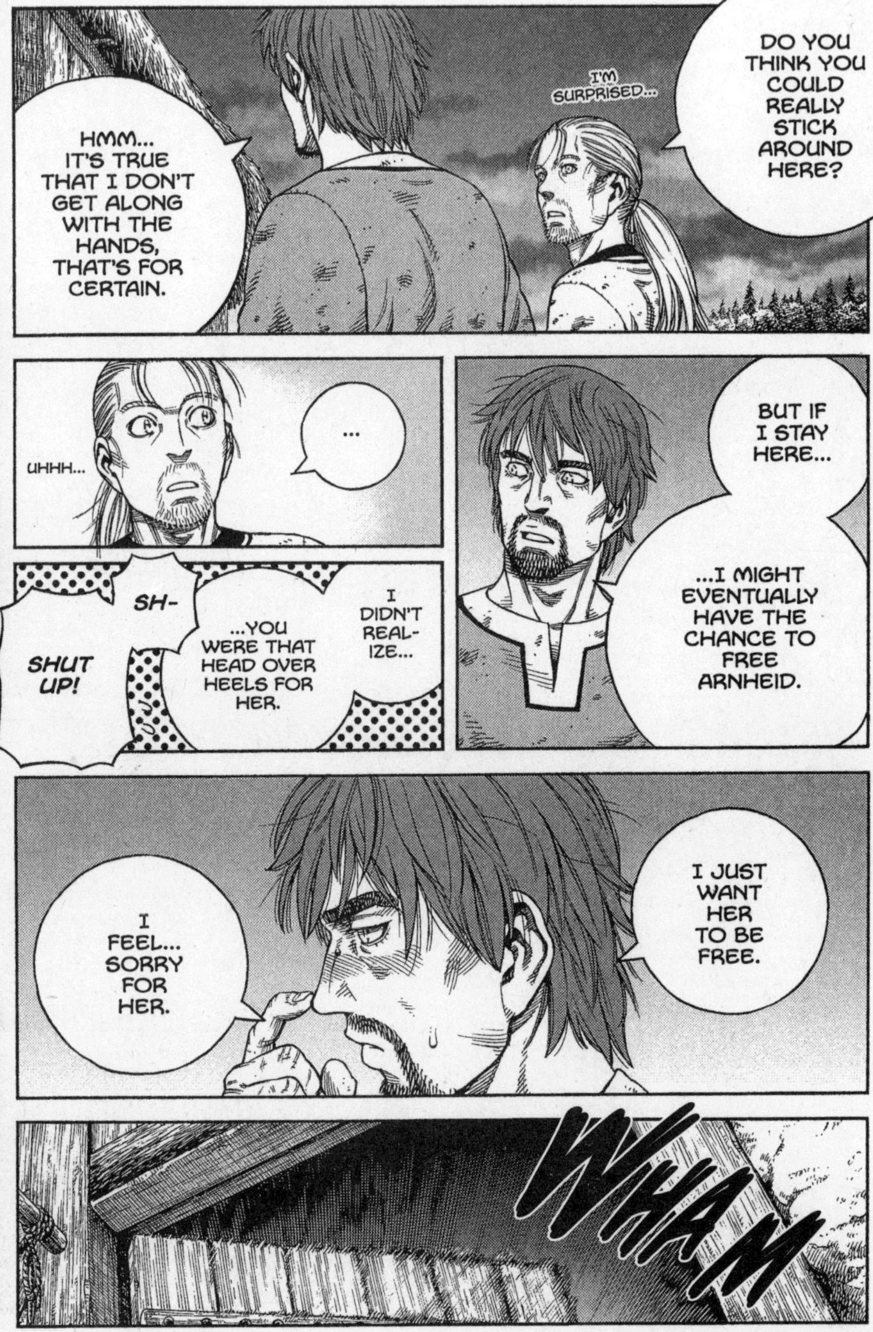
DO YOU THINK YOU COULD REALLY STICK AROUND HERE?
I'M SURPRISED...
HMM... IT'S TRUE THAT I DON'T GET ALONG WITH THE HANDS, THAT'S FOR CERTAIN.
BUT IF I STAY HERE...
...I MIGHT EVENTUALLY HAVE THE CHANCE TO FREE ARNHEID.
...
UHHH...
I DIDN'T REAL-IZE...
...YOU WERE THAT HEAD OVER HEELS FOR HER.
SH-
SHUT UP!
I JUST WANT HER TO BE FREE.
I FEEL... SORRY FOR HER.
WHAM

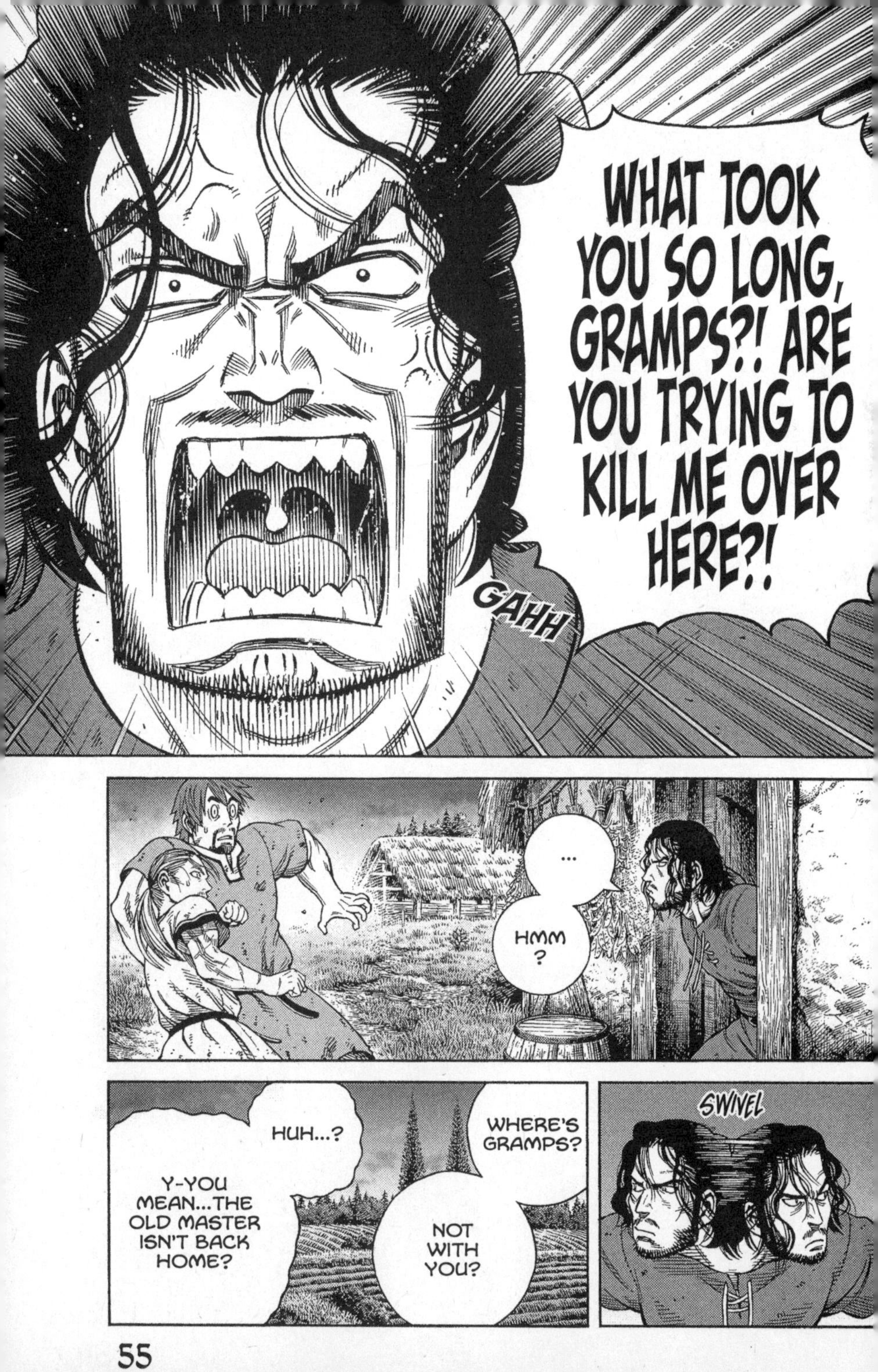
WHAT TOOK YOU SO LONG, GRAMPS?! ARE YOU TRYING TO KILL ME OVER HERE?!
GAHH
...
HMM?
SWIVEL
WHERE'S GRAMPS?
NOT WITH YOU?
HUH...?
Y-YOU MEAN...THE OLD MASTER ISN'T BACK HOME?

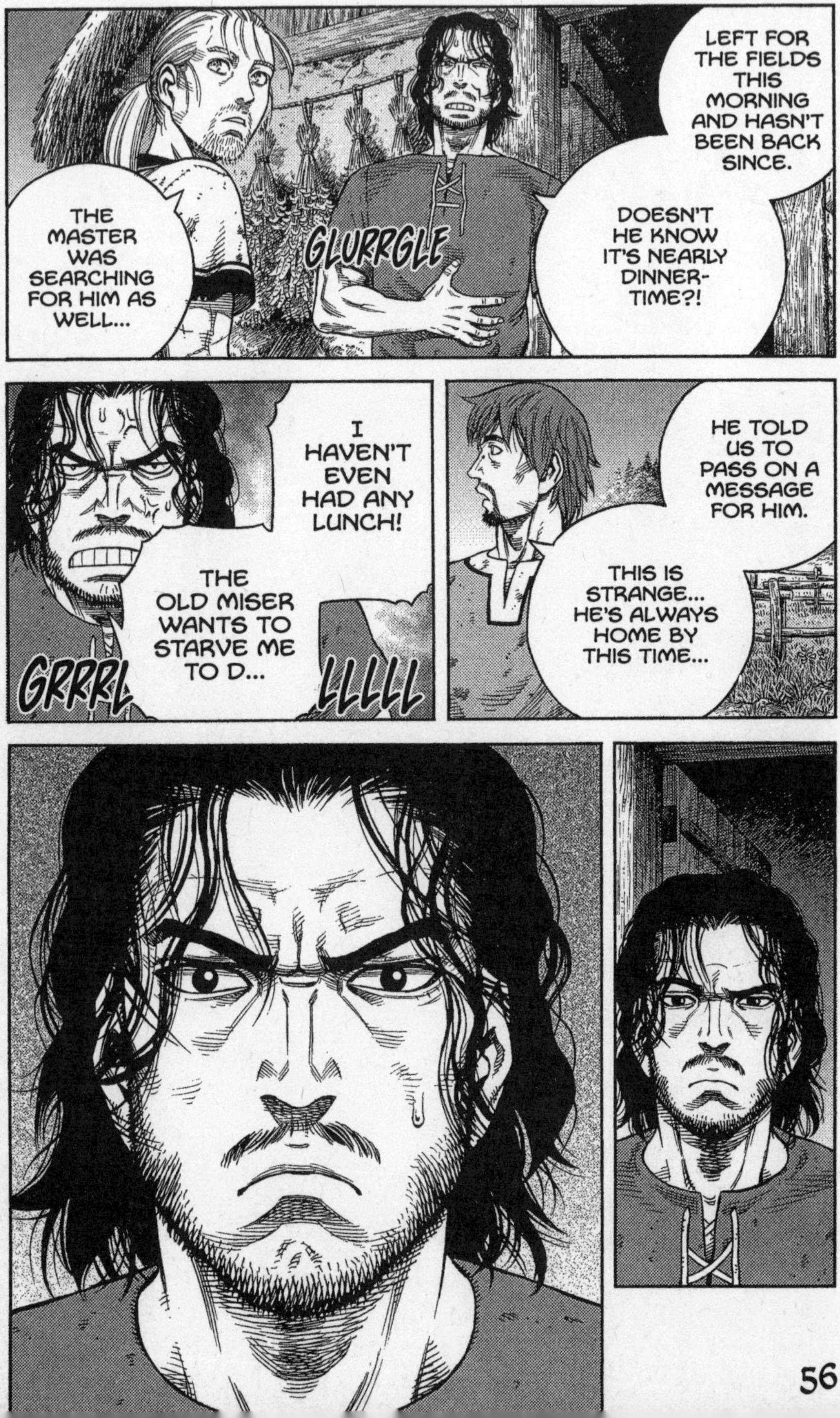
LEFT FOR THE FIELDS THIS MORNING AND HASN'T BEEN BACK SINCE.
DOESN'T HE KNOW IT'S NEARLY DINNER-TIME?!
GLURRGLE
THE MASTER WAS SEARCHING FOR HIM AS WELL...
HE TOLD US TO PASS ON A MESSAGE FOR HIM.
THIS IS STRANGE... HE'S ALWAYS HOME BY THIS TIME...
I HAVEN'T EVEN HAD ANY LUNCH!
THE OLD MISER WANTS TO STARVE ME TO D...
GRRRL
LLLLL

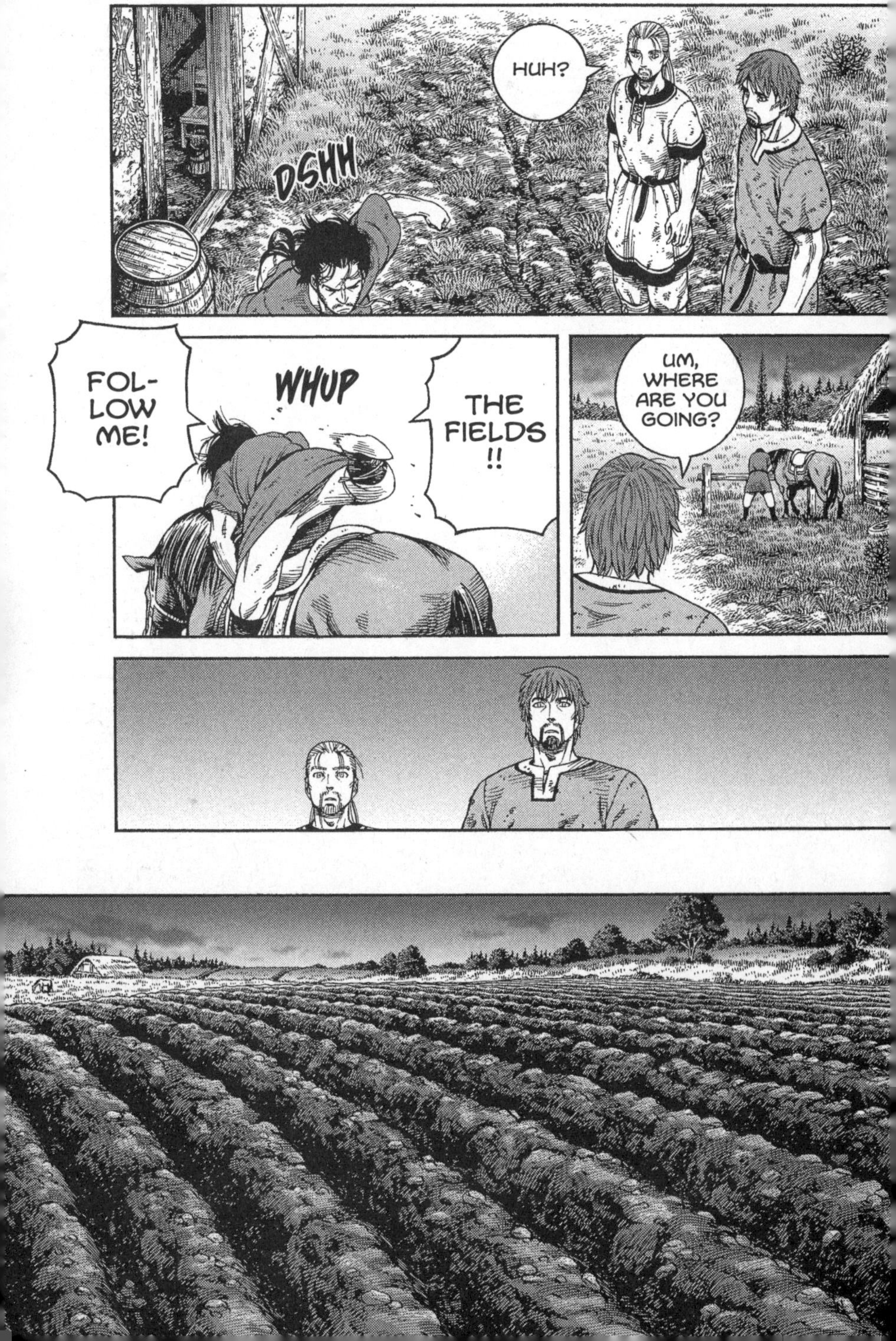
HUH?
DSHH
UM, WHERE ARE YOU GOING?
THE FIELDS !!
WHUP
FOL-LOW ME!

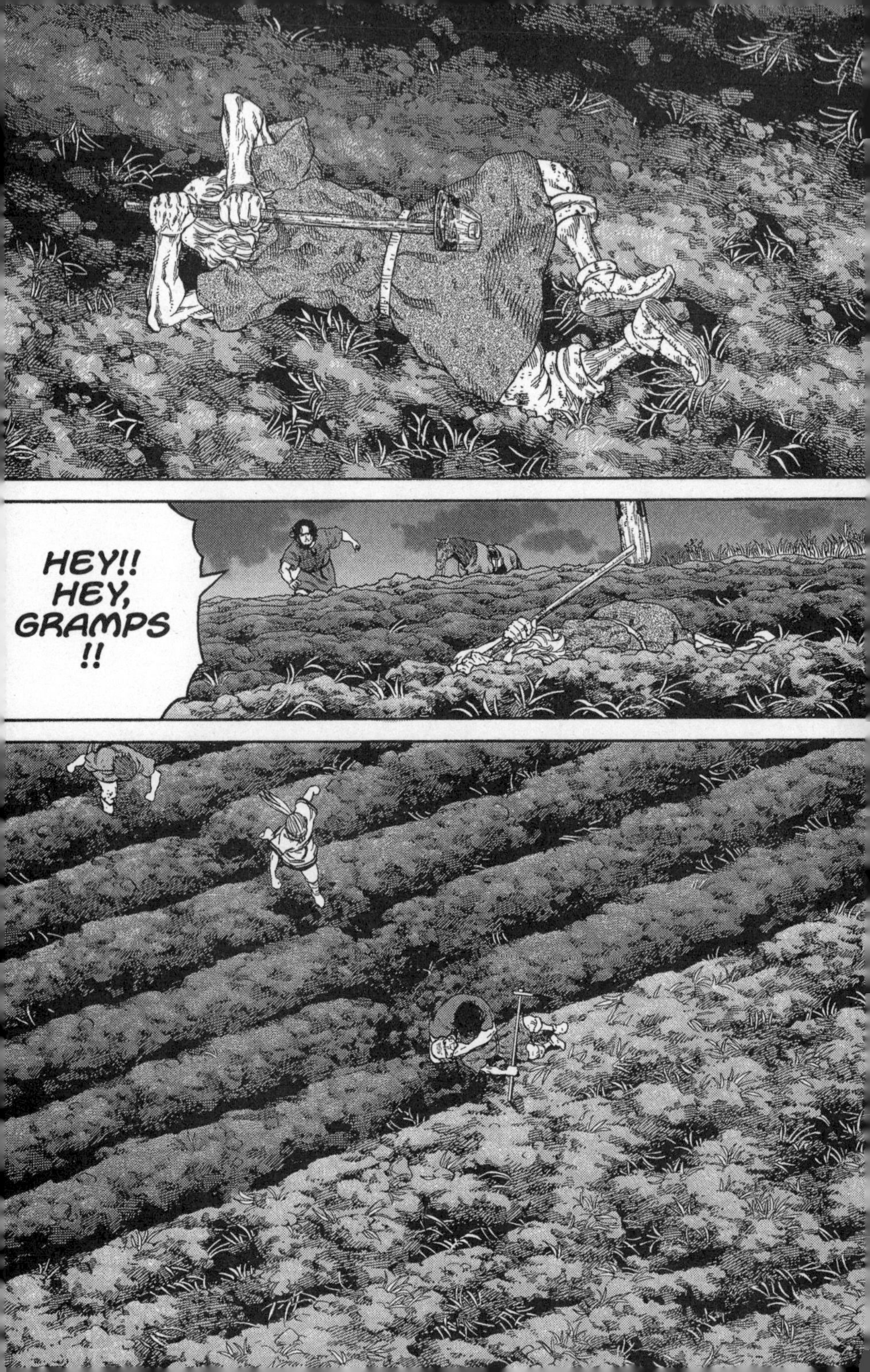
HEY!! HEY, GRAMPS !!

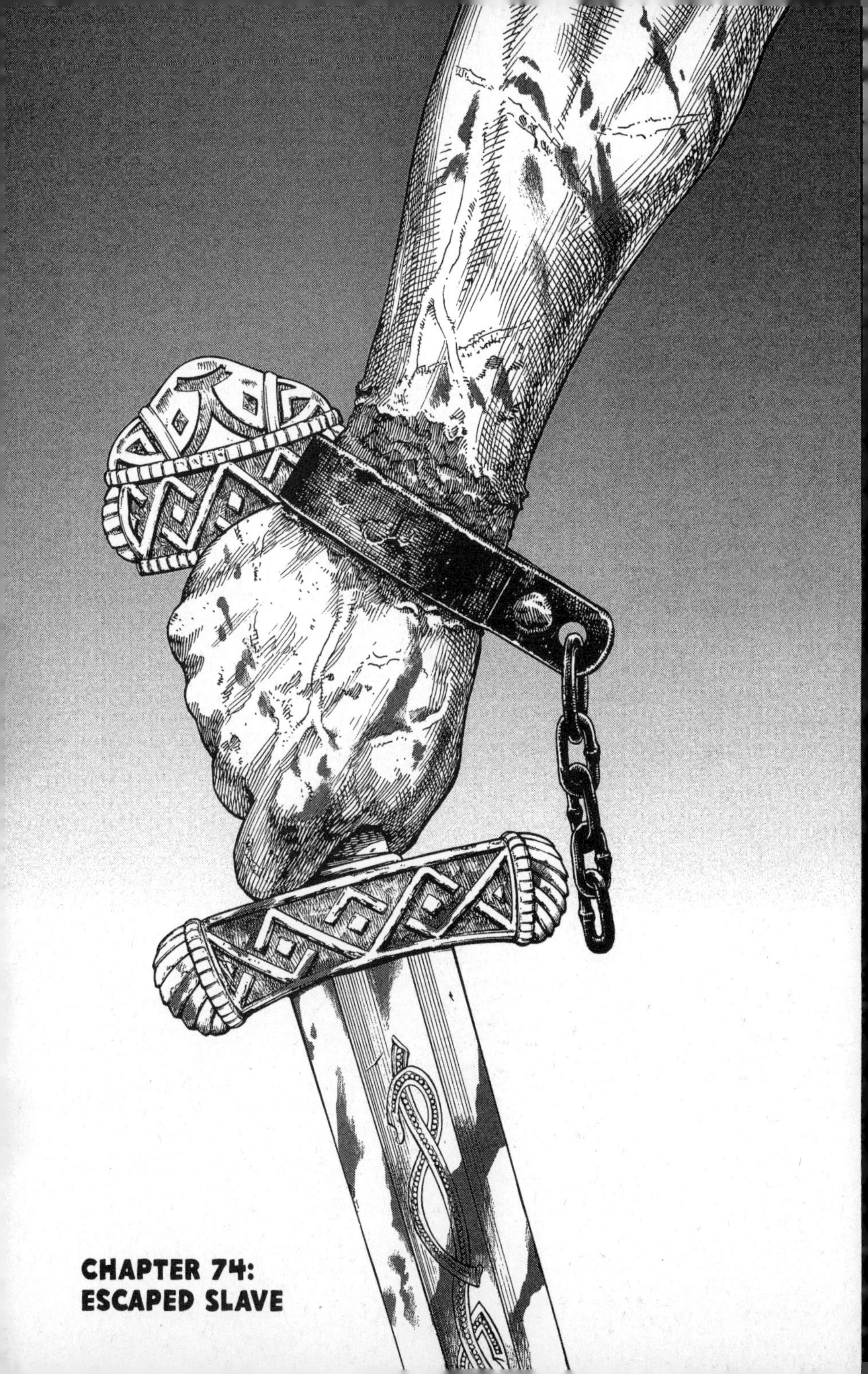

CHAPTER 74: ESCAPED SLAVE

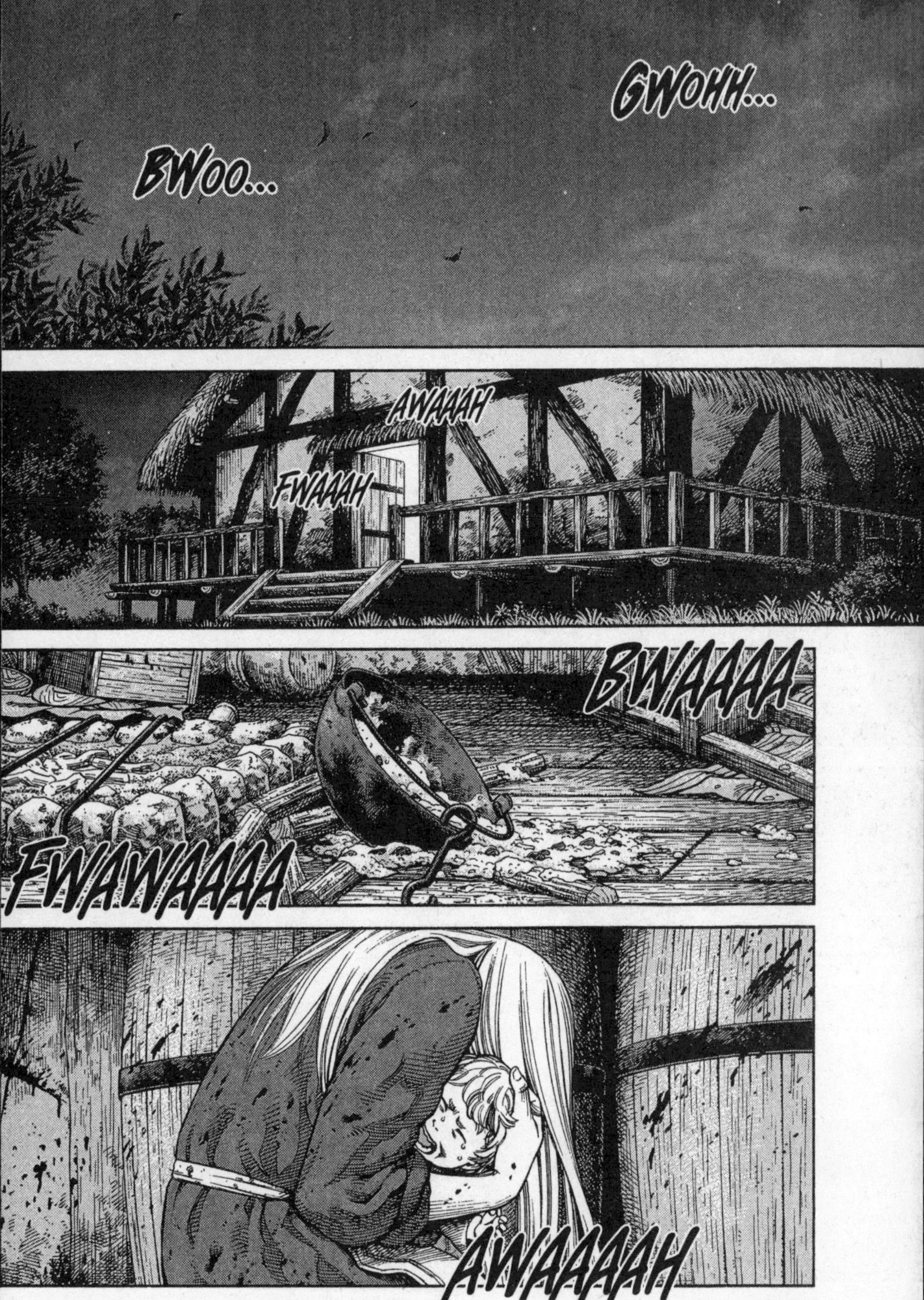
GWOHH...
BWOO...
AWAAAH
FWAAAH
BWAAAA
FWAWAAAA
AWAAAAH

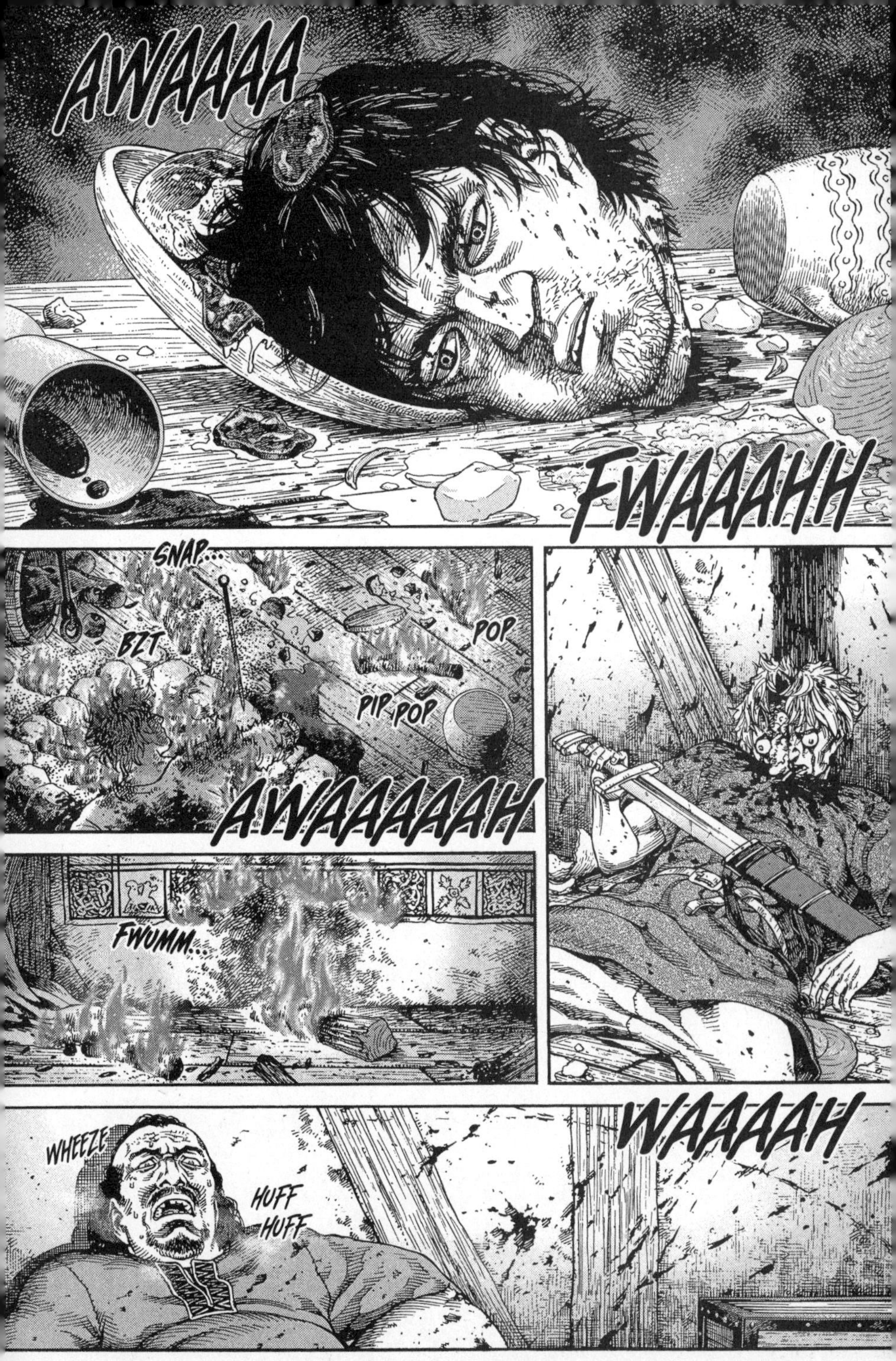
AWAAAA
FWAAAAH
SNAP...
POP
BZT
PIP POP
AWAAAAAAH
FWUMM...
WAAAAH
WHEEZE
HUFF
HUFF

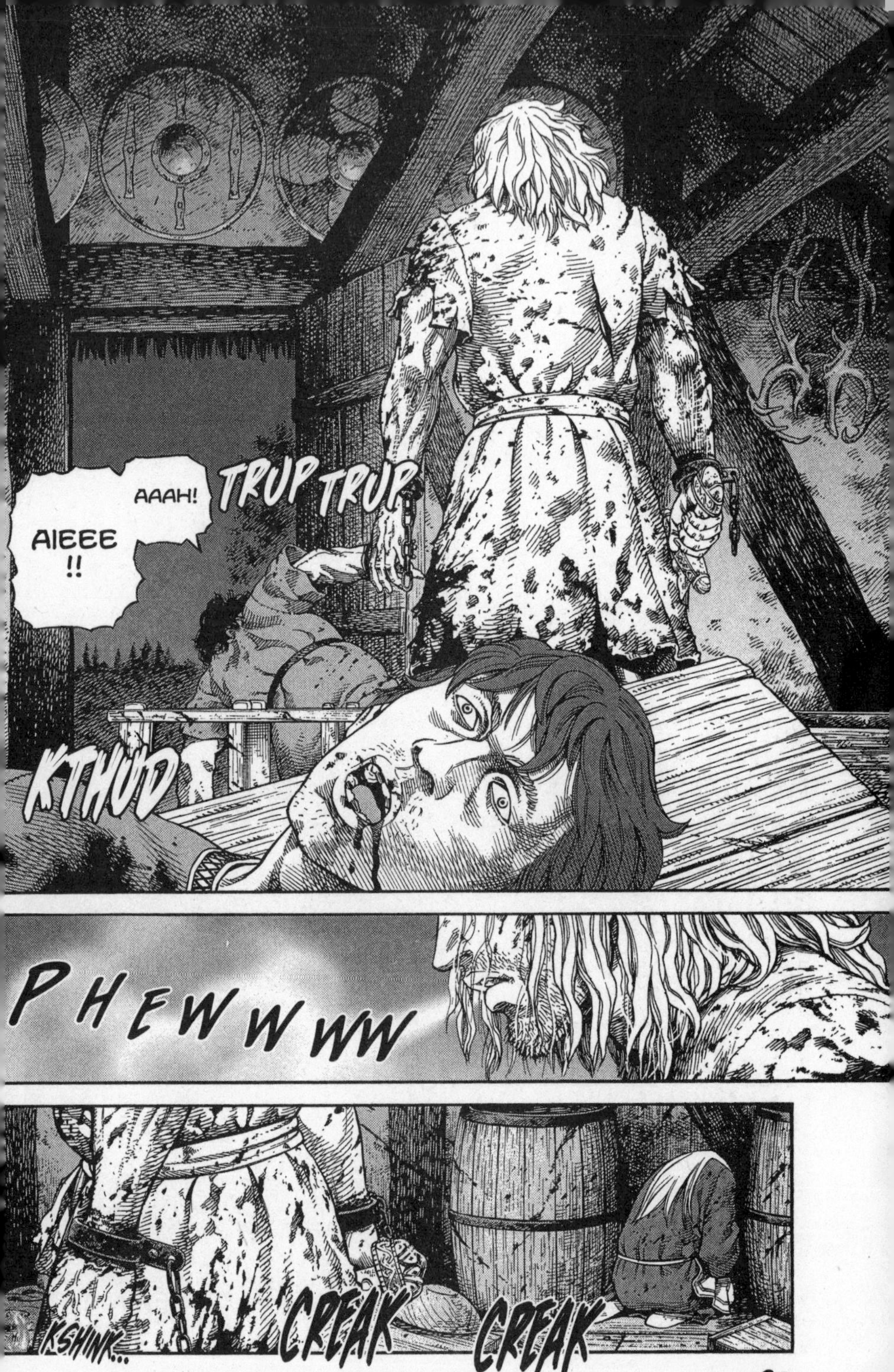
TRUP TRUP
AAAH! AIEEE !!
KTHUD
PHEWWWW
CREAK
CREAK
KSHINK...

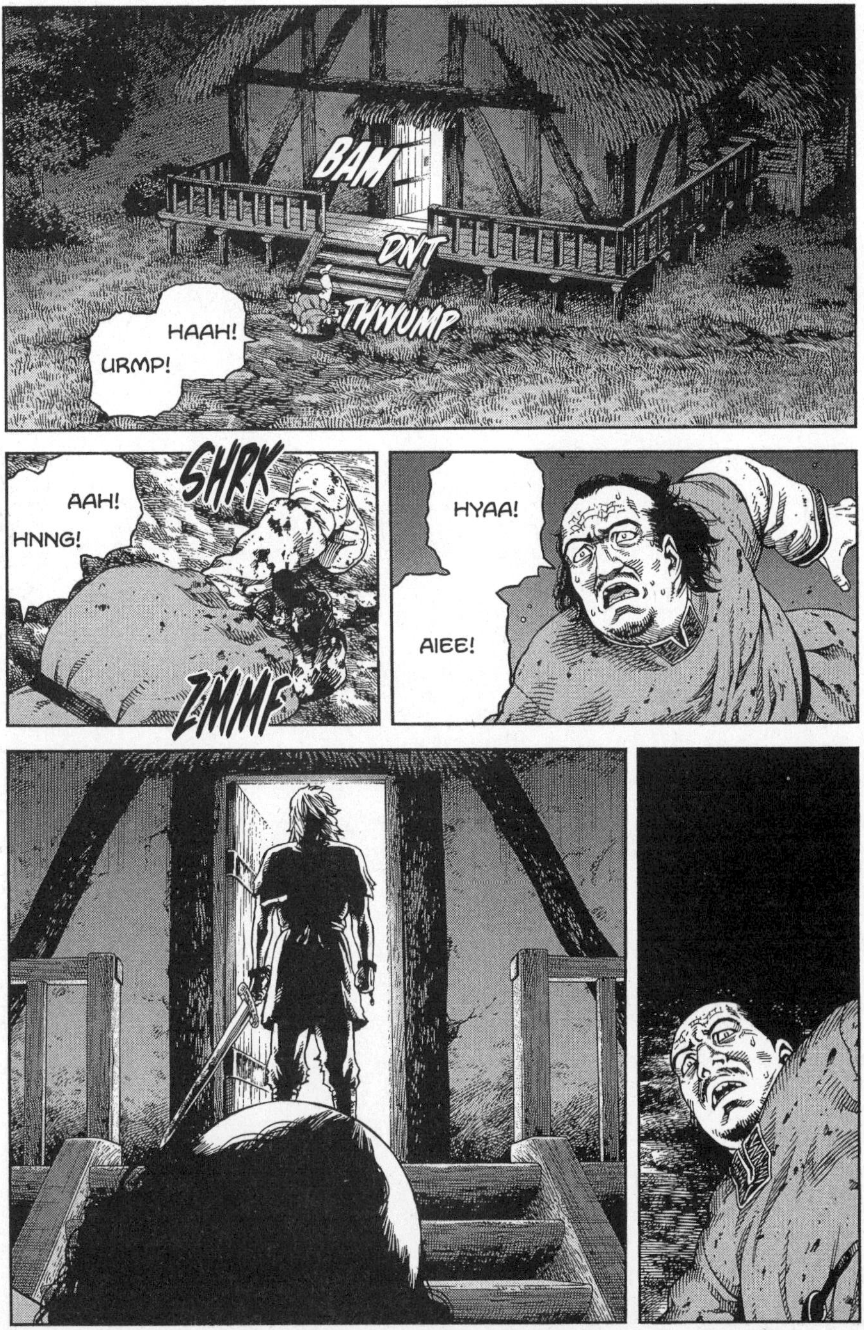
BAM
DNT
THWUMP
HAAH!
URMP!
HYAA!
AIEE!
SHRK
AAH!
HNNG!
ZMMF

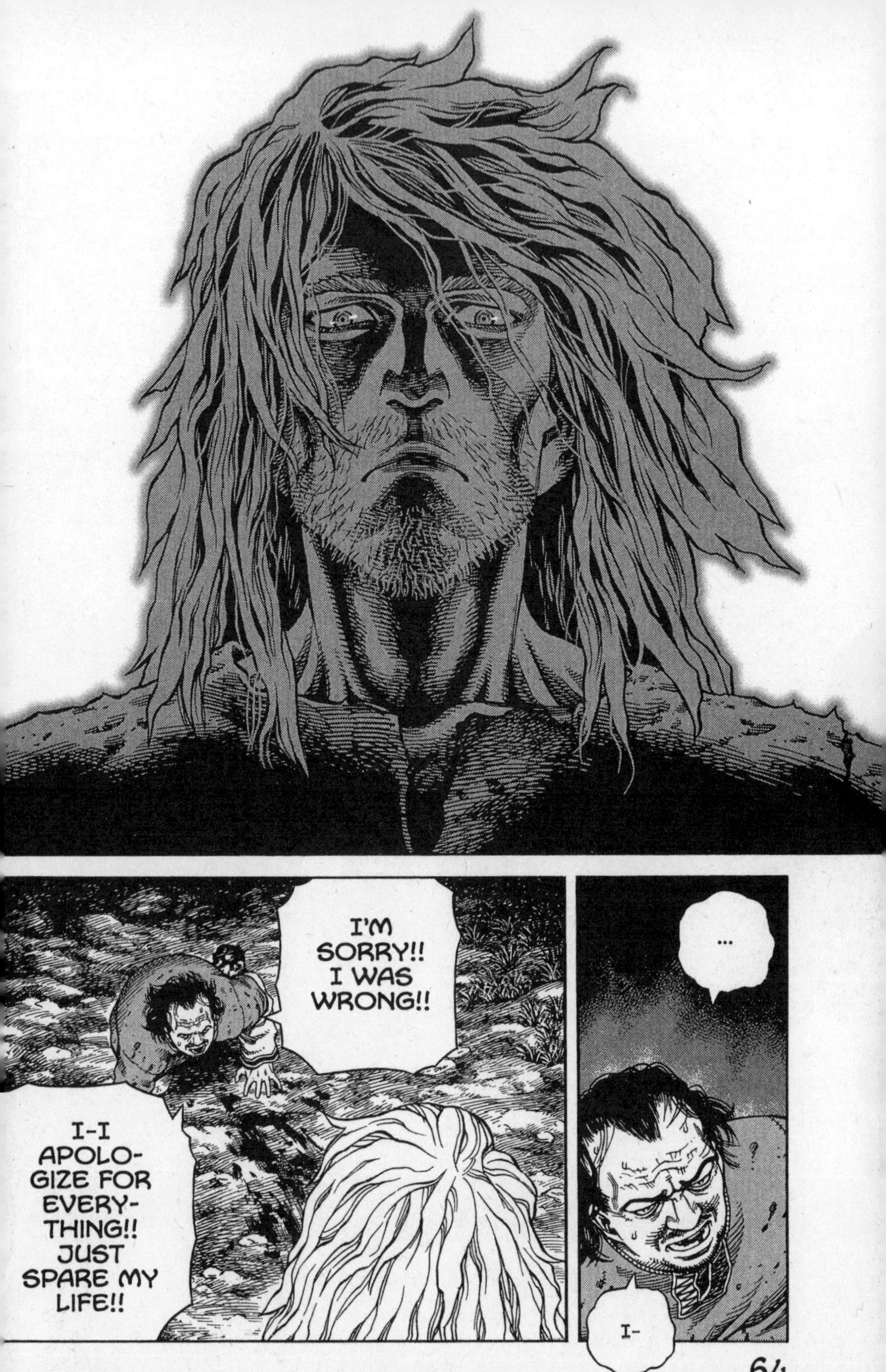
...
I-
I'M SORRY!! I WAS WRONG!!
I-I APOLOGIZE FOR EVERYTHING!! JUST SPARE MY LIFE!!

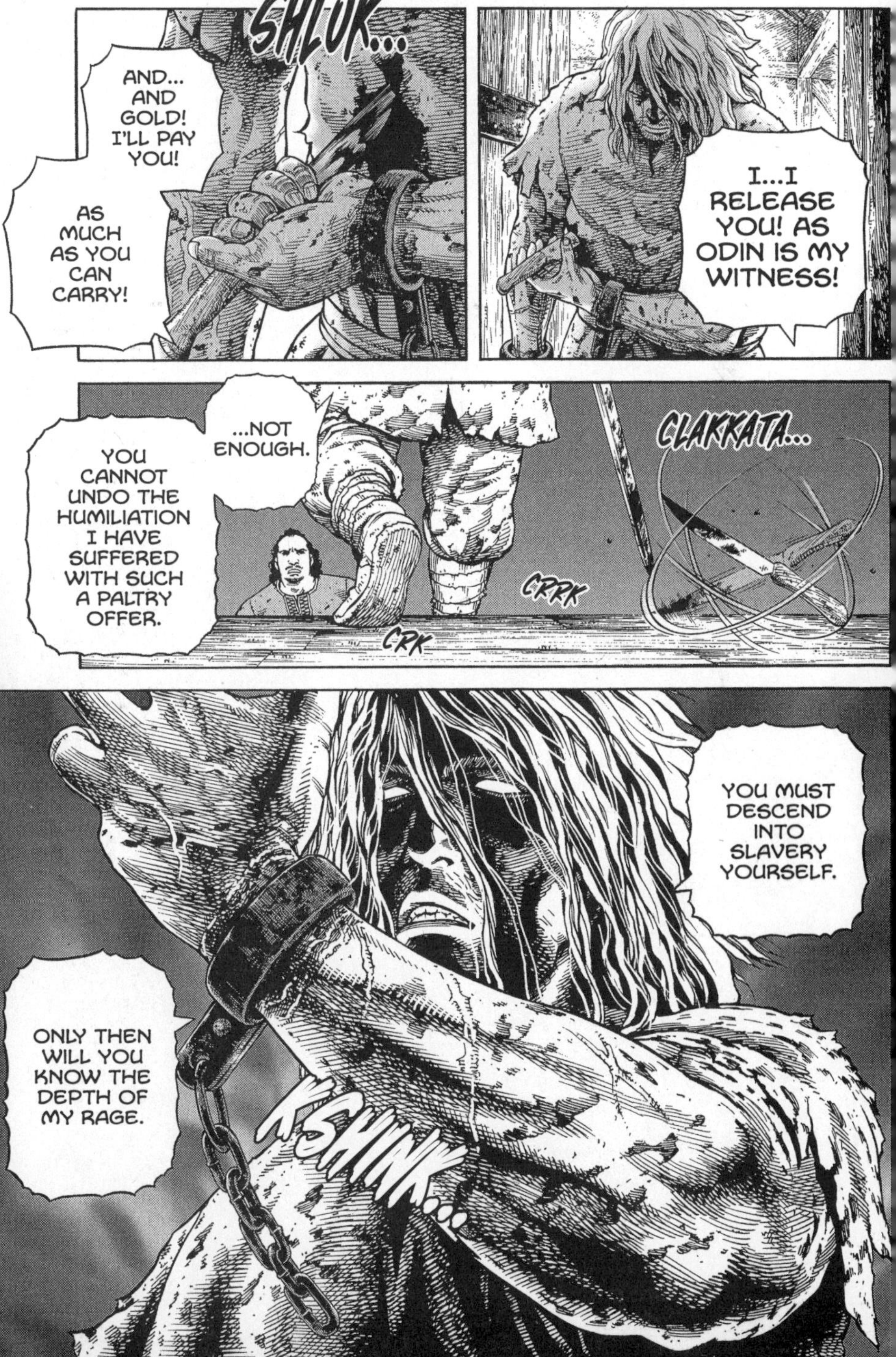
I...I RELEASE YOU! AS ODIN IS MY WITNESS!
SHLUK...
AND... AND GOLD! I'LL PAY YOU!
AS MUCH AS YOU CAN CARRY!
CLAKKATA...
...NOT ENOUGH.
YOU CANNOT UNDO THE HUMILIATION I HAVE SUFFERED WITH SUCH A PALTRY OFFER.
CRRK
CRK
YOU MUST DESCEND INTO SLAVERY YOURSELF.
ONLY THEN WILL YOU KNOW THE DEPTH OF MY RAGE.
K-SHINK...

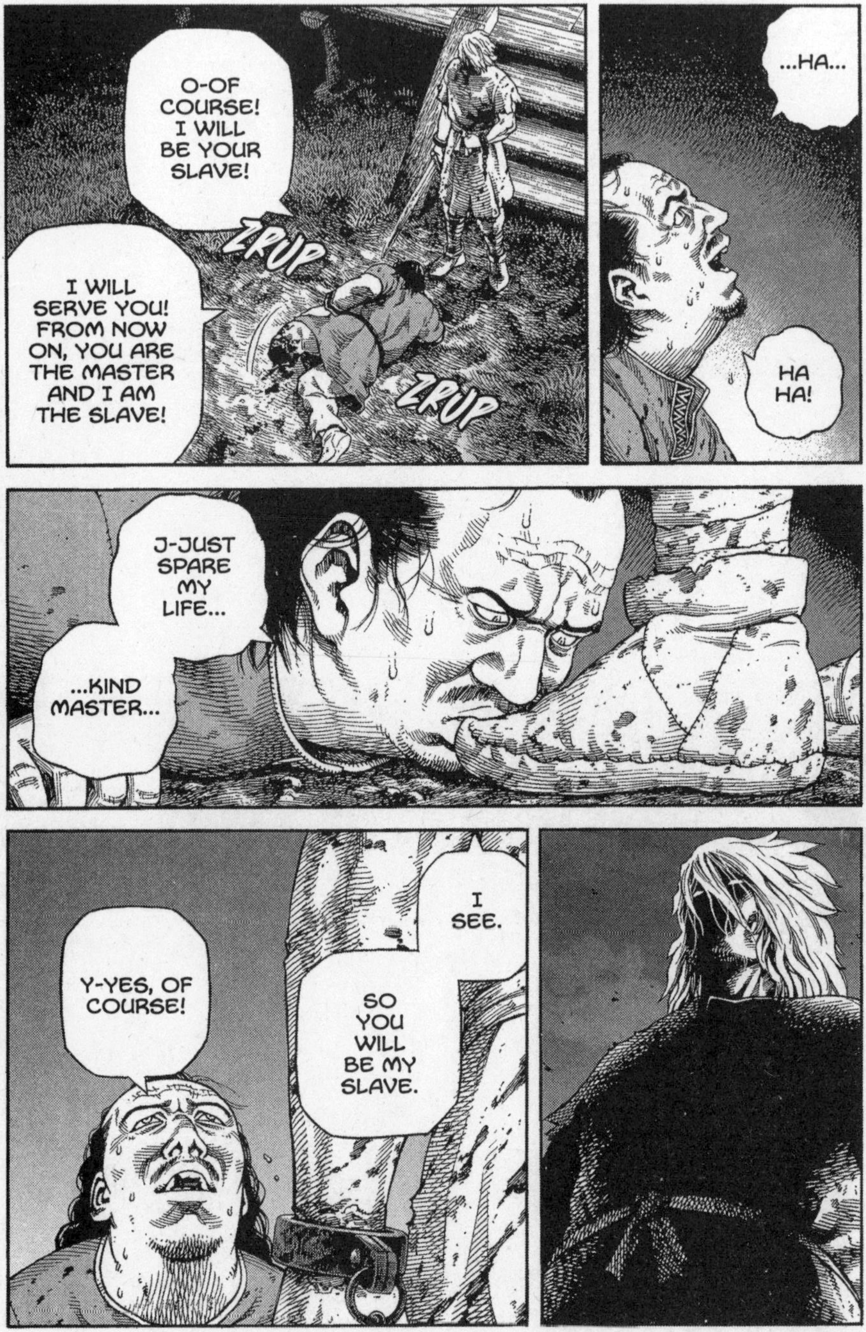
...HA...
HA HA!
O-OF COURSE! I WILL BE YOUR SLAVE!
ZRUP
I WILL SERVE YOU! FROM NOW ON, YOU ARE THE MASTER AND I AM THE SLAVE!
ZRUP
J-JUST SPARE MY LIFE...
...KIND MASTER...
I SEE.
SO YOU WILL BE MY SLAVE.
Y-YES, OF COURSE!

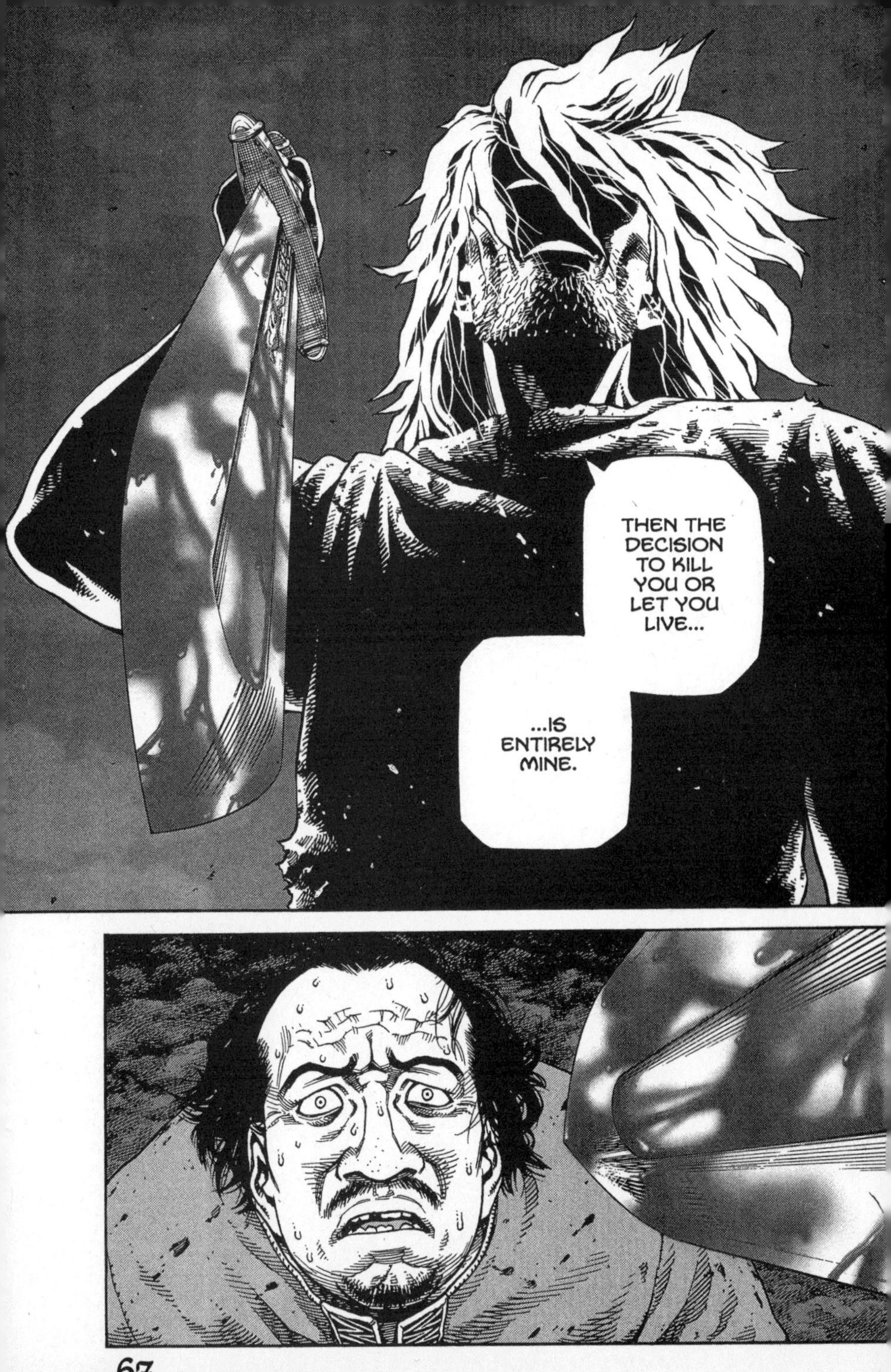
THEN THE DECISION TO KILL YOU OR LET YOU LIVE...
...IS ENTIRELY MINE.

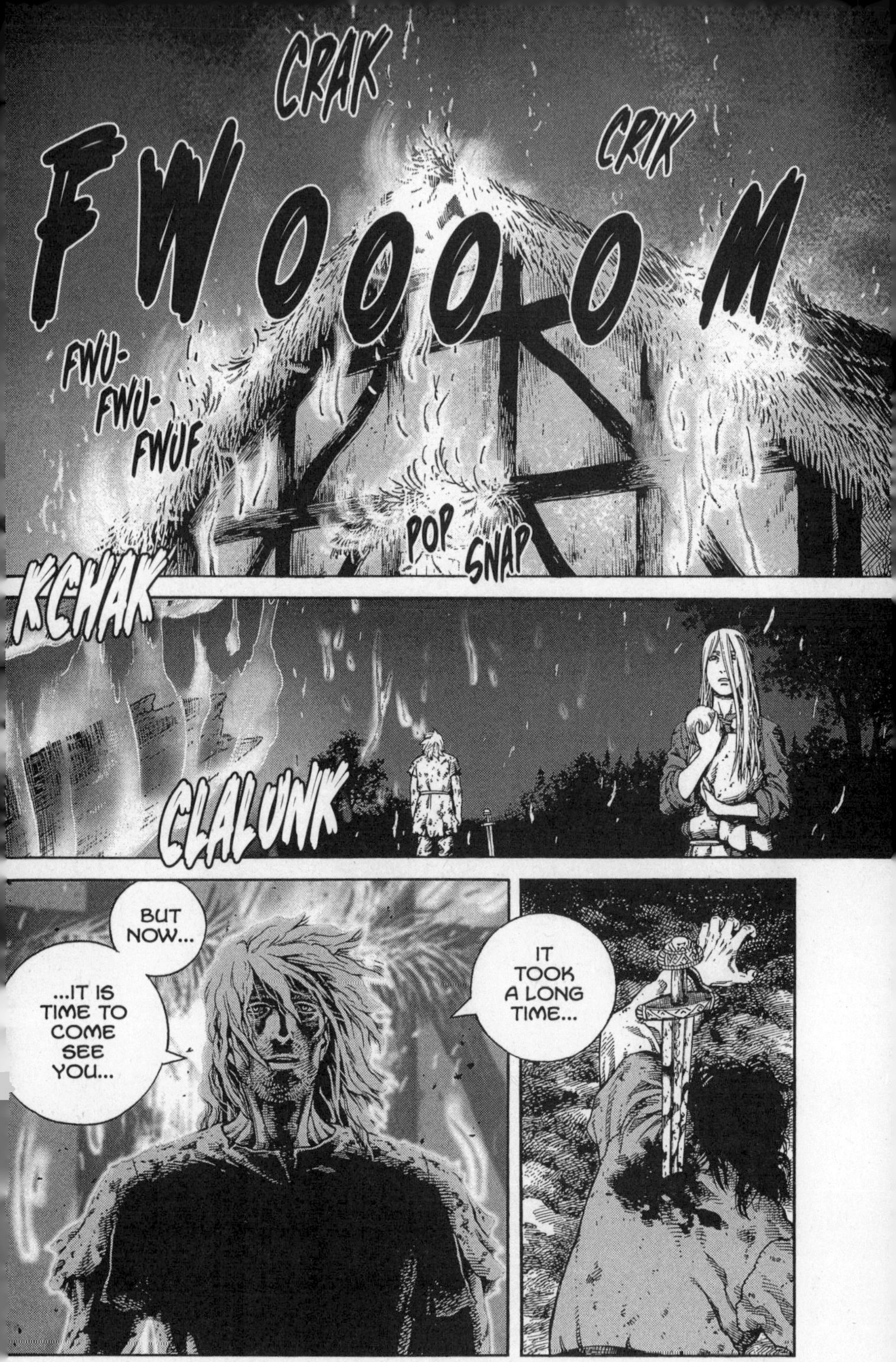
CRIK
CRAK
FWOOOOM
FWU-
FWU-
FWUF
SNAP
POP
KCHAK
CLALUNK
IT TOOK A LONG TIME...
BUT NOW...
...IT IS TIME TO COME SEE YOU...

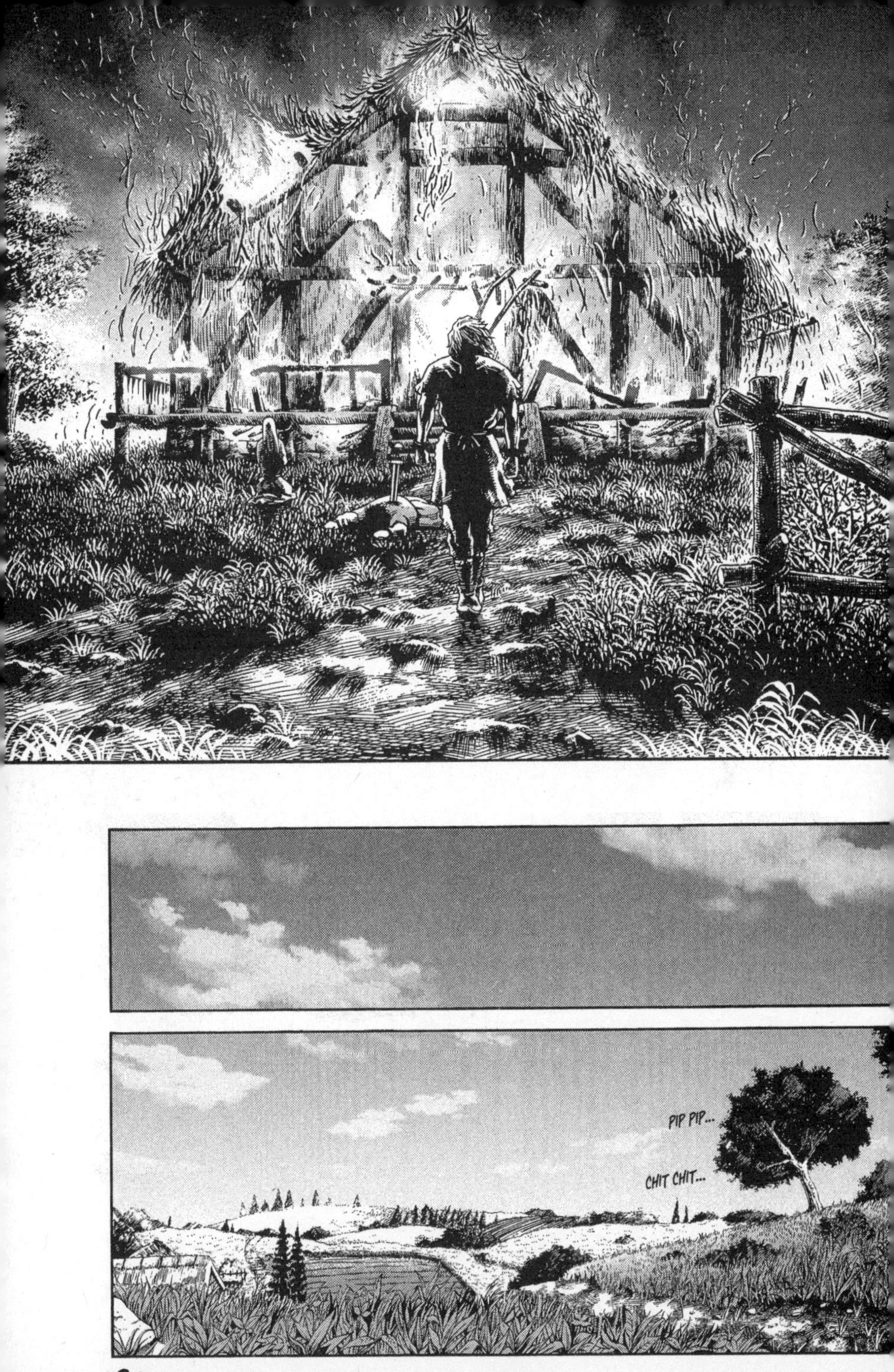
PIP PIP...
CHIT CHIT...

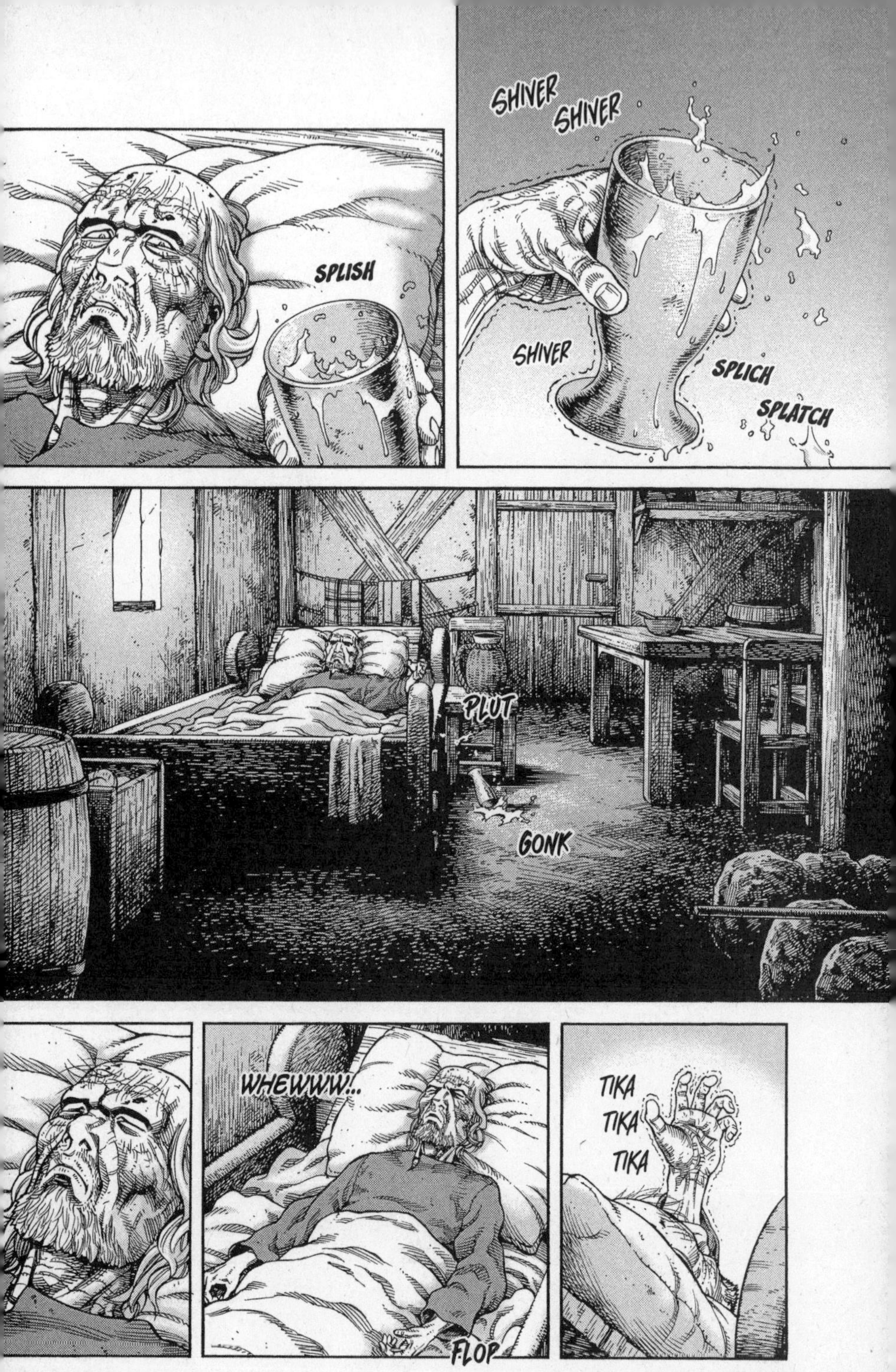
SHIVER
SHIVER
SHIVER
SPLICH
SPLATCH
SPLISH
PLUT
GONK
TIKA
TIKA
TIKA
WHEWWW...
FLOP

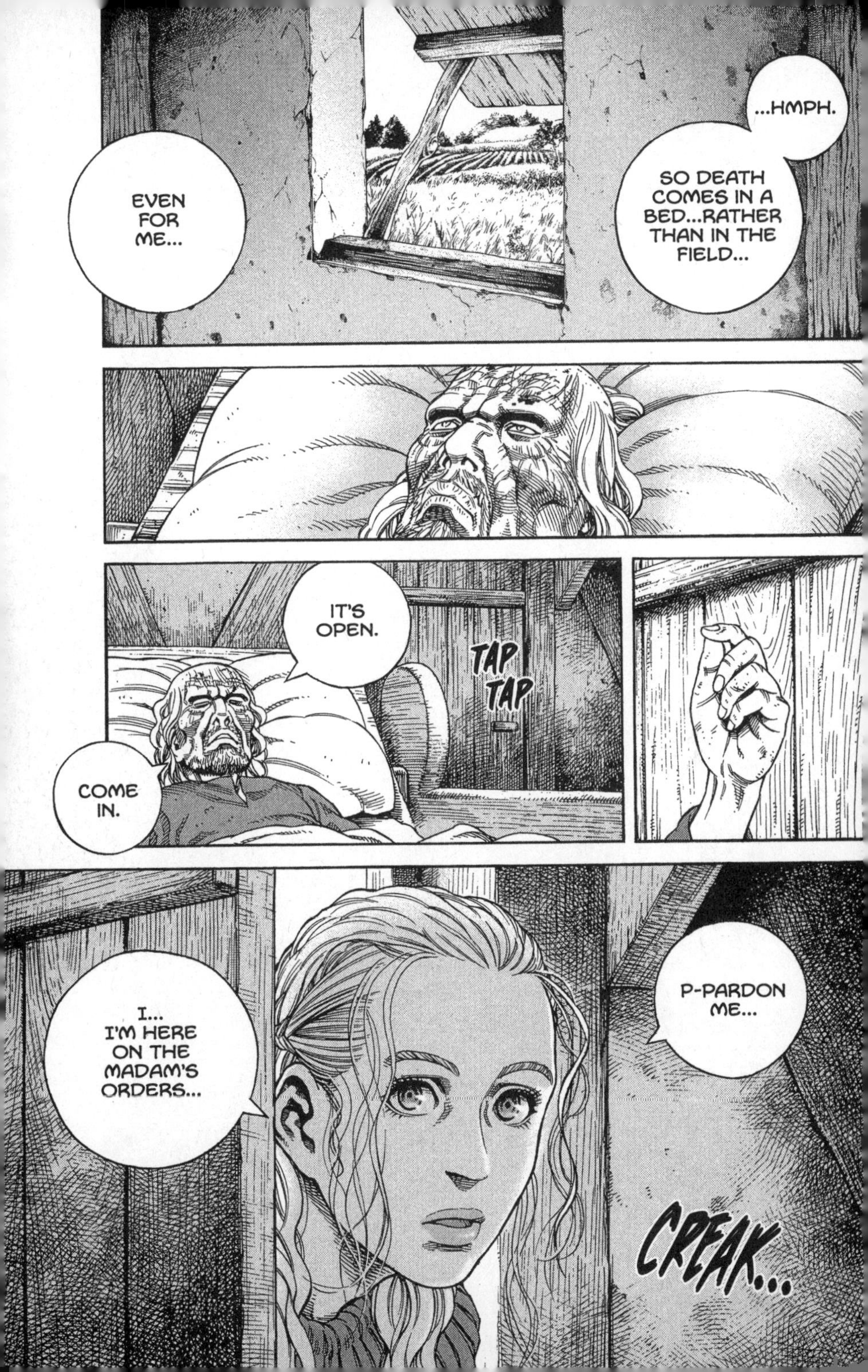
...HMPH.
SO DEATH COMES IN A BED...RATHER THAN IN THE FIELD...
EVEN FOR ME...
TAP TAP
IT'S OPEN.
COME IN.
CREAK...
P-PARDON ME...
I... I'M HERE ON THE MADAM'S ORDERS...

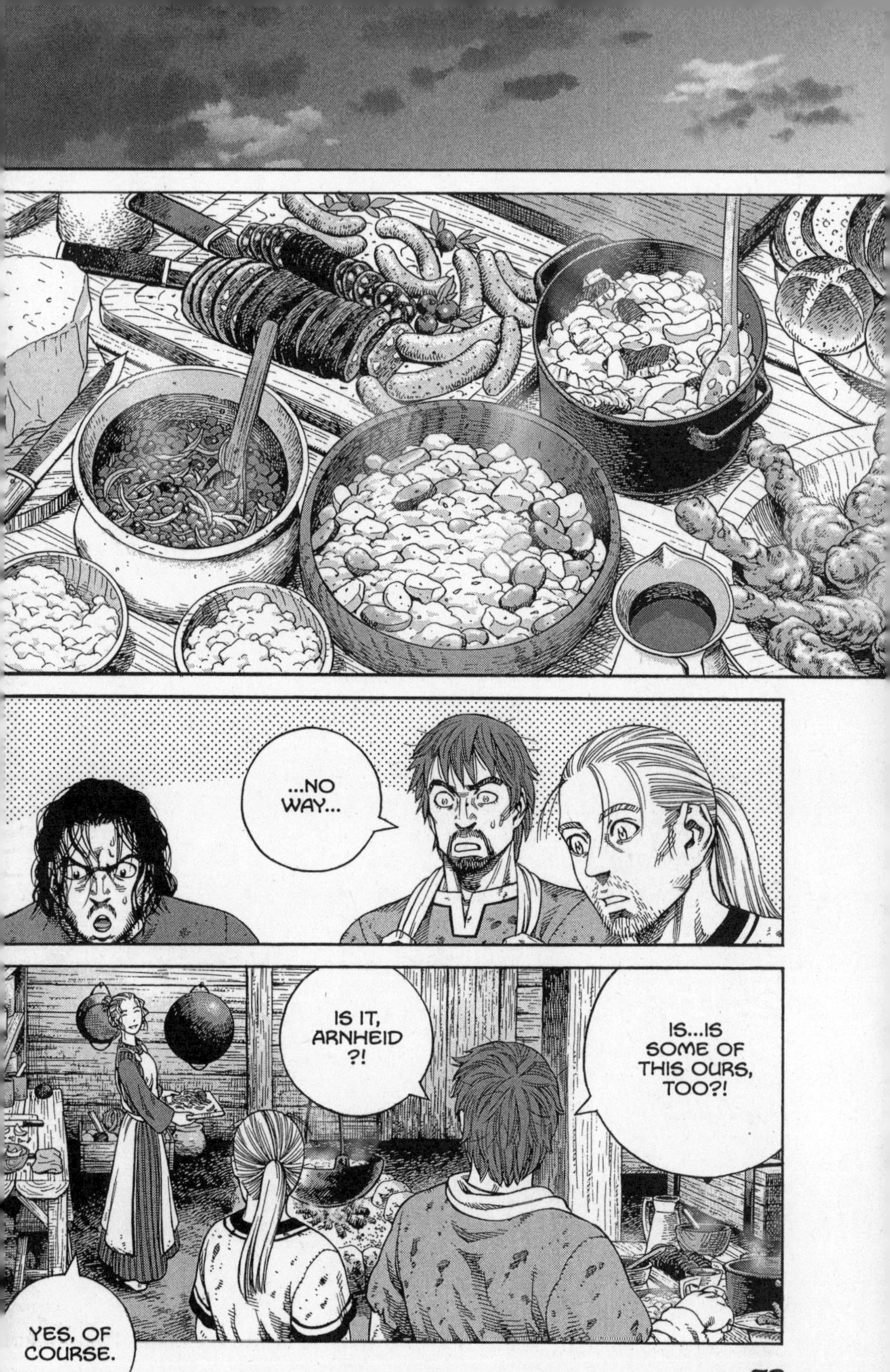
...NO WAY...
IS...IS SOME OF THIS OURS, TOO?!
IS IT, ARNHEID ?!
YES, OF COURSE.

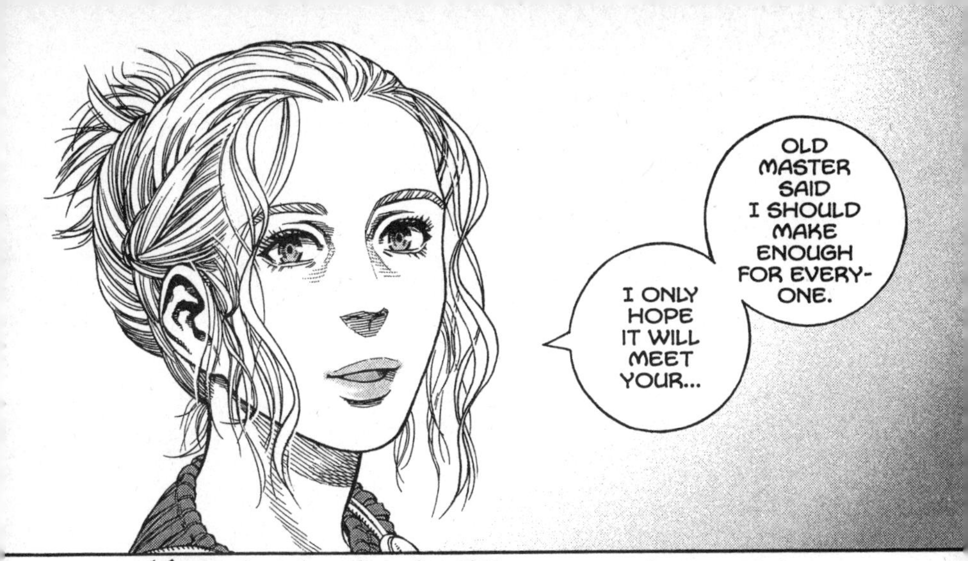
OLD MASTER SAID I SHOULD MAKE ENOUGH FOR EVERY-ONE.
I ONLY HOPE IT WILL MEET YOUR...

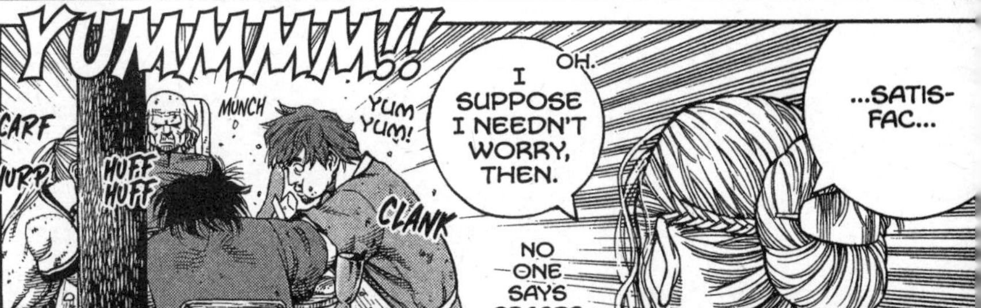
...SATIS-FAC...
OH.
I SUPPOSE I NEEDN'T WORRY, THEN.
NO ONE SAYS GRACE?
CLANK
YUM YUM!
MUNCH
HUFF HUFF
YUMMMMM!!
SCARF
CHURP

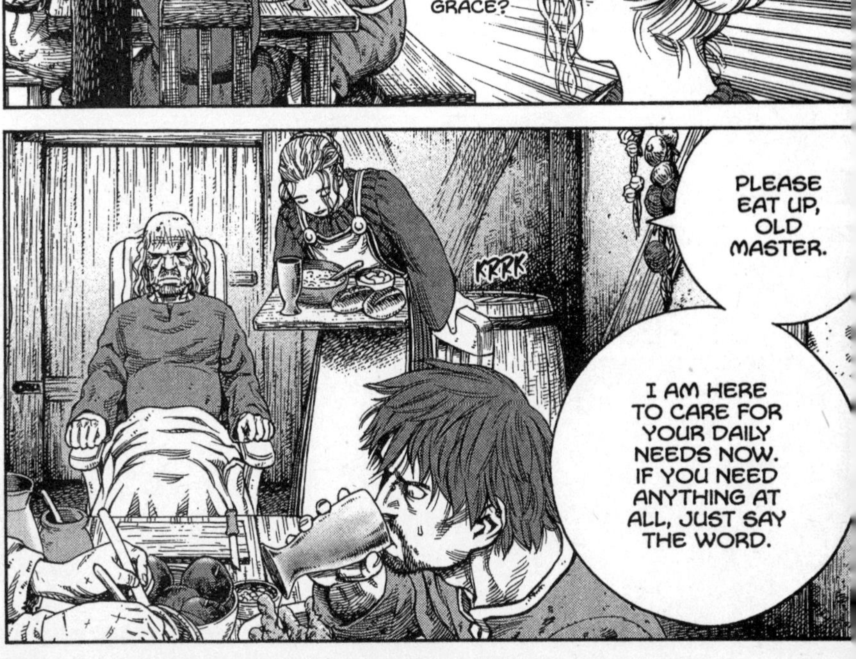
PLEASE EAT UP, OLD MASTER.
KRRK
I AM HERE TO CARE FOR YOUR DAILY NEEDS NOW. IF YOU NEED ANYTHING AT ALL, JUST SAY THE WORD.

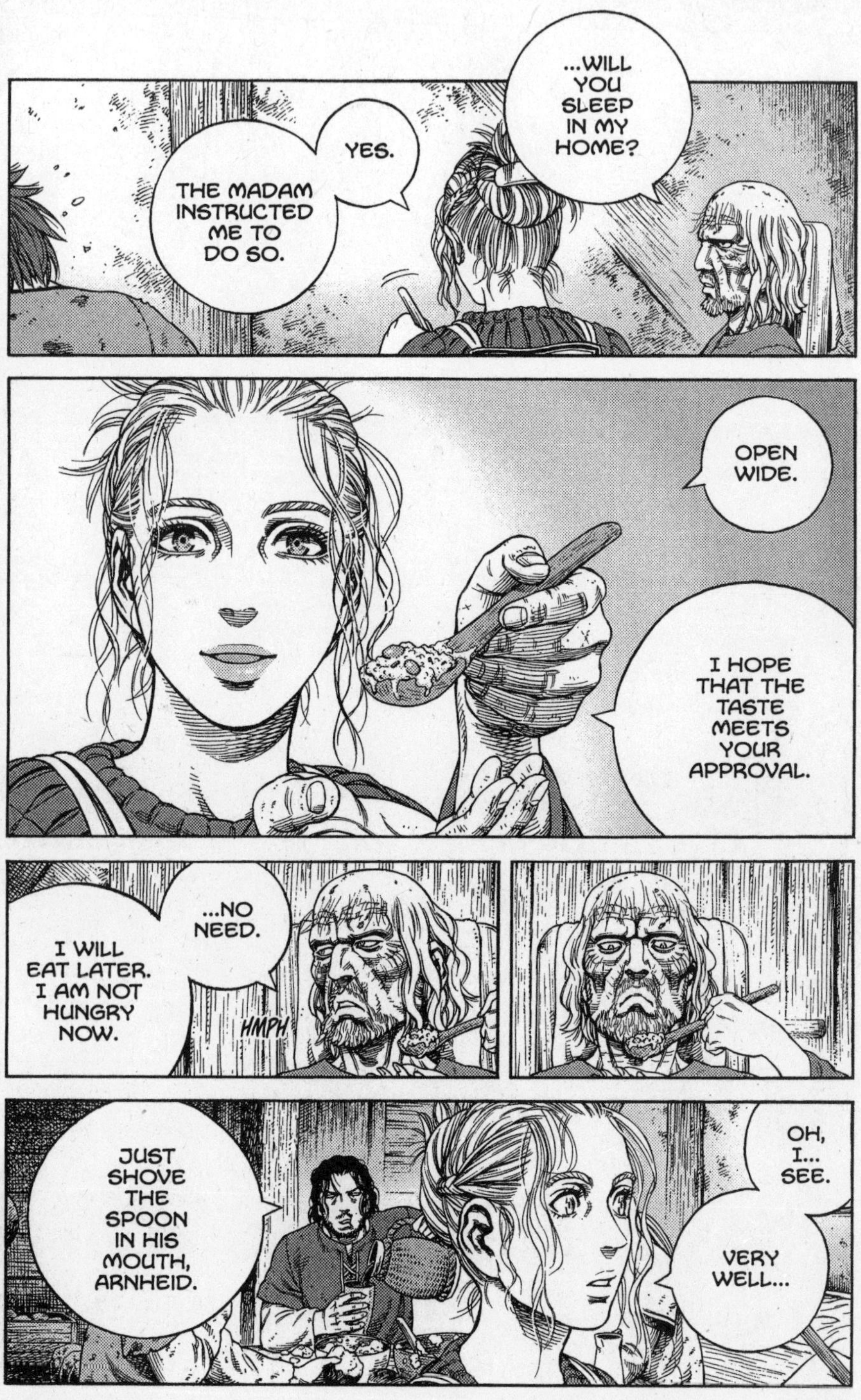
...WILL YOU SLEEP IN MY HOME?
YES.
THE MADAM INSTRUCTED ME TO DO SO.
OPEN WIDE.
I HOPE THAT THE TASTE MEETS YOUR APPROVAL.
...NO NEED.
I WILL EAT LATER. I AM NOT HUNGRY NOW.
HMPH
OH, I... SEE.
VERY WELL...
JUST SHOVE THE SPOON IN HIS MOUTH, ARNHEID.

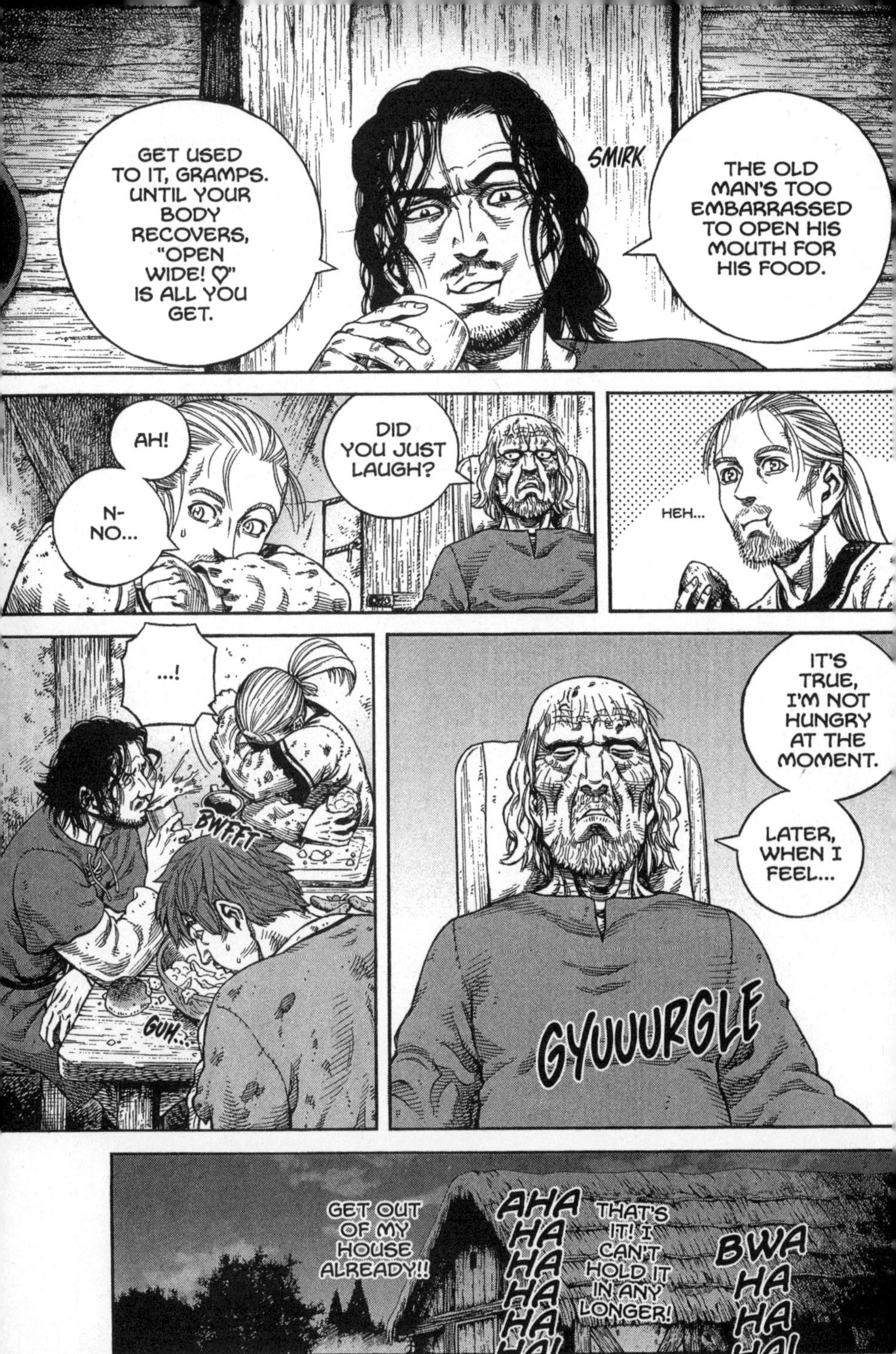
THE OLD MAN'S TOO EMBARRASSED TO OPEN HIS MOUTH FOR HIS FOOD.
SMIRK
GET USED TO IT, GRAMPS. UNTIL YOUR BODY RECOVERS, "OPEN WIDE! ♡" IS ALL YOU GET.
HEH...
DID YOU JUST LAUGH?
AH!
N- NO...
IT'S TRUE, I'M NOT HUNGRY AT THE MOMENT.
LATER, WHEN I FEEL...
GYUUURGLE
...!
BWFFT
GUH...
BWA HA HA HA!
THAT'S IT! I CAN'T HOLD IT IN ANY LONGER!
AHA HA HA HA HA HA HA!
GET OUT OF MY HOUSE ALREADY!!

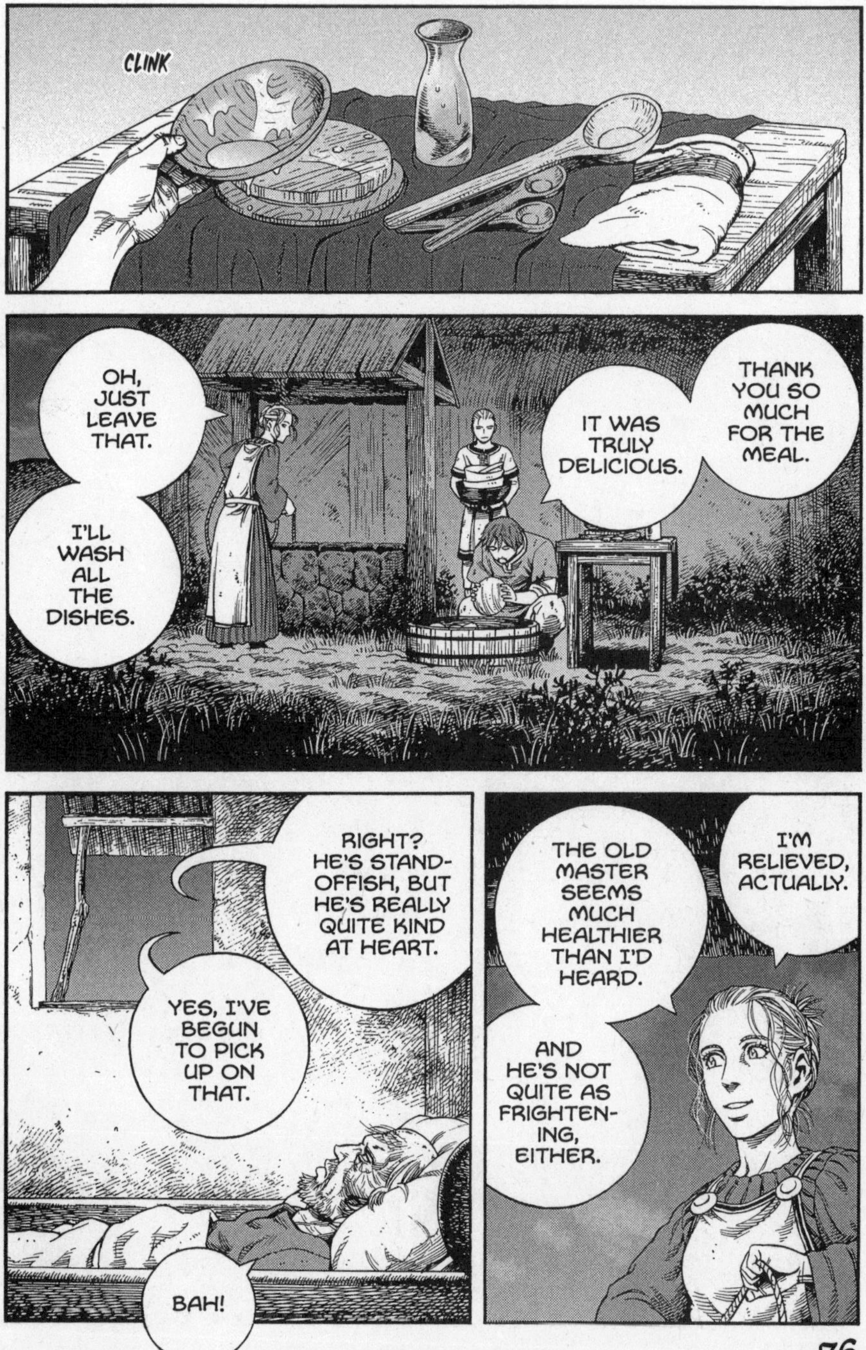
CLINK
THANK YOU SO MUCH FOR THE MEAL.
IT WAS TRULY DELICIOUS.
OH, JUST LEAVE THAT.
I'LL WASH ALL THE DISHES.
I'M RELIEVED, ACTUALLY.
THE OLD MASTER SEEMS MUCH HEALTHIER THAN I'D HEARD.
AND HE'S NOT QUITE AS FRIGHTEN-ING, EITHER.
RIGHT? HE'S STAND-OFFISH, BUT HE'S REALLY QUITE KIND AT HEART.
YES, I'VE BEGUN TO PICK UP ON THAT.
BAH!

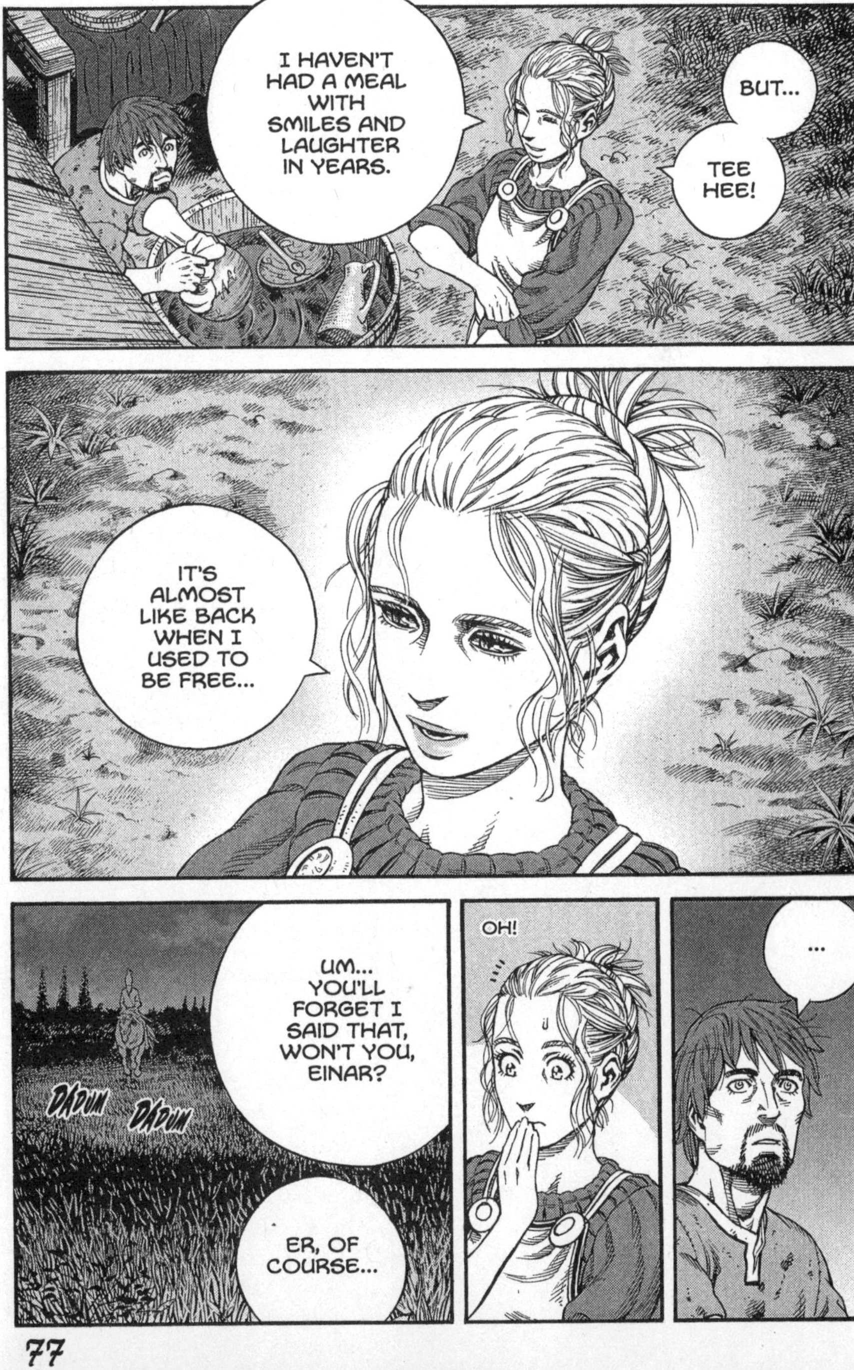
BUT...
TEE HEE!
I HAVEN'T HAD A MEAL WITH SMILES AND LAUGHTER IN YEARS.
IT'S ALMOST LIKE BACK WHEN I USED TO BE FREE...
...
OH!
UM... YOU'LL FORGET I SAID THAT, WON'T YOU, EINAR?
DADUM
DADUM
ER, OF COURSE...

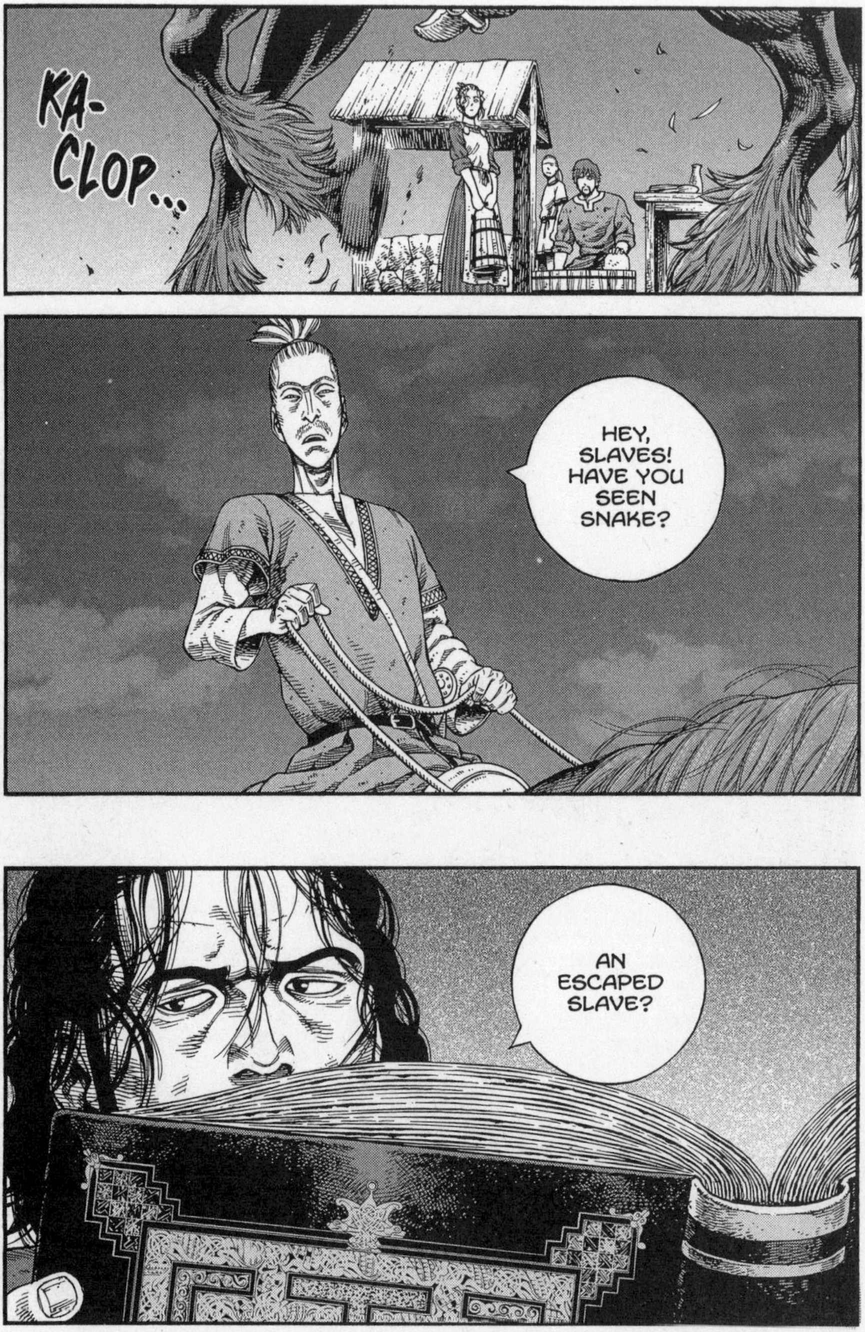
KA-CLOP...
HEY, SLAVES! HAVE YOU SEEN SNAKE?
AN ESCAPED SLAVE?

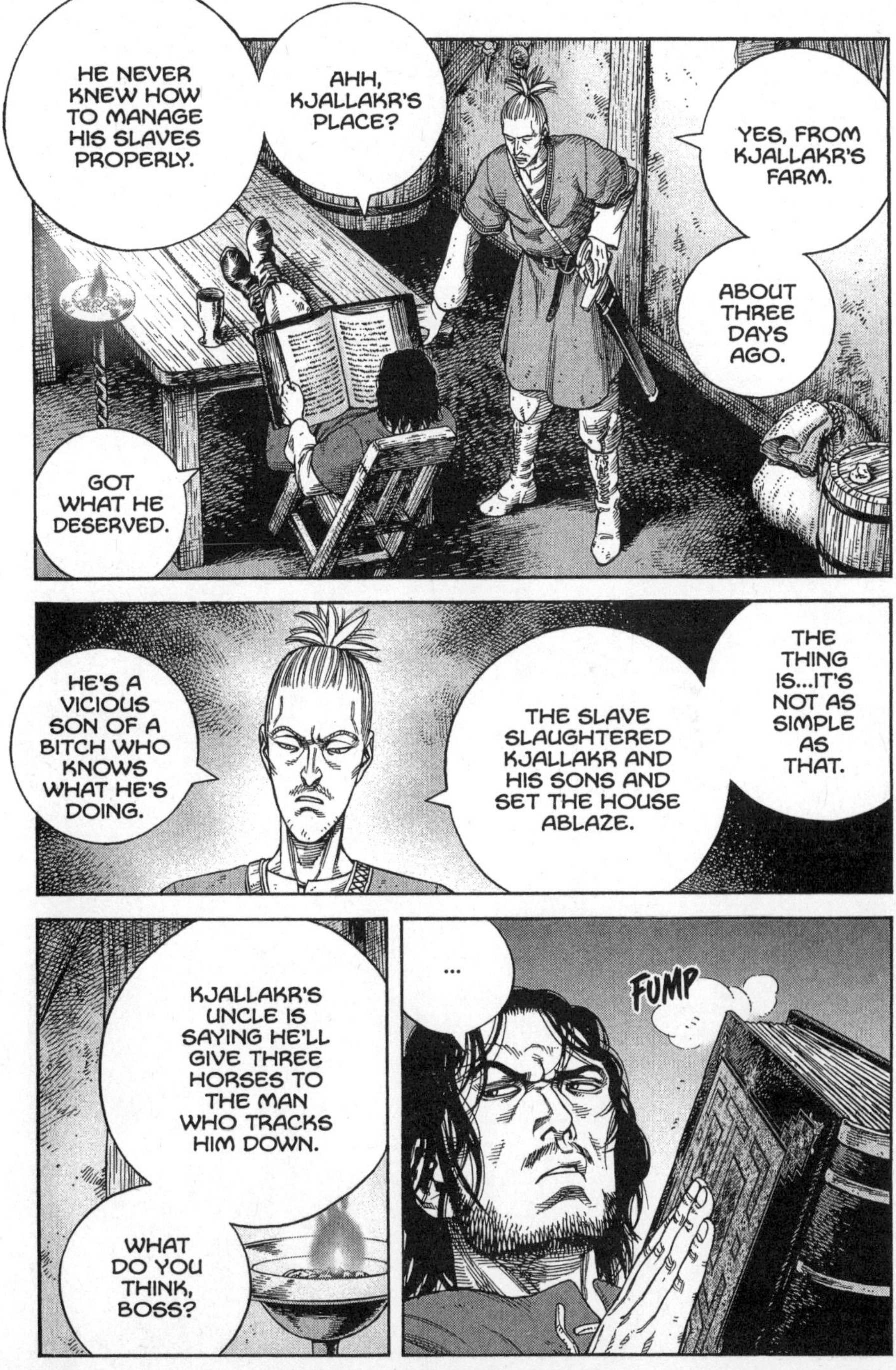
YES, FROM KJALLAKR'S FARM.
ABOUT THREE DAYS AGO.
AHH, KJALLAKR'S PLACE?
HE NEVER KNEW HOW TO MANAGE HIS SLAVES PROPERLY.
GOT WHAT HE DESERVED.
THE THING IS...IT'S NOT AS SIMPLE AS THAT.
THE SLAVE SLAUGHTERED KJALLAKR AND HIS SONS AND SET THE HOUSE ABLAZE.
HE'S A VICIOUS SON OF A BITCH WHO KNOWS WHAT HE'S DOING.
...
FUMP
KJALLAKR'S UNCLE IS SAYING HE'LL GIVE THREE HORSES TO THE MAN WHO TRACKS HIM DOWN.
WHAT DO YOU THINK, BOSS?

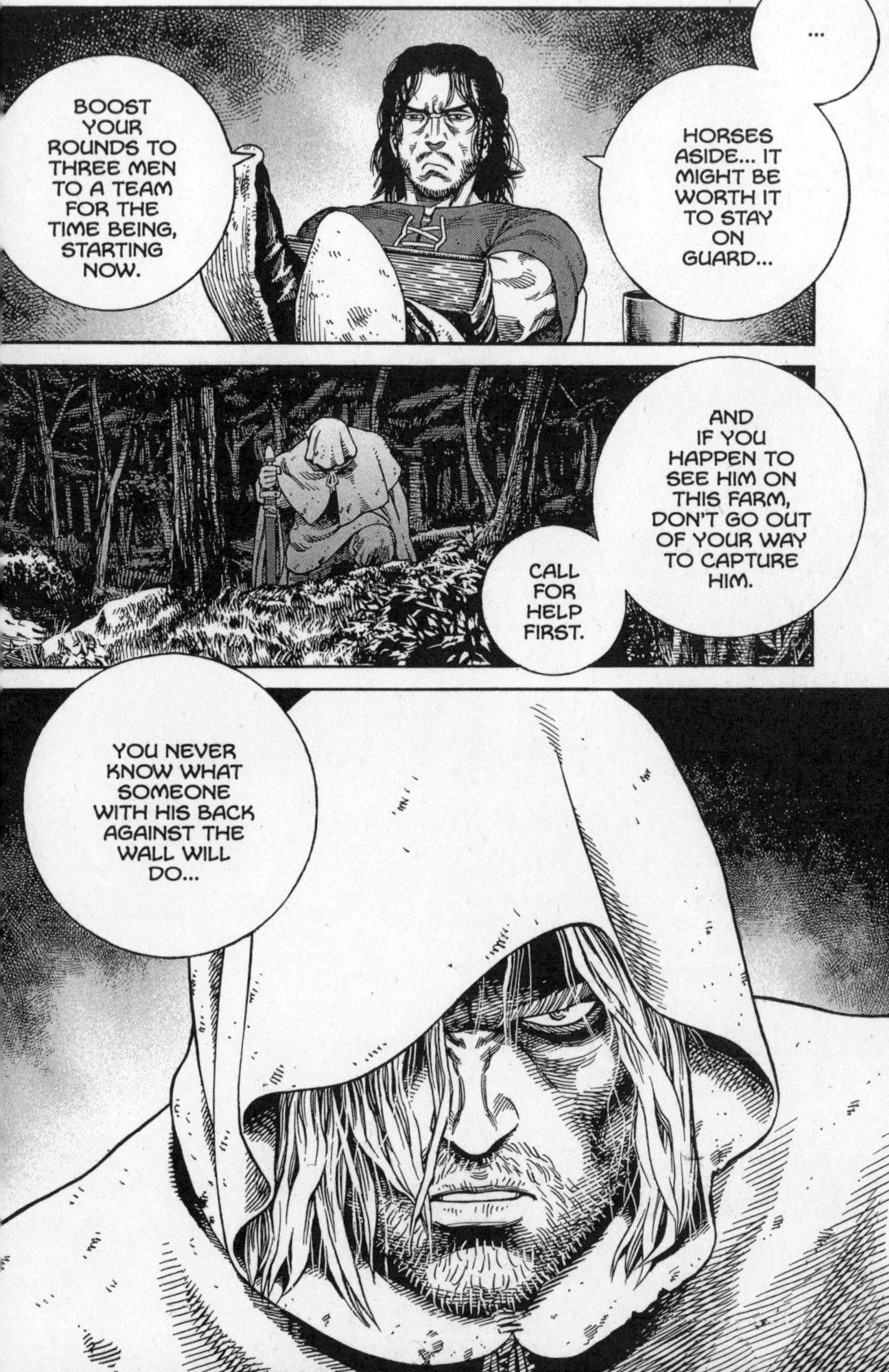
...
HORSES ASIDE... IT MIGHT BE WORTH IT TO STAY ON GUARD...
BOOST YOUR ROUNDS TO THREE MEN TO A TEAM FOR THE TIME BEING, STARTING NOW.
AND IF YOU HAPPEN TO SEE HIM ON THIS FARM, DON'T GO OUT OF YOUR WAY TO CAPTURE HIM.
CALL FOR HELP FIRST.
YOU NEVER KNOW WHAT SOMEONE WITH HIS BACK AGAINST THE WALL WILL DO...

CHAPTER 75: KING AND SWORD

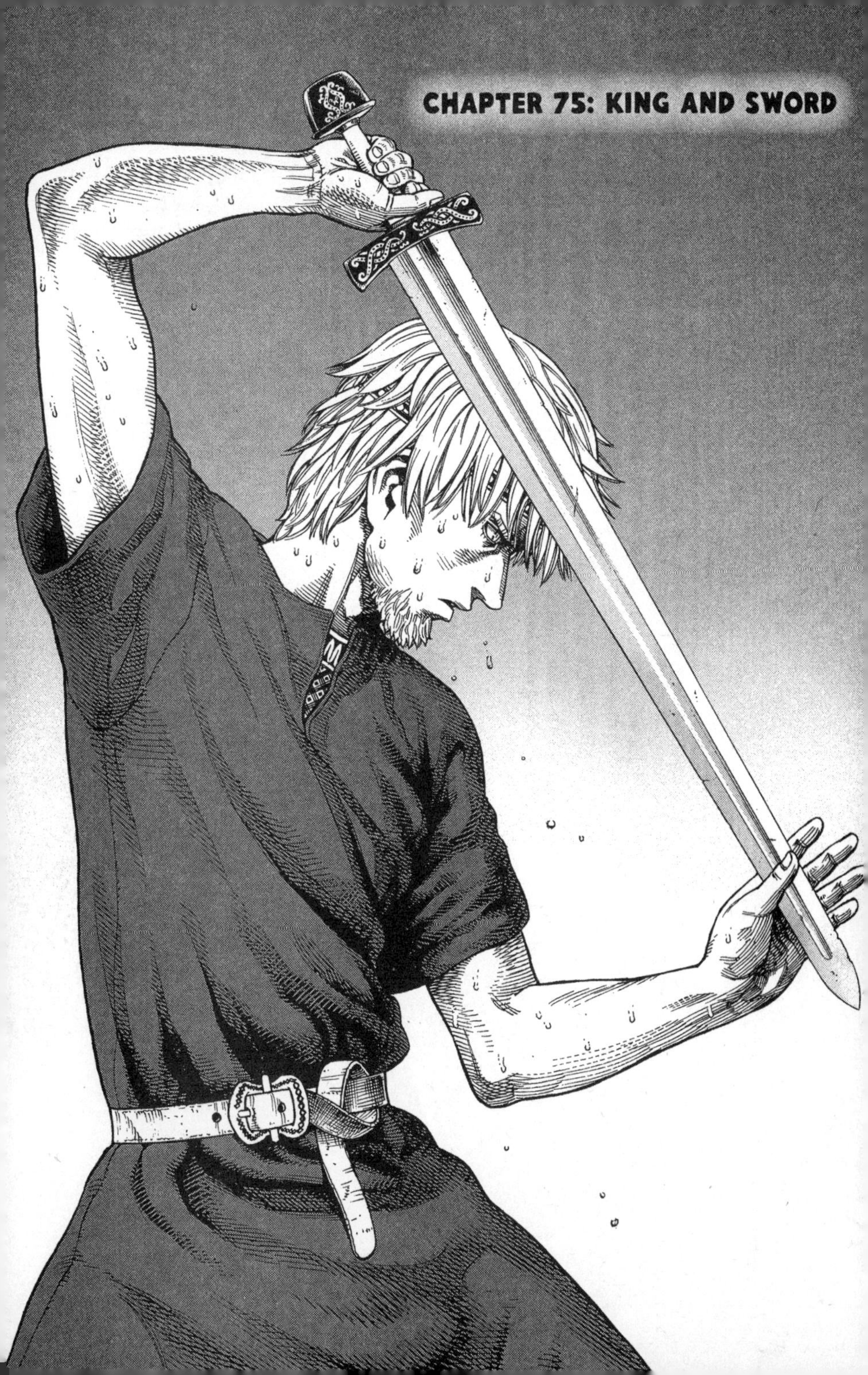

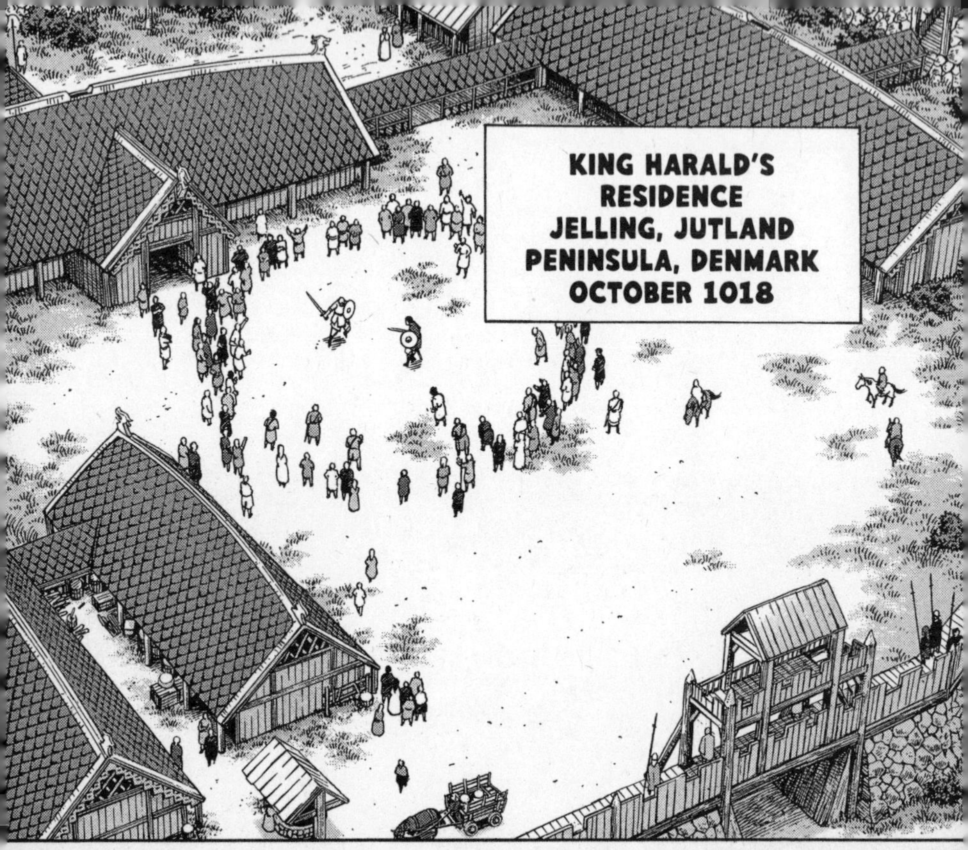
KING HARALD'S
RESIDENCE
JELLING, JUTLAND
PENINSULA, DENMARK
OCTOBER 1018

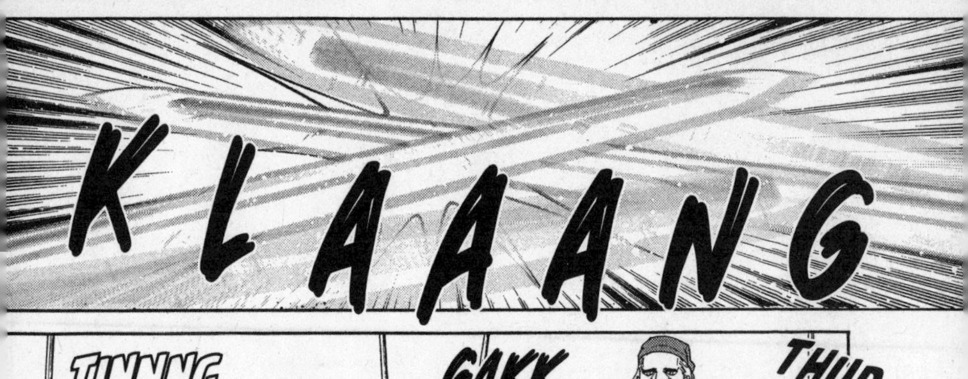
KLAAANG

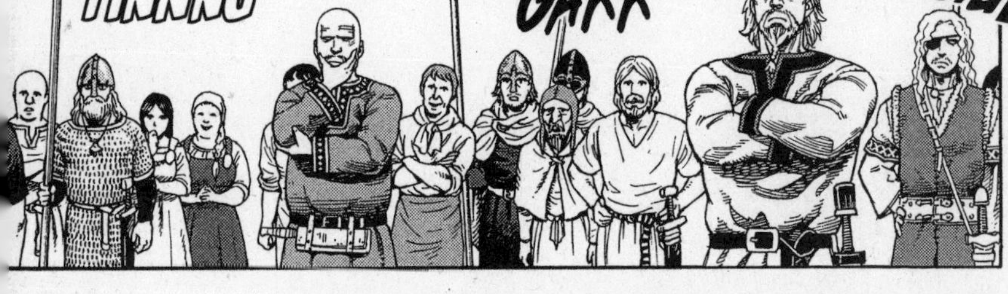
THUD
GAKK
TINNNG

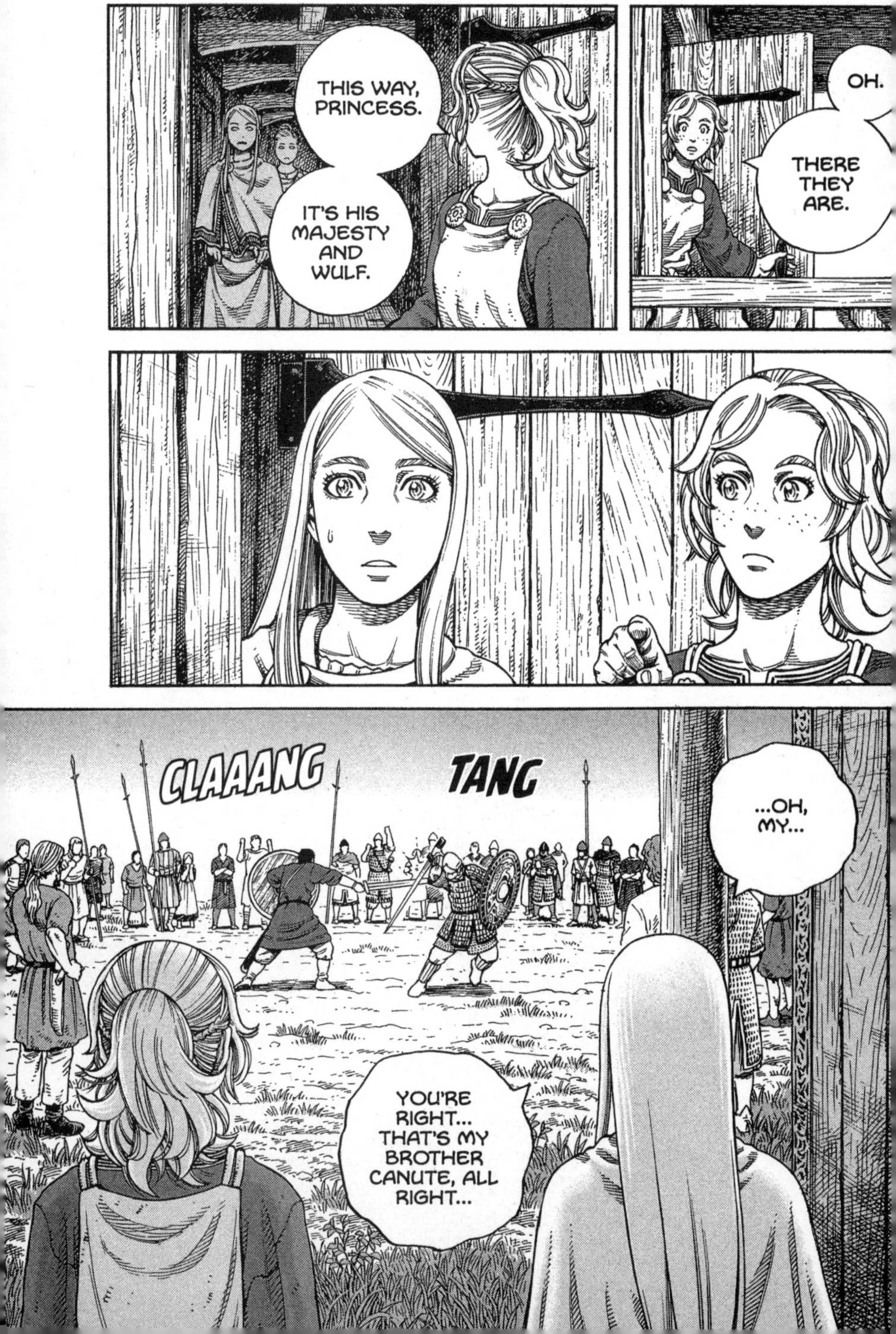
OH.
THERE THEY ARE.
THIS WAY, PRINCESS.
IT'S HIS MAJESTY AND WULF.
...OH, MY...
TANG
CLAAANG
YOU'RE RIGHT... THAT'S MY BROTHER CANUTE, ALL RIGHT...

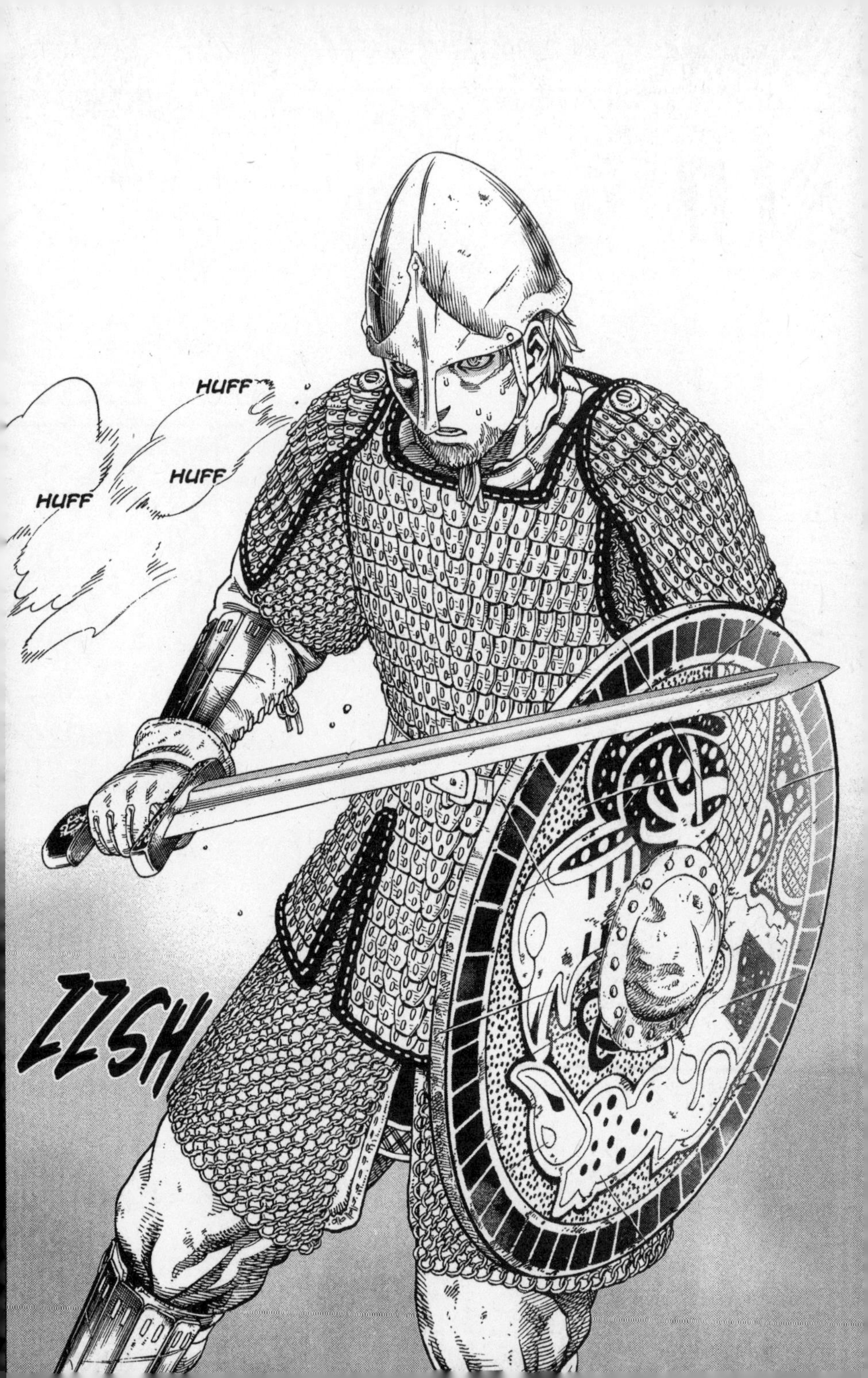
HUFF
HUFF
HUFF
ZZSH

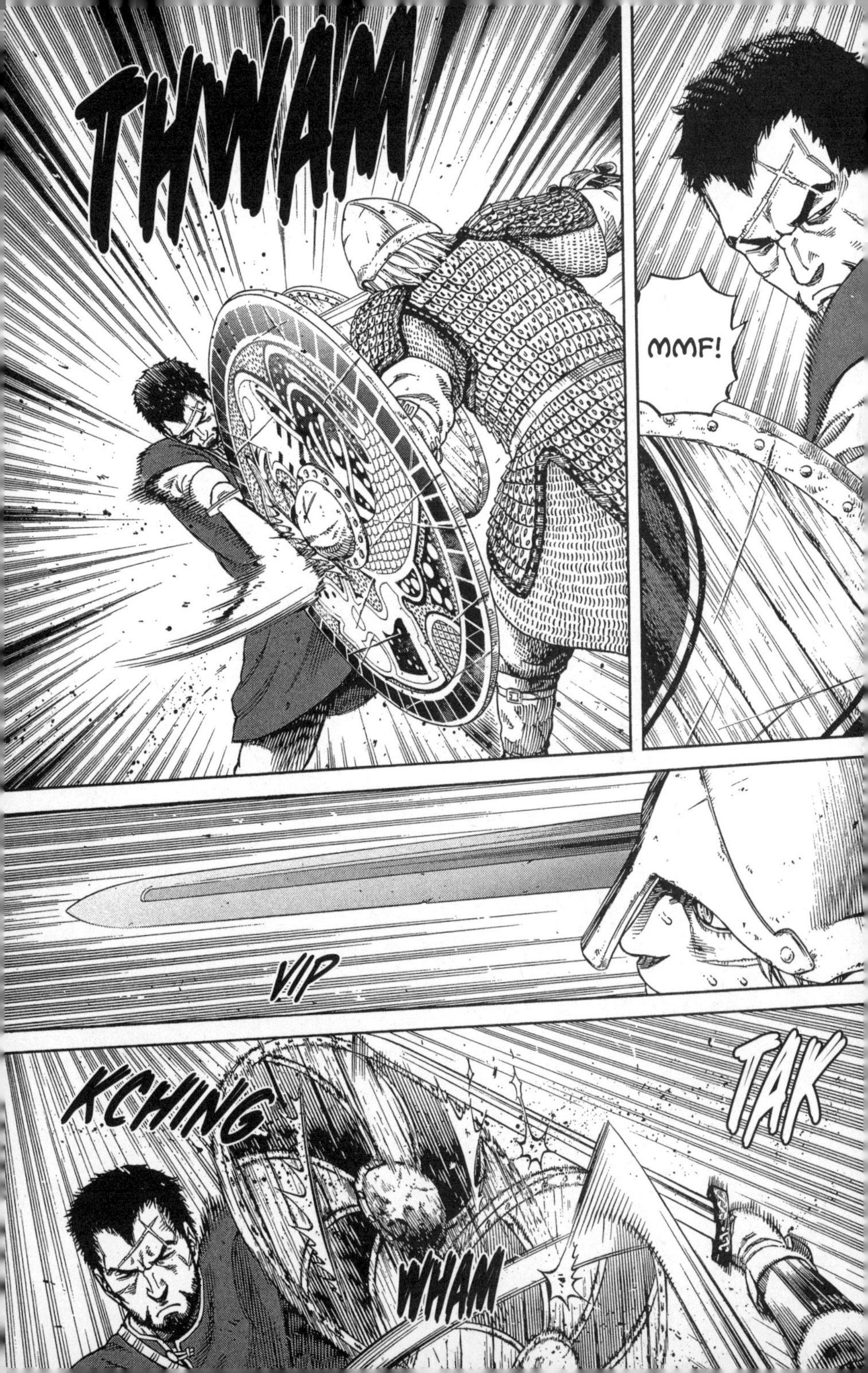
MMF!
THWAM
VIP
TAK
KCHING
WHAM

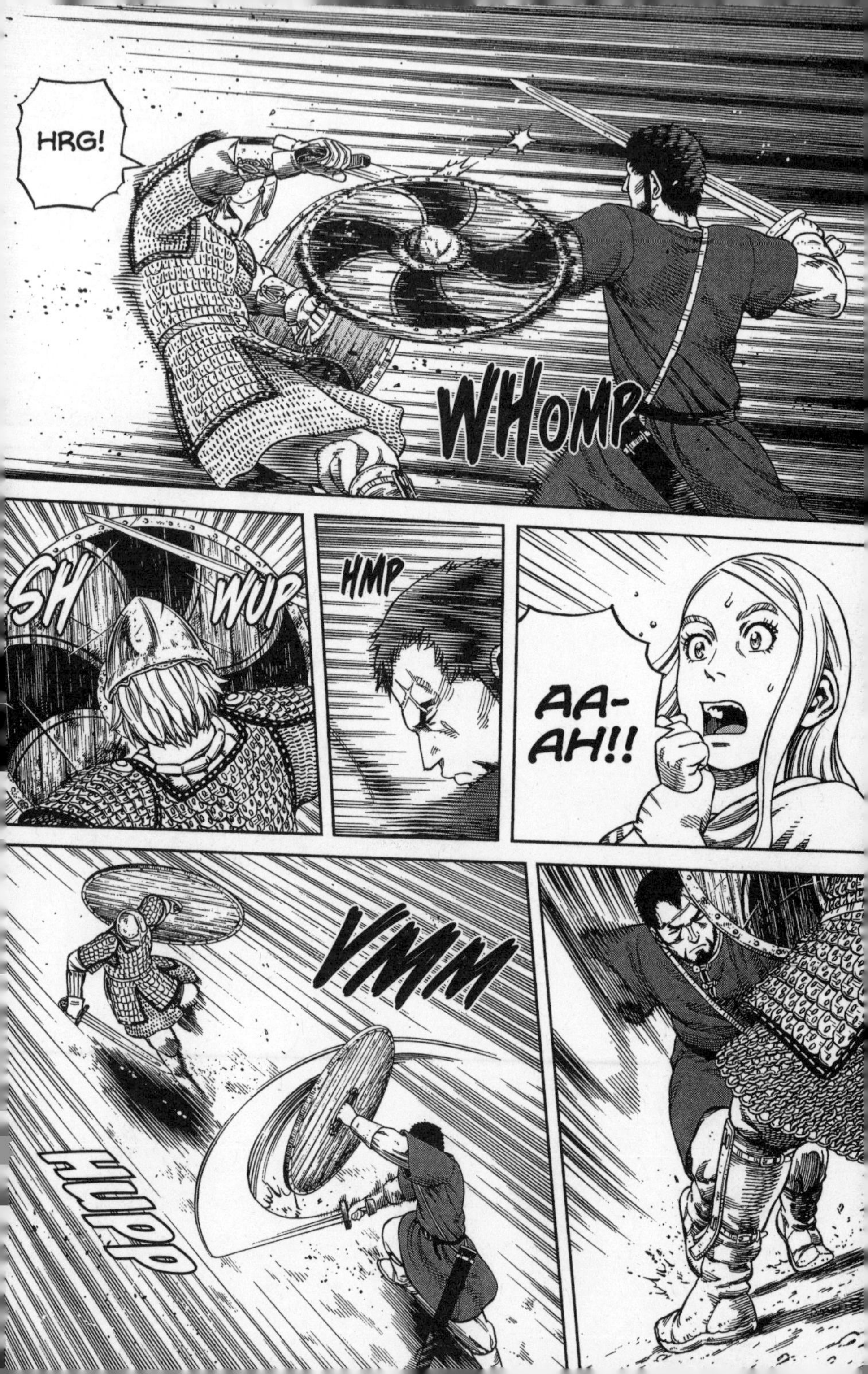
HRG!
WHOMP
AA-AH!!
HMP
SH WUP
VMM
HUPP

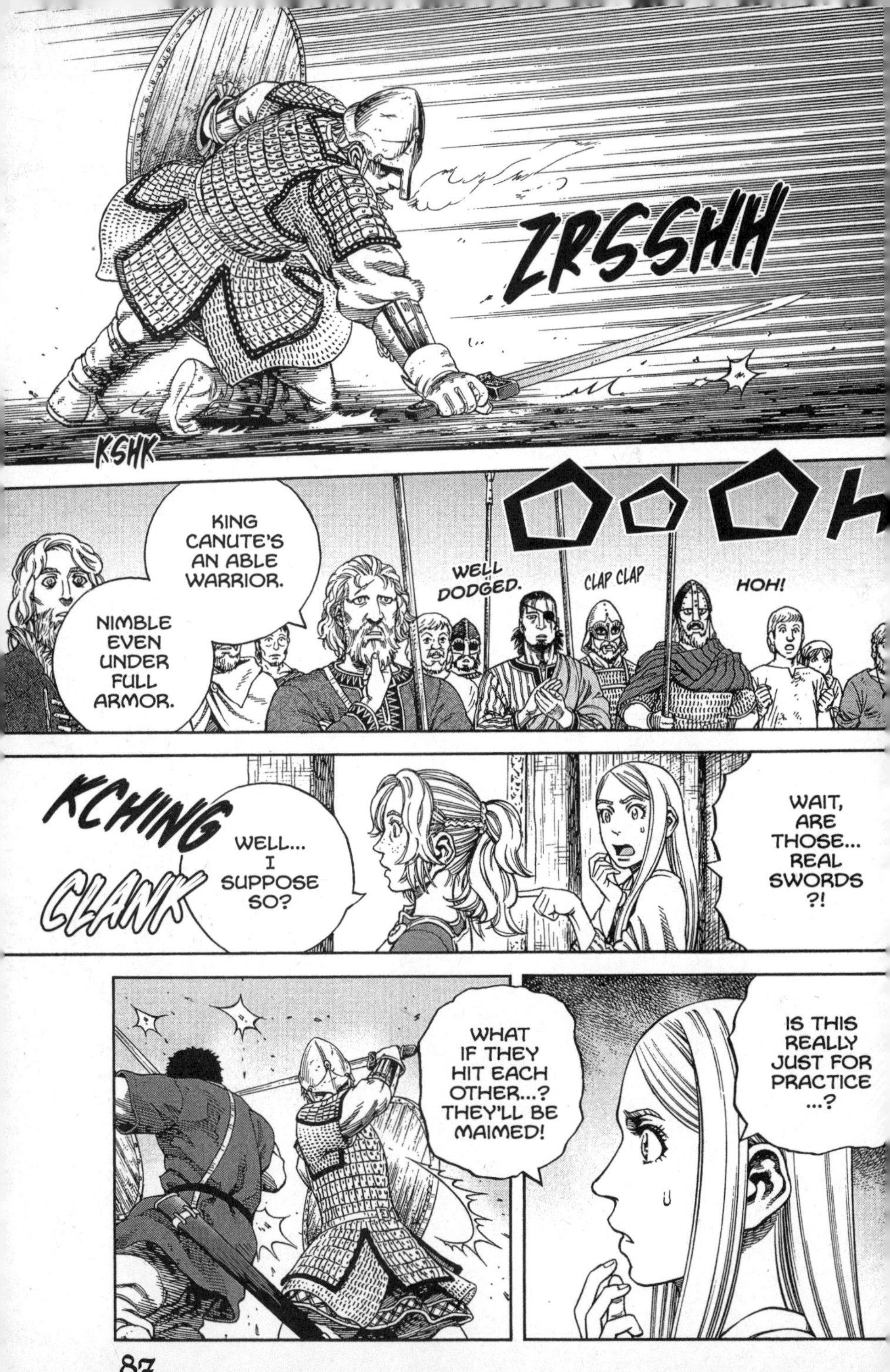
ZRSSHH
KSHK
OOOH
HOH!
CLAP CLAP
WELL DODGED.
KING CANUTE'S AN ABLE WARRIOR.
NIMBLE EVEN UNDER FULL ARMOR.
WAIT, ARE THOSE... REAL SWORDS?!
WELL... I SUPPOSE SO?
KCHING
CLANK
IS THIS REALLY JUST FOR PRACTICE...?
WHAT IF THEY HIT EACH OTHER...? THEY'LL BE MAIMED!

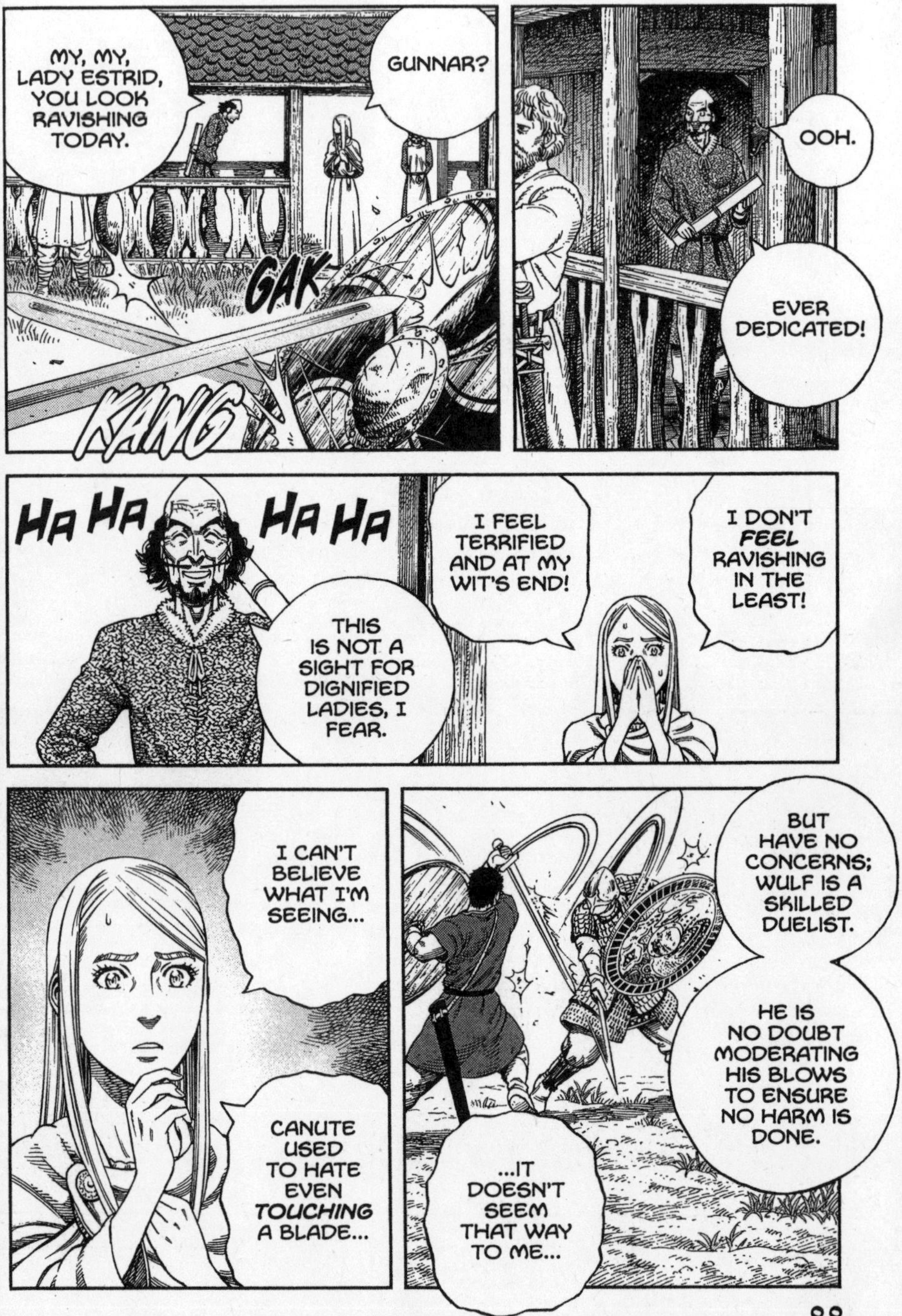
OOH.
EVER DEDICATED!
GUNNAR?
MY, MY, LADY ESTRID, YOU LOOK RAVISHING TODAY.
GAK
KANG
I DON'T *FEEL* RAVISHING IN THE LEAST!
I FEEL TERRIFIED AND AT MY WIT'S END!
HA HA HA HA
THIS IS NOT A SIGHT FOR DIGNIFIED LADIES, I FEAR.
BUT HAVE NO CONCERNS; WULF IS A SKILLED DUELIST.
HE IS NO DOUBT MODERATING HIS BLOWS TO ENSURE NO HARM IS DONE.
...IT DOESN'T SEEM THAT WAY TO ME...
I CAN'T BELIEVE WHAT I'M SEEING...
CANUTE USED TO HATE EVEN *TOUCHING* A BLADE...

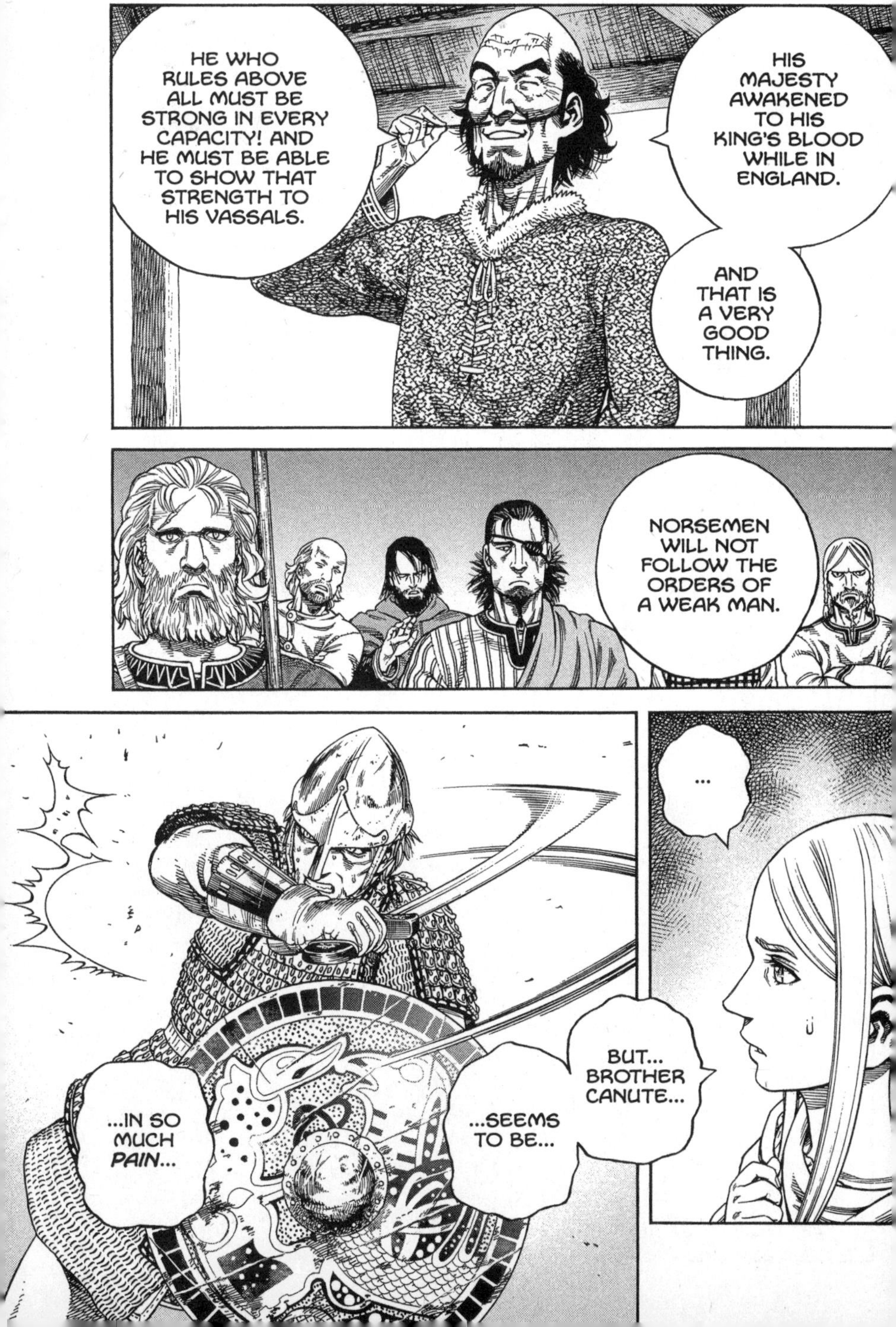
HIS MAJESTY AWAKENED TO HIS KING'S BLOOD WHILE IN ENGLAND.
AND THAT IS A VERY GOOD THING.
HE WHO RULES ABOVE ALL MUST BE STRONG IN EVERY CAPACITY! AND HE MUST BE ABLE TO SHOW THAT STRENGTH TO HIS VASSALS.
NORSEMEN WILL NOT FOLLOW THE ORDERS OF A WEAK MAN.
...
BUT... BROTHER CANUTE...
...SEEMS TO BE...
...IN SO MUCH *PAIN*...

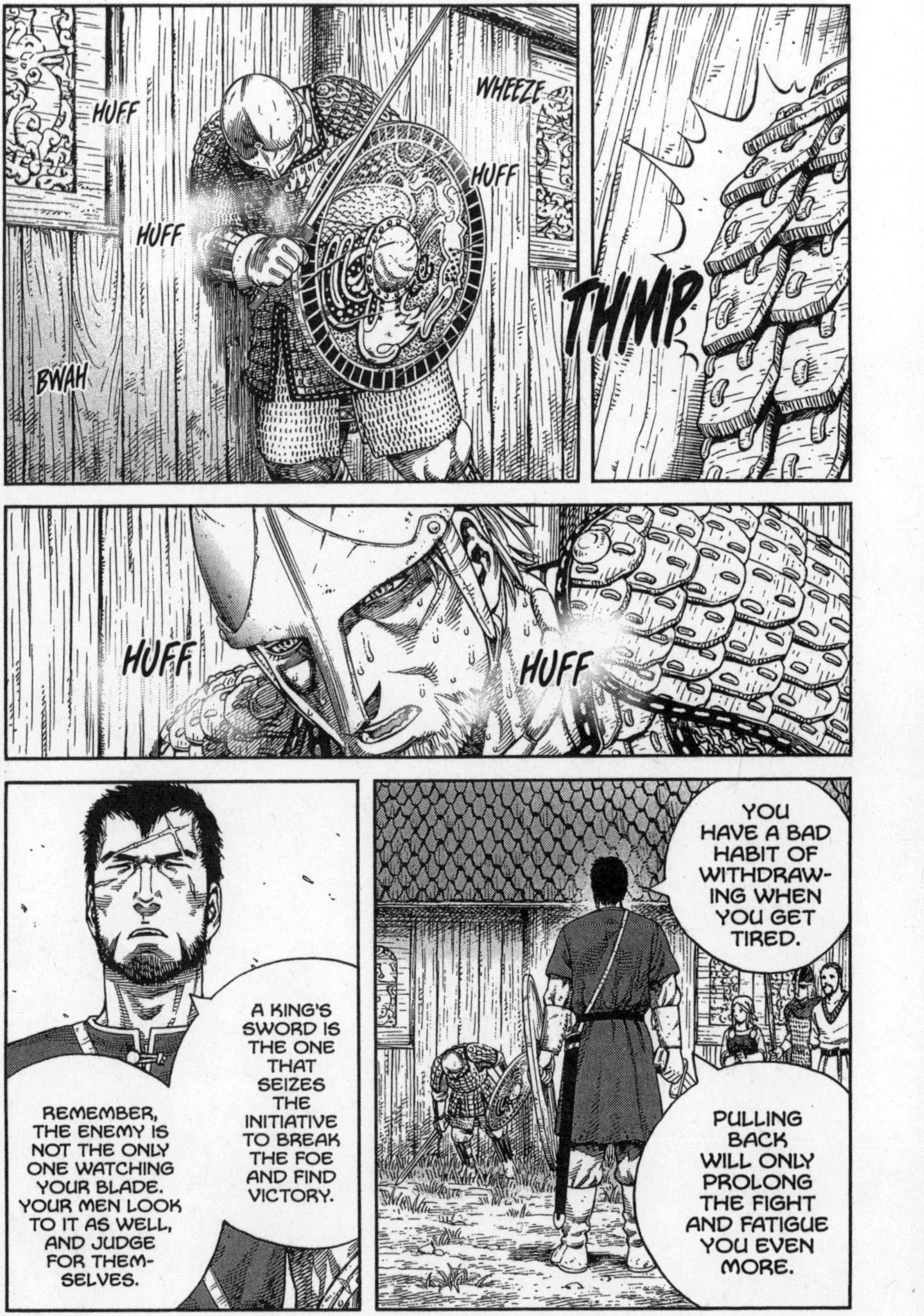
THMP
WHEEZE
HUFF
HUFF
HUFF
BWAH
HUFF
HUFF
YOU HAVE A BAD HABIT OF WITHDRAWING WHEN YOU GET TIRED.
PULLING BACK WILL ONLY PROLONG THE FIGHT AND FATIGUE YOU EVEN MORE.
A KING'S SWORD IS THE ONE THAT SEIZES THE INITIATIVE TO BREAK THE FOE AND FIND VICTORY.
REMEMBER, THE ENEMY IS NOT THE ONLY ONE WATCHING YOUR BLADE. YOUR MEN LOOK TO IT AS WELL, AND JUDGE FOR THEMSELVES.

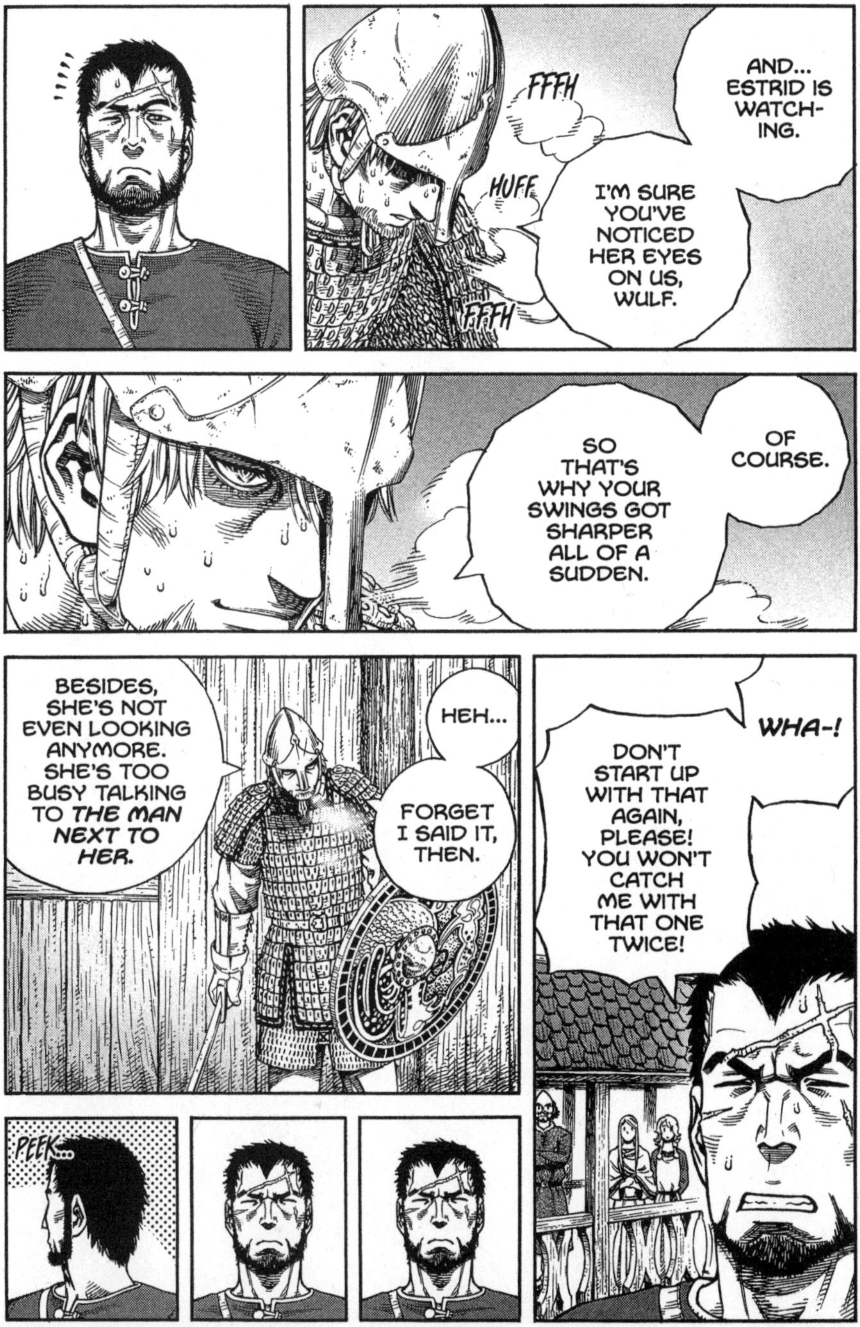
AND... ESTRID IS WATCHING-ING.
FFFH
HUFF
I'M SURE YOU'VE NOTICED HER EYES ON US, WULF.
FFFH
OF COURSE.
SO THAT'S WHY YOUR SWINGS GOT SHARPER ALL OF A SUDDEN.
WHA-!
DON'T START UP WITH THAT AGAIN, PLEASE! YOU WON'T CATCH ME WITH THAT ONE TWICE!
HEH...
FORGET I SAID IT, THEN.
BESIDES, SHE'S NOT EVEN LOOKING ANYMORE. SHE'S TOO BUSY TALKING TO *THE MAN NEXT TO HER*.
PEEK...

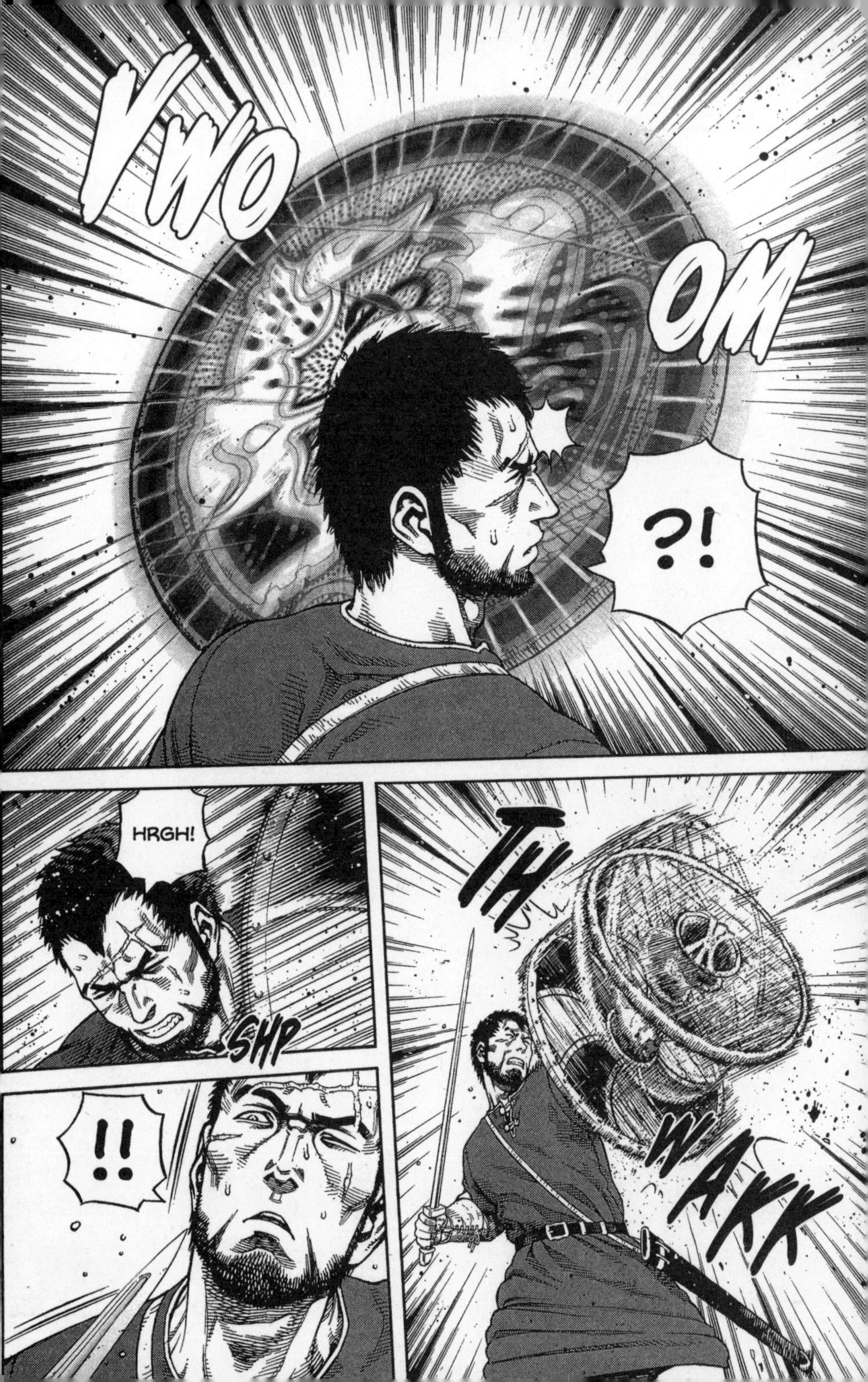
VWO
OM
?!
TH
WAKK
HRGH!
SHP
!!

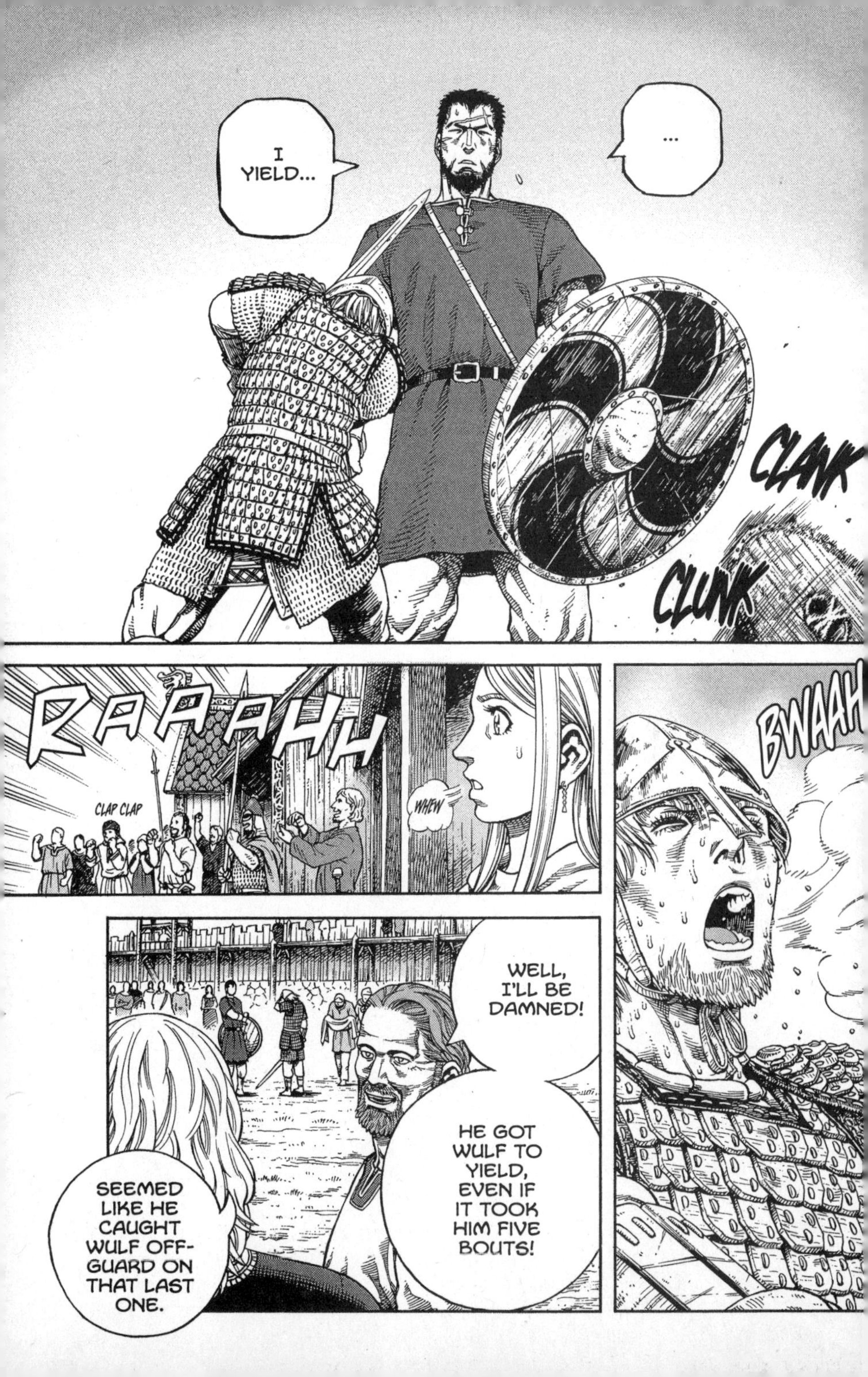
...
I YIELD...
CLANK
CLUNK
BWAAH
WHEW
RAAAHH
CLAP CLAP
WELL, I'LL BE DAMNED!
HE GOT WULF TO YIELD, EVEN IF IT TOOK HIM FIVE BOUTS!
SEEMED LIKE HE CAUGHT WULF OFF-GUARD ON THAT LAST ONE.

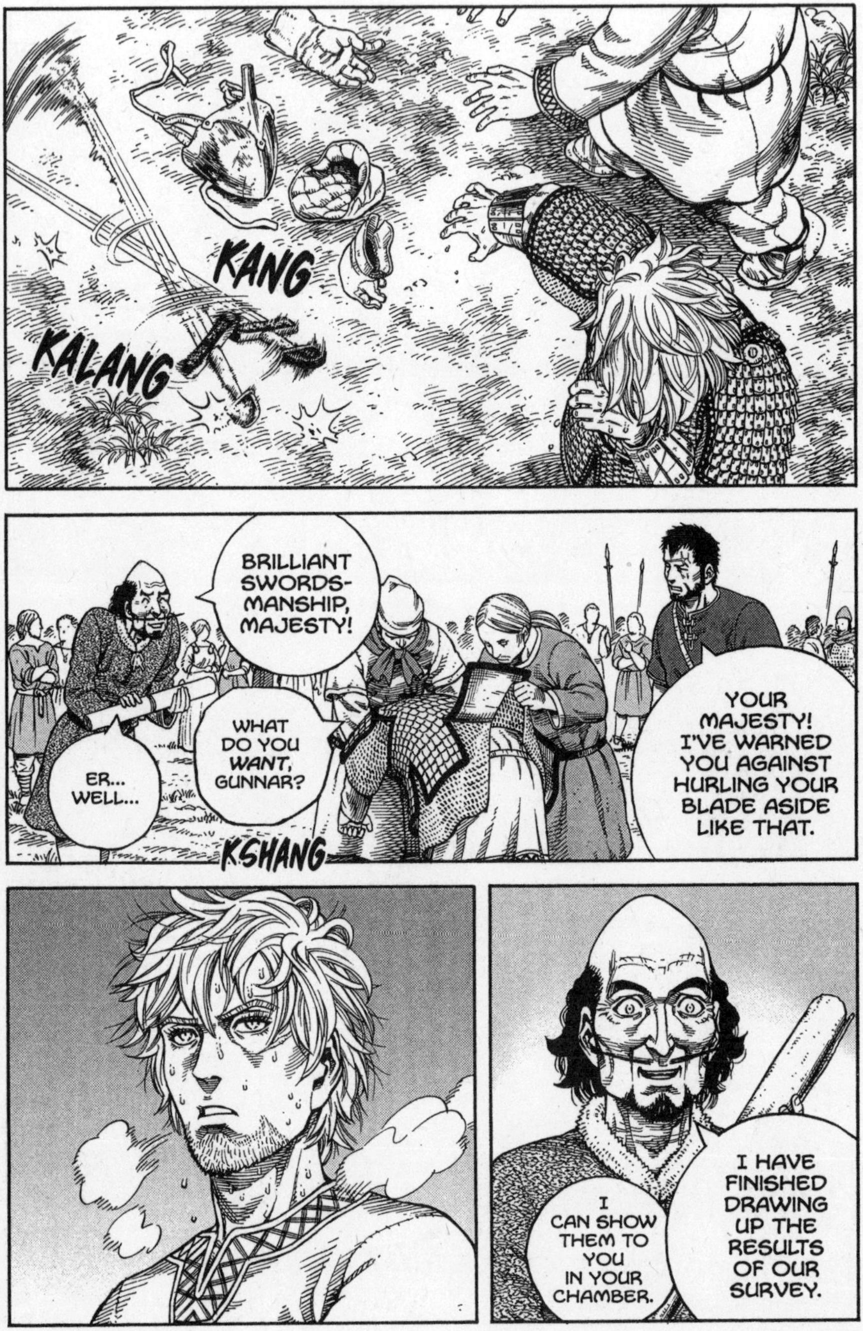
KANG
KALANG
BRILLIANT SWORDS-MANSHIP, MAJESTY!
YOUR MAJESTY! I'VE WARNED YOU AGAINST HURLING YOUR BLADE ASIDE LIKE THAT.
WHAT DO YOU *WANT*, GUNNAR?
ER... WELL...
KSHANG
I HAVE FINISHED DRAWING UP THE RESULTS OF OUR SURVEY.
I CAN SHOW THEM TO YOU IN YOUR CHAMBER.

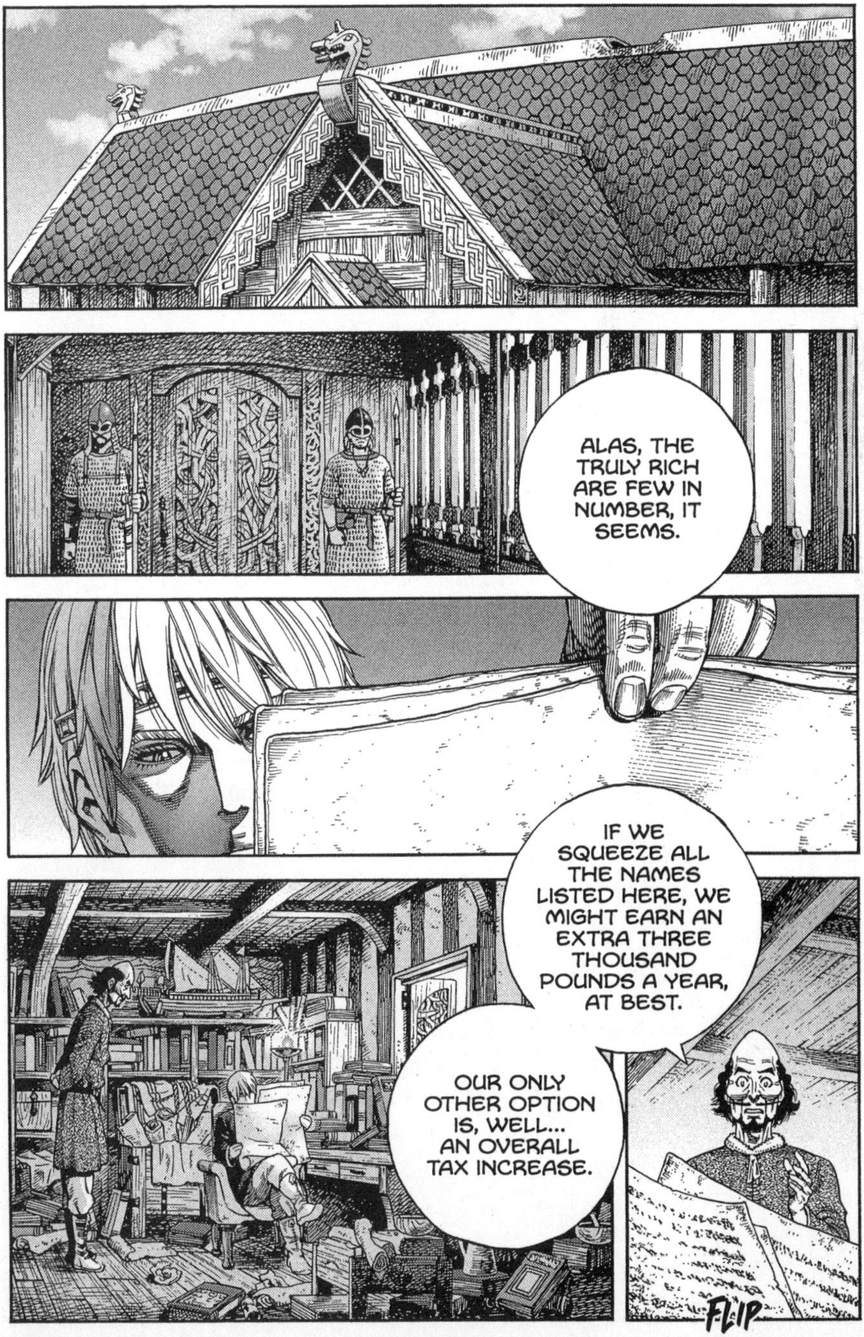
ALAS, THE TRULY RICH ARE FEW IN NUMBER, IT SEEMS.
IF WE SQUEEZE ALL THE NAMES LISTED HERE, WE MIGHT EARN AN EXTRA THREE THOUSAND POUNDS A YEAR, AT BEST.
OUR ONLY OTHER OPTION IS, WELL... AN OVERALL TAX INCREASE.
FLIP

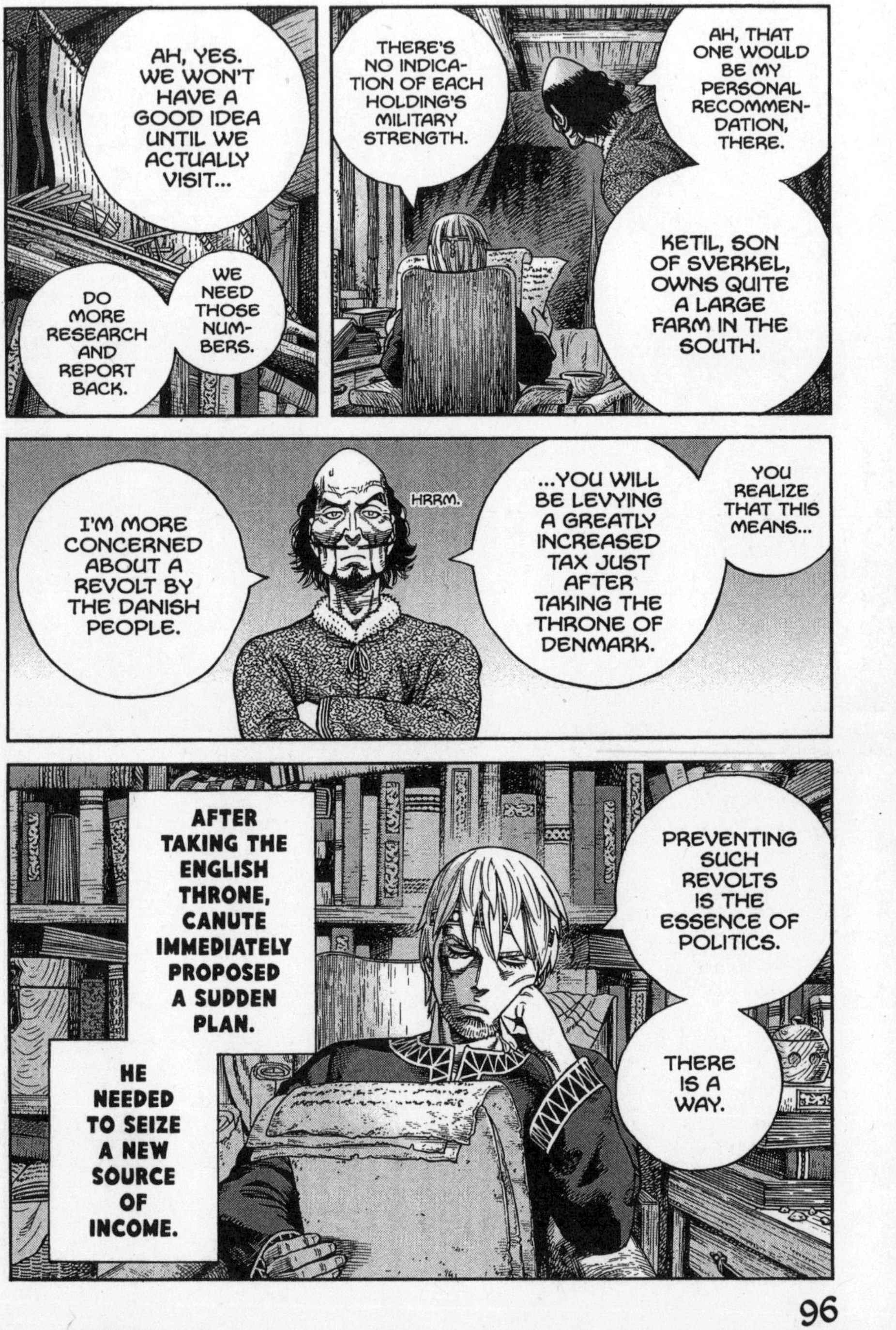
AH, THAT ONE WOULD BE MY PERSONAL RECOMMENDATION, THERE.
KETIL, SON OF SVERKEL, OWNS QUITE A LARGE FARM IN THE SOUTH.
THERE'S NO INDICATION OF EACH HOLDING'S MILITARY STRENGTH.
AH, YES. WE WON'T HAVE A GOOD IDEA UNTIL WE ACTUALLY VISIT...
WE NEED THOSE NUMBERS.
DO MORE RESEARCH AND REPORT BACK.
YOU REALIZE THAT THIS MEANS...
...YOU WILL BE LEVYING A GREATLY INCREASED TAX JUST AFTER TAKING THE THRONE OF DENMARK.
HRRM.
I'M MORE CONCERNED ABOUT A REVOLT BY THE DANISH PEOPLE.
PREVENTING SUCH REVOLTS IS THE ESSENCE OF POLITICS.
THERE IS A WAY.
AFTER TAKING THE ENGLISH THRONE, CANUTE IMMEDIATELY PROPOSED A SUDDEN PLAN.
HE NEEDED TO SEIZE A NEW SOURCE OF INCOME.

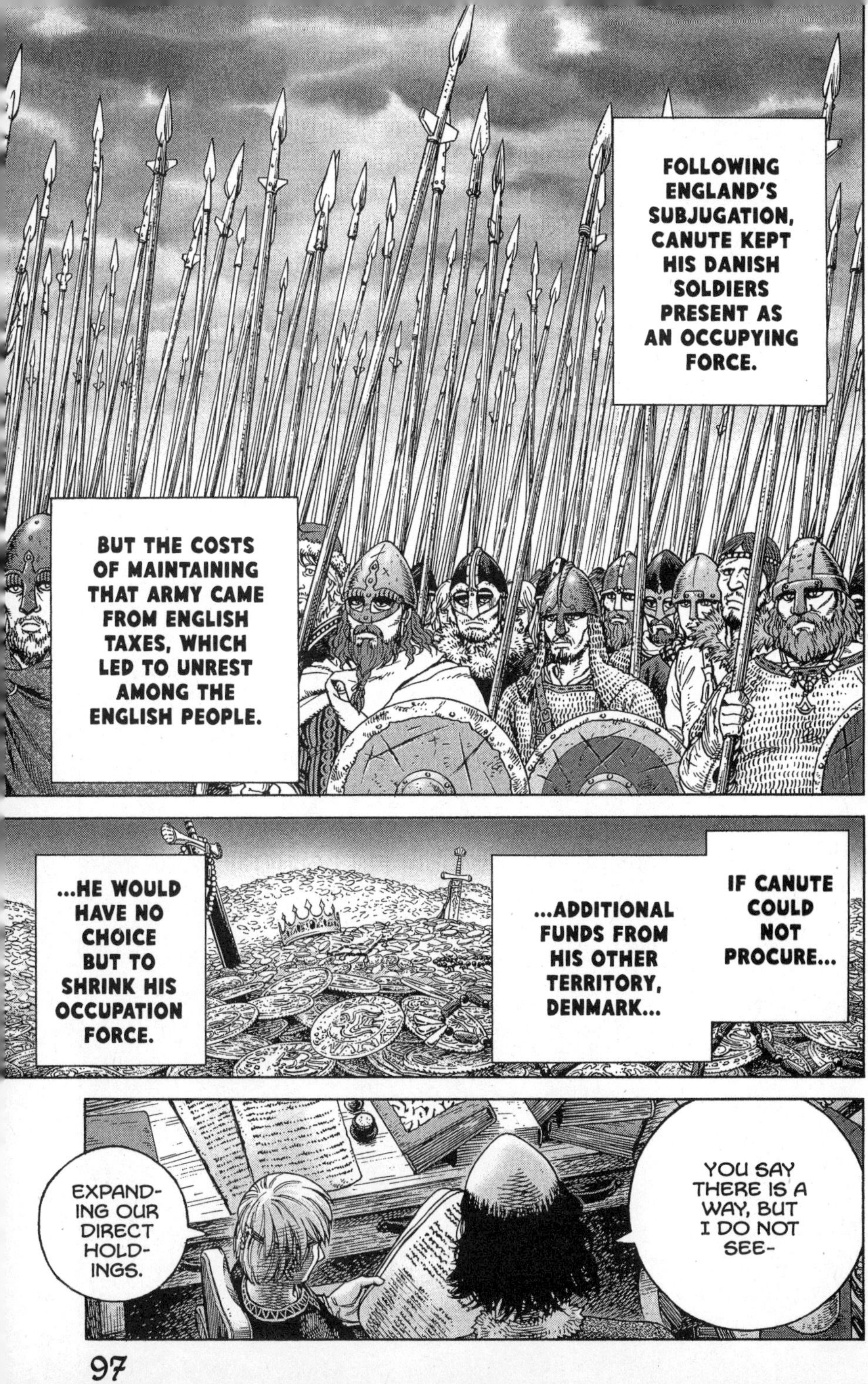
FOLLOWING ENGLAND'S SUBJUGATION, CANUTE KEPT HIS DANISH SOLDIERS PRESENT AS AN OCCUPYING FORCE.
BUT THE COSTS OF MAINTAINING THAT ARMY CAME FROM ENGLISH TAXES, WHICH LED TO UNREST AMONG THE ENGLISH PEOPLE.
IF CANUTE COULD NOT PROCURE...
...ADDITIONAL FUNDS FROM HIS OTHER TERRITORY, DENMARK...
...HE WOULD HAVE NO CHOICE BUT TO SHRINK HIS OCCUPATION FORCE.
YOU SAY THERE IS A WAY, BUT I DO NOT SEE-
EXPANDING OUR DIRECT HOLDINGS.

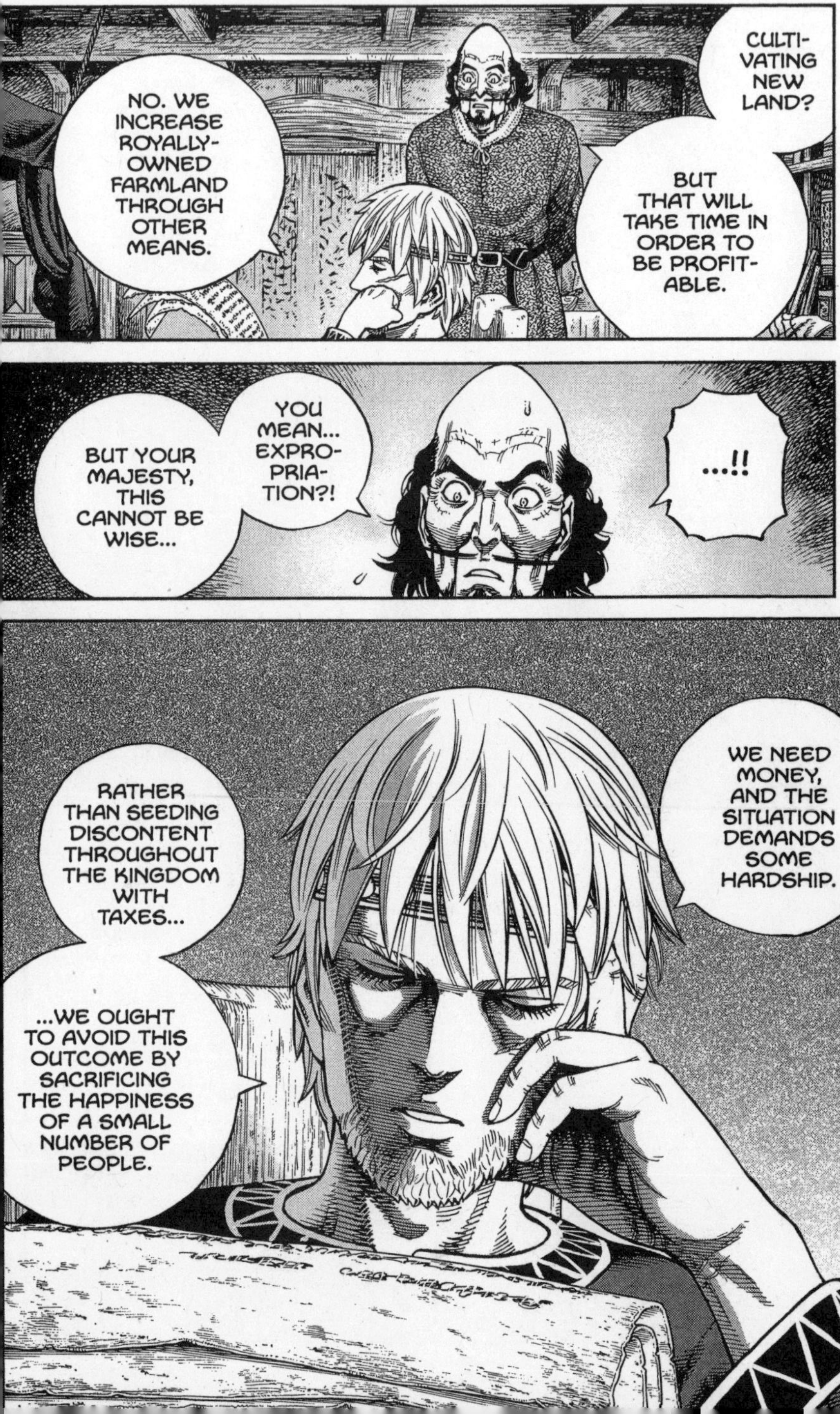
CULTI-VATING NEW LAND?
BUT THAT WILL TAKE TIME IN ORDER TO BE PROFIT-ABLE.
NO. WE INCREASE ROYALLY-OWNED FARMLAND THROUGH OTHER MEANS.
...!!
YOU MEAN... EXPRO-PRIA-TION?!
BUT YOUR MAJESTY, THIS CANNOT BE WISE...
WE NEED MONEY, AND THE SITUATION DEMANDS SOME HARDSHIP.
RATHER THAN SEEDING DISCONTENT THROUGHOUT THE KINGDOM WITH TAXES...
...WE OUGHT TO AVOID THIS OUTCOME BY SACRIFICING THE HAPPINESS OF A SMALL NUMBER OF PEOPLE.

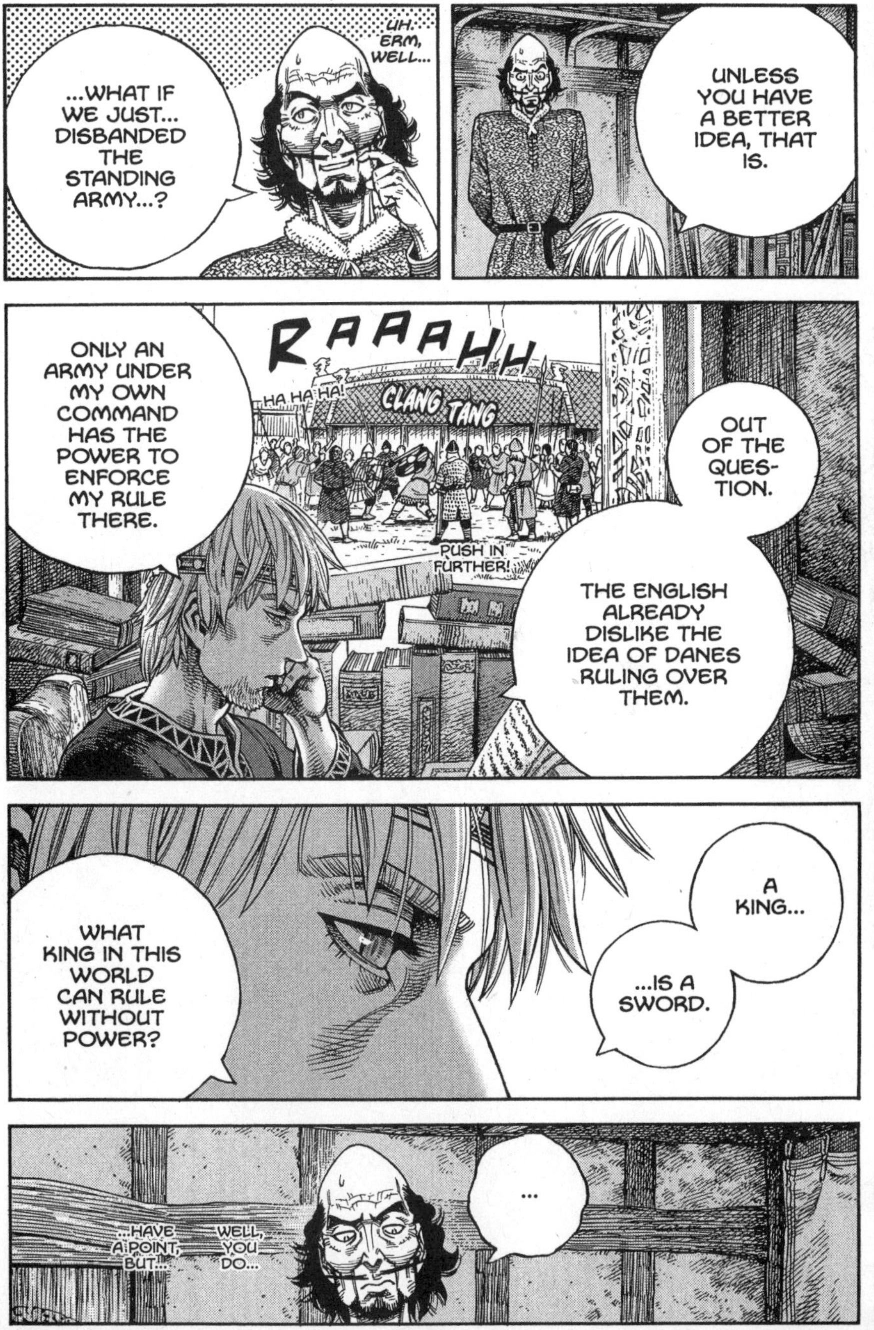
UNLESS YOU HAVE A BETTER IDEA, THAT IS.
UH. ERM, WELL...
...WHAT IF WE JUST... DISBANDED THE STANDING ARMY...?
RAAAHH
HA HA HA!
CLANG TANG
OUT OF THE QUES-TION.
THE ENGLISH ALREADY DISLIKE THE IDEA OF DANES RULING OVER THEM.
ONLY AN ARMY UNDER MY OWN COMMAND HAS THE POWER TO ENFORCE MY RULE THERE.
PUSH IN FURTHER!
A KING...
...IS A SWORD.
WHAT KING IN THIS WORLD CAN RULE WITHOUT POWER?
...
WELL, YOU DO...
...HAVE A POINT, BUT...

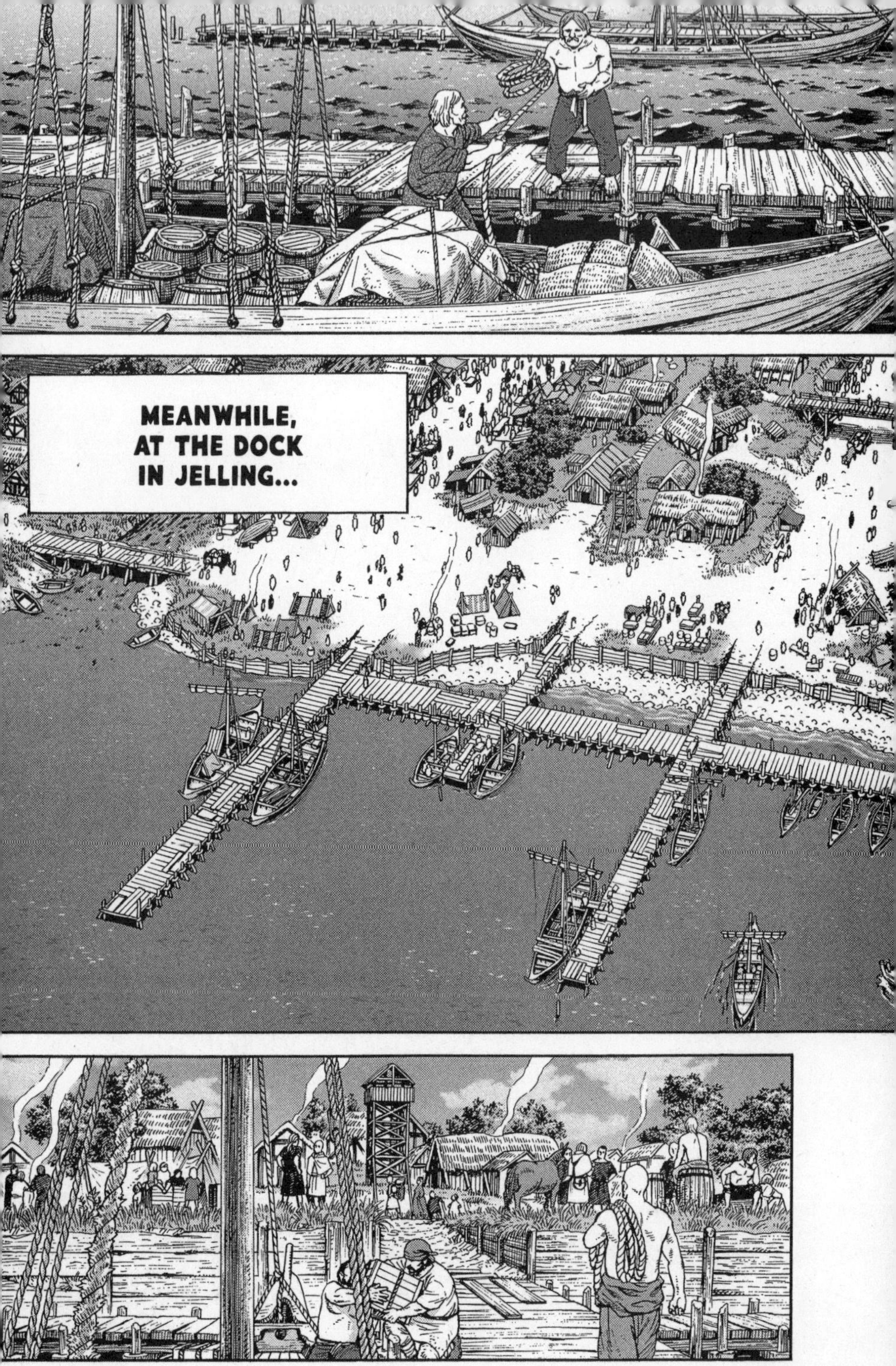
MEANWHILE, AT THE DOCK IN JELLING...

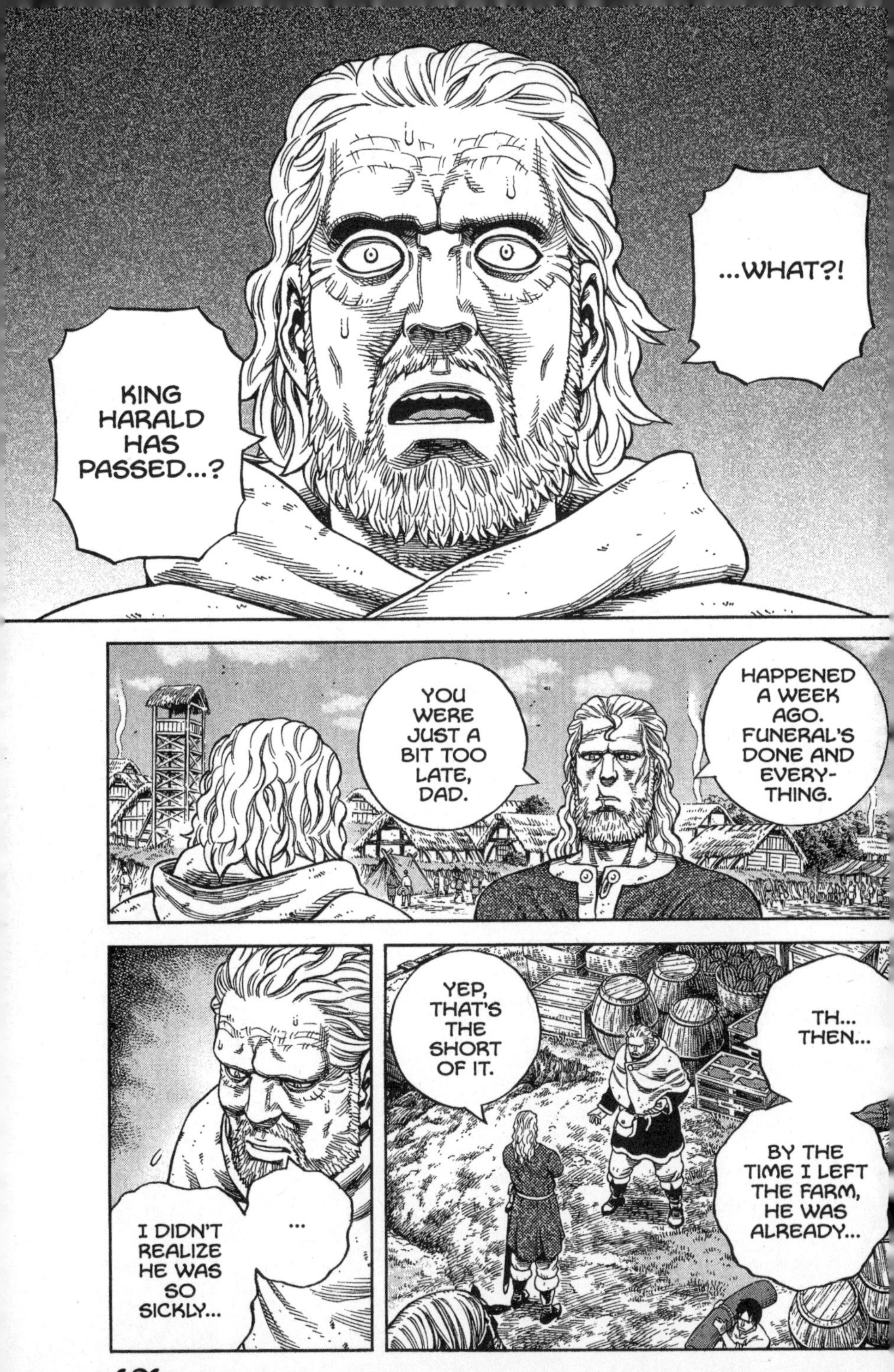
...WHAT?!
KING HARALD HAS PASSED...?
HAPPENED A WEEK AGO. FUNERAL'S DONE AND EVERY-THING.
YOU WERE JUST A BIT TOO LATE, DAD.
TH... THEN...
BY THE TIME I LEFT THE FARM, HE WAS ALREADY...
YEP, THAT'S THE SHORT OF IT.
...
I DIDN'T REALIZE HE WAS SO SICKLY...

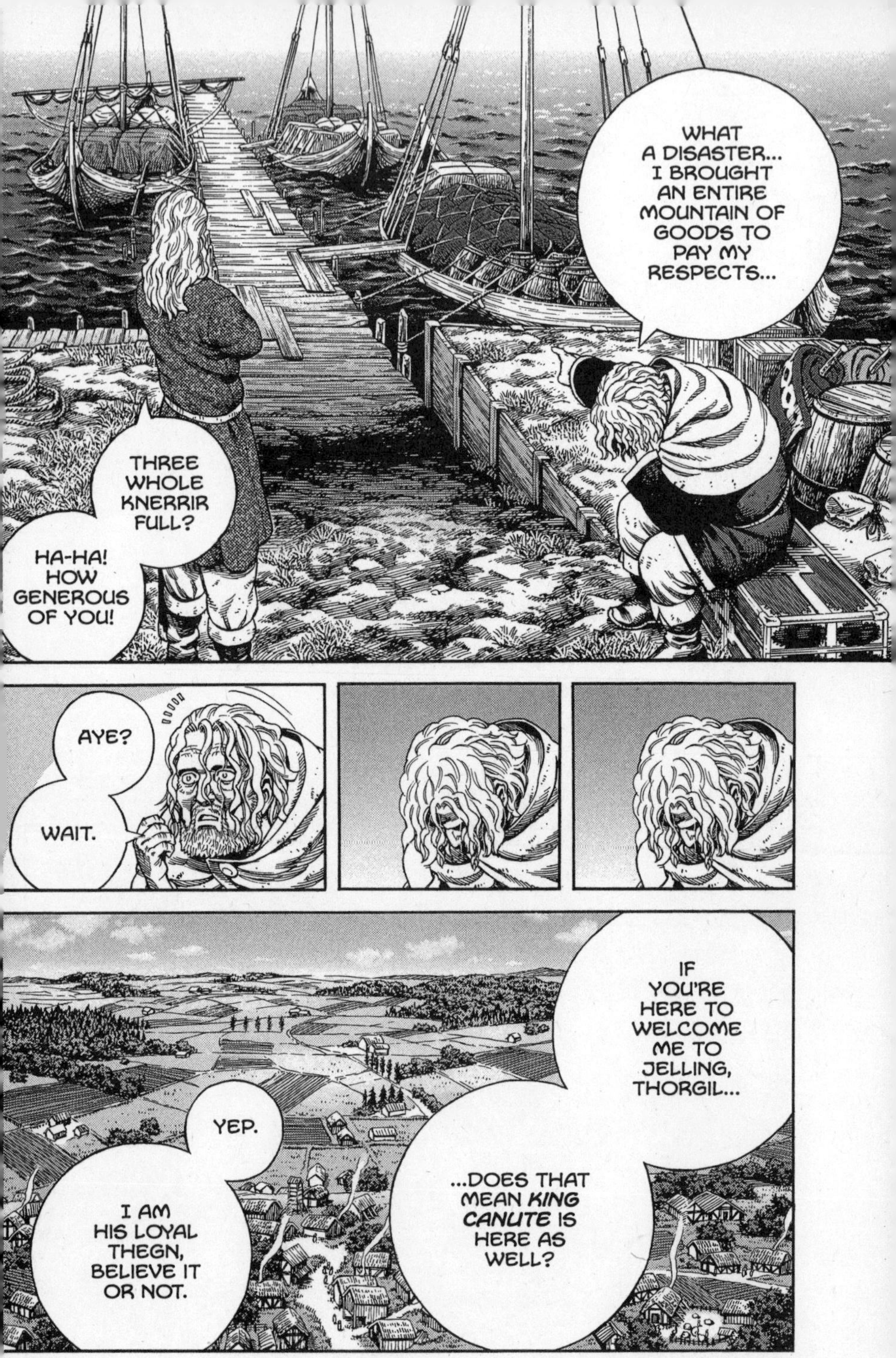
WHAT A DISASTER... I BROUGHT AN ENTIRE MOUNTAIN OF GOODS TO PAY MY RESPECTS...
THREE WHOLE KNERRIR FULL?
HA-HA! HOW GENEROUS OF YOU!
AYE?
WAIT.
IF YOU'RE HERE TO WELCOME ME TO JELLING, THORGIL...
...DOES THAT MEAN *KING CANUTE* IS HERE AS WELL?
YEP.
I AM HIS LOYAL THEGN, BELIEVE IT OR NOT.

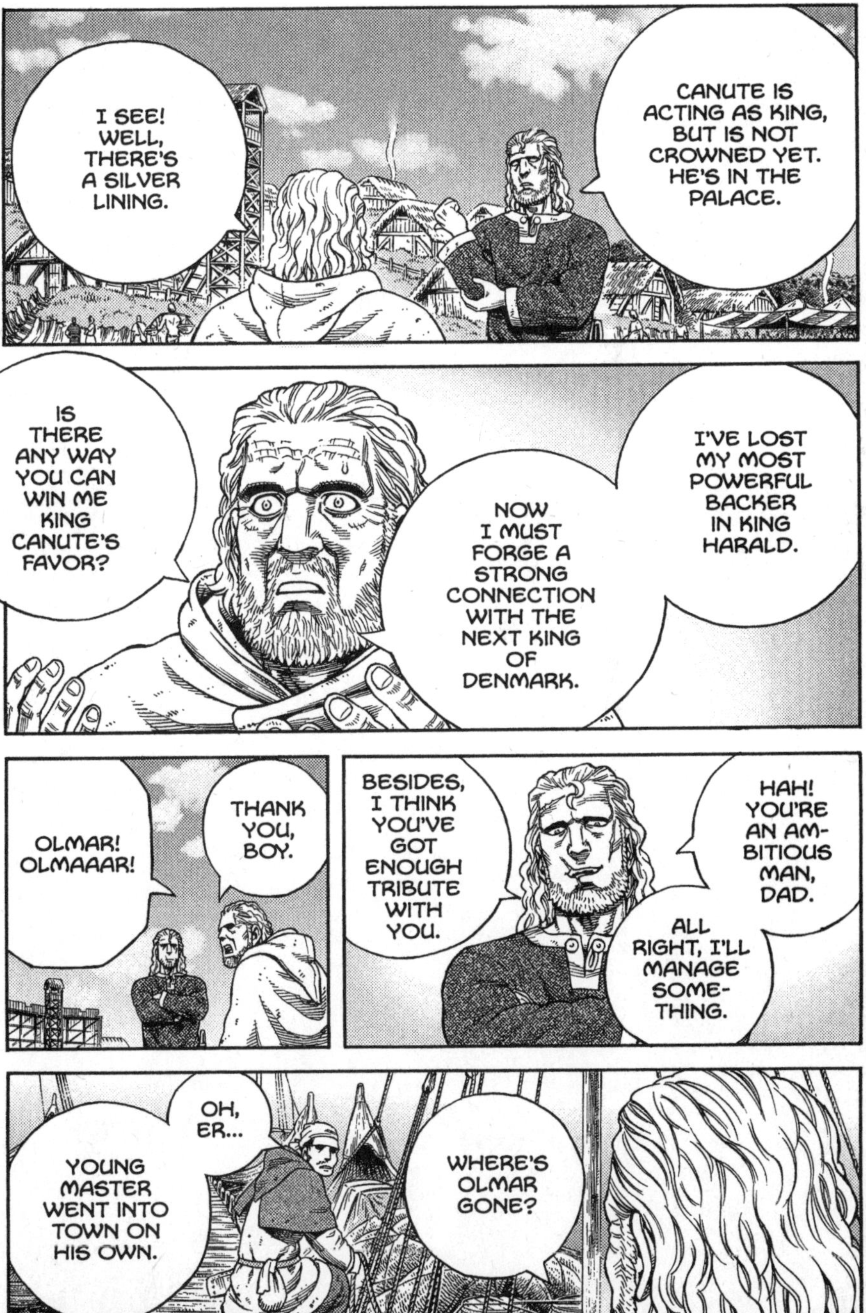
CANUTE IS ACTING AS KING, BUT IS NOT CROWNED YET. HE'S IN THE PALACE.
I SEE! WELL, THERE'S A SILVER LINING.
I'VE LOST MY MOST POWERFUL BACKER IN KING HARALD.
NOW I MUST FORGE A STRONG CONNECTION WITH THE NEXT KING OF DENMARK.
IS THERE ANY WAY YOU CAN WIN ME KING CANUTE'S FAVOR?
HAH! YOU'RE AN AM-BITIOUS MAN, DAD.
BESIDES, I THINK YOU'VE GOT ENOUGH TRIBUTE WITH YOU.
ALL RIGHT, I'LL MANAGE SOME-THING.
THANK YOU, BOY.
OLMAR! OLMAAAR!
WHERE'S OLMAR GONE?
OH, ER...
YOUNG MASTER WENT INTO TOWN ON HIS OWN.

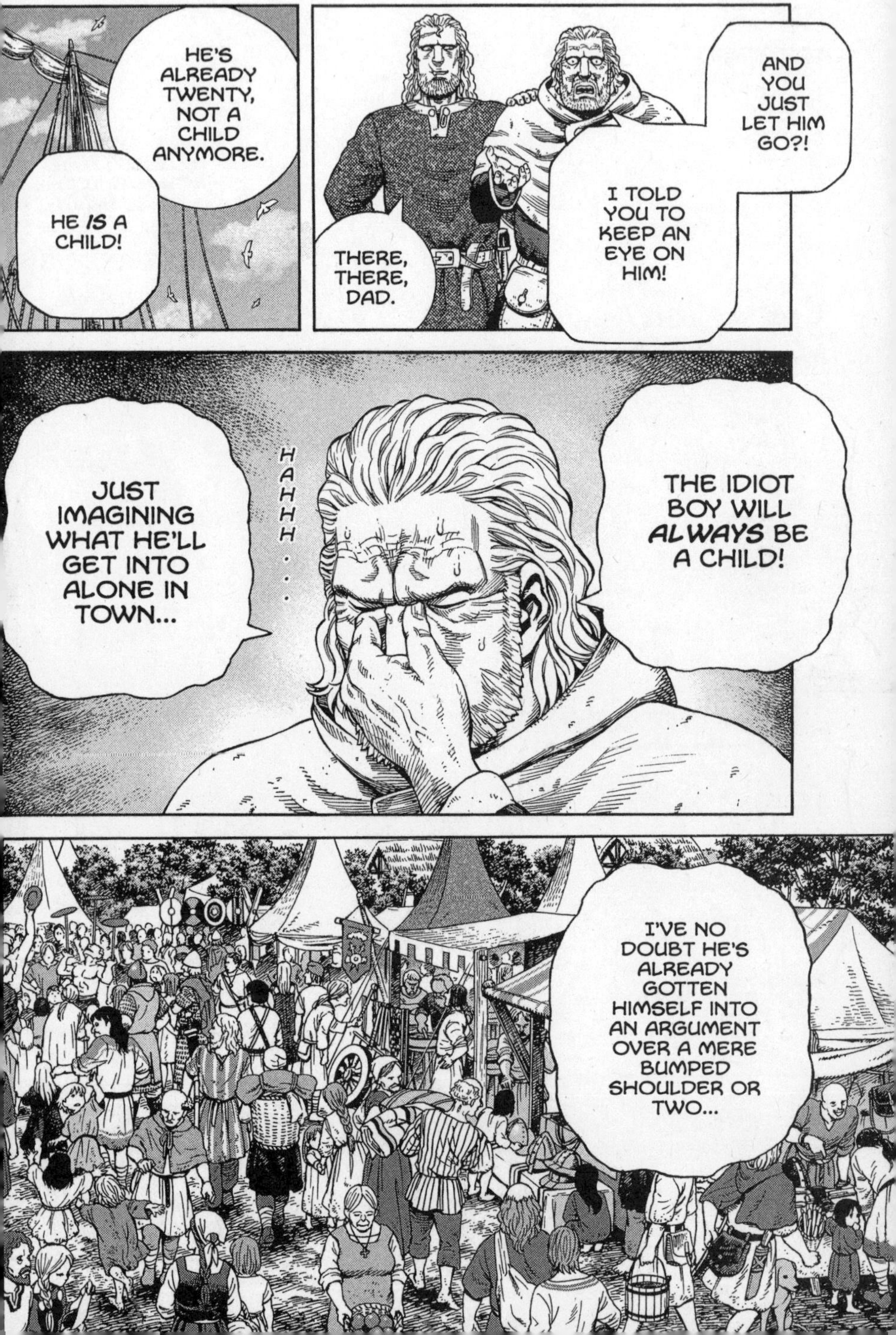
AND YOU JUST LET HIM GO?!
I TOLD YOU TO KEEP AN EYE ON HIM!
THERE, THERE, DAD.
HE'S ALREADY TWENTY, NOT A CHILD ANYMORE.
HE *IS* A CHILD!
THE IDIOT BOY WILL *ALWAYS* BE A CHILD!
HAHHH...
JUST IMAGINING WHAT HE'LL GET INTO ALONE IN TOWN...
I'VE NO DOUBT HE'S ALREADY GOTTEN HIMSELF INTO AN ARGUMENT OVER A MERE BUMPED SHOULDER OR TWO...

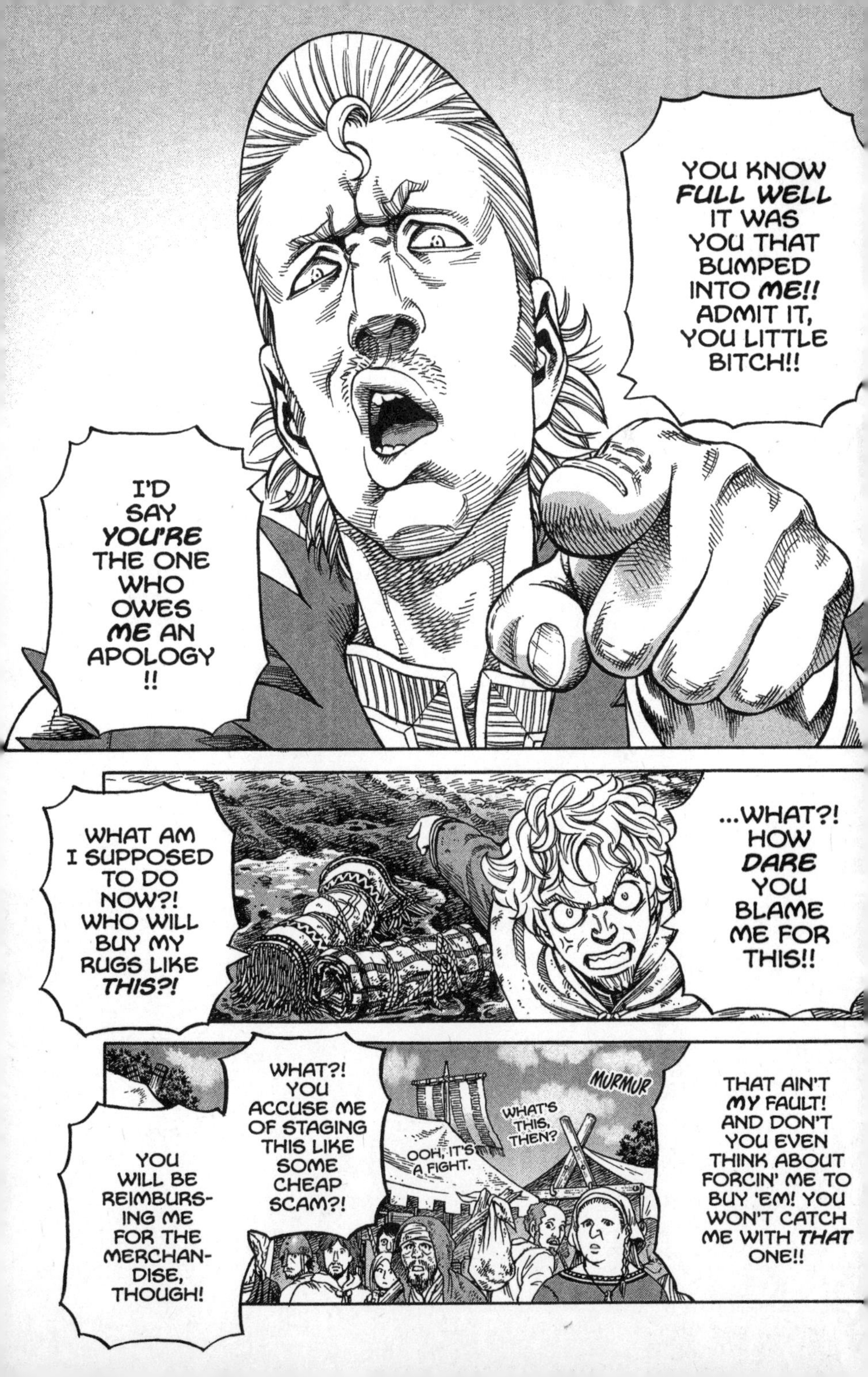
YOU KNOW FULL WELL IT WAS YOU THAT BUMPED INTO ME!! ADMIT IT, YOU LITTLE BITCH!!
I'D SAY YOU'RE THE ONE WHO OWES ME AN APOLOGY !!
...WHAT?! HOW DARE YOU BLAME ME FOR THIS!!
WHAT AM I SUPPOSED TO DO NOW?! WHO WILL BUY MY RUGS LIKE THIS?!
THAT AIN'T MY FAULT! AND DON'T YOU EVEN THINK ABOUT FORCIN' ME TO BUY 'EM! YOU WON'T CATCH ME WITH THAT ONE!!
MURMUR
WHAT'S THIS, THEN?
WHAT?! YOU ACCUSE ME OF STAGING THIS LIKE SOME CHEAP SCAM?!
OOH, IT'S A FIGHT.
YOU WILL BE REIMBURSING ME FOR THE MERCHANDISE, THOUGH!

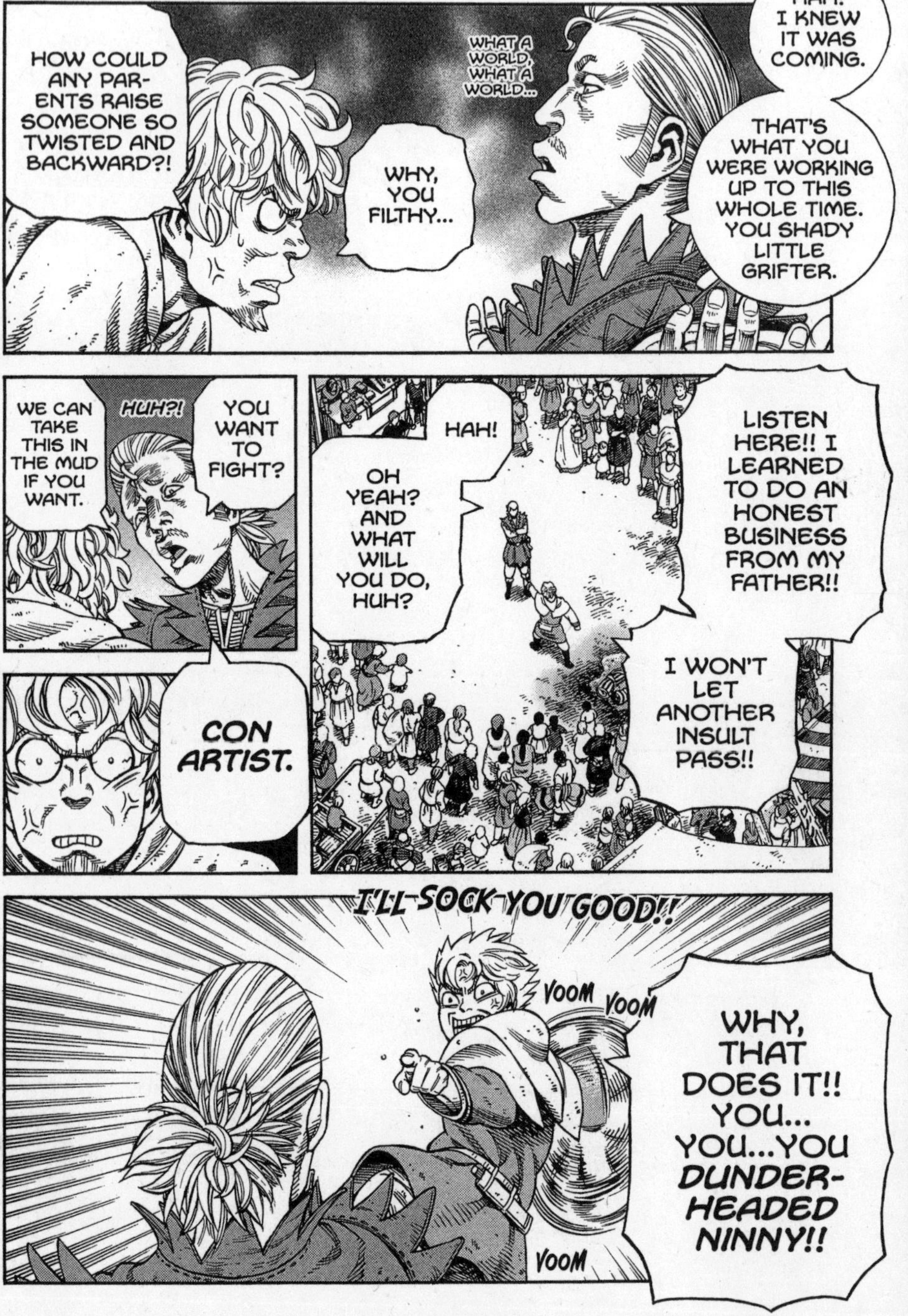
HAH! I KNEW IT WAS COMING.
THAT'S WHAT YOU WERE WORKING UP TO THIS WHOLE TIME. YOU SHADY LITTLE GRIFTER.
WHAT A WORLD, WHAT A WORLD...
WHY, YOU FILTHY...
HOW COULD ANY PAR-ENTS RAISE SOMEONE SO TWISTED AND BACKWARD?!
LISTEN HERE!! I LEARNED TO DO AN HONEST BUSINESS FROM MY FATHER!!
I WON'T LET ANOTHER INSULT PASS!!
HAH!
OH YEAH? AND WHAT WILL YOU DO, HUH?
YOU WANT TO FIGHT?
HUH?!
WE CAN TAKE THIS IN THE MUD IF YOU WANT.
CON ARTIST.
I'LL SOCK YOU GOOD!!
WHY, THAT DOES IT!! YOU... YOU...YOU DUNDER-HEADED NINNY!!
VOOM VOOM
VOOM

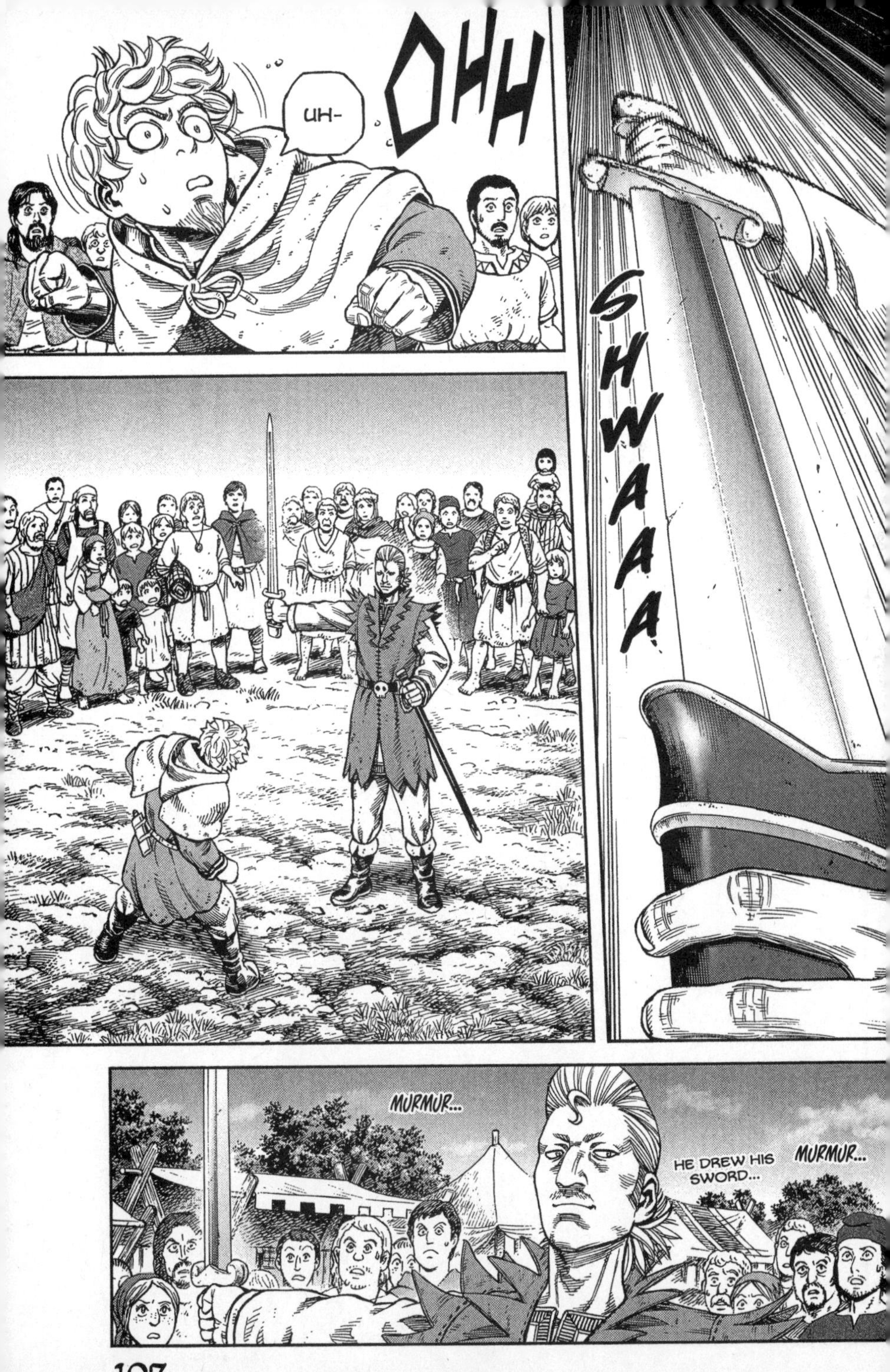
SHWAAAA
OHH
UH-
MURMUR...
HE DREW HIS SWORD...
MURMUR...

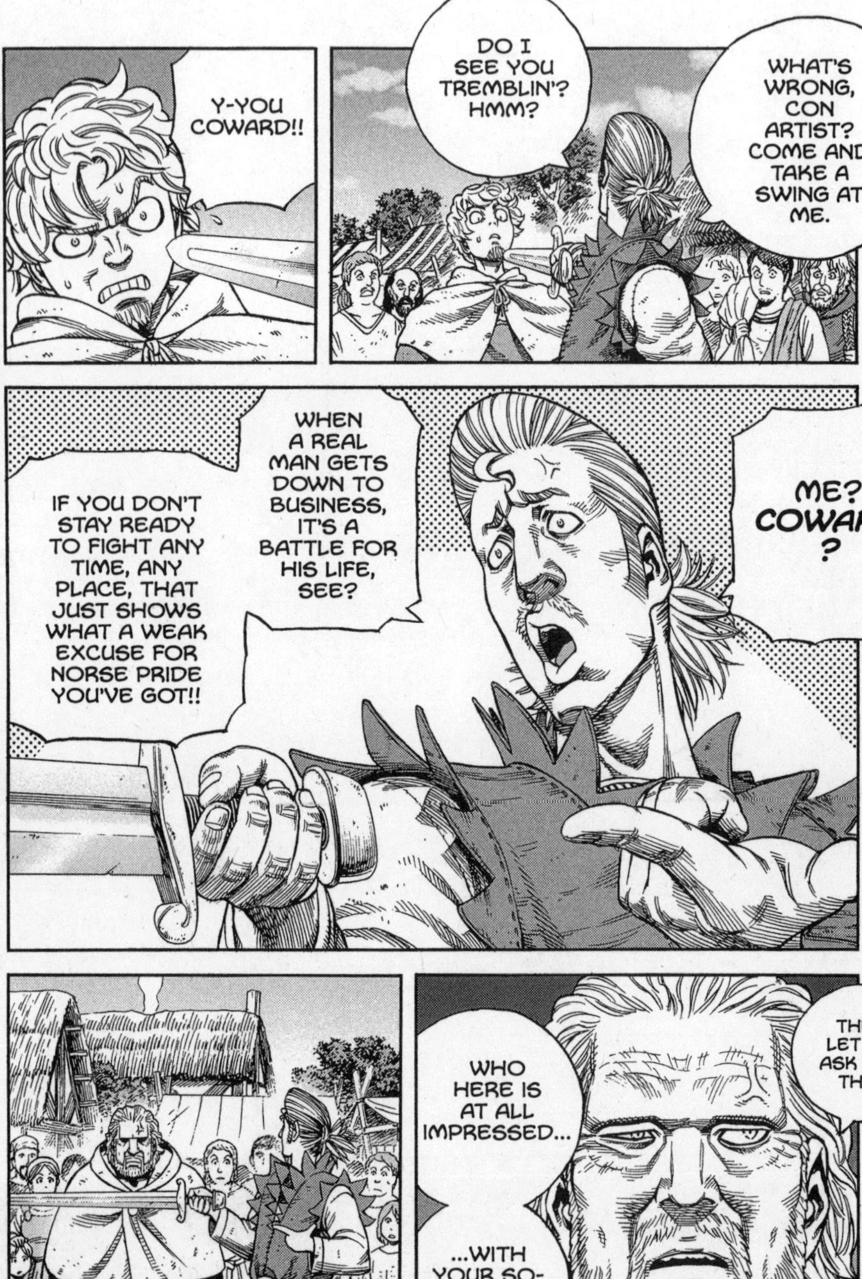
WHAT'S WRONG, CON ARTIST? COME AND TAKE A SWING AT ME.
DO I SEE YOU TREMBLIN'? HMM?
Y-YOU COWARD!!
ME? COWARD?
WHEN A REAL MAN GETS DOWN TO BUSINESS, IT'S A BATTLE FOR HIS LIFE, SEE?
IF YOU DON'T STAY READY TO FIGHT ANY TIME, ANY PLACE, THAT JUST SHOWS WHAT A WEAK EXCUSE FOR NORSE PRIDE YOU'VE GOT!!
THEN LET ME ASK YOU THIS.
WHO HERE IS AT ALL IMPRESSED...
...WITH YOUR SO-CALLED "PRIDE"?

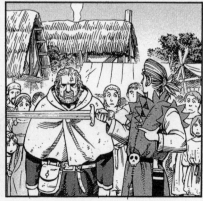

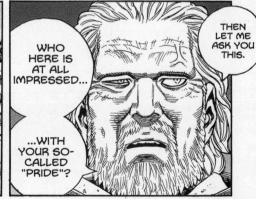

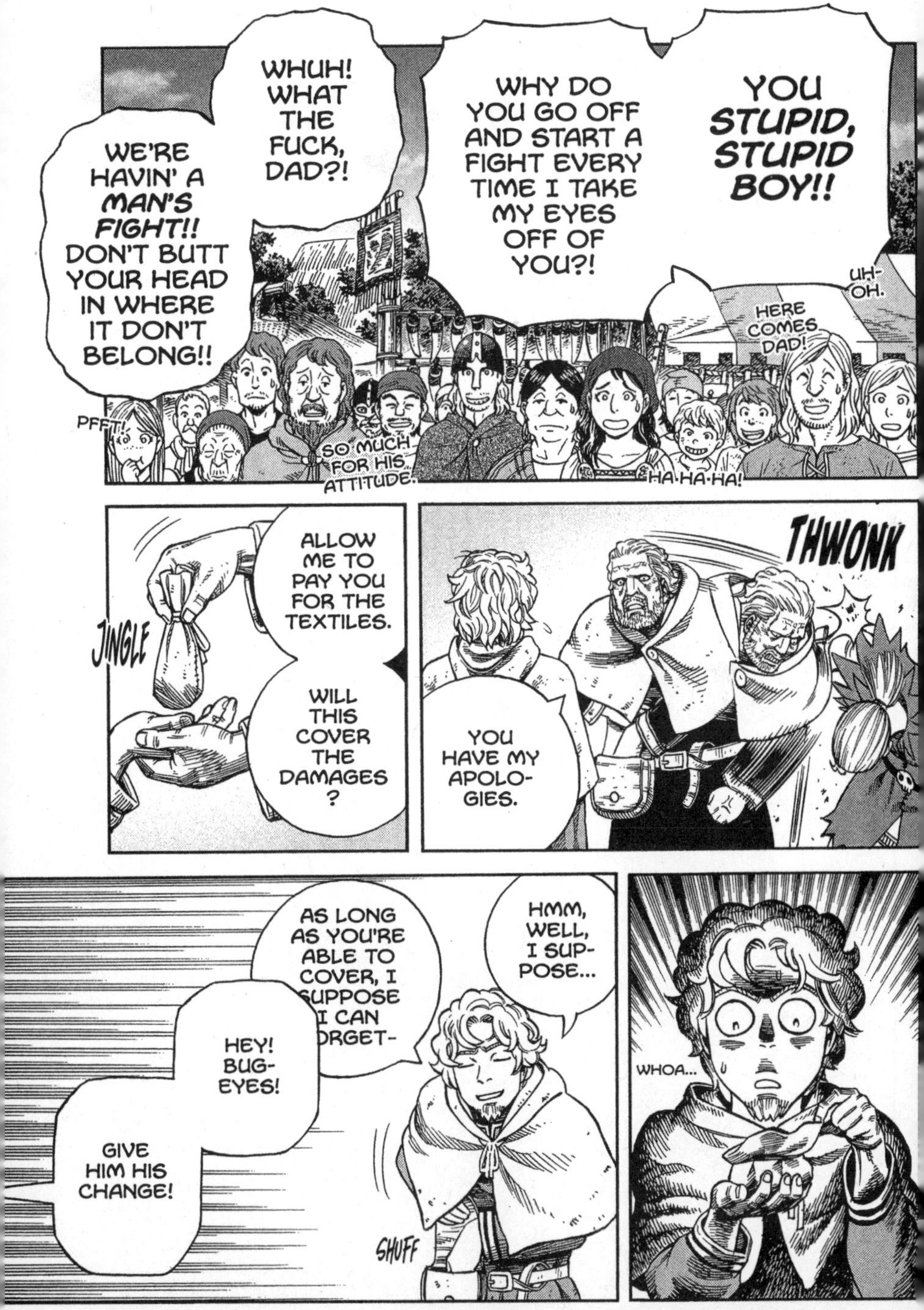
YOU STUPID, STUPID BOY!!
WHY DO YOU GO OFF AND START A FIGHT EVERY TIME I TAKE MY EYES OFF OF YOU?!
WHUH! WHAT THE FUCK, DAD?!
WE'RE HAVIN' A MAN'S FIGHT!! DON'T BUTT YOUR HEAD IN WHERE IT DON'T BELONG!!
UH-OH.
HERE COMES DAD!
HA-HA-HA!
SO MUCH FOR HIS ATTITUDE.
PFFT!
THWONK
YOU HAVE MY APOLOGIES.
ALLOW ME TO PAY YOU FOR THE TEXTILES.
WILL THIS COVER THE DAMAGES?
JINGLE
WHOA...
HMM, WELL, I SUPPOSE...
AS LONG AS YOU'RE ABLE TO COVER, I SUPPOSE I CAN FORGET-
HEY! BUG-EYES!
GIVE HIM HIS CHANGE!
SHUFF

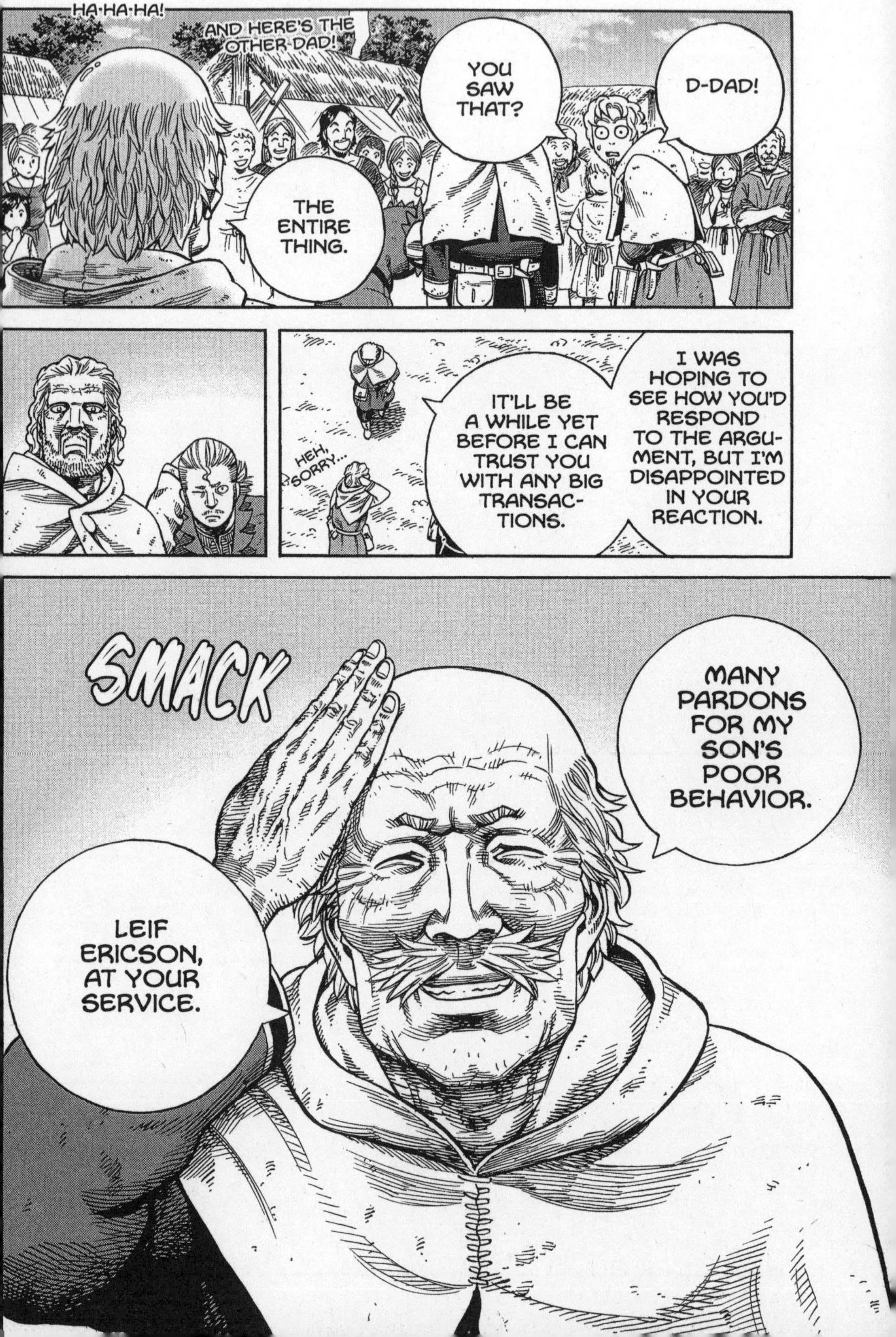
D-DAD!
YOU SAW THAT?
AND HERE'S THE OTHER DAD!
HA-HA-HA!
THE ENTIRE THING.
I WAS HOPING TO SEE HOW YOU'D RESPOND TO THE ARGUMENT, BUT I'M DISAPPOINTED IN YOUR REACTION.
IT'LL BE A WHILE YET BEFORE I CAN TRUST YOU WITH ANY BIG TRANSACTIONS.
HEH, SORRY...
MANY PARDONS FOR MY SON'S POOR BEHAVIOR.
SMACK
LEIF ERICSON, AT YOUR SERVICE.

CHAPTER 76: OLMAR'S FINEST HOUR

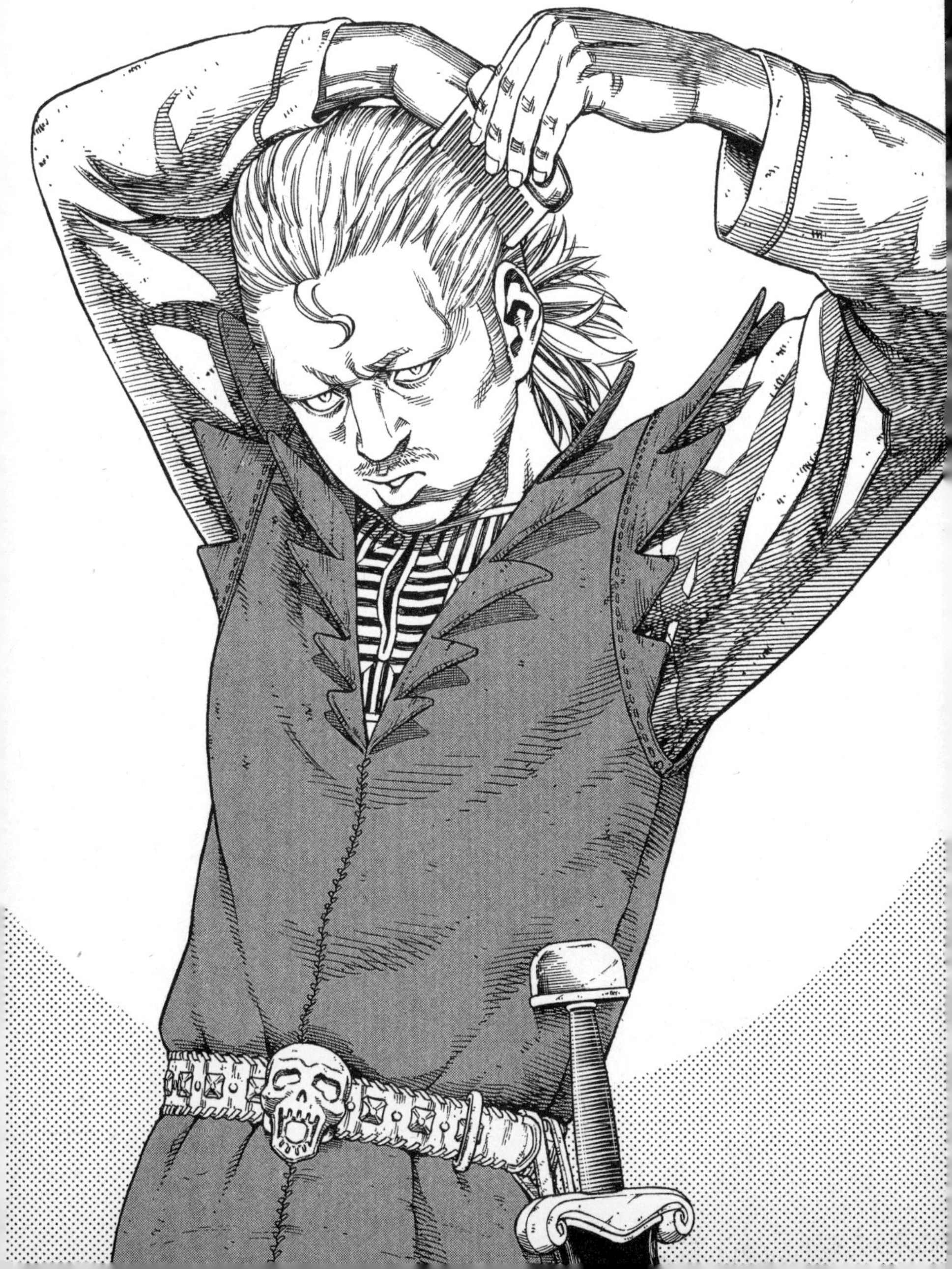

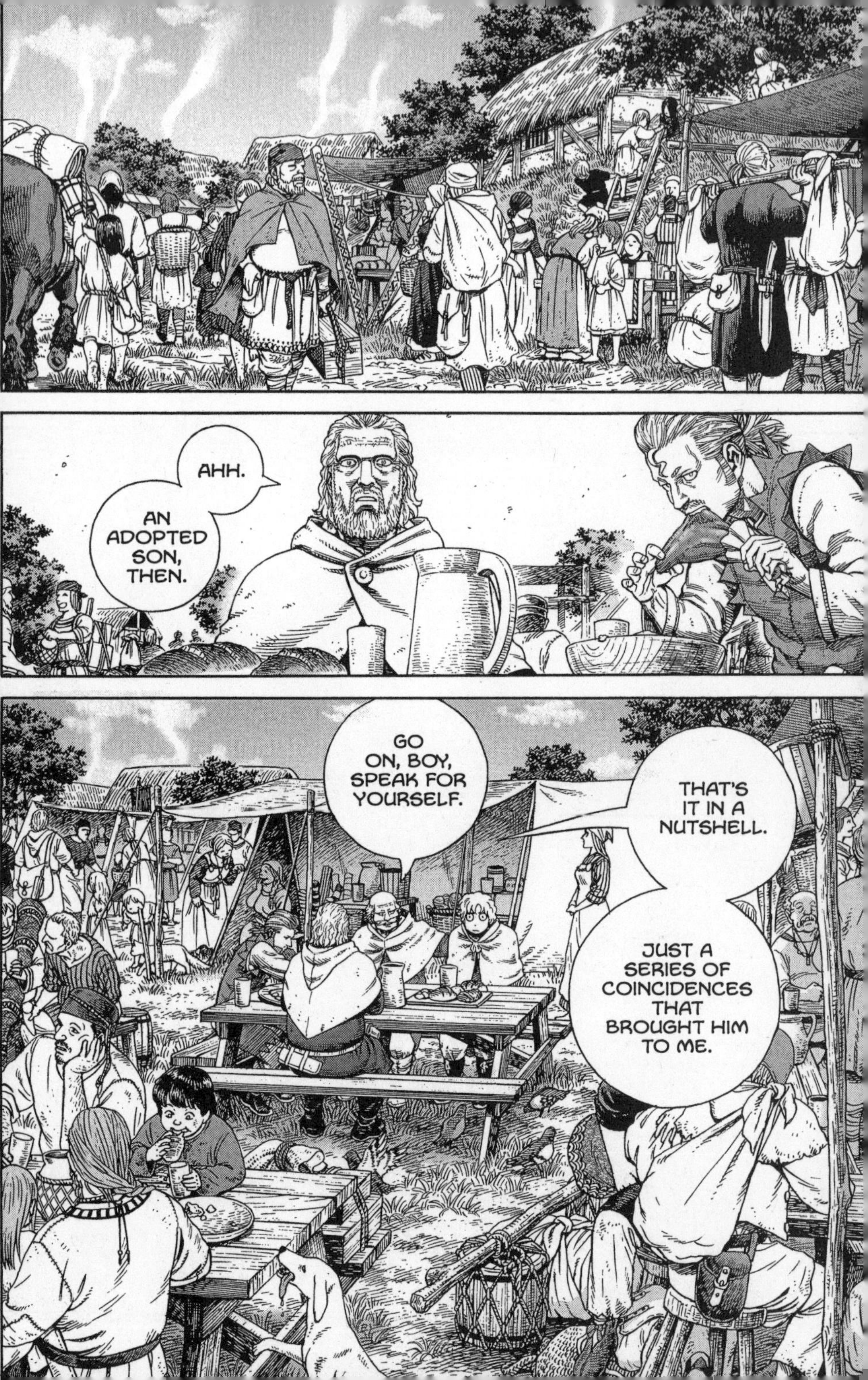
AHH.
AN ADOPTED SON, THEN.
THAT'S IT IN A NUTSHELL.
JUST A SERIES OF COINCIDENCES THAT BROUGHT HIM TO ME.
GO ON, BOY, SPEAK FOR YOURSELF.

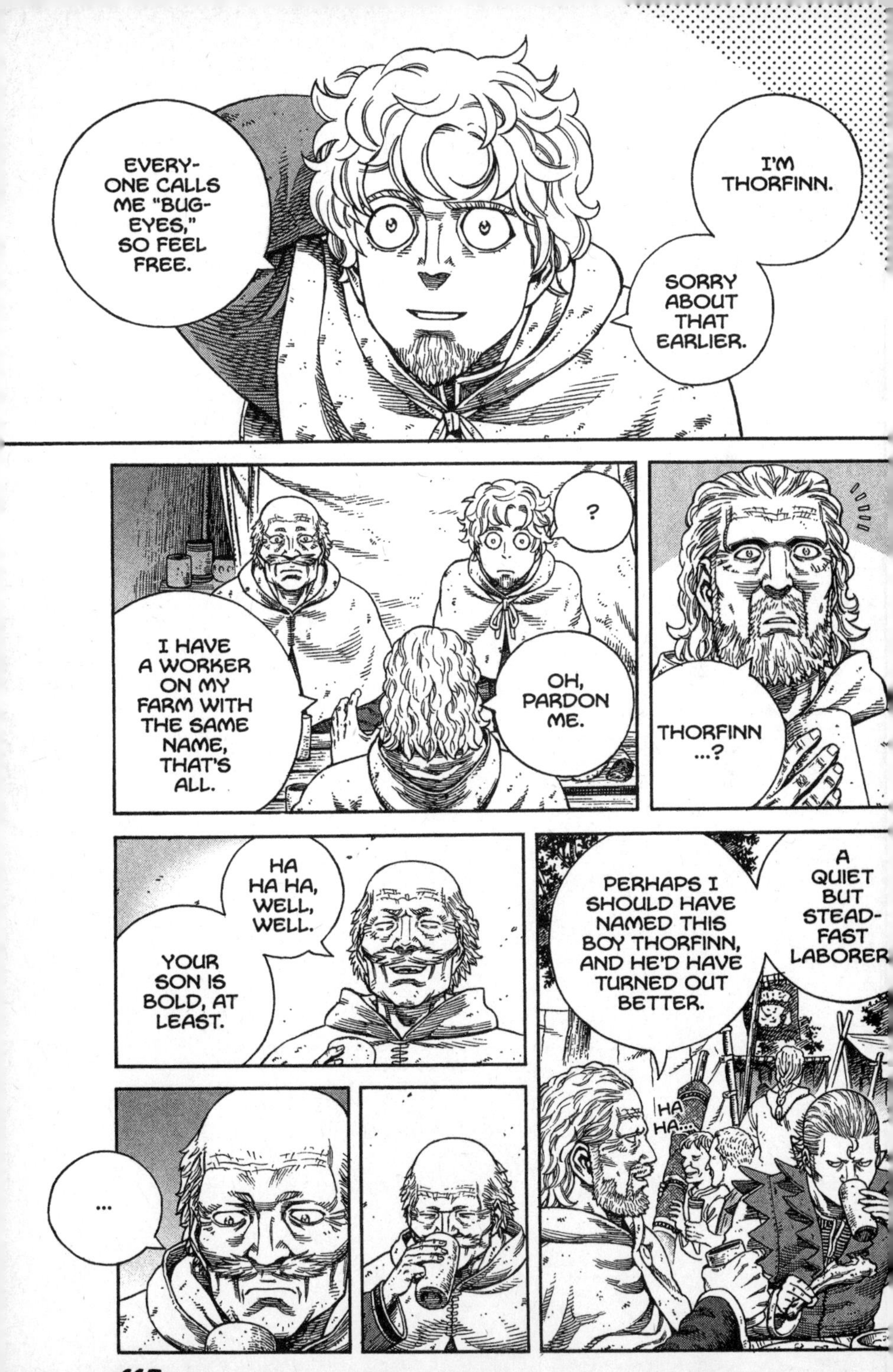
I'M THORFINN.
SORRY ABOUT THAT EARLIER.
EVERY-ONE CALLS ME "BUG-EYES," SO FEEL FREE.
THORFINN ...?
?
OH, PARDON ME.
I HAVE A WORKER ON MY FARM WITH THE SAME NAME, THAT'S ALL.
A QUIET BUT STEAD-FAST LABORER
PERHAPS I SHOULD HAVE NAMED THIS BOY THORFINN, AND HE'D HAVE TURNED OUT BETTER.
HA HA...
HA HA HA, WELL, WELL.
YOUR SON IS BOLD, AT LEAST.
...

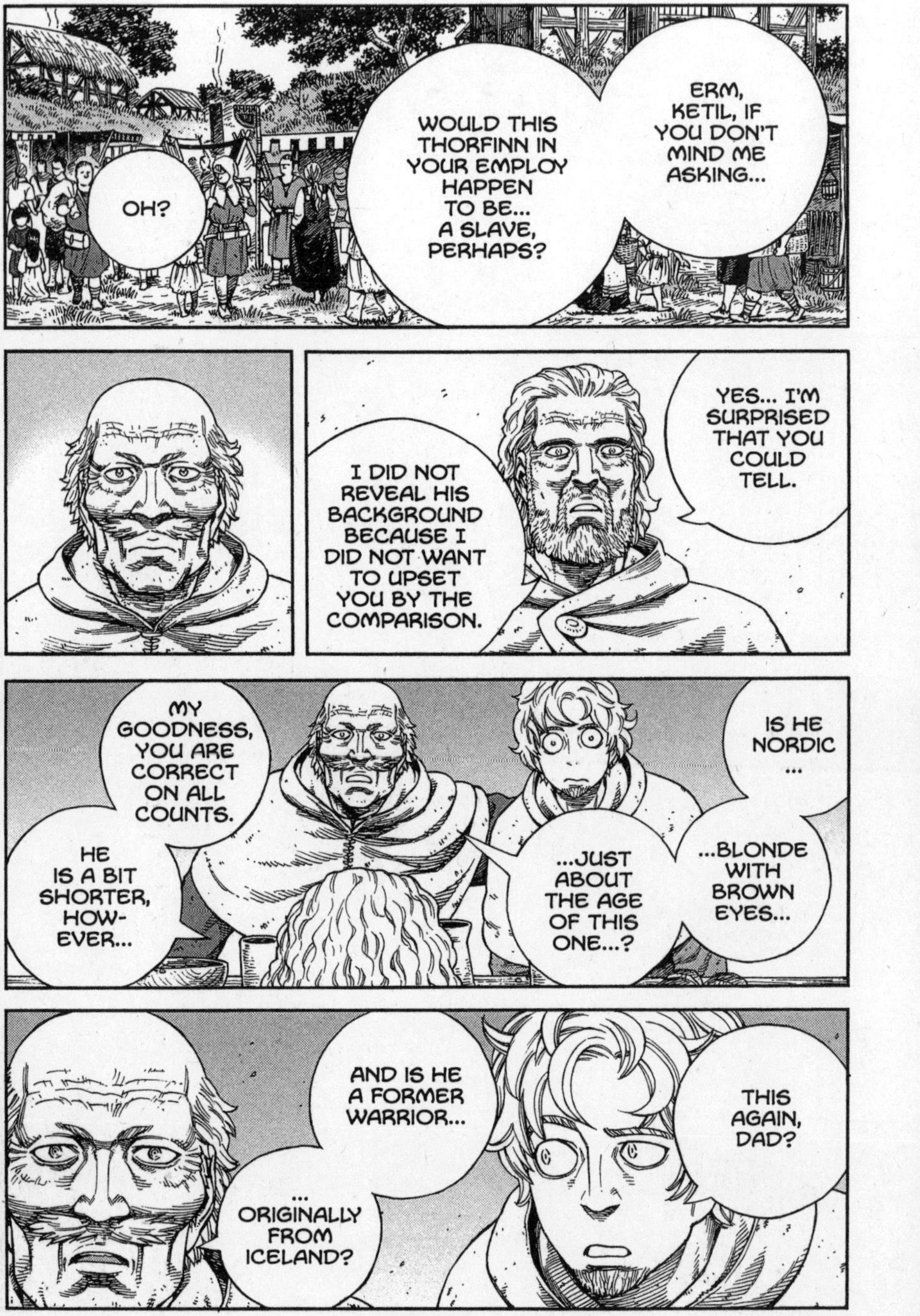
ERM, KETIL, IF YOU DON'T MIND ME ASKING...
WOULD THIS THORFINN IN YOUR EMPLOY HAPPEN TO BE... A SLAVE, PERHAPS?
OH?
YES... I'M SURPRISED THAT YOU COULD TELL.
I DID NOT REVEAL HIS BACKGROUND BECAUSE I DID NOT WANT TO UPSET YOU BY THE COMPARISON.
IS HE NORDIC ...
...BLONDE WITH BROWN EYES...
...JUST ABOUT THE AGE OF THIS ONE...?
MY GOODNESS, YOU ARE CORRECT ON ALL COUNTS.
HE IS A BIT SHORTER, HOW-EVER...
THIS AGAIN, DAD?
AND IS HE A FORMER WARRIOR...
... ORIGINALLY FROM ICELAND?

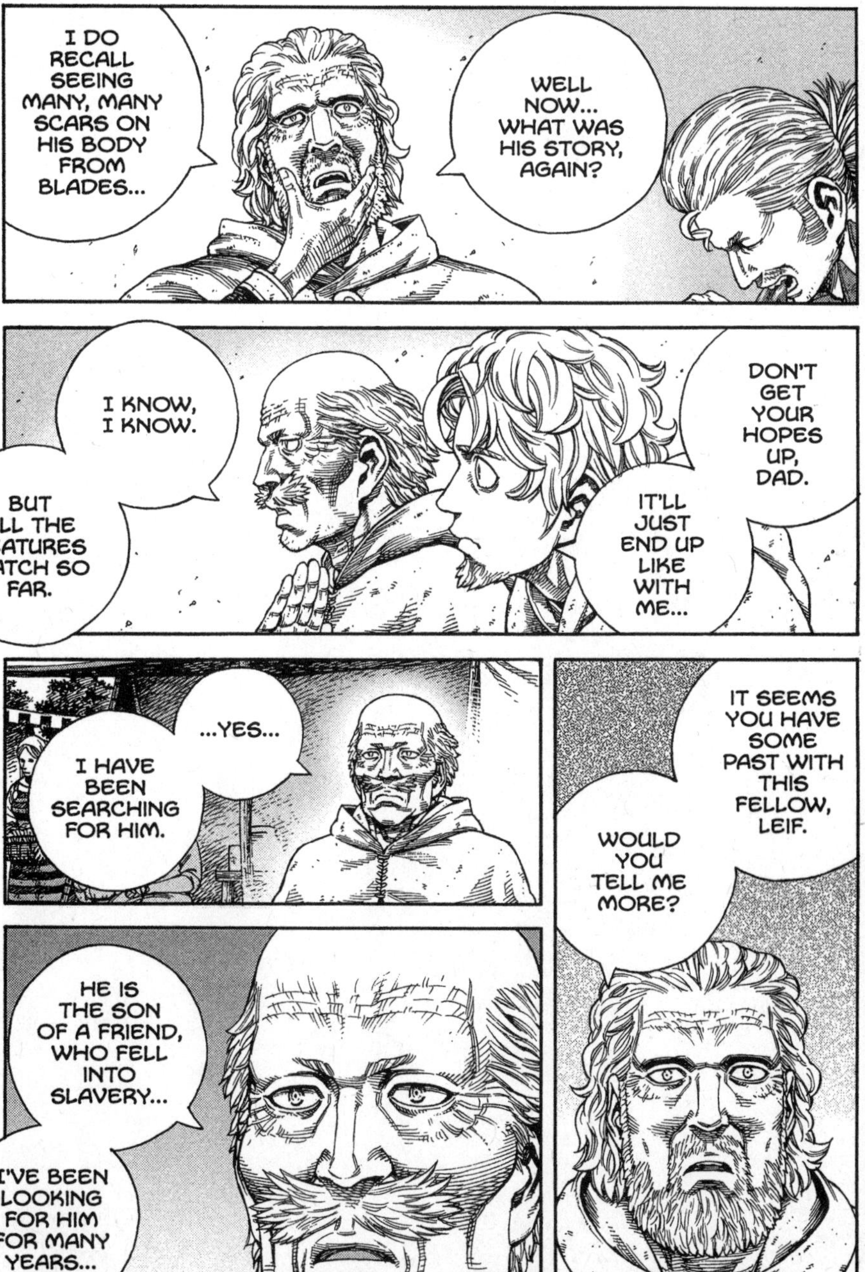
WELL NOW... WHAT WAS HIS STORY, AGAIN?
I DO RECALL SEEING MANY, MANY SCARS ON HIS BODY FROM BLADES...
DON'T GET YOUR HOPES UP, DAD.
IT'LL JUST END UP LIKE WITH ME...
I KNOW, I KNOW.
BUT ALL THE FEATURES MATCH SO FAR.
IT SEEMS YOU HAVE SOME PAST WITH THIS FELLOW, LEIF.
WOULD YOU TELL ME MORE?
...YES...
I HAVE BEEN SEARCHING FOR HIM.
HE IS THE SON OF A FRIEND, WHO FELL INTO SLAVERY...
I'VE BEEN LOOKING FOR HIM FOR MANY YEARS...

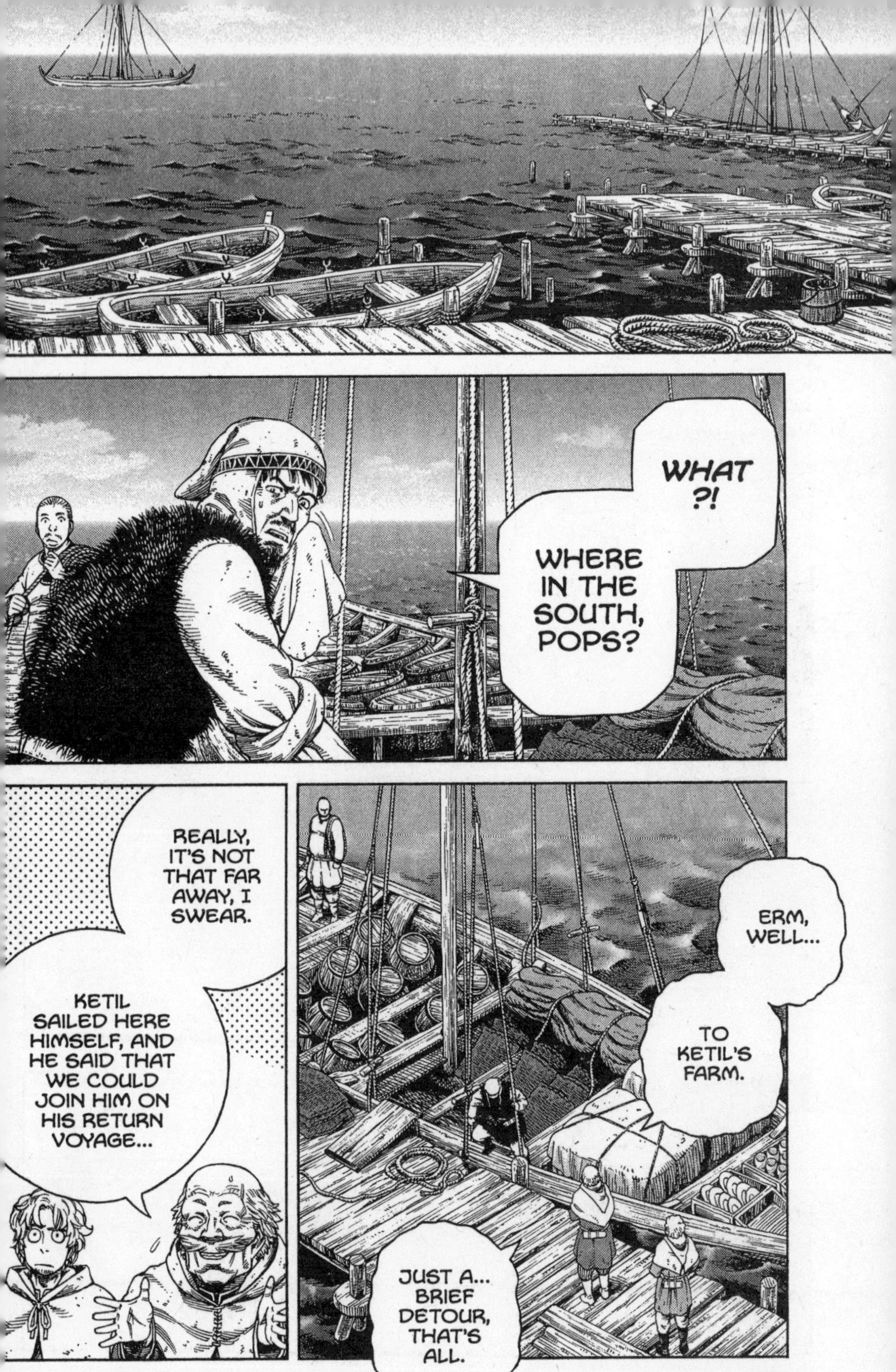
WHAT ?!
WHERE IN THE SOUTH, POPS?
ERM, WELL...
TO KETIL'S FARM.
JUST A... BRIEF DETOUR, THAT'S ALL.
REALLY, IT'S NOT THAT FAR AWAY, I SWEAR.
KETIL SAILED HERE HIMSELF, AND HE SAID THAT WE COULD JOIN HIM ON HIS RETURN VOYAGE...

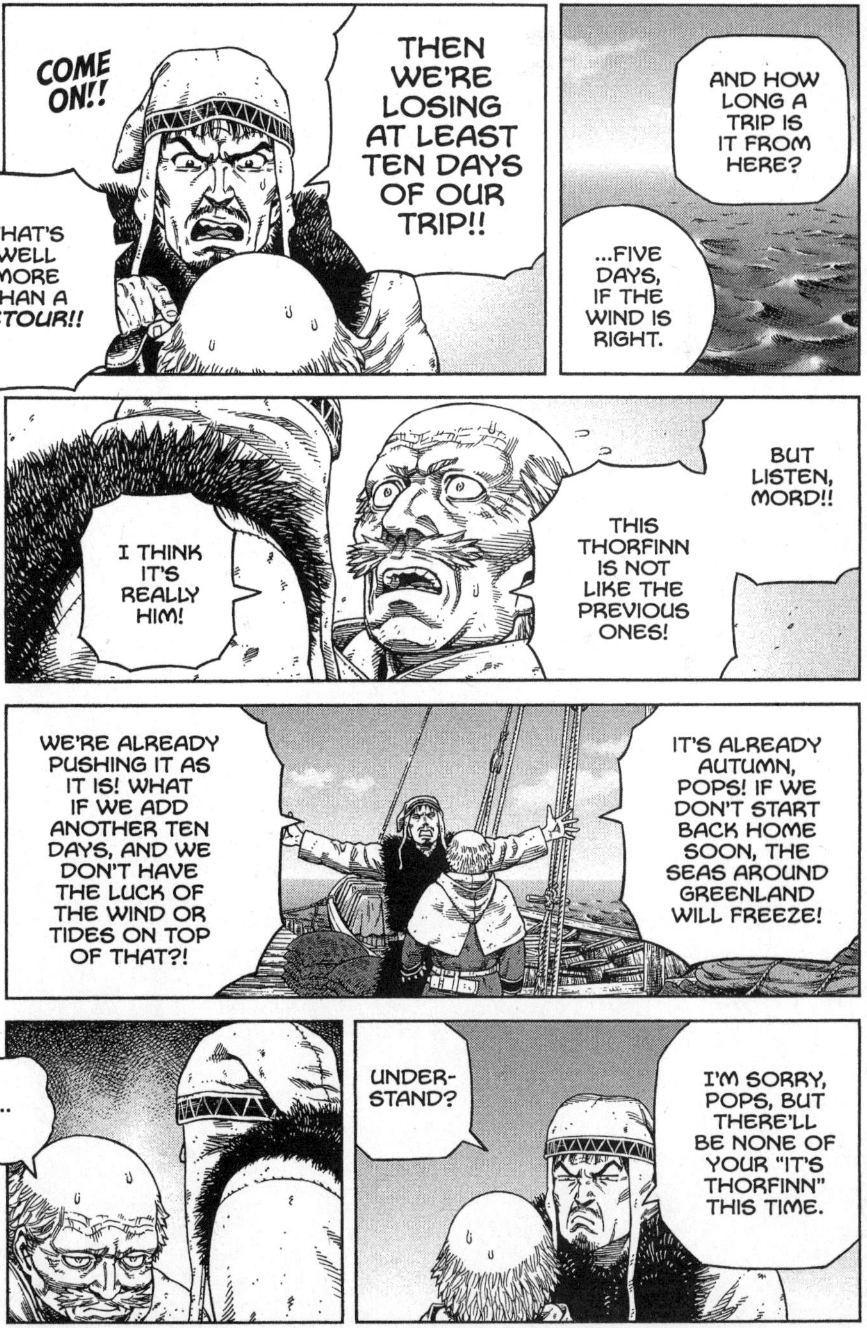
AND HOW LONG A TRIP IS IT FROM HERE?
...FIVE DAYS, IF THE WIND IS RIGHT.
THEN WE'RE LOSING AT LEAST TEN DAYS OF OUR TRIP!!
COME ON!!
THAT'S WELL MORE THAN A *DETOUR*!!
BUT LISTEN, MORD!!
THIS THORFINN IS NOT LIKE THE PREVIOUS ONES!
I THINK IT'S REALLY HIM!
IT'S ALREADY AUTUMN, POPS! IF WE DON'T START BACK HOME SOON, THE SEAS AROUND GREENLAND WILL FREEZE!
WE'RE ALREADY PUSHING IT AS IT IS! WHAT IF WE ADD ANOTHER TEN DAYS, AND WE DON'T HAVE THE LUCK OF THE WIND OR TIDES ON TOP OF THAT?!
I'M SORRY, POPS, BUT THERE'LL BE NONE OF YOUR "IT'S THORFINN" THIS TIME.
UNDER-STAND?
...

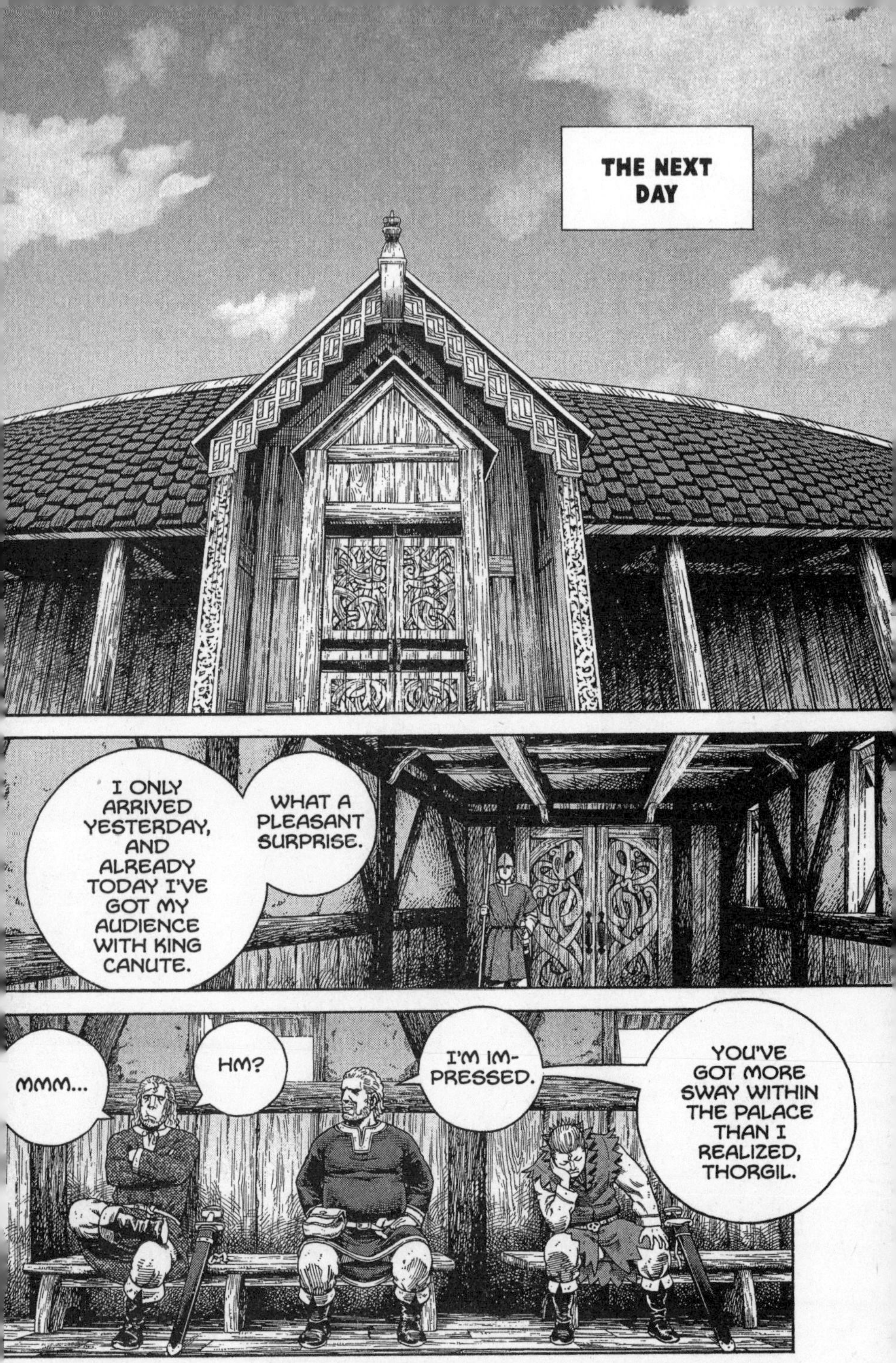
THE NEXT DAY
WHAT A PLEASANT SURPRISE.
I ONLY ARRIVED YESTERDAY, AND ALREADY TODAY I'VE GOT MY AUDIENCE WITH KING CANUTE.
YOU'VE GOT MORE SWAY WITHIN THE PALACE THAN I REALIZED, THORGIL.
I'M IM-PRESSED.
HM?
MMM...

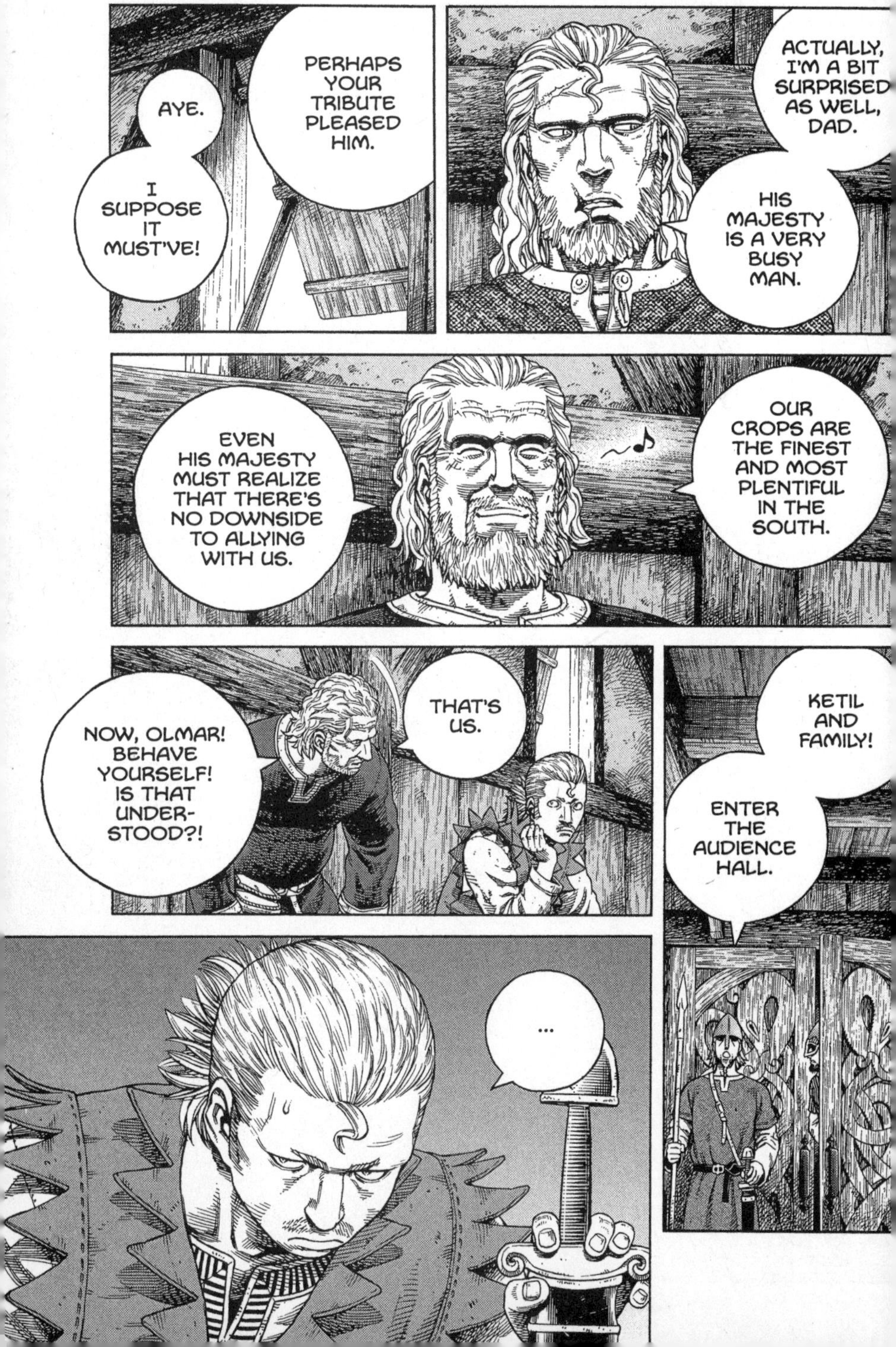
ACTUALLY, I'M A BIT SURPRISED AS WELL, DAD.
HIS MAJESTY IS A VERY BUSY MAN.
PERHAPS YOUR TRIBUTE PLEASED HIM.
AYE.
I SUPPOSE IT MUST'VE!
OUR CROPS ARE THE FINEST AND MOST PLENTIFUL IN THE SOUTH.
EVEN HIS MAJESTY MUST REALIZE THAT THERE'S NO DOWNSIDE TO ALLYING WITH US.
KETIL AND FAMILY!
ENTER THE AUDIENCE HALL.
THAT'S US.
NOW, OLMAR! BEHAVE YOURSELF! IS THAT UNDER-STOOD?!
...

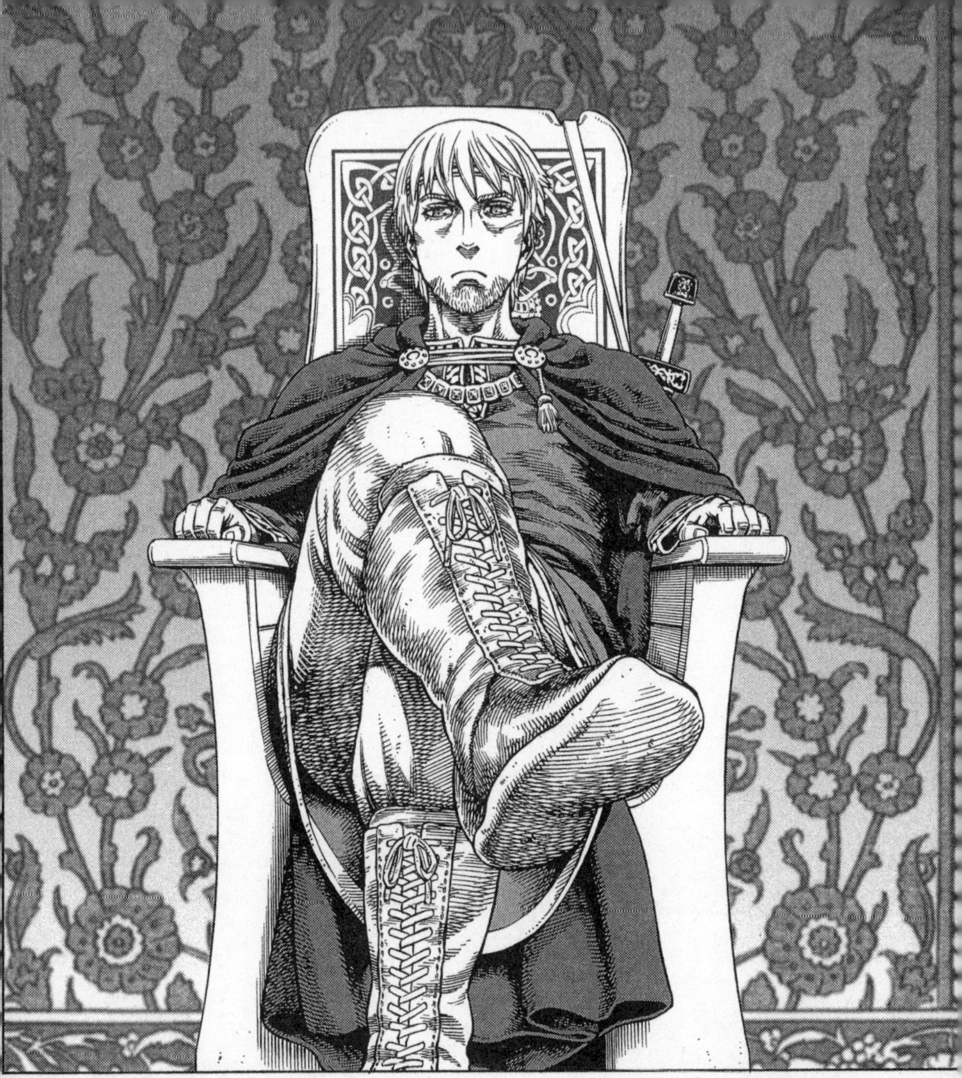

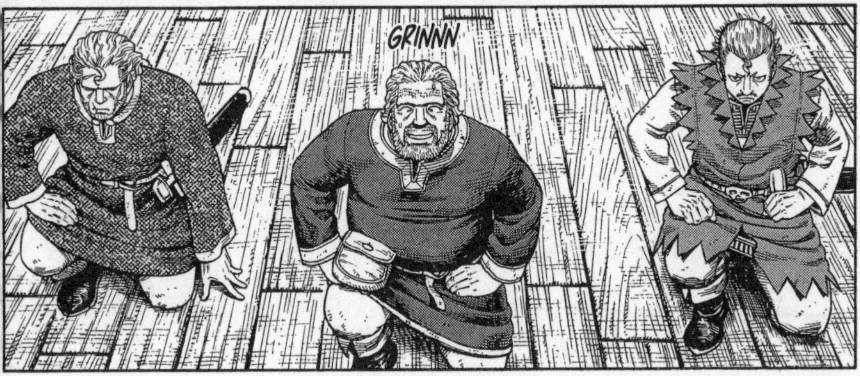
GRINNN

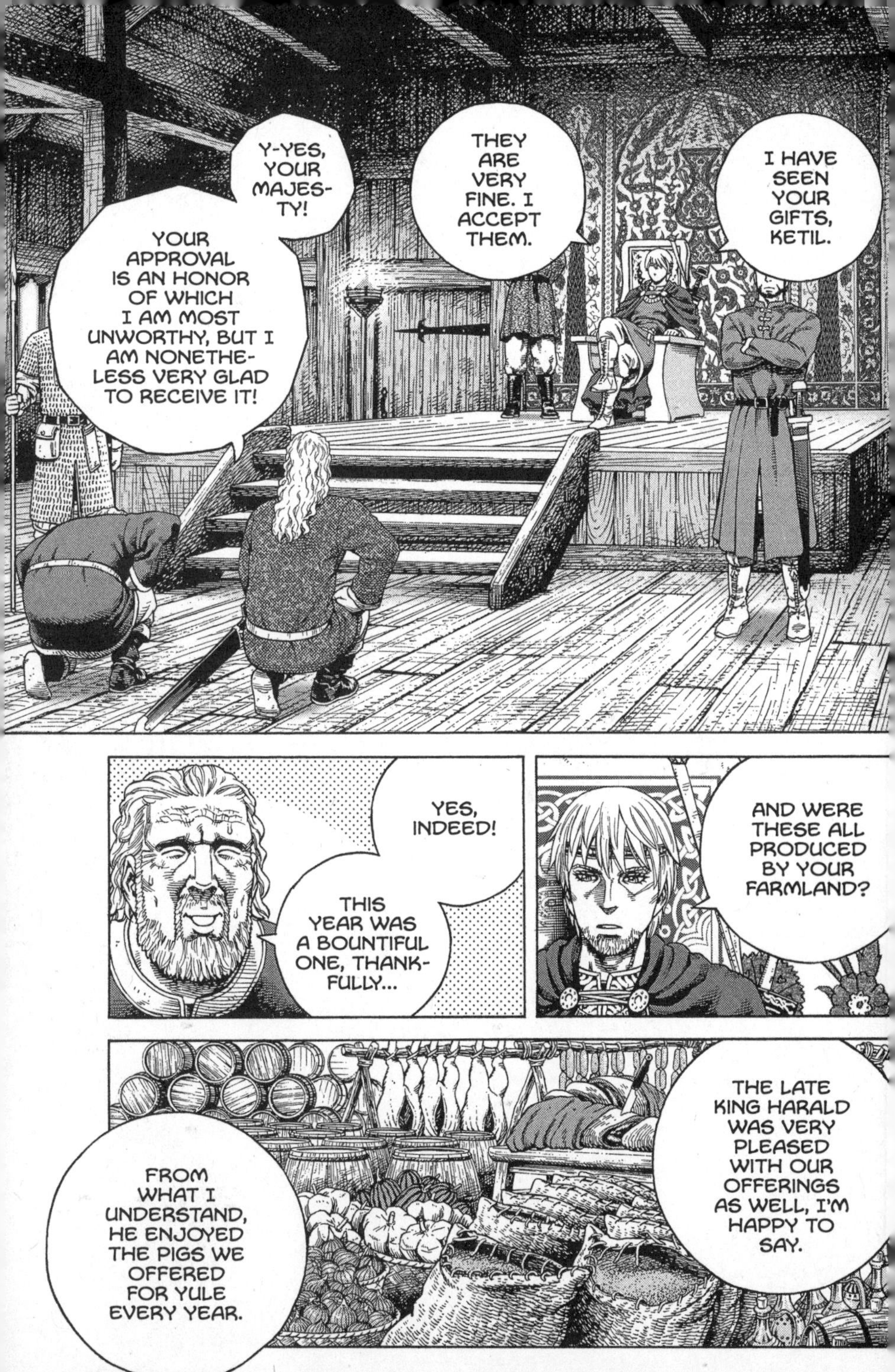
I HAVE SEEN YOUR GIFTS, KETIL.
THEY ARE VERY FINE. I ACCEPT THEM.
Y-YES, YOUR MAJESTY!
YOUR APPROVAL IS AN HONOR OF WHICH I AM MOST UNWORTHY, BUT I AM NONETHELESS VERY GLAD TO RECEIVE IT!
AND WERE THESE ALL PRODUCED BY YOUR FARMLAND?
YES, INDEED!
THIS YEAR WAS A BOUNTIFUL ONE, THANKFULLY...
THE LATE KING HARALD WAS VERY PLEASED WITH OUR OFFERINGS AS WELL, I'M HAPPY TO SAY.
FROM WHAT I UNDERSTAND, HE ENJOYED THE PIGS WE OFFERED FOR YULE EVERY YEAR.

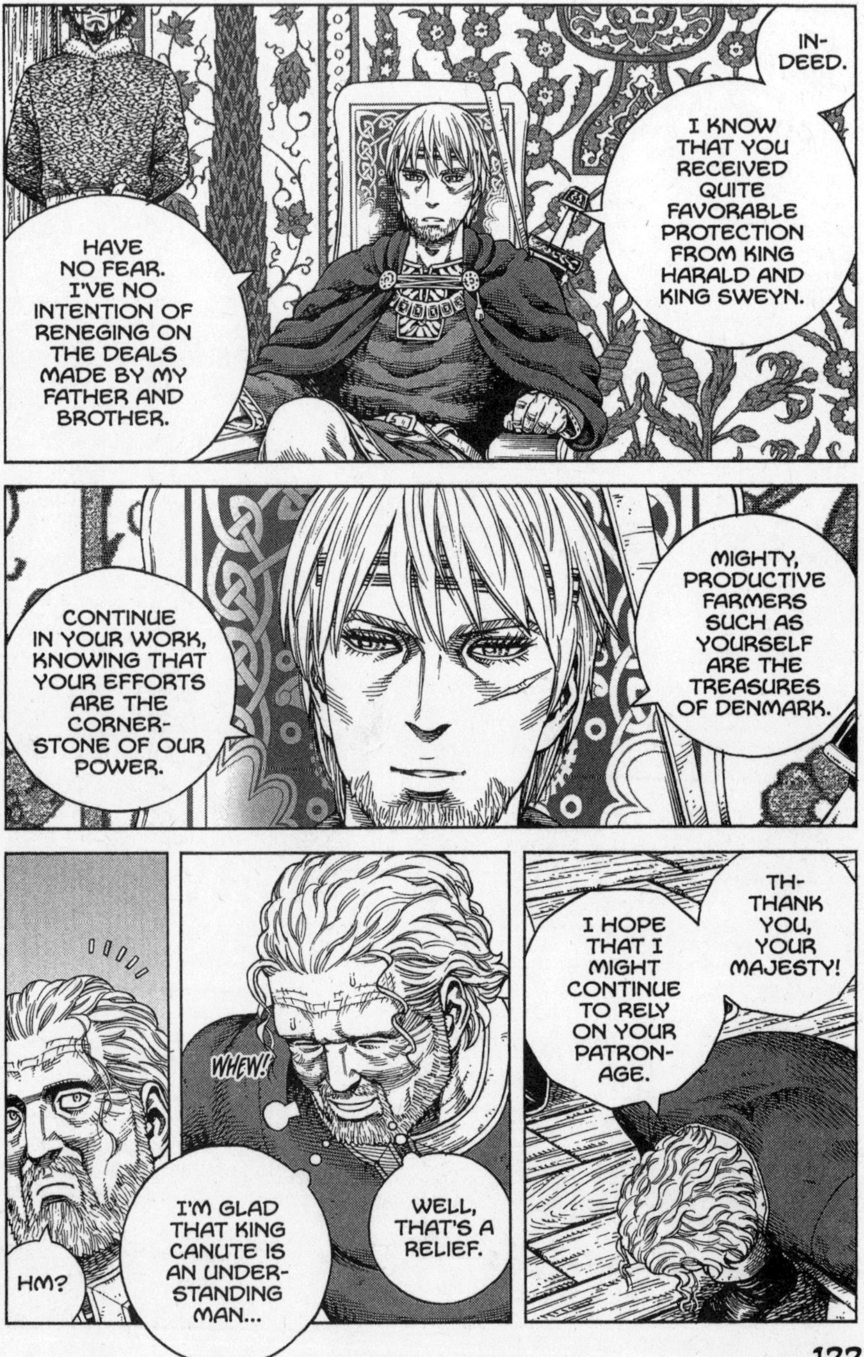
IN-DEED.
I KNOW THAT YOU RECEIVED QUITE FAVORABLE PROTECTION FROM KING HARALD AND KING SWEYN.
HAVE NO FEAR. I'VE NO INTENTION OF RENEGING ON THE DEALS MADE BY MY FATHER AND BROTHER.
MIGHTY, PRODUCTIVE FARMERS SUCH AS YOURSELF ARE THE TREASURES OF DENMARK.
CONTINUE IN YOUR WORK, KNOWING THAT YOUR EFFORTS ARE THE CORNER-STONE OF OUR POWER.
TH-THANK YOU, YOUR MAJESTY!
I HOPE THAT I MIGHT CONTINUE TO RELY ON YOUR PATRON-AGE.
WHEW!
WELL, THAT'S A RELIEF.
I'M GLAD THAT KING CANUTE IS AN UNDER-STANDING MAN...
HM?

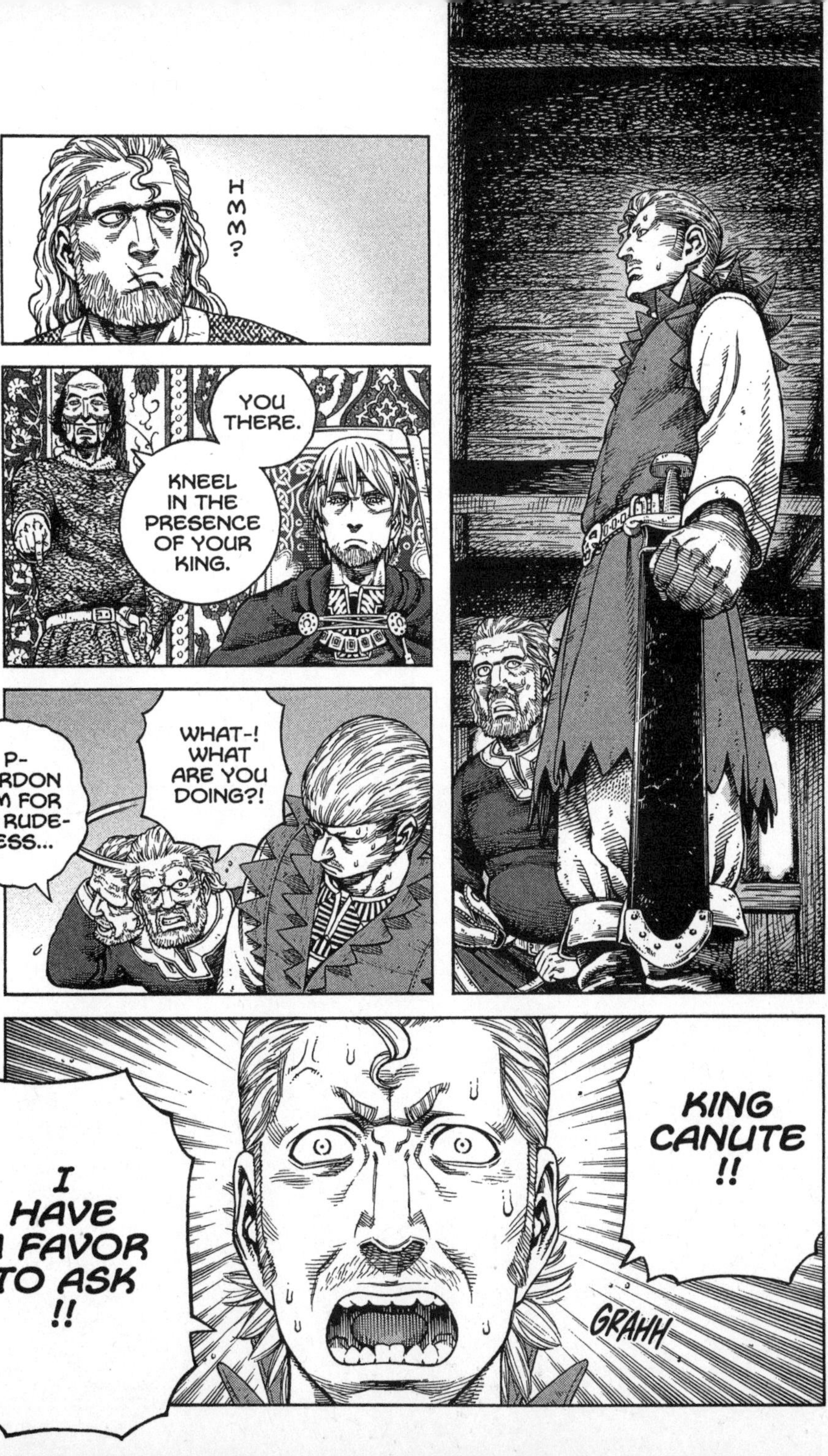
HMM?
YOU THERE.
KNEEL IN THE PRESENCE OF YOUR KING.
WHAT-! WHAT ARE YOU DOING?!
P-PARDON HIM FOR HIS RUDENESS...
KING CANUTE!!
GRAHH
I HAVE A FAVOR TO ASK!!

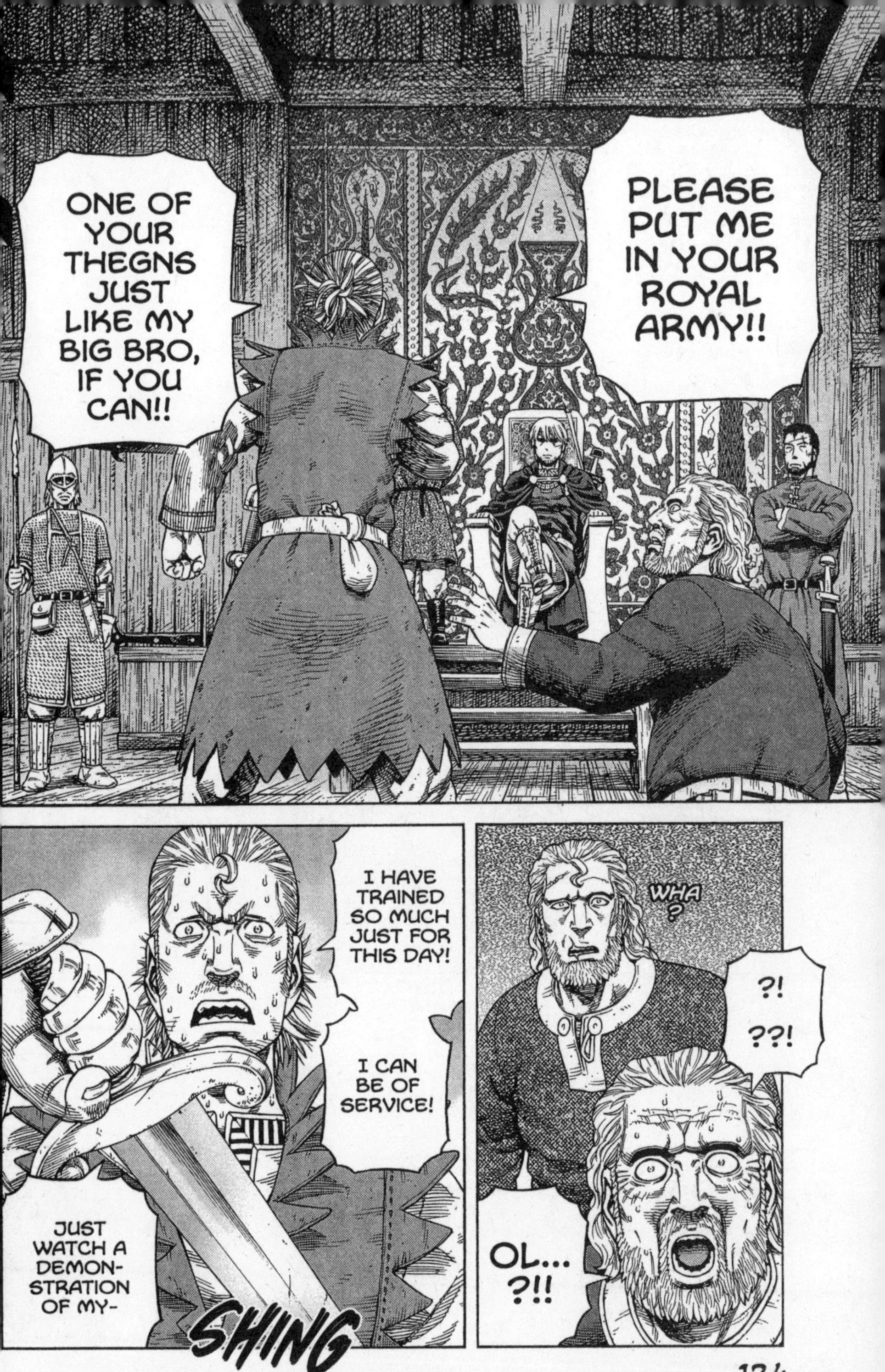
PLEASE PUT ME IN YOUR ROYAL ARMY!!
ONE OF YOUR THEGNS JUST LIKE MY BIG BRO, IF YOU CAN!!
WHA ?
?! ??!
OL... ?!!
I HAVE TRAINED SO MUCH JUST FOR THIS DAY!
I CAN BE OF SERVICE!
JUST WATCH A DEMON-STRATION OF MY-
SHING

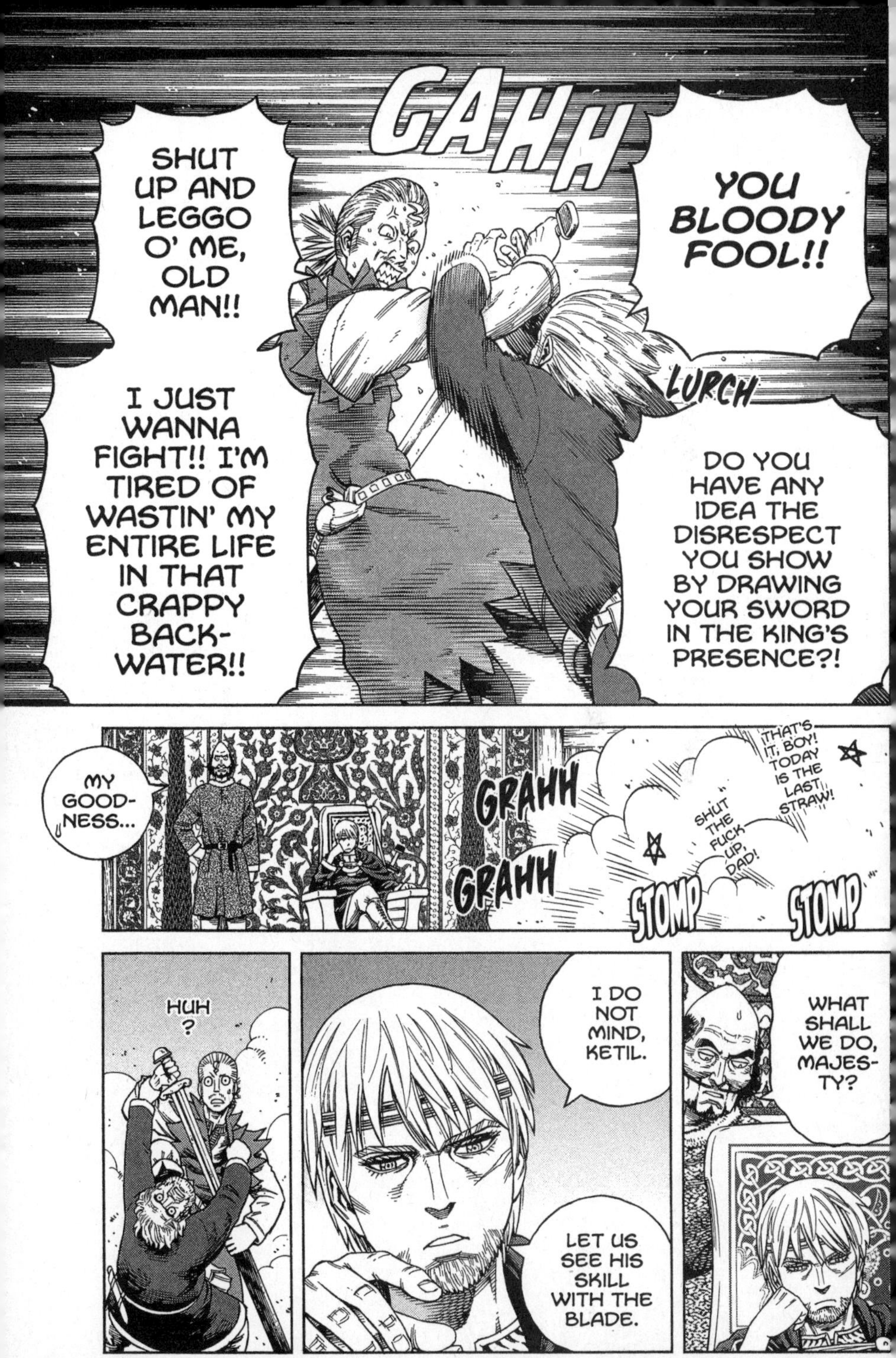
GAHH
YOU BLOODY FOOL!!
LURCH
DO YOU HAVE ANY IDEA THE DISRESPECT YOU SHOW BY DRAWING YOUR SWORD IN THE KING'S PRESENCE?!
SHUT UP AND LEGGO O' ME, OLD MAN!!
I JUST WANNA FIGHT!! I'M TIRED OF WASTIN' MY ENTIRE LIFE IN THAT CRAPPY BACK-WATER!!
THAT'S IT, BOY! TODAY IS THE LAST STRAW!
SHUT THE FUCK UP, DAD!
STOMP
STOMP
GRAHH
GRAHH
MY GOOD-NESS...
WHAT SHALL WE DO, MAJES-TY?
I DO NOT MIND, KETIL.
LET US SEE HIS SKILL WITH THE BLADE.
HUH ?

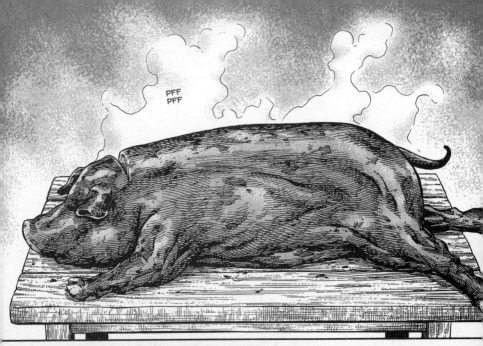

PFF
PFF

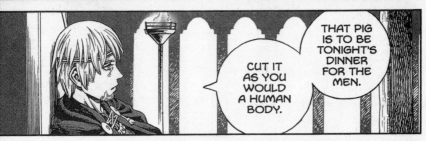

THAT PIG IS TO BE TONIGHT'S DINNER FOR THE MEN.

CUT IT AS YOU WOULD A HUMAN BODY.

126

ONE GOOD WHACK, THEN...

ERM, YES.

SHH...

KIYEI-YAAA-AAH!!

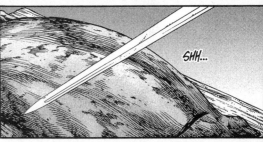

FFFH...

HAAAA

PHEWWW...

TAP TAP

ZZT

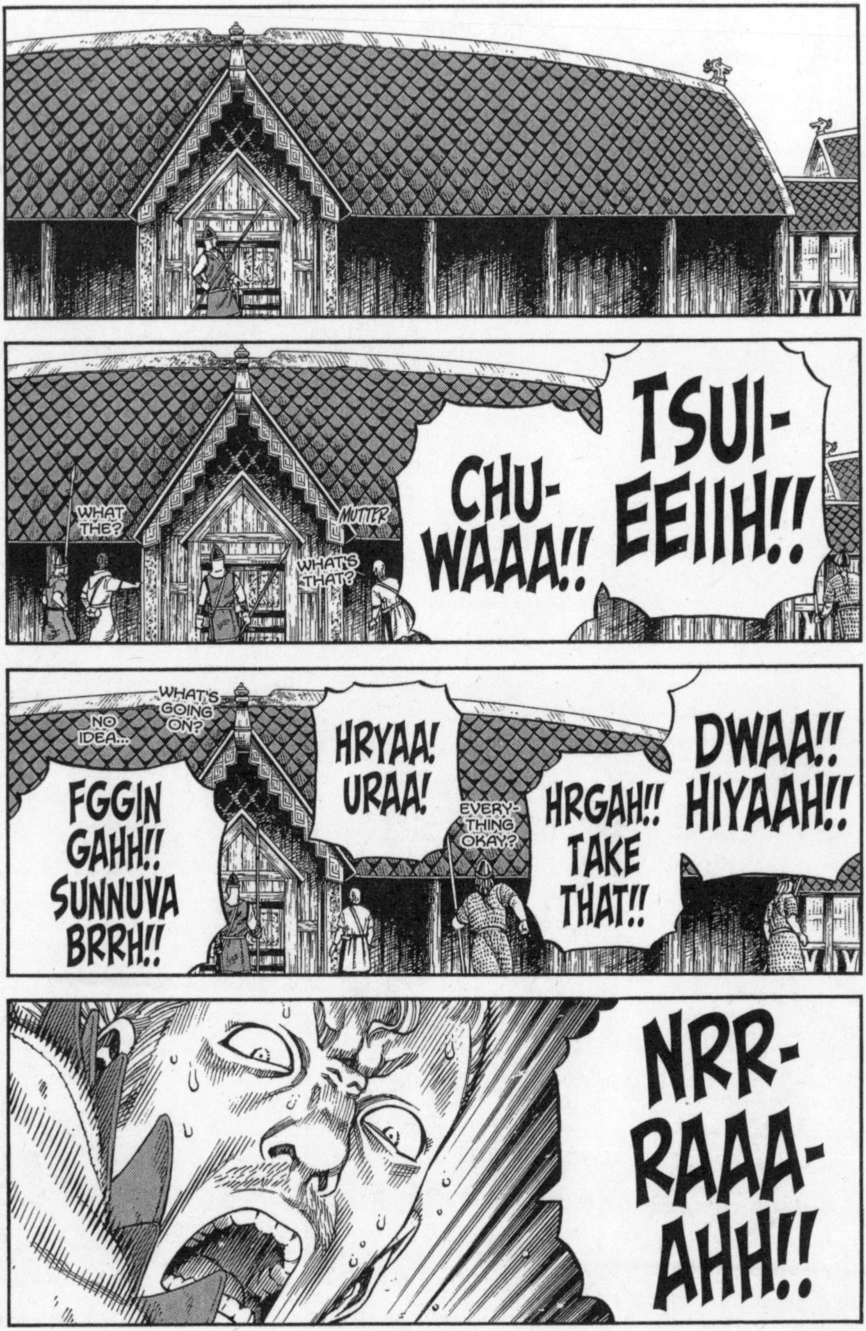
TSUI-EEIIH!!
CHU-WAAA!!
MUTTER
WHAT'S THAT?
WHAT THE?
DWAA!! HIYAAH!!
HRGAH!! TAKE THAT!!
EVERY-THING OKAY?
HRYAA! URAA!
WHAT'S GOING ON?
NO IDEA...
FGGIN GAHH!! SUNNUVA BRRH!!
NRR-RAAA-AHH!!

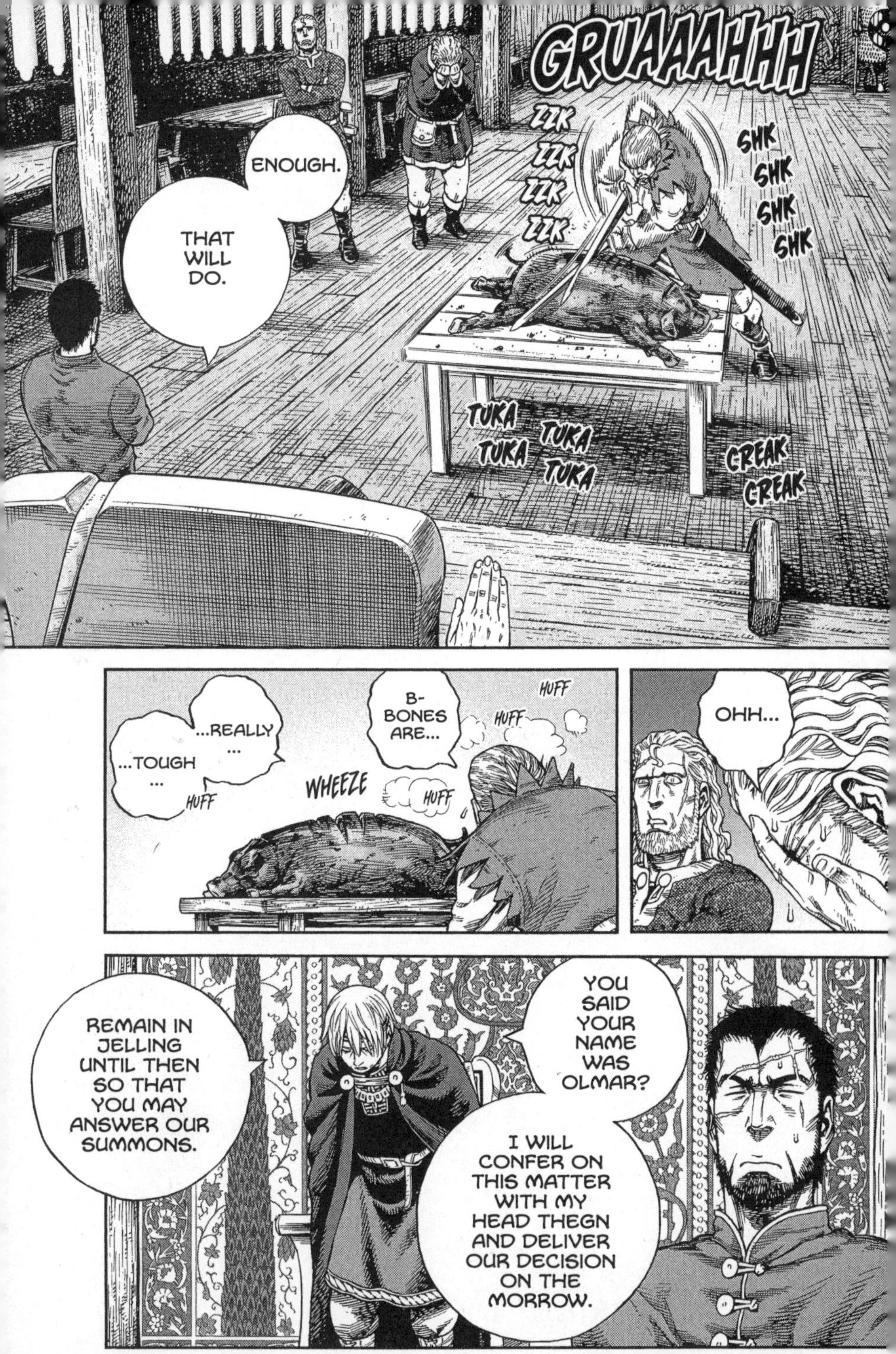
GRUAAAHHH
SHK SHK SHK SHK
ZZK ZZK ZZK ZZK
ENOUGH.
THAT WILL DO.
CREAK CREAK
TUKA TUKA
TUKA TUKA
OHH...
HUFF
HUFF
B- BONES ARE...
...REALLY ...
...TOUGH ...
HUFF
WHEEZE
HUFF
YOU SAID YOUR NAME WAS OLMAR?
I WILL CONFER ON THIS MATTER WITH MY HEAD THEGN AND DELIVER OUR DECISION ON THE MORROW.
REMAIN IN JELLING UNTIL THEN SO THAT YOU MAY ANSWER OUR SUMMONS.

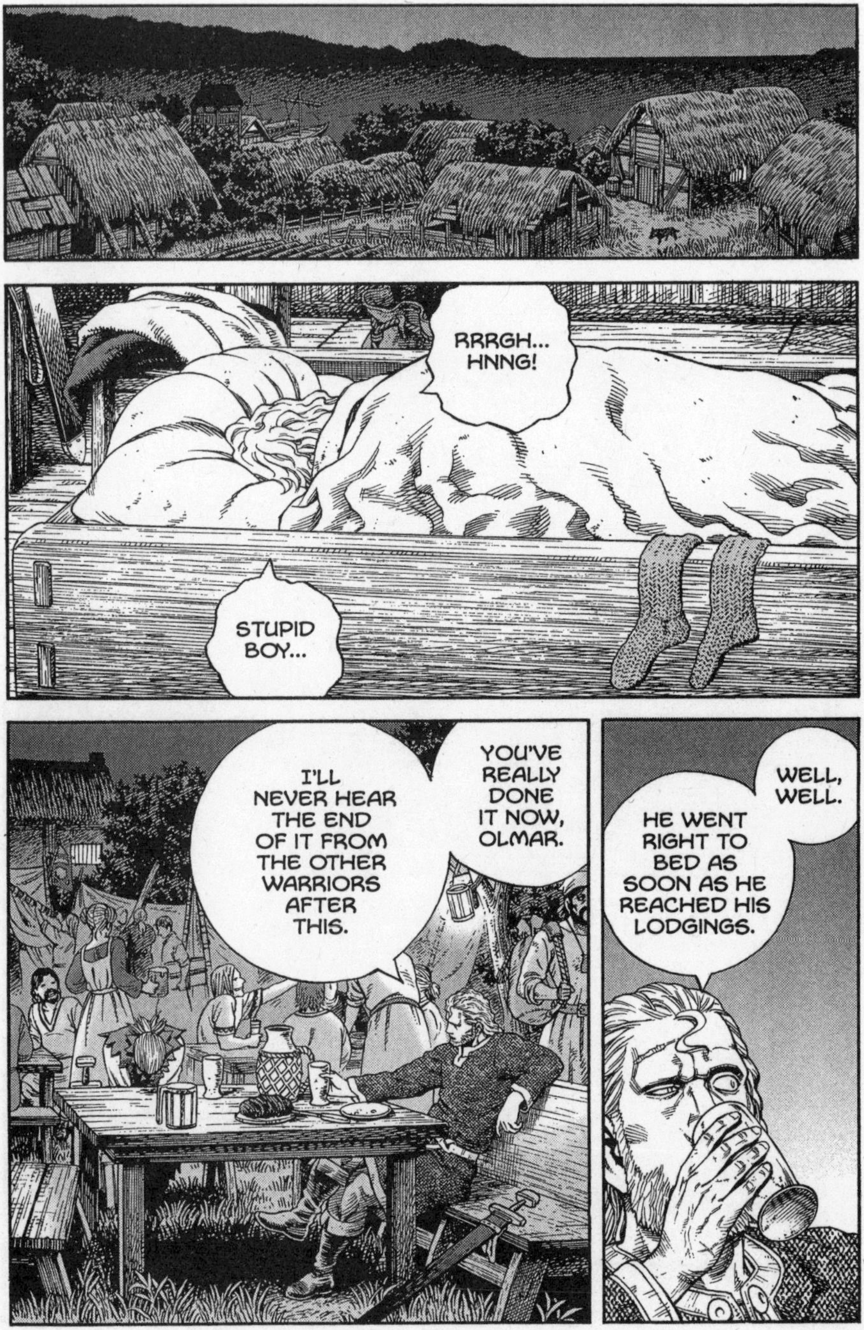
RRRGH... HNNG!
STUPID BOY...
WELL, WELL.
HE WENT RIGHT TO BED AS SOON AS HE REACHED HIS LODGINGS.
YOU'VE REALLY DONE IT NOW, OLMAR.
I'LL NEVER HEAR THE END OF IT FROM THE OTHER WARRIORS AFTER THIS.

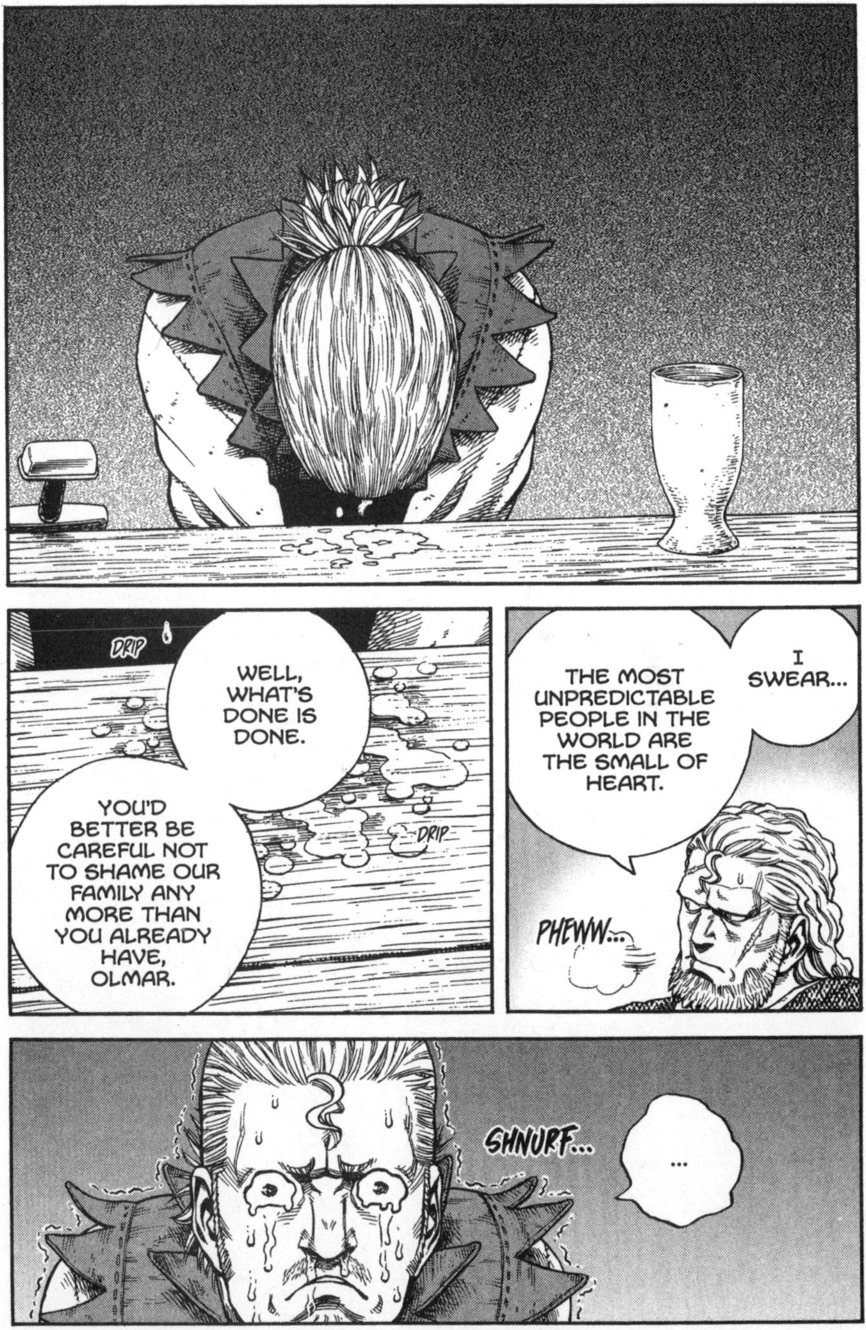
I SWEAR...
THE MOST UNPREDICTABLE PEOPLE IN THE WORLD ARE THE SMALL OF HEART.
PHEWW...
DRIP
WELL, WHAT'S DONE IS DONE.
YOU'D BETTER BE CAREFUL NOT TO SHAME OUR FAMILY ANY MORE THAN YOU ALREADY HAVE, OLMAR.
DRIP
...
SHNURF...

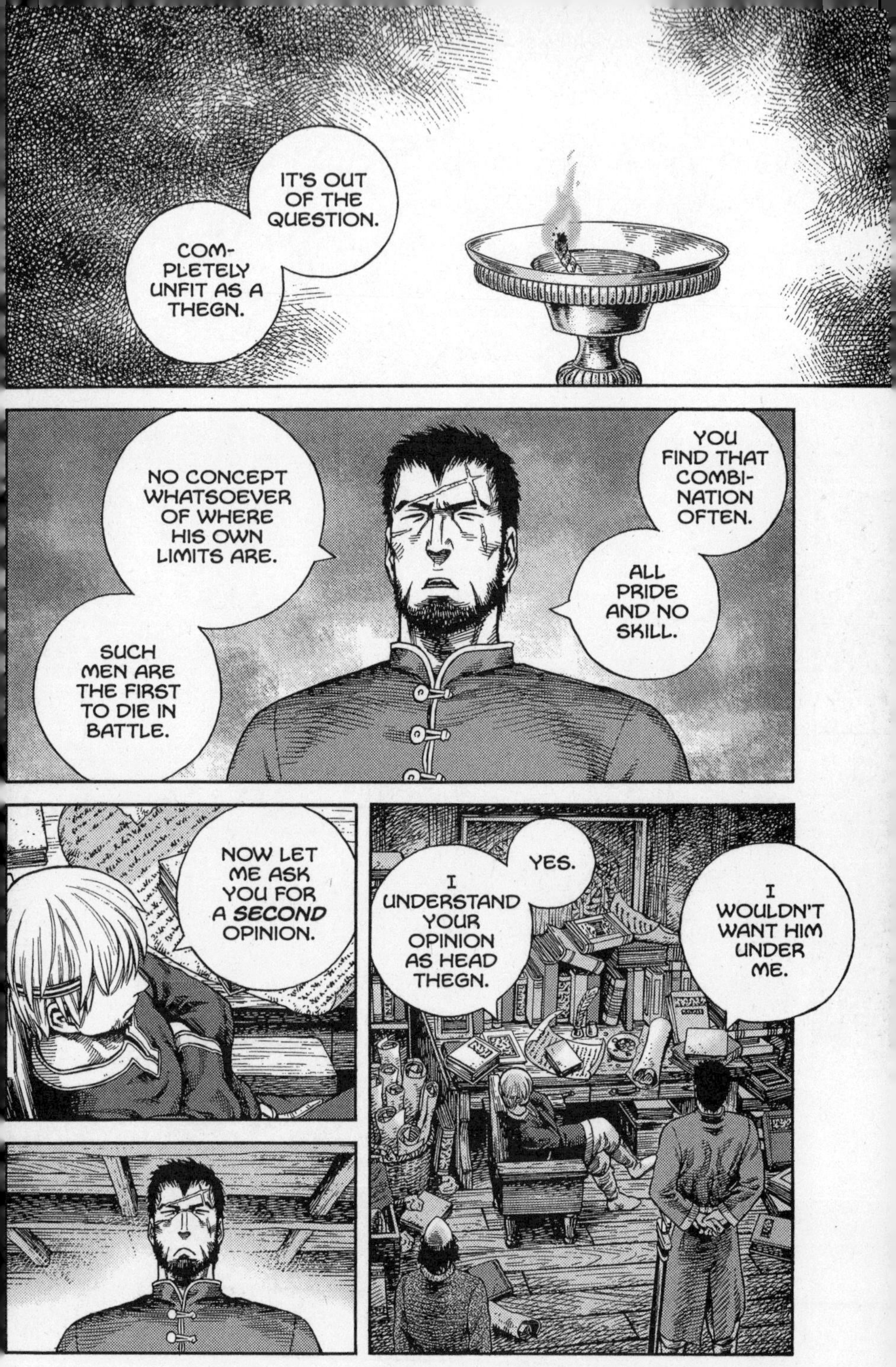
IT'S OUT OF THE QUESTION.
COM-PLETELY UNFIT AS A THEGN.
YOU FIND THAT COMBI-NATION OFTEN.
ALL PRIDE AND NO SKILL.
NO CONCEPT WHATSOEVER OF WHERE HIS OWN LIMITS ARE.
SUCH MEN ARE THE FIRST TO DIE IN BATTLE.
I WOULDN'T WANT HIM UNDER ME.
YES.
I UNDERSTAND YOUR OPINION AS HEAD THEGN.
NOW LET ME ASK YOU FOR A *SECOND* OPINION.

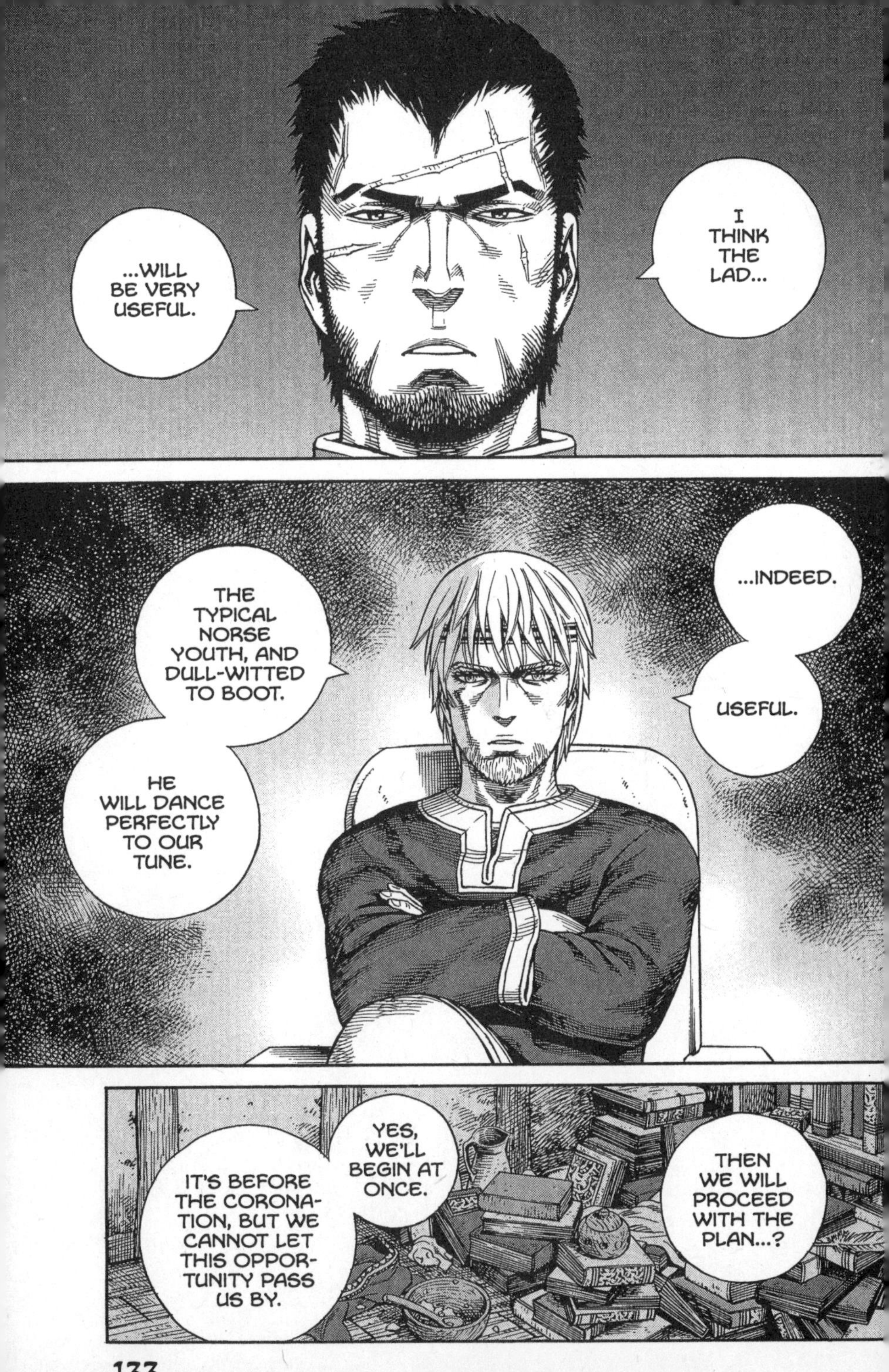
I THINK THE LAD...
...WILL BE VERY USEFUL.
...INDEED.
USEFUL.
THE TYPICAL NORSE YOUTH, AND DULL-WITTED TO BOOT.
HE WILL DANCE PERFECTLY TO OUR TUNE.
THEN WE WILL PROCEED WITH THE PLAN...?
YES, WE'LL BEGIN AT ONCE.
IT'S BEFORE THE CORONATION, BUT WE CANNOT LET THIS OPPORTUNITY PASS US BY.

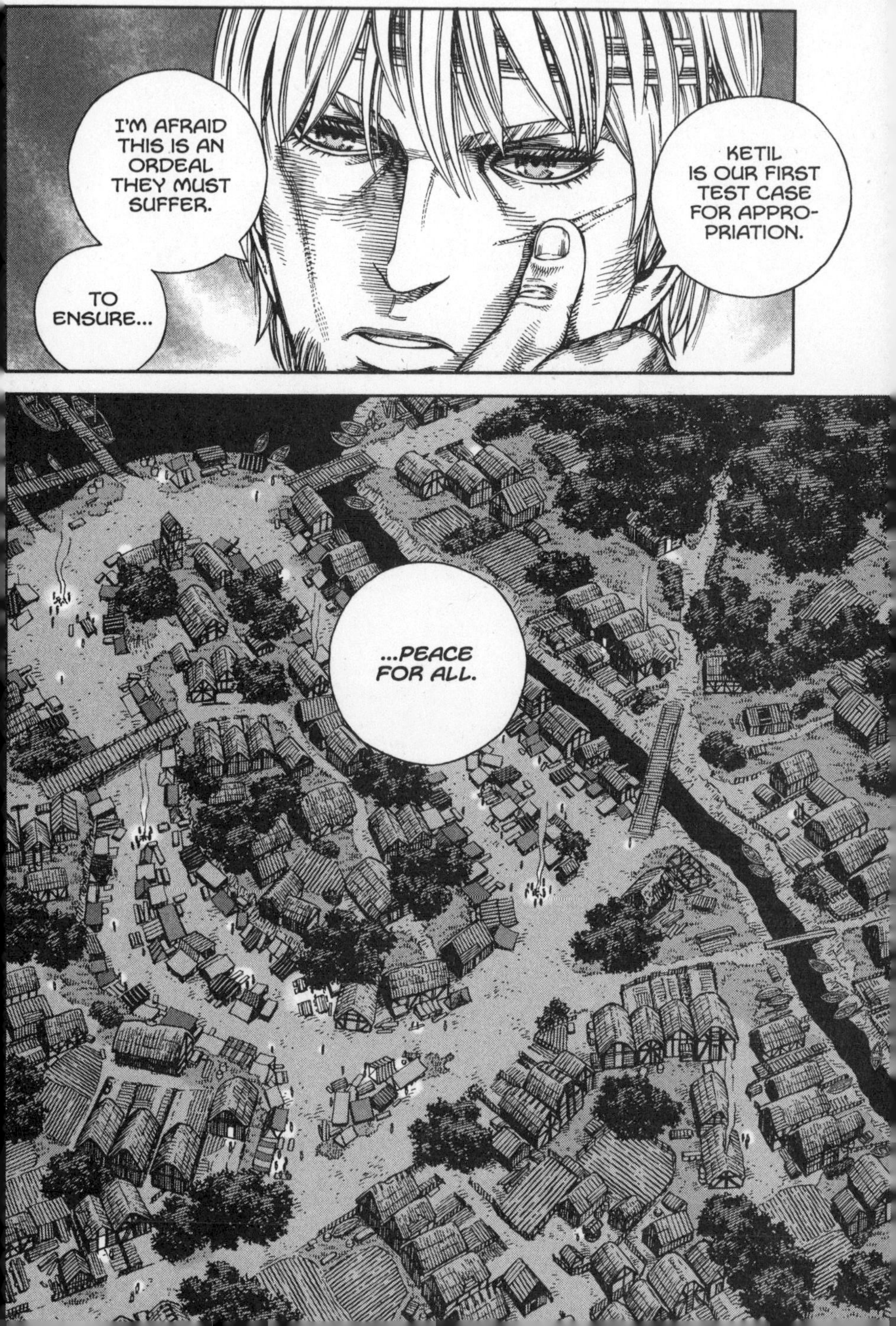
KETIL IS OUR FIRST TEST CASE FOR APPRO-PRIATION.
I'M AFRAID THIS IS AN ORDEAL THEY MUST SUFFER.
TO ENSURE...
...PEACE FOR ALL.

CHAPTER 77: DISGRACE

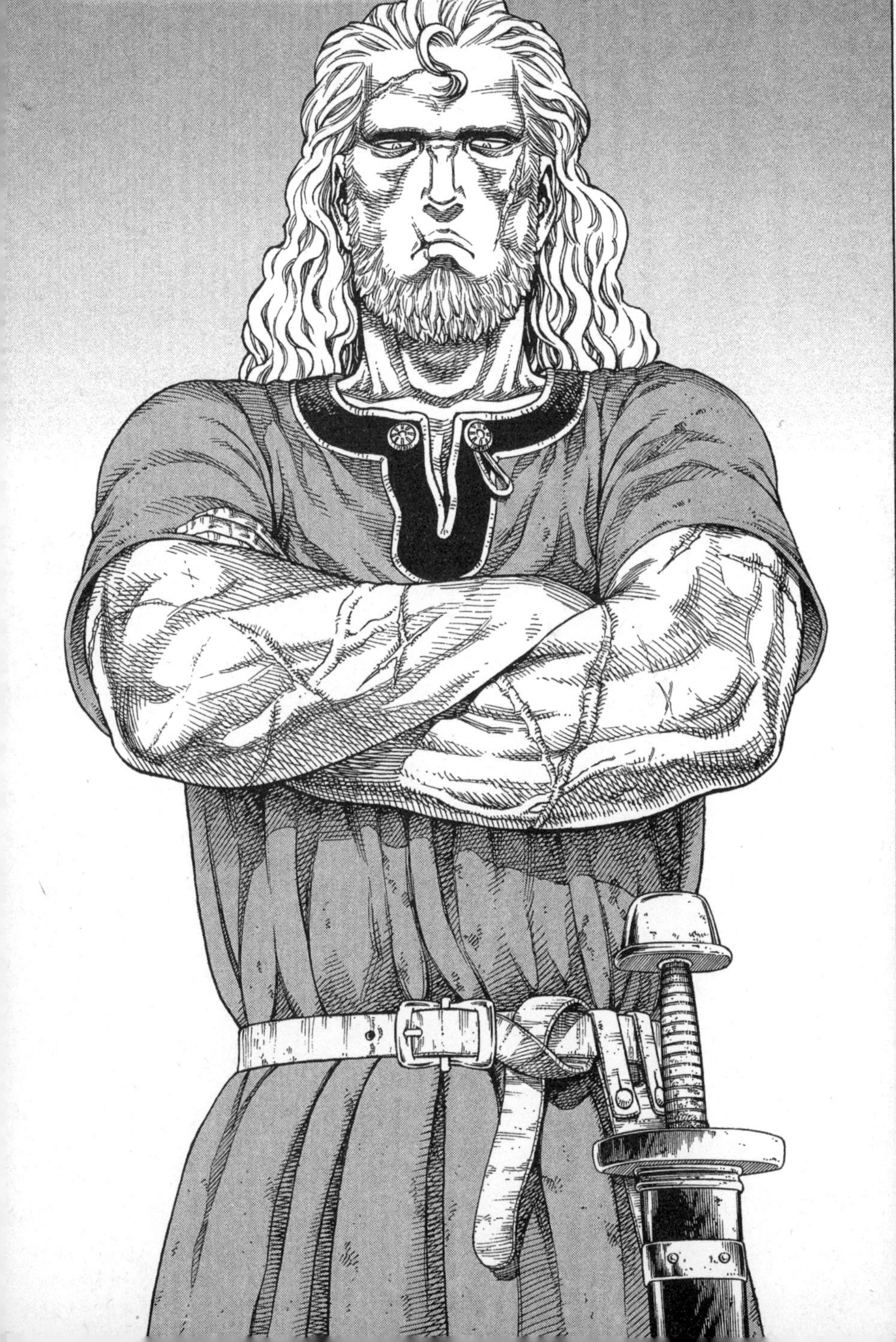

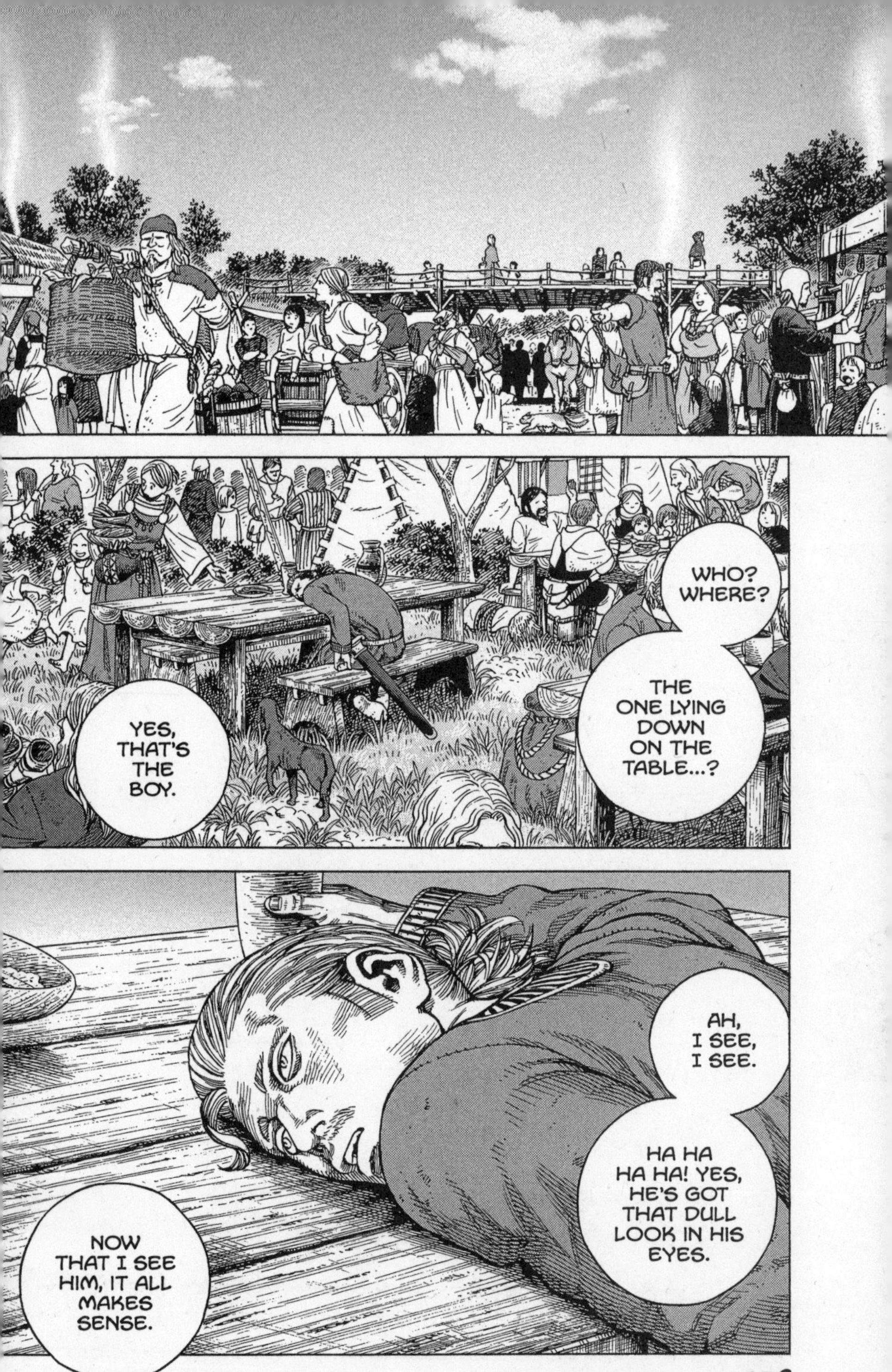
WHO? WHERE?
THE ONE LYING DOWN ON THE TABLE...?
YES, THAT'S THE BOY.
AH, I SEE, I SEE.
HA HA HA HA! YES, HE'S GOT THAT DULL LOOK IN HIS EYES.
NOW THAT I SEE HIM, IT ALL MAKES SENSE.

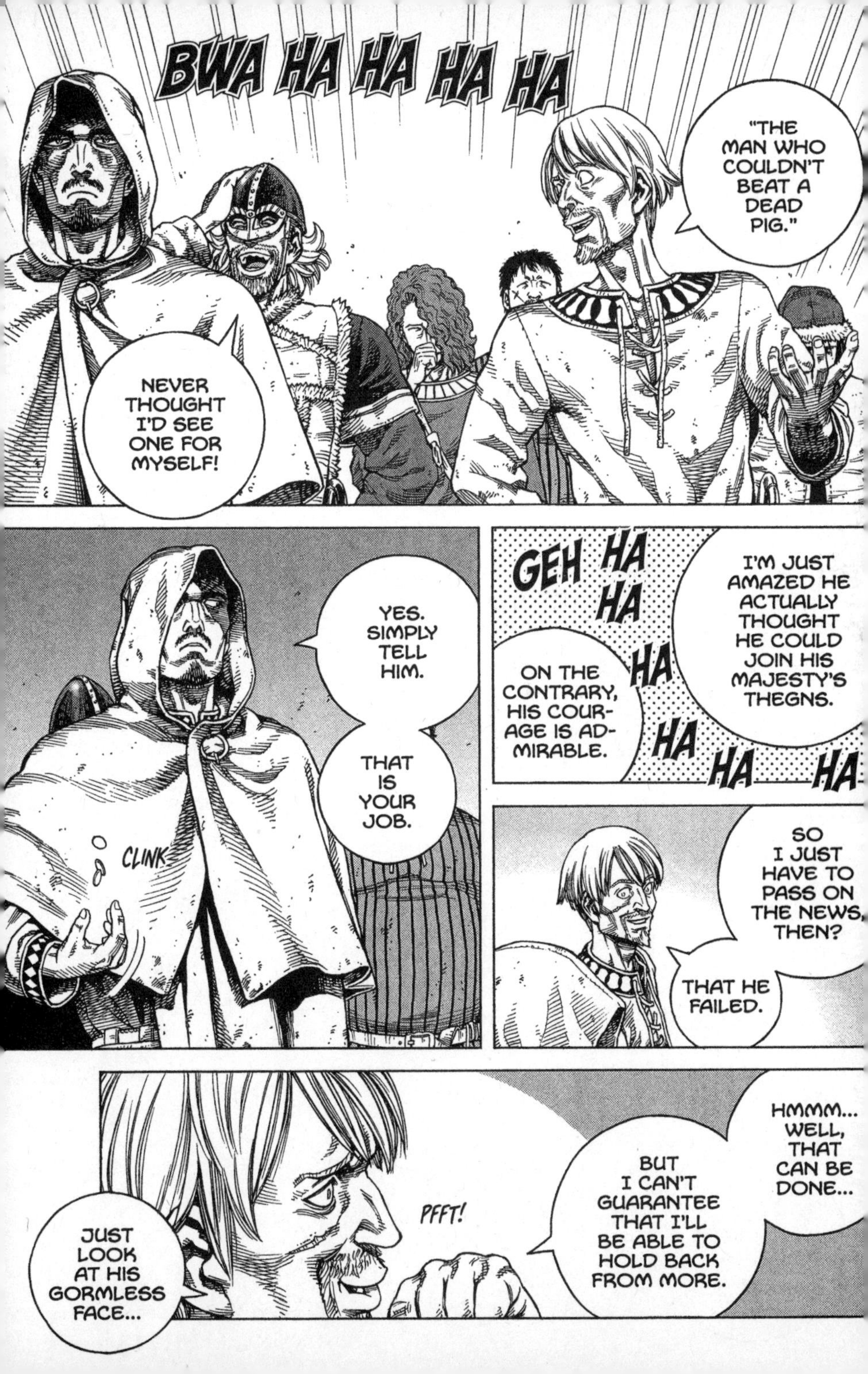
BWA HA HA HA HA
"THE MAN WHO COULDN'T BEAT A DEAD PIG."
NEVER THOUGHT I'D SEE ONE FOR MYSELF!
I'M JUST AMAZED HE ACTUALLY THOUGHT HE COULD JOIN HIS MAJESTY'S THEGNS.
GEH HA HA HA HA HA HA HA
ON THE CONTRARY, HIS COURAGE IS ADMIRABLE.
SO I JUST HAVE TO PASS ON THE NEWS, THEN?
THAT HE FAILED.
YES. SIMPLY TELL HIM.
THAT IS YOUR JOB.
CLINK
HMMM... WELL, THAT CAN BE DONE...
BUT I CAN'T GUARANTEE THAT I'LL BE ABLE TO HOLD BACK FROM MORE.
PFFT!
JUST LOOK AT HIS GORMLESS FACE...

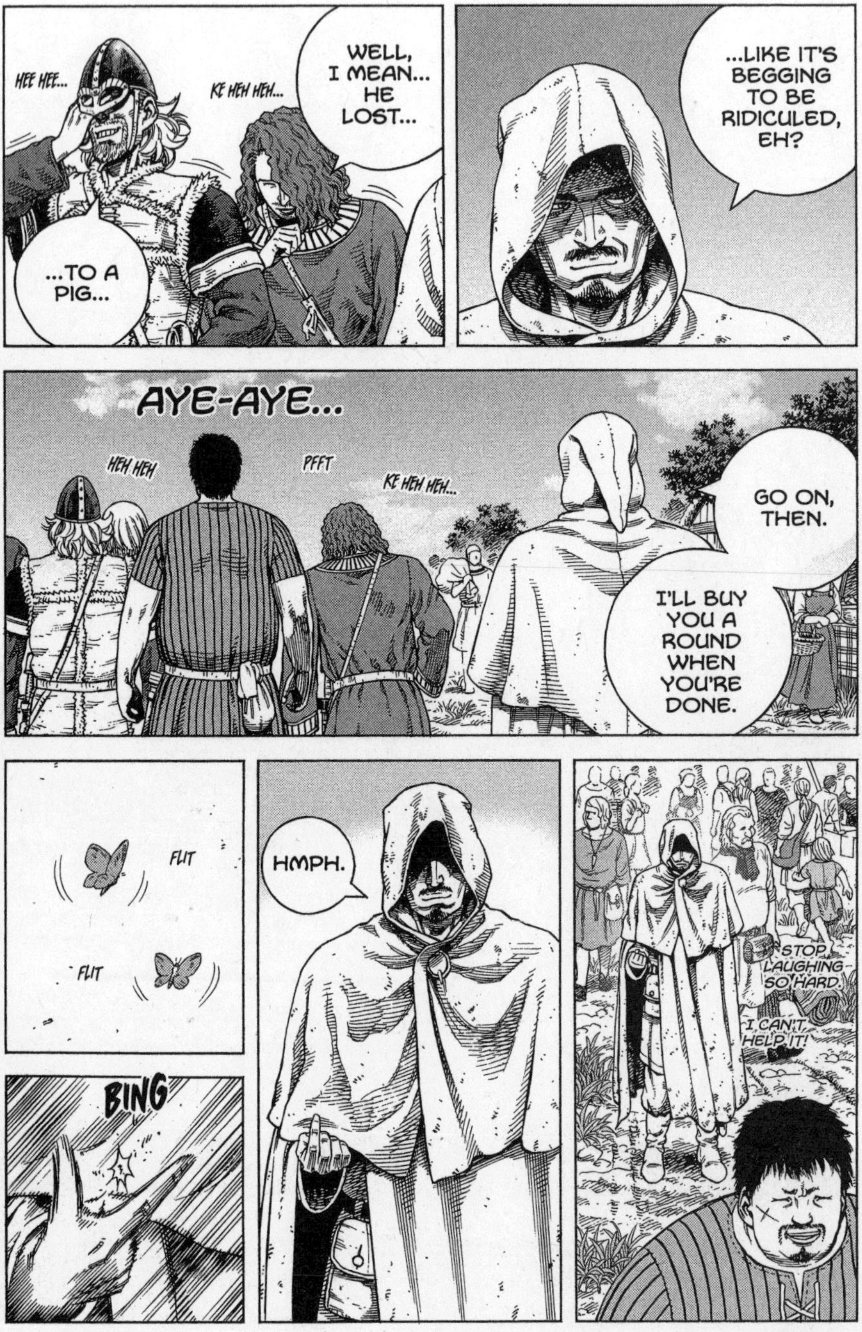
...LIKE IT'S BEGGING TO BE RIDICULED, EH?
WELL, I MEAN... HE LOST...
KE HEH HEH...
HEE HEE...
...TO A PIG...
GO ON, THEN.
I'LL BUY YOU A ROUND WHEN YOU'RE DONE.
KE HEH HEH...
PFFT
HEH HEH
AYE-AYE...
STOP LAUGHING SO HARD.
I CAN'T HELP IT!
HMPH.
FLIT
FLIT
BING

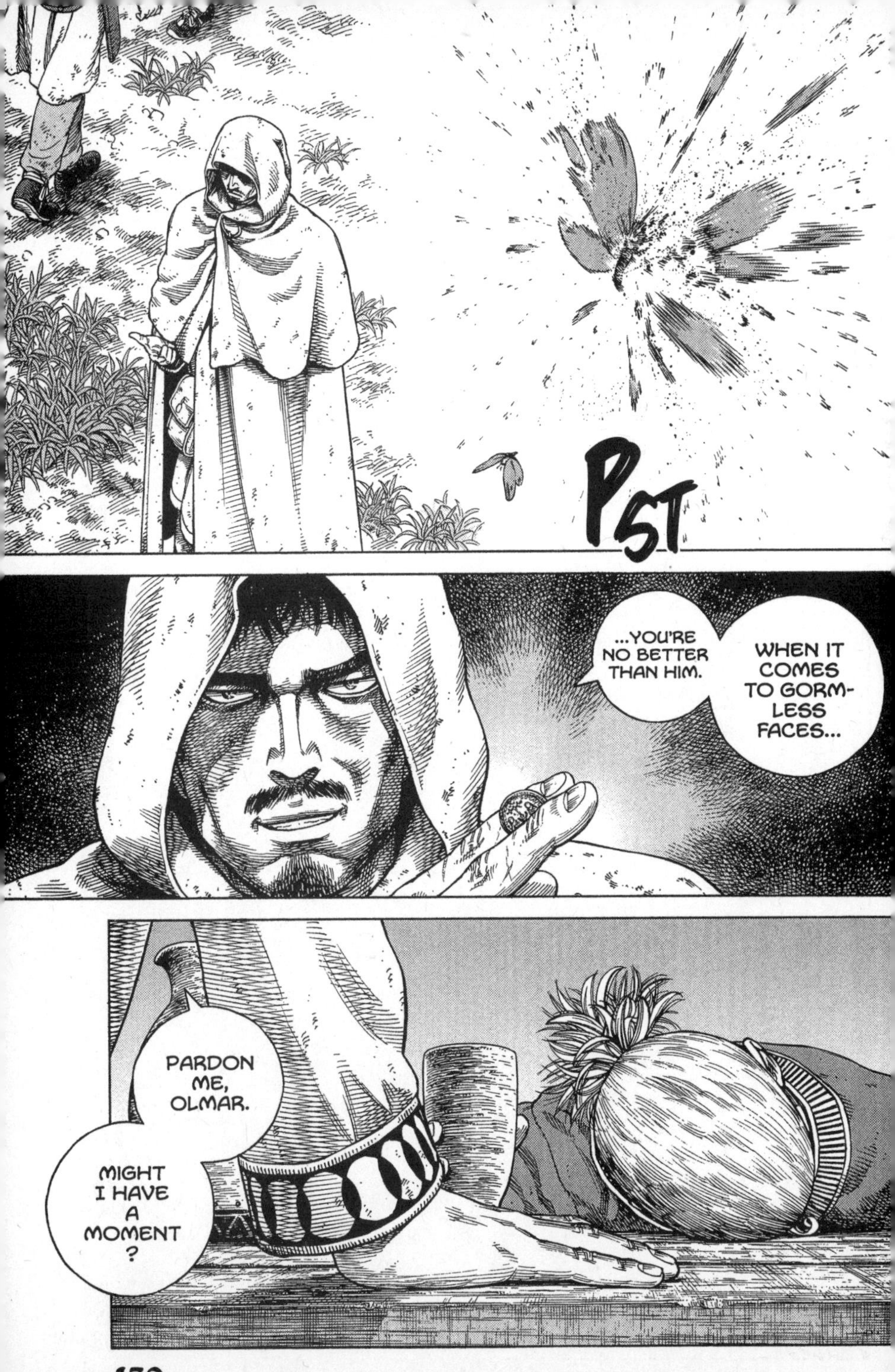
PST
WHEN IT COMES TO GORMLESS FACES...
...YOU'RE NO BETTER THAN HIM.
PARDON ME, OLMAR.
MIGHT I HAVE A MOMENT?

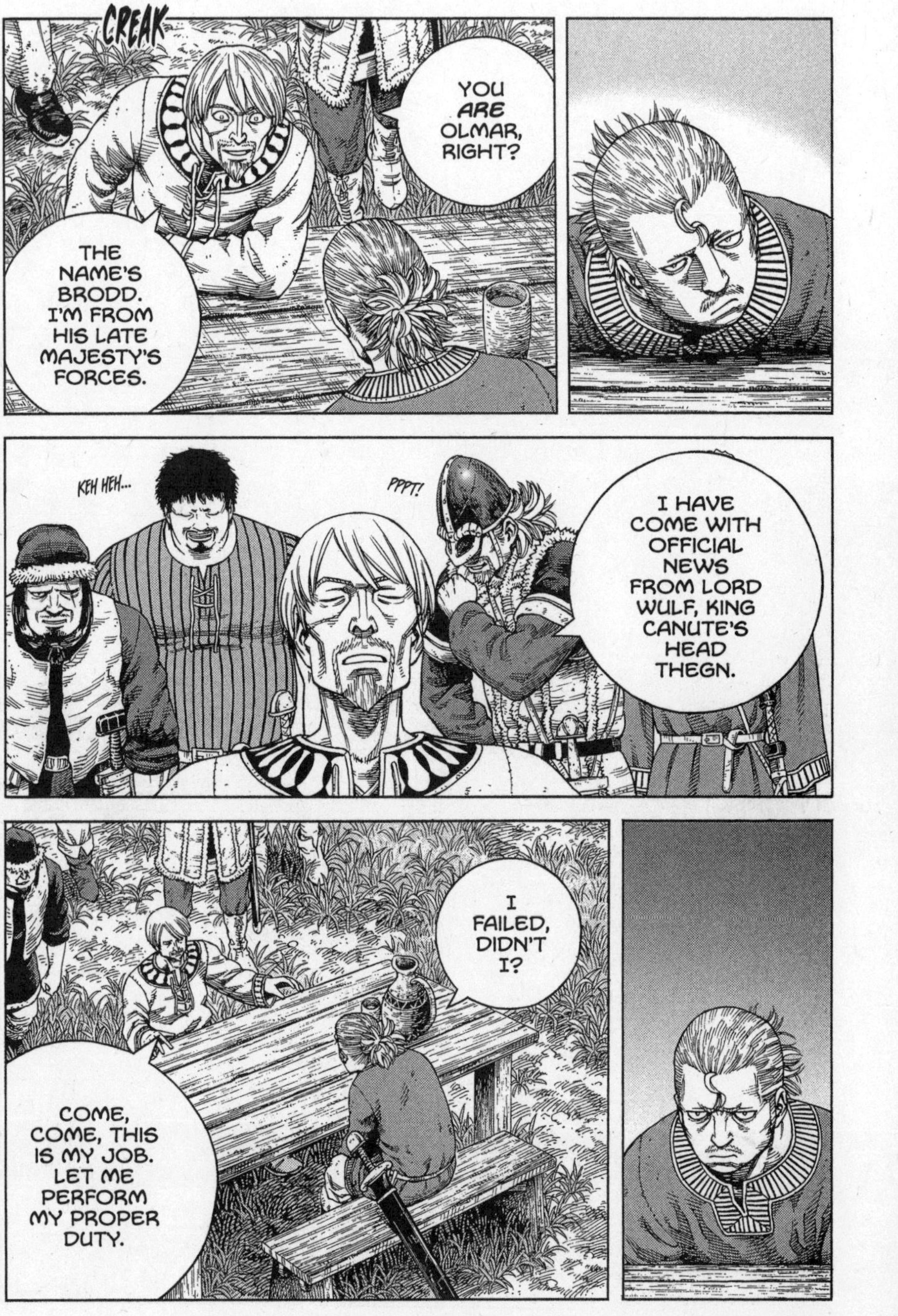
CREAK
YOU ARE OLMAR, RIGHT?
THE NAME'S BRODD. I'M FROM HIS LATE MAJESTY'S FORCES.
I HAVE COME WITH OFFICIAL NEWS FROM LORD WULF, KING CANUTE'S HEAD THEGN.
PPPT!
KEH HEH...
I FAILED, DIDN'T I?
COME, COME, THIS IS MY JOB. LET ME PERFORM MY PROPER DUTY.

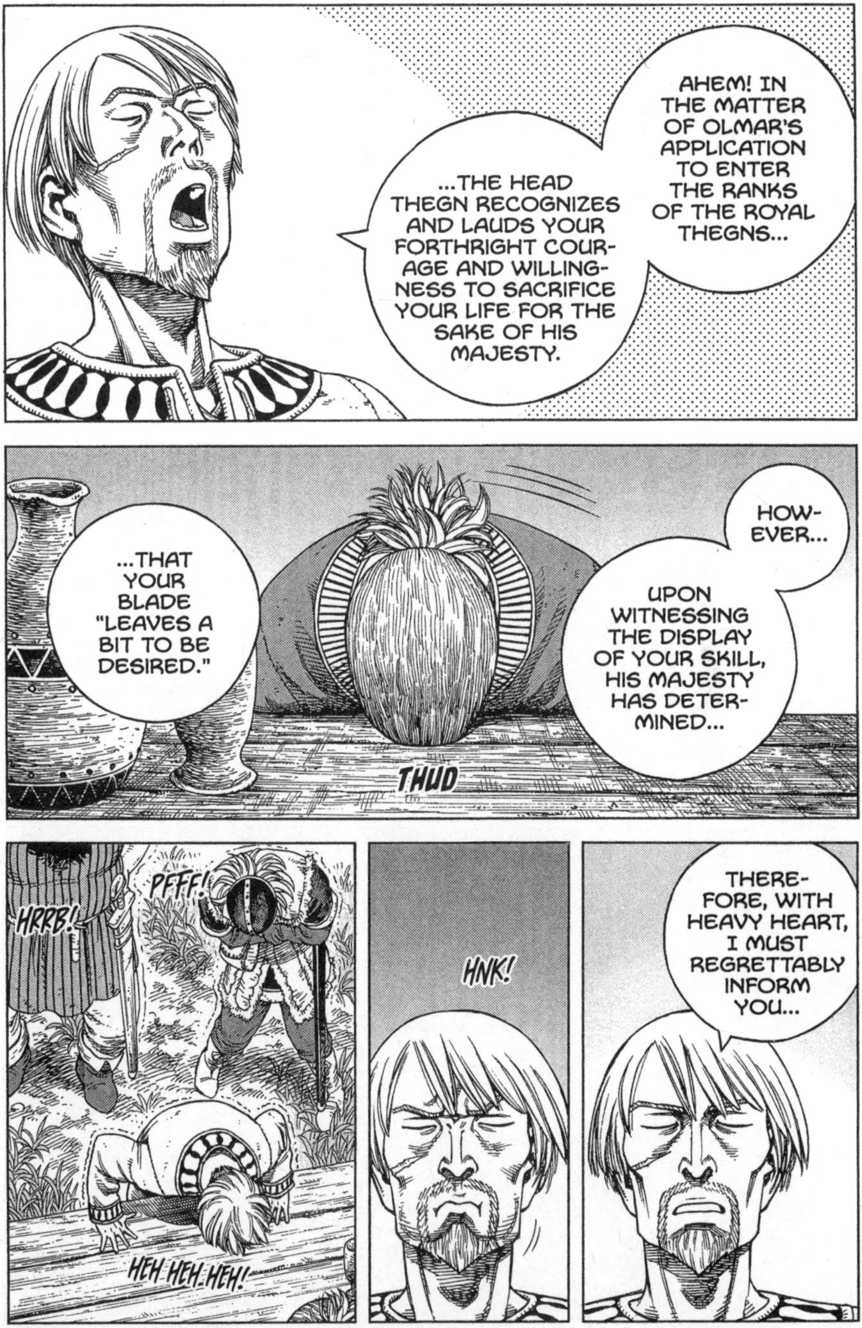
AHEM! IN THE MATTER OF OLMAR'S APPLICATION TO ENTER THE RANKS OF THE ROYAL THEGNS...
...THE HEAD THEGN RECOGNIZES AND LAUDS YOUR FORTHRIGHT COURAGE AND WILLINGNESS TO SACRIFICE YOUR LIFE FOR THE SAKE OF HIS MAJESTY.
HOW-EVER...
UPON WITNESSING THE DISPLAY OF YOUR SKILL, HIS MAJESTY HAS DETERMINED...
...THAT YOUR BLADE "LEAVES A BIT TO BE DESIRED."
THUD
THEREFORE, WITH HEAVY HEART, I MUST REGRETTABLY INFORM YOU...
HNK!
PFFF!
HRRB!
HEH HEH HEH!

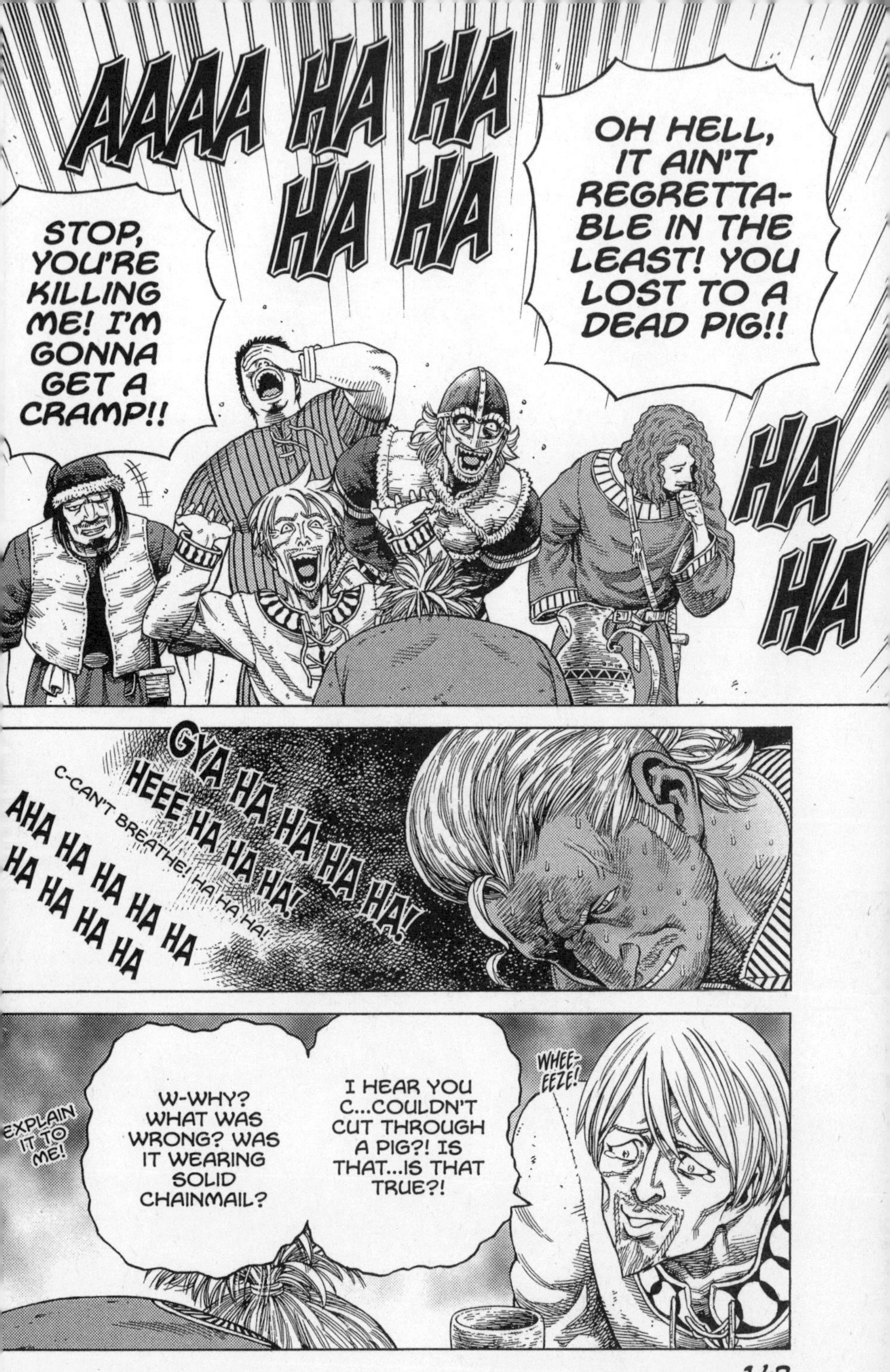
OH HELL, IT AIN'T REGRETTA-BLE IN THE LEAST! YOU LOST TO A DEAD PIG!!
AAAA HA HA HA HA HA HA
STOP, YOU'RE KILLING ME! I'M GONNA GET A CRAMP!!
HA HA HA
GYA HA HA HA HA HA HA!
HEEE HA HA HA!
C-CAN'T BREATHE! HA HA HA!
AHA HA HA HA HA HA HA HA HA HA
WHEEE-EEZE!
I HEAR YOU C...COULDN'T CUT THROUGH A PIG?! IS THAT...IS THAT TRUE?!
W-WHY? WHAT WAS WRONG? WAS IT WEARING SOLID CHAINMAIL?
EXPLAIN IT TO ME!

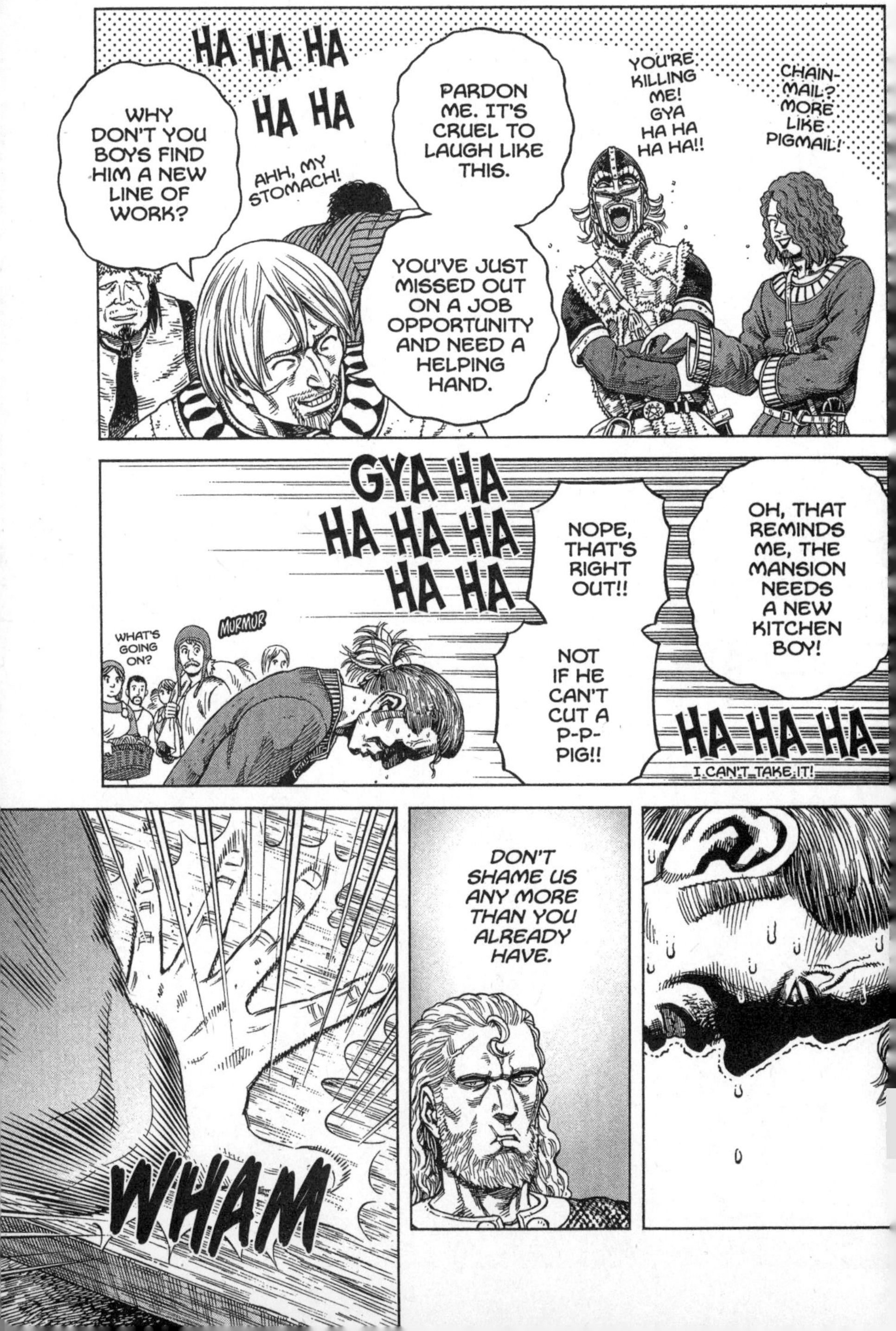
CHAIN-MAIL? MORE LIKE PIGMAIL!
YOU'RE KILLING ME! GYA HA HA HA HA!!
PARDON ME. IT'S CRUEL TO LAUGH LIKE THIS.
YOU'VE JUST MISSED OUT ON A JOB OPPORTUNITY AND NEED A HELPING HAND.
HA HA HA HA HA
AHH, MY STOMACH!
WHY DON'T YOU BOYS FIND HIM A NEW LINE OF WORK?
OH, THAT REMINDS ME, THE MANSION NEEDS A NEW KITCHEN BOY!
HA HA HA
I CAN'T TAKE IT!
NOPE, THAT'S RIGHT OUT!!
NOT IF HE CAN'T CUT A P-P-PIG!!
GYA HA HA HA HA HA HA
MURMUR
WHAT'S GOING ON?
DON'T SHAME US ANY MORE THAN YOU ALREADY HAVE.
WHAM

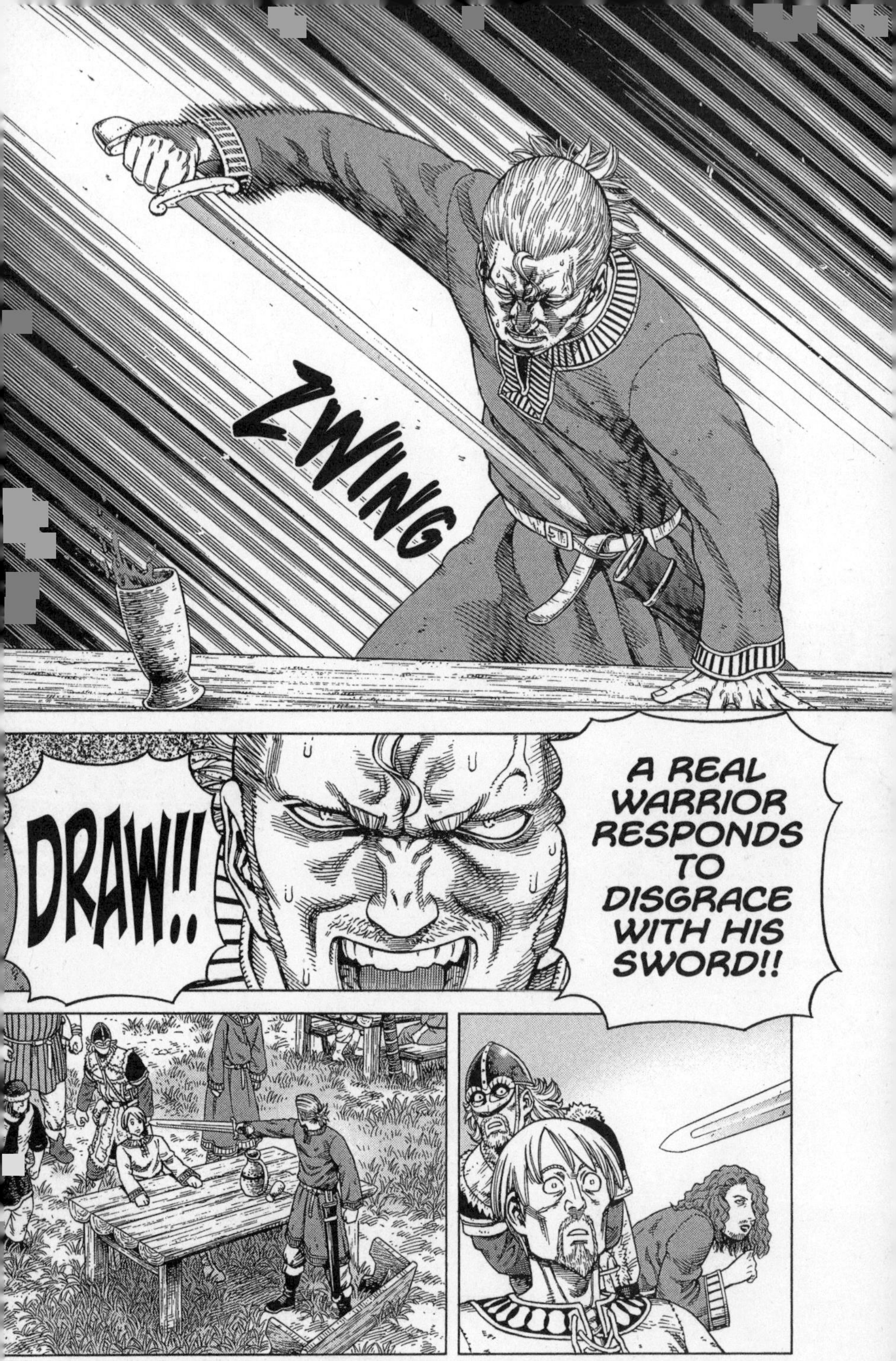
ZWING
A REAL WARRIOR RESPONDS TO DISGRACE WITH HIS SWORD!!
DRAW!!

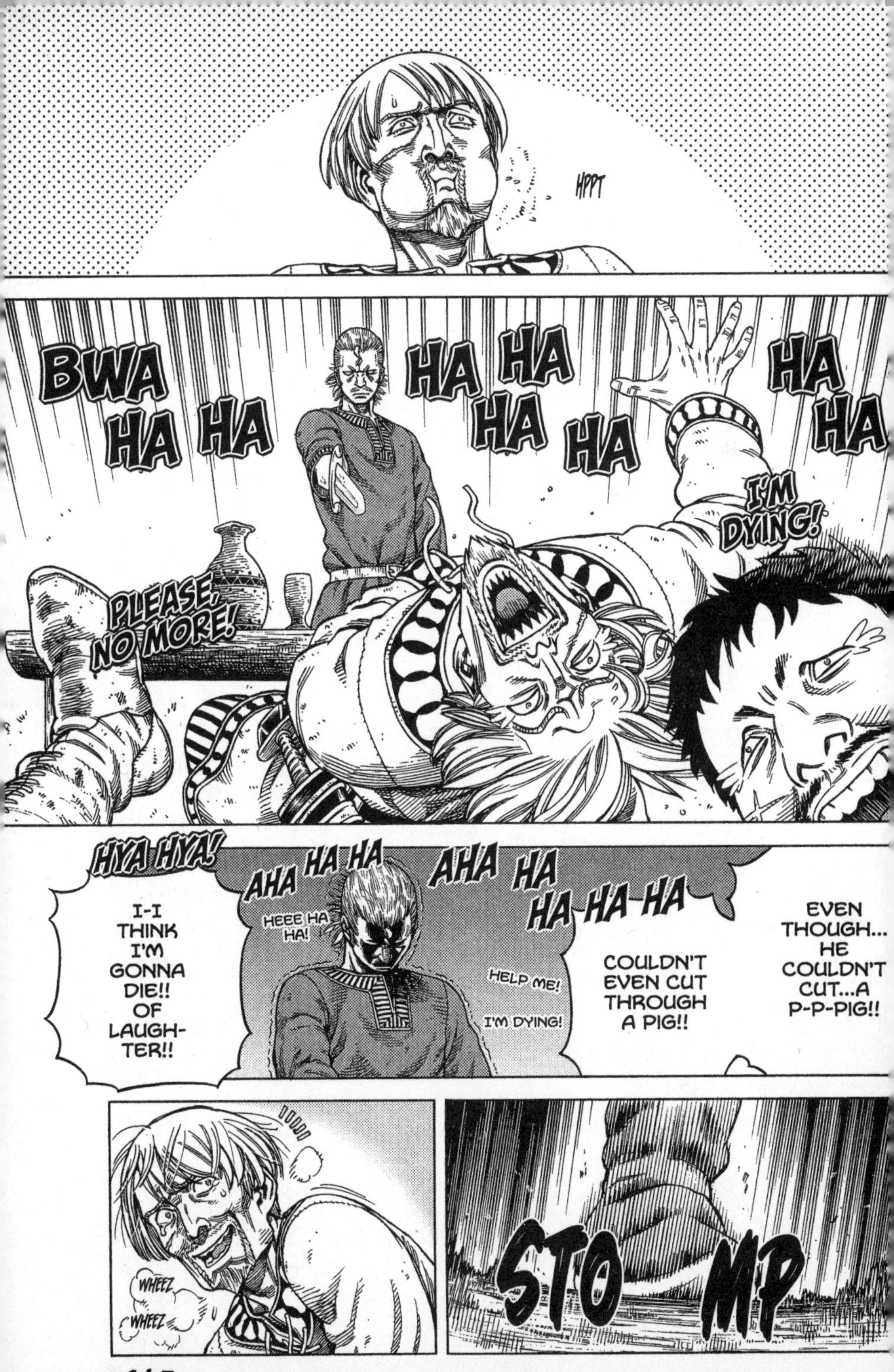
HPPT
HA HA
I'M DYING!
HA HA HA HA
BWA HA HA
PLEASE, NO MORE!
EVEN THOUGH... HE COULDN'T CUT...A P-P-PIG!!
COULDN'T EVEN CUT THROUGH A PIG!!
AHA HA HA-HA-HA
HELP ME!
I'M DYING!
AHA HA HA
HEEE HA HA!
HYA HYA!
I-I THINK I'M GONNA DIE!! OF LAUGHTER!!
STOMP
WHEEZ
WHEEZ

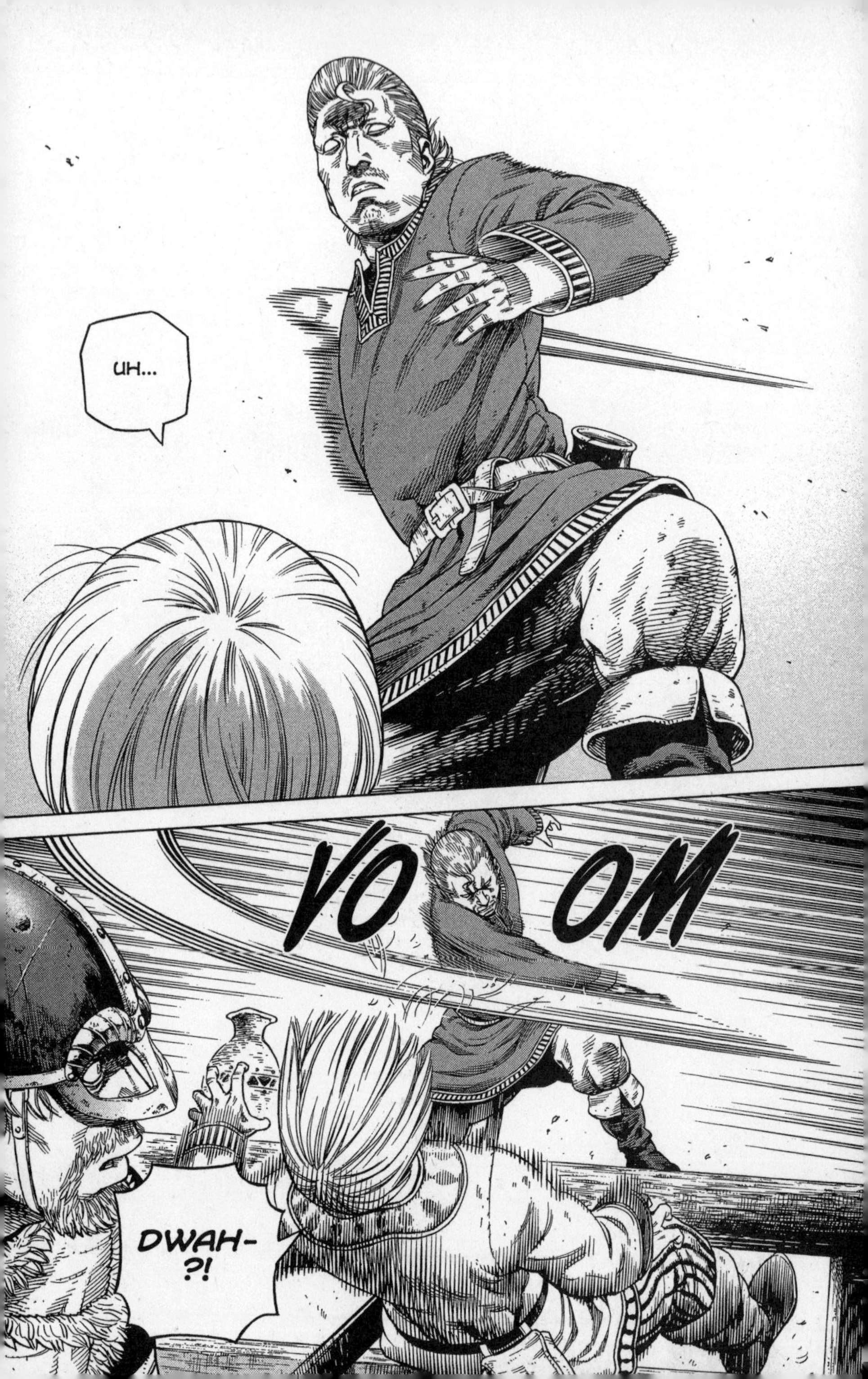
UH...
VO OM
DWAH-?!

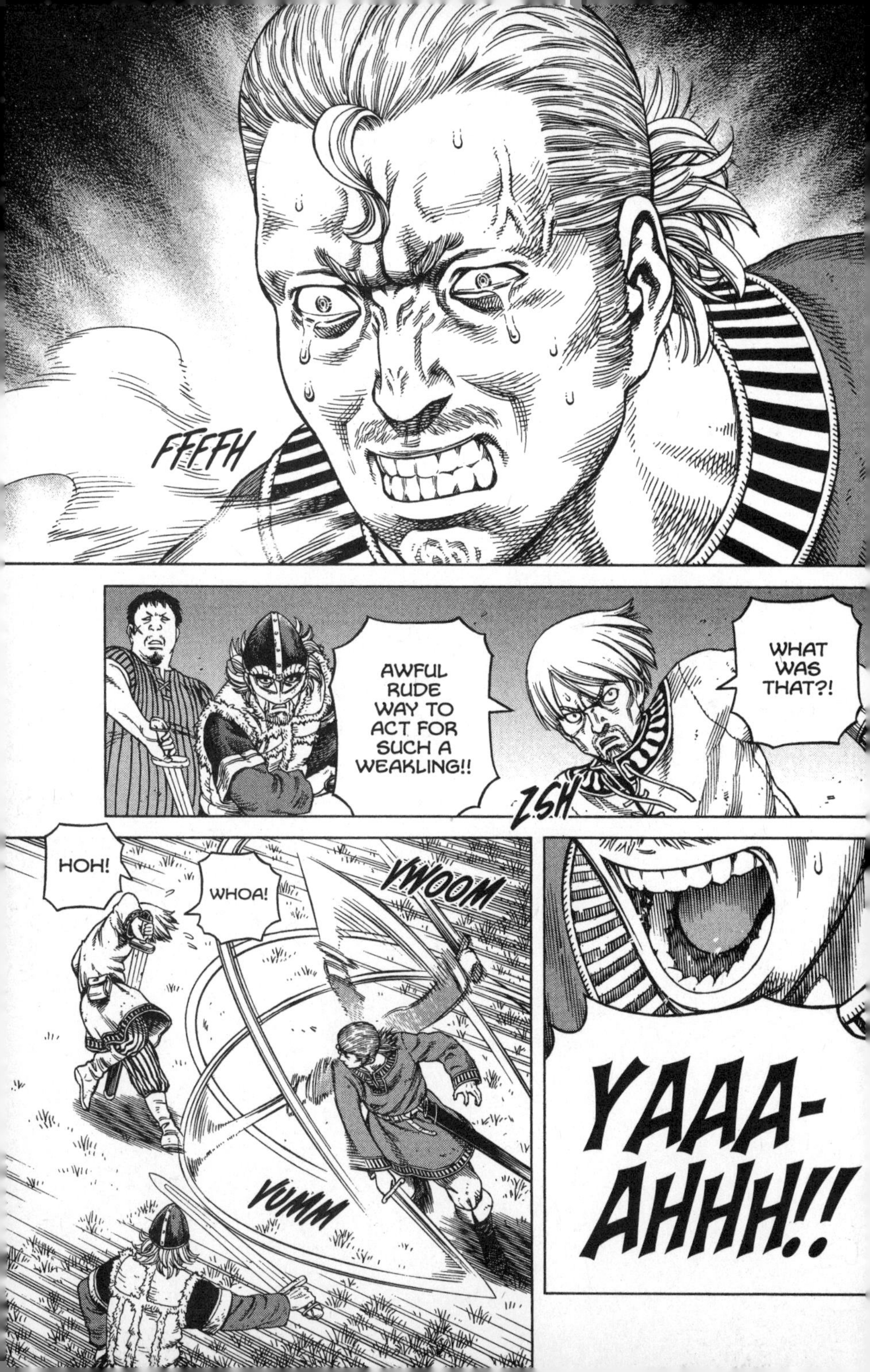
FFFFH
WHAT WAS THAT?!
AWFUL RUDE WAY TO ACT FOR SUCH A WEAKLING!!
ZSH
YAAA-AHHH!!
VWOOM
WHOA!
HOH!
VUMM

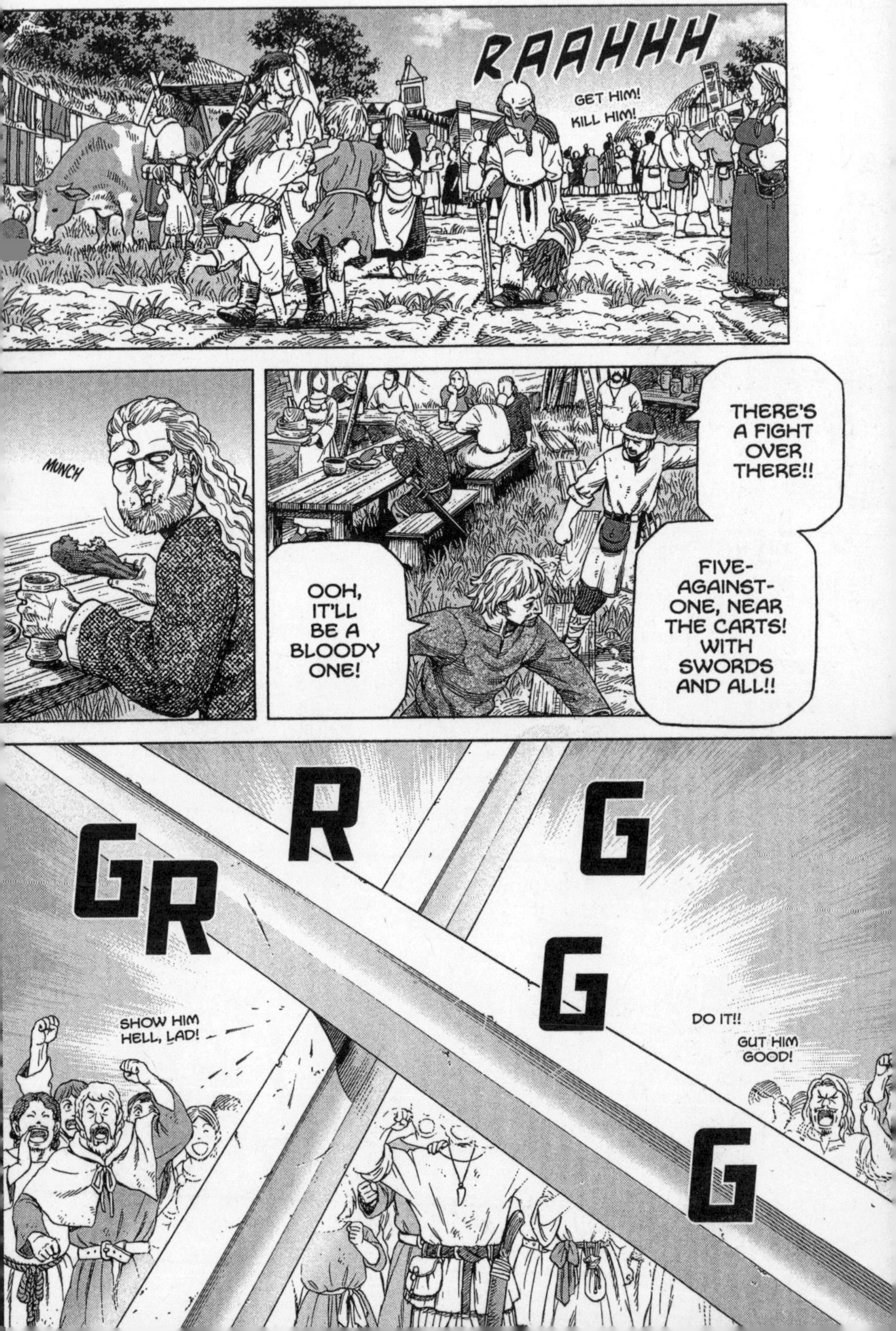
RAAHHH
GET HIM!
KILL HIM!
THERE'S A FIGHT OVER THERE!!
FIVE-AGAINST-ONE, NEAR THE CARTS! WITH SWORDS AND ALL!!
OOH, IT'LL BE A BLOODY ONE!
MUNCH
GRRGGG
DO IT!!
GUT HIM GOOD!
SHOW HIM HELL, LAD!

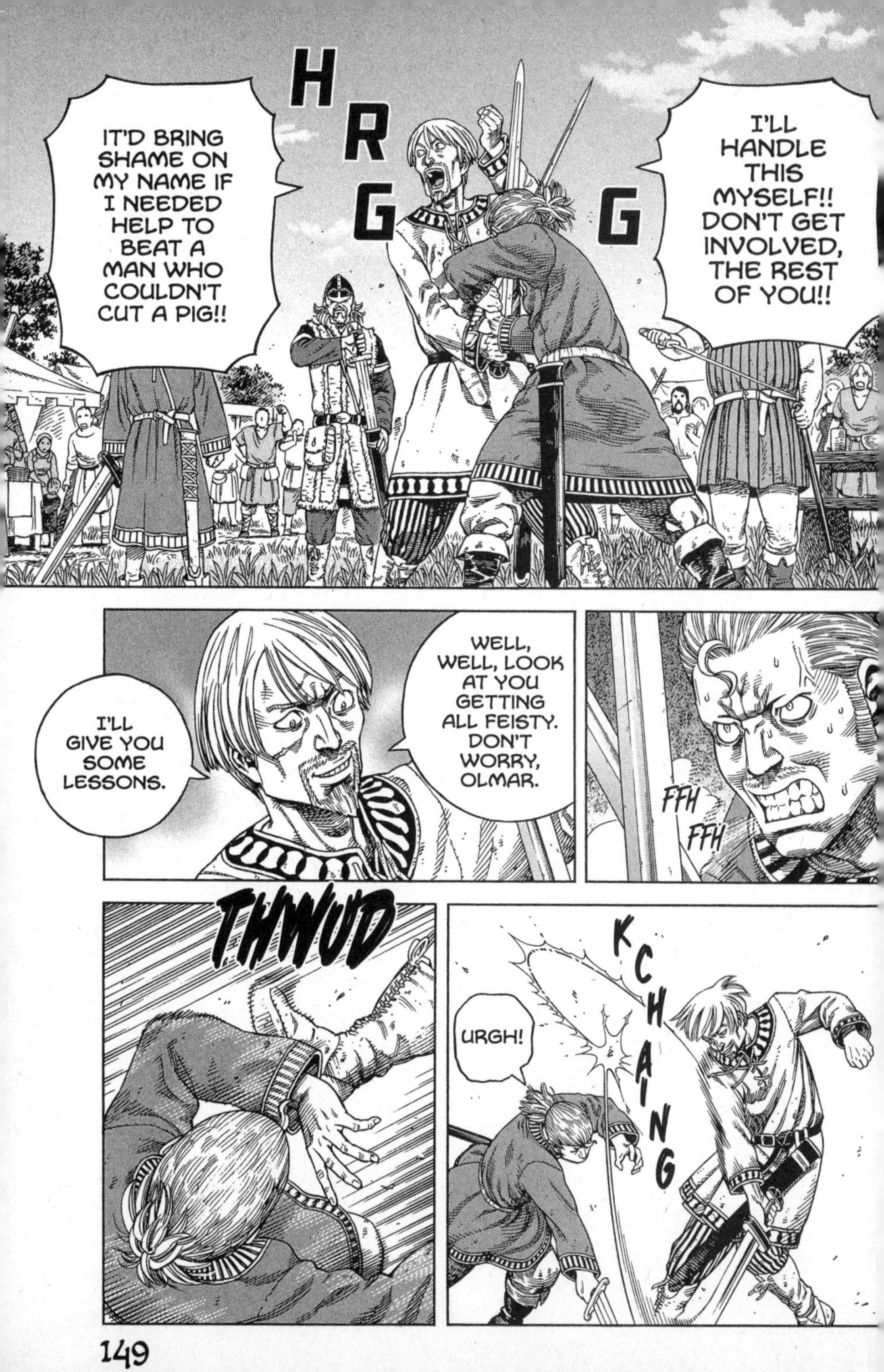
I'LL HANDLE THIS MYSELF!! DON'T GET INVOLVED, THE REST OF YOU!!
HRGG
IT'D BRING SHAME ON MY NAME IF I NEEDED HELP TO BEAT A MAN WHO COULDN'T CUT A PIG!!
FFH FFH
WELL, WELL, LOOK AT YOU GETTING ALL FEISTY. DON'T WORRY, OLMAR.
I'LL GIVE YOU SOME LESSONS.
KCHAING
URGH!
THWUD

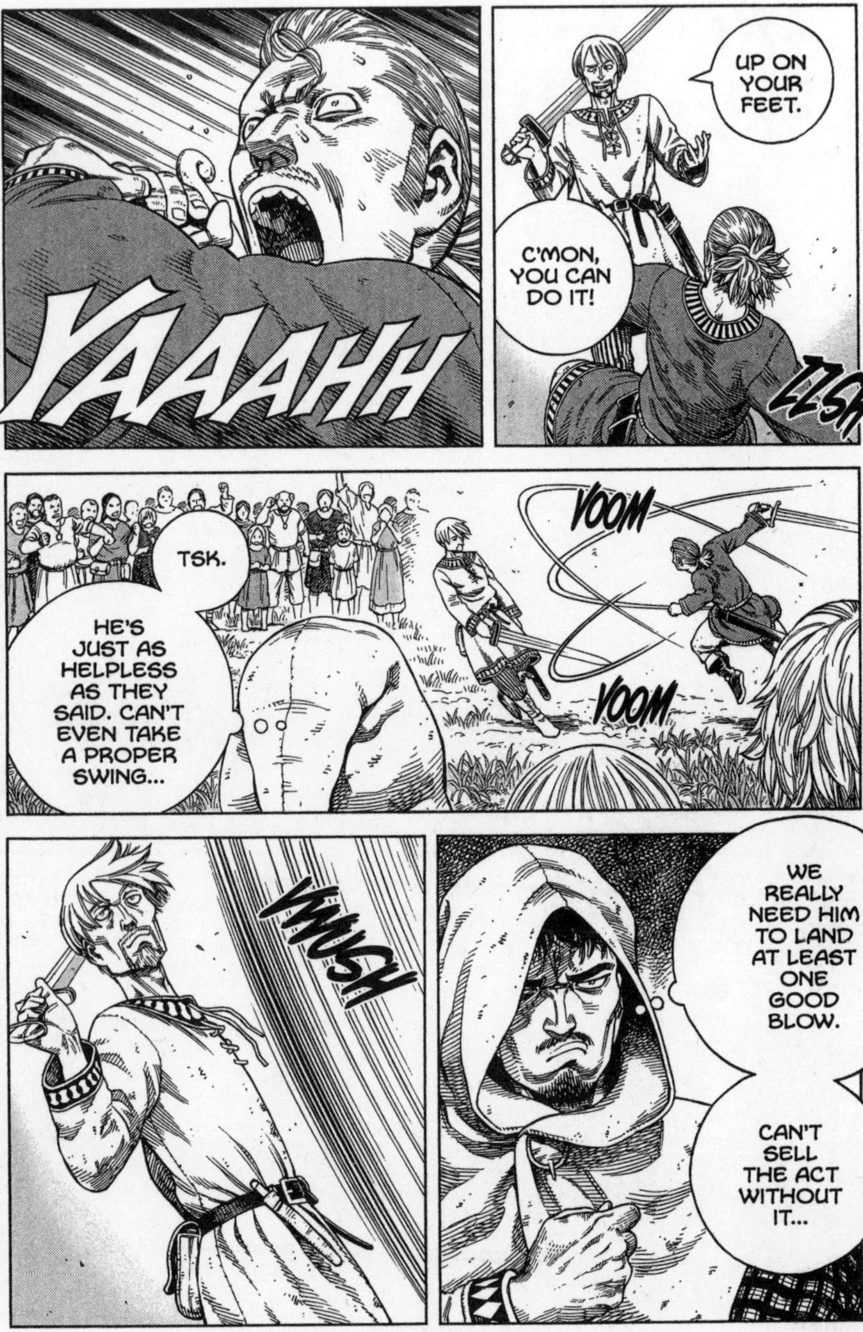
UP ON YOUR FEET.
C'MON, YOU CAN DO IT!
ZZSH
YAAAHH
VOOM
TSK.
HE'S JUST AS HELPLESS AS THEY SAID. CAN'T EVEN TAKE A PROPER SWING...
VOOM
WE REALLY NEED HIM TO LAND AT LEAST ONE GOOD BLOW.
CAN'T SELL THE ACT WITHOUT IT...
VWUSH

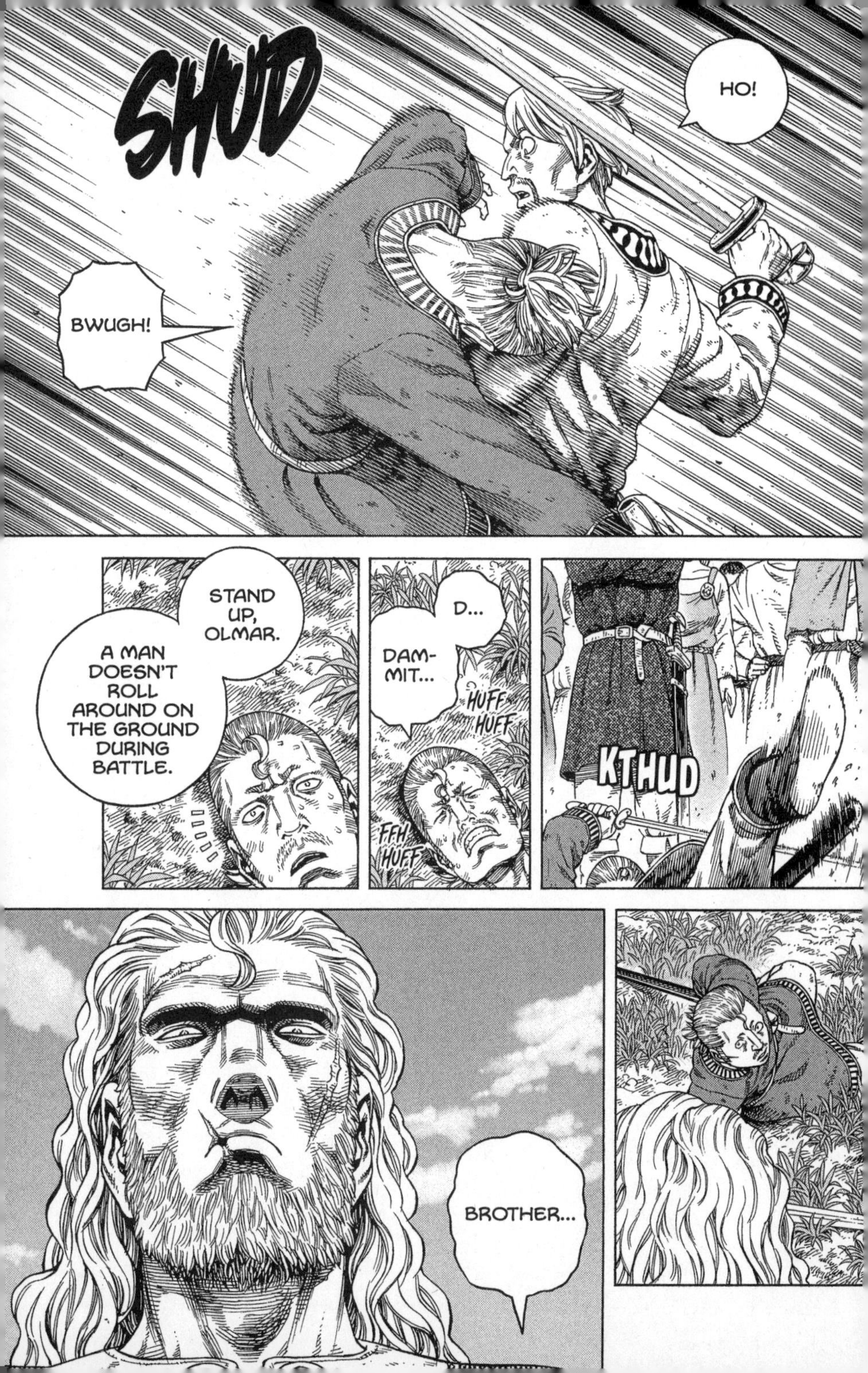
HO!
SHUD
BWUGH!
KTHUD
D...
DAM-MIT...
HUFF HUFF
FFH HUFF
STAND UP, OLMAR.
A MAN DOESN'T ROLL AROUND ON THE GROUND DURING BATTLE.
BROTHER...

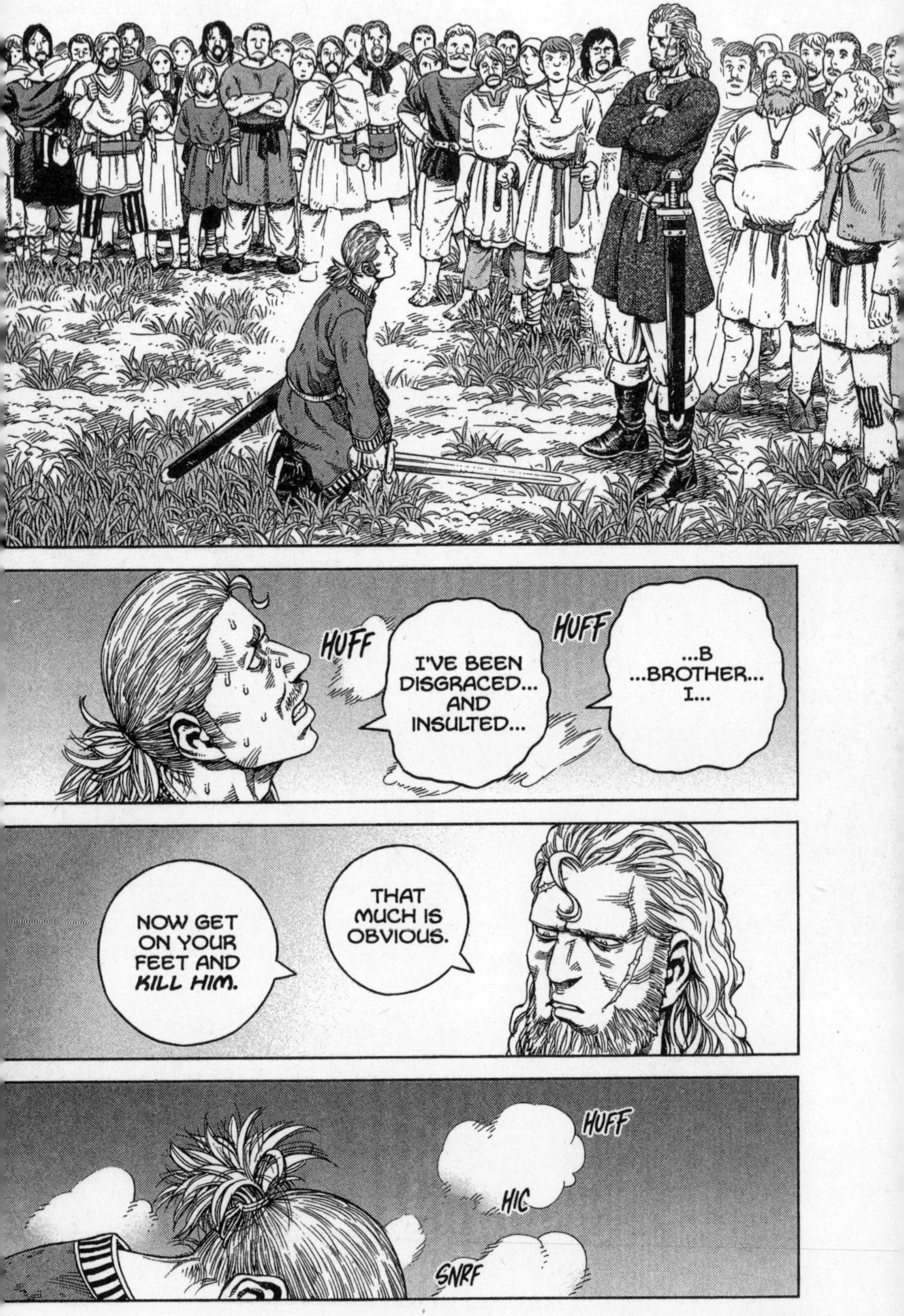
HUFF
...B ...BROTHER... I...
HUFF
I'VE BEEN DISGRACED... AND INSULTED...
THAT MUCH IS OBVIOUS.
NOW GET ON YOUR FEET AND *KILL HIM.*
HUFF
HIC
SNRF

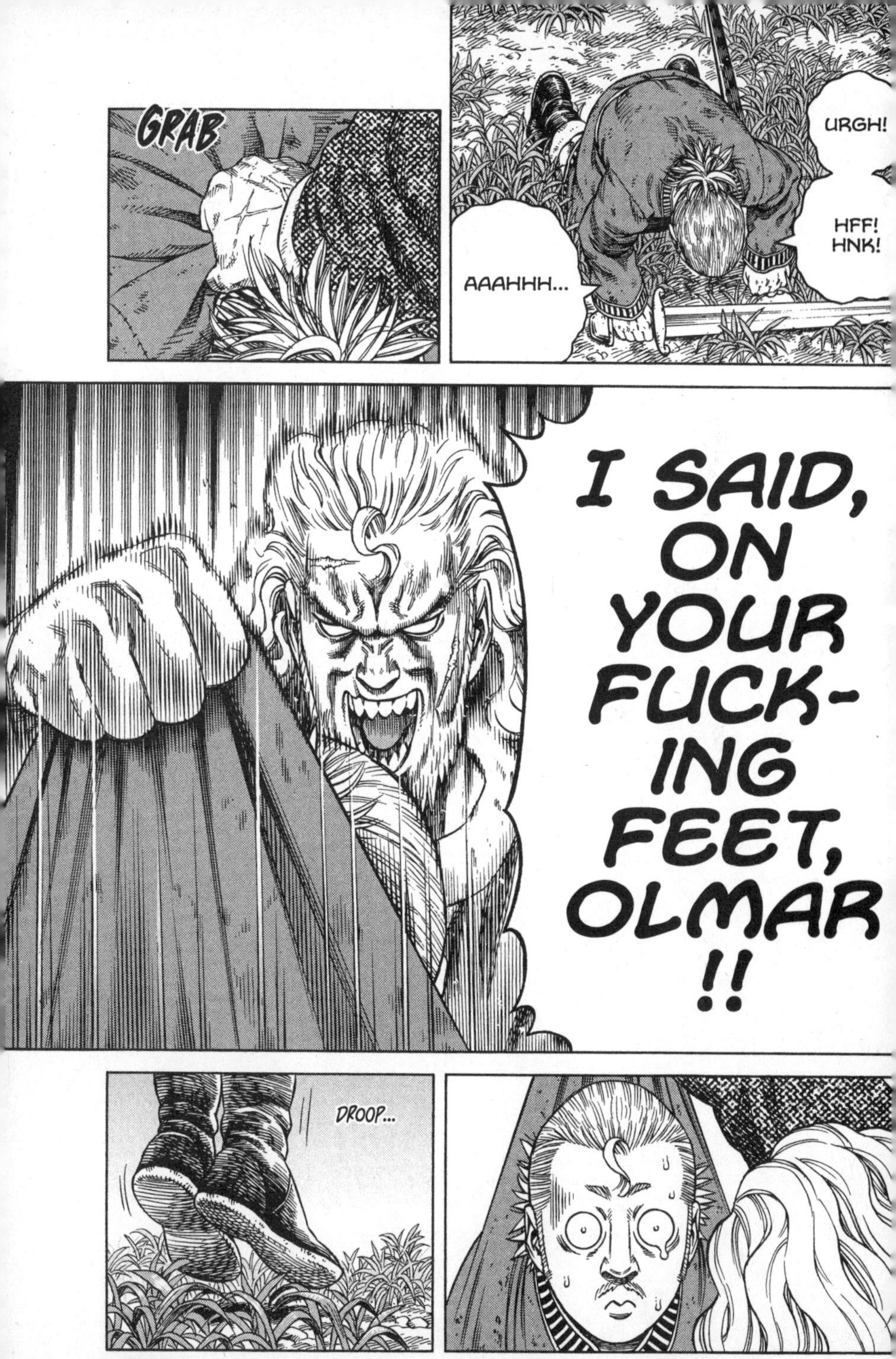
URGH!
HFF! HNK!
AAAHHH...
GRAB
I SAID, ON YOUR FUCKING FEET, OLMAR!!
DROOP...

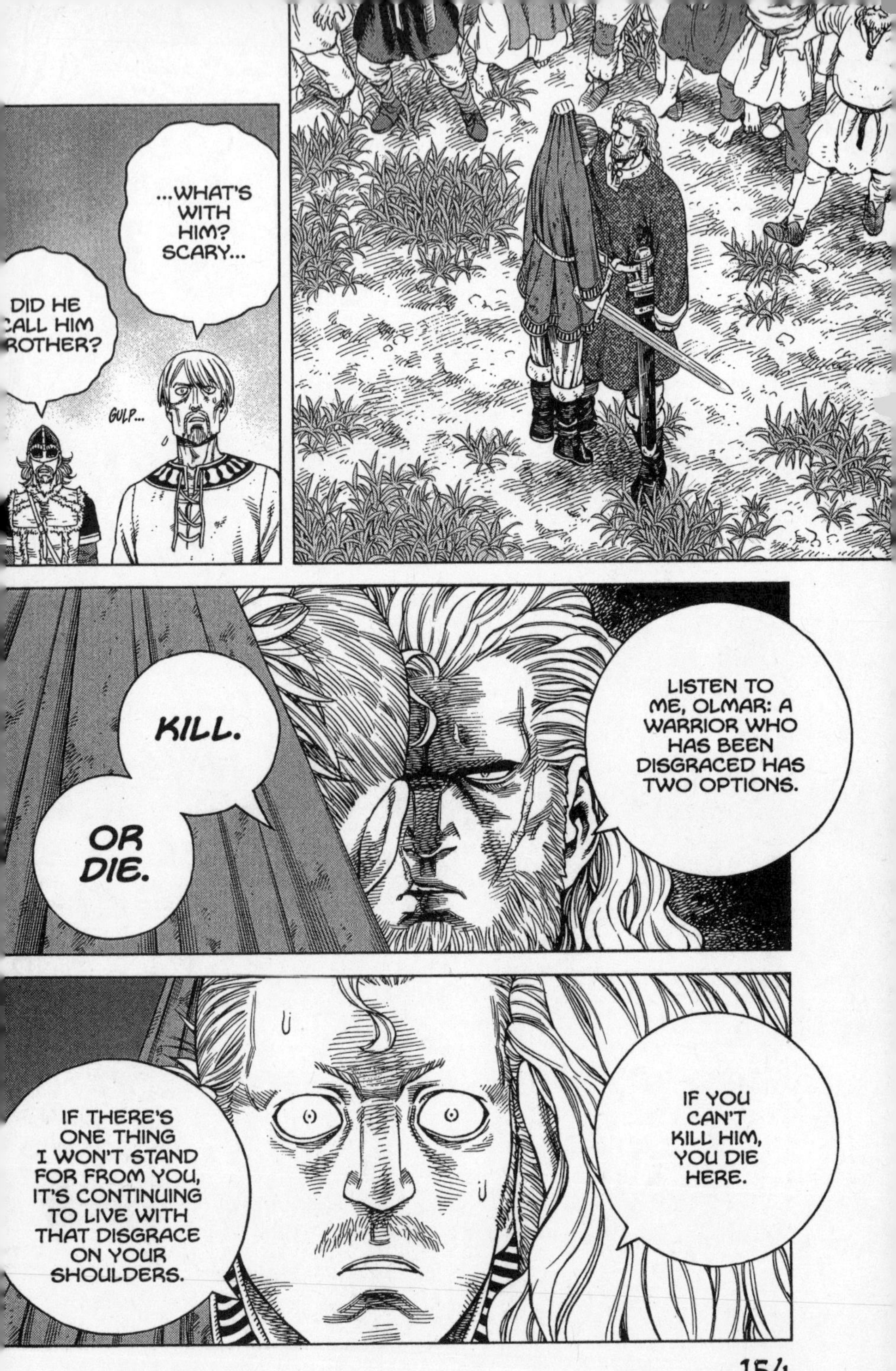
...WHAT'S WITH HIM? SCARY...
DID HE CALL HIM ROTHER?
GULP...
LISTEN TO ME, OLMAR: A WARRIOR WHO HAS BEEN DISGRACED HAS TWO OPTIONS.
KILL.
OR DIE.
IF YOU CAN'T KILL HIM, YOU DIE HERE.
IF THERE'S ONE THING I WON'T STAND FOR FROM YOU, IT'S CONTINUING TO LIVE WITH THAT DISGRACE ON YOUR SHOULDERS.

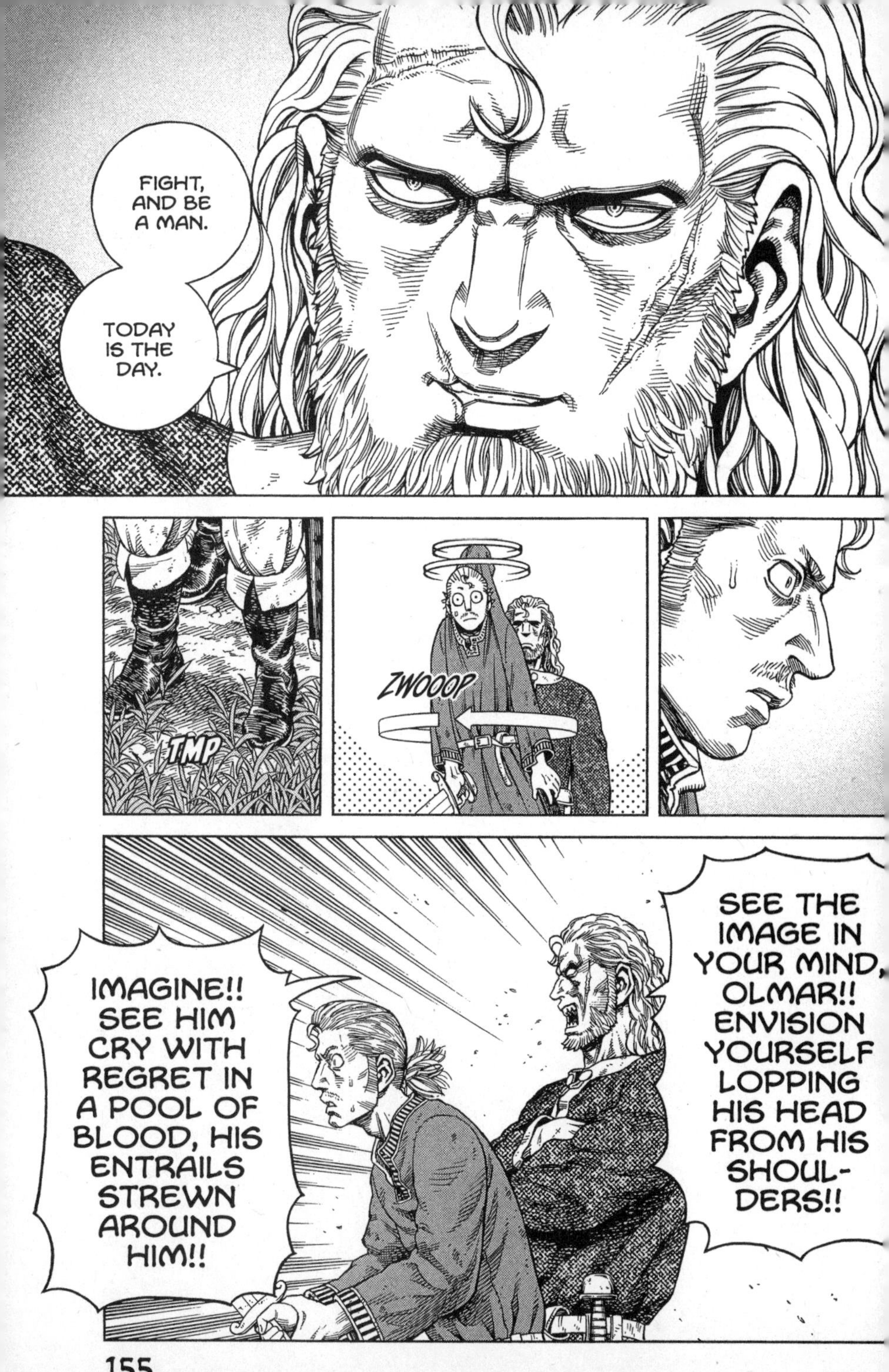
FIGHT, AND BE A MAN.
TODAY IS THE DAY.
ZWOOOP
TMP
SEE THE IMAGE IN YOUR MIND, OLMAR!! ENVISION YOURSELF LOPPING HIS HEAD FROM HIS SHOUL-DERS!!
IMAGINE!! SEE HIM CRY WITH REGRET IN A POOL OF BLOOD, HIS ENTRAILS STREWN AROUND HIM!!

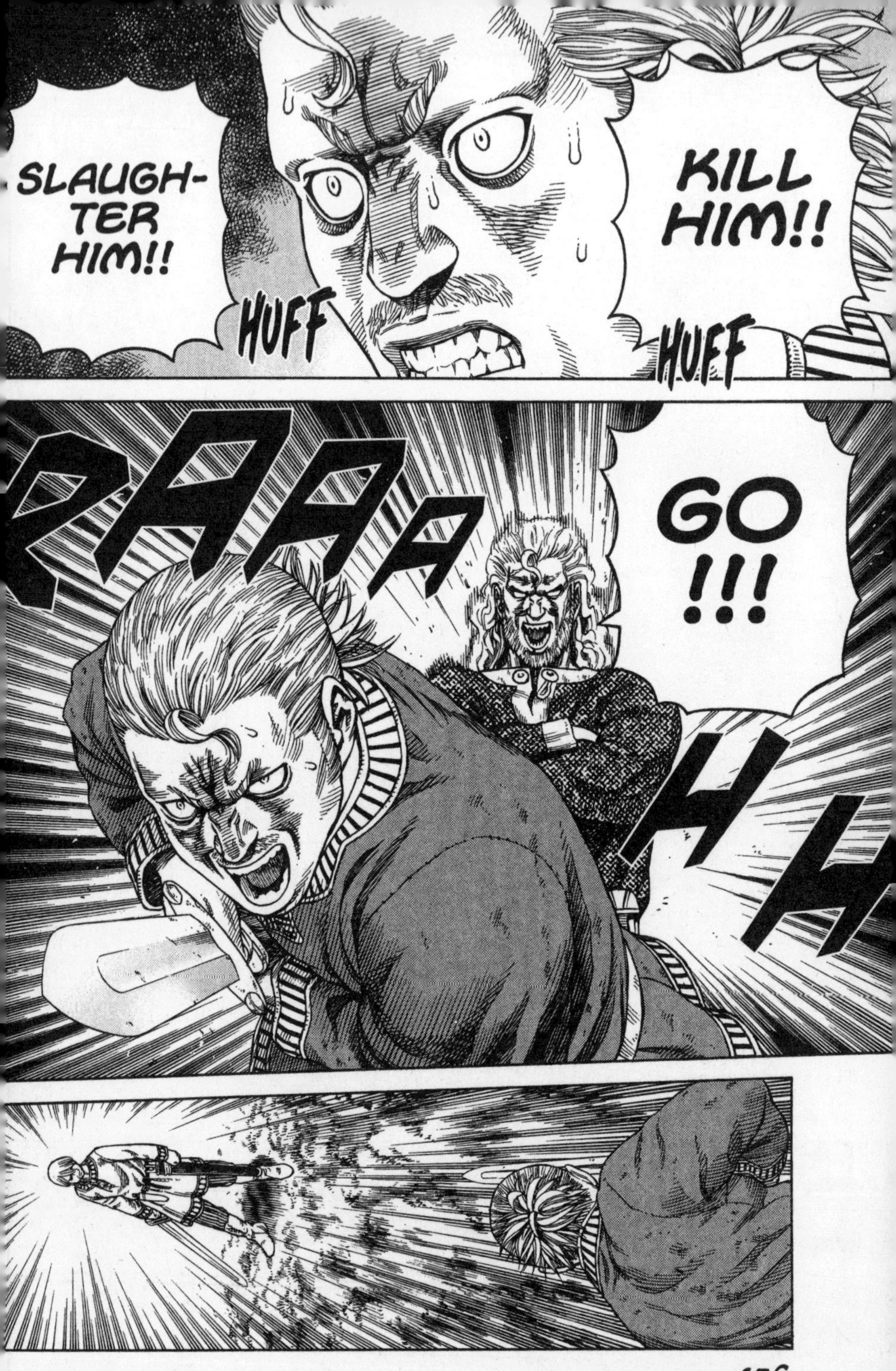
KILL HIM!!
HUFF
SLAUGH-TER HIM!!
HUFF
GO!!!
RAAAAHHH

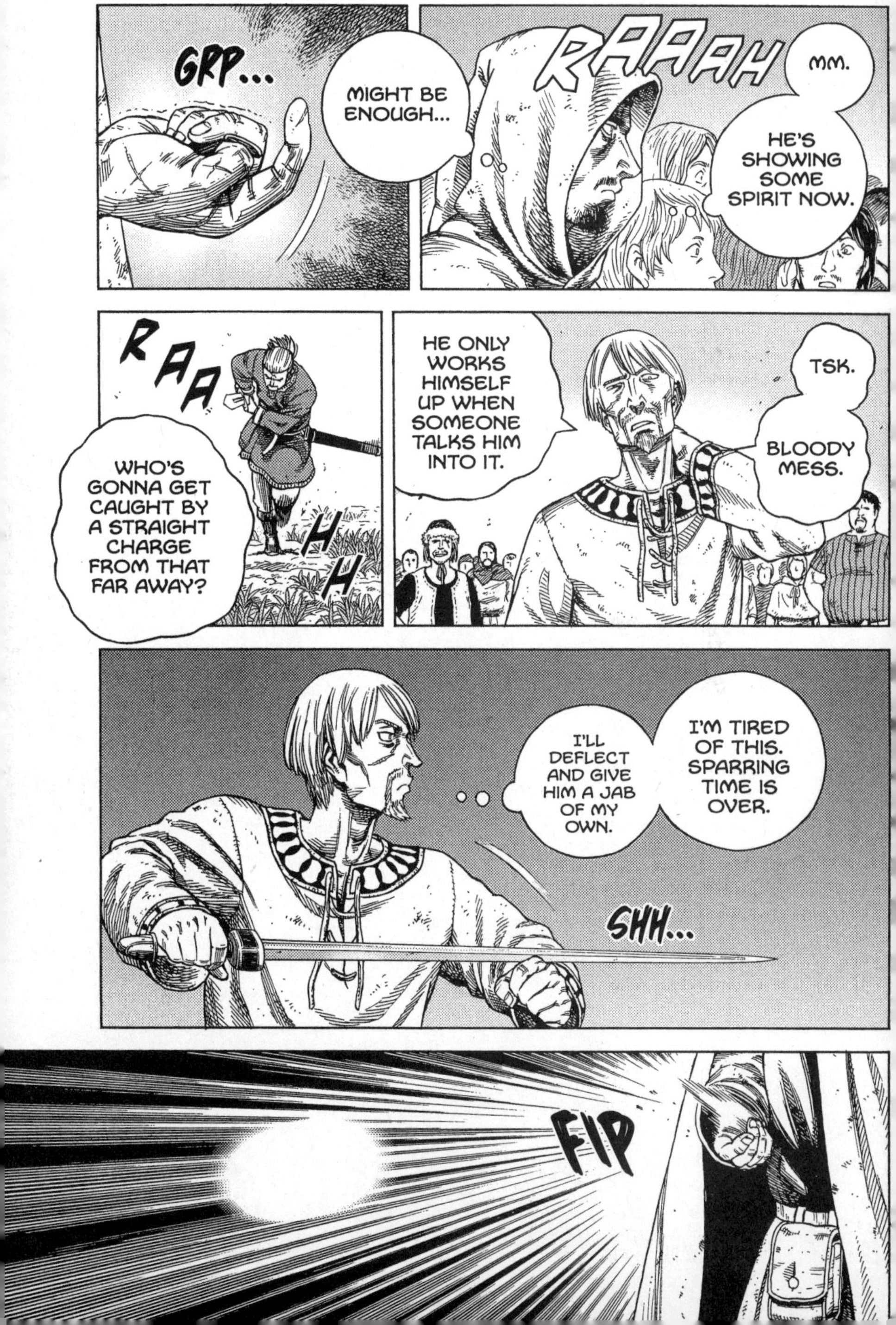
MM.
HE'S SHOWING SOME SPIRIT NOW.
RAAAAH
MIGHT BE ENOUGH...
GRP...
TSK.
BLOODY MESS.
HE ONLY WORKS HIMSELF UP WHEN SOMEONE TALKS HIM INTO IT.
RAA
HH
WHO'S GONNA GET CAUGHT BY A STRAIGHT CHARGE FROM THAT FAR AWAY?
I'M TIRED OF THIS. SPARRING TIME IS OVER.
I'LL DEFLECT AND GIVE HIM A JAB OF MY OWN.
SHH...
FIP

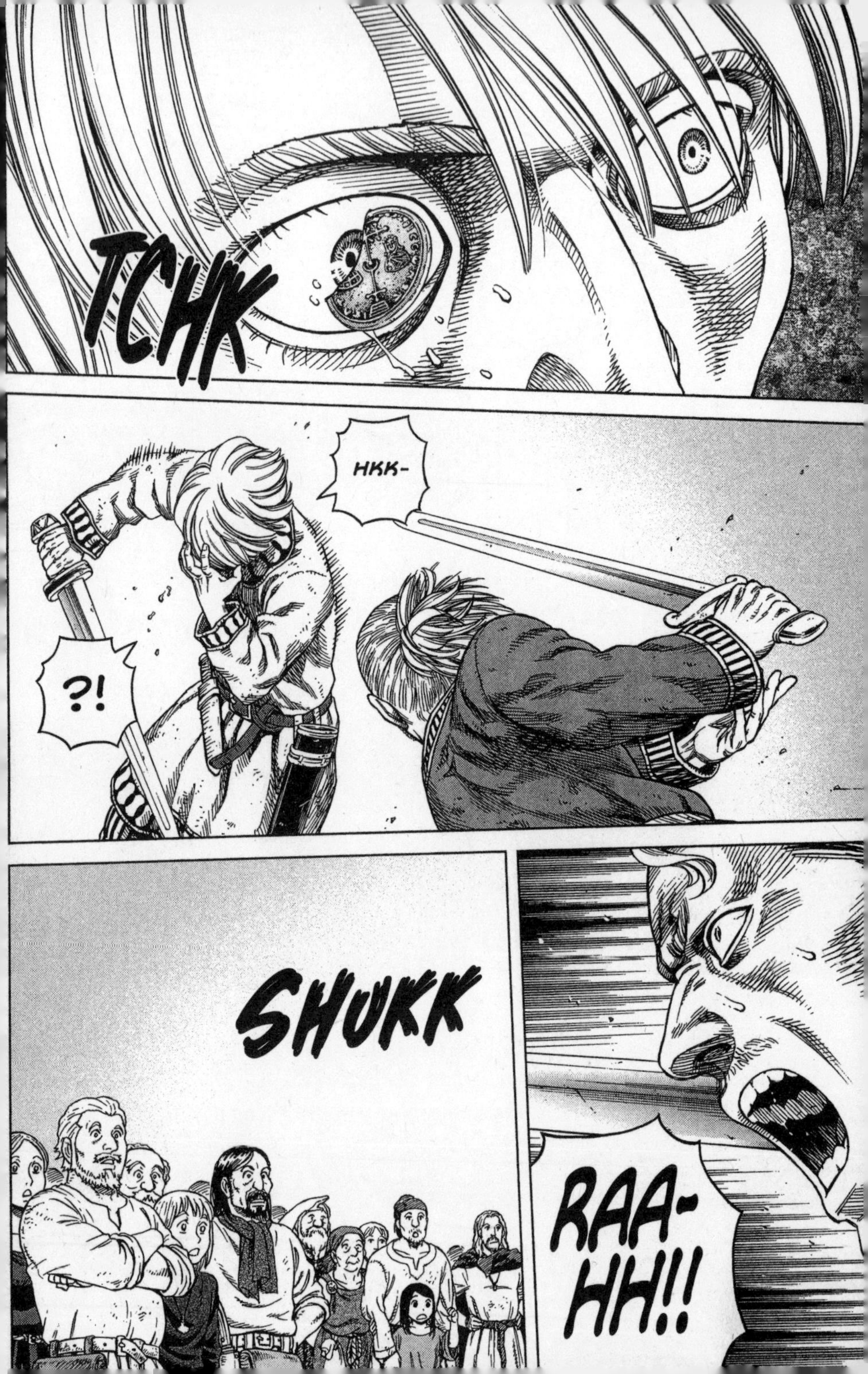
TCHK
HKK-
?!
RAA-HH!!
SHUKK

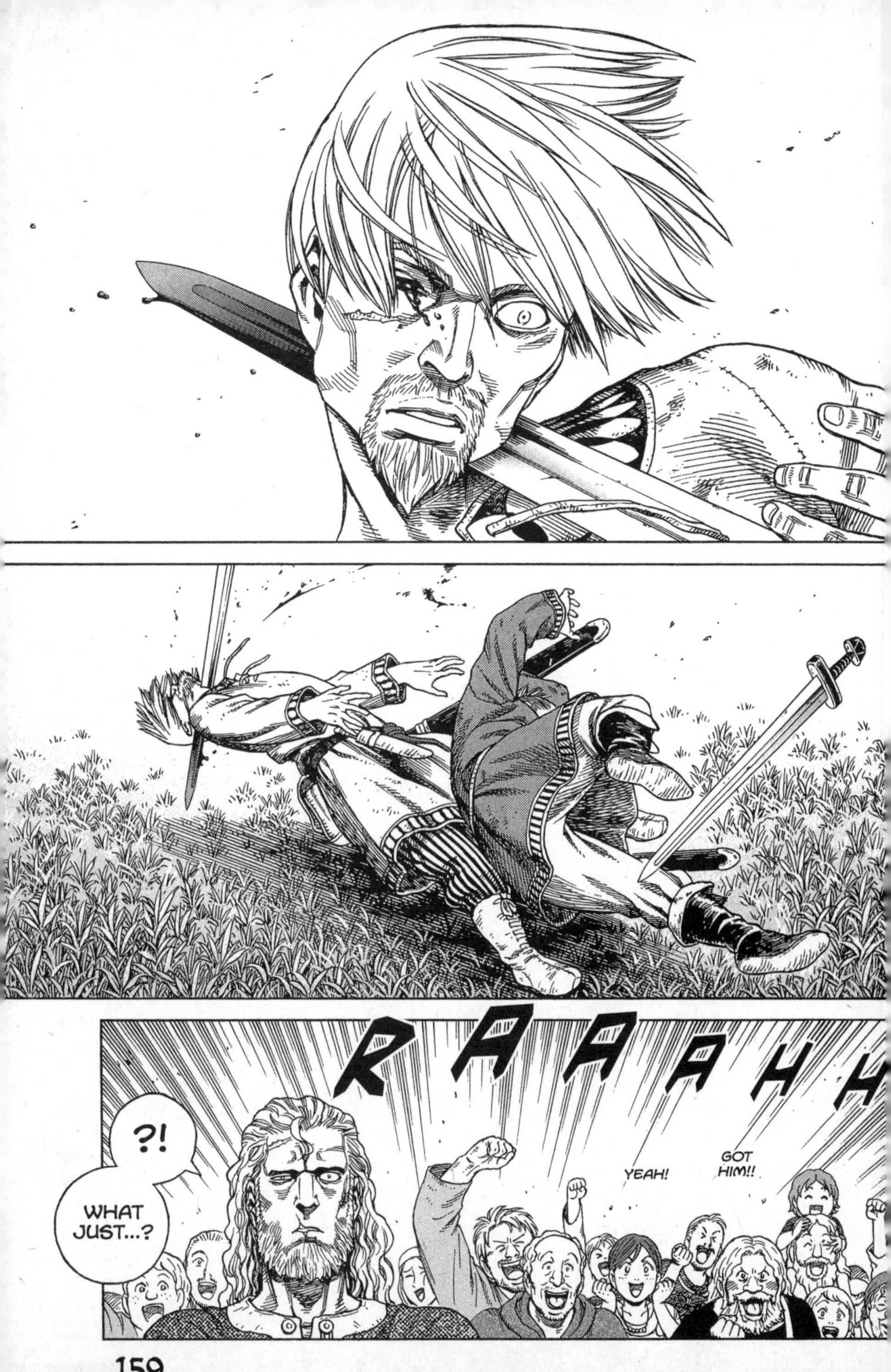
RAAAAHH
GOT HIM!!
YEAH!
?!
WHAT JUST...?

RAAAAHH
YAAH!
...
NO WAY!
YOU SERIOUS ...?
EUGH, NASTY!
HUFF
HUFF
HUFF
PUFF
... WHAT ...?
OOOHH

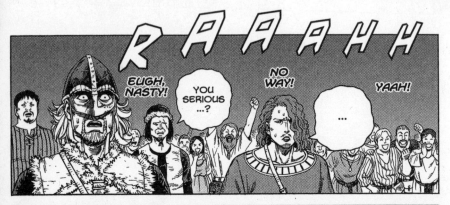

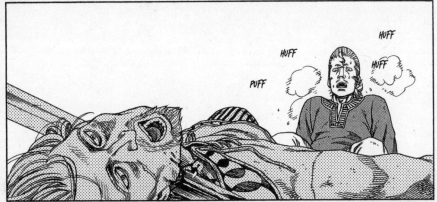

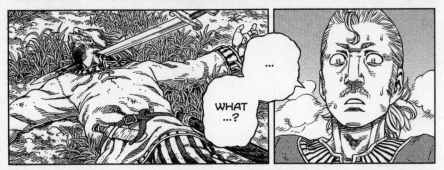

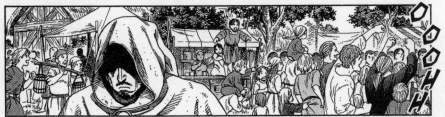

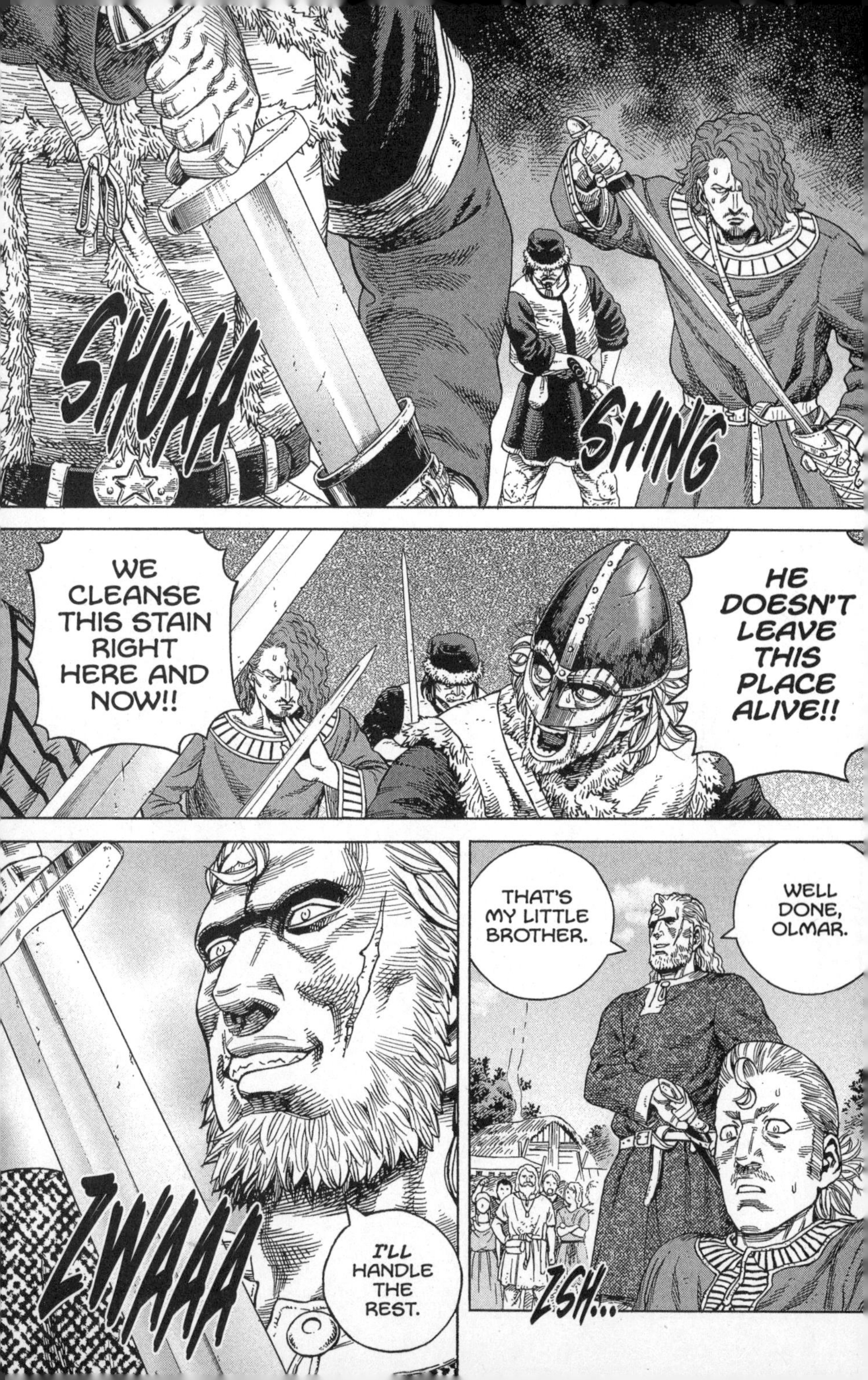
SHING
SHUAA
HE DOESN'T LEAVE THIS PLACE ALIVE!!
WE CLEANSE THIS STAIN RIGHT HERE AND NOW!!
WELL DONE, OLMAR.
THAT'S MY LITTLE BROTHER.
ZSH...
ZWAAA
I'LL HANDLE THE REST.

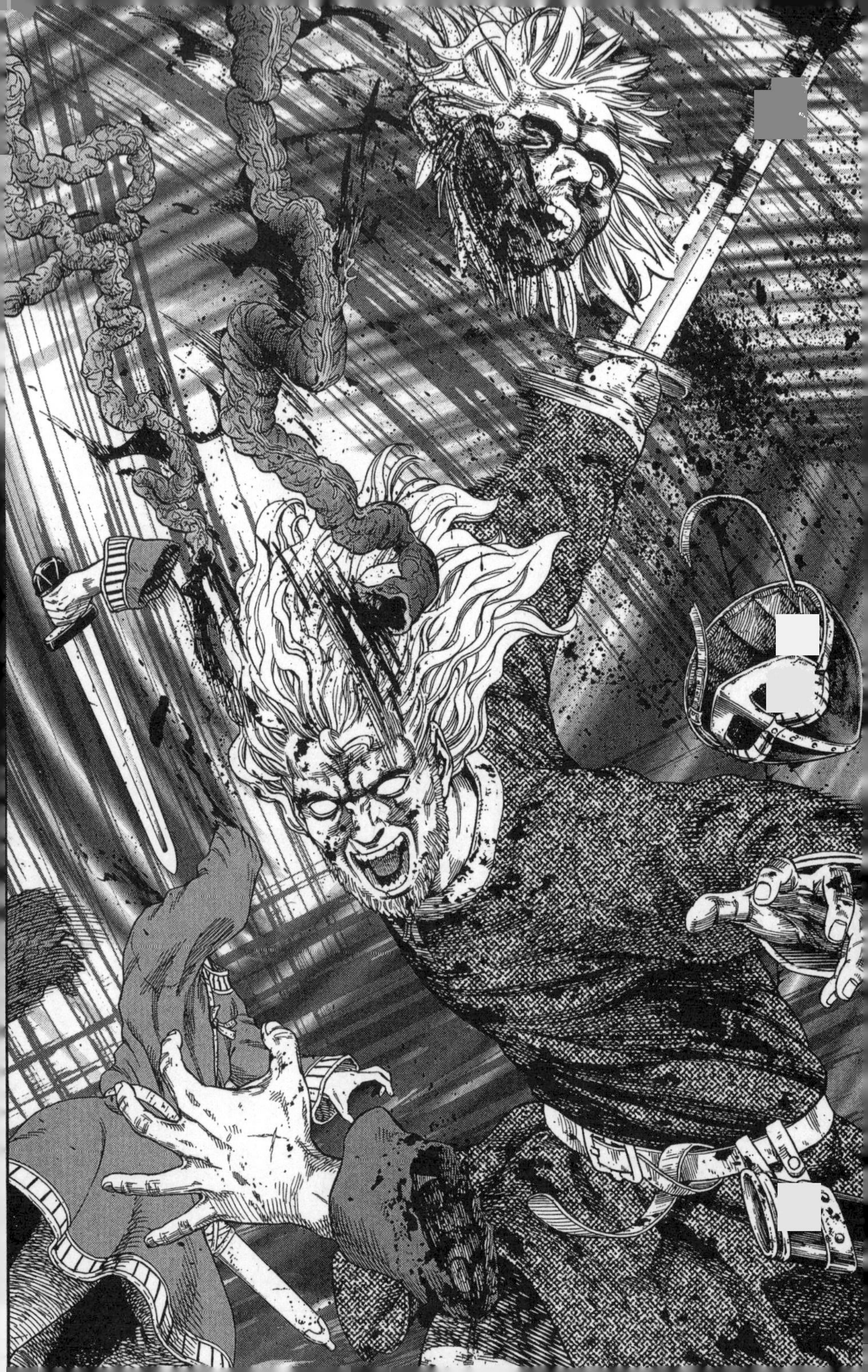

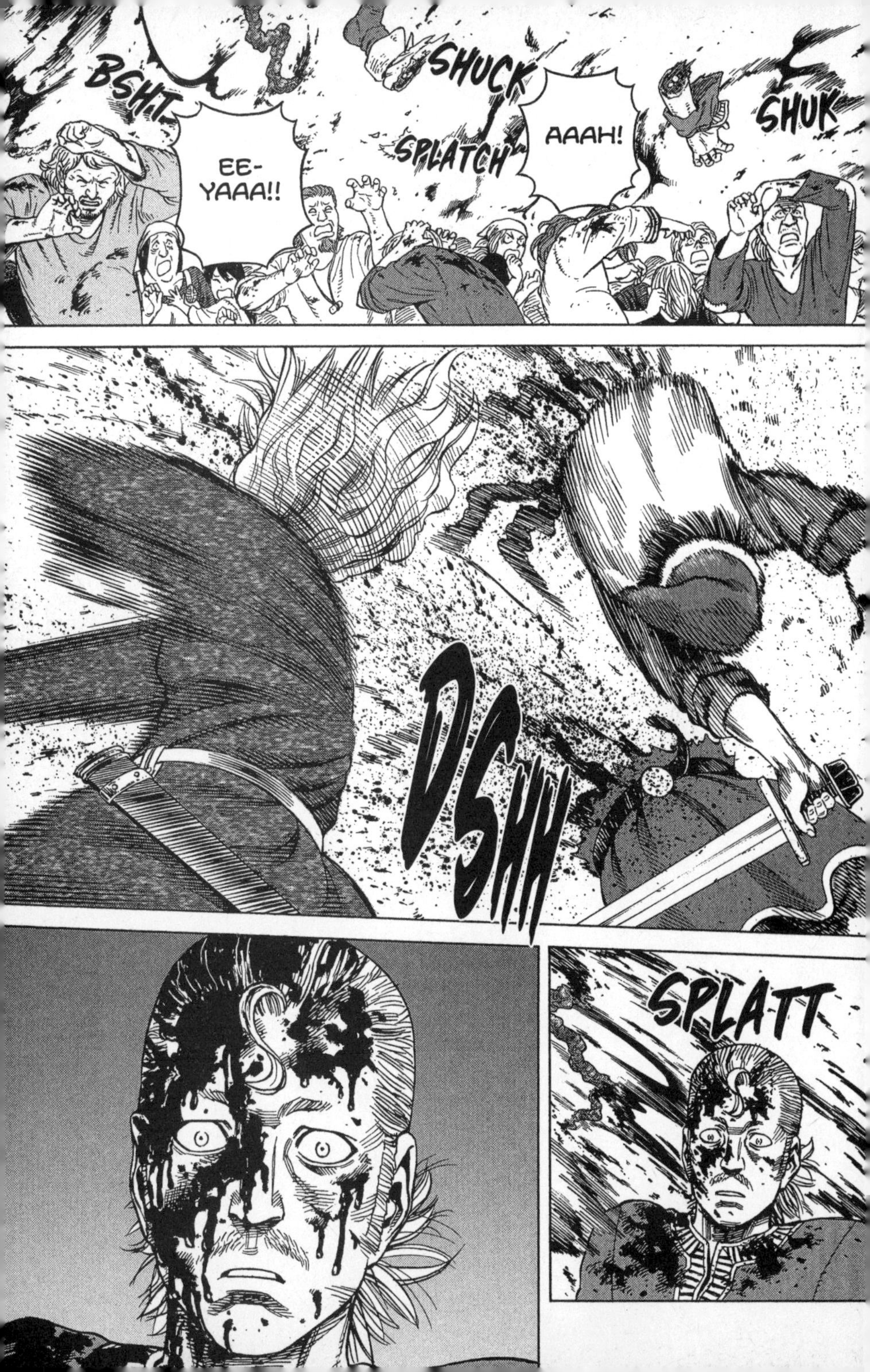
SHUK
AAAH!
SPLATCH
SHUCK
EE-YAAA!!
BSHT
DSHH
SPLATT

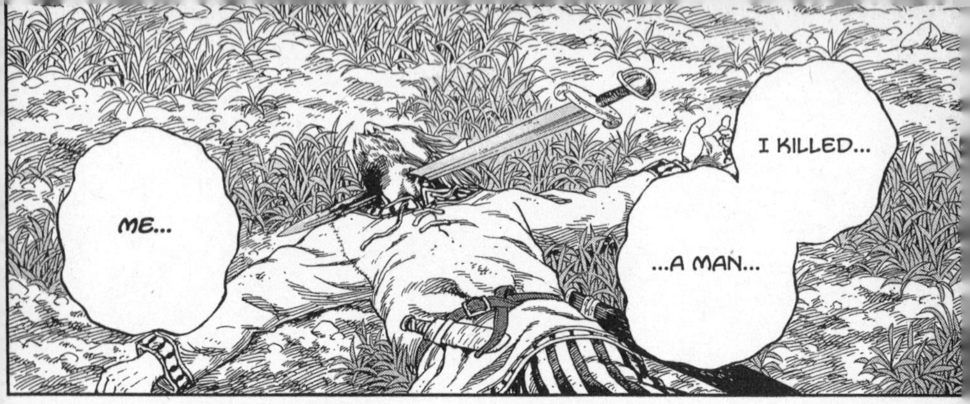
I KILLED...
...A MAN...
ME...
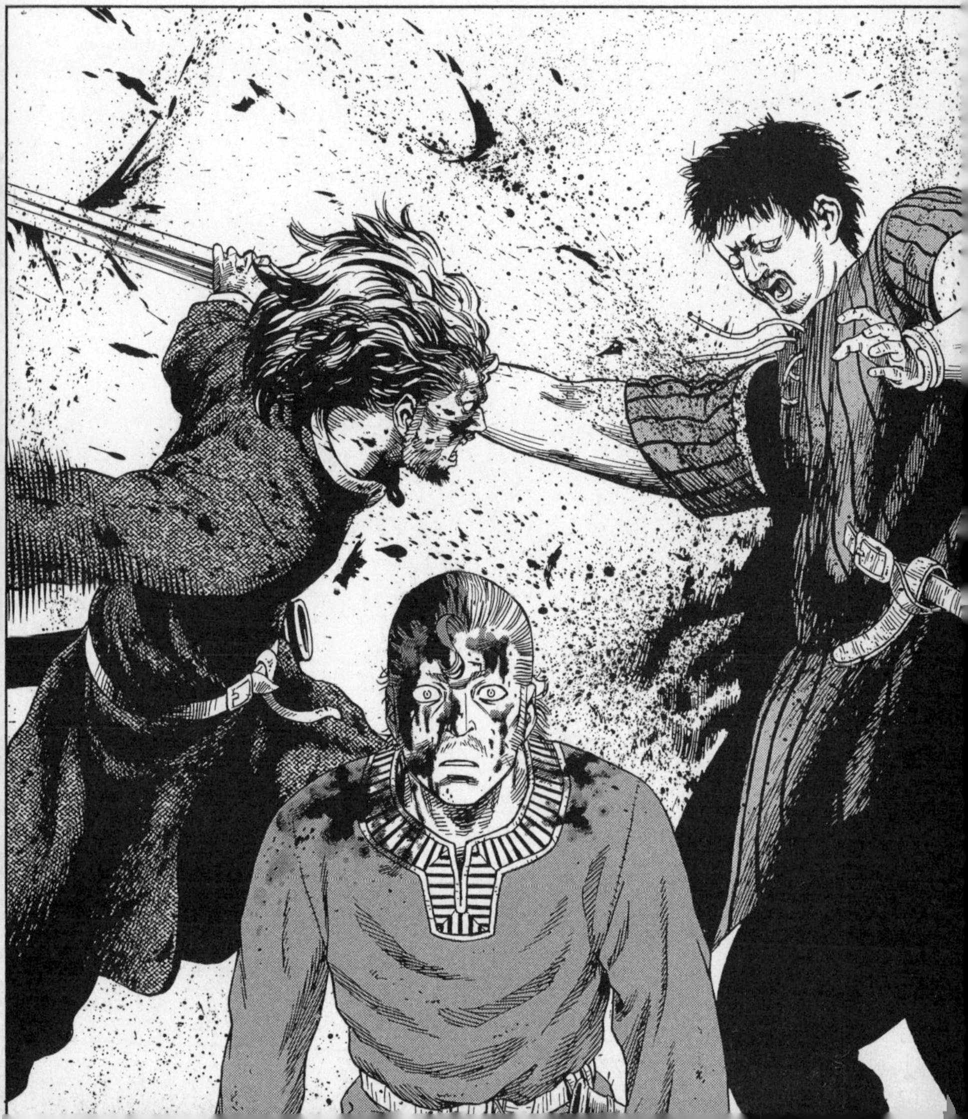

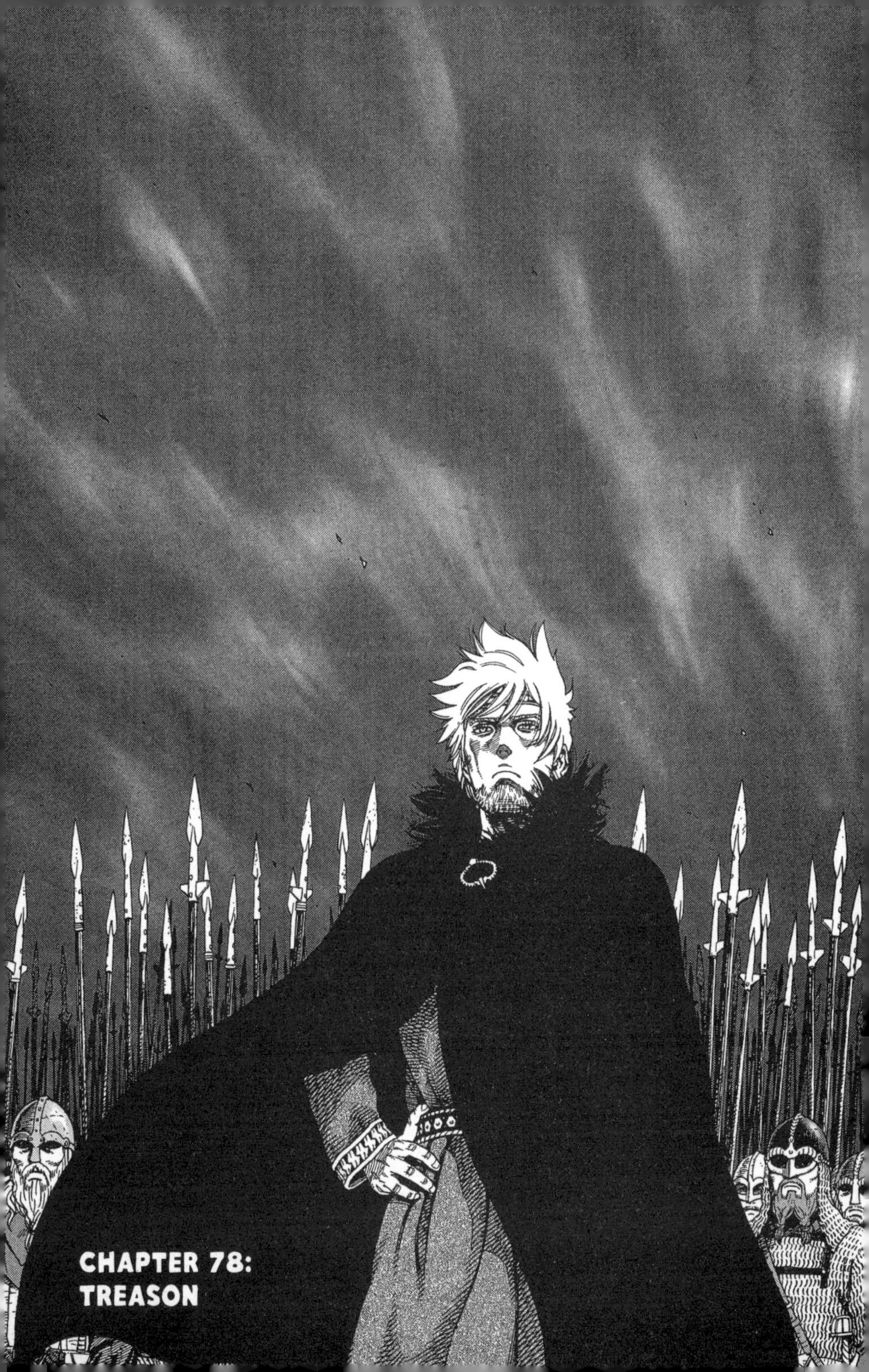
CHAPTER 78:
TREASON

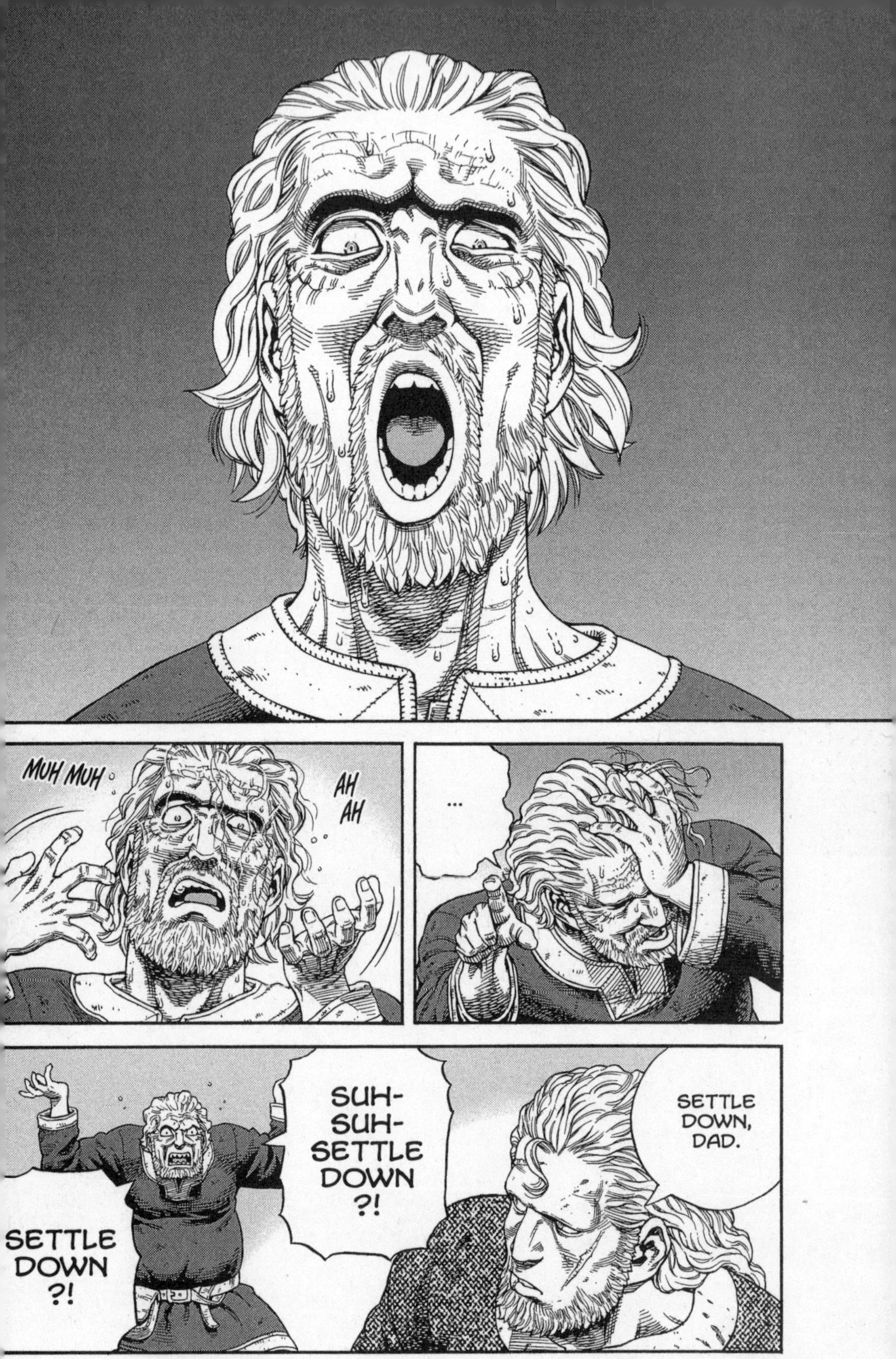
...
MUH MUH
AH AH
SETTLE DOWN, DAD.
SUH-SUH-SETTLE DOWN?!
SETTLE DOWN?!

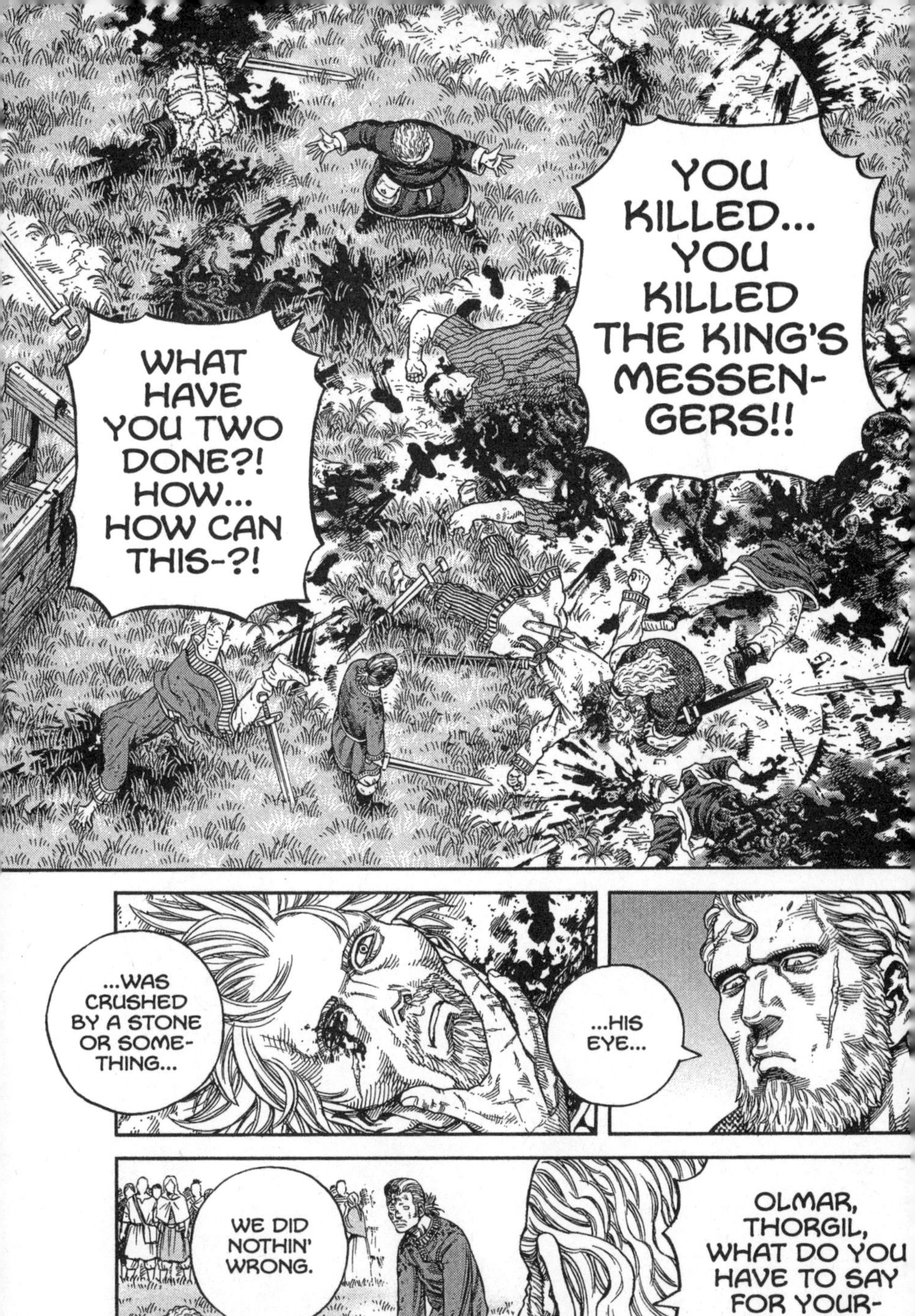
YOU KILLED... YOU KILLED THE KING'S MESSEN-GERS!!
WHAT HAVE YOU TWO DONE?! HOW... HOW CAN THIS-?!
...HIS EYE...
...WAS CRUSHED BY A STONE OR SOME-THING...
OLMAR, THORGIL, WHAT DO YOU HAVE TO SAY FOR YOUR-SELVES?!
WE DID NOTHIN' WRONG.

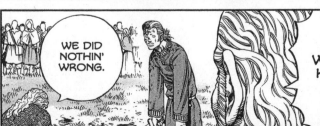

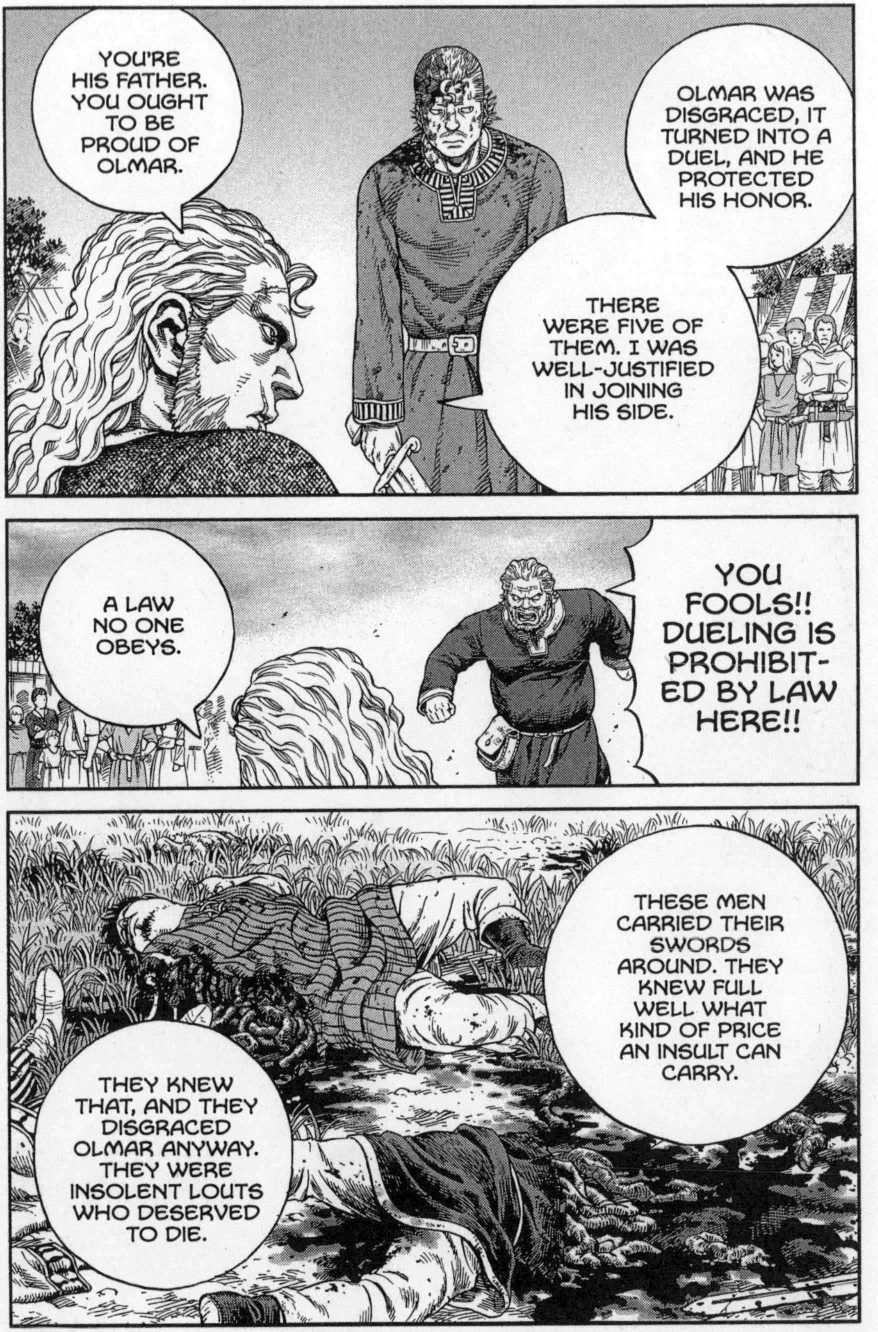
OLMAR WAS DISGRACED, IT TURNED INTO A DUEL, AND HE PROTECTED HIS HONOR.
THERE WERE FIVE OF THEM. I WAS WELL-JUSTIFIED IN JOINING HIS SIDE.
YOU'RE HIS FATHER. YOU OUGHT TO BE PROUD OF OLMAR.
YOU FOOLS!! DUELING IS PROHIBITED BY LAW HERE!!
A LAW NO ONE OBEYS.
THESE MEN CARRIED THEIR SWORDS AROUND. THEY KNEW FULL WELL WHAT KIND OF PRICE AN INSULT CAN CARRY.
THEY KNEW THAT, AND THEY DISGRACED OLMAR ANYWAY. THEY WERE INSOLENT LOUTS WHO DESERVED TO DIE.

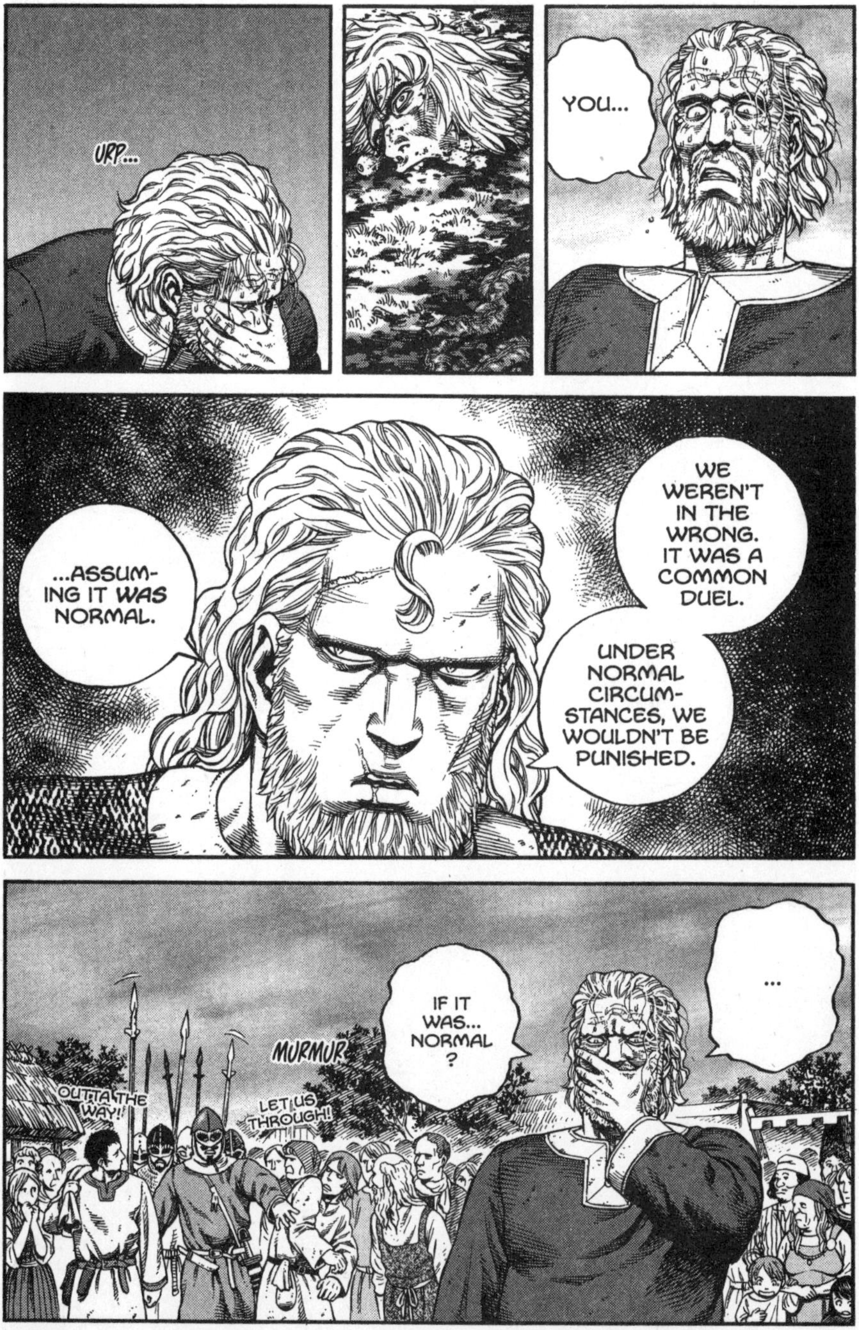
YOU...
URP...
WE WEREN'T IN THE WRONG. IT WAS A COMMON DUEL.
UNDER NORMAL CIRCUMSTANCES, WE WOULDN'T BE PUNISHED.
...ASSUMING IT WAS NORMAL.
...
IF IT WAS... NORMAL ?
MURMUR
LET US THROUGH!
OUTTA THE WAY!

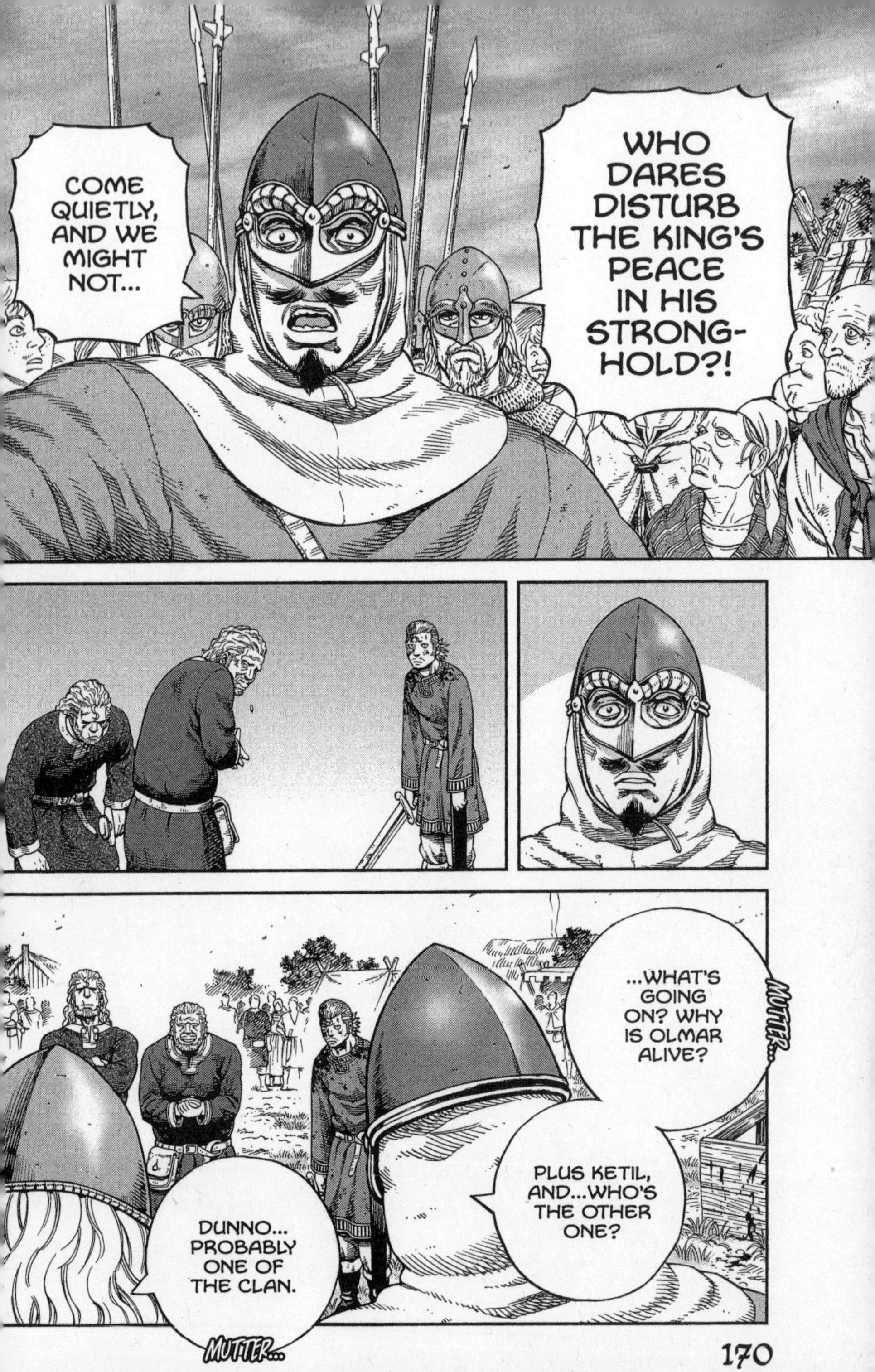
WHO DARES DISTURB THE KING'S PEACE IN HIS STRONG-HOLD?!
COME QUIETLY, AND WE MIGHT NOT...
...WHAT'S GOING ON? WHY IS OLMAR ALIVE?
MUTTER...
PLUS KETIL, AND...WHO'S THE OTHER ONE?
DUNNO... PROBABLY ONE OF THE CLAN.
MUTTER...

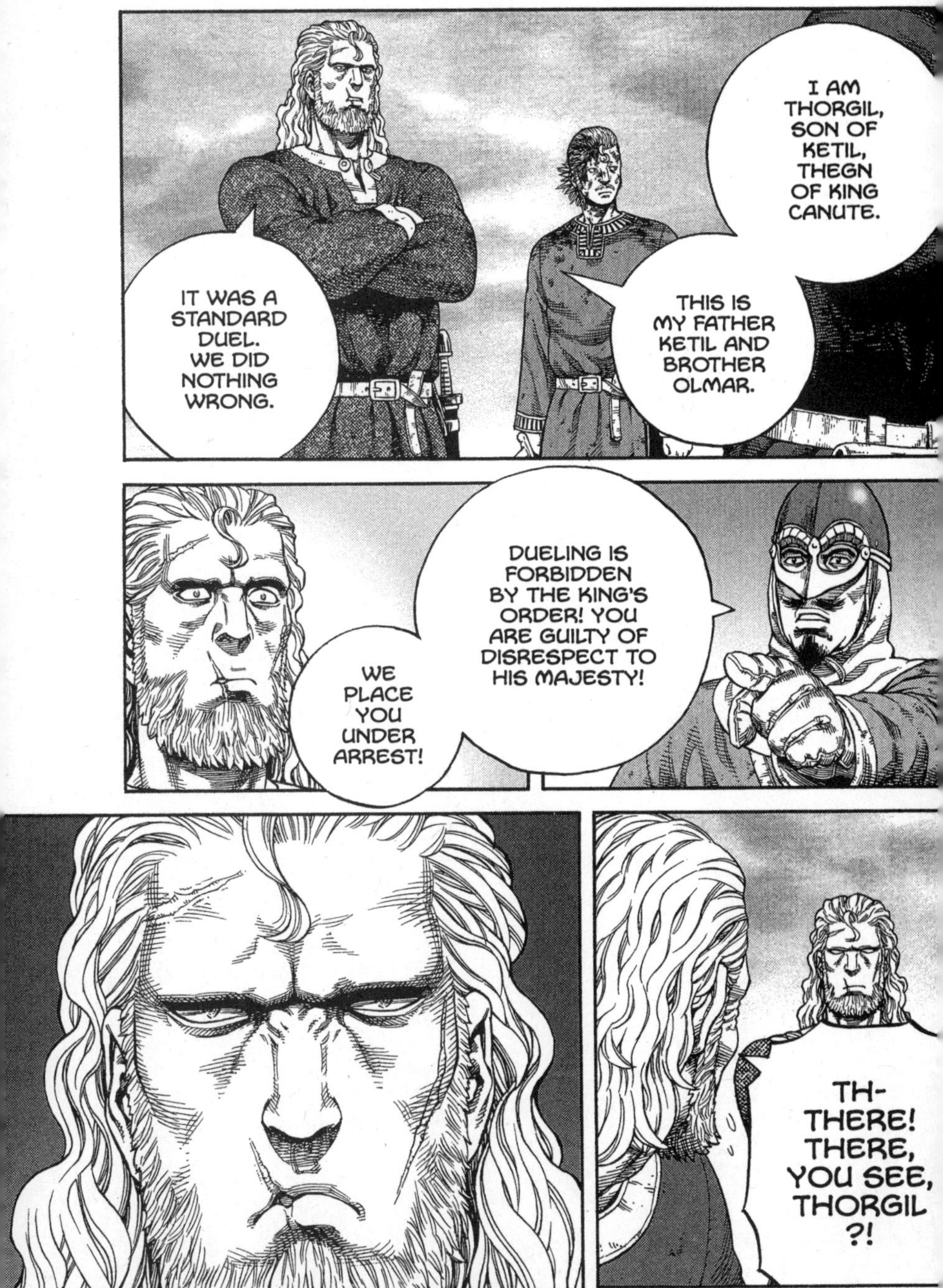
I AM THORGIL, SON OF KETIL, THEGN OF KING CANUTE.
THIS IS MY FATHER KETIL AND BROTHER OLMAR.
IT WAS A STANDARD DUEL. WE DID NOTHING WRONG.
DUELING IS FORBIDDEN BY THE KING'S ORDER! YOU ARE GUILTY OF DISRESPECT TO HIS MAJESTY!
WE PLACE YOU UNDER ARREST!
TH- THERE! THERE, YOU SEE, THORGIL ?!

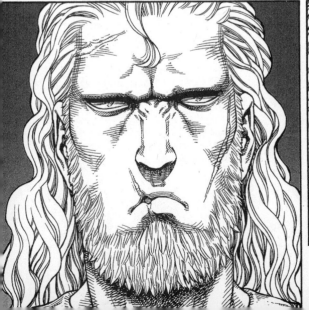

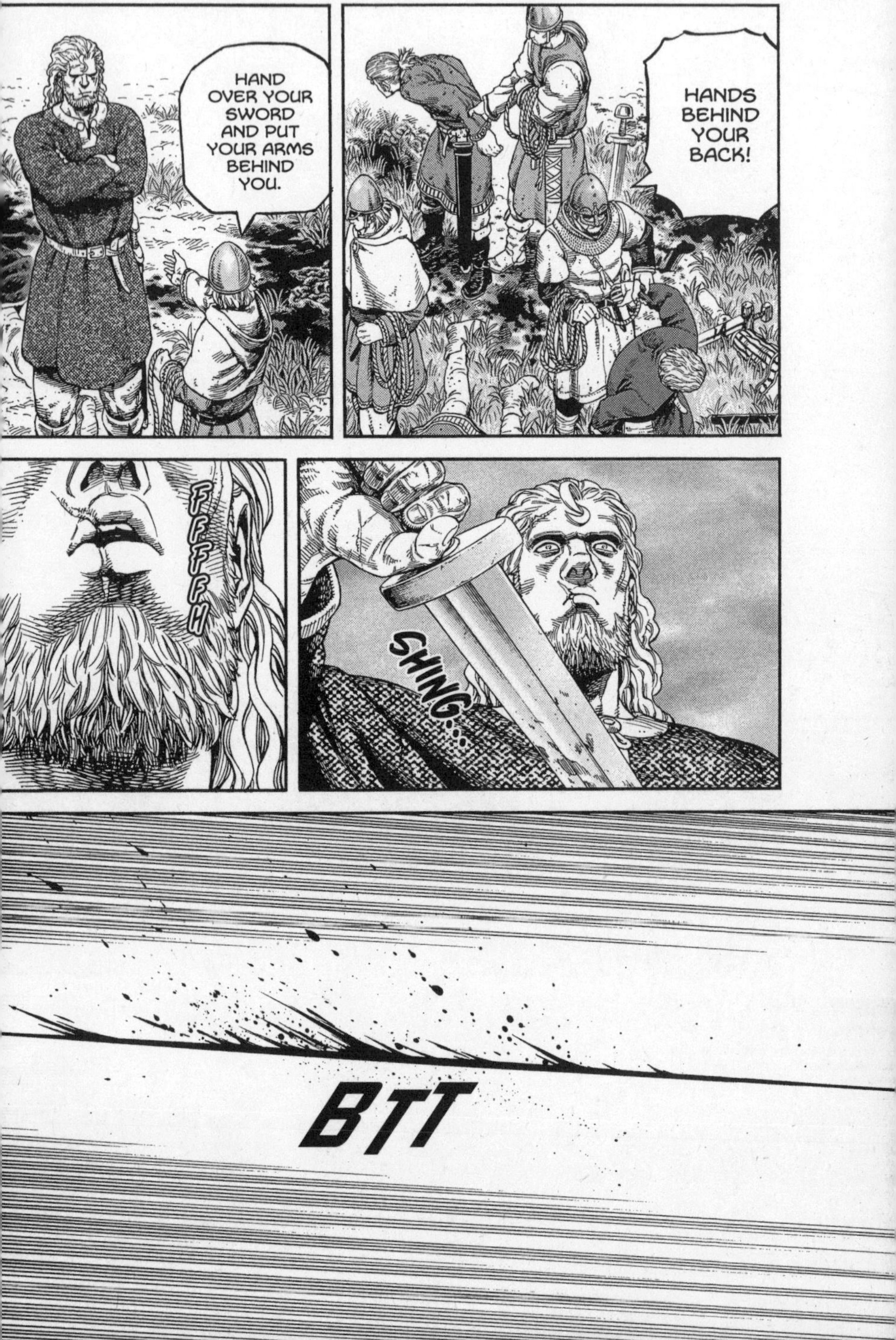

HANDS BEHIND YOUR BACK!
HAND OVER YOUR SWORD AND PUT YOUR ARMS BEHIND YOU.
SHING...
FFFFFH
BTT

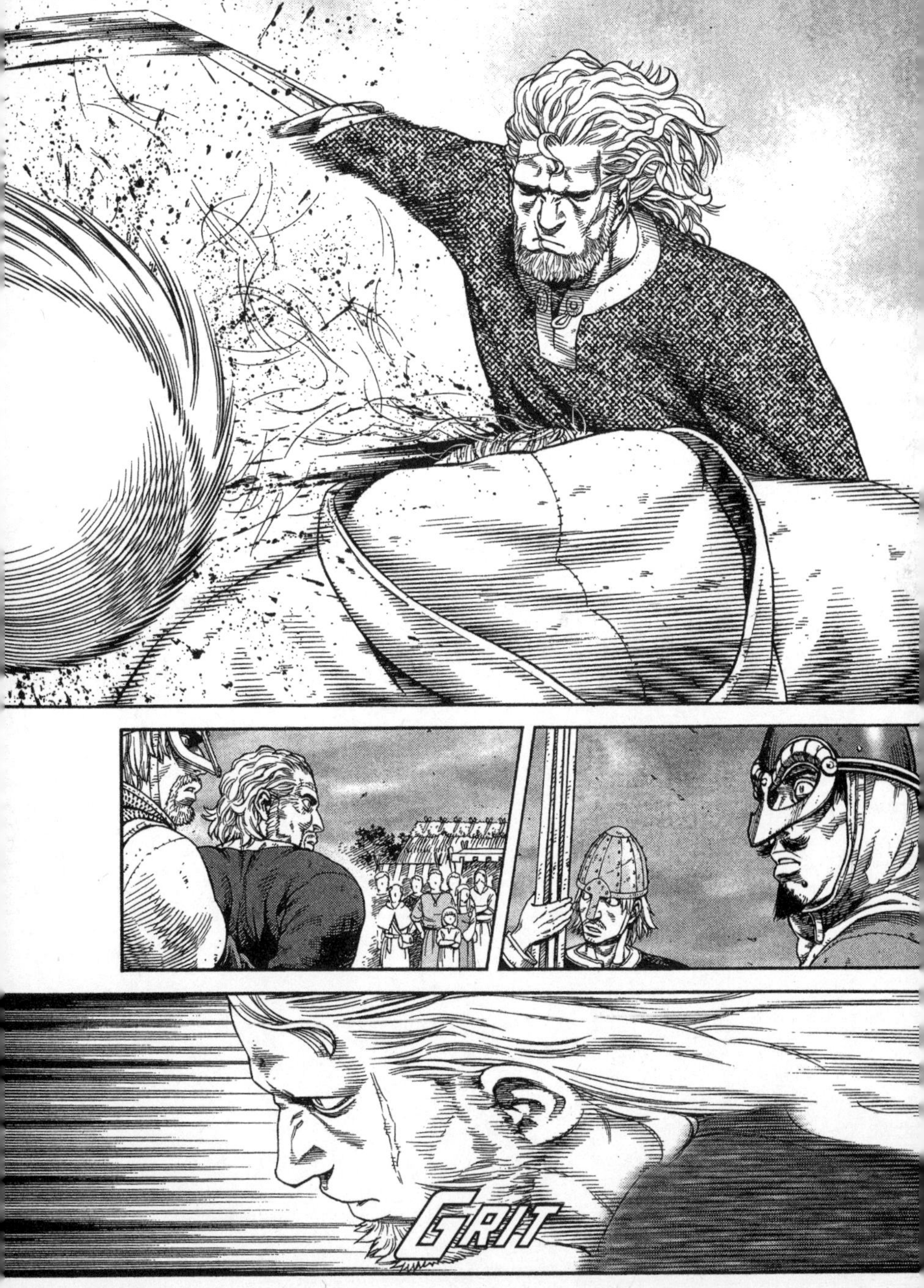
GRIT

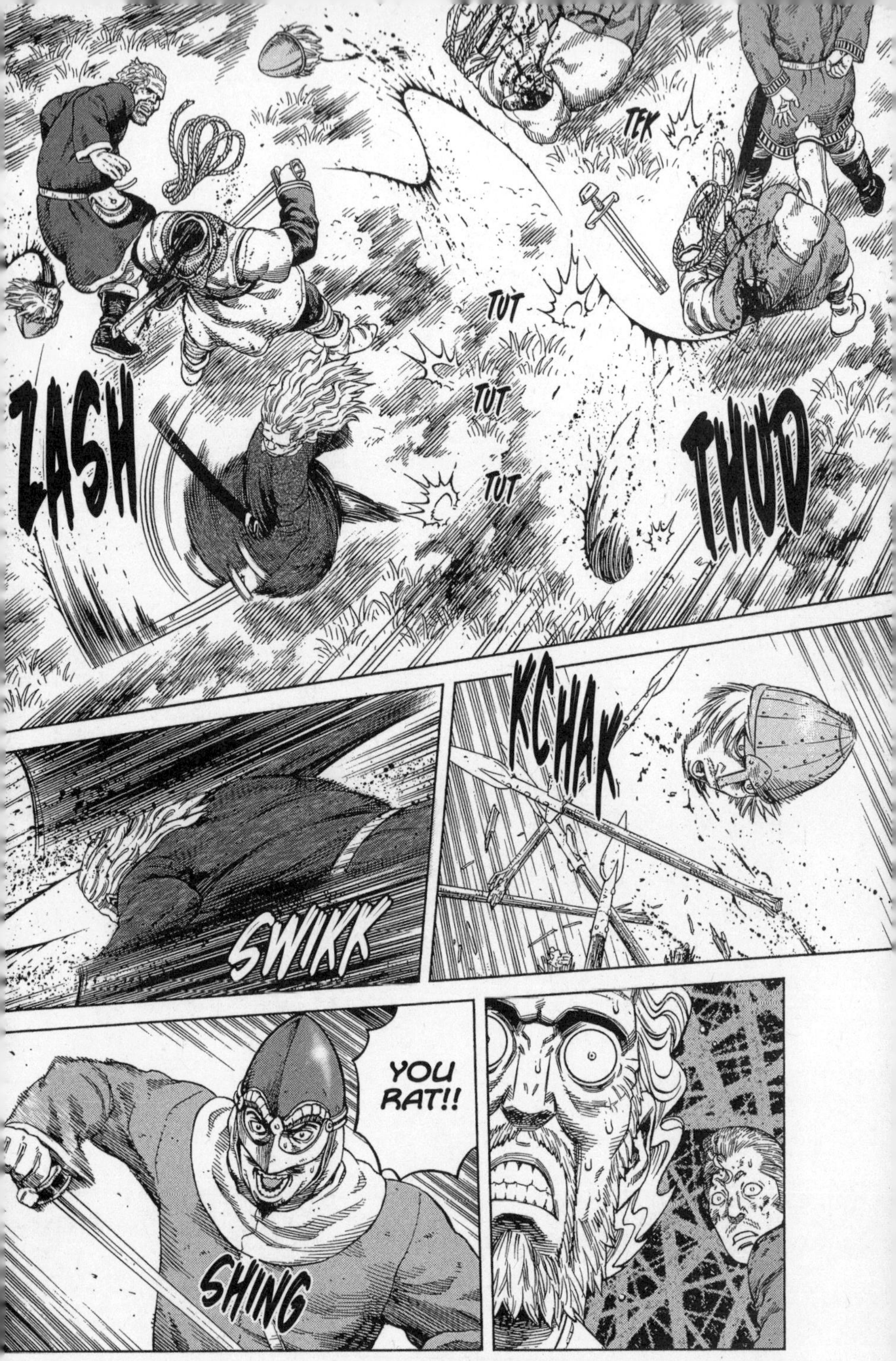
TEK
THUD
TUT
TUT
TUT
ZASH
KCHAK
SWIKK
YOU RAT!!
SHING

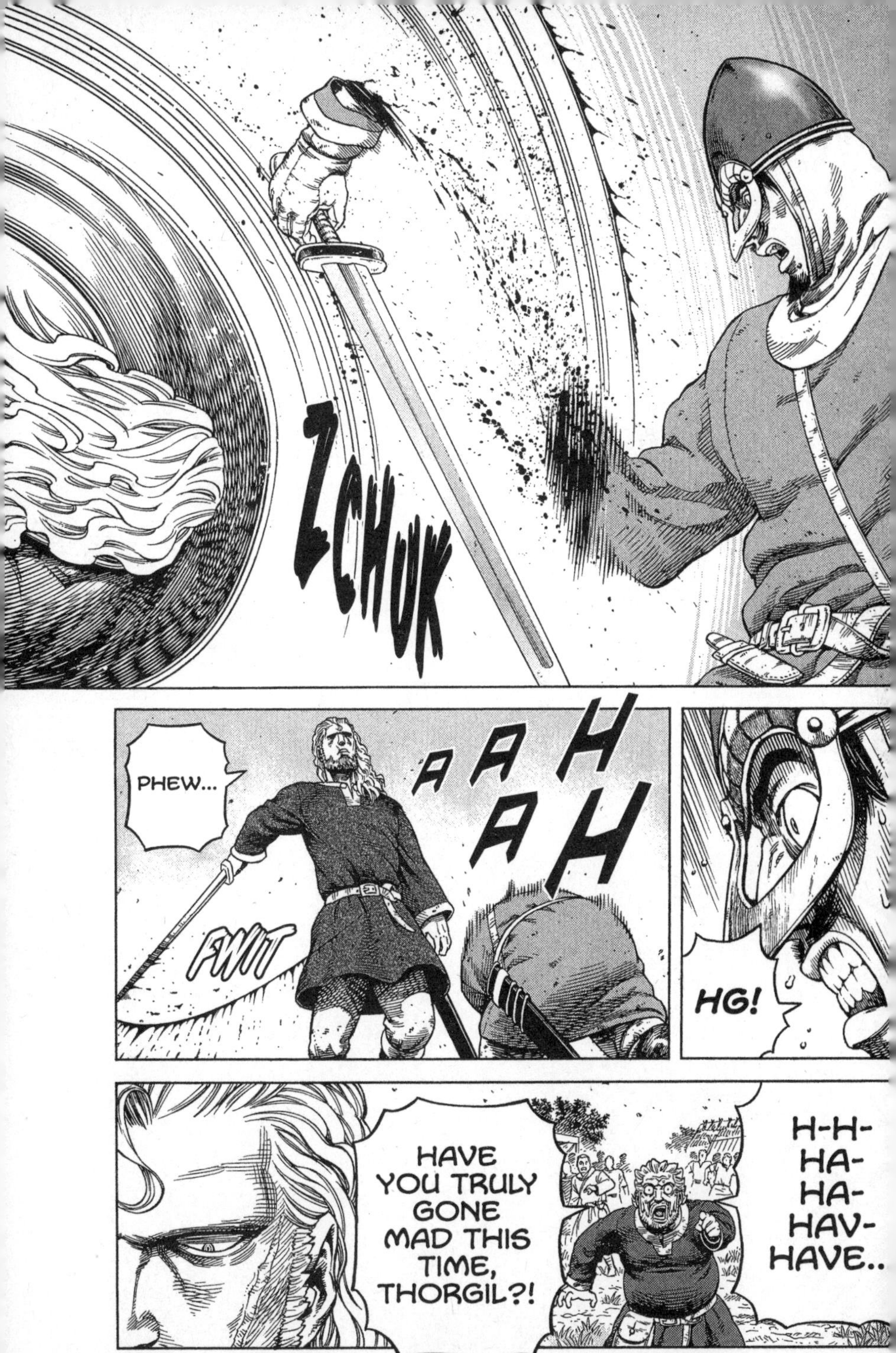

ZCHUK
HG!
AAAHH
PHEW...
FWIT
H-H-HA-HA-HAV-HAVE..
HAVE YOU TRULY GONE MAD THIS TIME, THORGIL?!

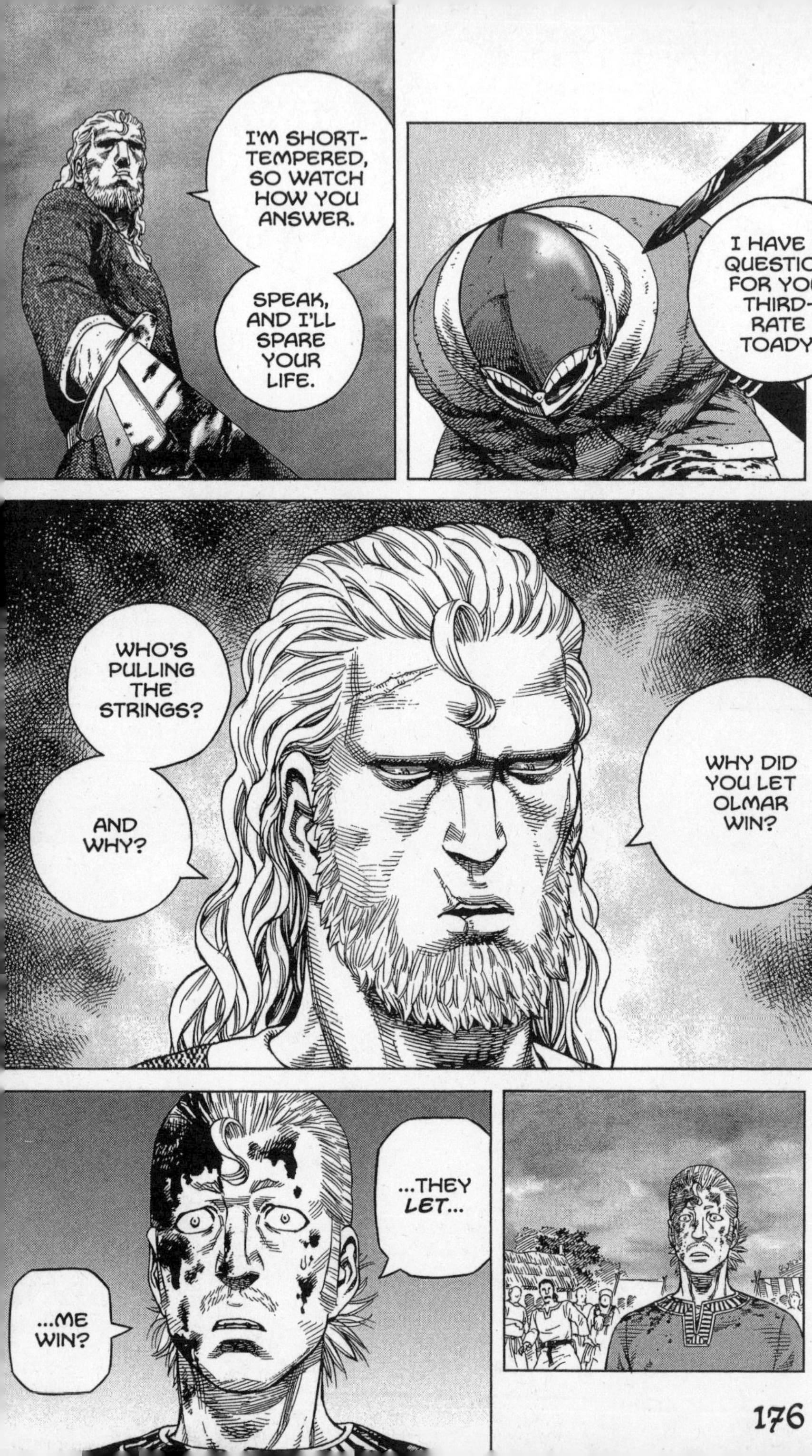
I HAVE A QUESTION FOR YOU, THIRD-RATE TOADY.
I'M SHORT-TEMPERED, SO WATCH HOW YOU ANSWER.
SPEAK, AND I'LL SPARE YOUR LIFE.
WHY DID YOU LET OLMAR WIN?
WHO'S PULLING THE STRINGS?
AND WHY?
...THEY *LET*...
...ME WIN?

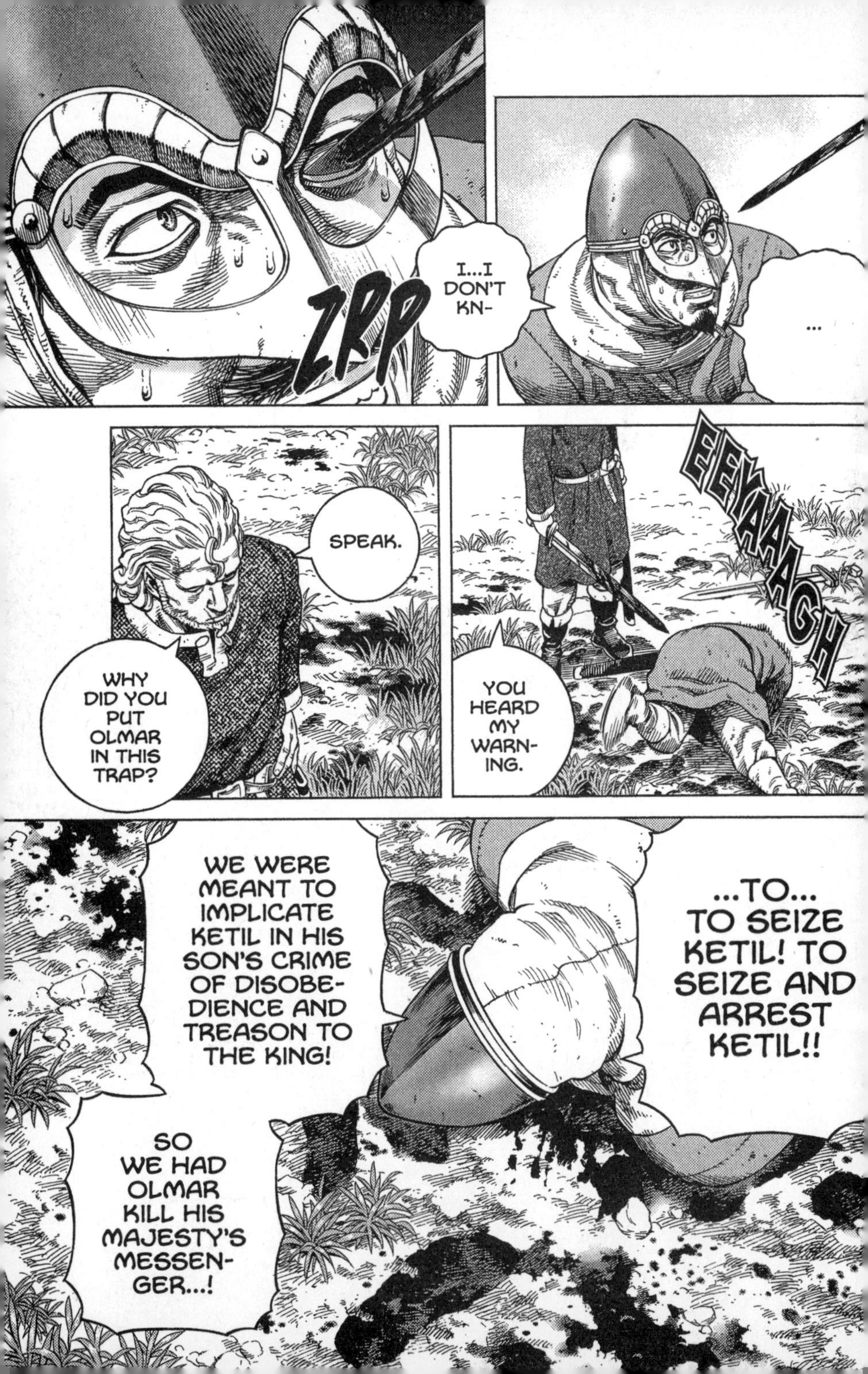
I...I DON'T KN-
...
ZRP
EEYAAAGH
YOU HEARD MY WARNING.
SPEAK.
WHY DID YOU PUT OLMAR IN THIS TRAP?
...TO... TO SEIZE KETIL! TO SEIZE AND ARREST KETIL!!
WE WERE MEANT TO IMPLICATE KETIL IN HIS SON'S CRIME OF DISOBEDIENCE AND TREASON TO THE KING!
SO WE HAD OLMAR KILL HIS MAJESTY'S MESSENGER...!

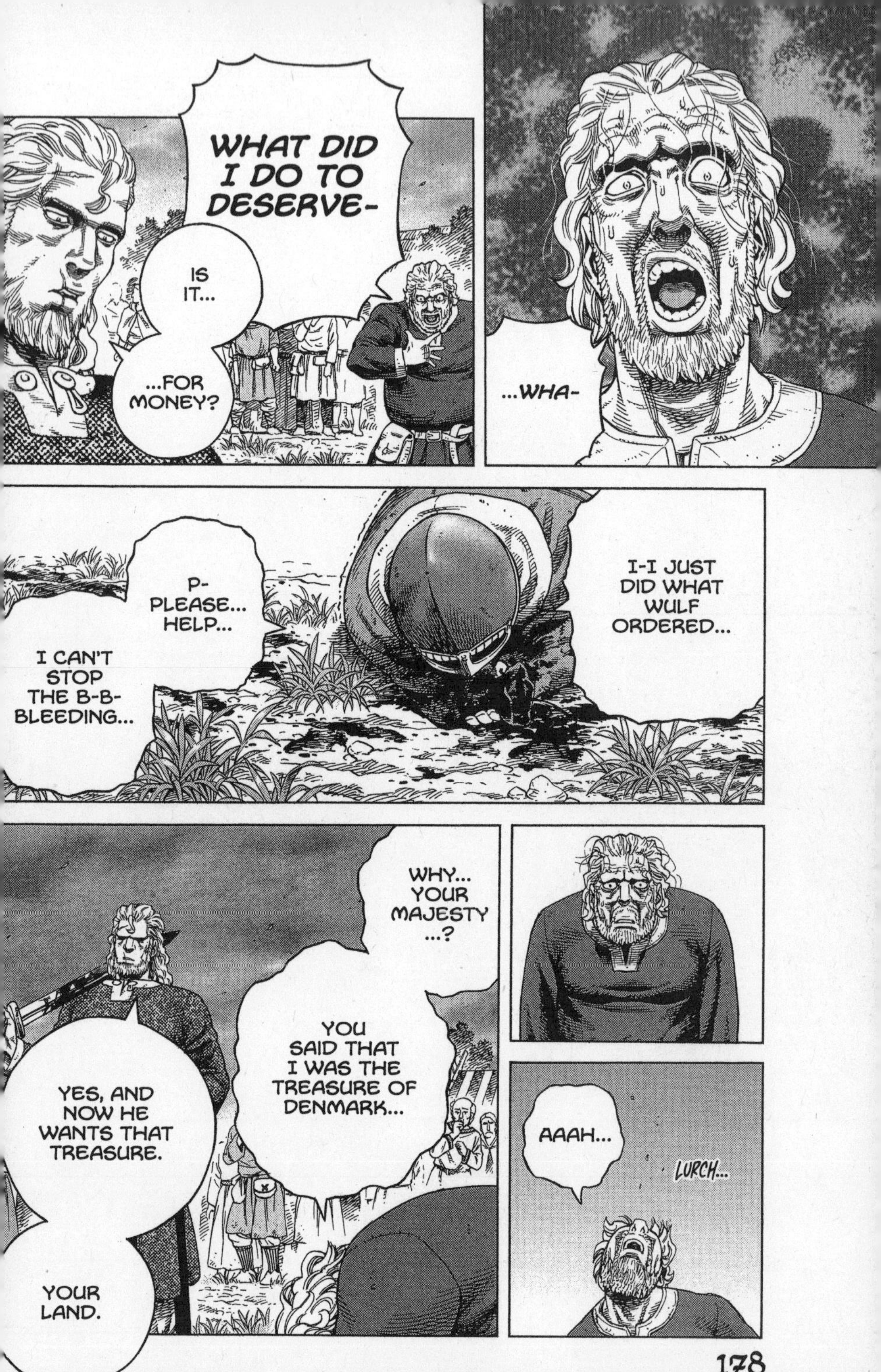
...WHA-
WHAT DID I DO TO DESERVE-
IS IT...
...FOR MONEY?
I-I JUST DID WHAT WULF ORDERED...
P- PLEASE... HELP...
I CAN'T STOP THE B-B-BLEEDING...
AAAH...
LURCH...
WHY... YOUR MAJESTY ...?
YOU SAID THAT I WAS THE TREASURE OF DENMARK...
YES, AND NOW HE WANTS THAT TREASURE.
YOUR LAND.

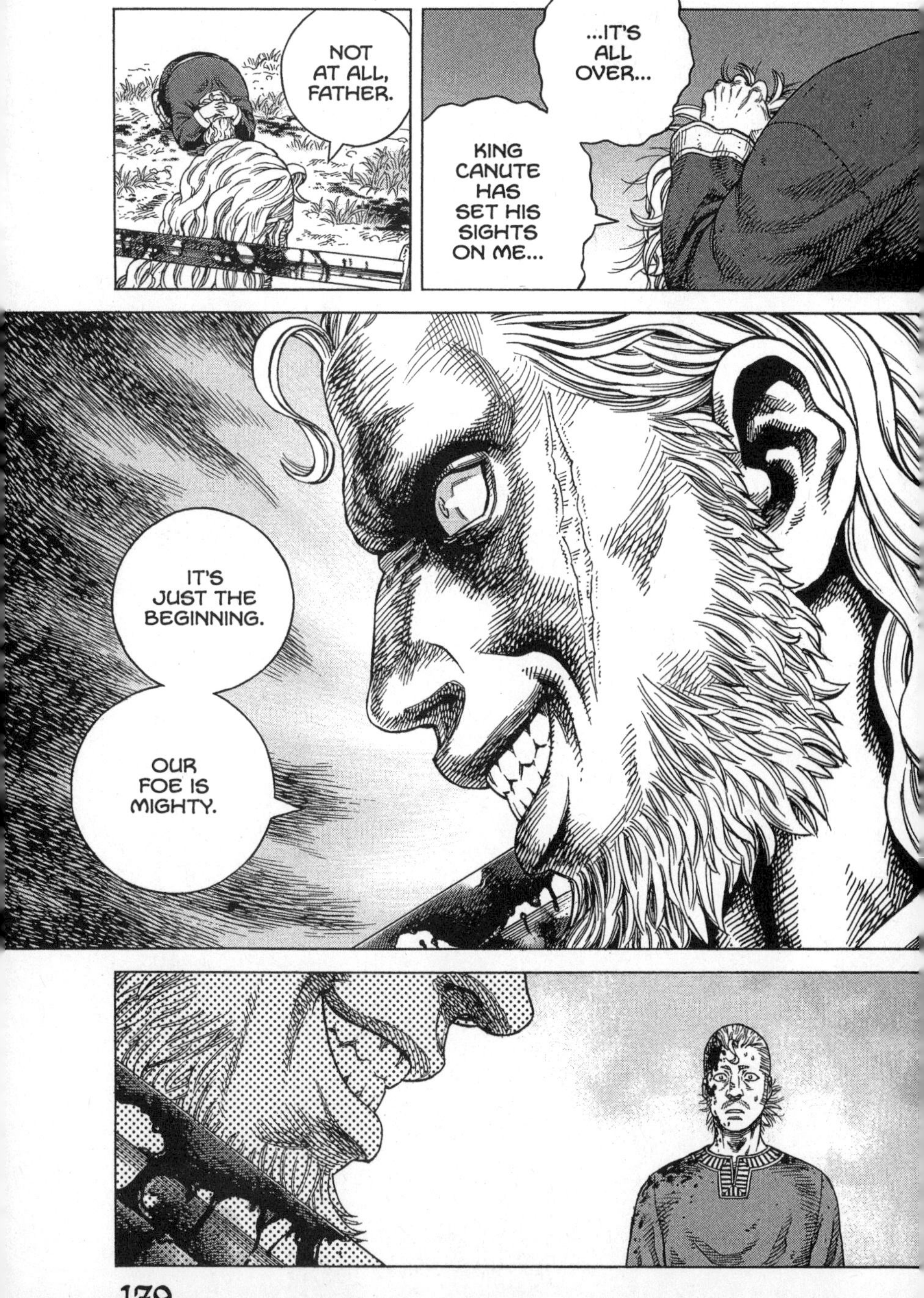
...IT'S ALL OVER...
KING CANUTE HAS SET HIS SIGHTS ON ME...
NOT AT ALL, FATHER.
IT'S JUST THE BEGINNING.
OUR FOE IS MIGHTY.

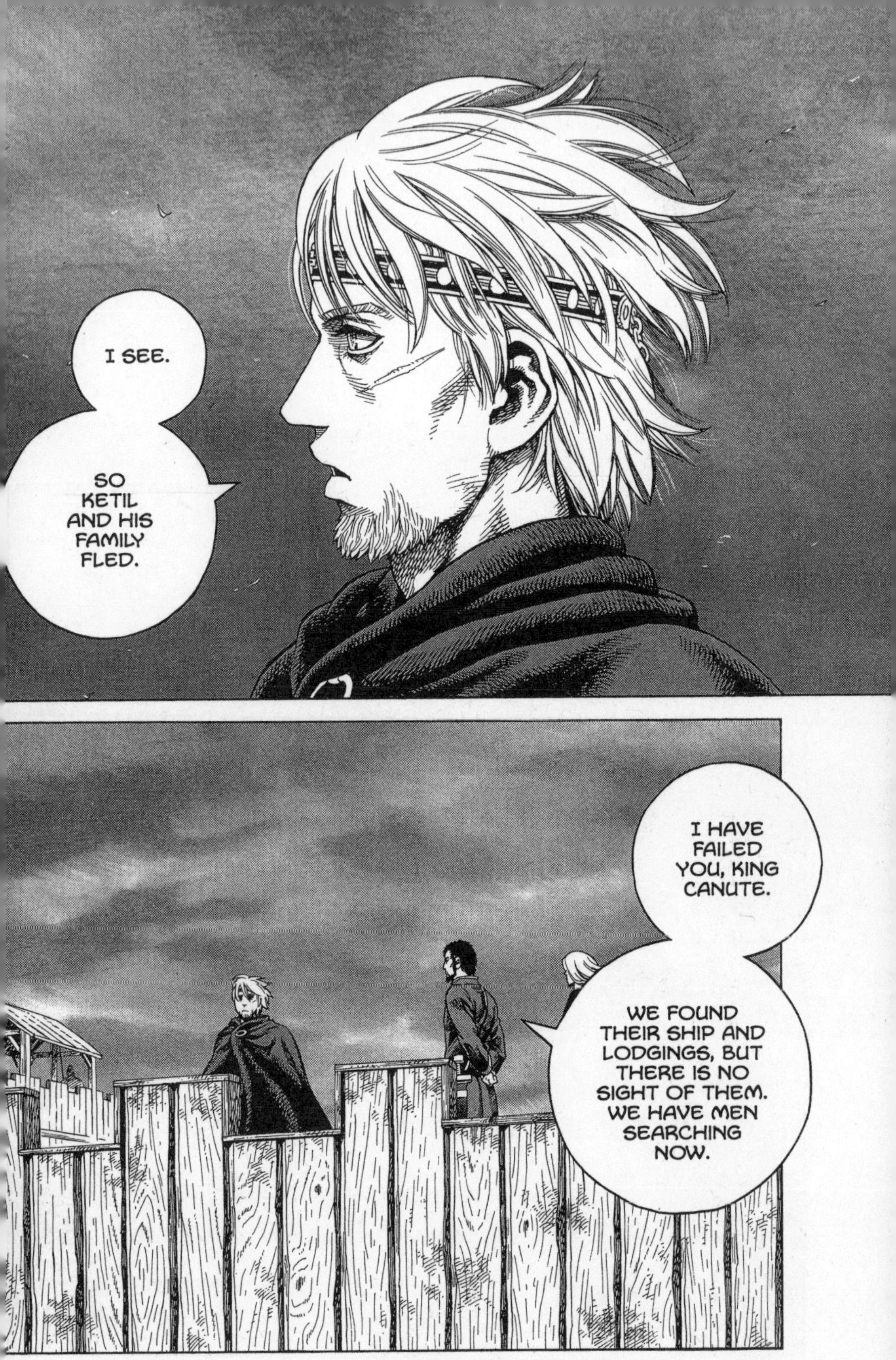
I SEE.
SO KETIL AND HIS FAMILY FLED.
I HAVE FAILED YOU, KING CANUTE.
WE FOUND THEIR SHIP AND LODGINGS, BUT THERE IS NO SIGHT OF THEM. WE HAVE MEN SEARCHING NOW.

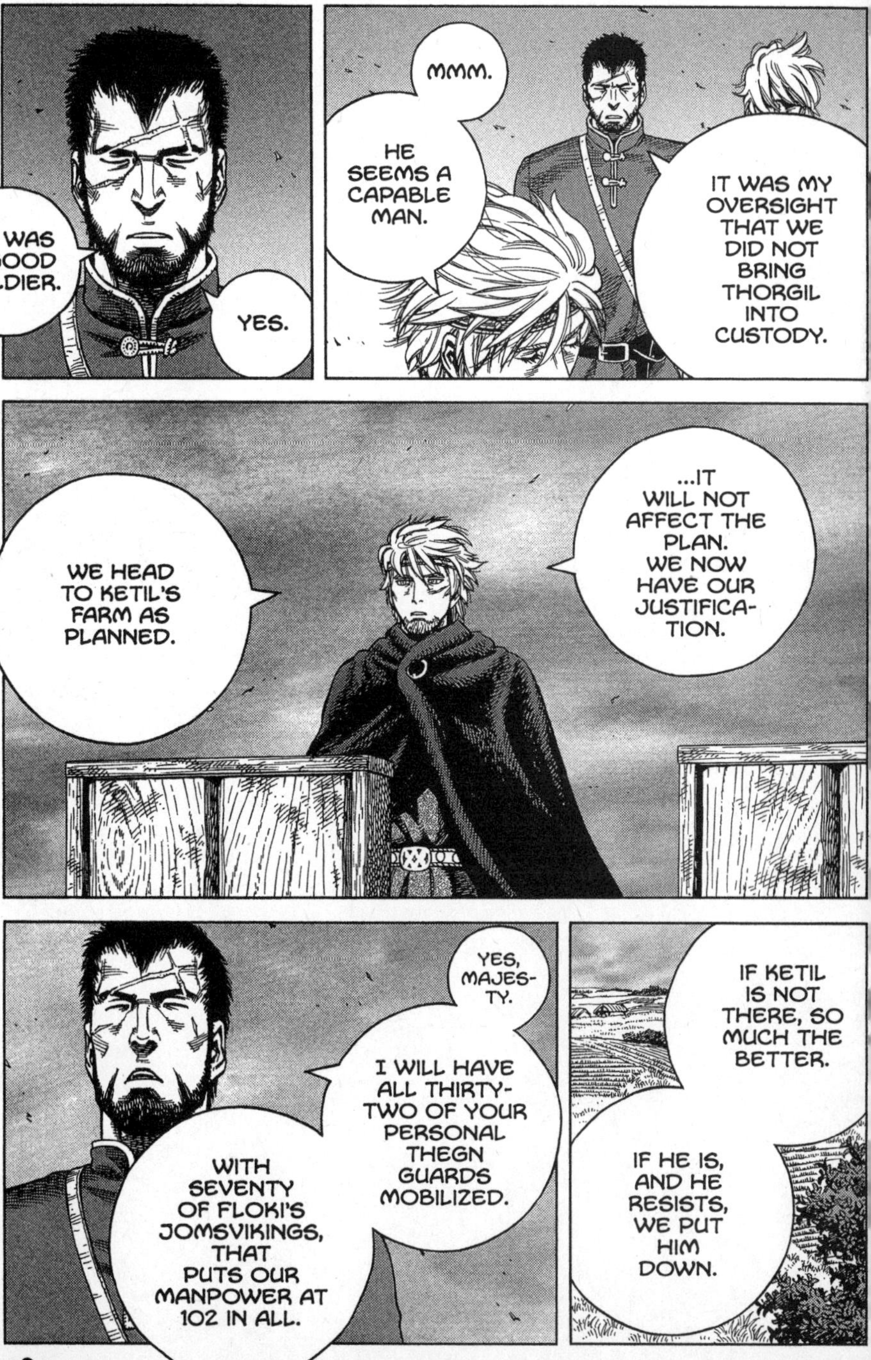

IT WAS MY OVERSIGHT THAT WE DID NOT BRING THORGIL INTO CUSTODY.
MMM.
HE SEEMS A CAPABLE MAN.
YES.
HE WAS A GOOD SOLDIER.
...IT WILL NOT AFFECT THE PLAN. WE NOW HAVE OUR JUSTIFICATION.
WE HEAD TO KETIL'S FARM AS PLANNED.
IF KETIL IS NOT THERE, SO MUCH THE BETTER.
IF HE IS, AND HE RESISTS, WE PUT HIM DOWN.
YES, MAJESTY.
I WILL HAVE ALL THIRTY-TWO OF YOUR PERSONAL THEGN GUARDS MOBILIZED.
WITH SEVENTY OF FLOKI'S JOMSVIKINGS, THAT PUTS OUR MANPOWER AT 102 IN ALL.

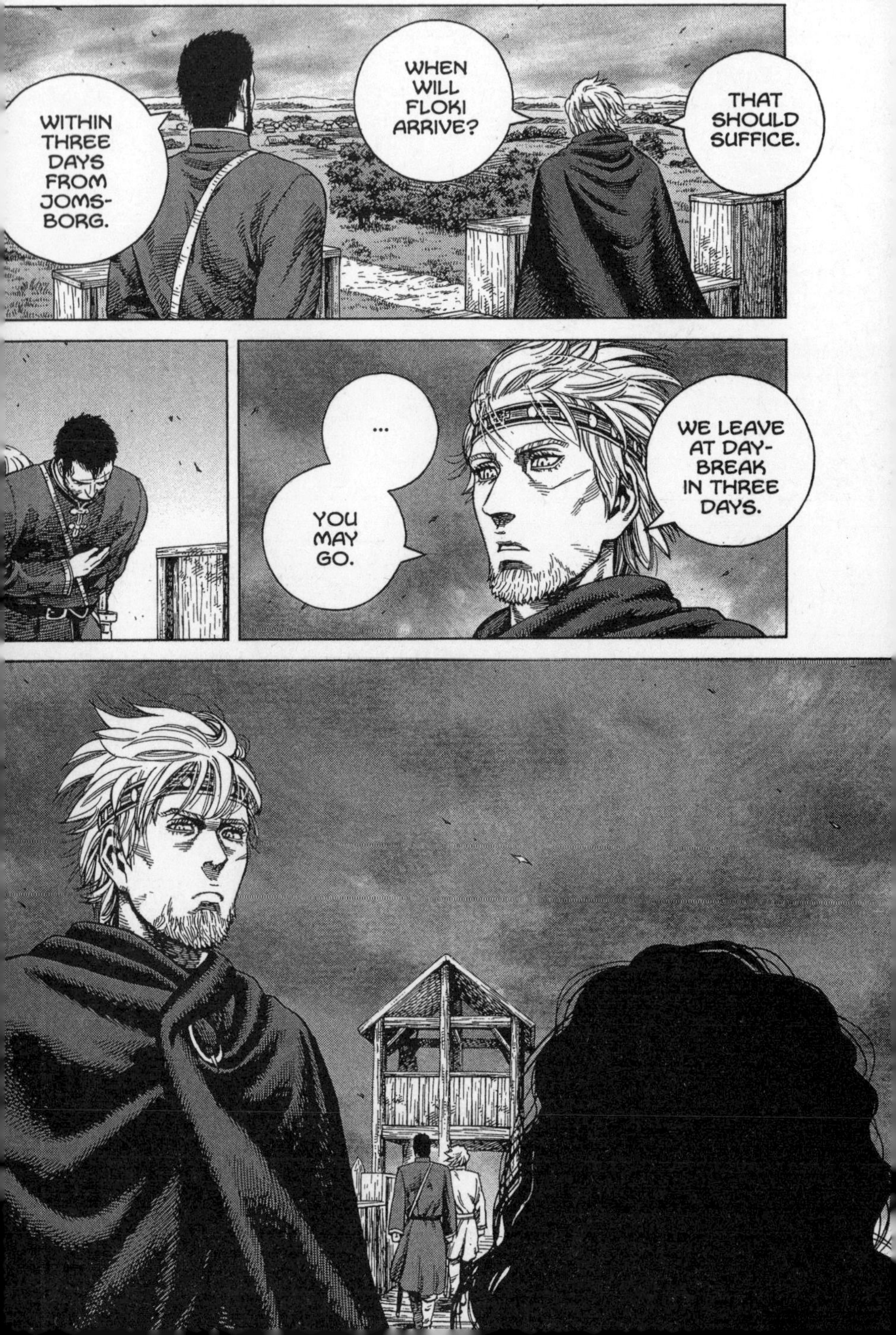
THAT SHOULD SUFFICE.
WHEN WILL FLOKI ARRIVE?
WITHIN THREE DAYS FROM JOMS-BORG.
WE LEAVE AT DAY-BREAK IN THREE DAYS.
...
YOU MAY GO.

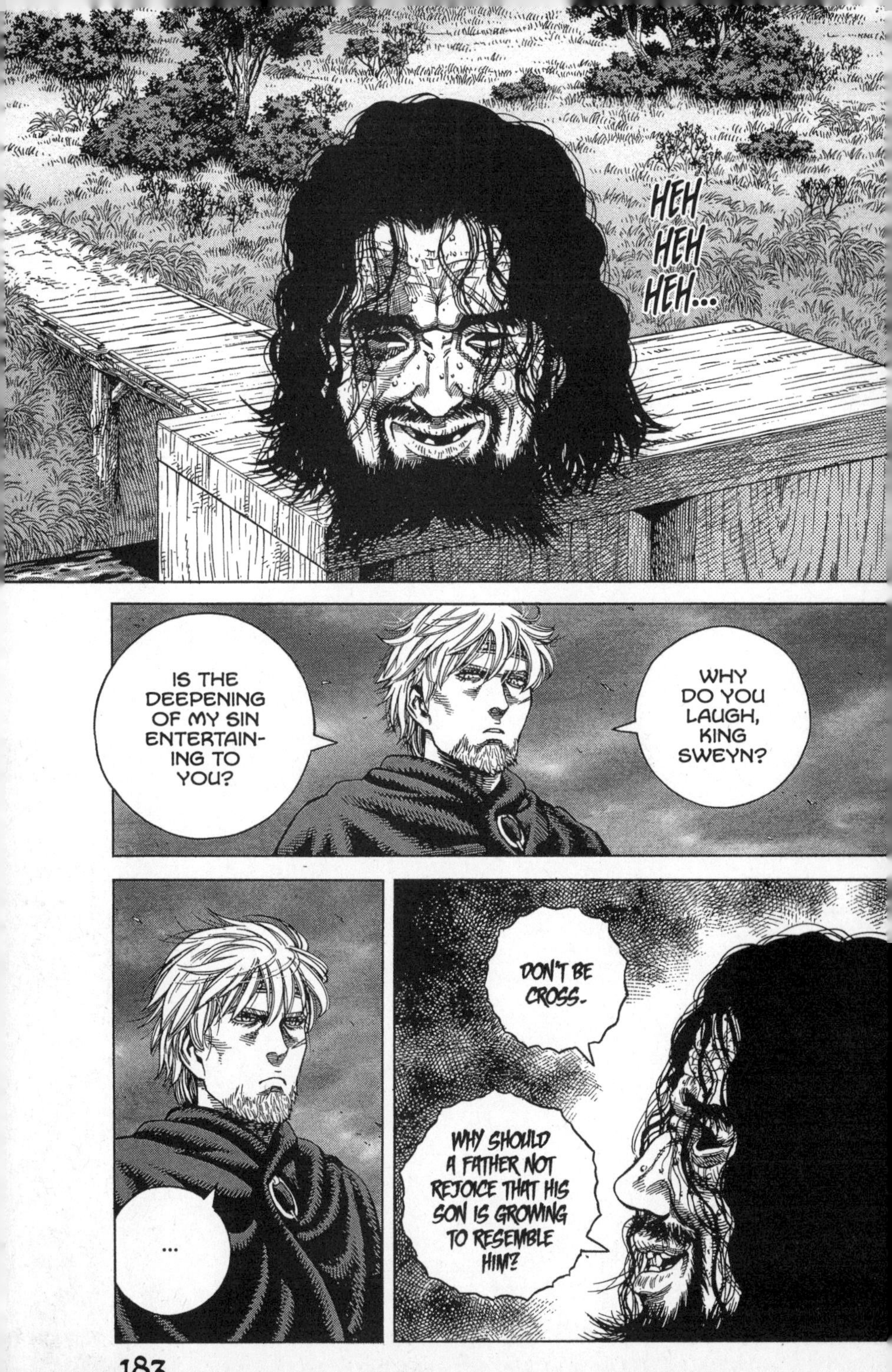
HEH HEH HEH...
WHY DO YOU LAUGH, KING SWEYN?
IS THE DEEPENING OF MY SIN ENTERTAINING TO YOU?
DON'T BE CROSS.
WHY SHOULD A FATHER NOT REJOICE THAT HIS SON IS GROWING TO RESEMBLE HIM?
...

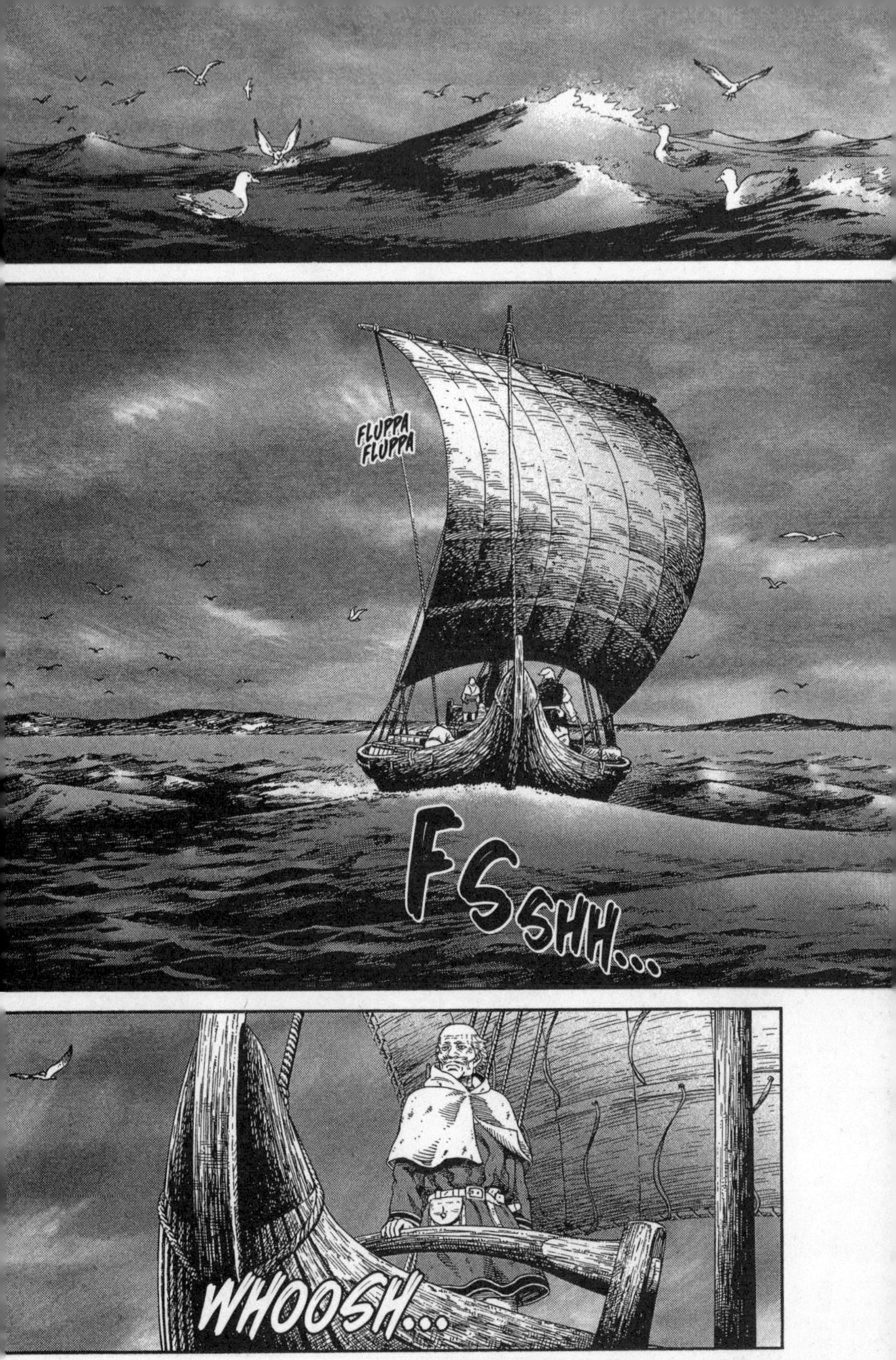
FLUPPA FLUPPA
FSSHH...
WHOOSH...

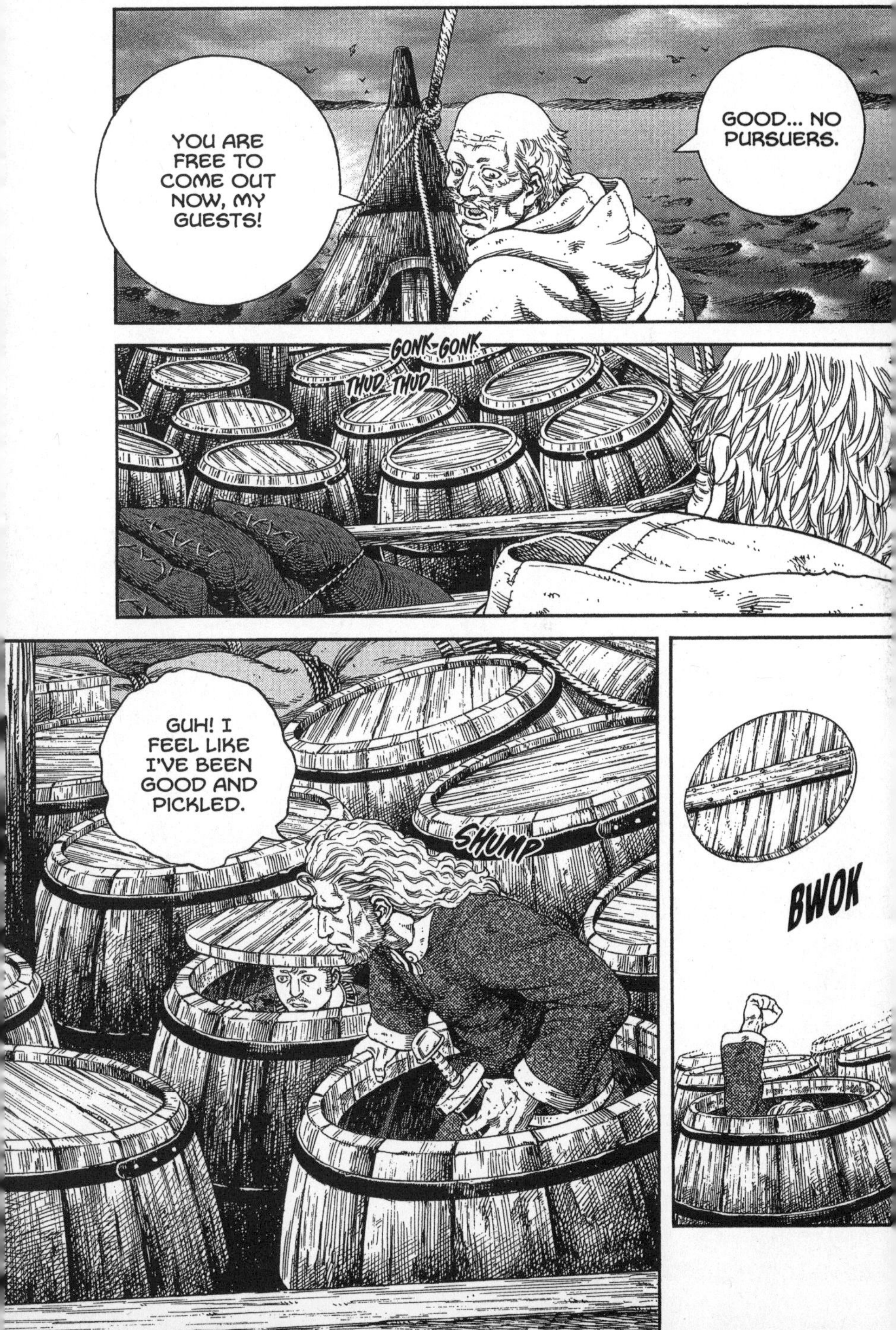
GOOD... NO PURSUERS.
YOU ARE FREE TO COME OUT NOW, MY GUESTS!
GONK-GONK
THUD THUD
BWOK
GUH! I FEEL LIKE I'VE BEEN GOOD AND PICKLED.
SHUMP

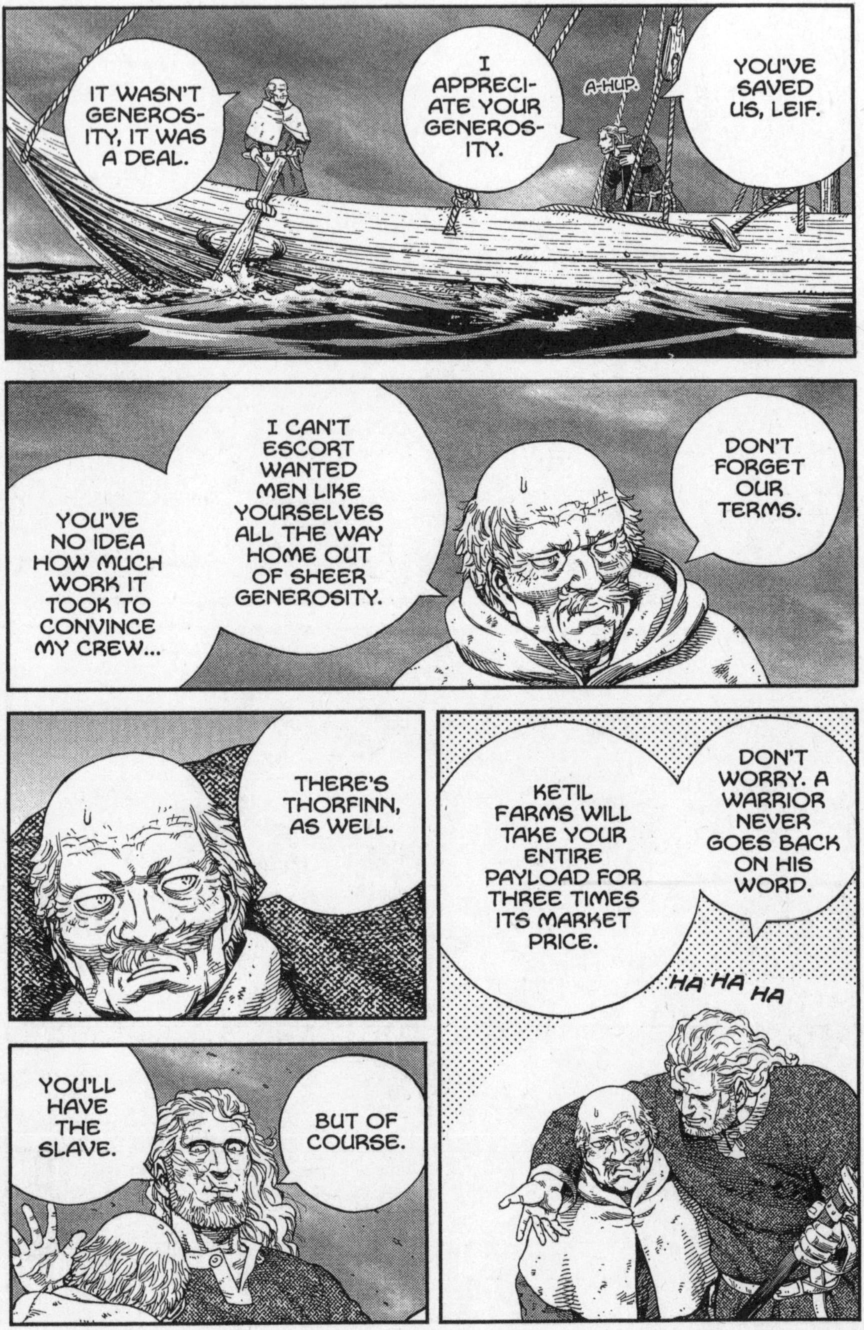
YOU'VE SAVED US, LEIF.
A-HUP.
I APPRECIATE YOUR GENEROSITY.
IT WASN'T GENEROSITY, IT WAS A DEAL.
DON'T FORGET OUR TERMS.
I CAN'T ESCORT WANTED MEN LIKE YOURSELVES ALL THE WAY HOME OUT OF SHEER GENEROSITY.
YOU'VE NO IDEA HOW MUCH WORK IT TOOK TO CONVINCE MY CREW...
DON'T WORRY. A WARRIOR NEVER GOES BACK ON HIS WORD.
KETIL FARMS WILL TAKE YOUR ENTIRE PAYLOAD FOR THREE TIMES ITS MARKET PRICE.
HA HA HA
THERE'S THORFINN, AS WELL.
BUT OF COURSE.
YOU'LL HAVE THE SLAVE.

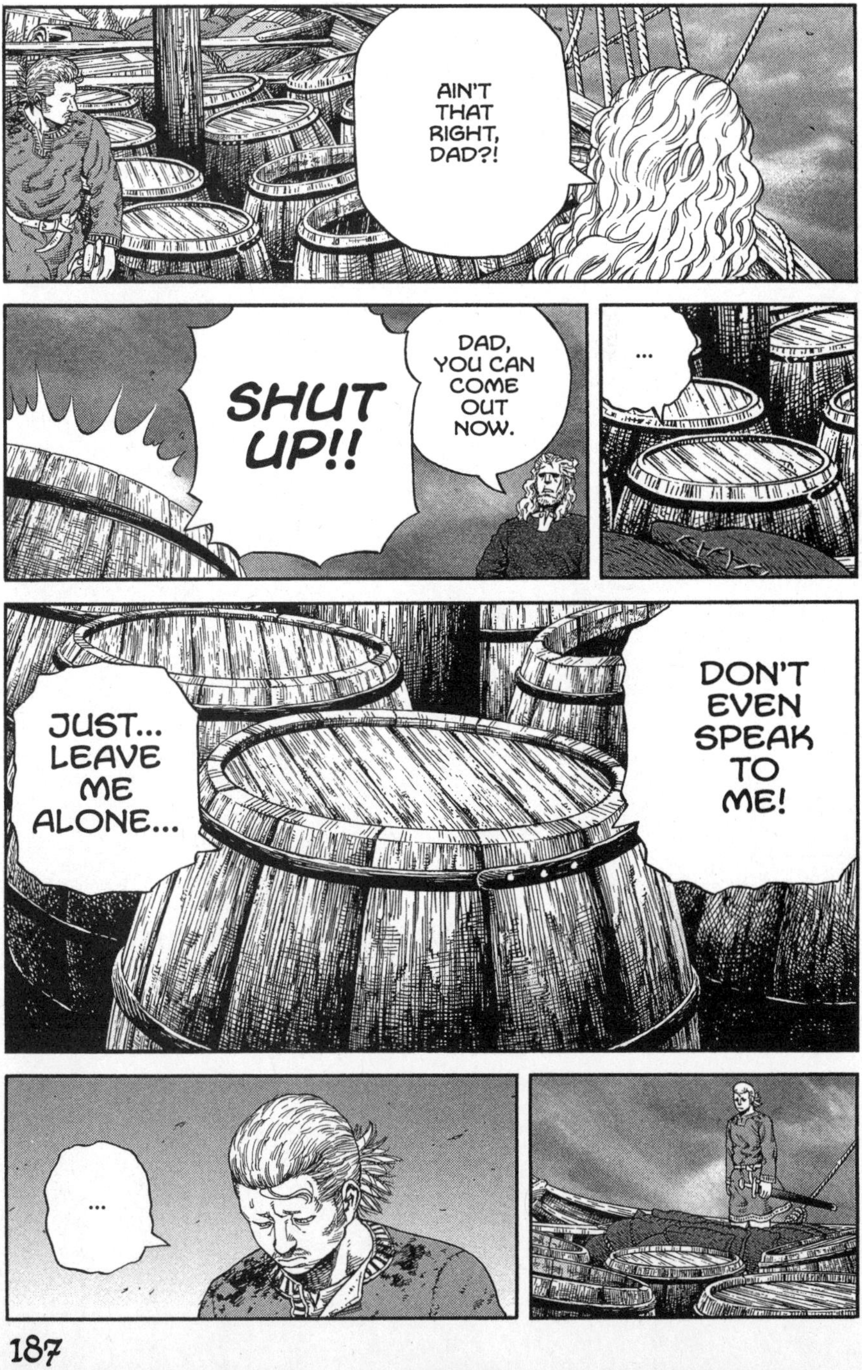
AIN'T THAT RIGHT, DAD?!
...
DAD, YOU CAN COME OUT NOW.
SHUT UP!!
DON'T EVEN SPEAK TO ME!
JUST... LEAVE ME ALONE...
...

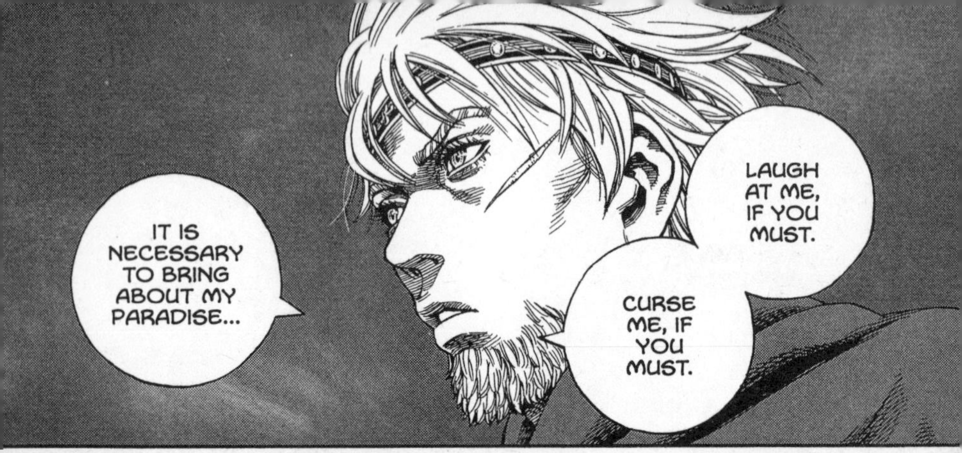
LAUGH AT ME, IF YOU MUST.
CURSE ME, IF YOU MUST.
IT IS NECESSARY TO BRING ABOUT MY PARADISE...
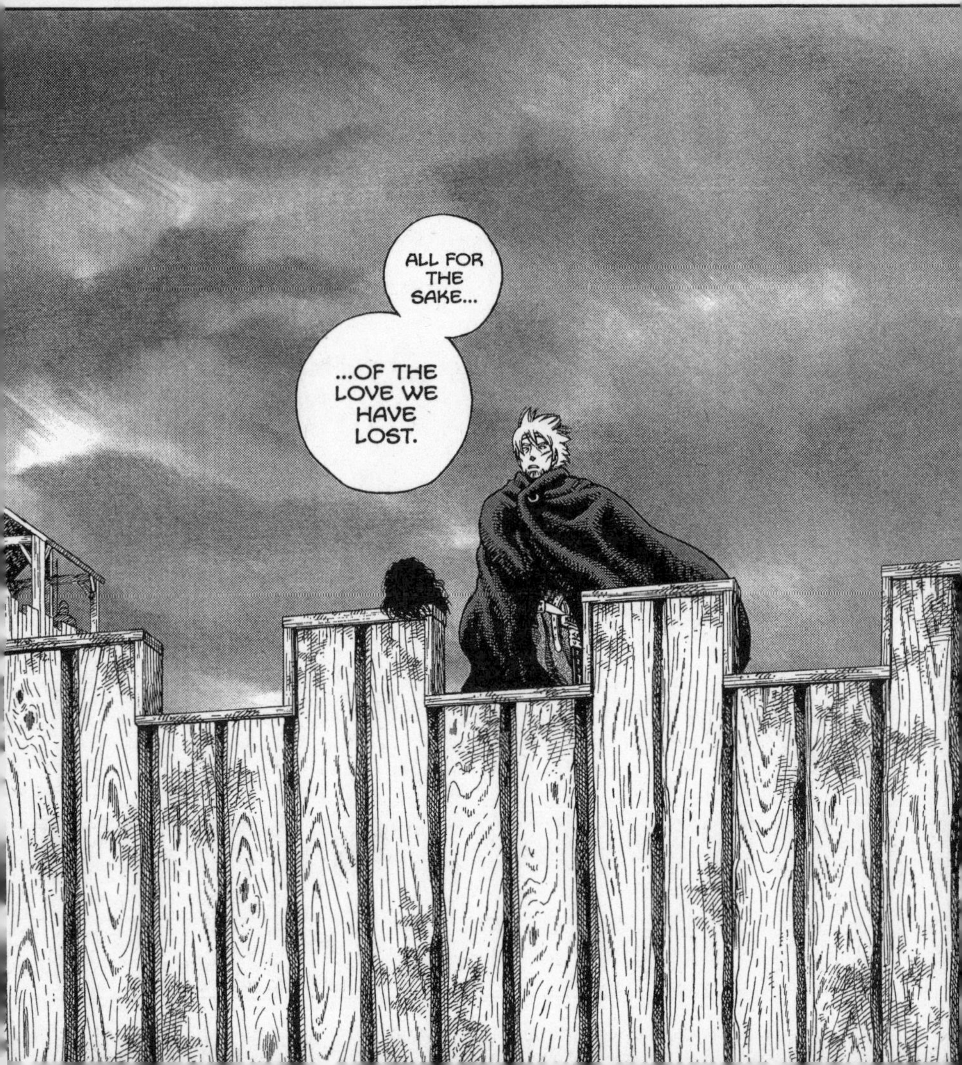
ALL FOR THE SAKE...
...OF THE LOVE WE HAVE LOST.

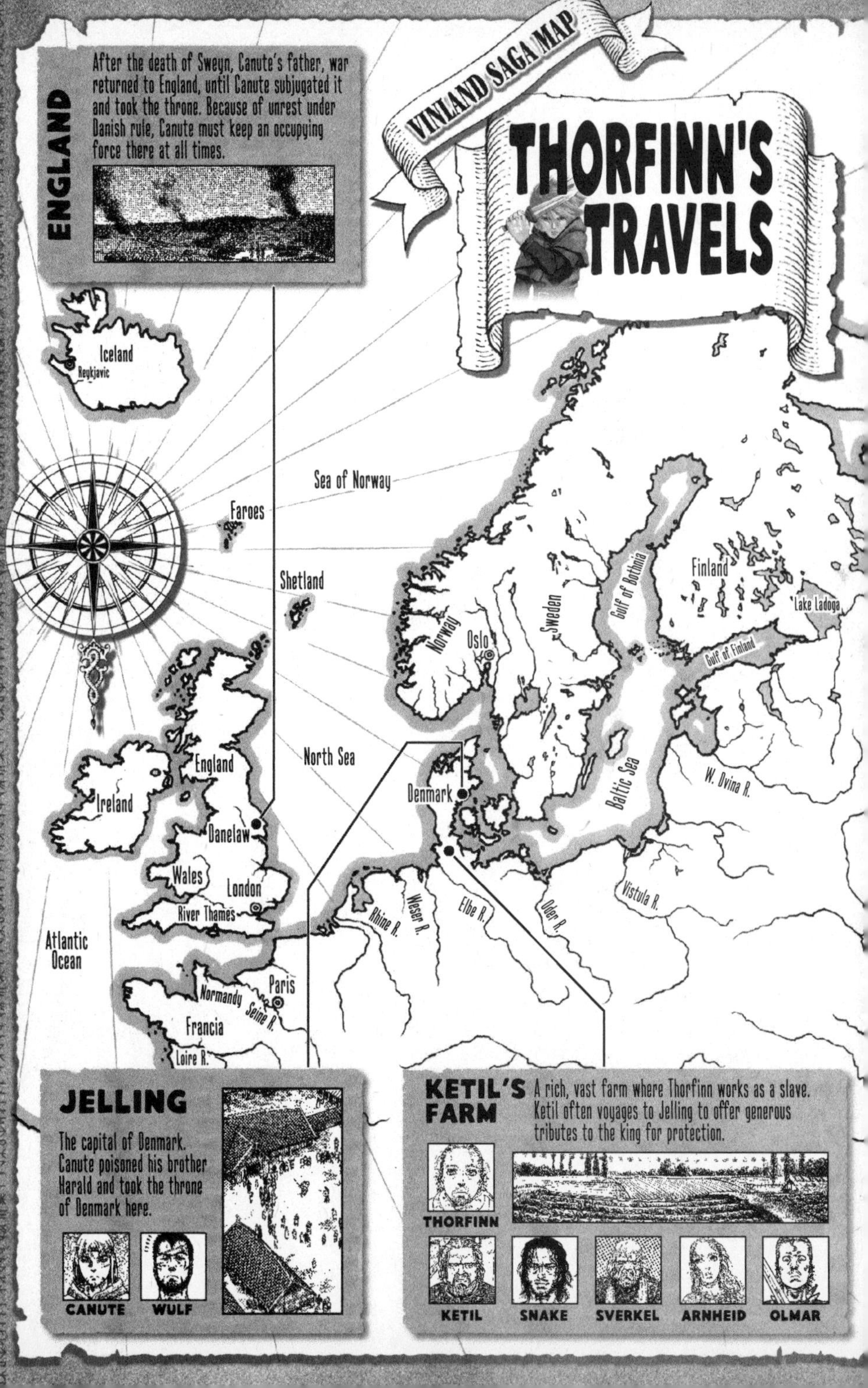
VINLAND SAGA MAP
THORFINN'S TRAVELS
ENGLAND
After the death of Sweyn, Canute's father, war returned to England, until Canute subjugated it and took the throne. Because of unrest under Danish rule, Canute must keep an occupying force there at all times.
Iceland
Reykjavic
Sea of Norway
Faroes
Shetland
Norway
Oslo
Sweden
Gulf of Bothnia
Finland
Lake Ladoga
Gulf of Finland
North Sea
Denmark
Baltic Sea
W. Dvina R.
England
Ireland
Danelaw
Wales
London
River Thames
Rhine R.
Weser R.
Elbe R.
Oder R.
Vistula R.
Atlantic Ocean
Paris
Normandy
Seine R.
Francia
Loire R.
JELLING
The capital of Denmark. Canute poisoned his brother Harald and took the throne of Denmark here.
CANUTE
WULF
KETIL'S FARM
A rich, vast farm where Thorfinn works as a slave. Ketil often voyages to Jelling to offer generous tributes to the king for protection.
THORFINN
KETIL
SNAKE
SVERKEL
ARNHEID
OLMAR

VINLAND SAGA FLIGHTS OF FANCY

I SWEAR, FOUR IS TOO MUCH!!

MAKOTO YUKIMURA

Because I drew it so well.

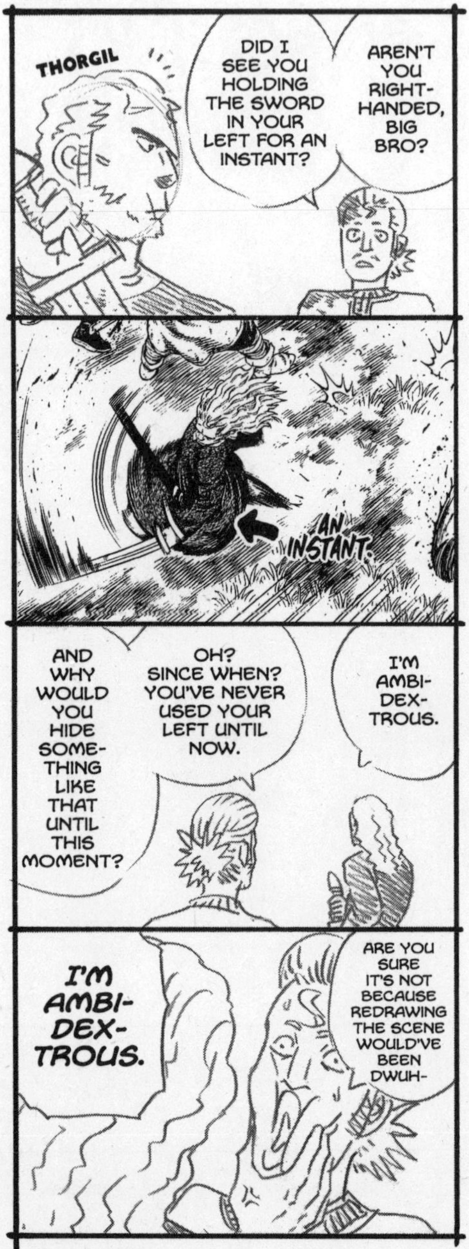
AREN'T YOU RIGHT-HANDED, BIG BRO?
DID I SEE YOU HOLDING THE SWORD IN YOUR LEFT FOR AN INSTANT?
THORGIL
AN INSTANT.
I'M AMBIDEXTROUS.
OH? SINCE WHEN? YOU'VE NEVER USED YOUR LEFT UNTIL NOW.
AND WHY WOULD YOU HIDE SOMETHING LIKE THAT UNTIL THIS MOMENT?
ARE YOU SURE IT'S NOT BECAUSE REDRAWING THE SCENE WOULD'VE BEEN DWUH-
I'M AMBIDEXTROUS.

...He's ambidextrous.

I'm so sorry.

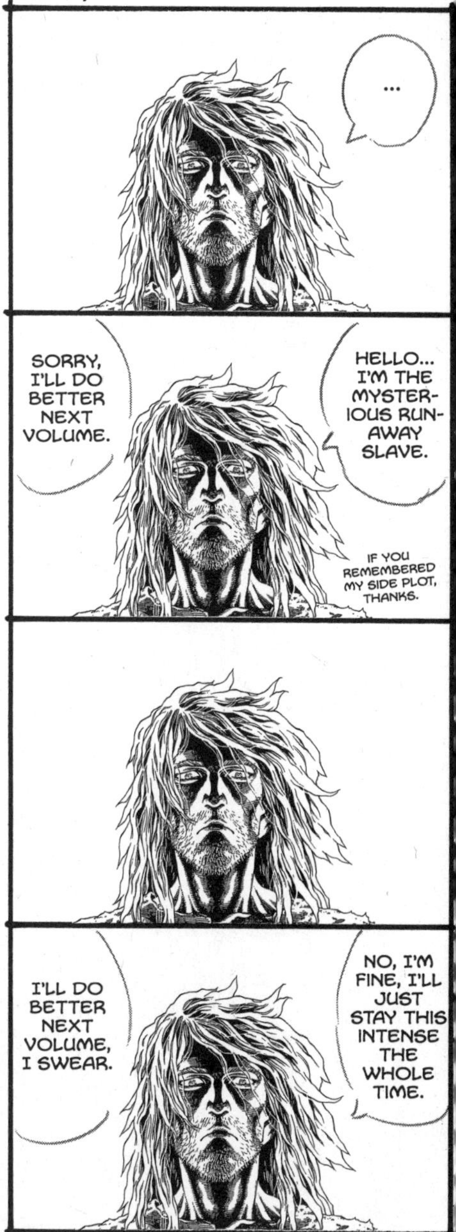
...
HELLO... I'M THE MYSTER-IOUS RUN-AWAY SLAVE.
SORRY, I'LL DO BETTER NEXT VOLUME.
IF YOU REMEMBERED MY SIDE PLOT, THANKS.
NO, I'M FINE, I'LL JUST STAY THIS INTENSE THE WHOLE TIME.
I'LL DO BETTER NEXT VOLUME, I SWEAR.

The Tragic Chains of Sin

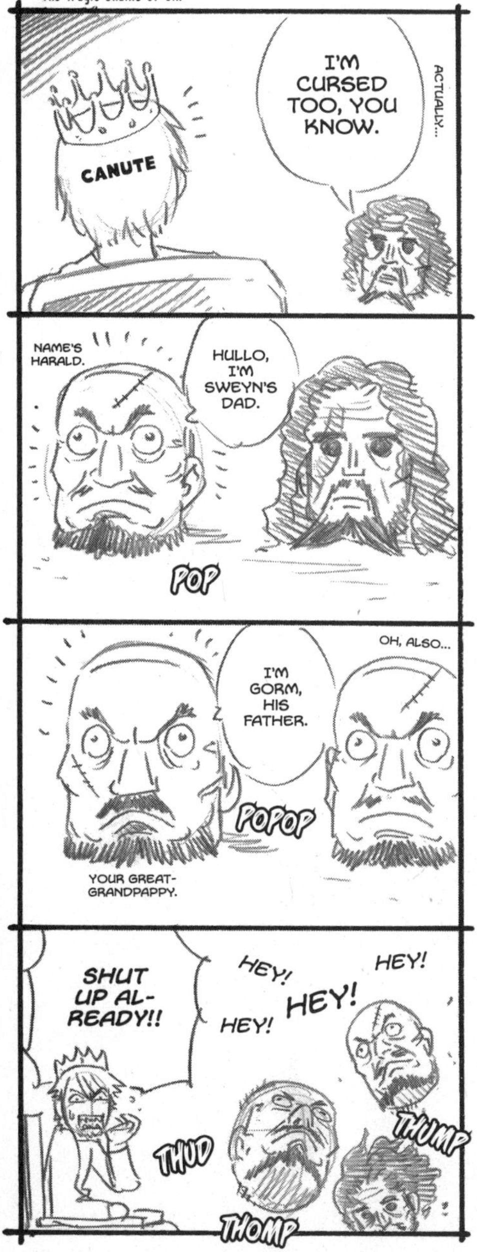
ACTUALLY...
I'M CURSED TOO, YOU KNOW.
CANUTE
HULLO, I'M SWEYN'S DAD.
NAME'S HARALD.
POP
OH, ALSO...
I'M GORM, HIS FATHER.
POPOP
YOUR GREAT-GRANDPAPPY.
HEY!
HEY!
HEY!
HEY!
SHUT UP AL-READY!!
THUMP
THUD
THOMP

SUPPLEMENTAL DESIGNS

OLD MASTER'S HOUSE (MAIN WING)

SEEMS LIKE SOMETHING'S MISSING...
DON'T KNOW WHAT, THOUGH...

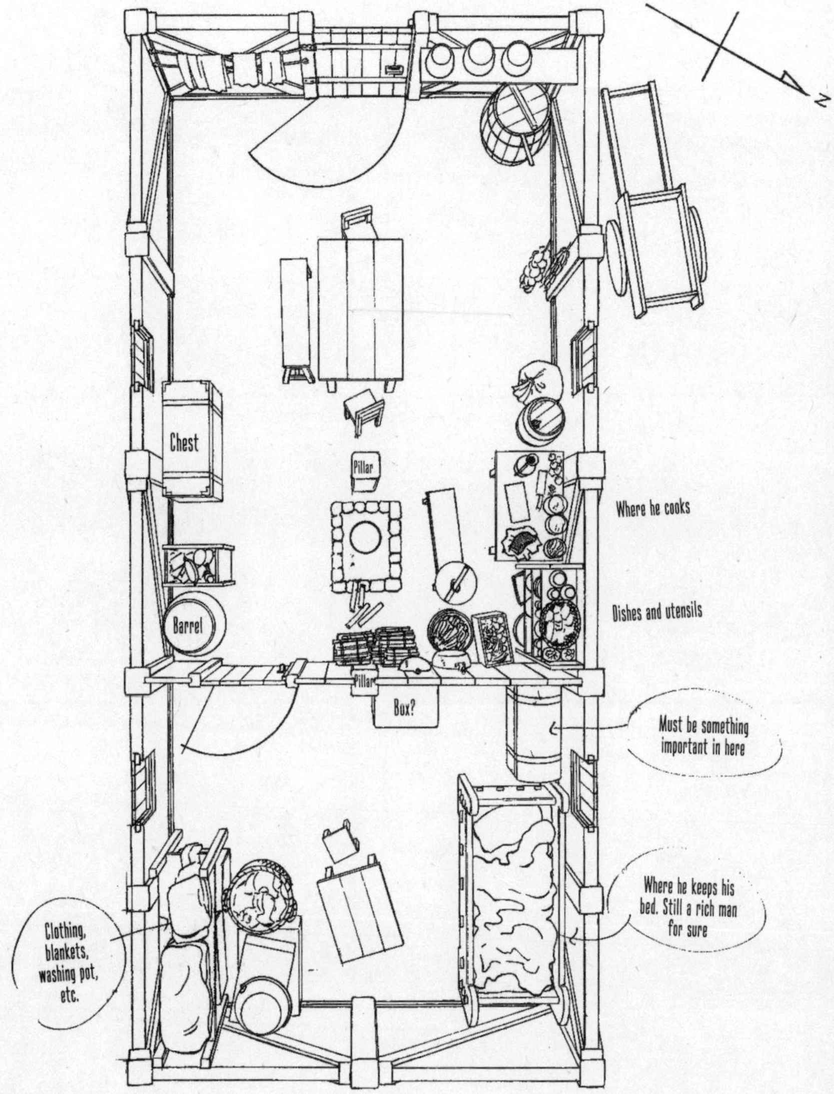
N
Chest
Pillar
Where he cooks
Barrel
Dishes and utensils
Pillar
Box?
Must be something important in here
Where he keeps his bed. Still a rich man for sure
Clothing, blankets, washing pot, etc.

It even surprises the author how many fathers and sons appear in this manga. Some are close, and others are not. My father is a strong and healthy judo athlete, a serious man who wore a crisp suit to work every morning and never caused trouble for our family with drinking or gambling. He's the perfect example of a good father, if I'm allowed to say so myself. I wanted to be independent from him as soon as possible. I felt ashamed to be under his care, didn't like having to follow his opinions, and swore that I wouldn't follow his influence. So I practiced kendo instead of judo. Of course, the fact that I would choose another combat style for my activity already says a lot, doesn't it? We didn't butt heads about things; if anything, we were close. But I wanted to be as far from him as I could be. That's what me and my father are like. I kind of hope that my sons are the same way with me. Grow up on your own, boys. Hmm...wait, doesn't that mean I have to be a perfect example of a good father, too? I don't know if I can live up to that...

MAKOTO YUKIMURA

VINLAND SAGA

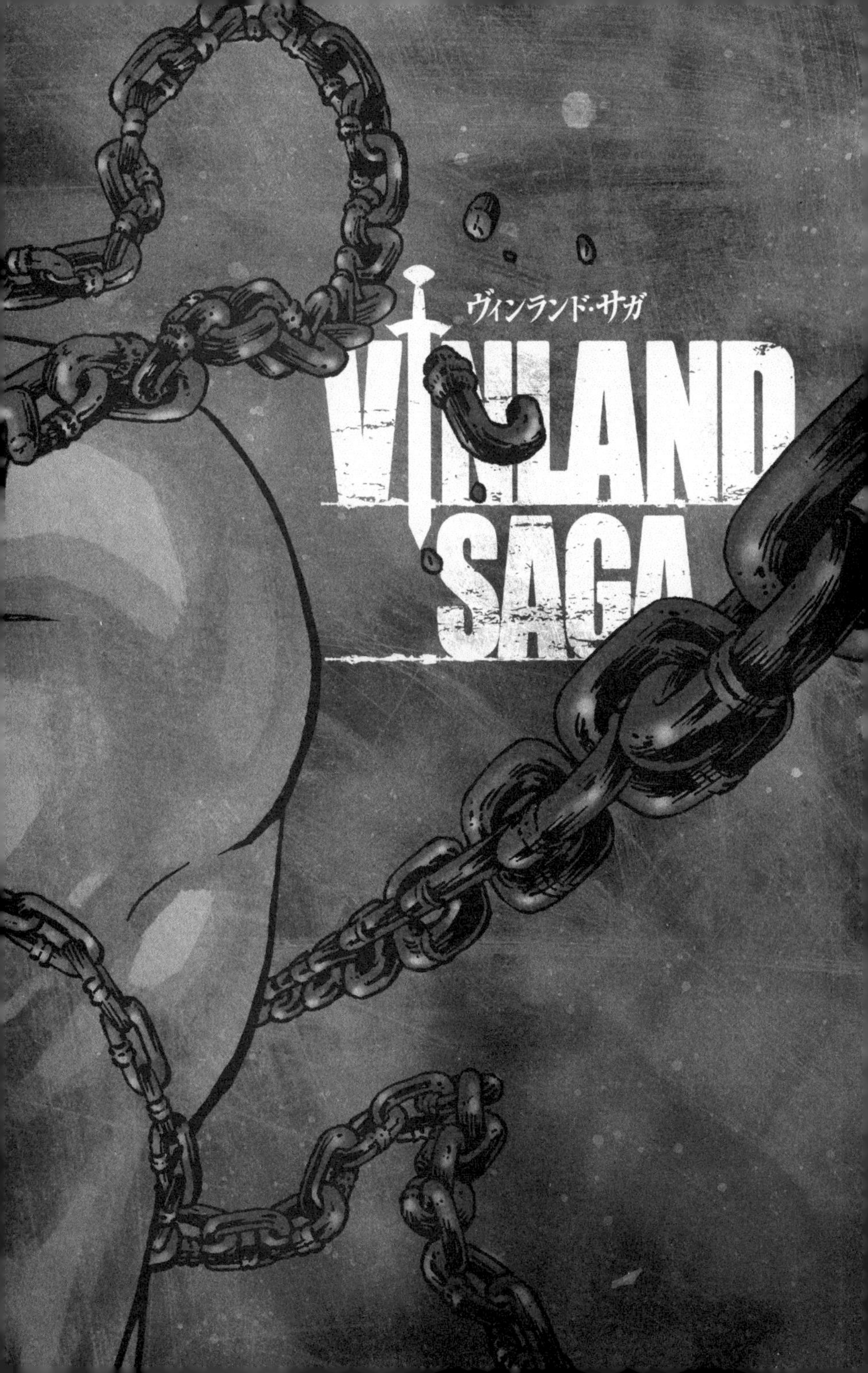
ヴィンランド・サガ
VINLAND SAGA

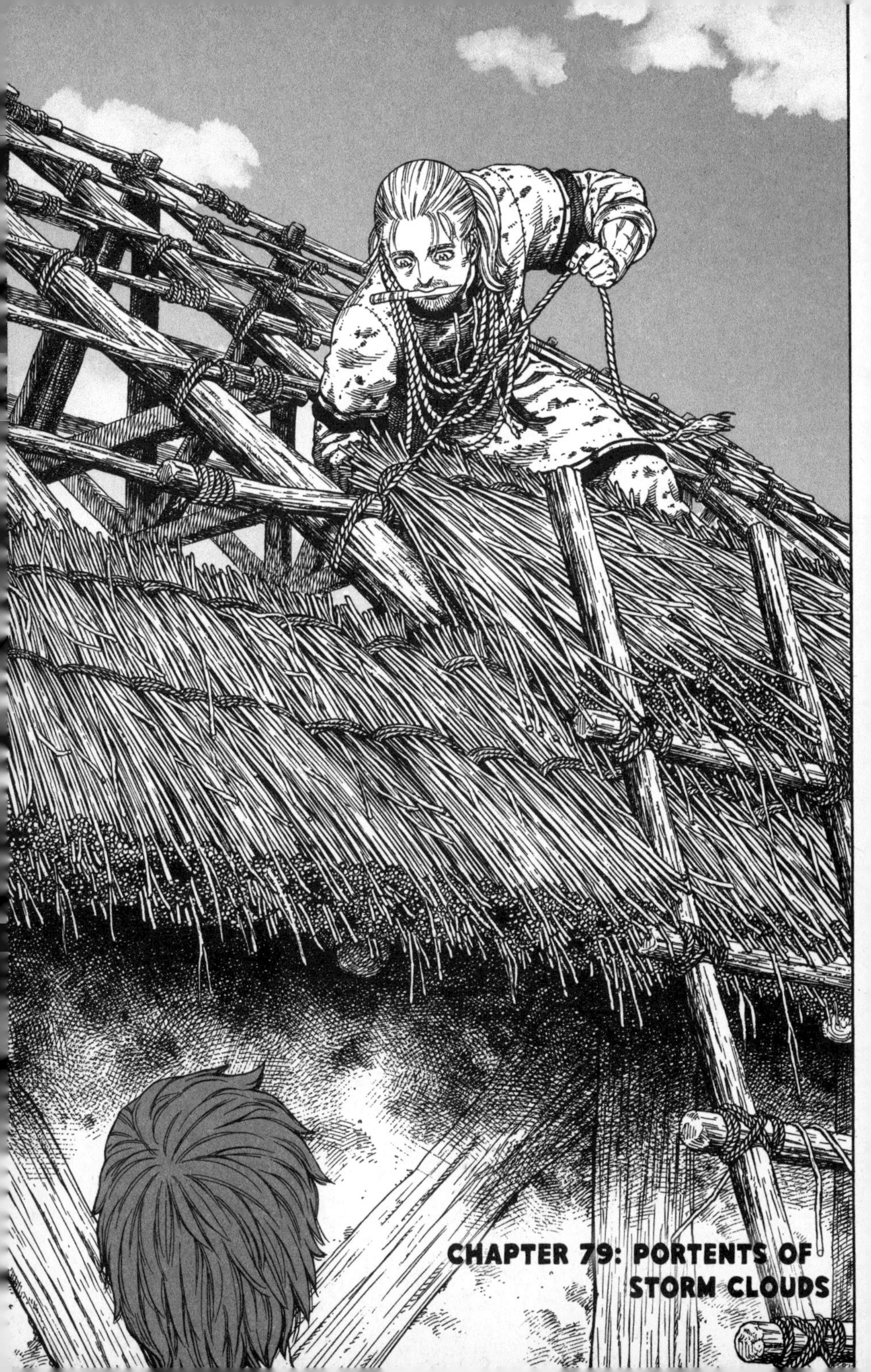
CHAPTER 79: PORTENTS OF
STORM CLOUDS

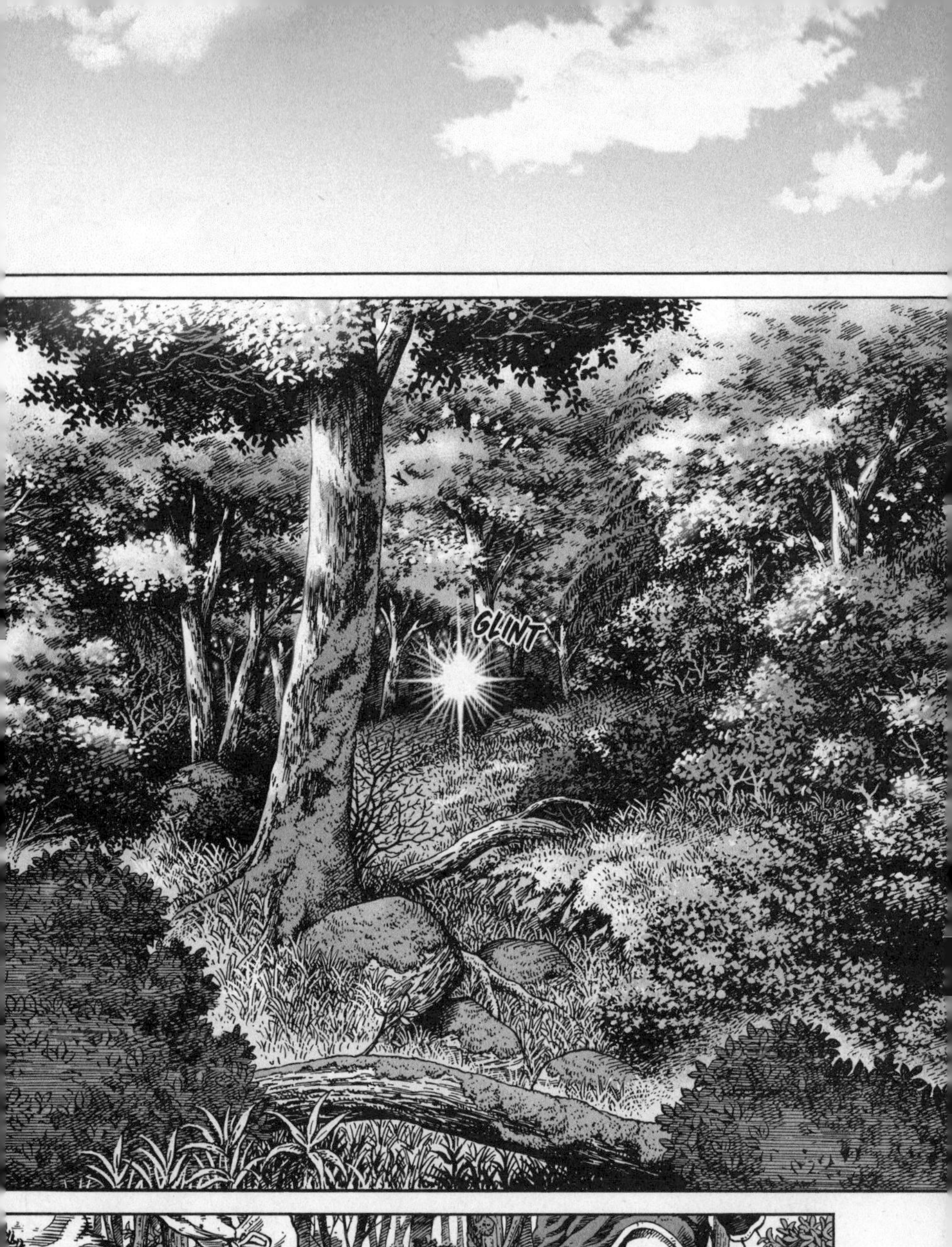
GLINT
KSHF
SHFF

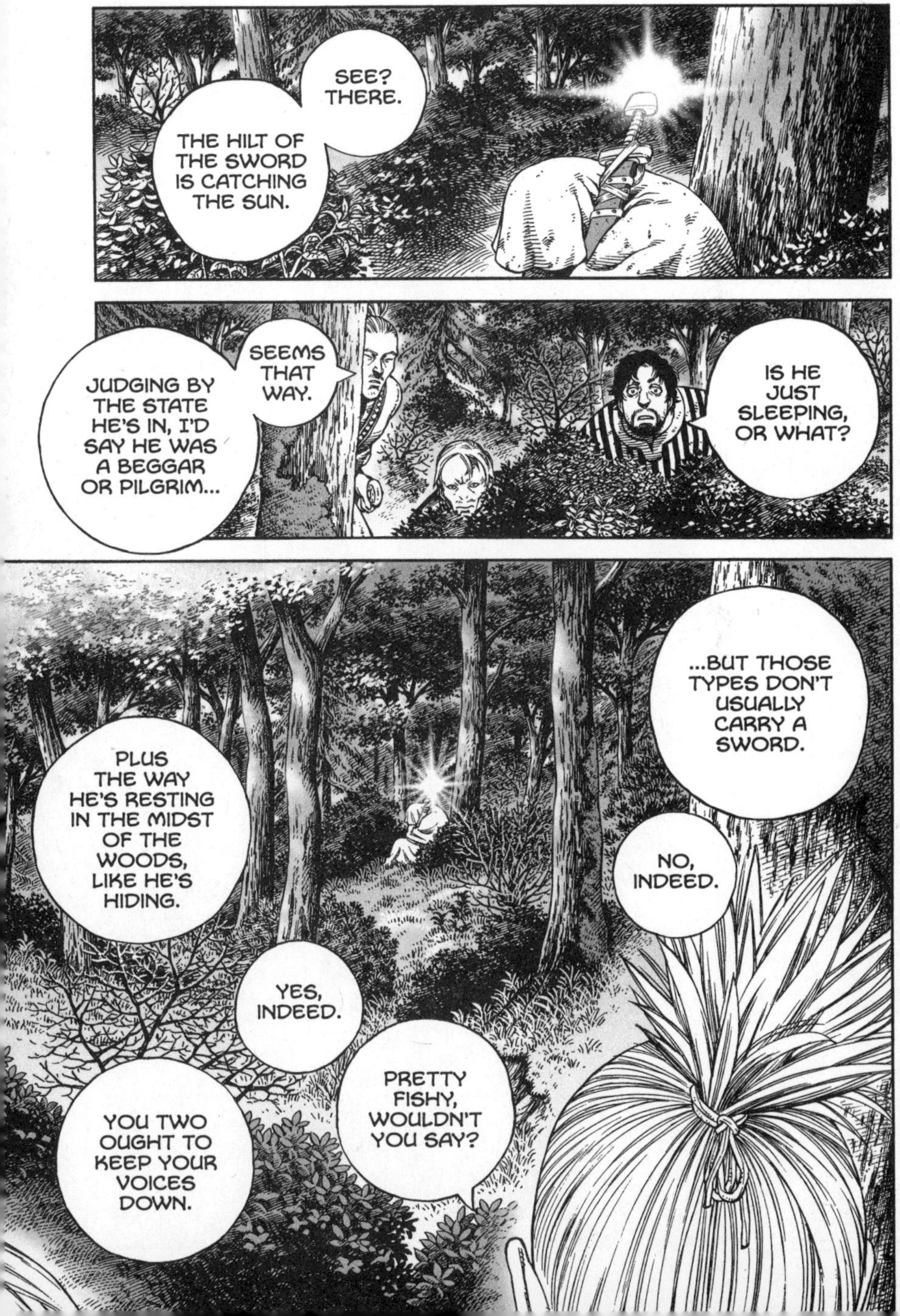
SEE? THERE.
THE HILT OF THE SWORD IS CATCHING THE SUN.
IS HE JUST SLEEPING, OR WHAT?
SEEMS THAT WAY.
JUDGING BY THE STATE HE'S IN, I'D SAY HE WAS A BEGGAR OR PILGRIM...
...BUT THOSE TYPES DON'T USUALLY CARRY A SWORD.
NO, INDEED.
PLUS THE WAY HE'S RESTING IN THE MIDST OF THE WOODS, LIKE HE'S HIDING.
YES, INDEED.
PRETTY FISHY, WOULDN'T YOU SAY?
YOU TWO OUGHT TO KEEP YOUR VOICES DOWN.

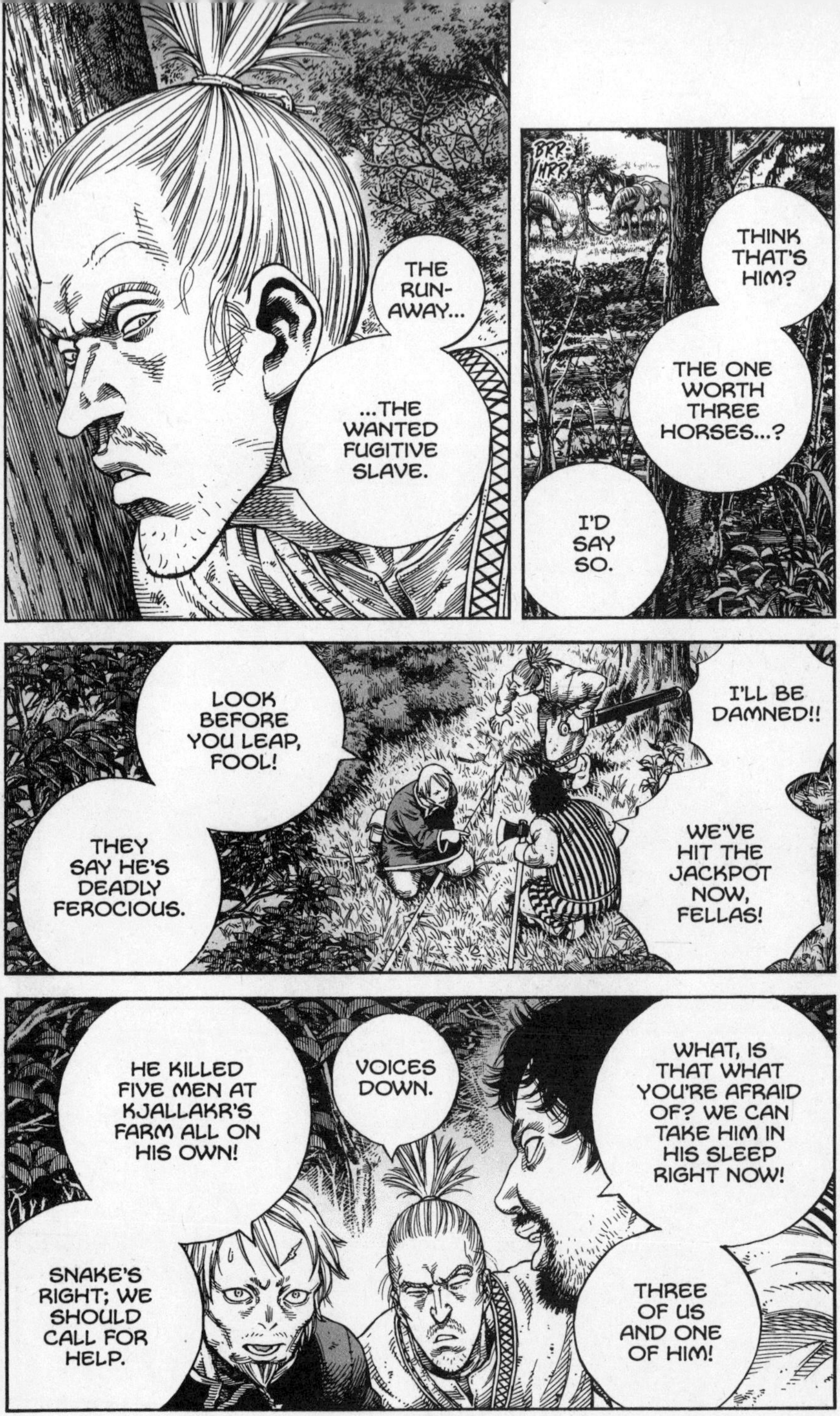
BRR-HRR
THINK THAT'S HIM?
THE ONE WORTH THREE HORSES...?
I'D SAY SO.
THE RUN-AWAY...
...THE WANTED FUGITIVE SLAVE.
I'LL BE DAMNED!!
WE'VE HIT THE JACKPOT NOW, FELLAS!
LOOK BEFORE YOU LEAP, FOOL!
THEY SAY HE'S DEADLY FEROCIOUS.
WHAT, IS THAT WHAT YOU'RE AFRAID OF? WE CAN TAKE HIM IN HIS SLEEP RIGHT NOW!
THREE OF US AND ONE OF HIM!
VOICES DOWN.
HE KILLED FIVE MEN AT KJALLAKR'S FARM ALL ON HIS OWN!
SNAKE'S RIGHT; WE SHOULD CALL FOR HELP.

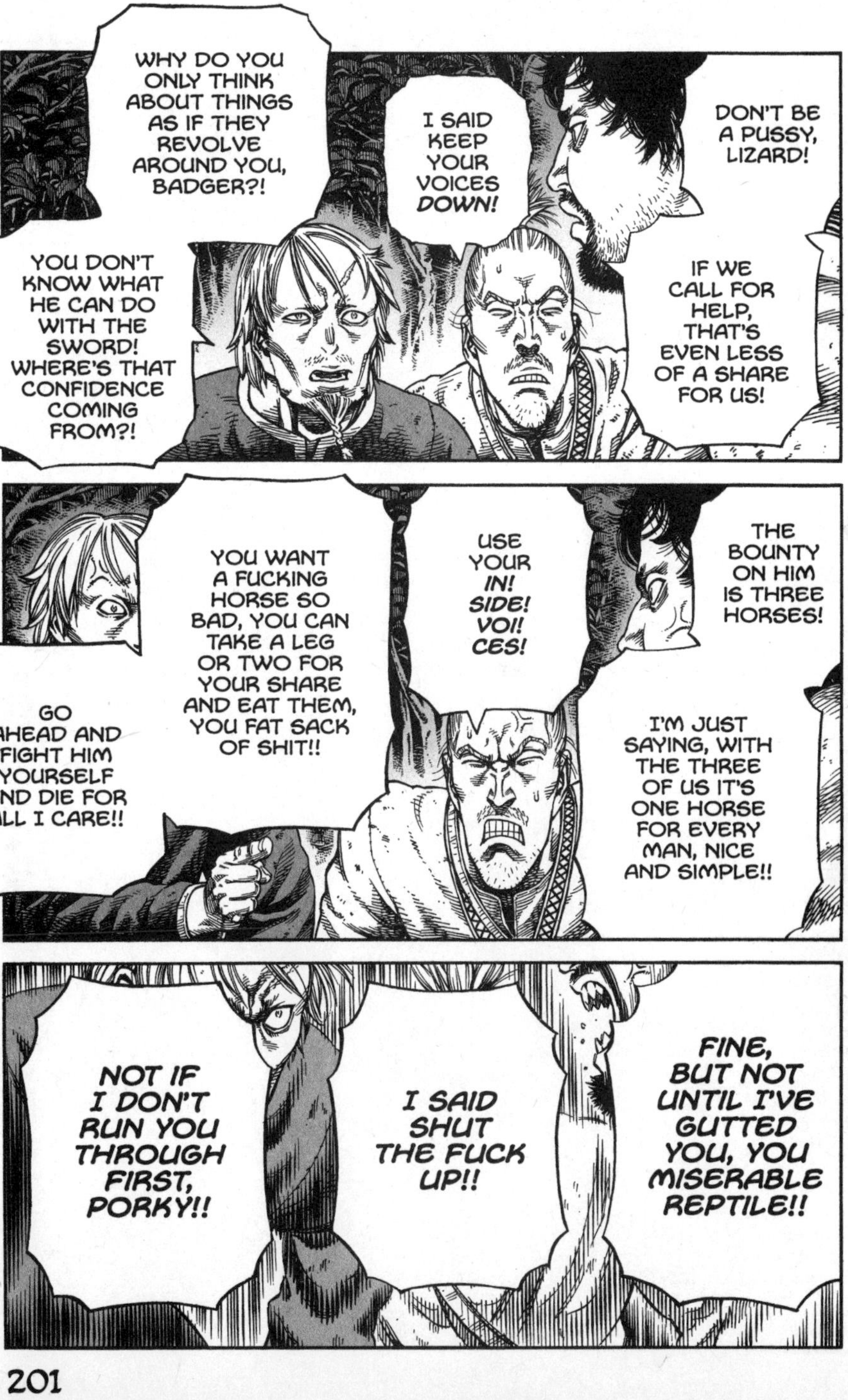
DON'T BE A PUSSY, LIZARD!
IF WE CALL FOR HELP, THAT'S EVEN LESS OF A SHARE FOR US!
I SAID KEEP YOUR VOICES *DOWN!*
WHY DO YOU ONLY THINK ABOUT THINGS AS IF THEY REVOLVE AROUND YOU, BADGER?!
YOU DON'T KNOW WHAT HE CAN DO WITH THE SWORD! WHERE'S THAT CONFIDENCE COMING FROM?!
THE BOUNTY ON HIM IS THREE HORSES!
I'M JUST SAYING, WITH THE THREE OF US IT'S ONE HORSE FOR EVERY MAN, NICE AND SIMPLE!!
USE YOUR *IN! SIDE! VOI! CES!*
YOU WANT A FUCKING HORSE SO BAD, YOU CAN TAKE A LEG OR TWO FOR YOUR SHARE AND EAT THEM, YOU FAT SACK OF SHIT!!
GO AHEAD AND FIGHT HIM YOURSELF AND DIE FOR ALL I CARE!!
FINE, BUT NOT UNTIL I'VE GUTTED YOU, YOU MISERABLE REPTILE!!
I SAID SHUT THE FUCK UP!!
NOT IF I DON'T RUN YOU THROUGH FIRST, PORKY!!

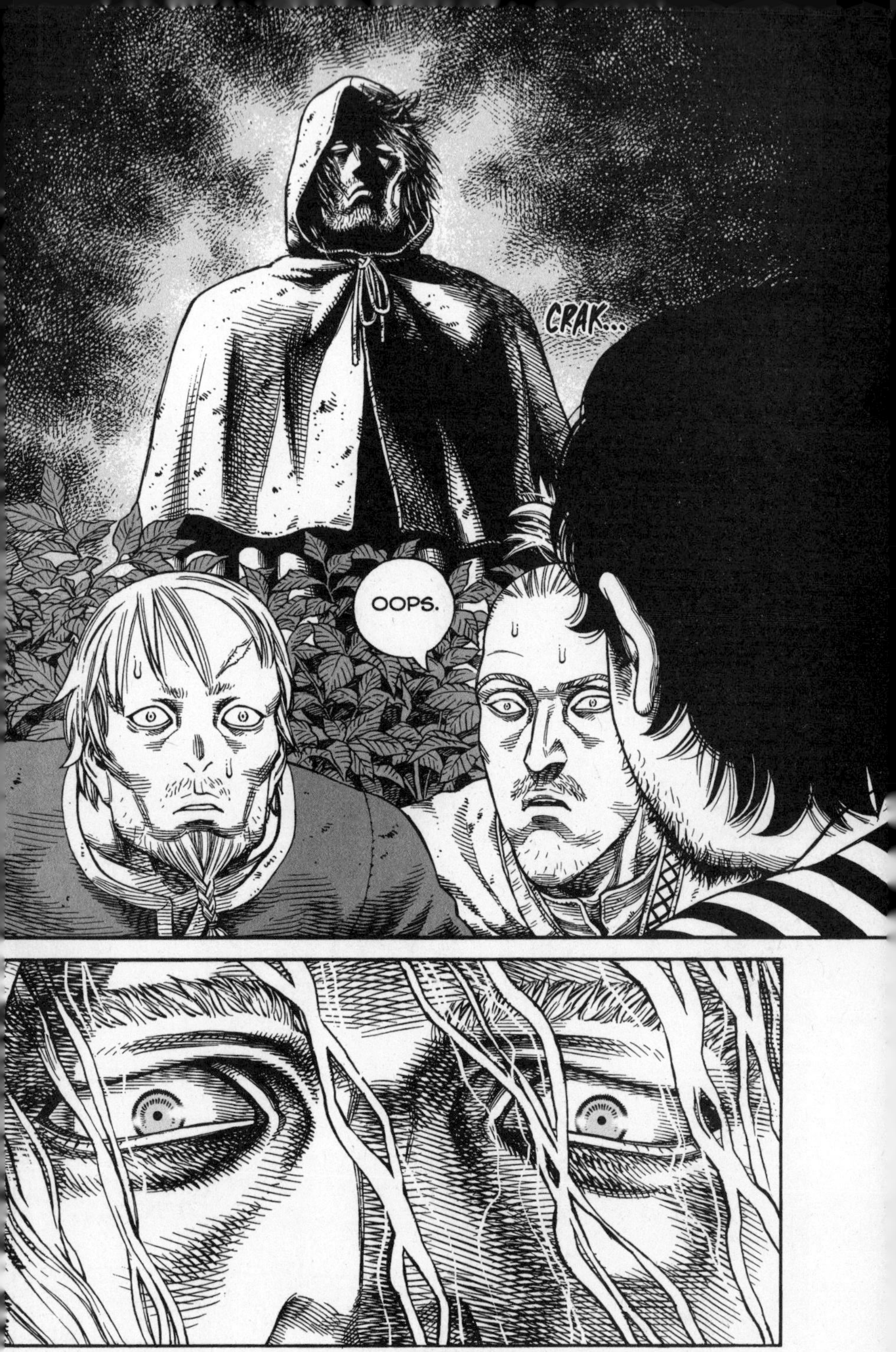
CRAK...
OOPS.

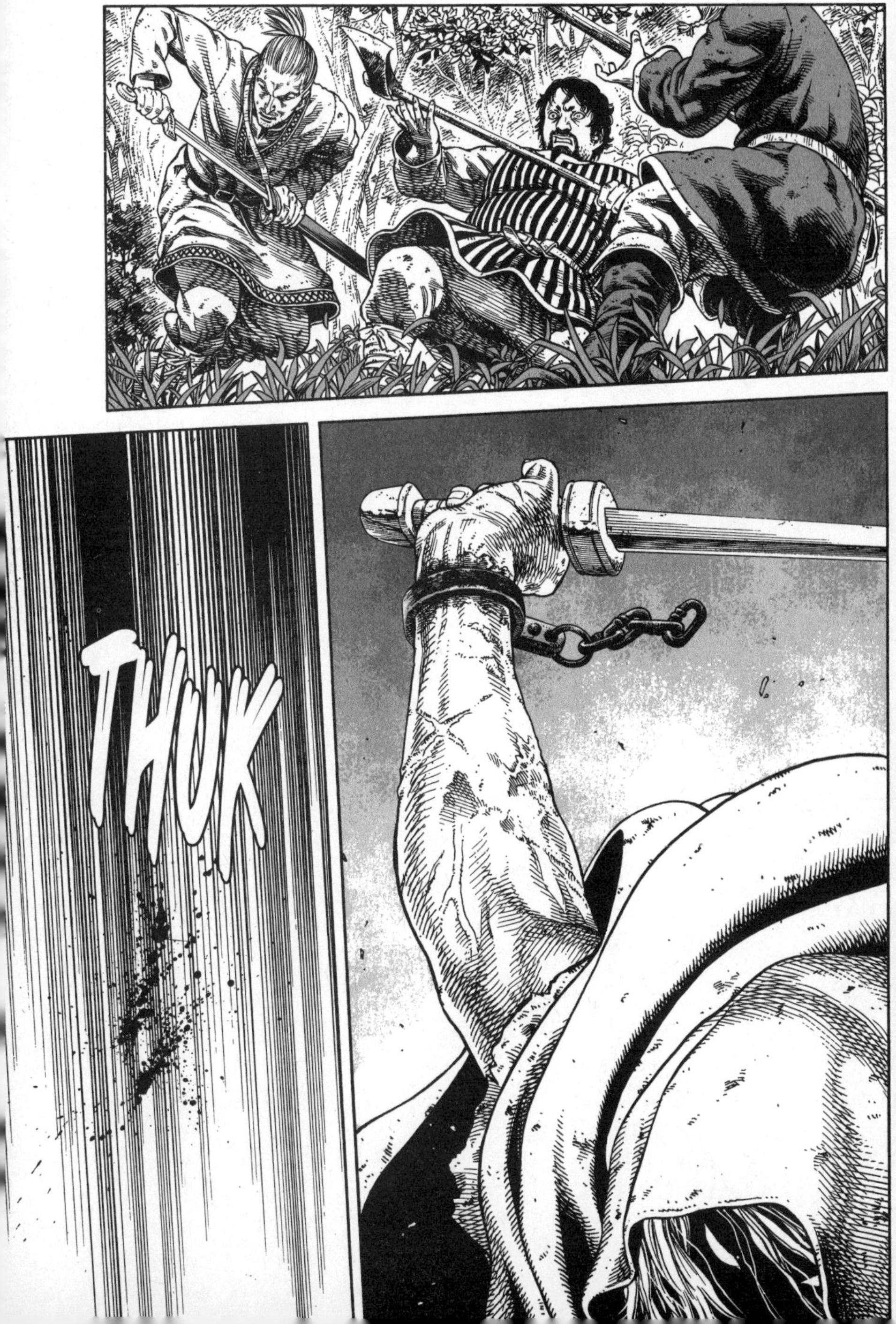
THUK

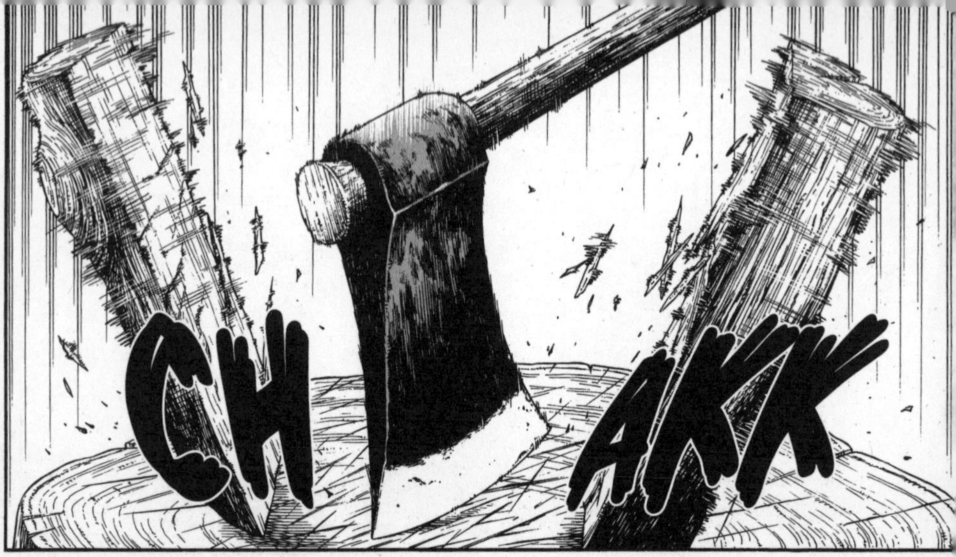
CHAKK
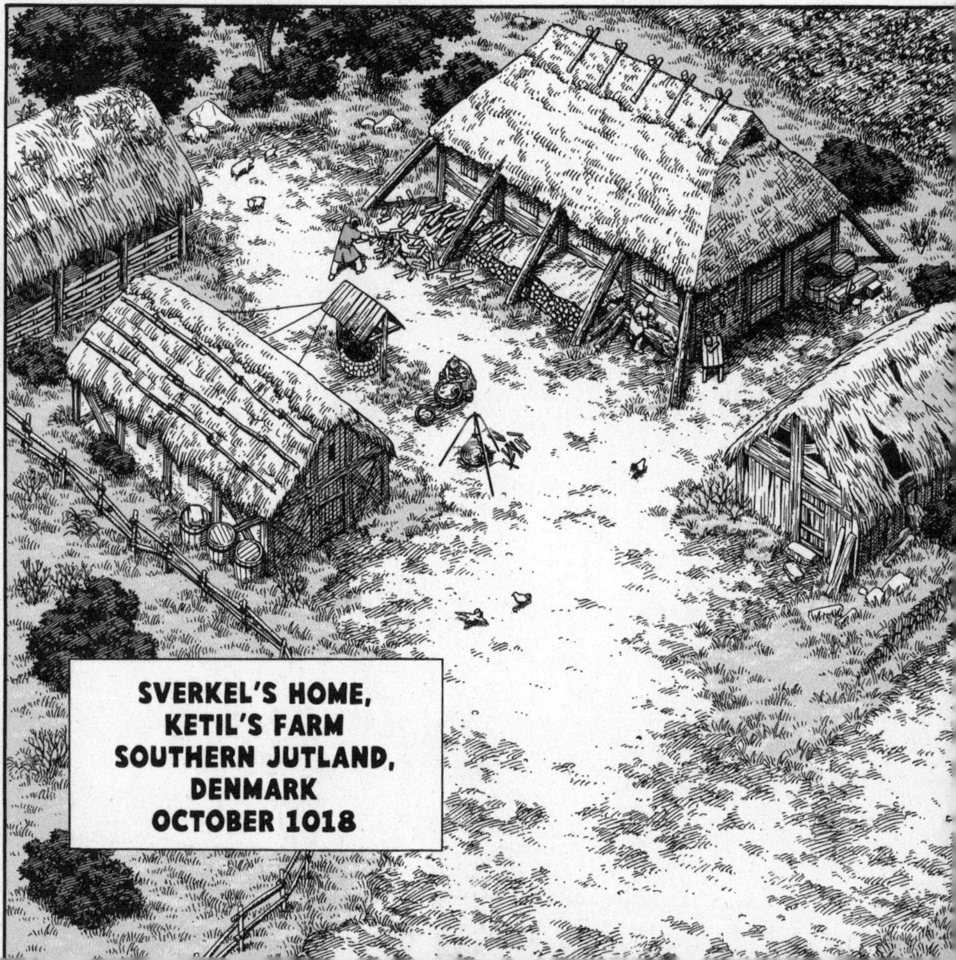
SVERKEL'S HOME,
KETIL'S FARM
SOUTHERN JUTLAND,
DENMARK
OCTOBER 1018

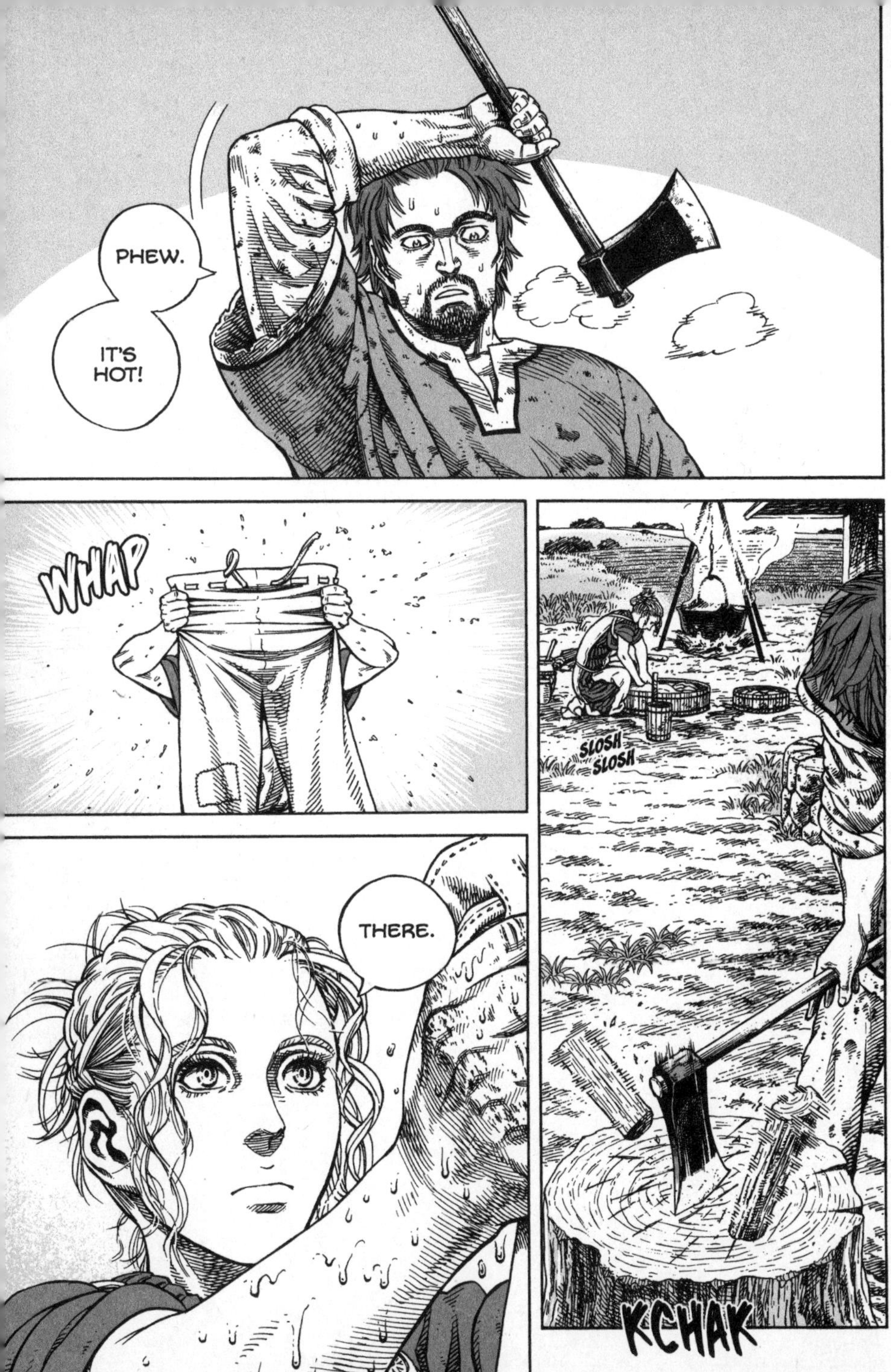
PHEW.
IT'S HOT!
SLOSH
SLOSH
KCHAK
WHAP
THERE.

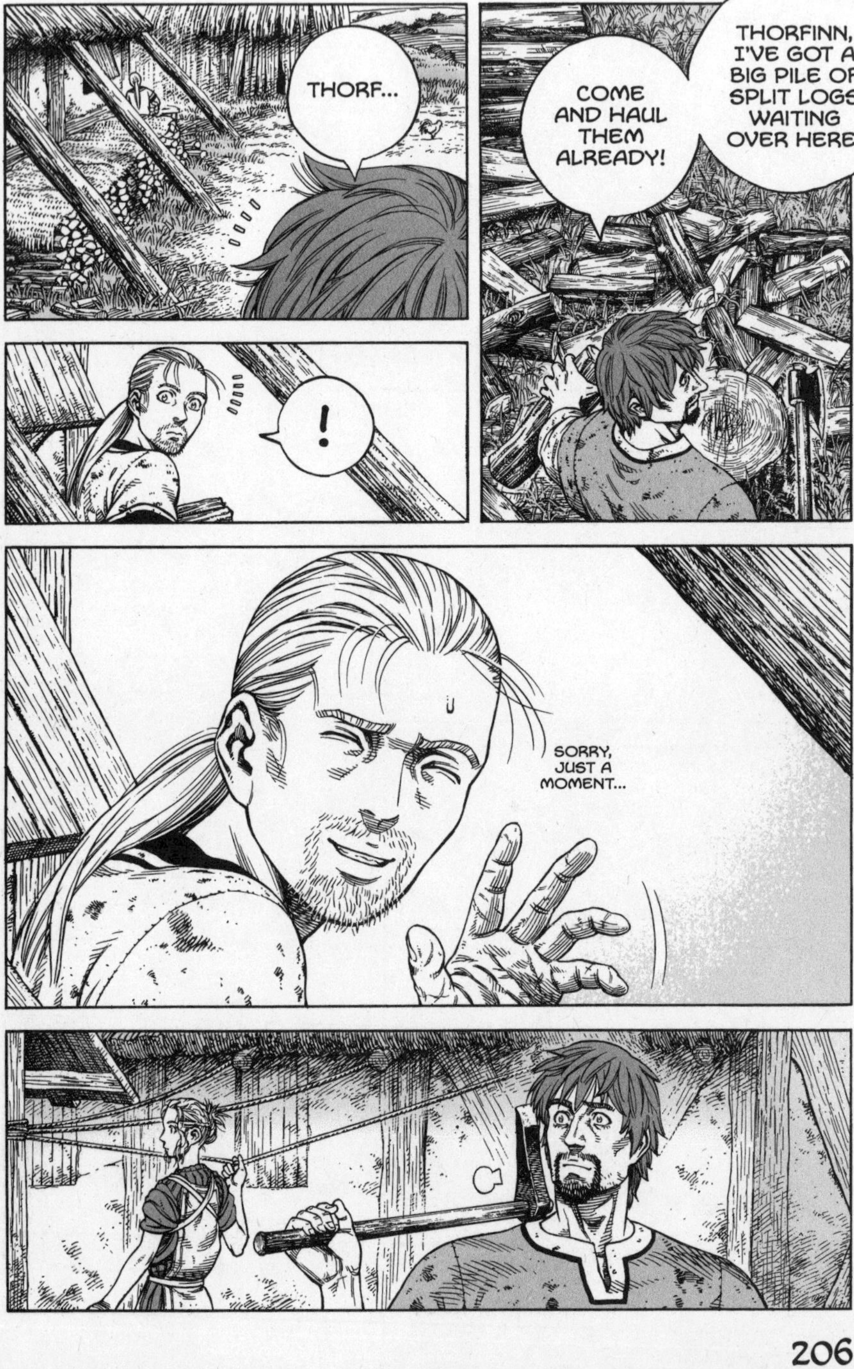
THORFINN, I'VE GOT A BIG PILE OF SPLIT LOGS WAITING OVER HERE!
COME AND HAUL THEM ALREADY!
THORF...
!
SORRY, JUST A MOMENT...

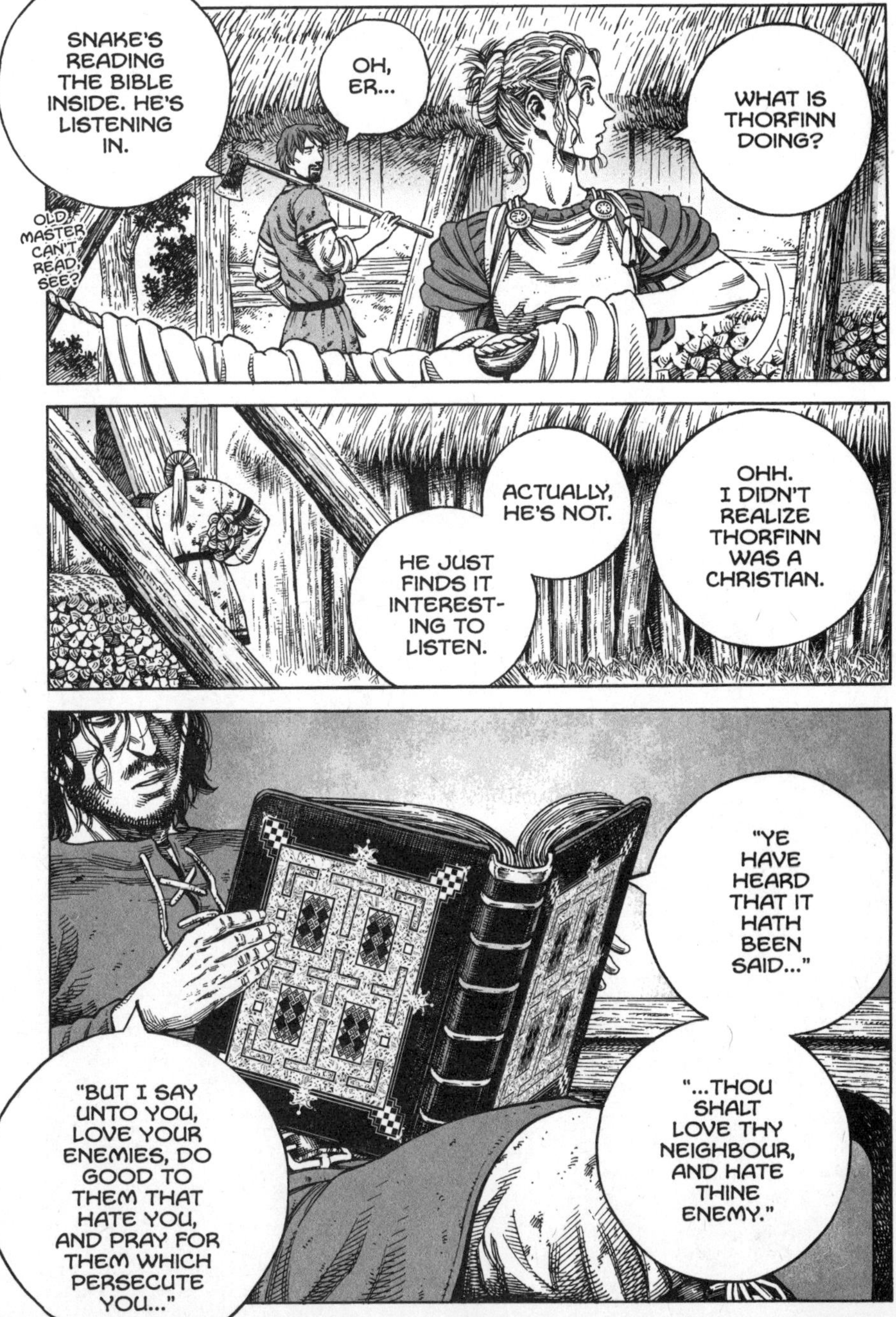
WHAT IS THORFINN DOING?
OH, ER...
SNAKE'S READING THE BIBLE INSIDE. HE'S LISTENING IN.
OLD MASTER CAN'T READ, SEE?
OHH. I DIDN'T REALIZE THORFINN WAS A CHRISTIAN.
ACTUALLY, HE'S NOT.
HE JUST FINDS IT INTEREST-ING TO LISTEN.
"YE HAVE HEARD THAT IT HATH BEEN SAID..."
"...THOU SHALT LOVE THY NEIGHBOUR, AND HATE THINE ENEMY."
"BUT I SAY UNTO YOU, LOVE YOUR ENEMIES, DO GOOD TO THEM THAT HATE YOU, AND PRAY FOR THEM WHICH PERSECUTE YOU..."

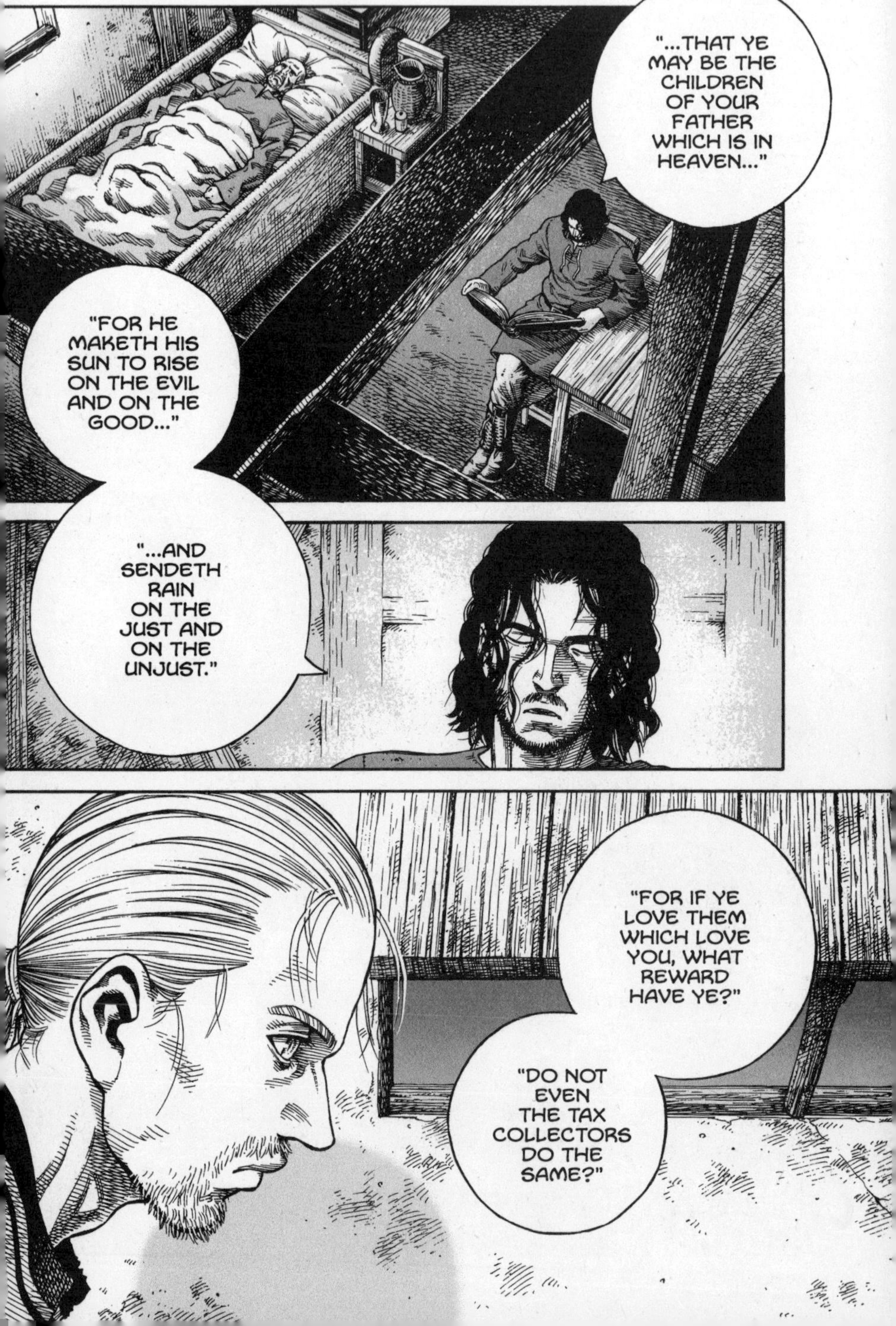
"...THAT YE MAY BE THE CHILDREN OF YOUR FATHER WHICH IS IN HEAVEN..."
"FOR HE MAKETH HIS SUN TO RISE ON THE EVIL AND ON THE GOOD..."
"...AND SENDETH RAIN ON THE JUST AND ON THE UNJUST."
"FOR IF YE LOVE THEM WHICH LOVE YOU, WHAT REWARD HAVE YE?"
"DO NOT EVEN THE TAX COLLECTORS DO THE SAME?"

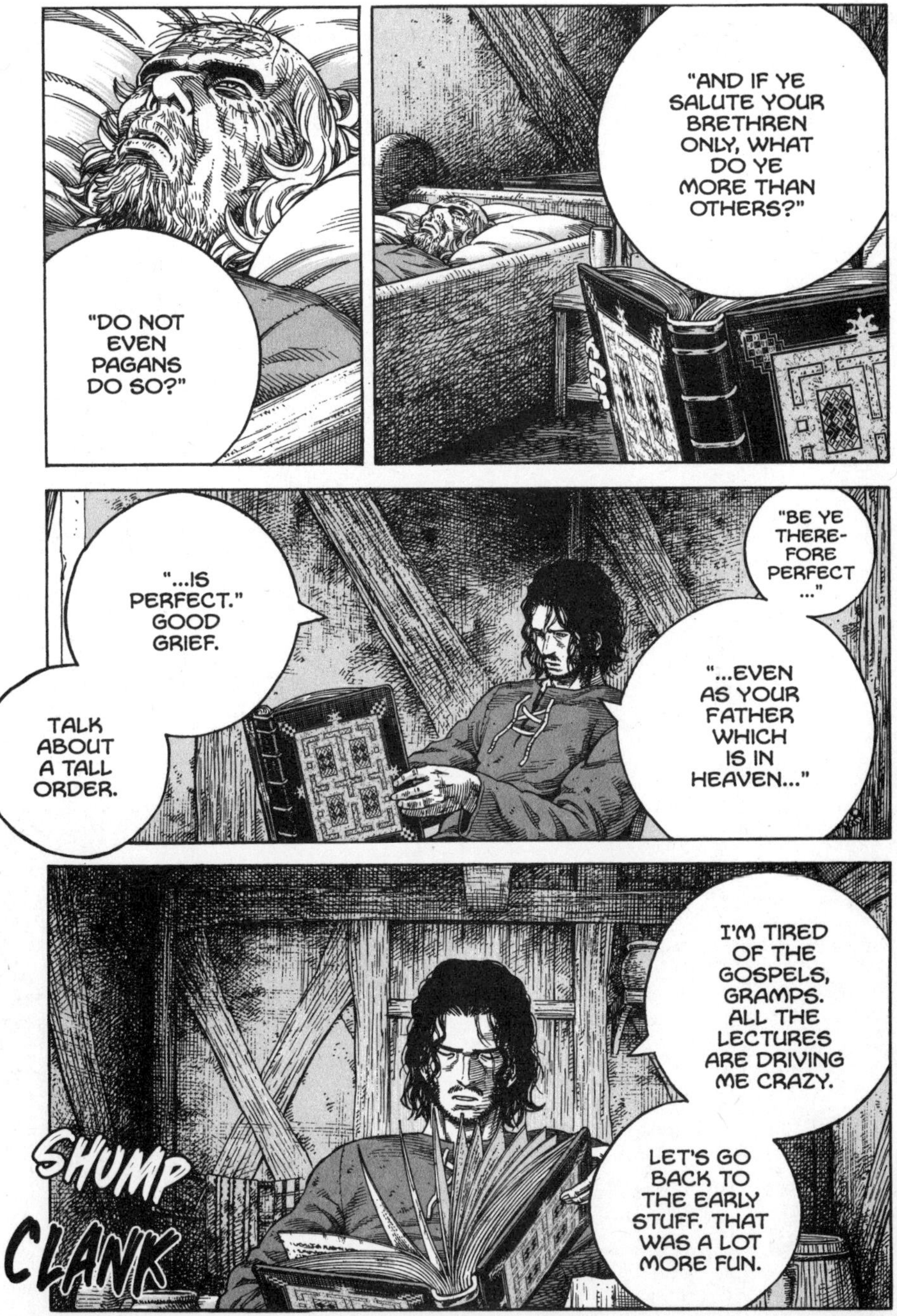
"AND IF YE SALUTE YOUR BRETHREN ONLY, WHAT DO YE MORE THAN OTHERS?"
"DO NOT EVEN PAGANS DO SO?"
"BE YE THERE-FORE PERFECT ..."
"...EVEN AS YOUR FATHER WHICH IS IN HEAVEN..."
"...IS PERFECT." GOOD GRIEF.
TALK ABOUT A TALL ORDER.
I'M TIRED OF THE GOSPELS, GRAMPS. ALL THE LECTURES ARE DRIVING ME CRAZY.
LET'S GO BACK TO THE EARLY STUFF. THAT WAS A LOT MORE FUN.
SHUMP
CLANK

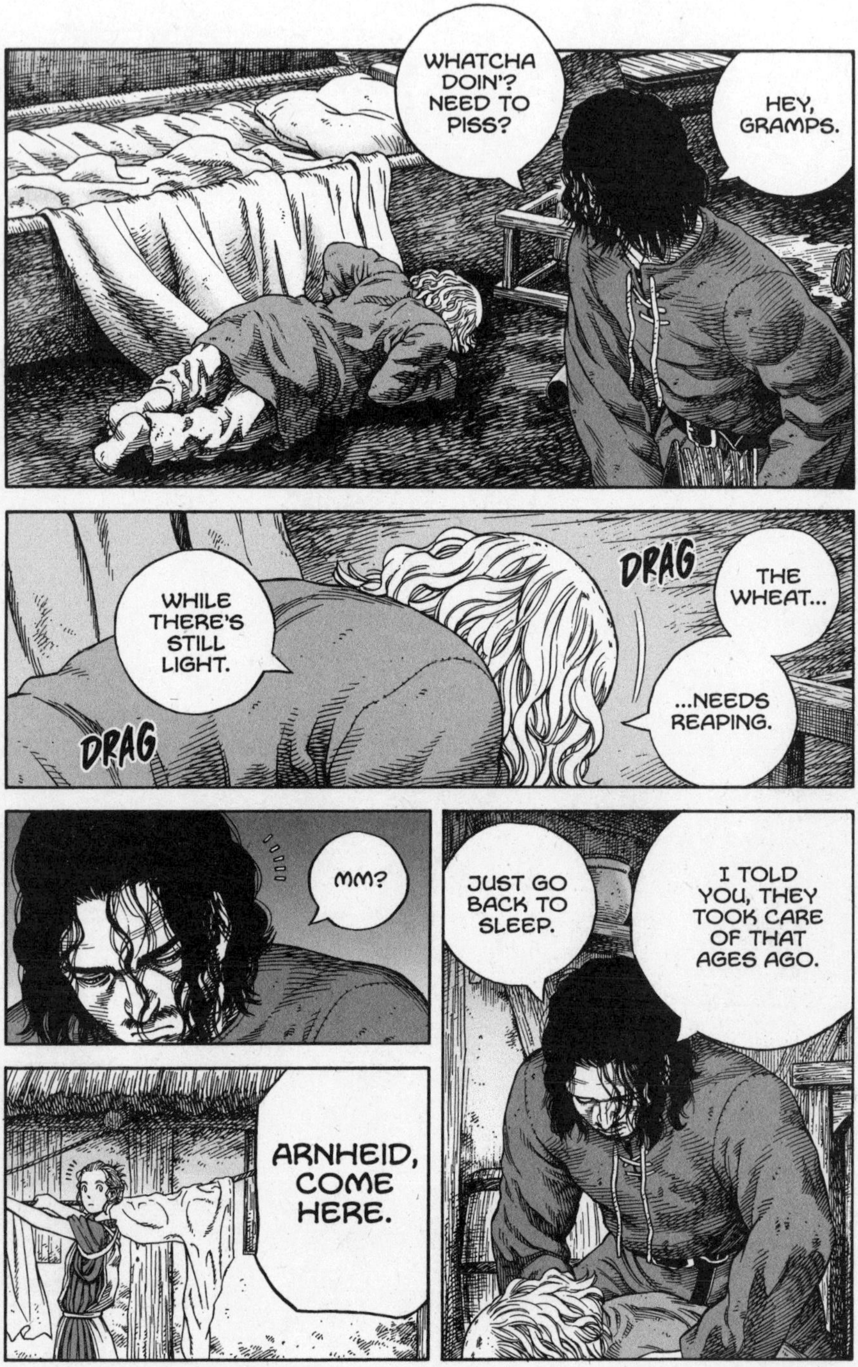
HEY, GRAMPS.
WHATCHA DOIN'? NEED TO PISS?
THE WHEAT...
...NEEDS REAPING.
DRAG
WHILE THERE'S STILL LIGHT.
DRAG
I TOLD YOU, THEY TOOK CARE OF THAT AGES AGO.
JUST GO BACK TO SLEEP.
MM?
ARNHEID, COME HERE.

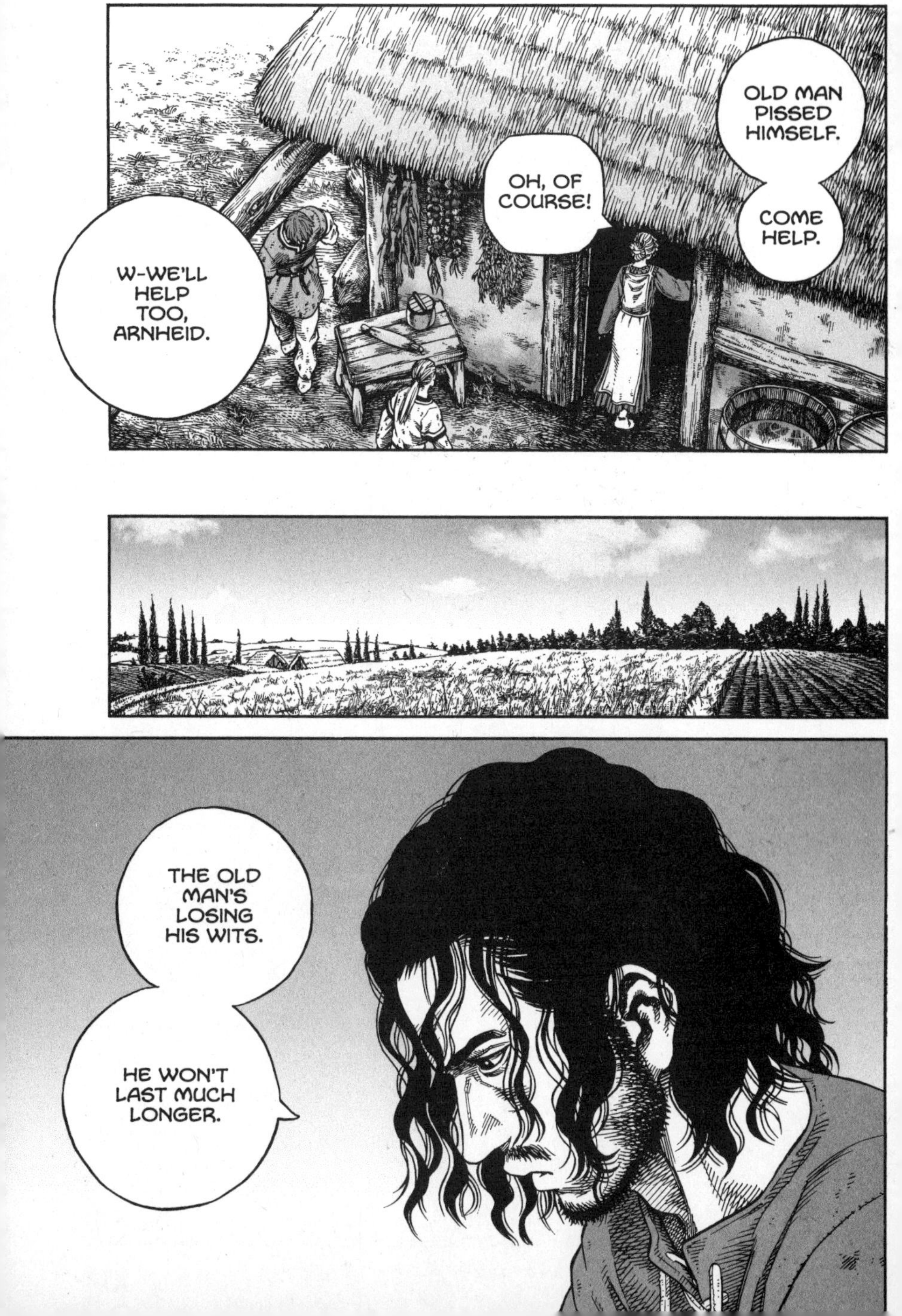
OLD MAN PISSED HIMSELF.
COME HELP.
OH, OF COURSE!
W-WE'LL HELP TOO, ARNHEID.
THE OLD MAN'S LOSING HIS WITS.
HE WON'T LAST MUCH LONGER.

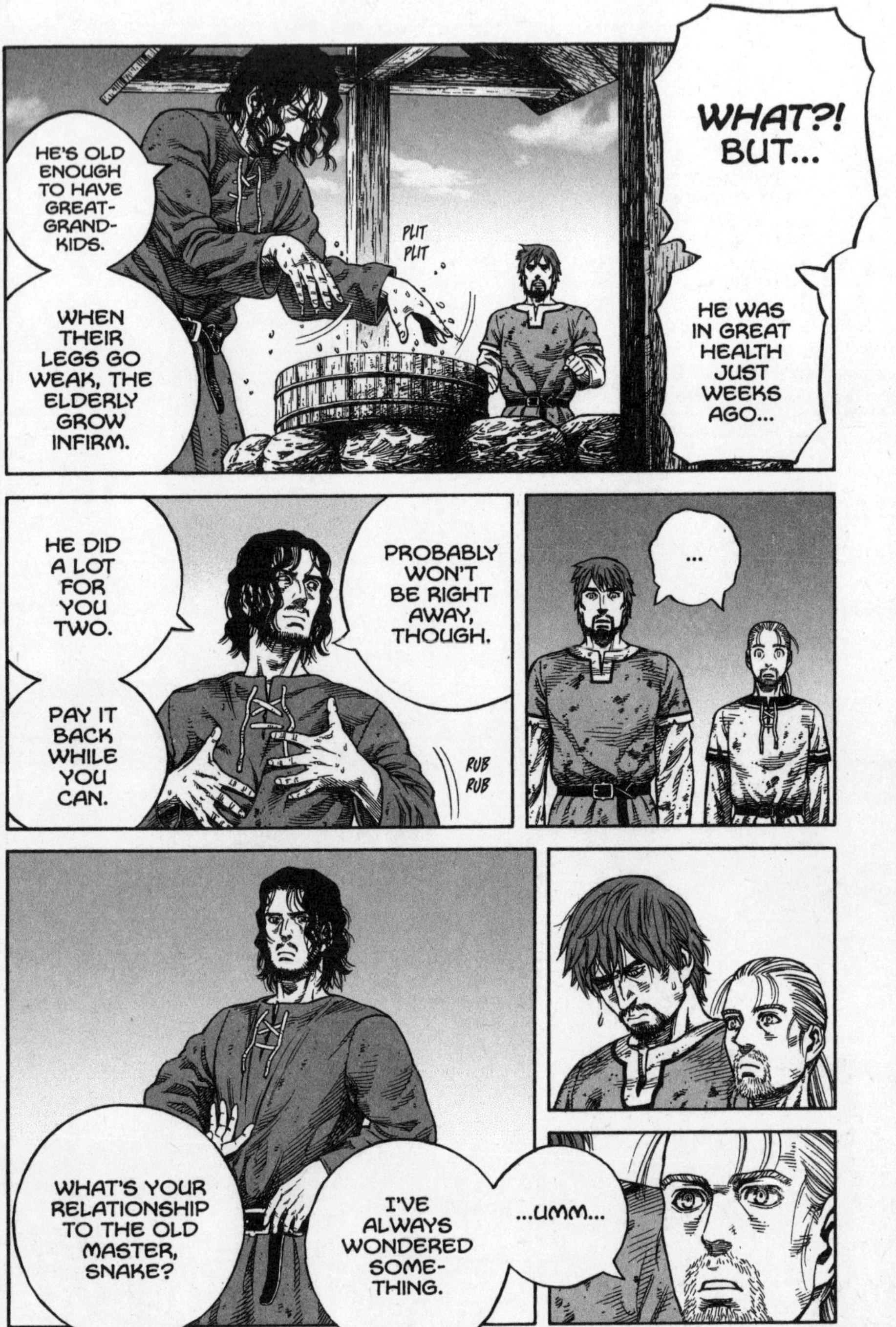
WHAT?! BUT...
HE WAS IN GREAT HEALTH JUST WEEKS AGO...
HE'S OLD ENOUGH TO HAVE GREAT-GRAND-KIDS.
PLIT PLIT
WHEN THEIR LEGS GO WEAK, THE ELDERLY GROW INFIRM.
...
PROBABLY WON'T BE RIGHT AWAY, THOUGH.
HE DID A LOT FOR YOU TWO.
RUB RUB
PAY IT BACK WHILE YOU CAN.
...UMM...
I'VE ALWAYS WONDERED SOME-THING.
WHAT'S YOUR RELATIONSHIP TO THE OLD MASTER, SNAKE?

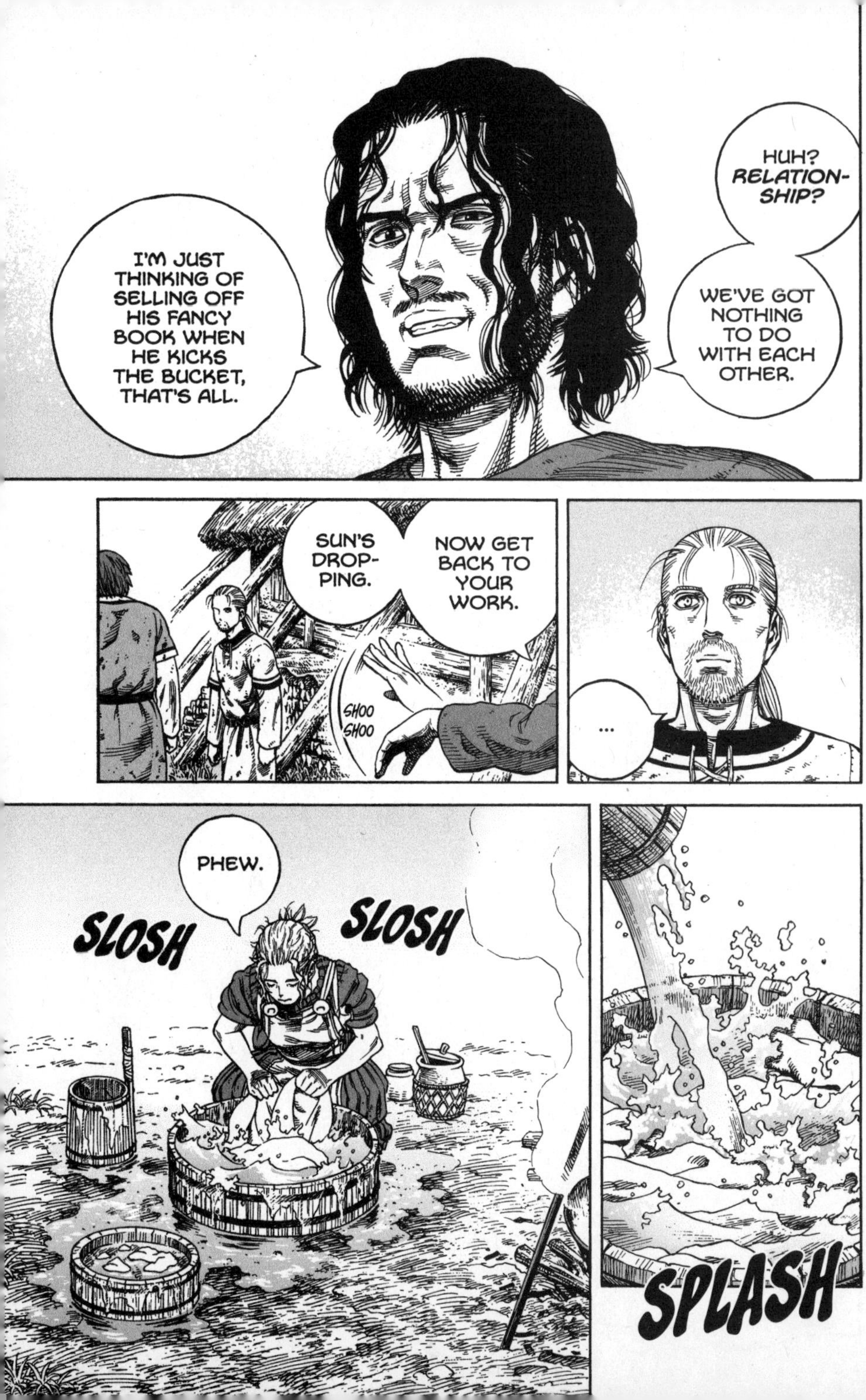
HUH? RELATIONSHIP?
WE'VE GOT NOTHING TO DO WITH EACH OTHER.
I'M JUST THINKING OF SELLING OFF HIS FANCY BOOK WHEN HE KICKS THE BUCKET, THAT'S ALL.
...
NOW GET BACK TO YOUR WORK.
SUN'S DROPPING.
SHOO SHOO
SPLASH
SLOSH
PHEW.
SLOSH

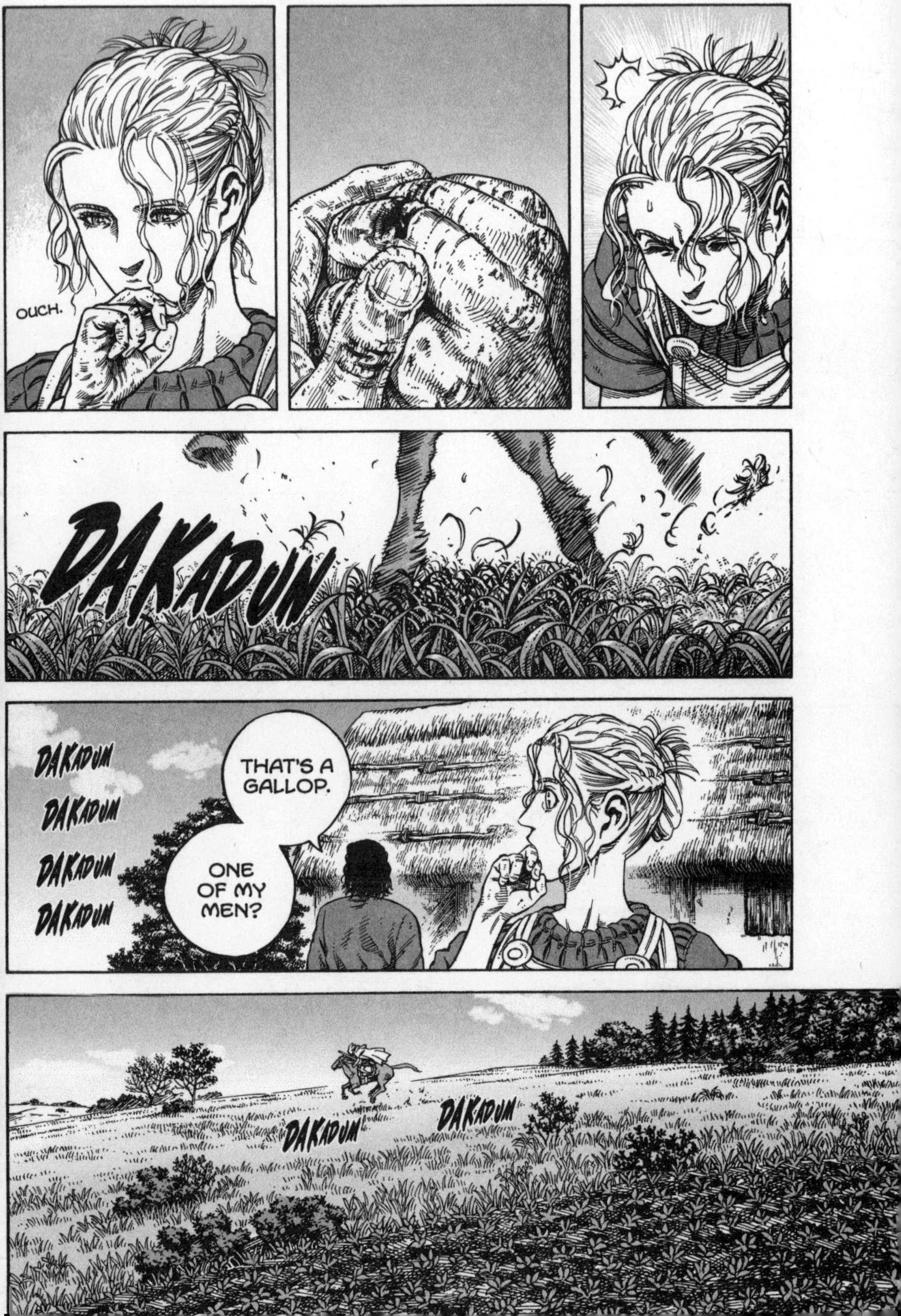
OUCH.
DAKADUN
THAT'S A GALLOP.
ONE OF MY MEN?
DAKADUM
DAKADUM
DAKADUM
DAKADUM
DAKADUM
DAKADUM

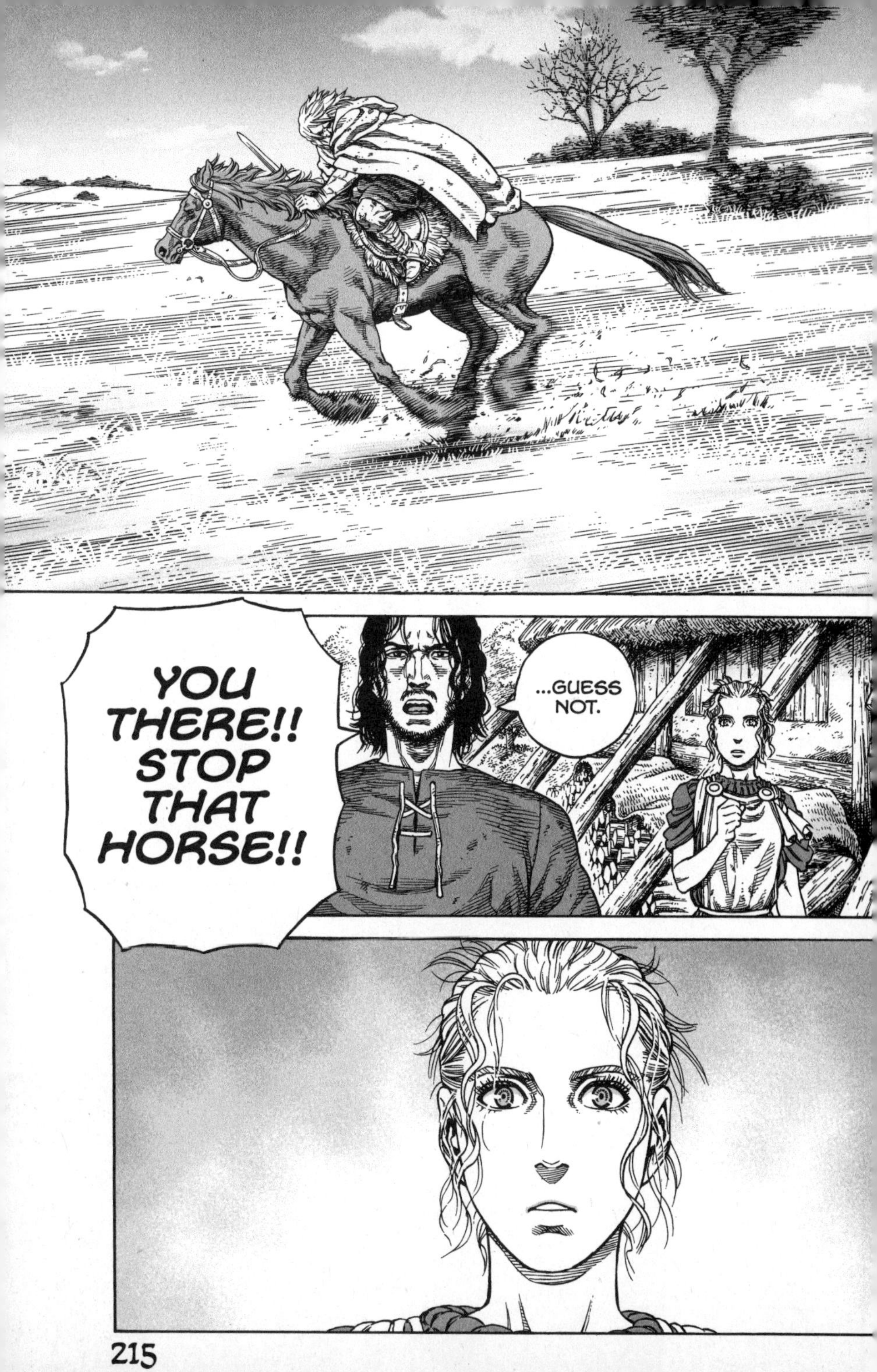
...GUESS NOT.
YOU THERE!! STOP THAT HORSE!!

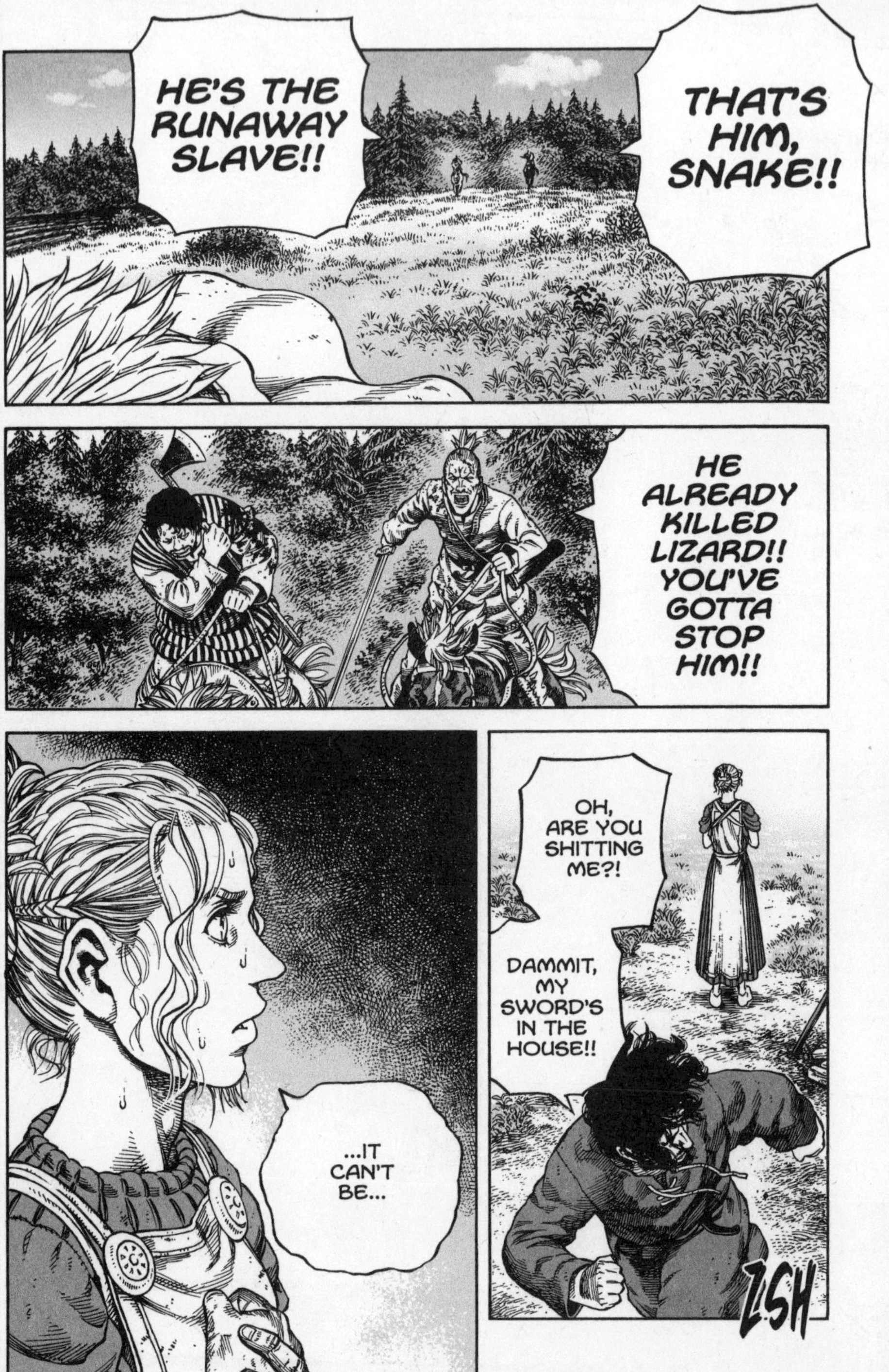
THAT'S HIM, SNAKE!!
HE'S THE RUNAWAY SLAVE!!
HE ALREADY KILLED LIZARD!! YOU'VE GOTTA STOP HIM!!
OH, ARE YOU SHITTING ME?!
DAMMIT, MY SWORD'S IN THE HOUSE!!
ZSH
...IT CAN'T BE...

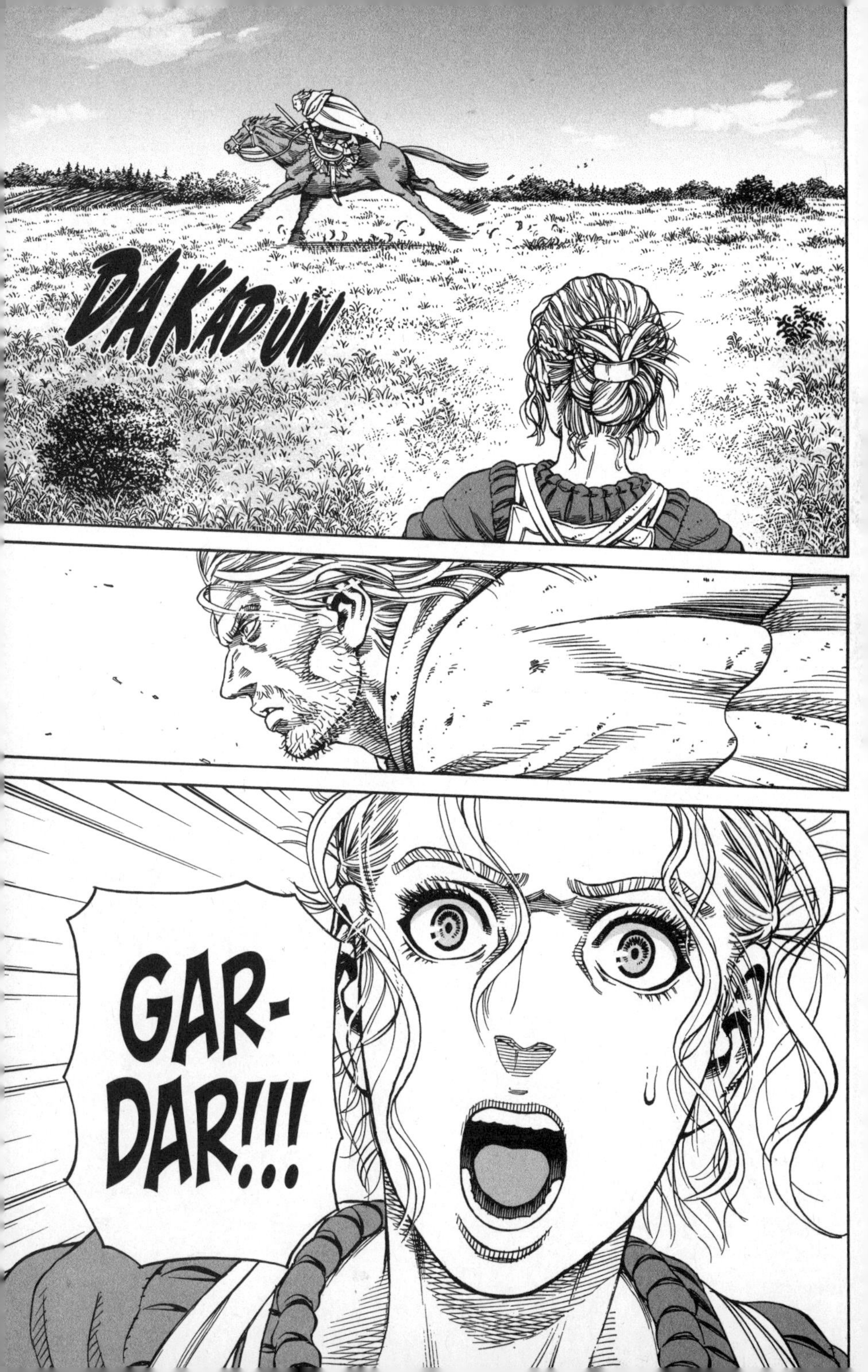
DAKADUN
GAR-
DAR!!!

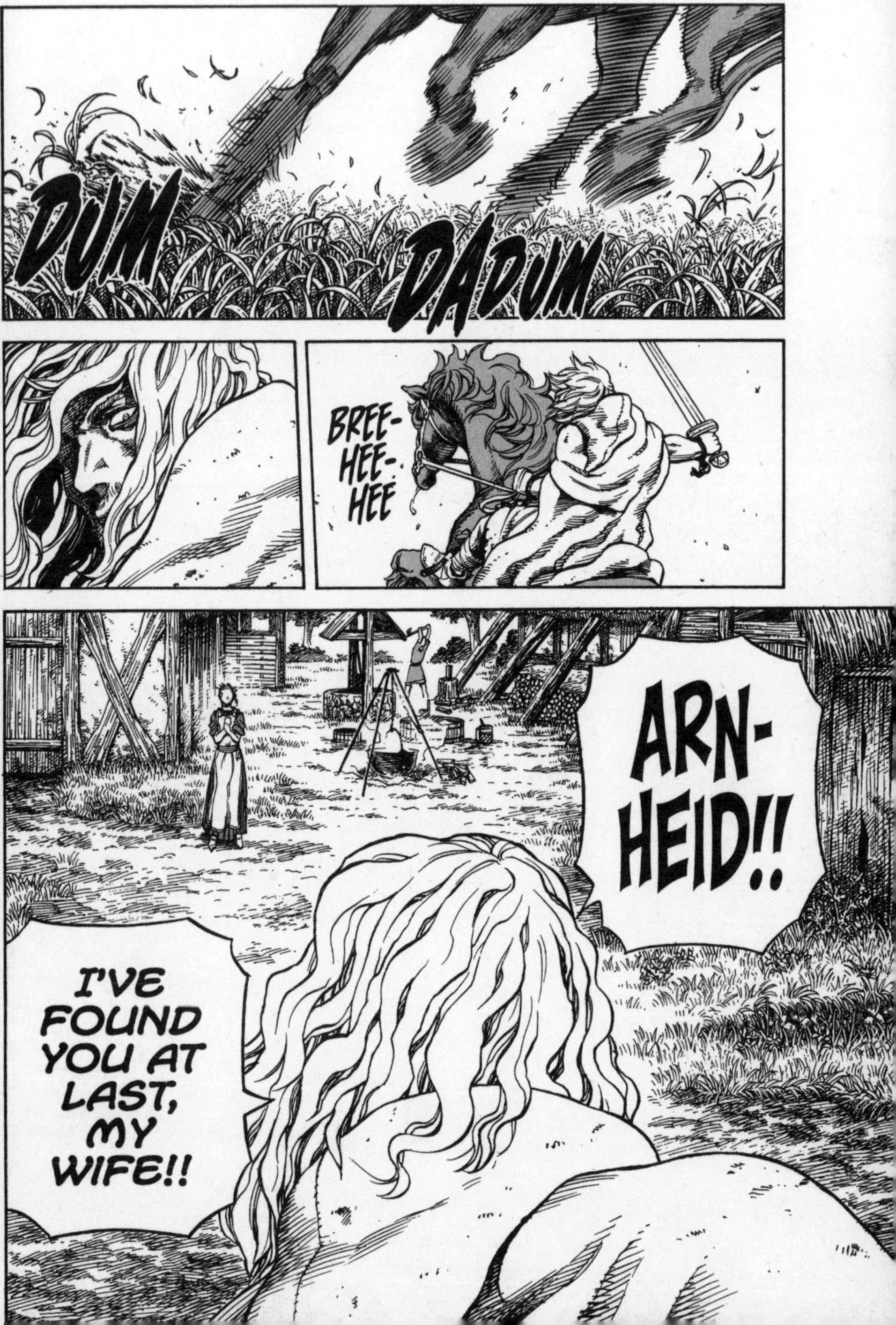
DUM
DADUM
BREE-HEE-HEE
ARN-HEID!!
I'VE FOUND YOU AT LAST, MY WIFE!!

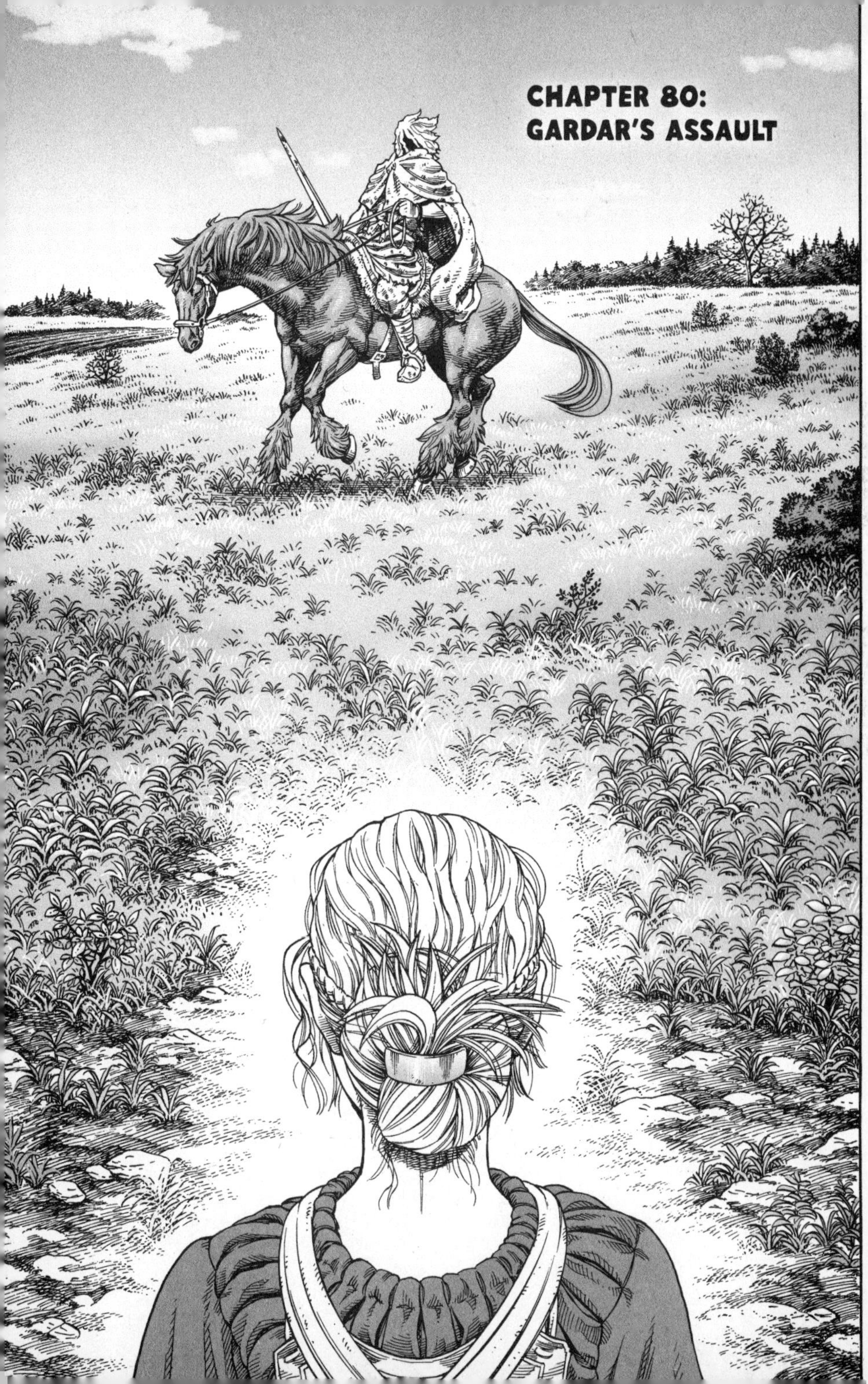
CHAPTER 80:
GARDAR'S ASSAULT

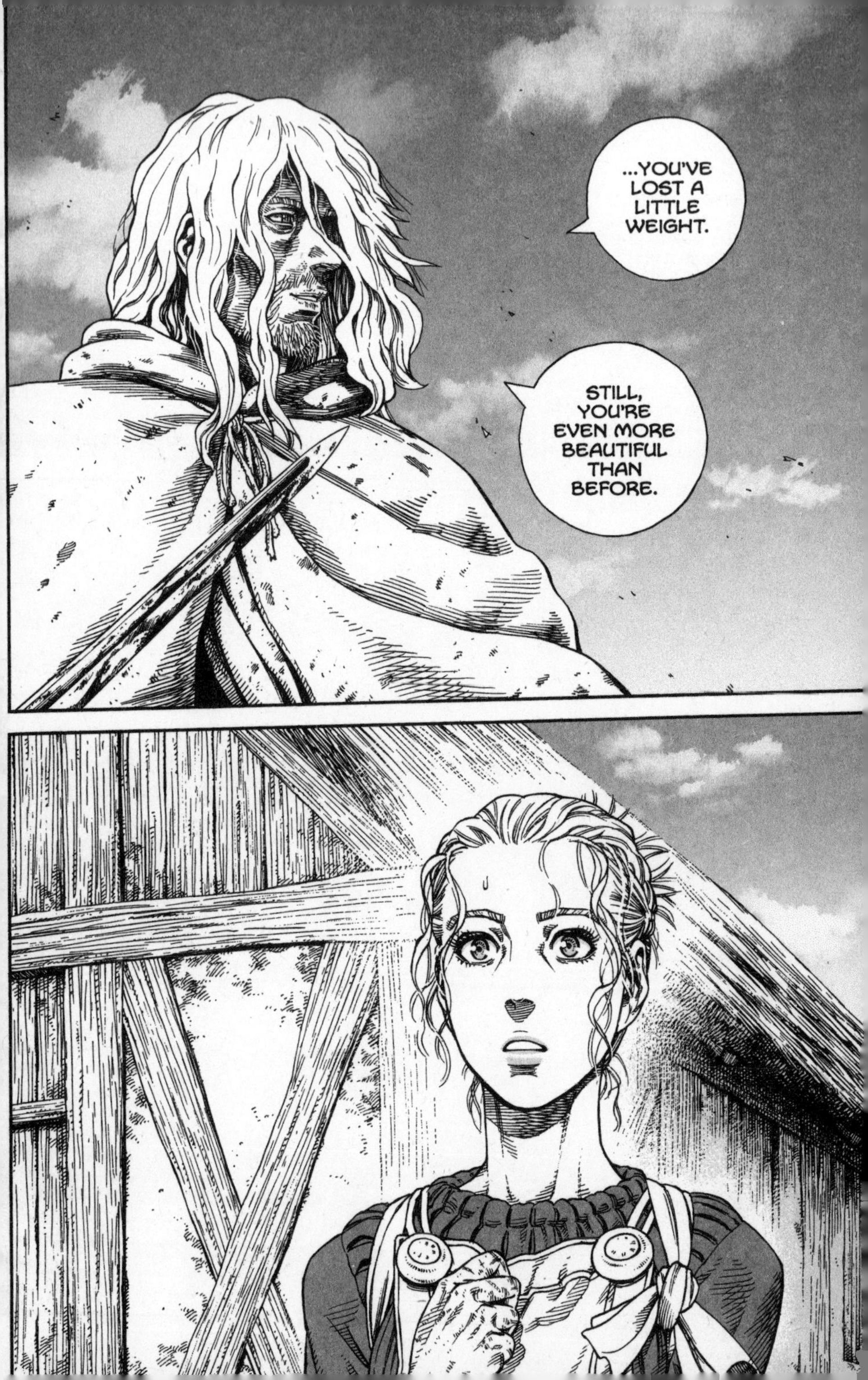
...YOU'VE LOST A LITTLE WEIGHT.
STILL, YOU'RE EVEN MORE BEAUTIFUL THAN BEFORE.

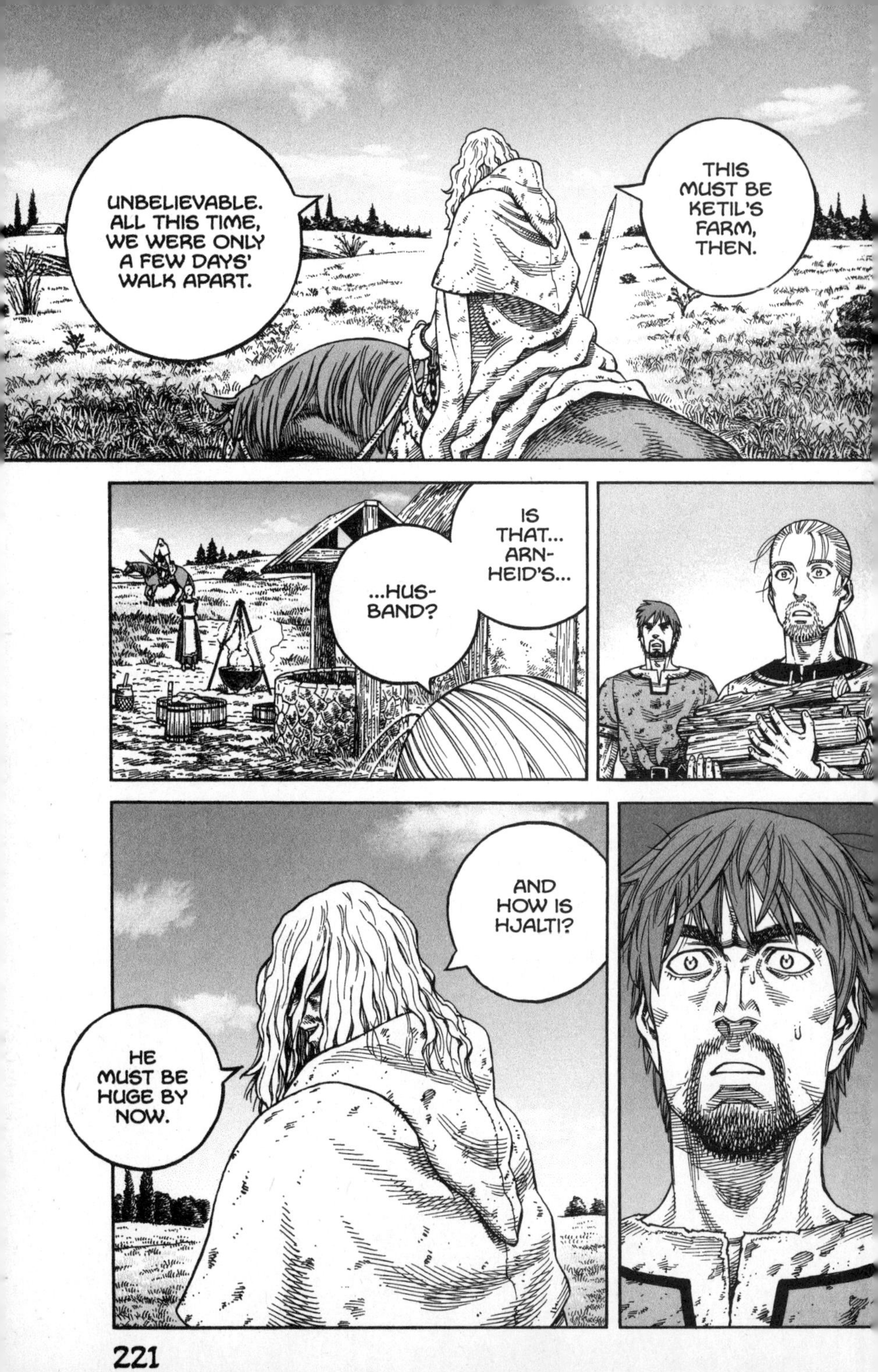
THIS MUST BE KETIL'S FARM, THEN.
UNBELIEVABLE. ALL THIS TIME, WE WERE ONLY A FEW DAYS' WALK APART.
IS THAT... ARN-HEID'S...
...HUS-BAND?
AND HOW IS HJALTI?
HE MUST BE HUGE BY NOW.

HJALTI IS...

...GARDAR...

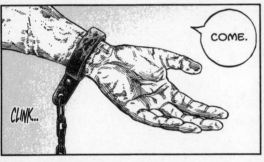

COME.

CLINK...

SHUK

SHLOP

LET'S GO BACK HOME.

THE THREE OF US.

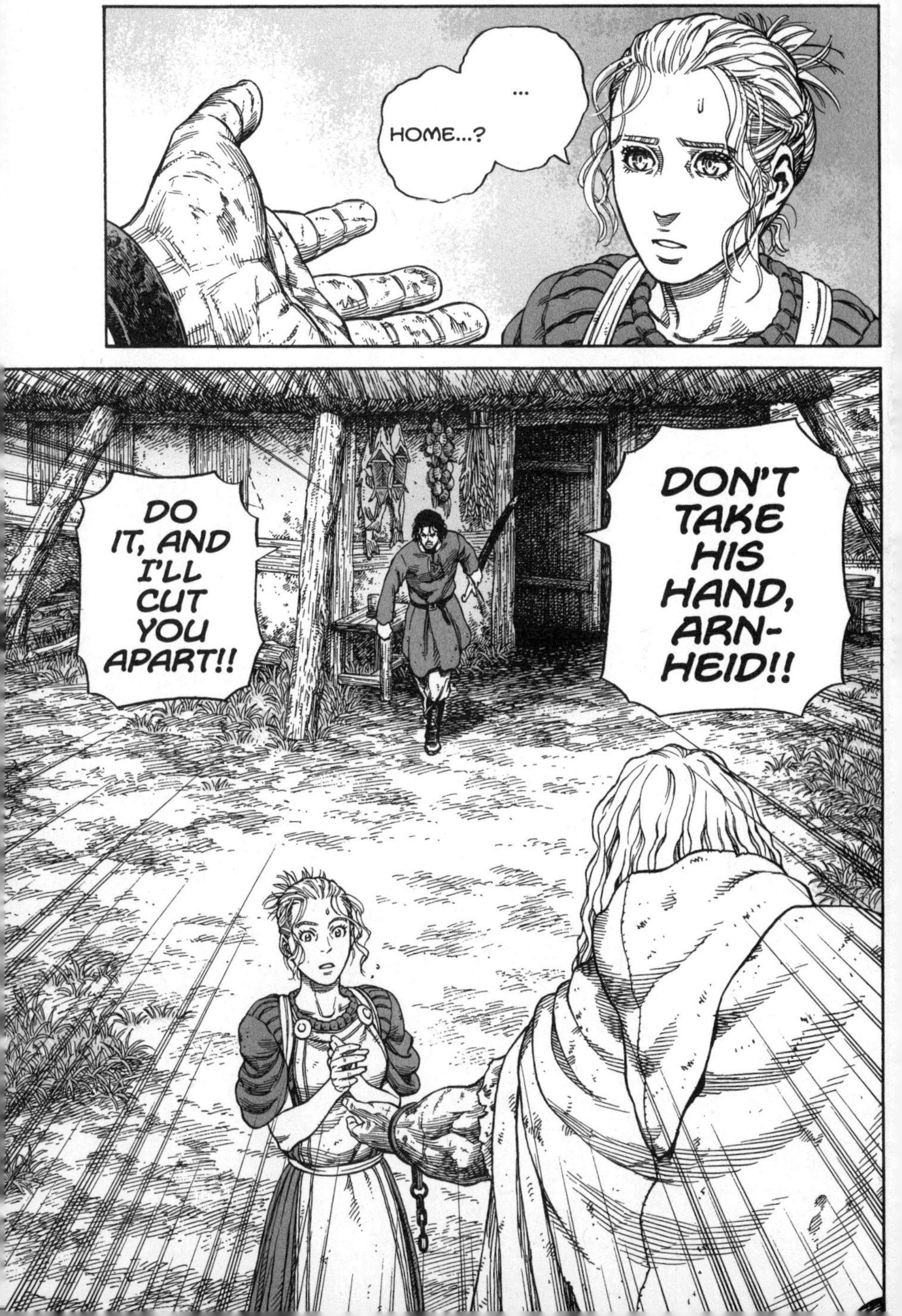
... HOME...?
DON'T TAKE HIS HAND, ARN-HEID!!
DO IT, AND I'LL CUT YOU APART!!

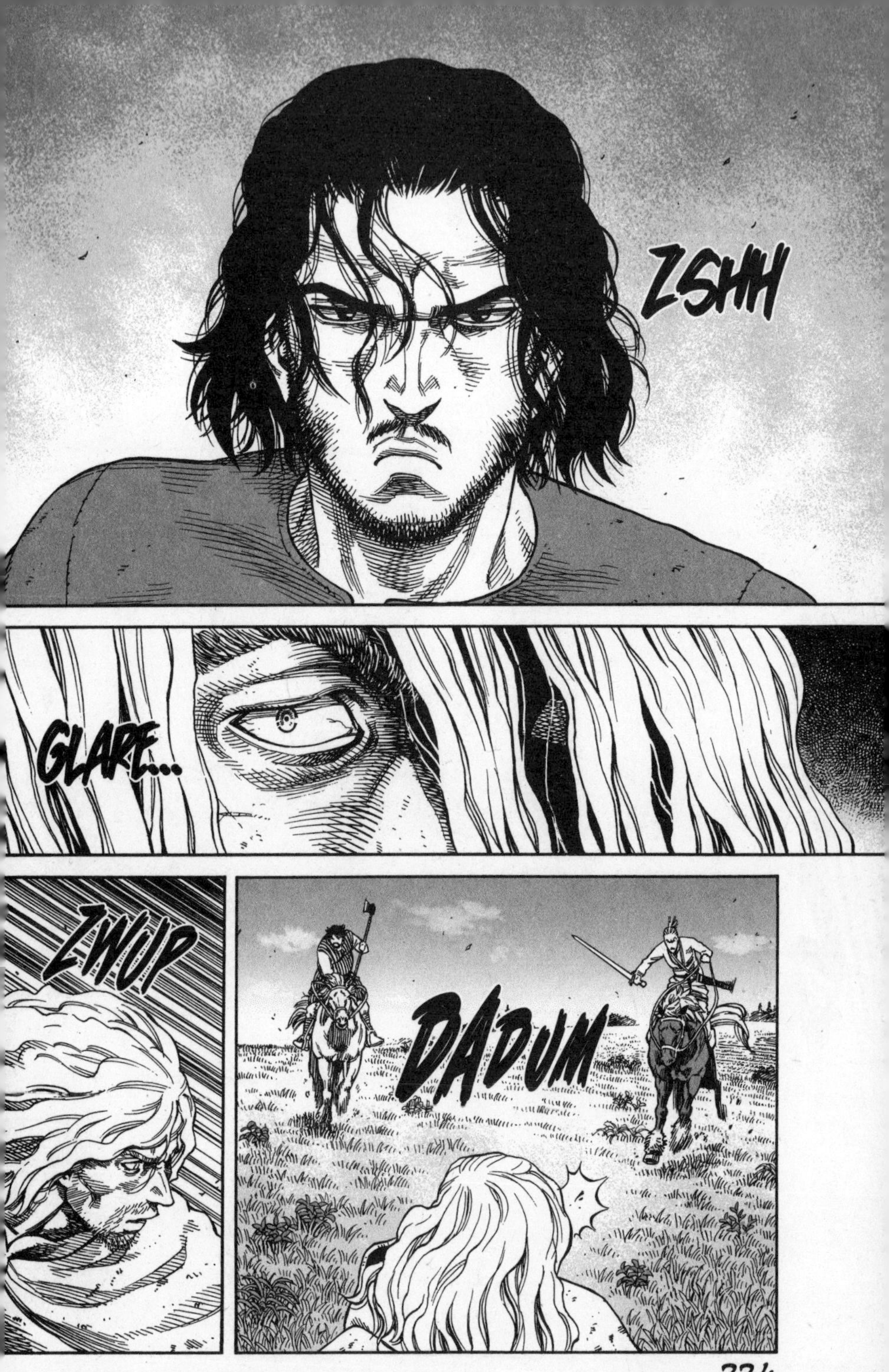
ZSHH
GLARE...
DADUM
ZWUP

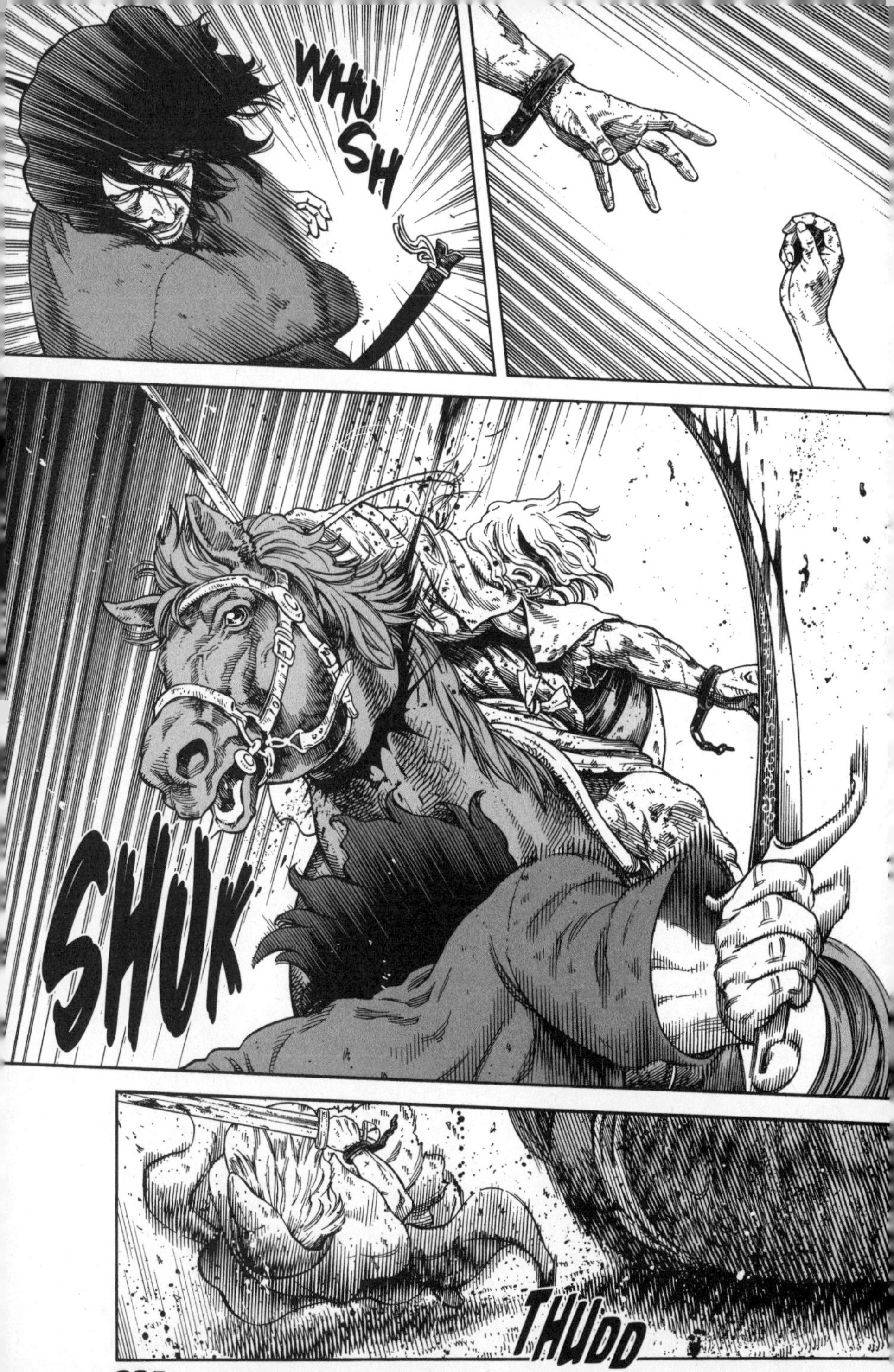
WHUSH
SHUK
THUDD

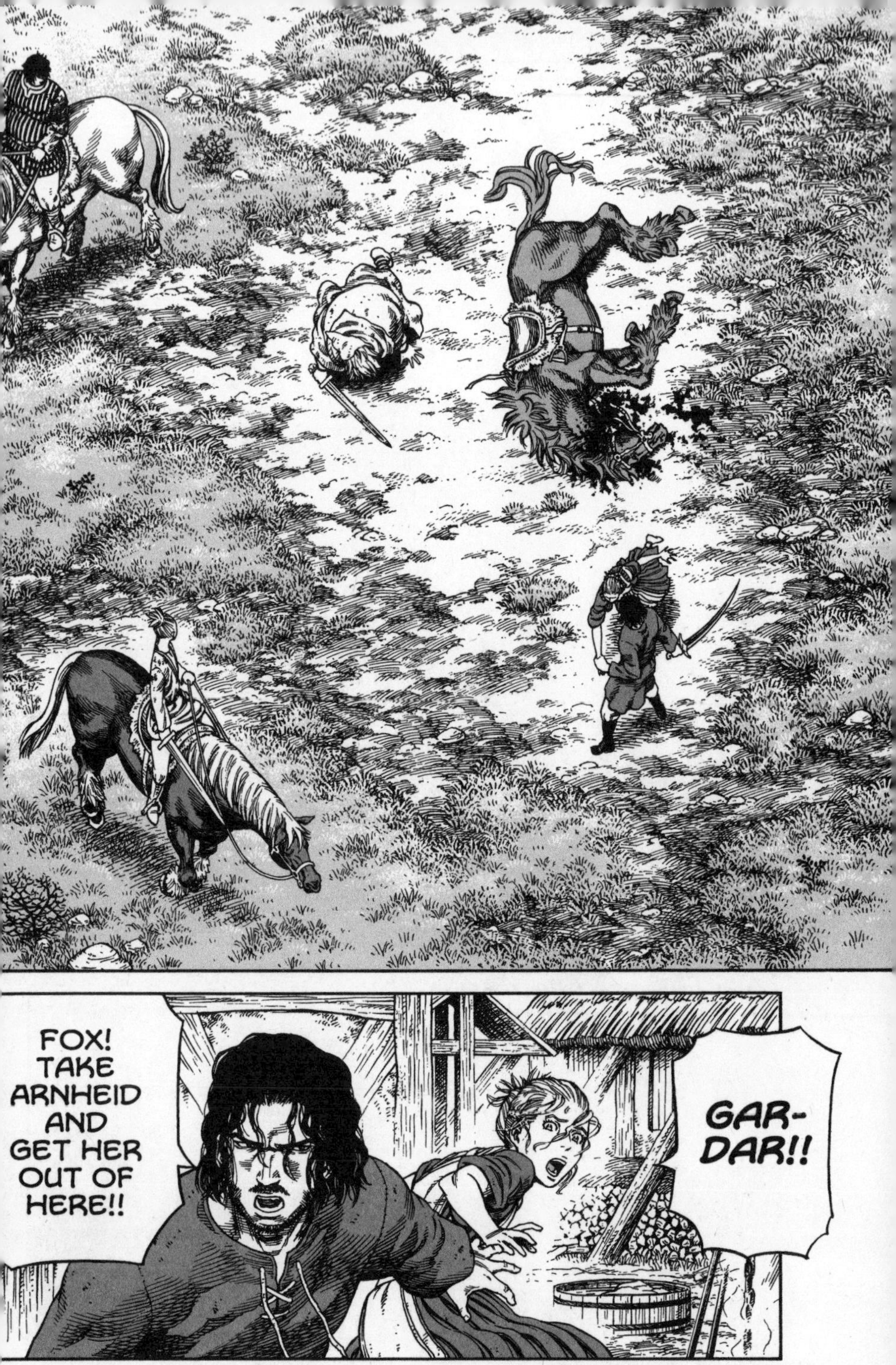
GAR-DAR!!
FOX! TAKE ARNHEID AND GET HER OUT OF HERE!!

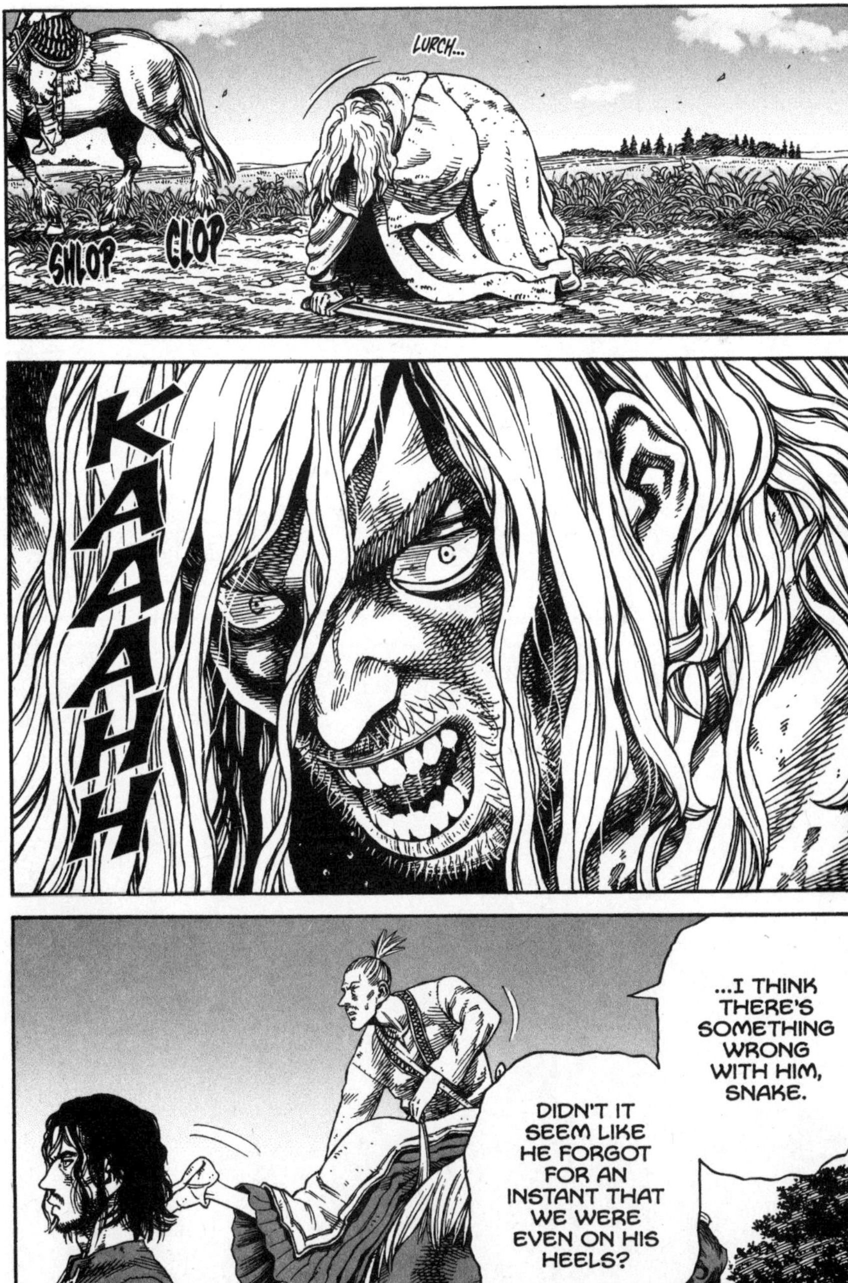
LURCH...
CLOP
SHLOP
KAAAAHH
...I THINK THERE'S SOMETHING WRONG WITH HIM, SNAKE.
DIDN'T IT SEEM LIKE HE FORGOT FOR AN INSTANT THAT WE WERE EVEN ON HIS HEELS?

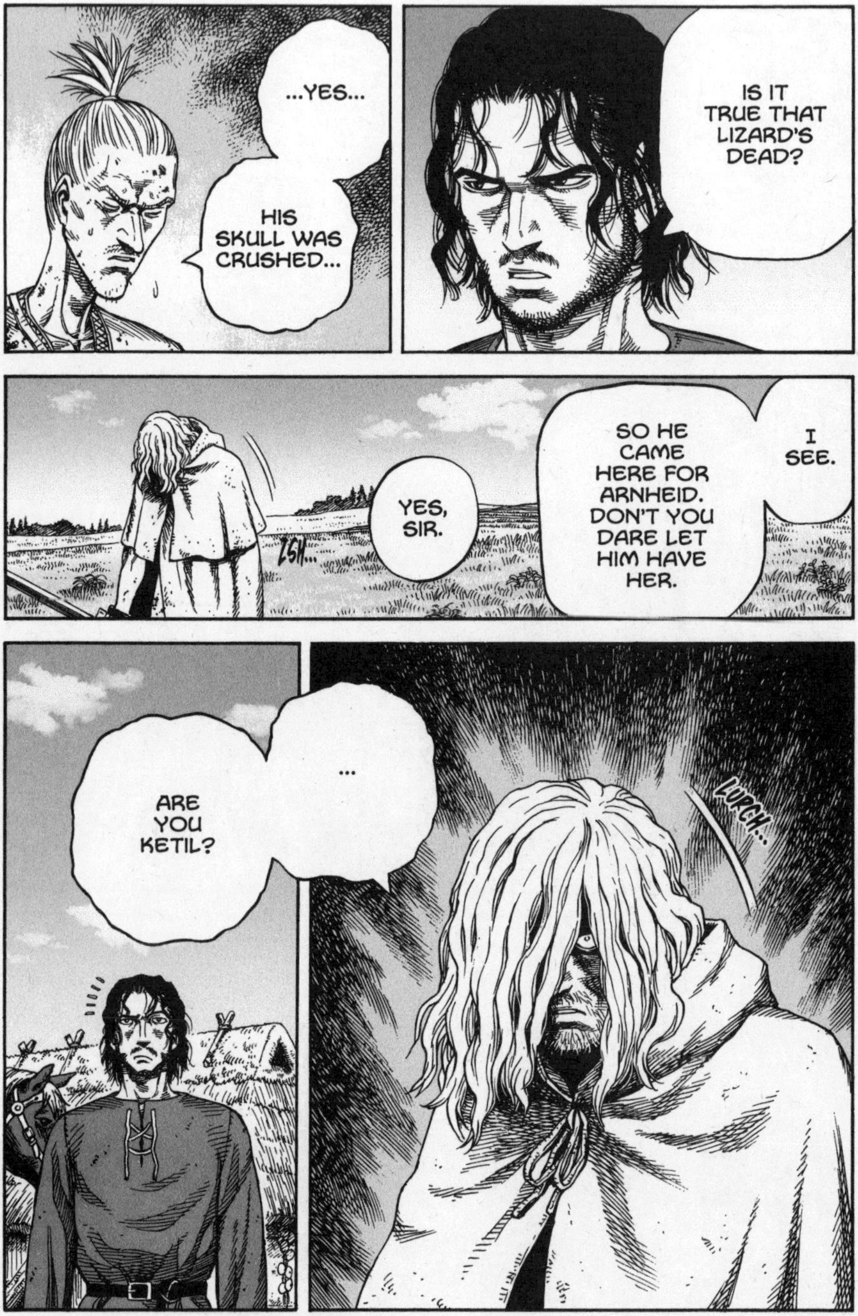
IS IT TRUE THAT LIZARD'S DEAD?
...YES...
HIS SKULL WAS CRUSHED...
I SEE.
SO HE CAME HERE FOR ARNHEID. DON'T YOU DARE LET HIM HAVE HER.
YES, SIR.
LURCH...
...
ARE YOU KETIL?

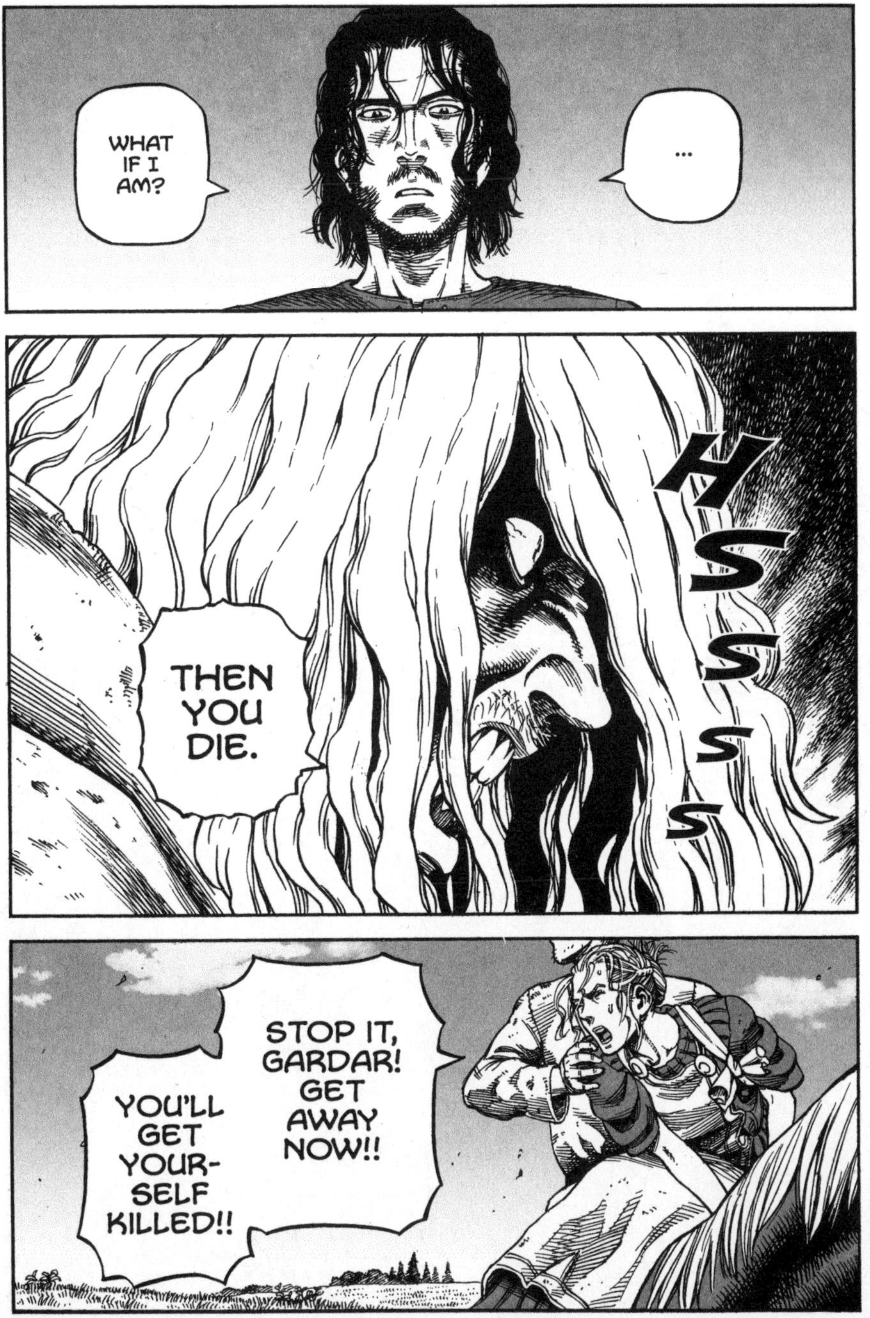
...
WHAT IF I AM?
HSSSS
THEN YOU DIE.
STOP IT, GARDAR! GET AWAY NOW!!
YOU'LL GET YOUR-SELF KILLED!!

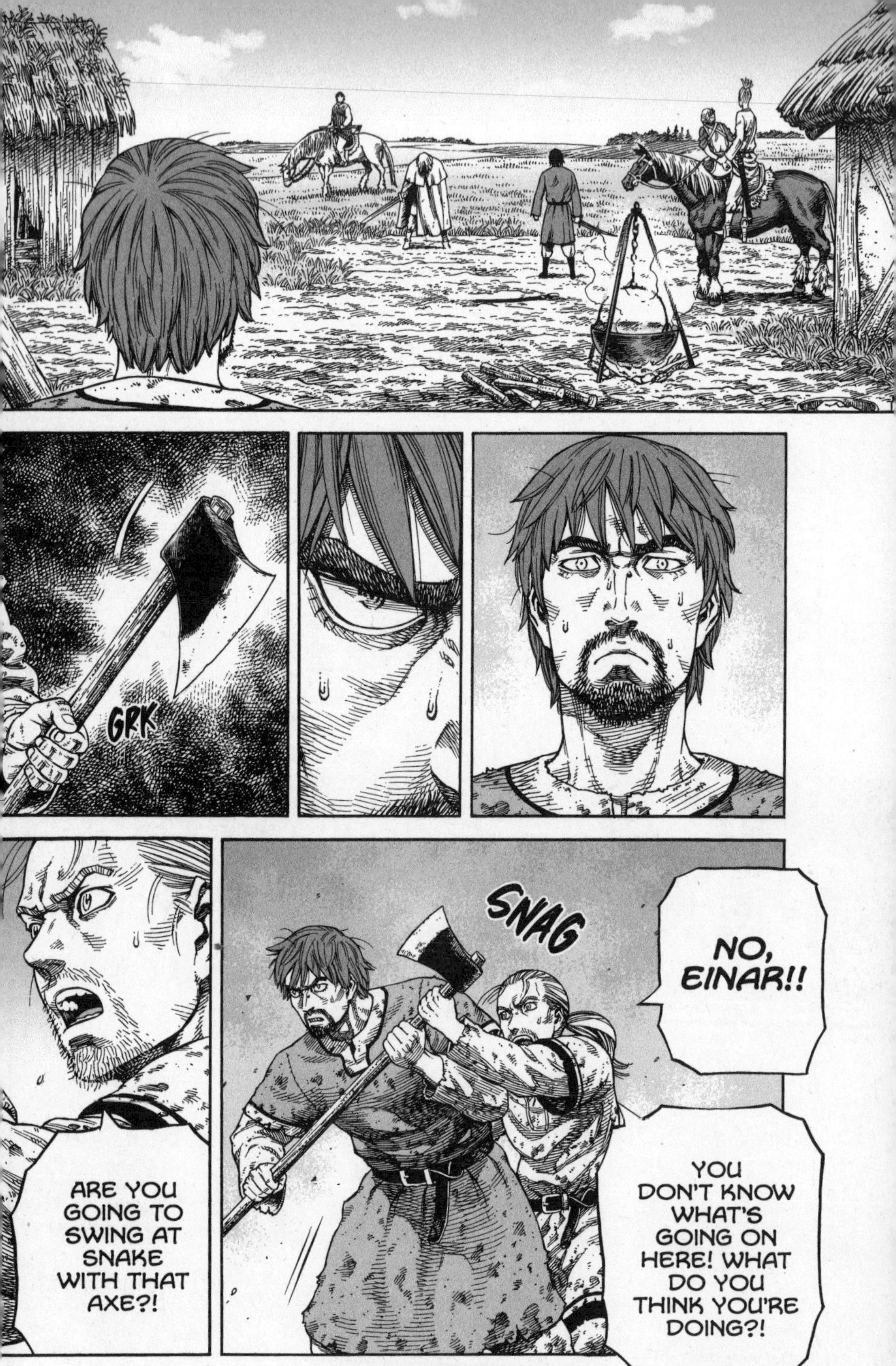
GRK
NO, EINAR!!
SNAG
YOU DON'T KNOW WHAT'S GOING ON HERE! WHAT DO YOU THINK YOU'RE DOING?!
ARE YOU GOING TO SWING AT SNAKE WITH THAT AXE?!

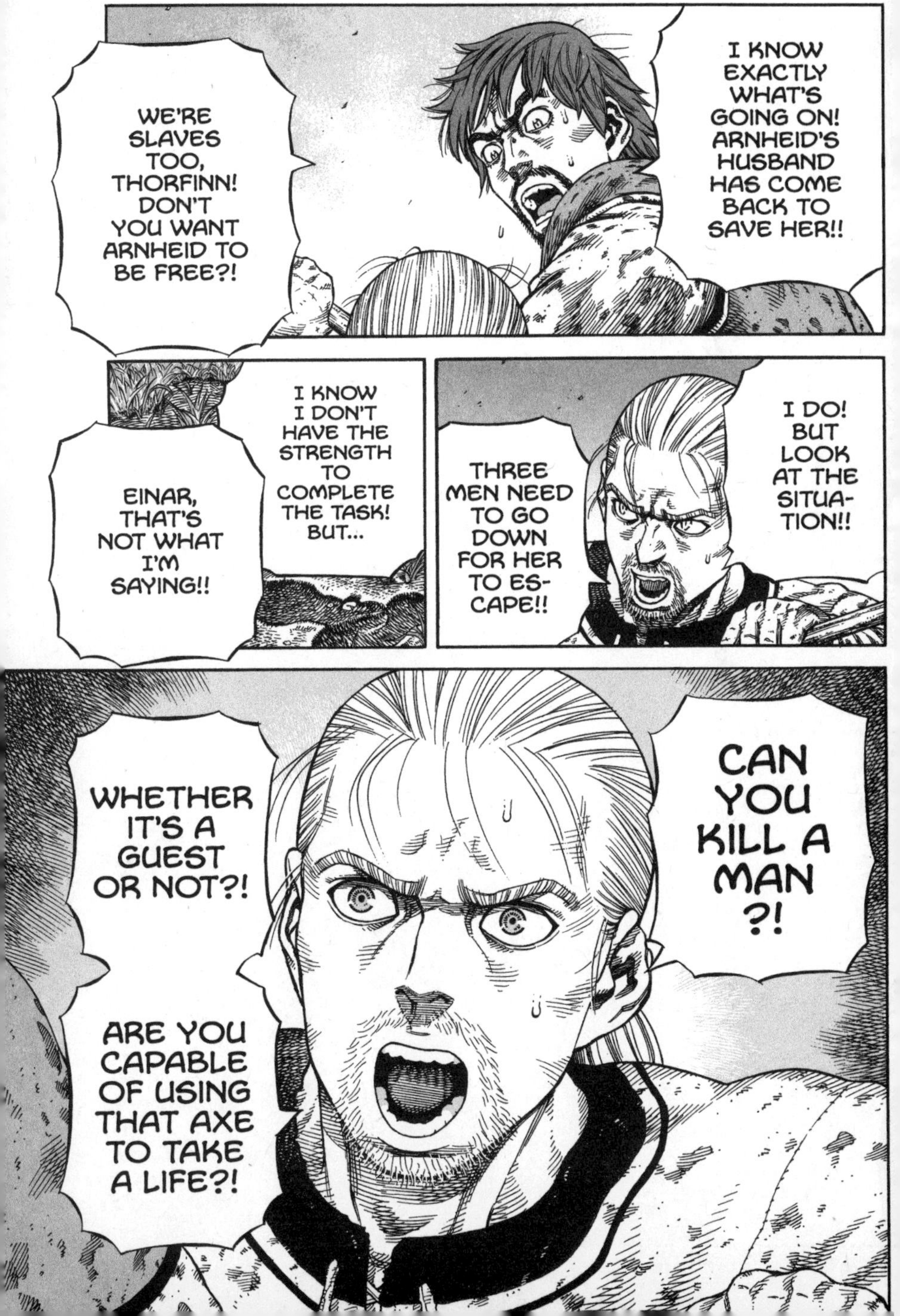
I KNOW EXACTLY WHAT'S GOING ON! ARNHEID'S HUSBAND HAS COME BACK TO SAVE HER!!
WE'RE SLAVES TOO, THORFINN! DON'T YOU WANT ARNHEID TO BE FREE?!
I DO! BUT LOOK AT THE SITUATION!!
THREE MEN NEED TO GO DOWN FOR HER TO ESCAPE!!
I KNOW I DON'T HAVE THE STRENGTH TO COMPLETE THE TASK! BUT...
EINAR, THAT'S NOT WHAT I'M SAYING!!
CAN YOU KILL A MAN?!
WHETHER IT'S A GUEST OR NOT?!
ARE YOU CAPABLE OF USING THAT AXE TO TAKE A LIFE?!

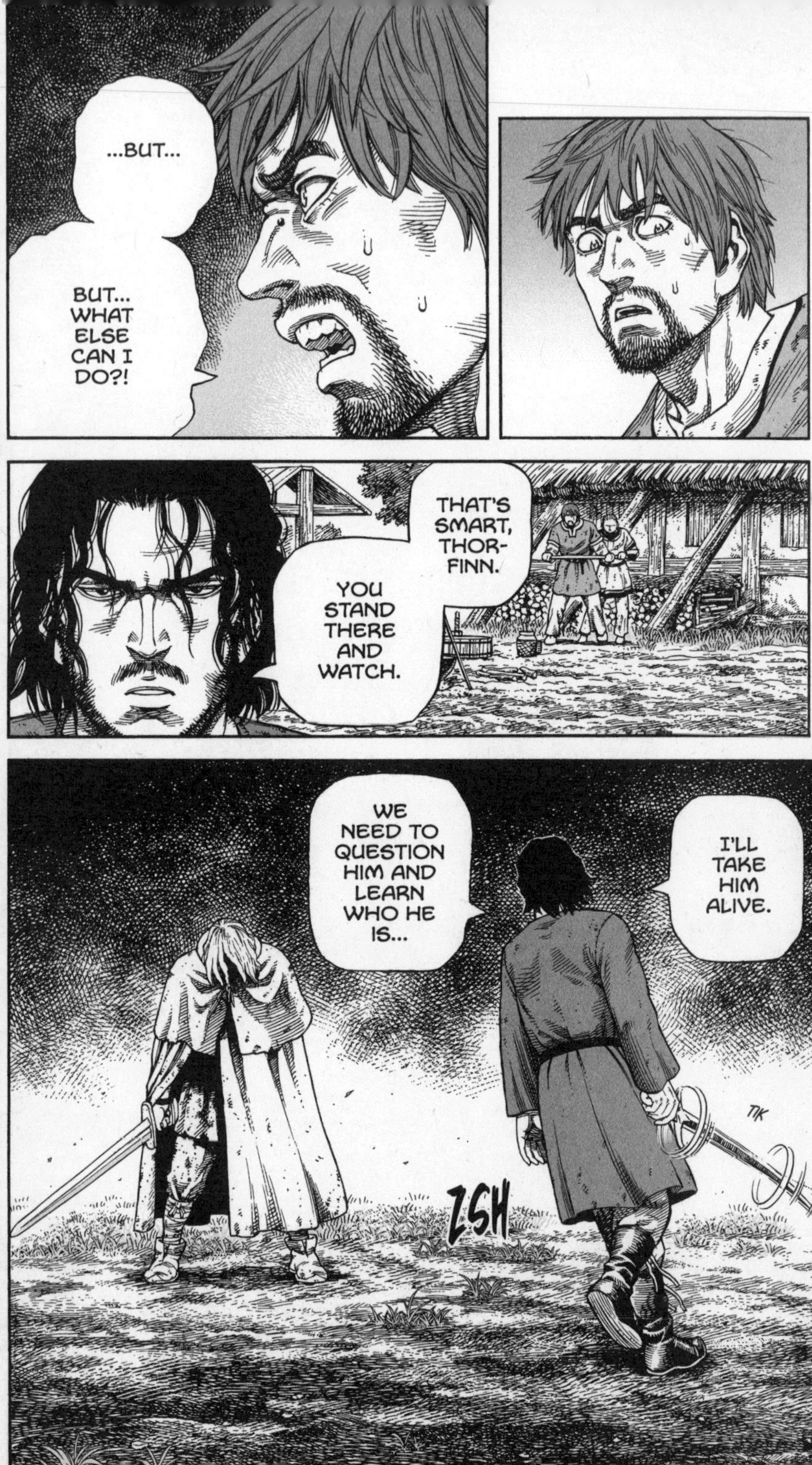
...BUT...
BUT... WHAT ELSE CAN I DO?!
THAT'S SMART, THORFINN.
YOU STAND THERE AND WATCH.
I'LL TAKE HIM ALIVE.
WE NEED TO QUESTION HIM AND LEARN WHO HE IS...
TIK
ZSH

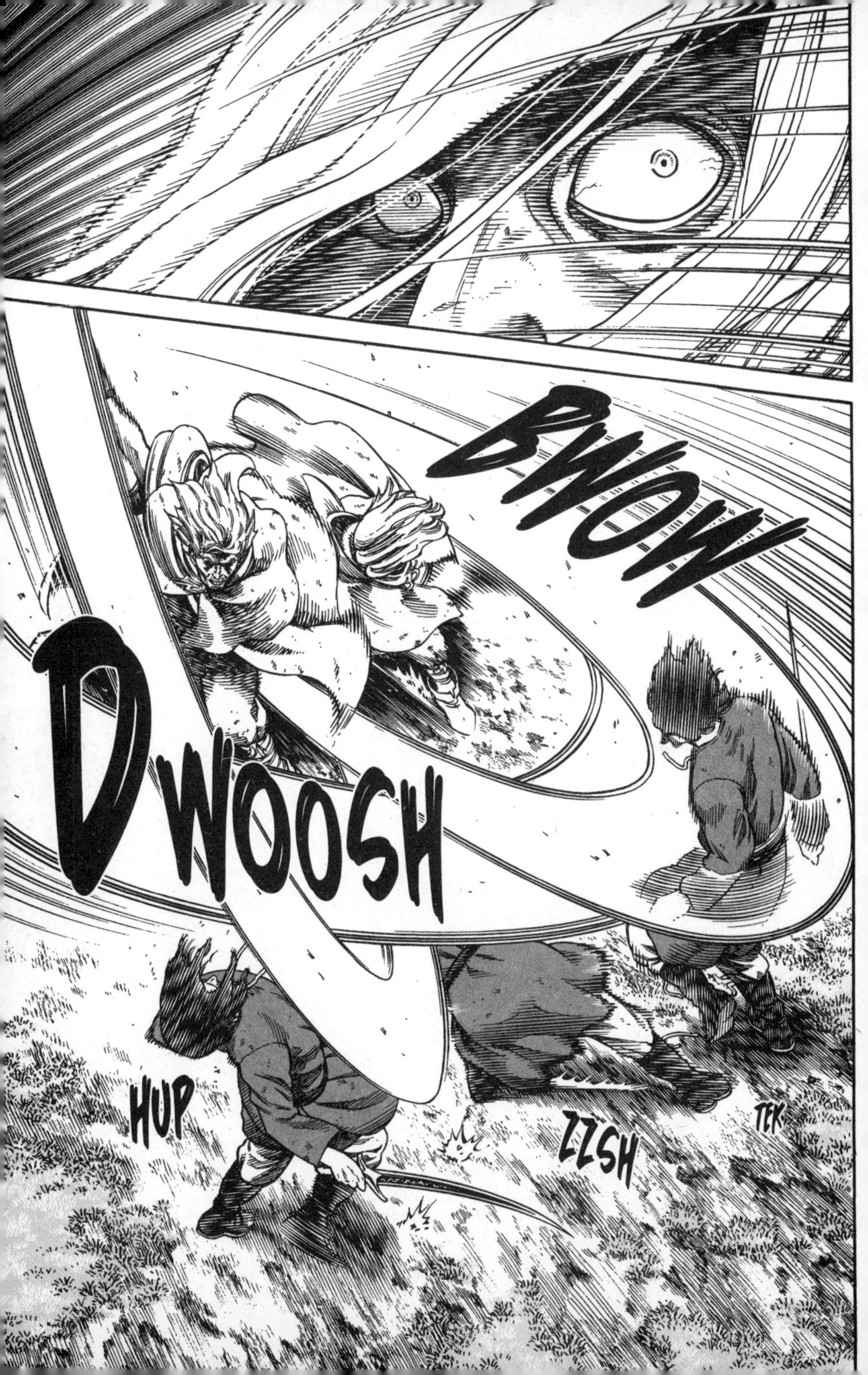
BWOW
DWOOSH
TEK
ZZSH
HUP

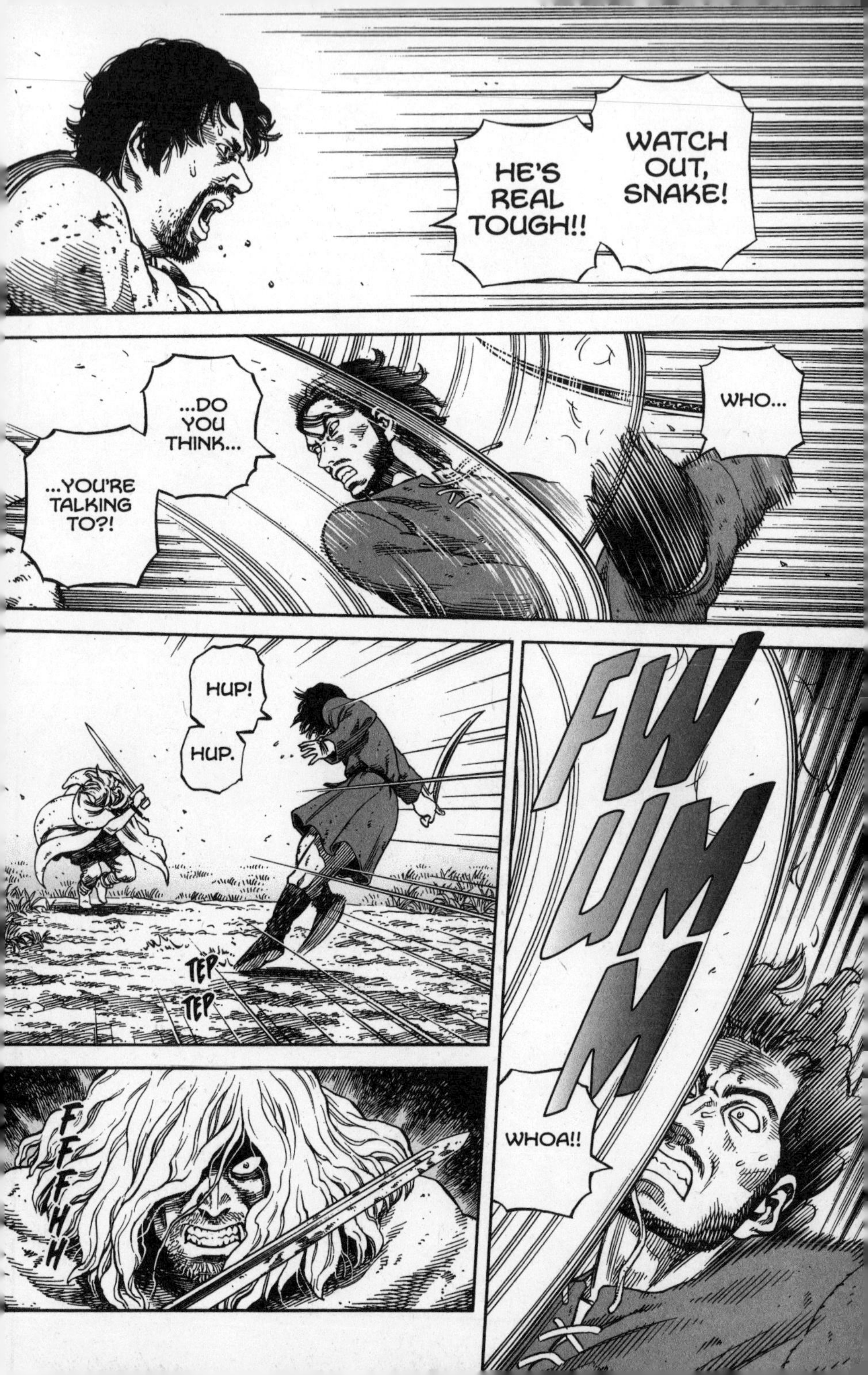
WATCH OUT, SNAKE!
HE'S REAL TOUGH!!
WHO...
...DO YOU THINK...
...YOU'RE TALKING TO?!
FWUMM
WHOA!!
HUP!
HUP.
TEP
TEP
FFFFHH

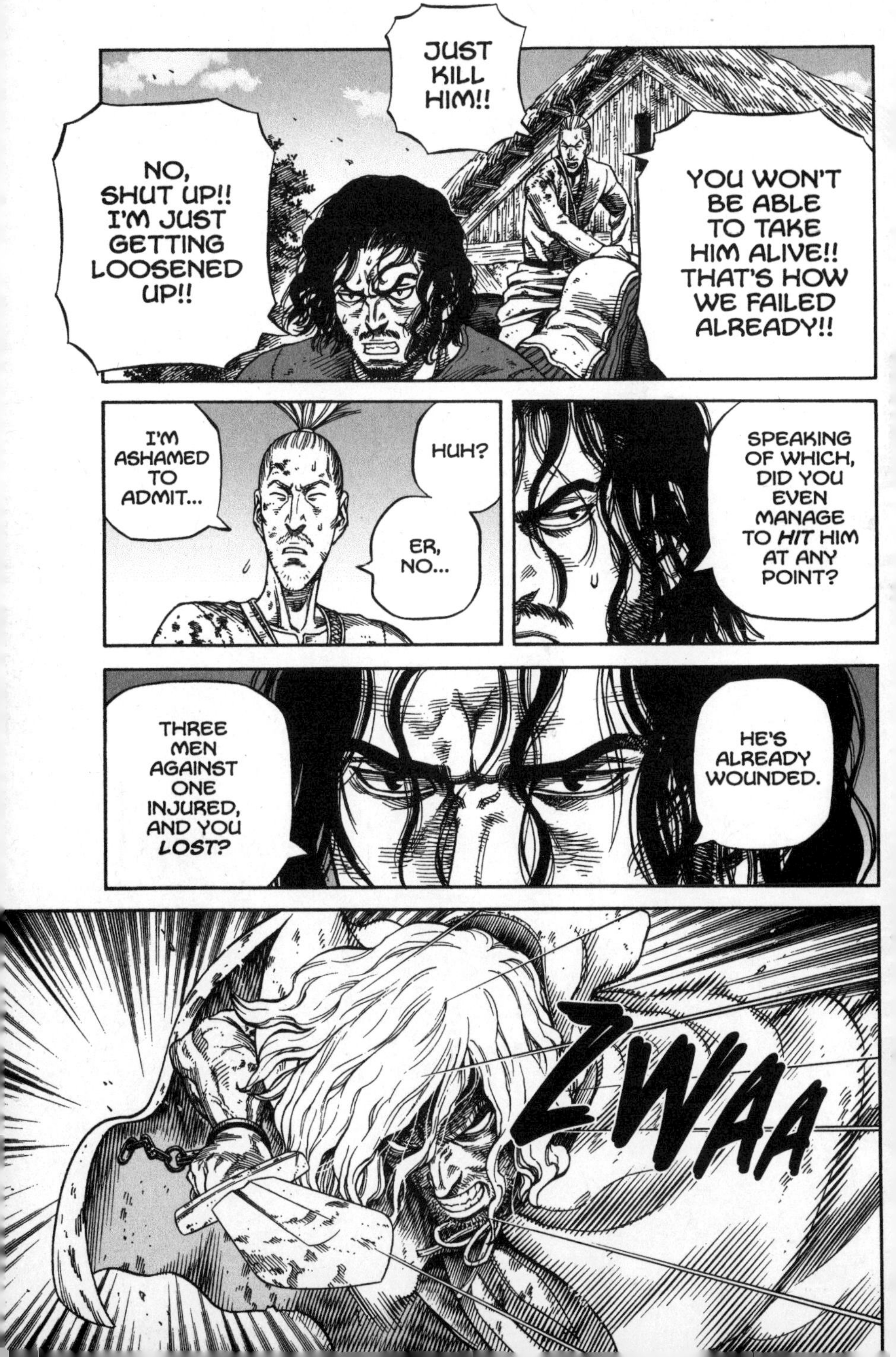
JUST KILL HIM!!
YOU WON'T BE ABLE TO TAKE HIM ALIVE!! THAT'S HOW WE FAILED ALREADY!!
NO, SHUT UP!! I'M JUST GETTING LOOSENED UP!!
SPEAKING OF WHICH, DID YOU EVEN MANAGE TO *HIT* HIM AT ANY POINT?
HUH?
ER, NO...
I'M ASHAMED TO ADMIT...
HE'S ALREADY WOUNDED.
THREE MEN AGAINST ONE INJURED, AND YOU *LOST*?
ZWAA

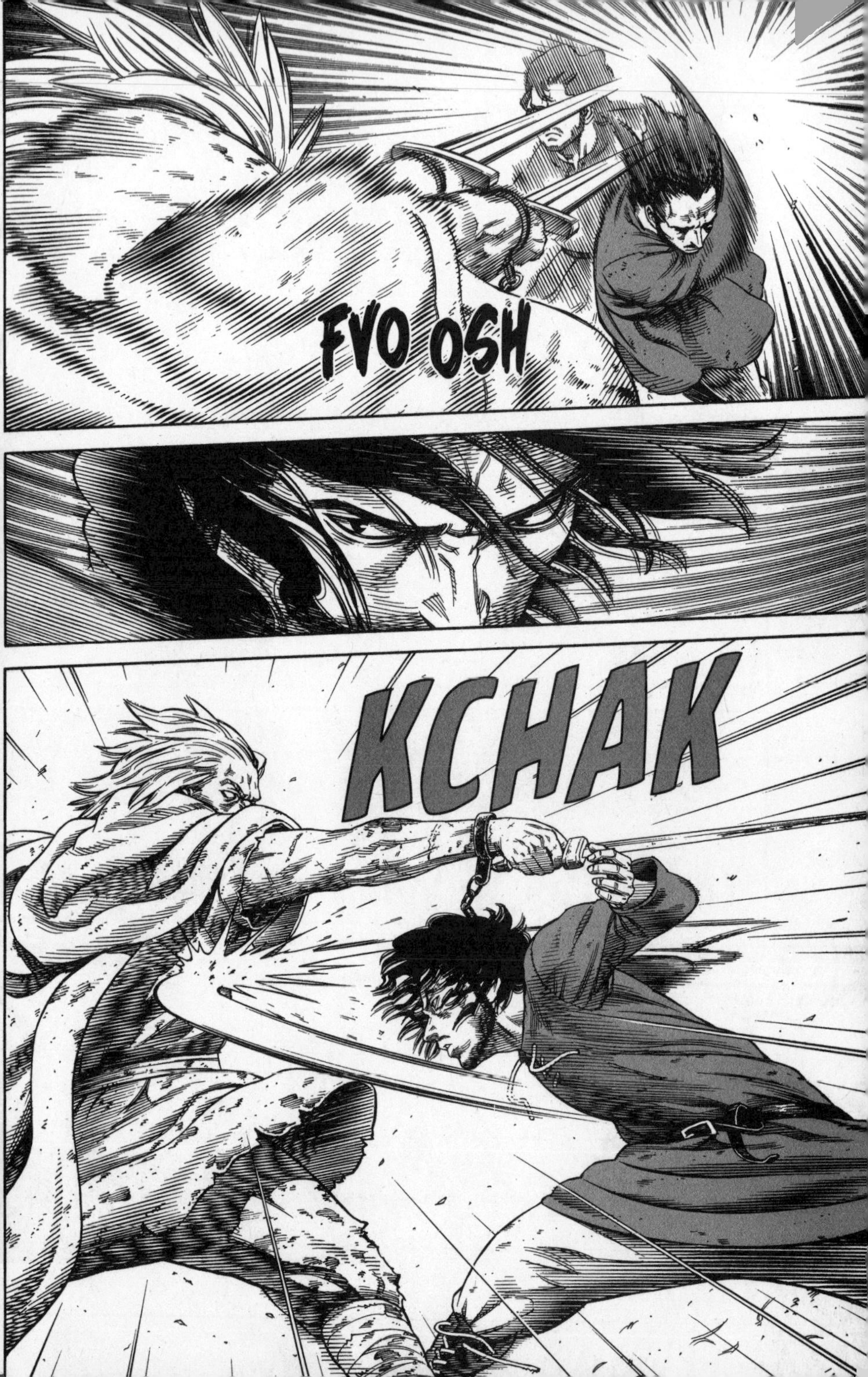
FVO OSH
KCHAK

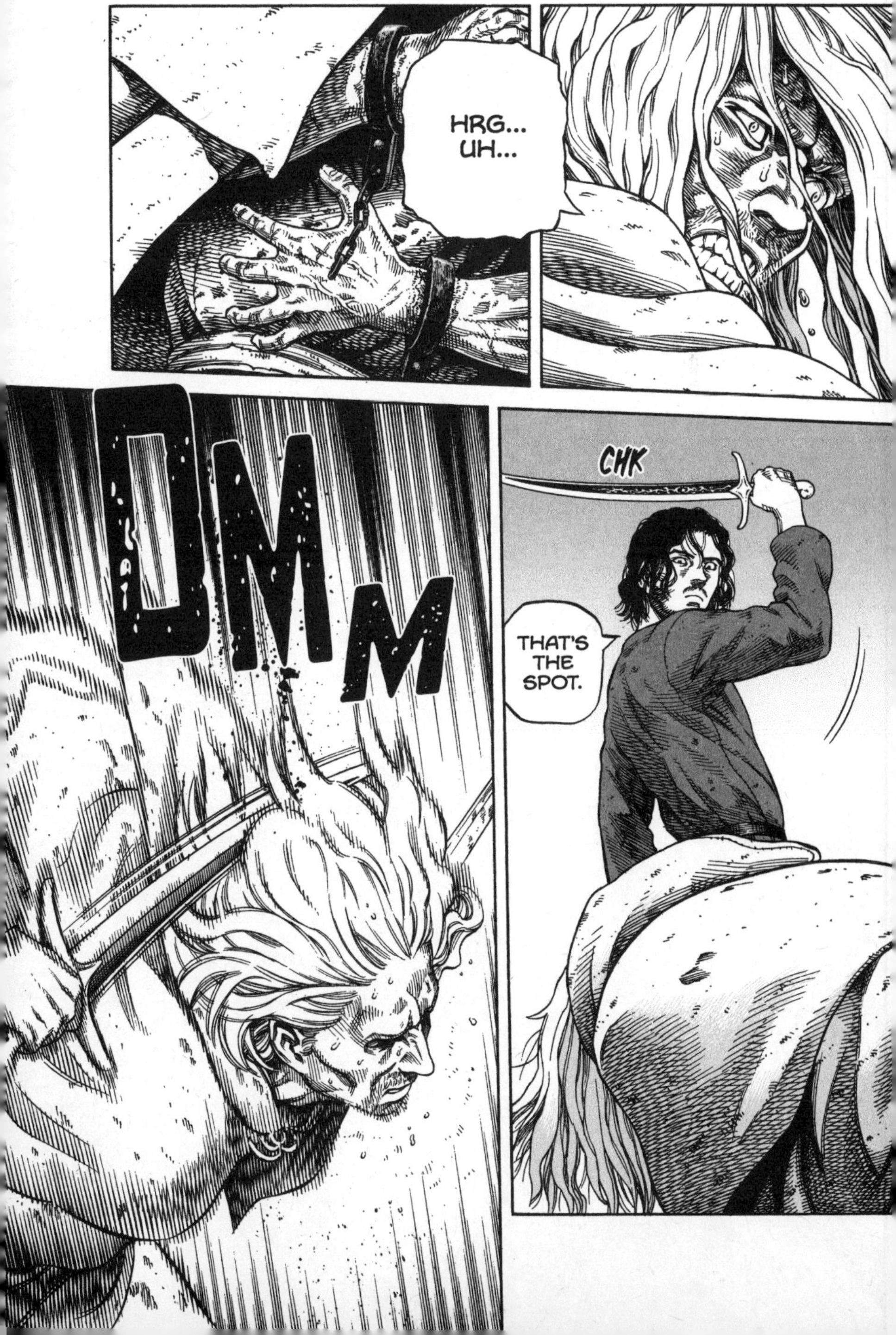
HRG... UH...
CHK
THAT'S THE SPOT.
DMM

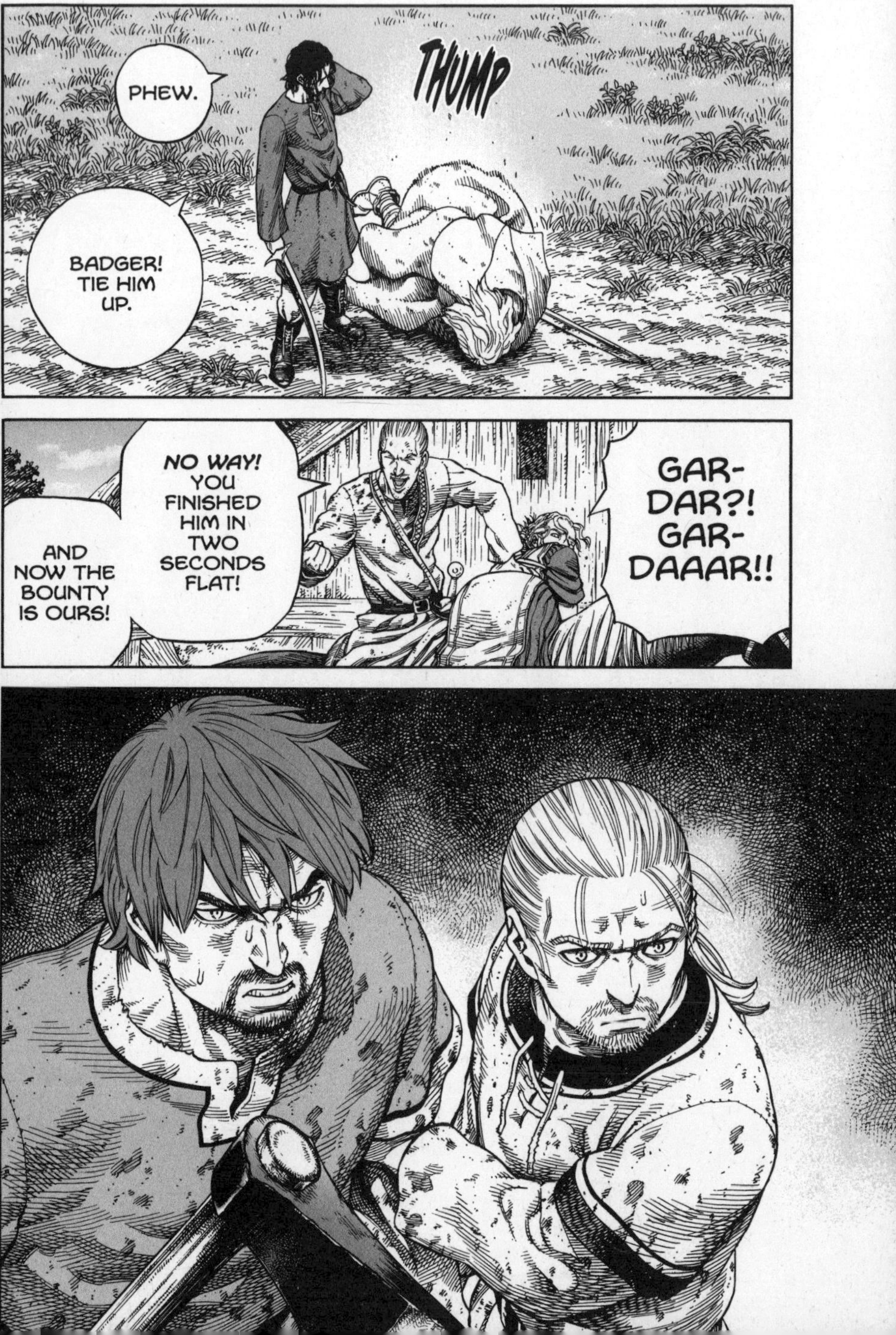
THUMP
PHEW.
BADGER! TIE HIM UP.
GAR-DAR?! GAR-DAAAR!!
NO WAY! YOU FINISHED HIM IN TWO SECONDS FLAT!
AND NOW THE BOUNTY IS OURS!

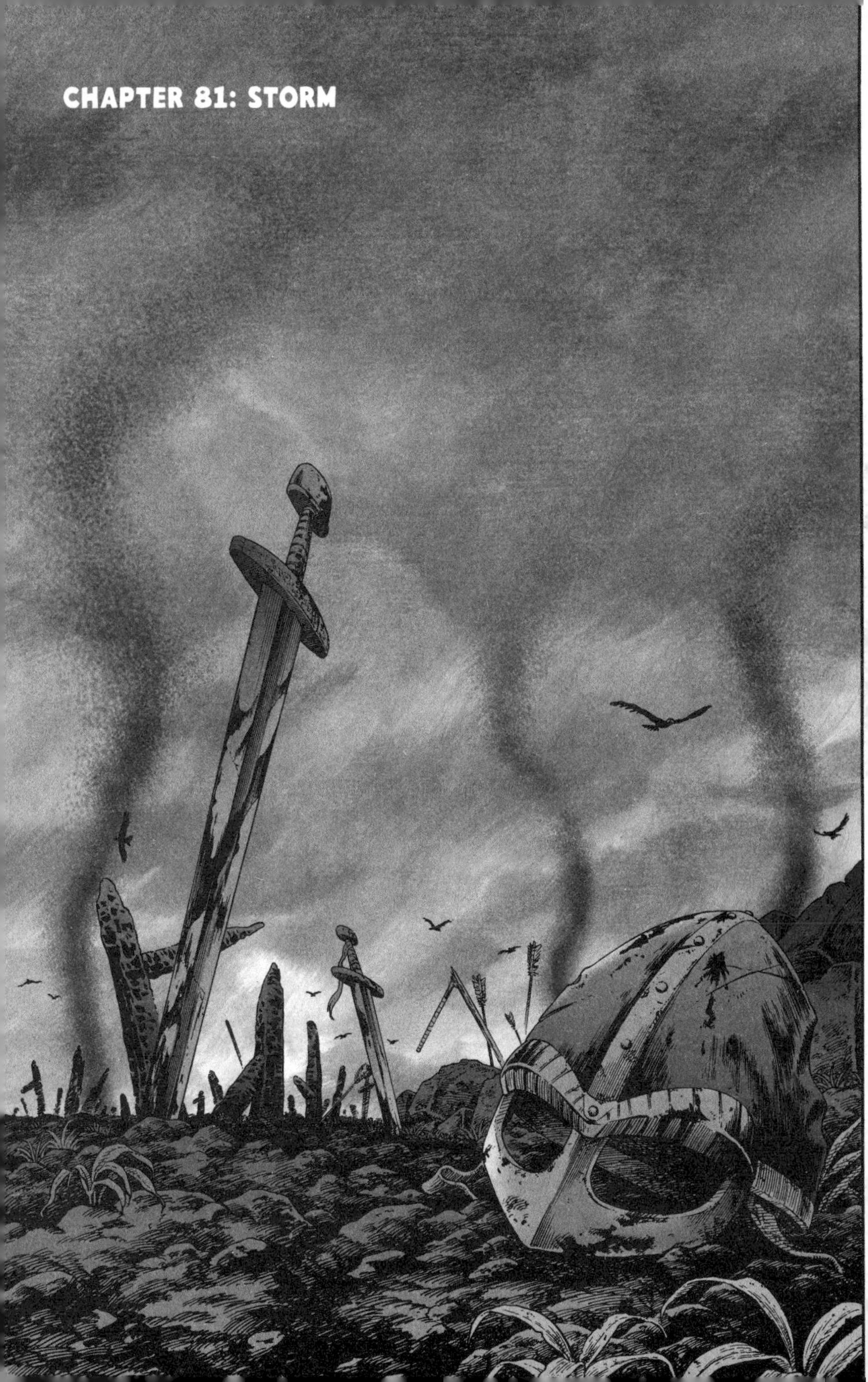
CHAPTER 81: STORM

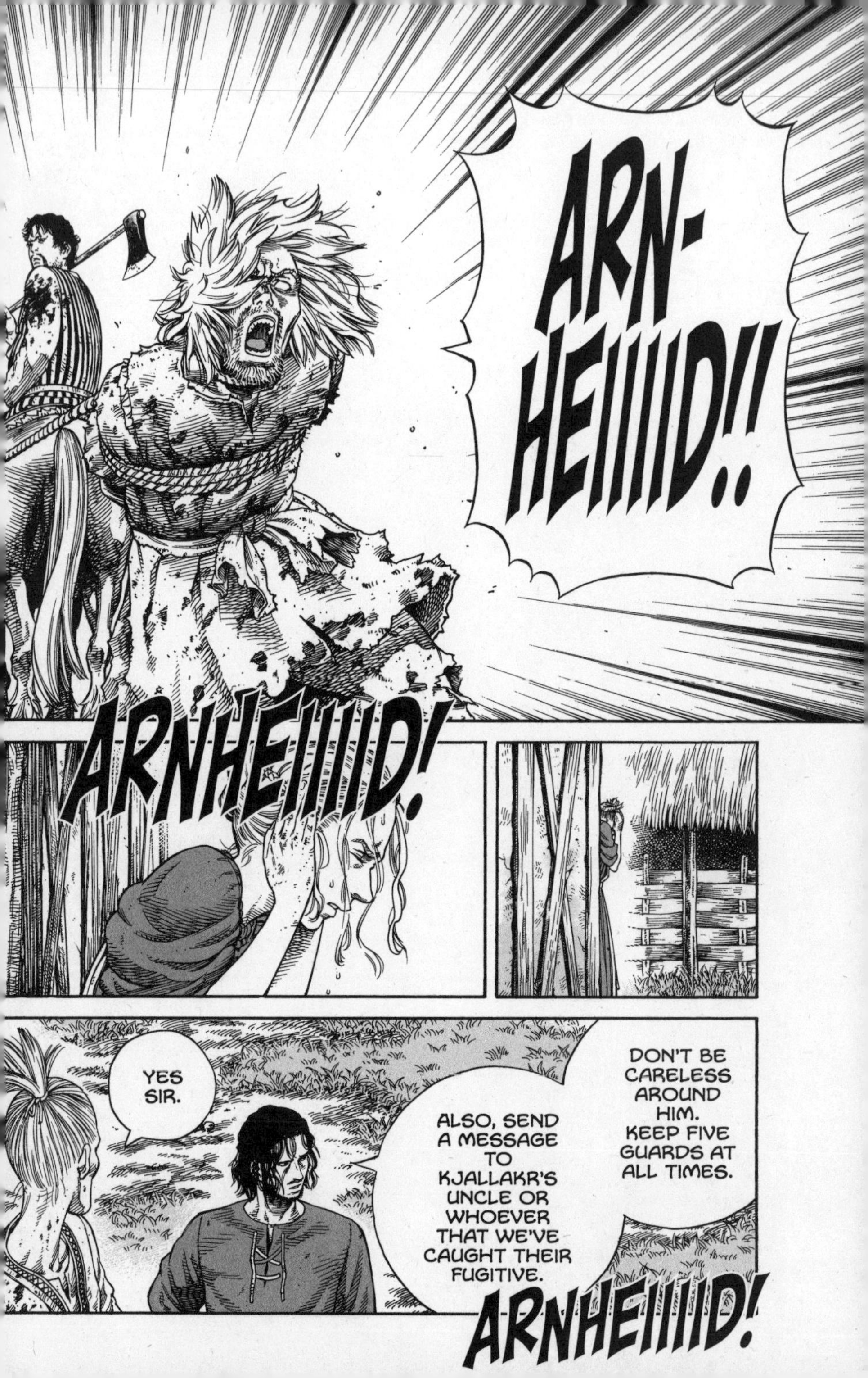

ARN-HEIIIID!!
ARNHEIIIID!
DON'T BE CARELESS AROUND HIM. KEEP FIVE GUARDS AT ALL TIMES.
ALSO, SEND A MESSAGE TO KJALLAKR'S UNCLE OR WHOEVER THAT WE'VE CAUGHT THEIR FUGITIVE.
YES SIR.
ARNHEIIIID!

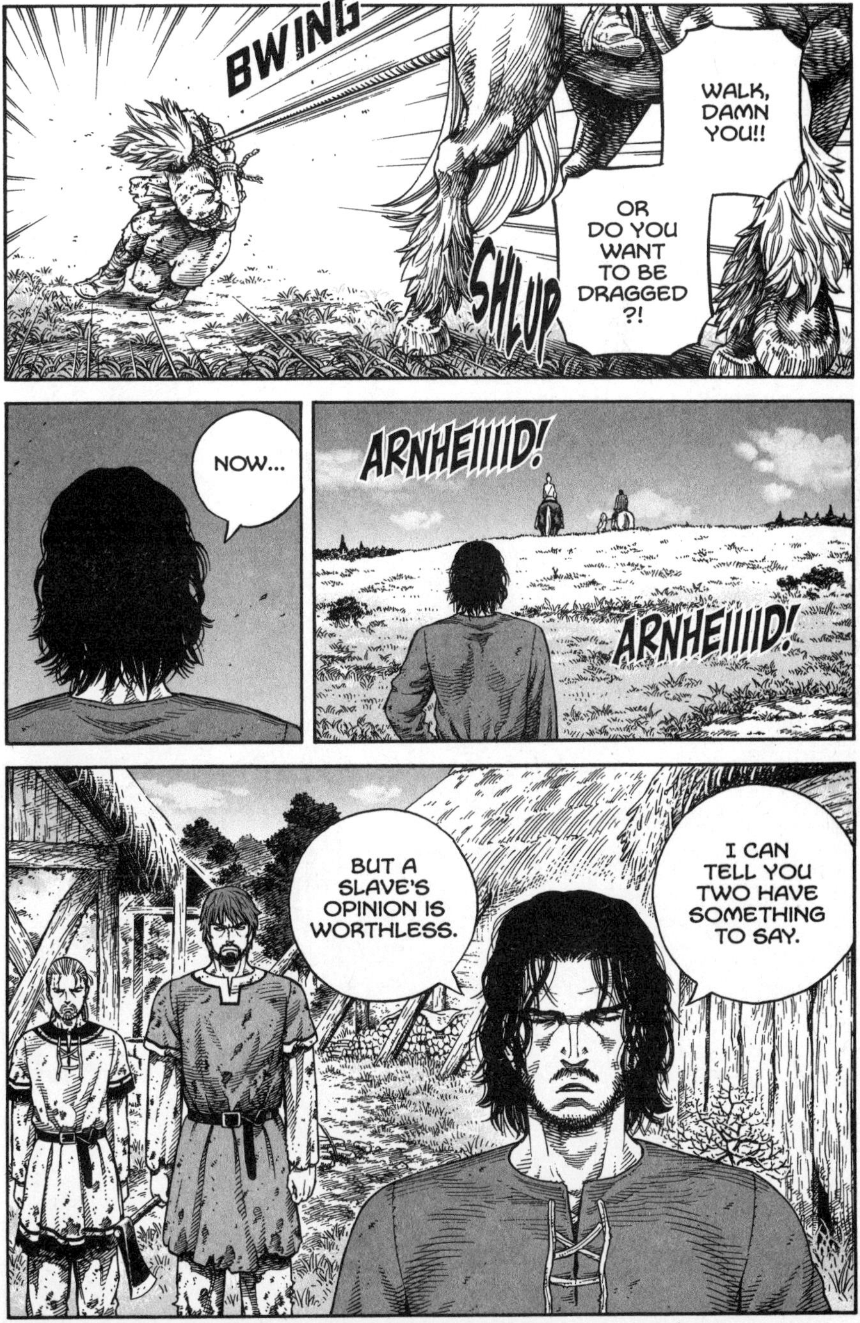
WALK, DAMN YOU!!
BWING
OR DO YOU WANT TO BE DRAGGED?!
SHLUP
ARNHEIIIIID!
ARNHEIIIIID!
NOW...
I CAN TELL YOU TWO HAVE SOMETHING TO SAY.
BUT A SLAVE'S OPINION IS WORTHLESS.

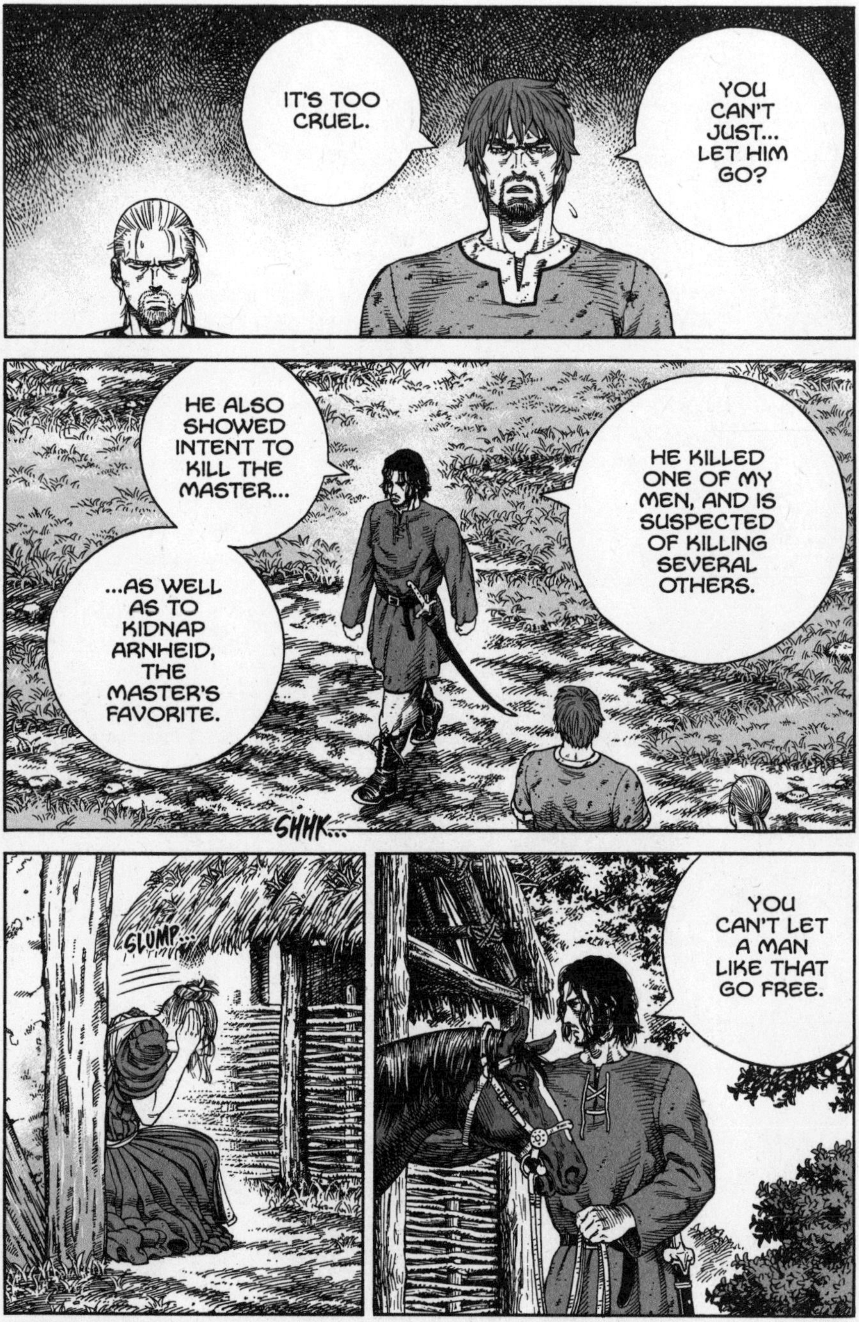
YOU CAN'T JUST... LET HIM GO?
IT'S TOO CRUEL.
HE KILLED ONE OF MY MEN, AND IS SUSPECTED OF KILLING SEVERAL OTHERS.
HE ALSO SHOWED INTENT TO KILL THE MASTER...
...AS WELL AS TO KIDNAP ARNHEID, THE MASTER'S FAVORITE.
SHHK...
YOU CAN'T LET A MAN LIKE THAT GO FREE.
SLUMP...

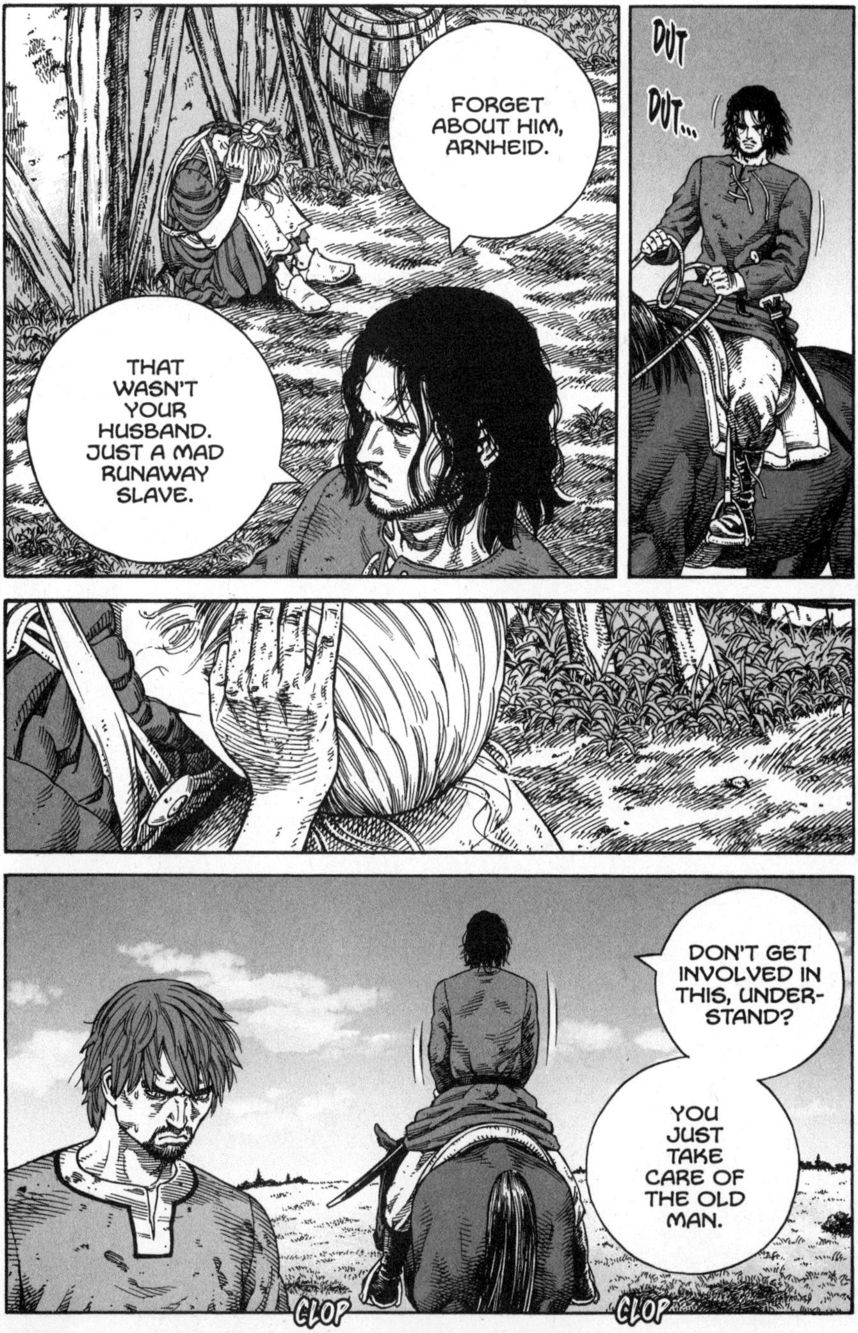
DUT DUT...
FORGET ABOUT HIM, ARNHEID.
THAT WASN'T YOUR HUSBAND. JUST A MAD RUNAWAY SLAVE.
DON'T GET INVOLVED IN THIS, UNDER-STAND?
YOU JUST TAKE CARE OF THE OLD MAN.
CLOP
CLOP

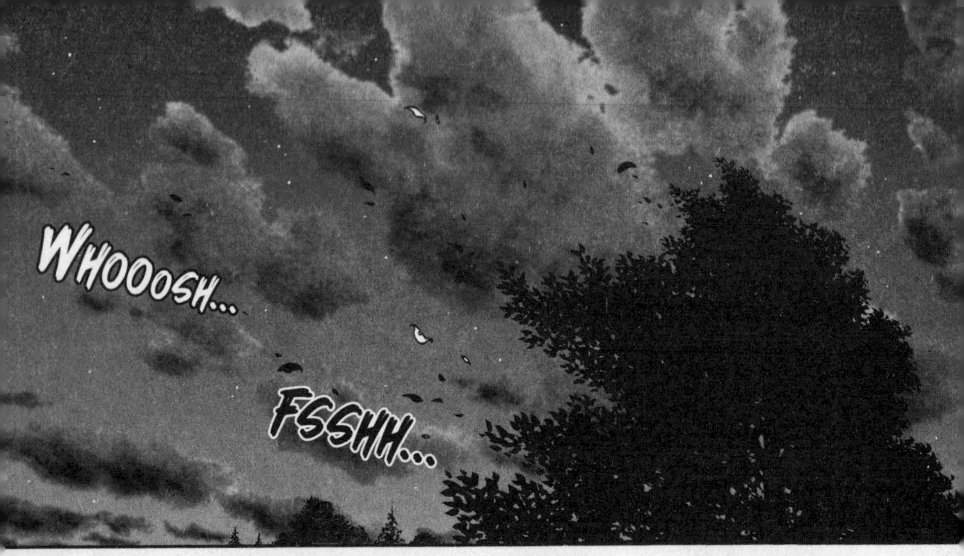
WHOOOSH...
FSSHH...

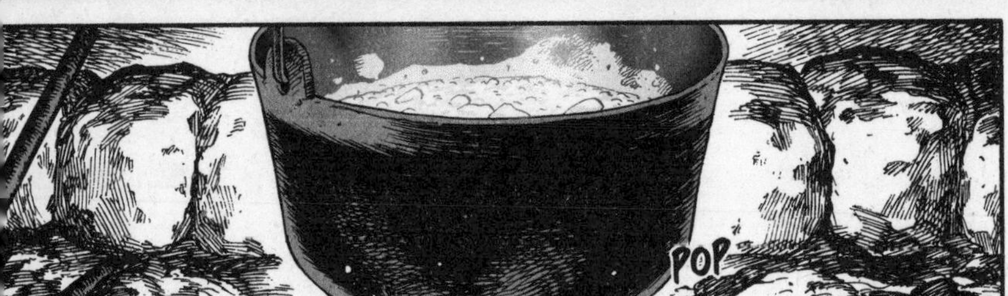
POP
SNAP

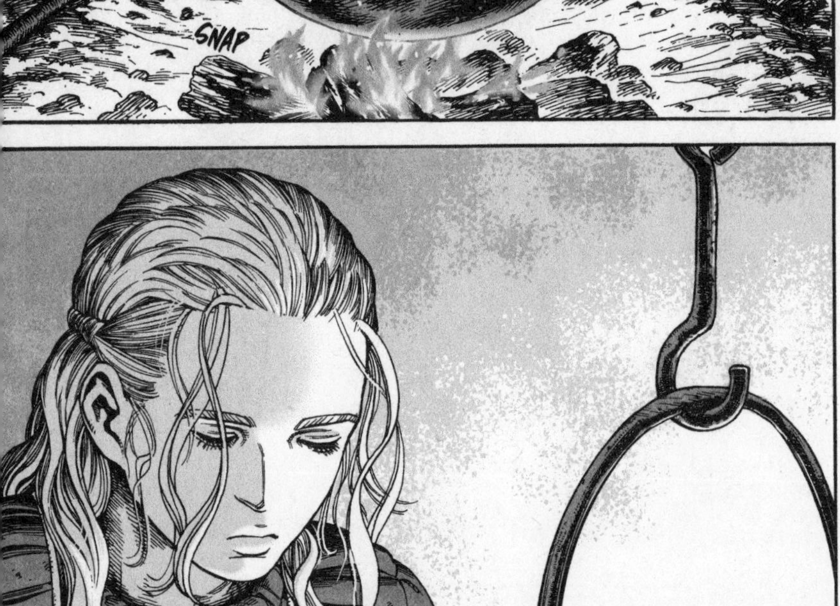

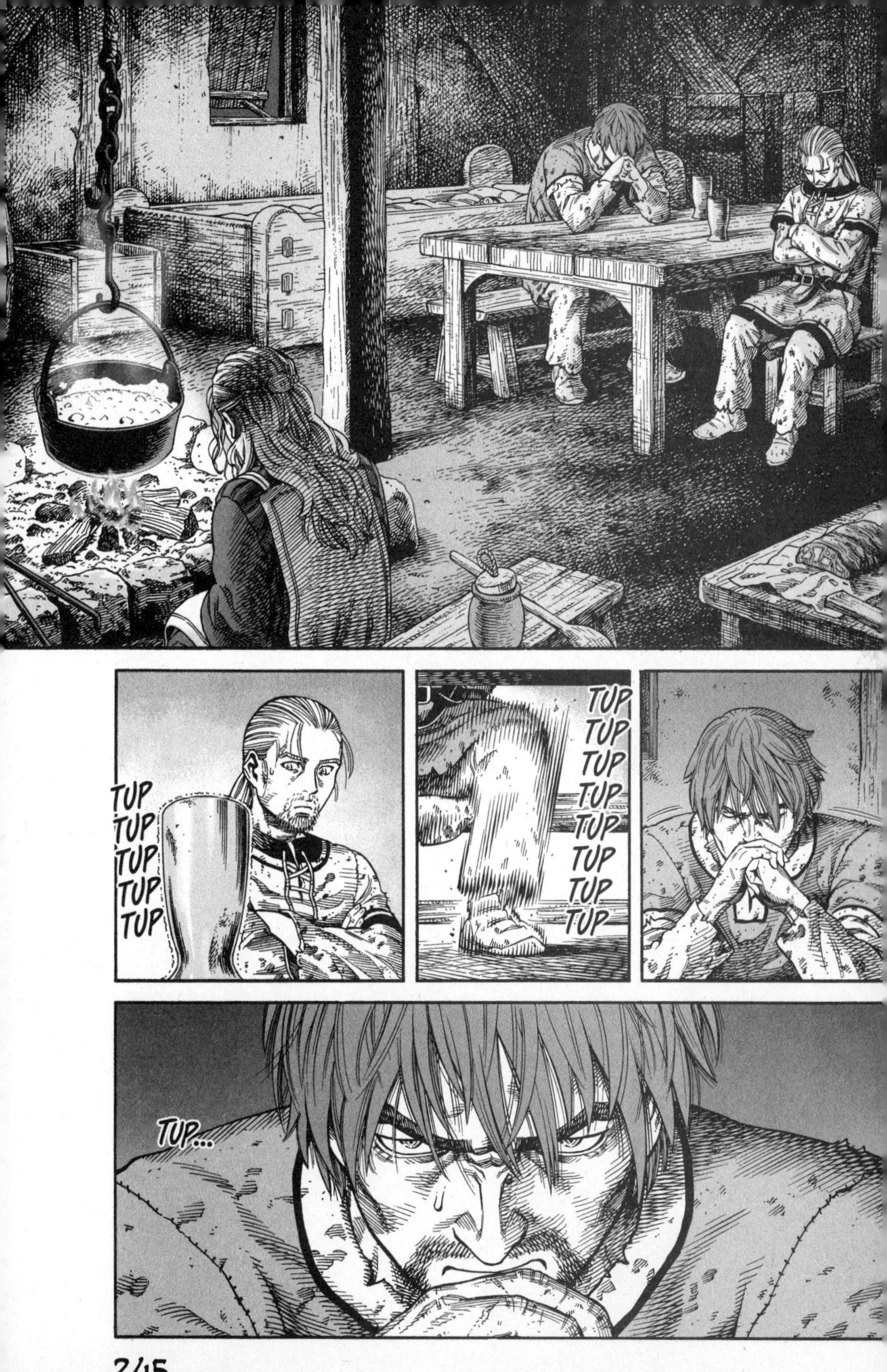
TUP
TUP
TUP
TUP
TUP
TUP
TUP
TUP
TUP
TUP
TUP
TUP
TUP
TUP...

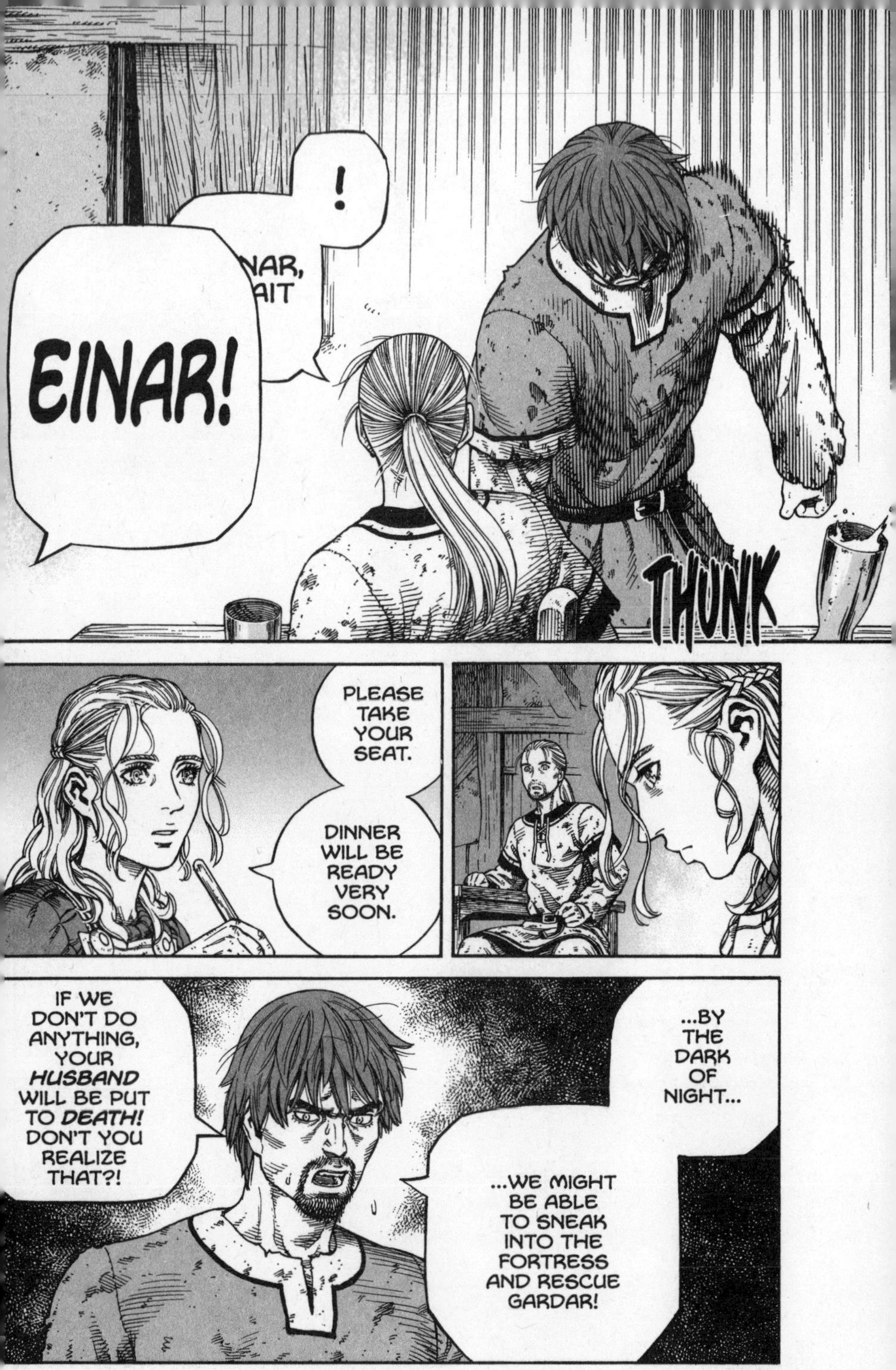
!
NAR, AIT
EINAR!
THUNK
PLEASE TAKE YOUR SEAT.
DINNER WILL BE READY VERY SOON.
IF WE DON'T DO ANYTHING, YOUR HUSBAND WILL BE PUT TO DEATH! DON'T YOU REALIZE THAT?!
...BY THE DARK OF NIGHT...
...WE MIGHT BE ABLE TO SNEAK INTO THE FORTRESS AND RESCUE GARDAR!

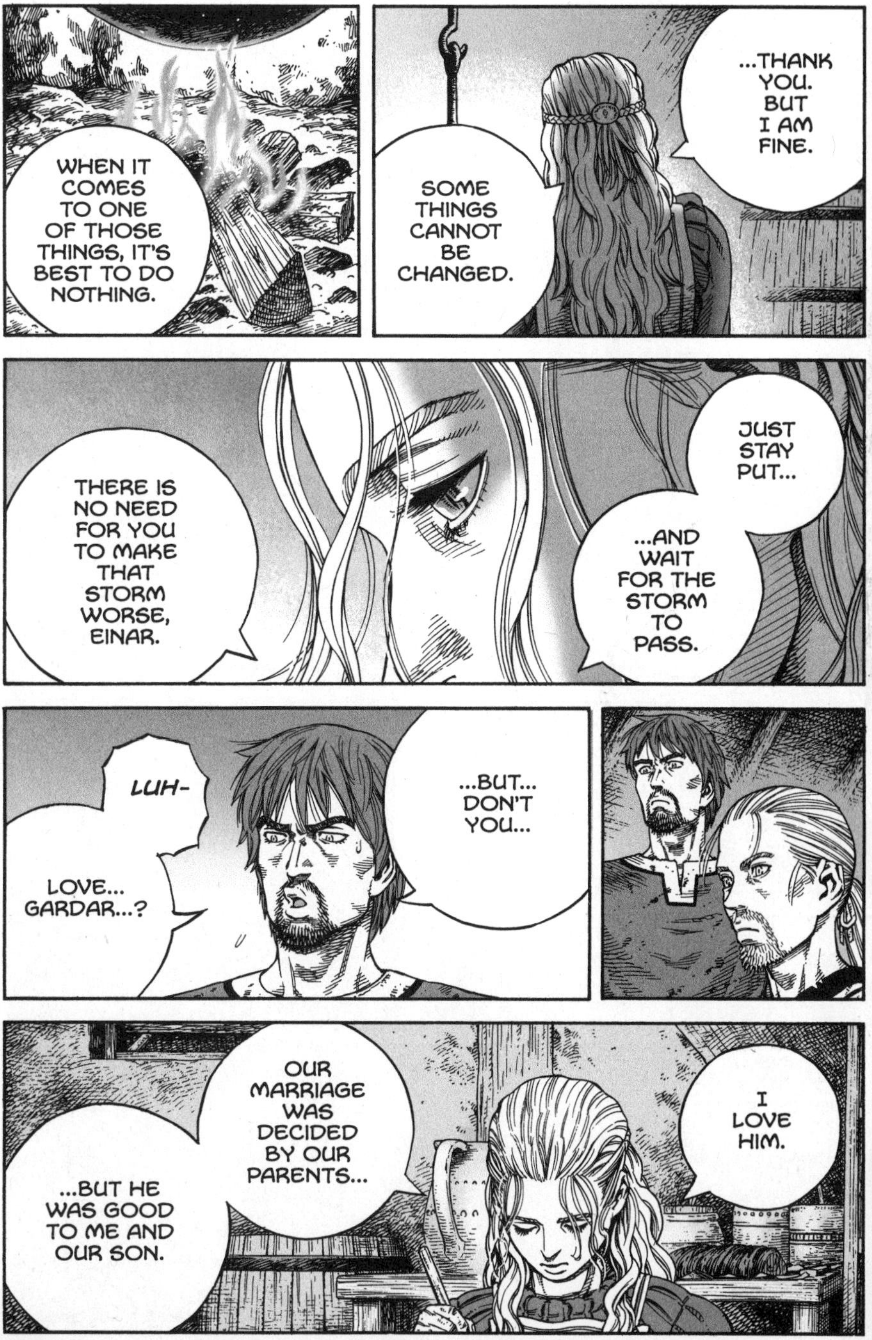
...THANK YOU. BUT I AM FINE.
SOME THINGS CANNOT BE CHANGED.
WHEN IT COMES TO ONE OF THOSE THINGS, IT'S BEST TO DO NOTHING.
JUST STAY PUT...
...AND WAIT FOR THE STORM TO PASS.
THERE IS NO NEED FOR YOU TO MAKE THAT STORM WORSE, EINAR.
...BUT... DON'T YOU...
LUH-
LOVE... GARDAR...?
I LOVE HIM.
OUR MARRIAGE WAS DECIDED BY OUR PARENTS...
...BUT HE WAS GOOD TO ME AND OUR SON.

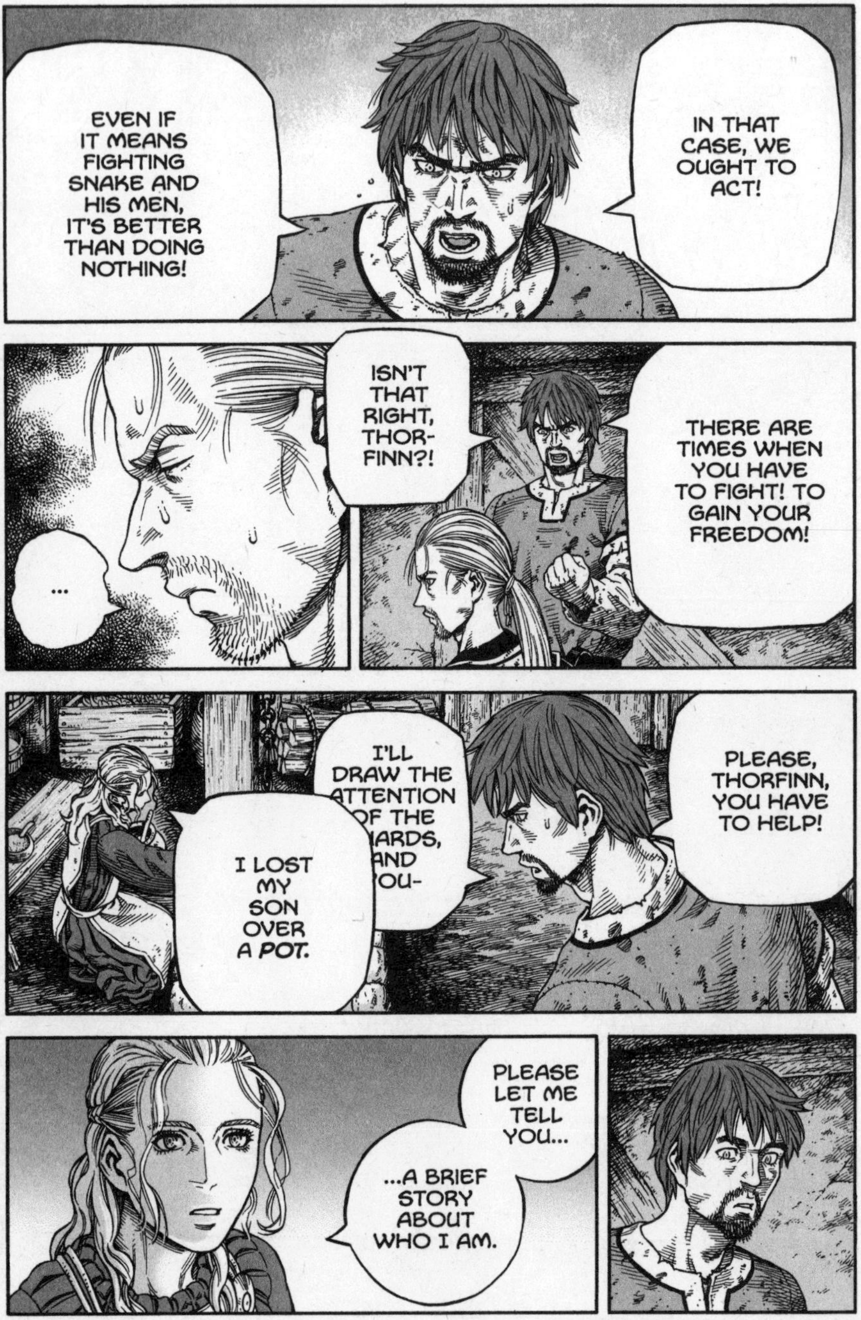

IN THAT CASE, WE OUGHT TO ACT!
EVEN IF IT MEANS FIGHTING SNAKE AND HIS MEN, IT'S BETTER THAN DOING NOTHING!
THERE ARE TIMES WHEN YOU HAVE TO FIGHT! TO GAIN YOUR FREEDOM!
ISN'T THAT RIGHT, THORFINN?!
...
PLEASE, THORFINN, YOU HAVE TO HELP!
I'LL DRAW THE ATTENTION OF THE GUARDS, AND YOU-
I LOST MY SON OVER A *POT*.
PLEASE LET ME TELL YOU...
...A BRIEF STORY ABOUT WHO I AM.

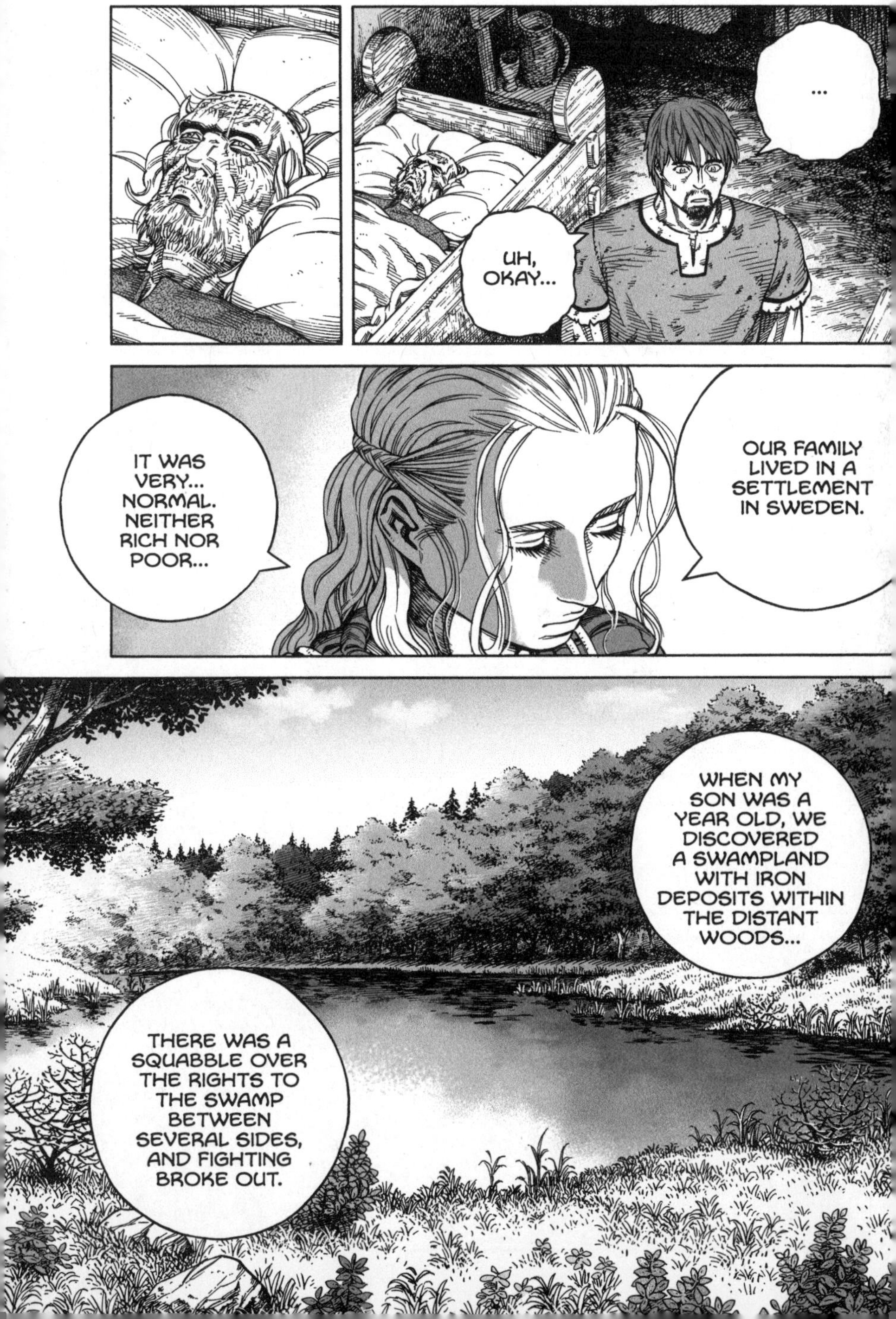
...
UH, OKAY...
OUR FAMILY LIVED IN A SETTLEMENT IN SWEDEN.
IT WAS VERY... NORMAL. NEITHER RICH NOR POOR...
WHEN MY SON WAS A YEAR OLD, WE DISCOVERED A SWAMPLAND WITH IRON DEPOSITS WITHIN THE DISTANT WOODS...
THERE WAS A SQUABBLE OVER THE RIGHTS TO THE SWAMP BETWEEN SEVERAL SIDES, AND FIGHTING BROKE OUT.

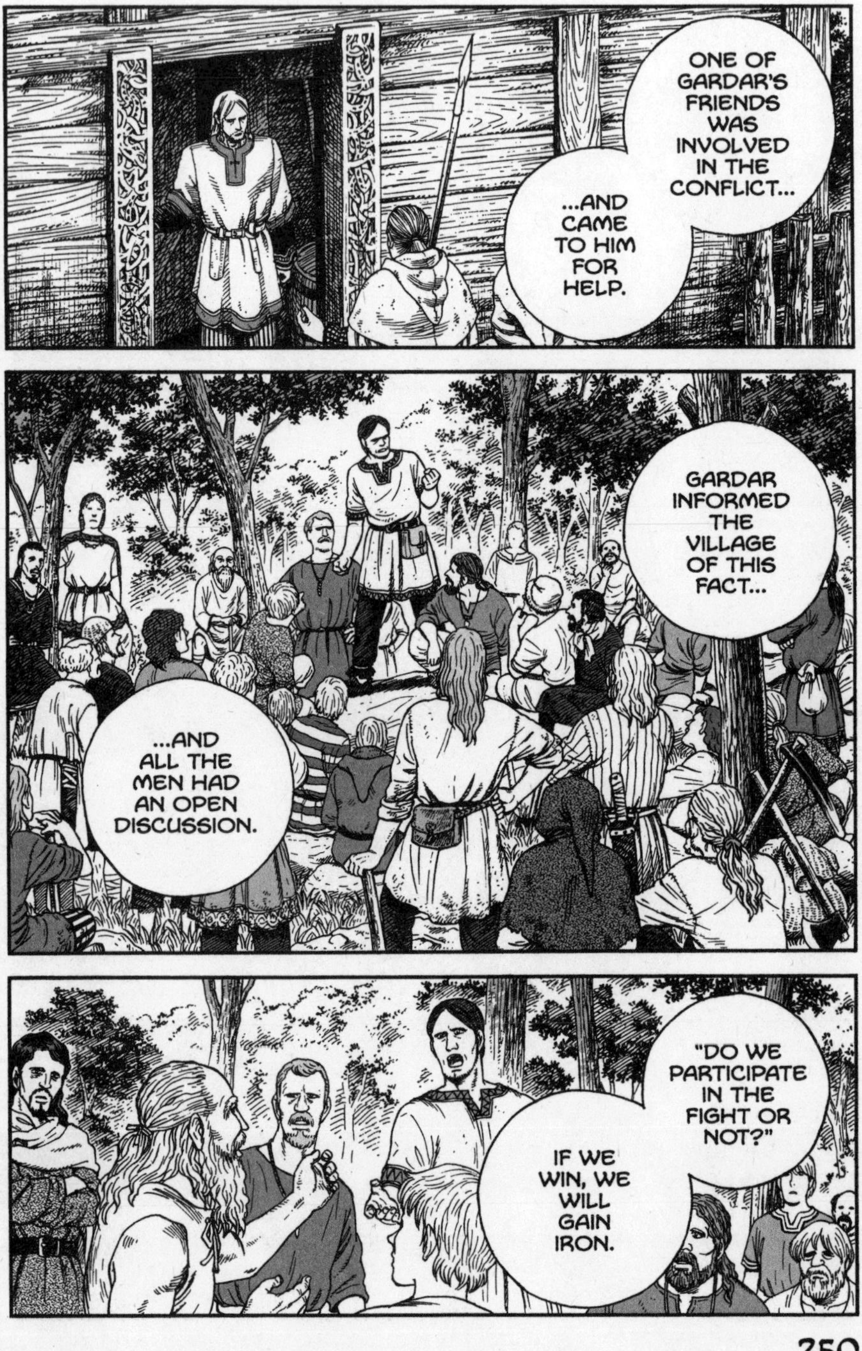
ONE OF GARDAR'S FRIENDS WAS INVOLVED IN THE CONFLICT...
...AND CAME TO HIM FOR HELP.
GARDAR INFORMED THE VILLAGE OF THIS FACT...
...AND ALL THE MEN HAD AN OPEN DISCUSSION.
"DO WE PARTICIPATE IN THE FIGHT OR NOT?"
IF WE WIN, WE WILL GAIN IRON.

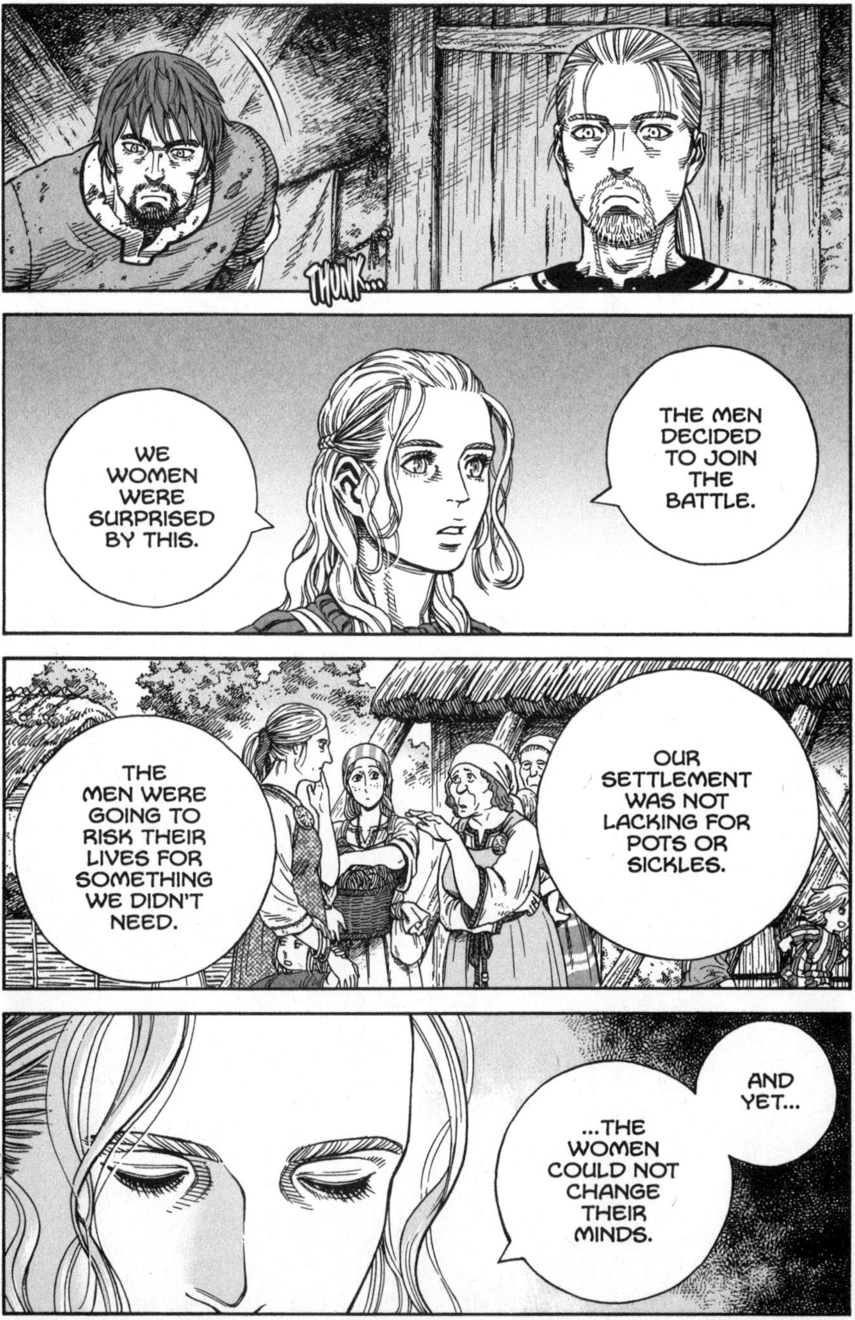
THUNK...
THE MEN DECIDED TO JOIN THE BATTLE.
WE WOMEN WERE SURPRISED BY THIS.
OUR SETTLEMENT WAS NOT LACKING FOR POTS OR SICKLES.
THE MEN WERE GOING TO RISK THEIR LIVES FOR SOMETHING WE DIDN'T NEED.
AND YET...
...THE WOMEN COULD NOT CHANGE THEIR MINDS.

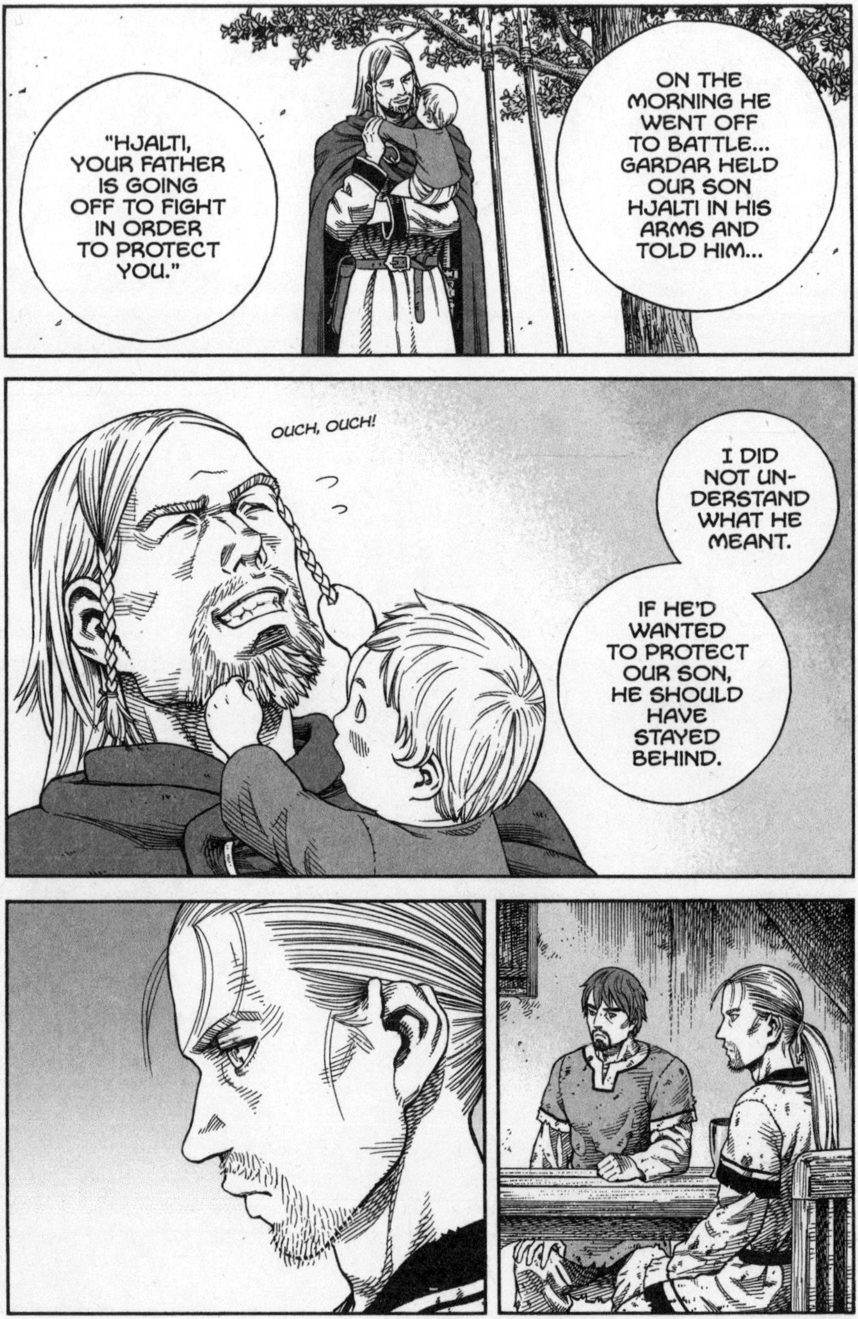
ON THE MORNING HE WENT OFF TO BATTLE... GARDAR HELD OUR SON HJALTI IN HIS ARMS AND TOLD HIM...
"HJALTI, YOUR FATHER IS GOING OFF TO FIGHT IN ORDER TO PROTECT YOU."
I DID NOT UN-DERSTAND WHAT HE MEANT.
IF HE'D WANTED TO PROTECT OUR SON, HE SHOULD HAVE STAYED BEHIND.
OUCH, OUCH!

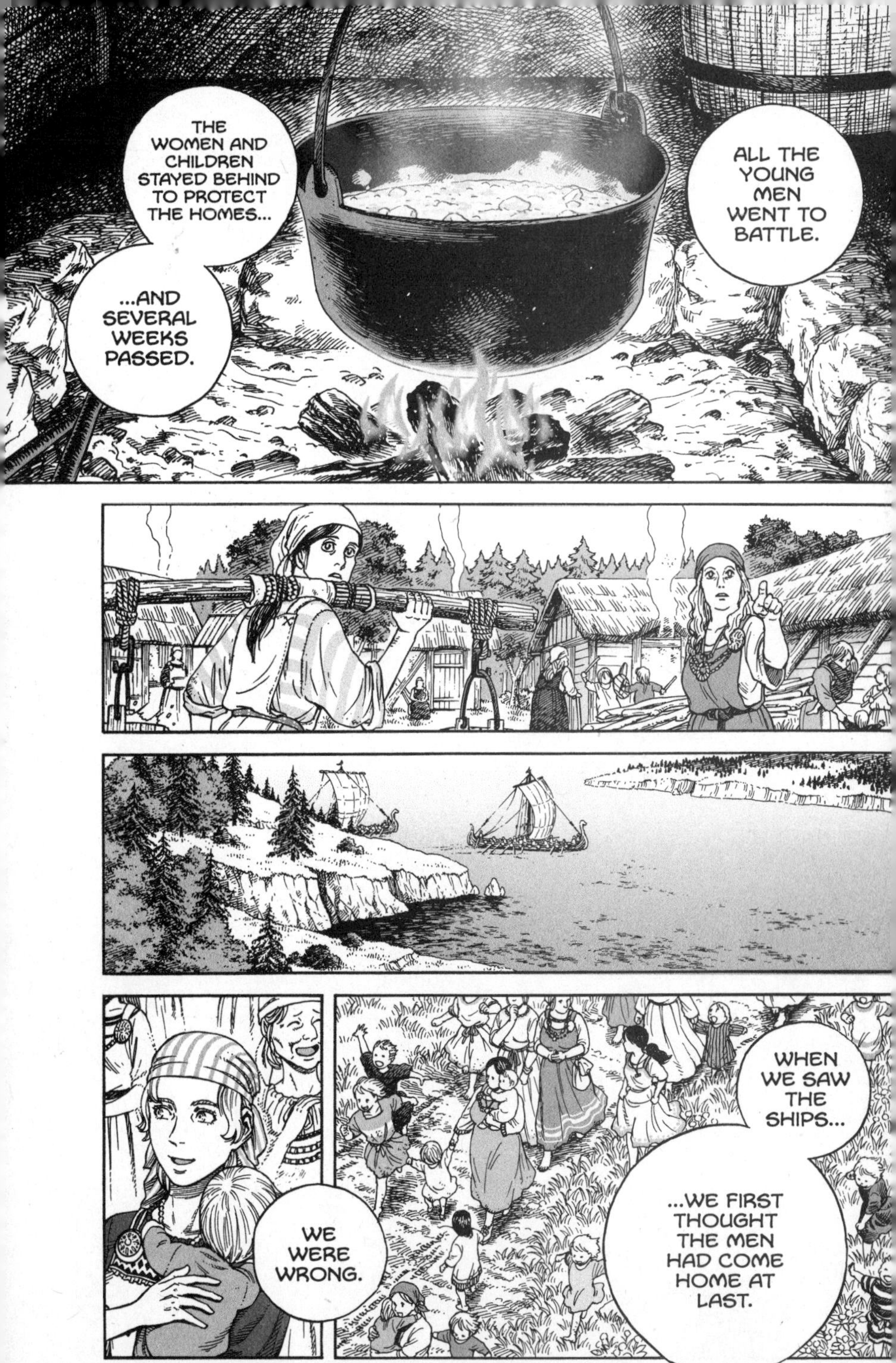
ALL THE YOUNG MEN WENT TO BATTLE.
THE WOMEN AND CHILDREN STAYED BEHIND TO PROTECT THE HOMES...
...AND SEVERAL WEEKS PASSED.
WHEN WE SAW THE SHIPS...
...WE FIRST THOUGHT THE MEN HAD COME HOME AT LAST.
WE WERE WRONG.

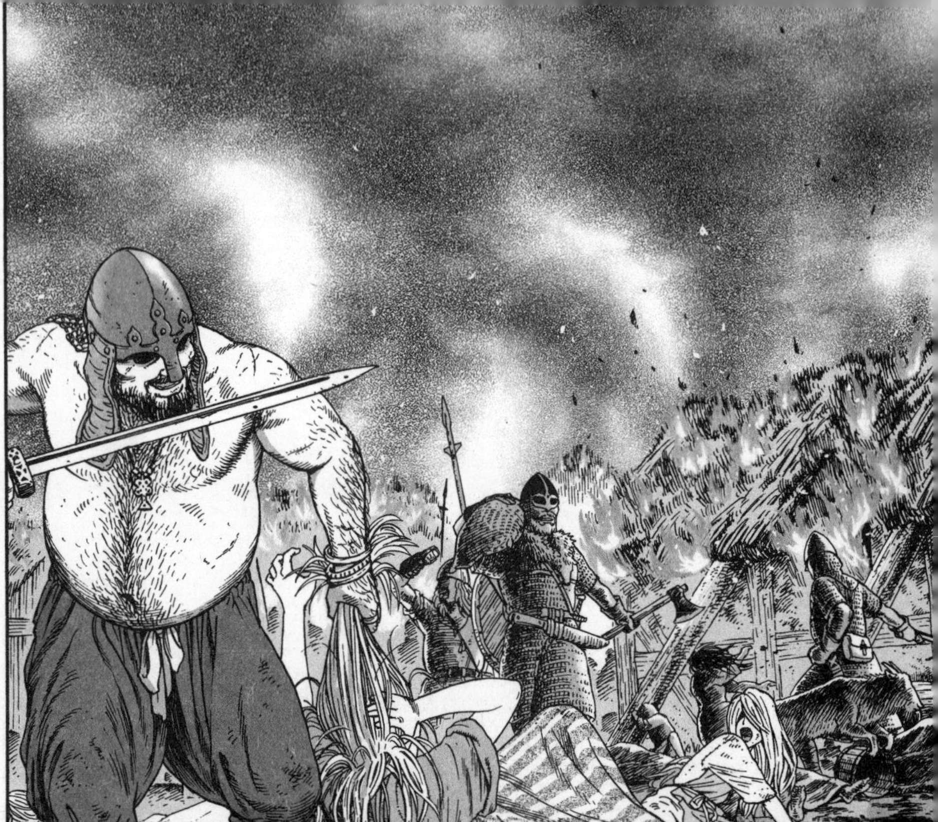

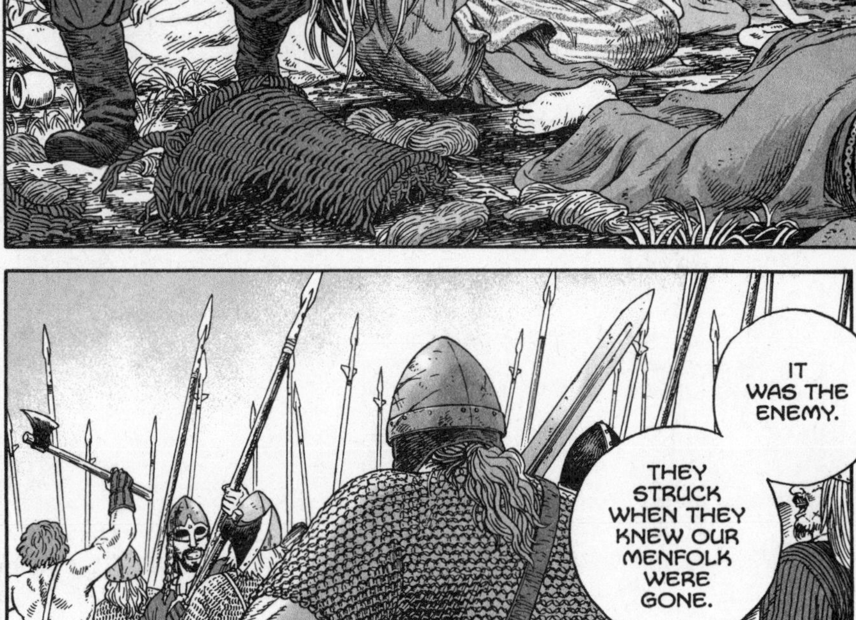
IT WAS THE ENEMY.
THEY STRUCK WHEN THEY KNEW OUR MENFOLK WERE GONE.

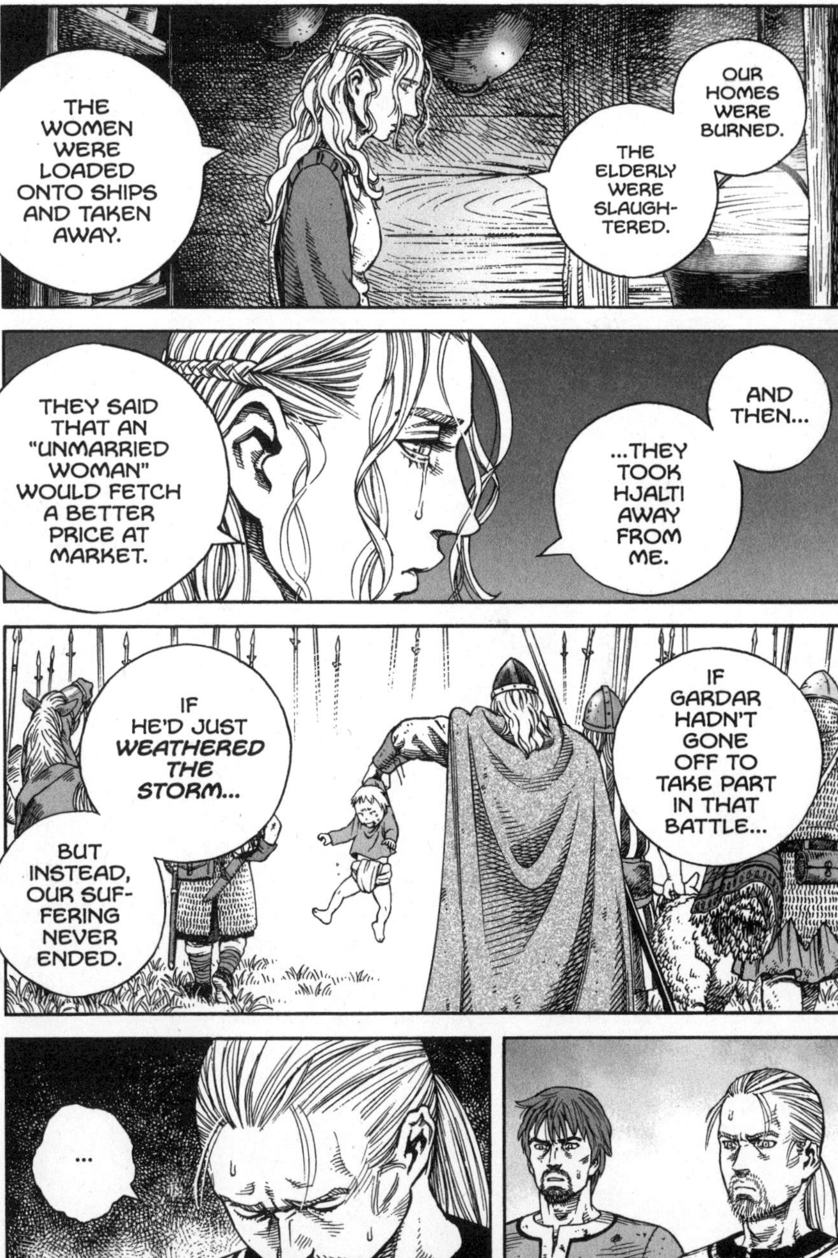
OUR HOMES WERE BURNED.
THE ELDERLY WERE SLAUGHTERED.
THE WOMEN WERE LOADED ONTO SHIPS AND TAKEN AWAY.
AND THEN...
...THEY TOOK HJALTI AWAY FROM ME.
THEY SAID THAT AN "UNMARRIED WOMAN" WOULD FETCH A BETTER PRICE AT MARKET.
IF GARDAR HADN'T GONE OFF TO TAKE PART IN THAT BATTLE...
IF HE'D JUST *WEATHERED THE STORM*...
BUT INSTEAD, OUR SUFFERING NEVER ENDED.
...

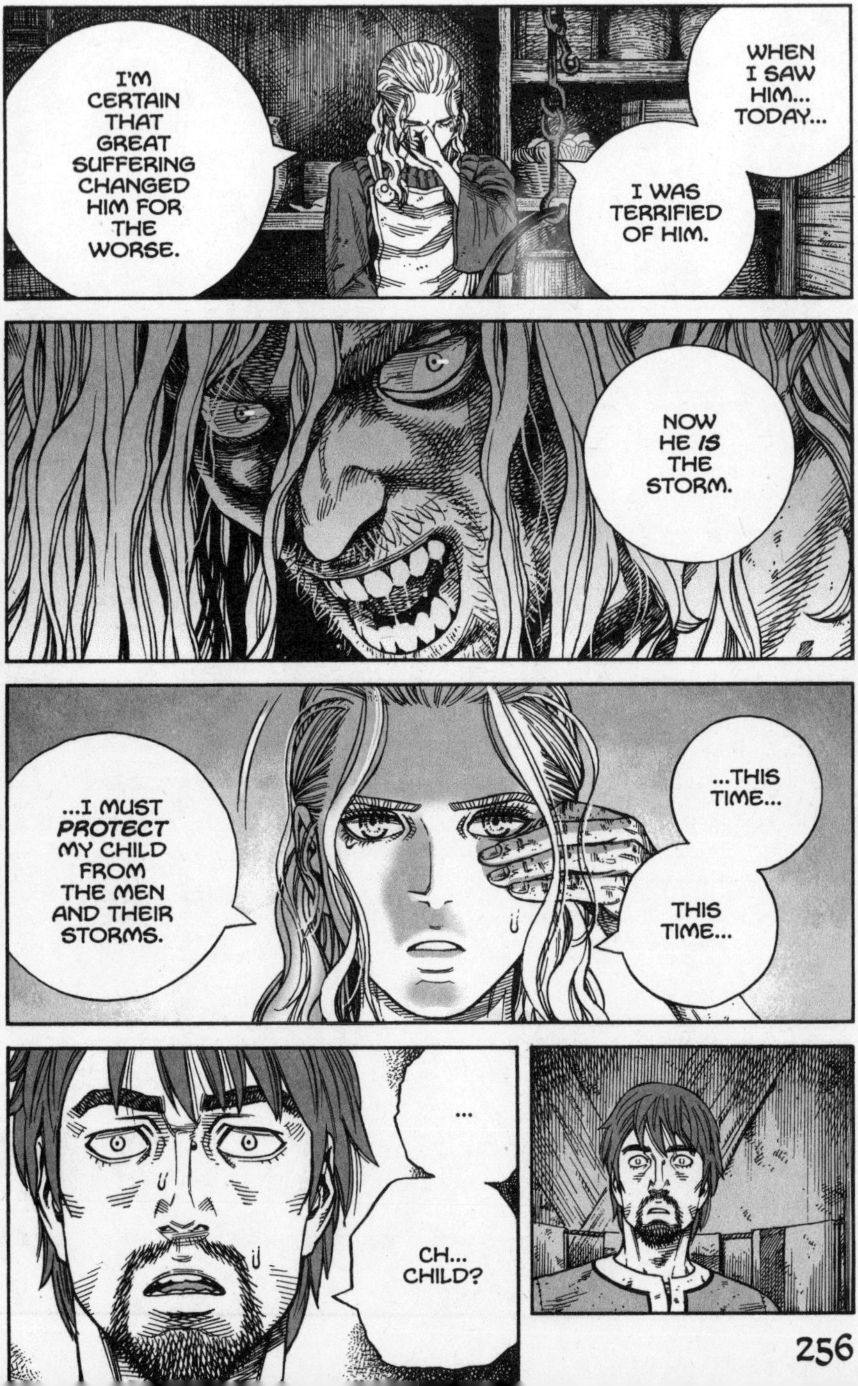
WHEN I SAW HIM... TODAY...
I WAS TERRIFIED OF HIM.
I'M CERTAIN THAT GREAT SUFFERING CHANGED HIM FOR THE WORSE.
NOW HE *IS* THE STORM.
...THIS TIME...
THIS TIME...
...I MUST *PROTECT* MY CHILD FROM THE MEN AND THEIR STORMS.
...
CH... CHILD?

I AM CARRYING THE CHILD OF THE MASTER NOW.

I LEARNED JUST DAYS AGO.

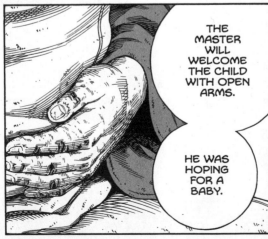

THE MASTER WILL WELCOME THE CHILD WITH OPEN ARMS.

HE WAS HOPING FOR A BABY.

...

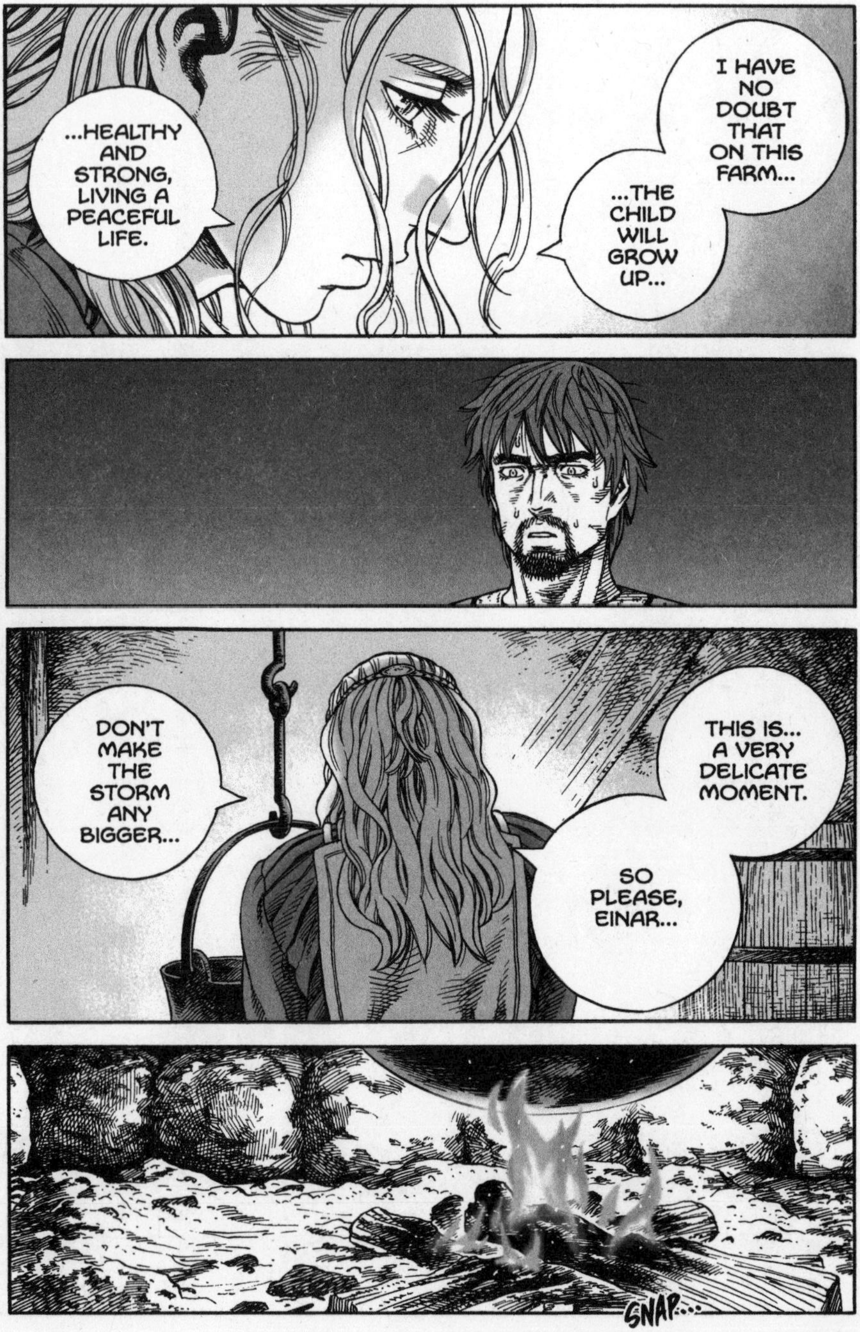
I HAVE NO DOUBT THAT ON THIS FARM...
...THE CHILD WILL GROW UP...
...HEALTHY AND STRONG, LIVING A PEACEFUL LIFE.
THIS IS... A VERY DELICATE MOMENT.
SO PLEASE, EINAR...
DON'T MAKE THE STORM ANY BIGGER...
SNAP...

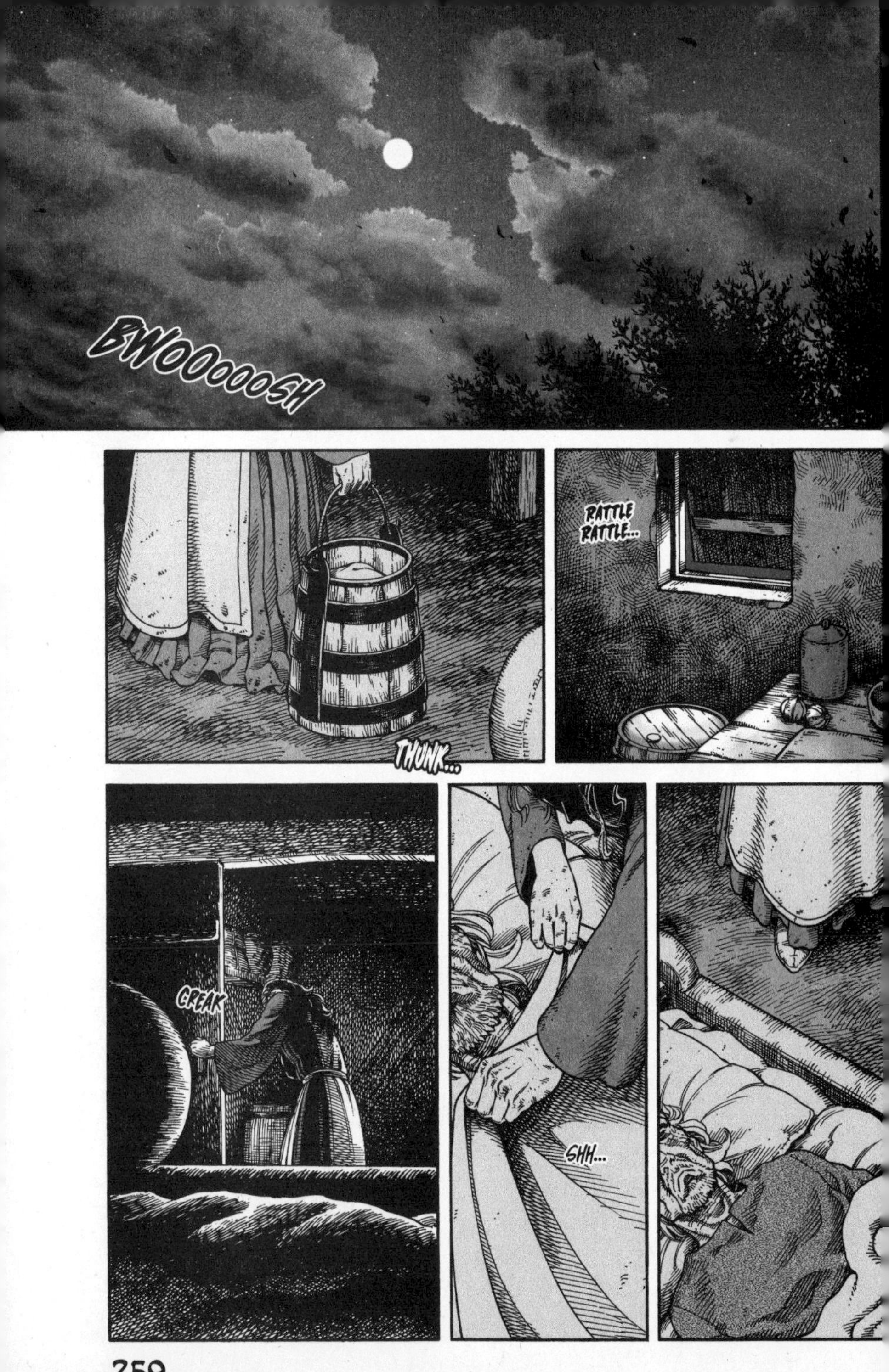
BWOOooosh
RATTLE RATTLE...
THUNK...
SHH...
CREAK

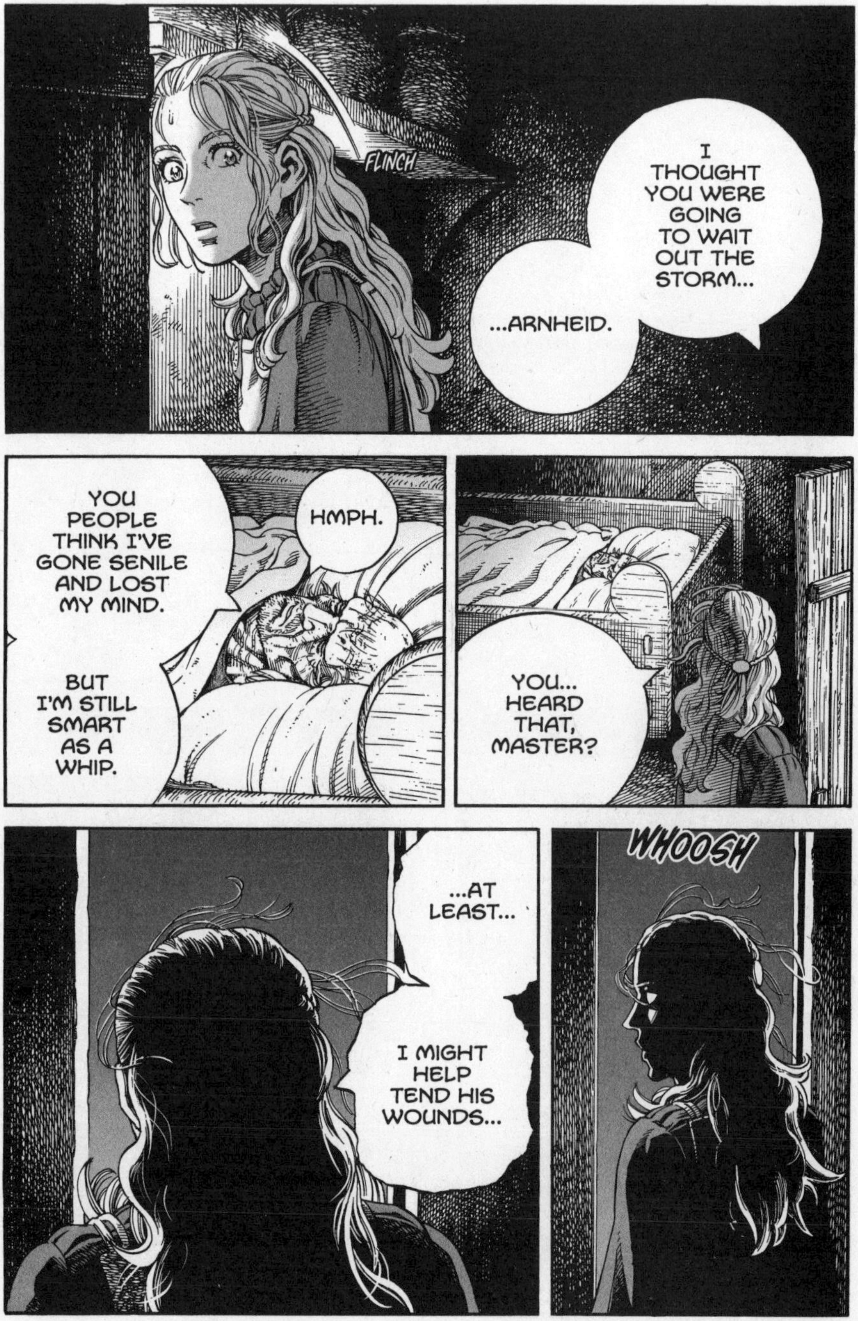
I THOUGHT YOU WERE GOING TO WAIT OUT THE STORM...
...ARNHEID.
FLINCH
YOU... HEARD THAT, MASTER?
HMPH.
YOU PEOPLE THINK I'VE GONE SENILE AND LOST MY MIND.
BUT I'M STILL SMART AS A WHIP.
WHOOSH
...AT LEAST...
I MIGHT HELP TEND HIS WOUNDS...

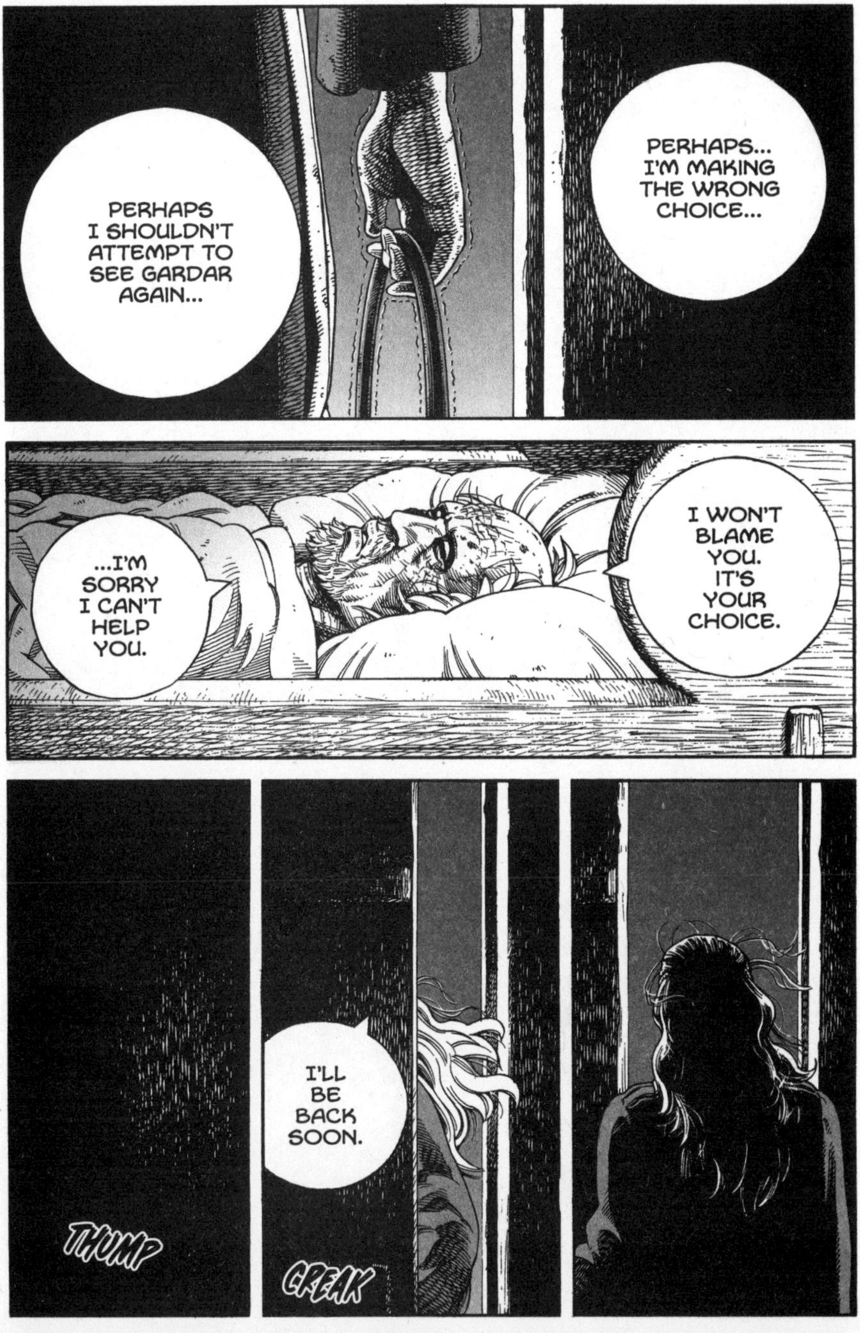
PERHAPS... I'M MAKING THE WRONG CHOICE...
PERHAPS I SHOULDN'T ATTEMPT TO SEE GARDAR AGAIN...
I WON'T BLAME YOU. IT'S YOUR CHOICE.
...I'M SORRY I CAN'T HELP YOU.
I'LL BE BACK SOON.
CREAK
THUMP

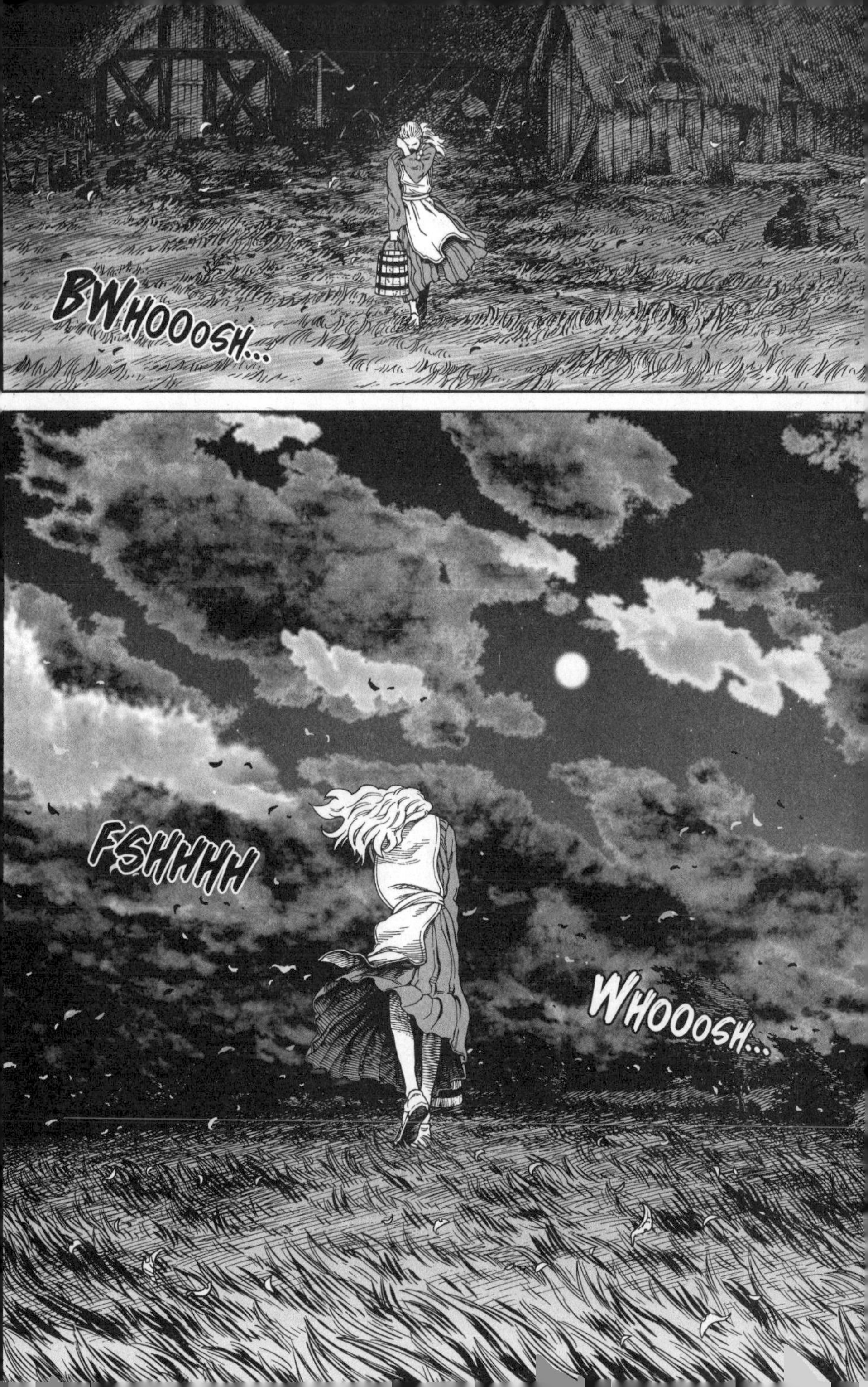
BWHOOOSH...
WHOOOSH...
FSHHHH

CHAPTER 82: BONDAGE

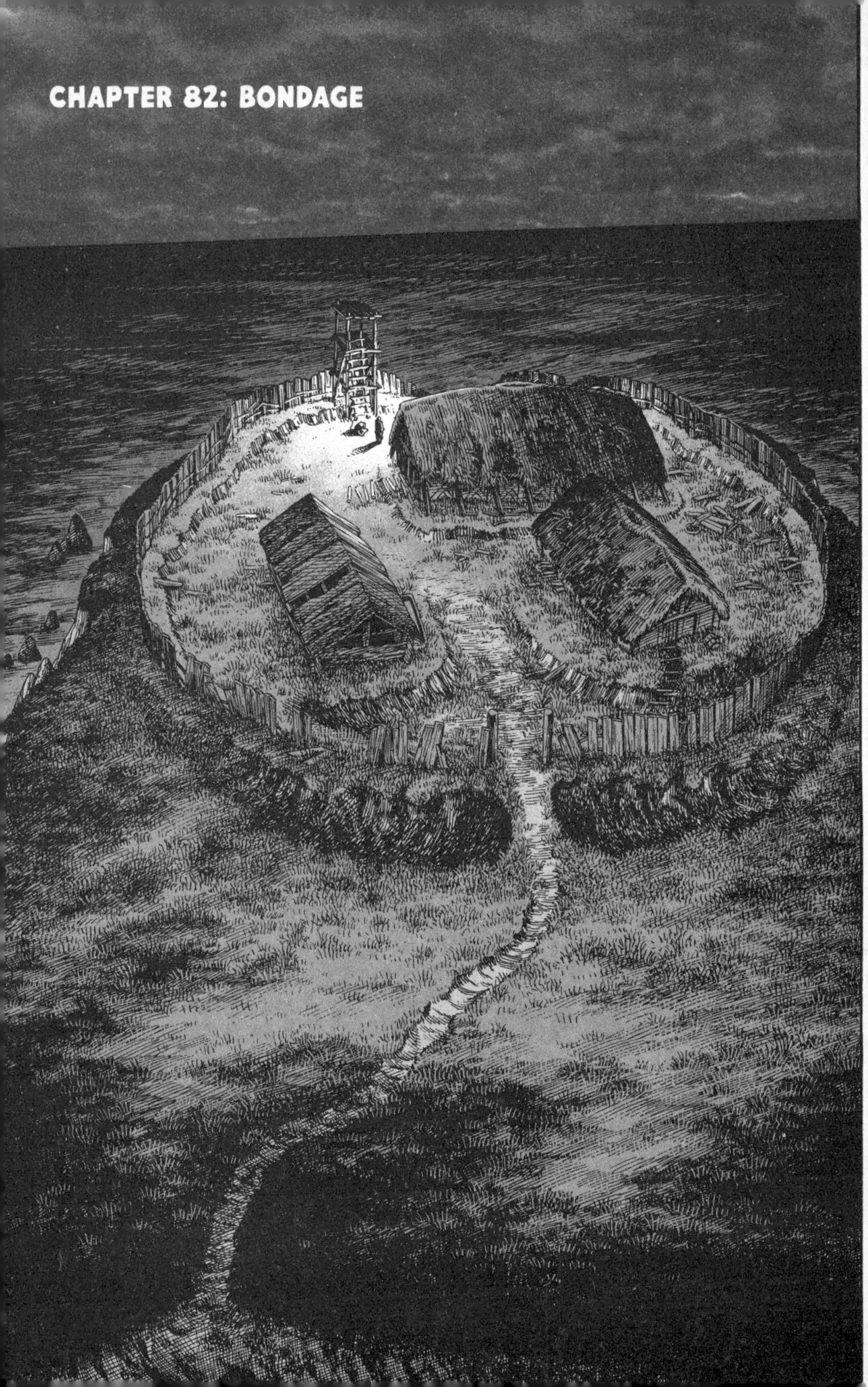

ZZSHHH

DSHH

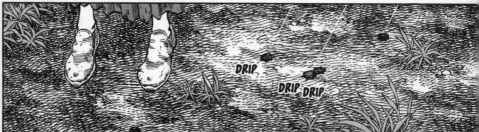

DRIP

DRIP DRIP

DSSHHH...

**GUEST
(BODYGUARD)
LODGING,
KETIL'S FARM**

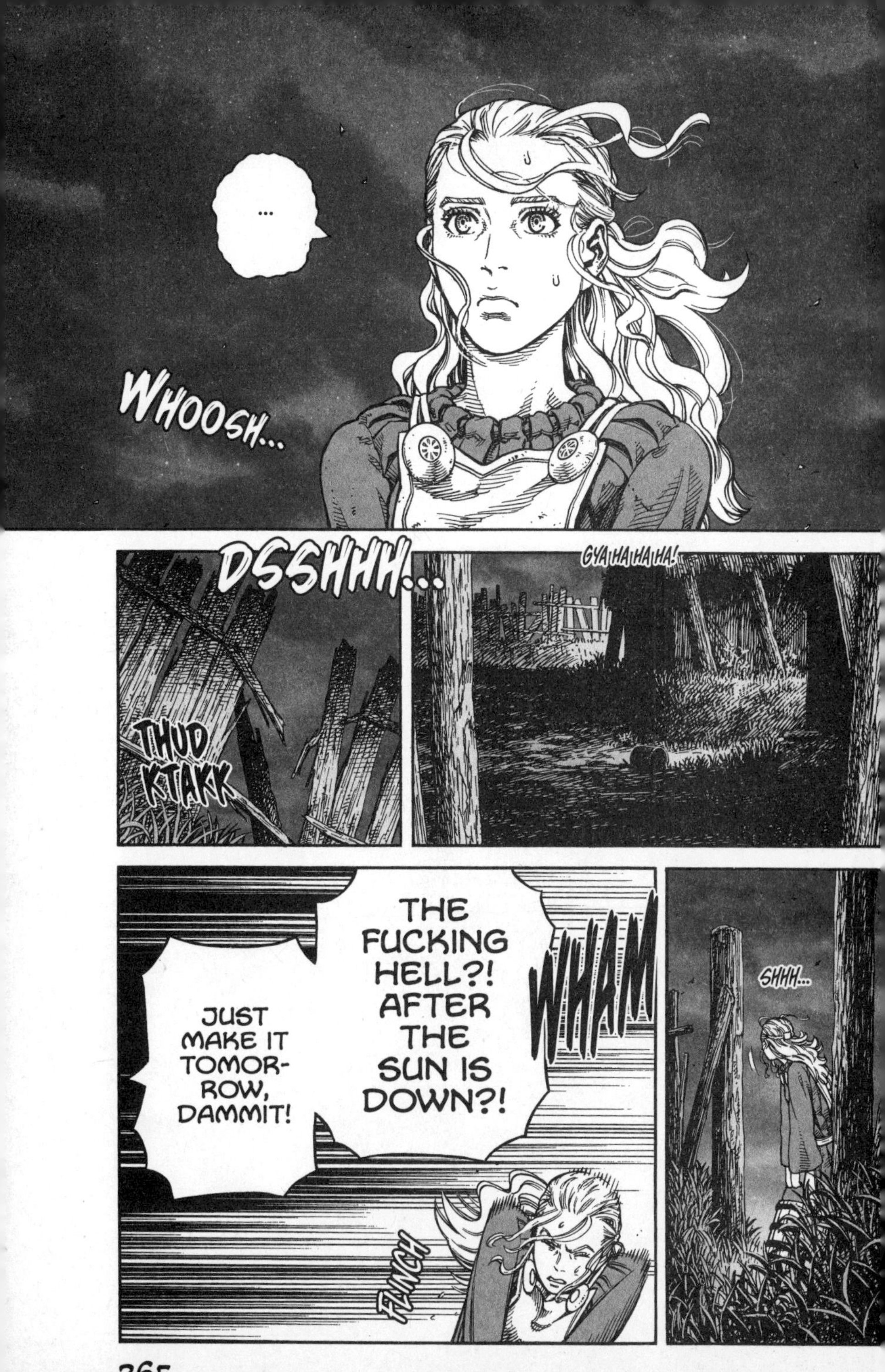
...
WHOOSH...
GYA HA HA HA!
DSSHHH...
THUD
KTAKK
SHHH...
WHAM
THE FUCKING HELL?! AFTER THE SUN IS DOWN?!
JUST MAKE IT TOMORROW, DAMMIT!
FLINCH

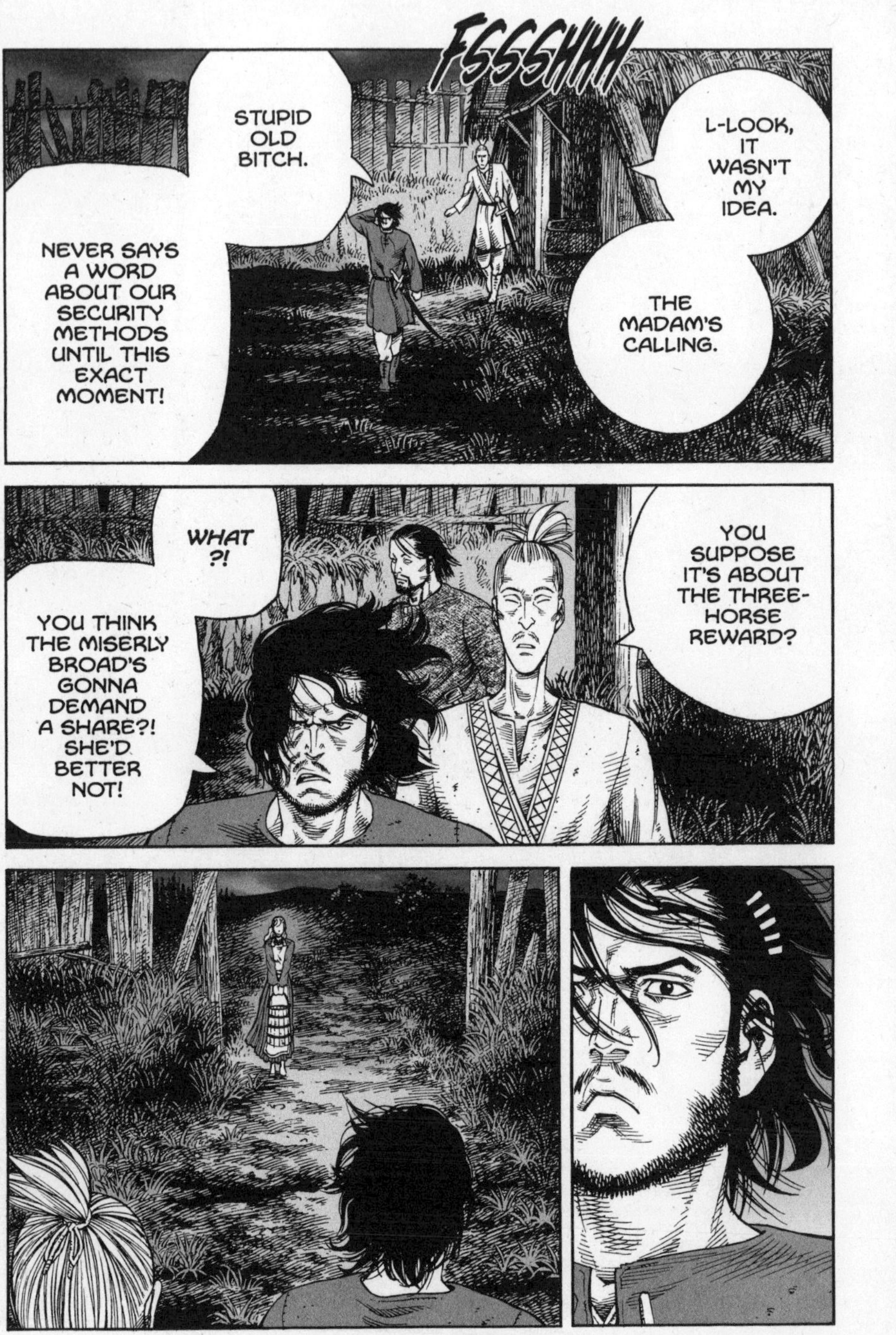
FSSSHHH
L-LOOK, IT WASN'T MY IDEA.
THE MADAM'S CALLING.
STUPID OLD BITCH.
NEVER SAYS A WORD ABOUT OUR SECURITY METHODS UNTIL THIS EXACT MOMENT!
YOU SUPPOSE IT'S ABOUT THE THREE-HORSE REWARD?
WHAT ?!
YOU THINK THE MISERLY BROAD'S GONNA DEMAND A SHARE?! SHE'D BETTER NOT!

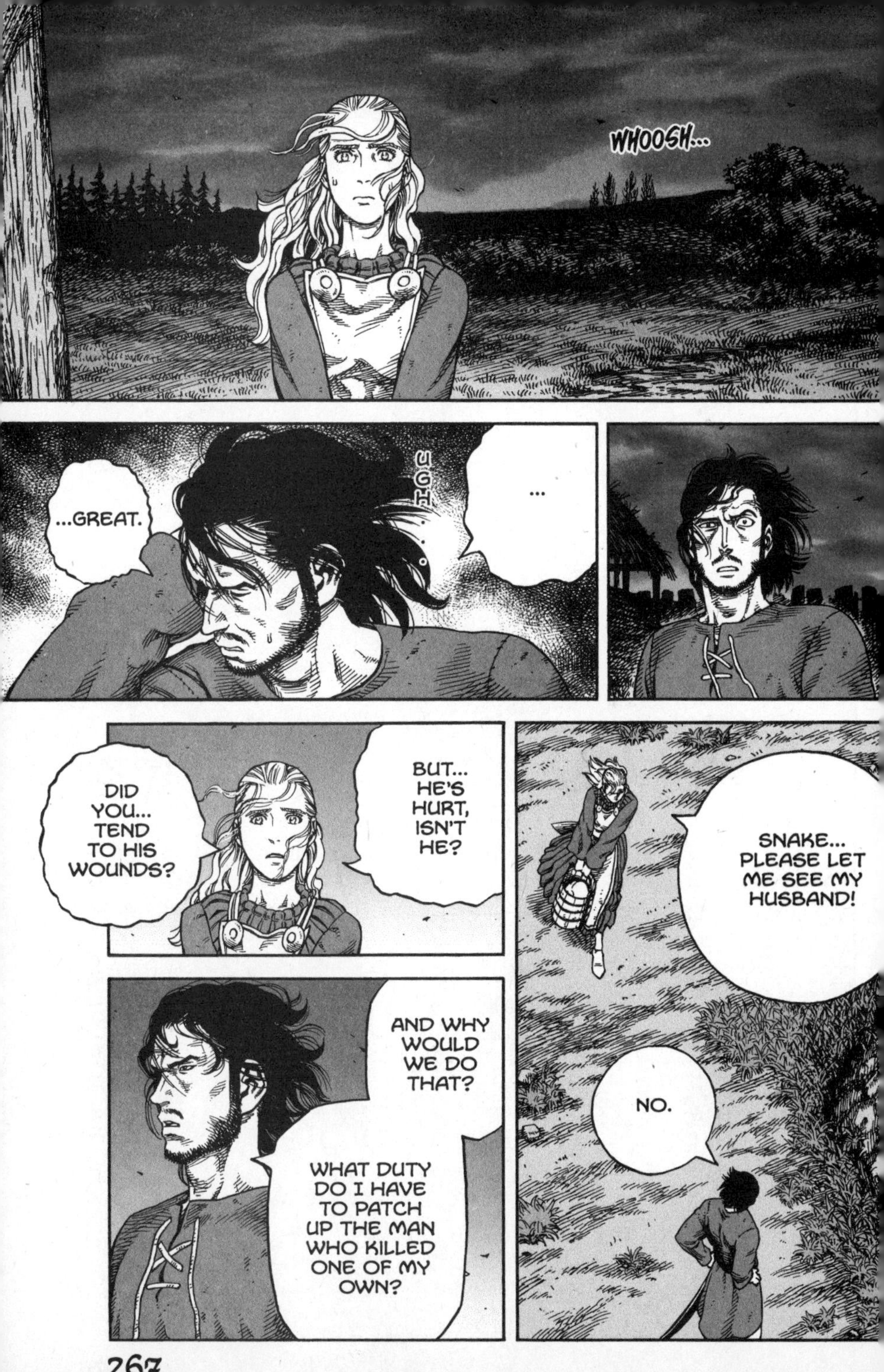
WHOOSH...
...
UGH...
...GREAT.
SNAKE... PLEASE LET ME SEE MY HUSBAND!
NO.
BUT... HE'S HURT, ISN'T HE?
DID YOU... TEND TO HIS WOUNDS?
AND WHY WOULD WE DO THAT?
WHAT DUTY DO I HAVE TO PATCH UP THE MAN WHO KILLED ONE OF MY OWN?

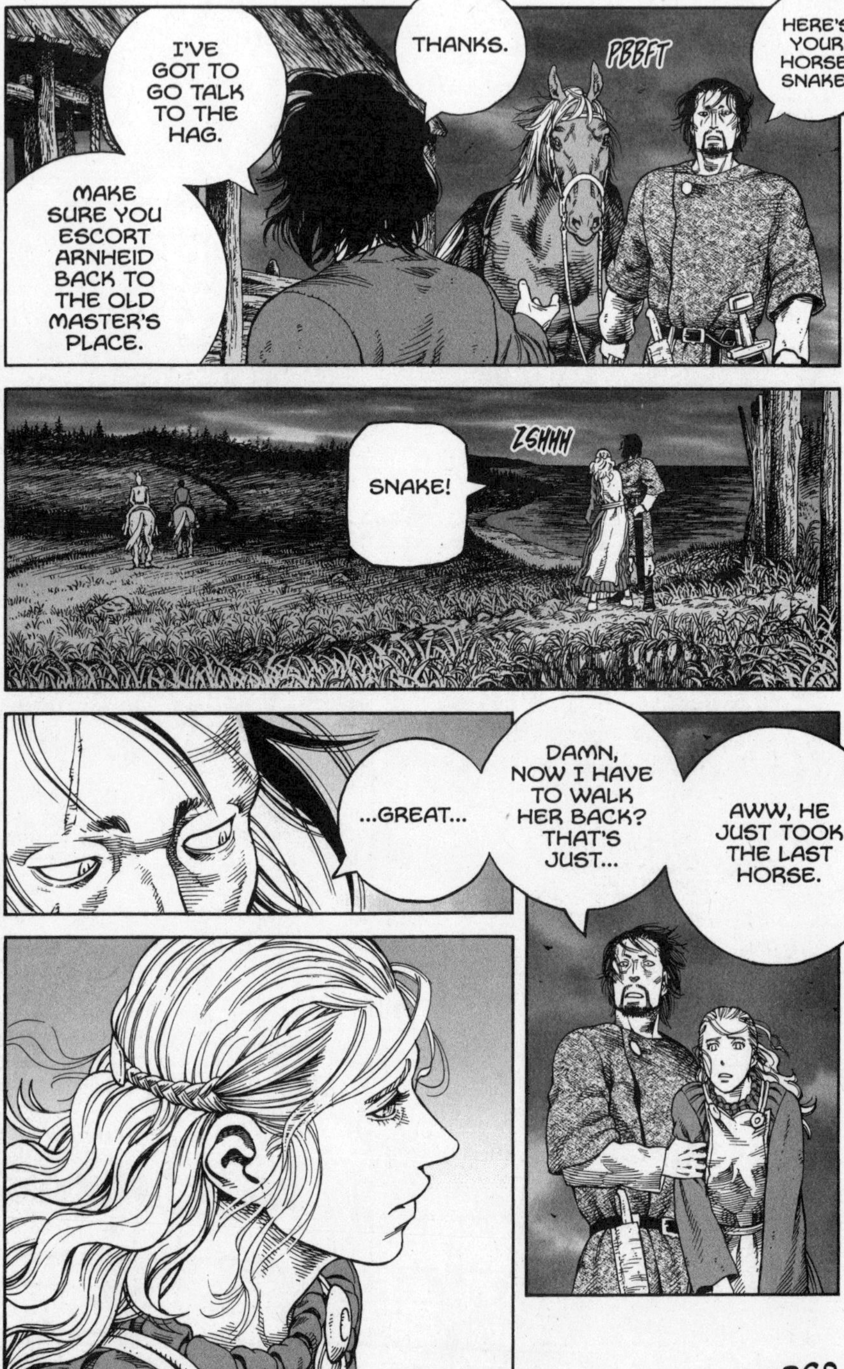
HERE'S YOUR HORSE, SNAKE.
PBBFT
THANKS.
I'VE GOT TO GO TALK TO THE HAG.
MAKE SURE YOU ESCORT ARNHEID BACK TO THE OLD MASTER'S PLACE.
ZSHHH
SNAKE!
OH!!
AWW, HE JUST TOOK THE LAST HORSE.
DAMN, NOW I HAVE TO WALK HER BACK? THAT'S JUST...
...GREAT...

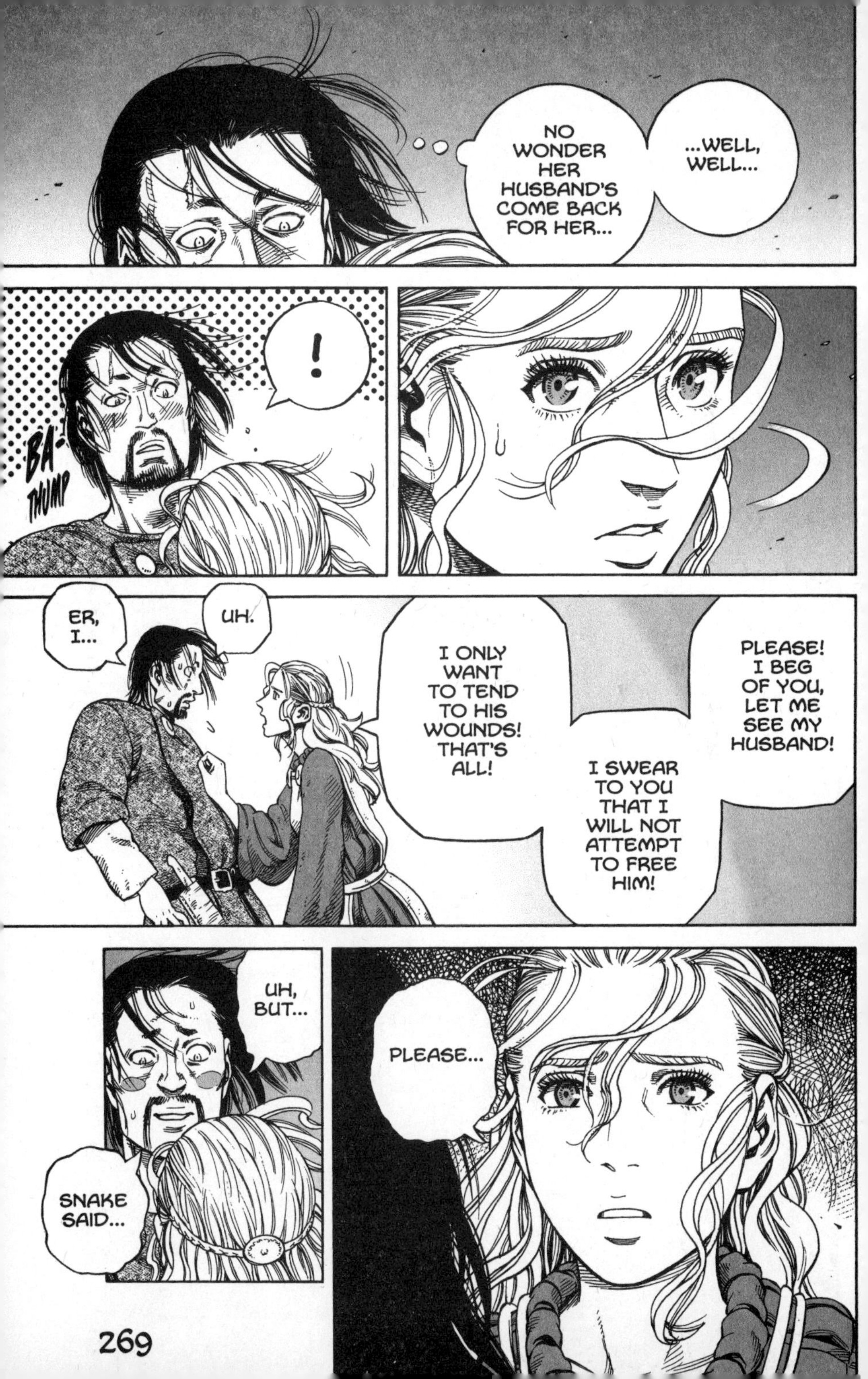
...WELL, WELL...
NO WONDER HER HUSBAND'S COME BACK FOR HER...
!
BA-THUMP
PLEASE! I BEG OF YOU, LET ME SEE MY HUSBAND!
I SWEAR TO YOU THAT I WILL NOT ATTEMPT TO FREE HIM!
I ONLY WANT TO TEND TO HIS WOUNDS! THAT'S ALL!
UH.
ER, I...
PLEASE...
UH, BUT...
SNAKE SAID...

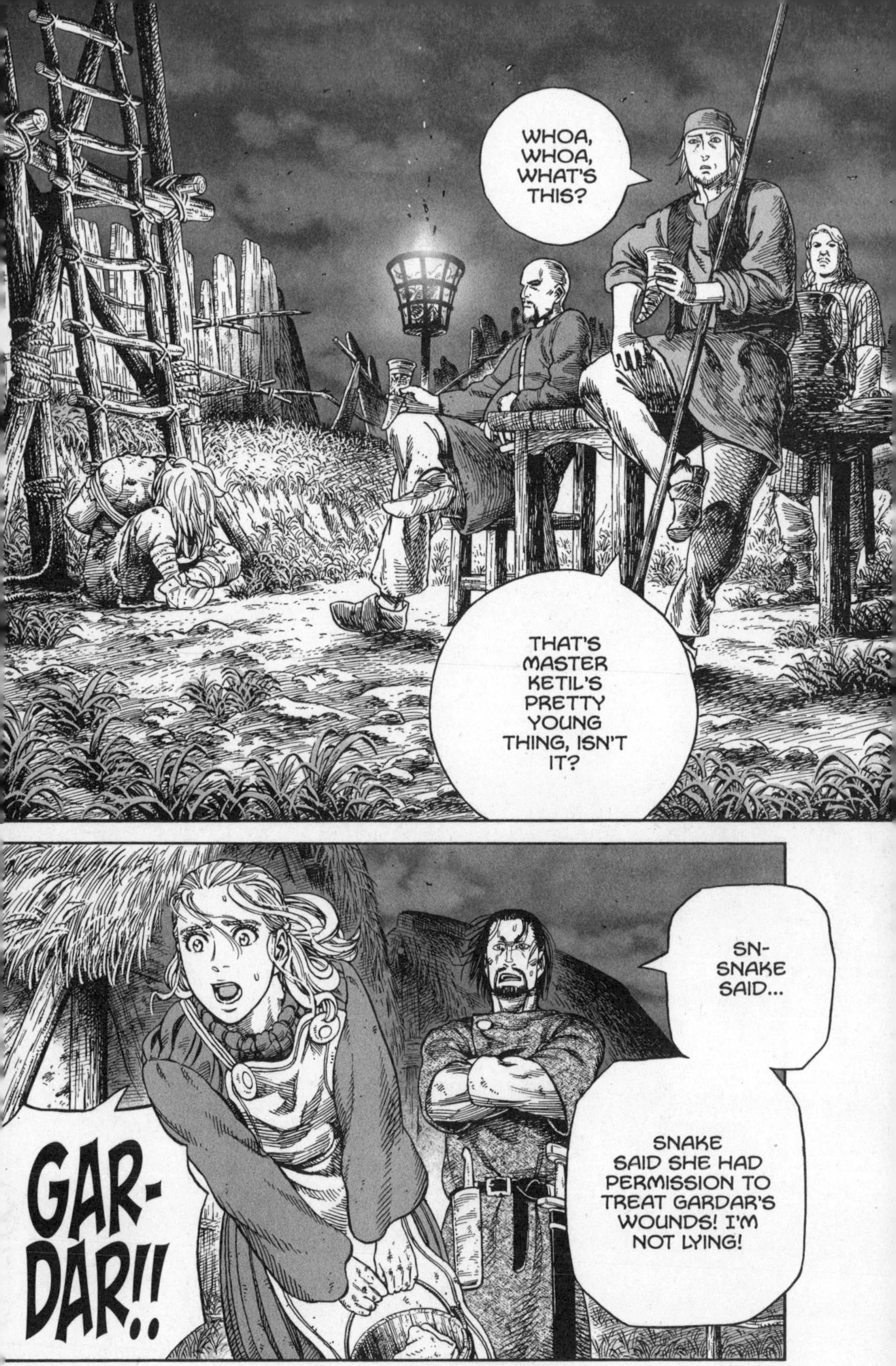
WHOA, WHOA, WHAT'S THIS?
THAT'S MASTER KETIL'S PRETTY YOUNG THING, ISN'T IT?
SN- SNAKE SAID...
SNAKE SAID SHE HAD PERMISSION TO TREAT GARDAR'S WOUNDS! I'M NOT LYING!
GAR- DAR!!

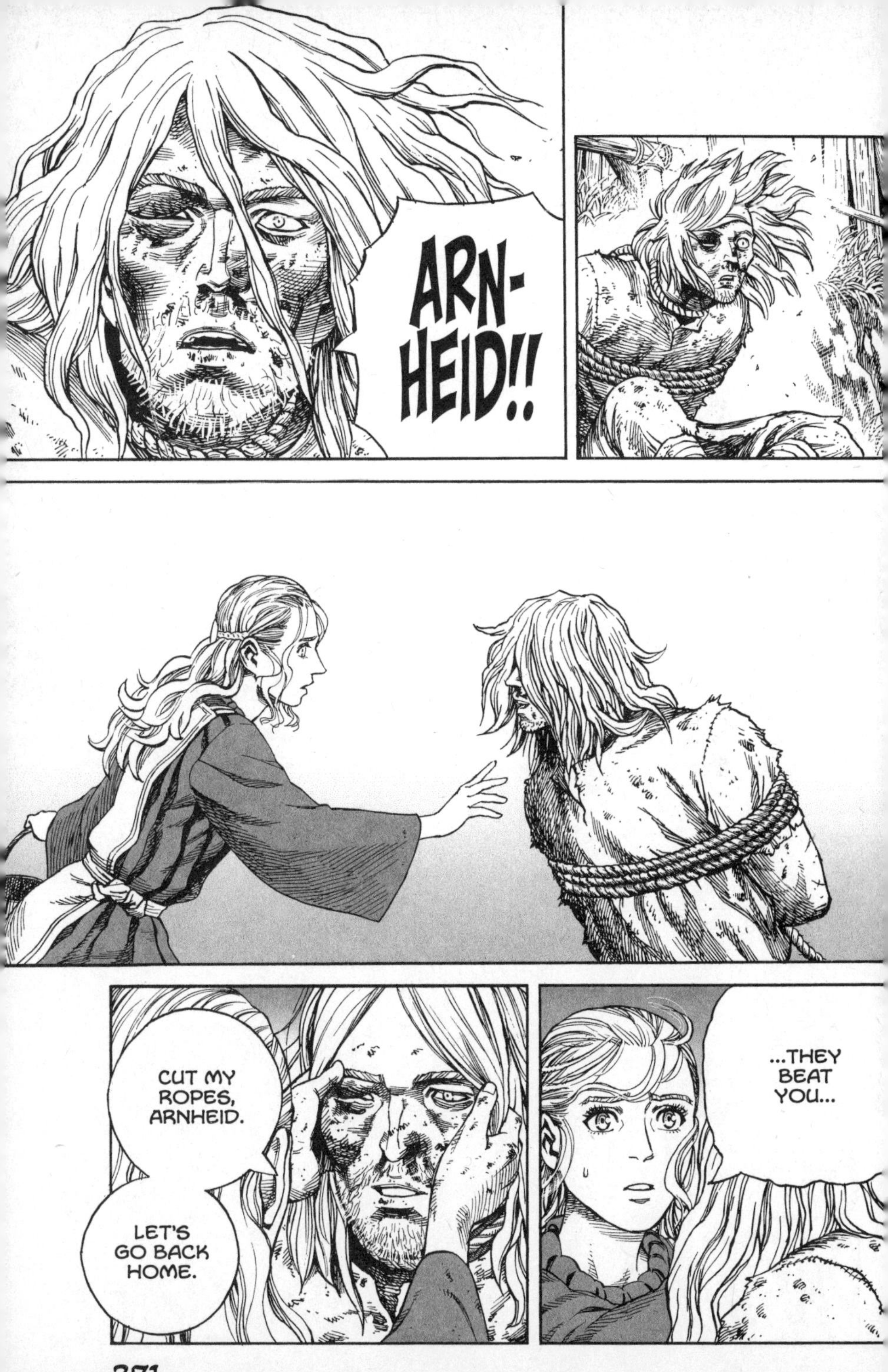
ARN-HEID!!
...THEY BEAT YOU...
CUT MY ROPES, ARNHEID.
LET'S GO BACK HOME.

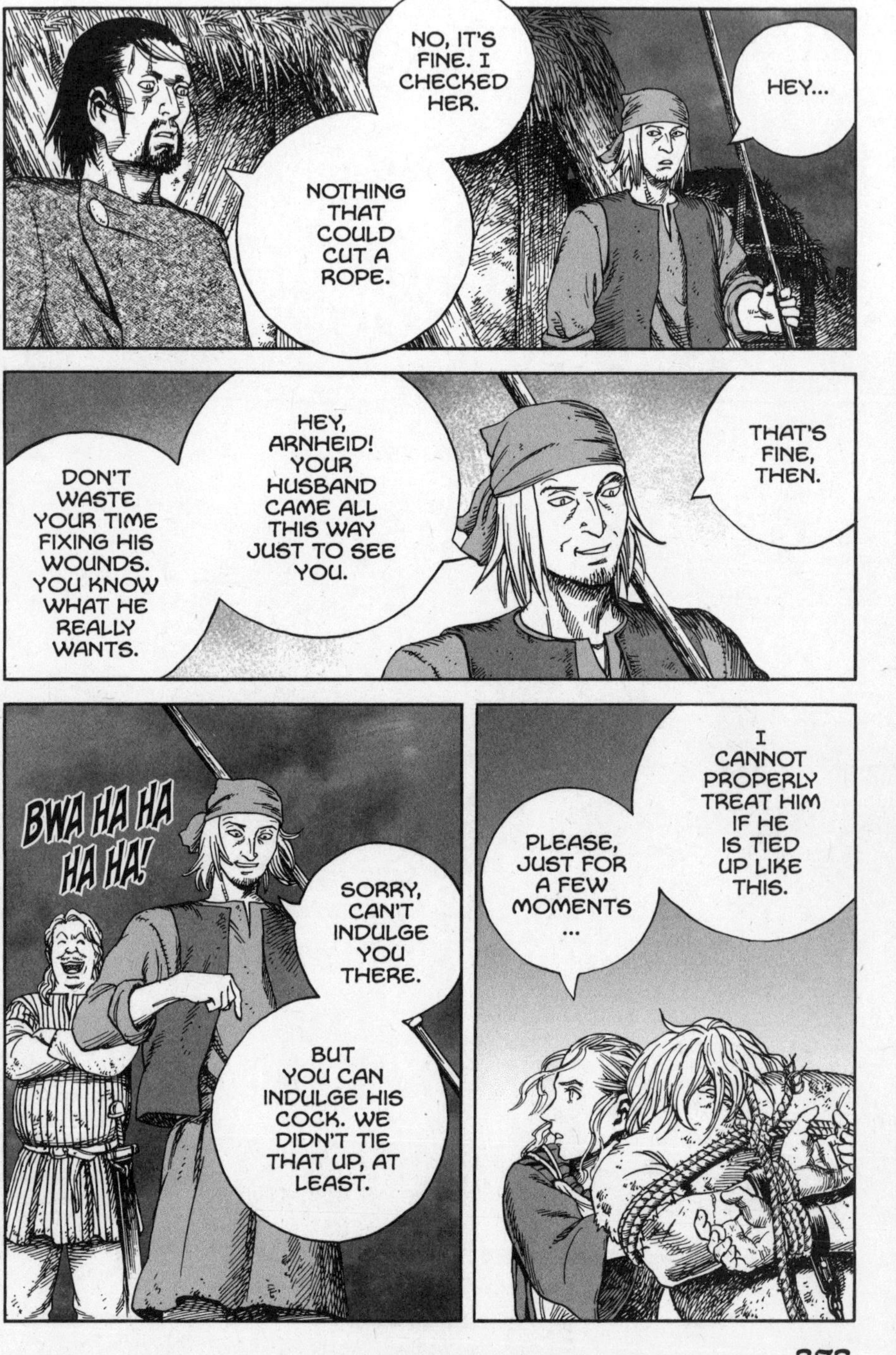
HEY...
NO, IT'S FINE. I CHECKED HER.
NOTHING THAT COULD CUT A ROPE.
THAT'S FINE, THEN.
HEY, ARNHEID! YOUR HUSBAND CAME ALL THIS WAY JUST TO SEE YOU.
DON'T WASTE YOUR TIME FIXING HIS WOUNDS. YOU KNOW WHAT HE REALLY WANTS.
I CANNOT PROPERLY TREAT HIM IF HE IS TIED UP LIKE THIS.
PLEASE, JUST FOR A FEW MOMENTS ...
SORRY, CAN'T INDULGE YOU THERE.
BUT YOU CAN INDULGE HIS COCK. WE DIDN'T TIE THAT UP, AT LEAST.
BWA HA HA HA HA!

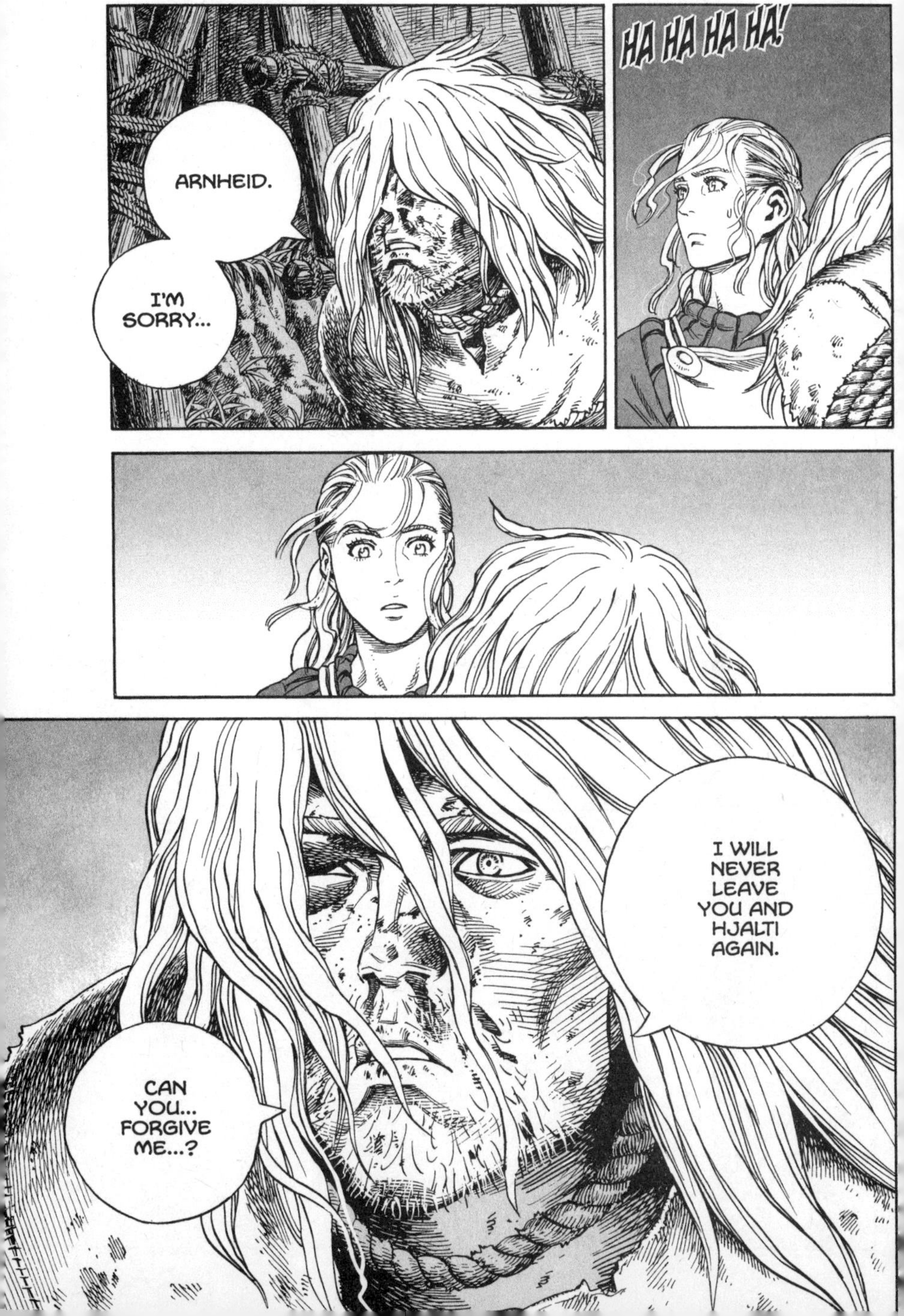
HA HA HA HA!
ARNHEID.
I'M SORRY...
I WILL NEVER LEAVE YOU AND HJALTI AGAIN.
CAN YOU... FORGIVE ME...?

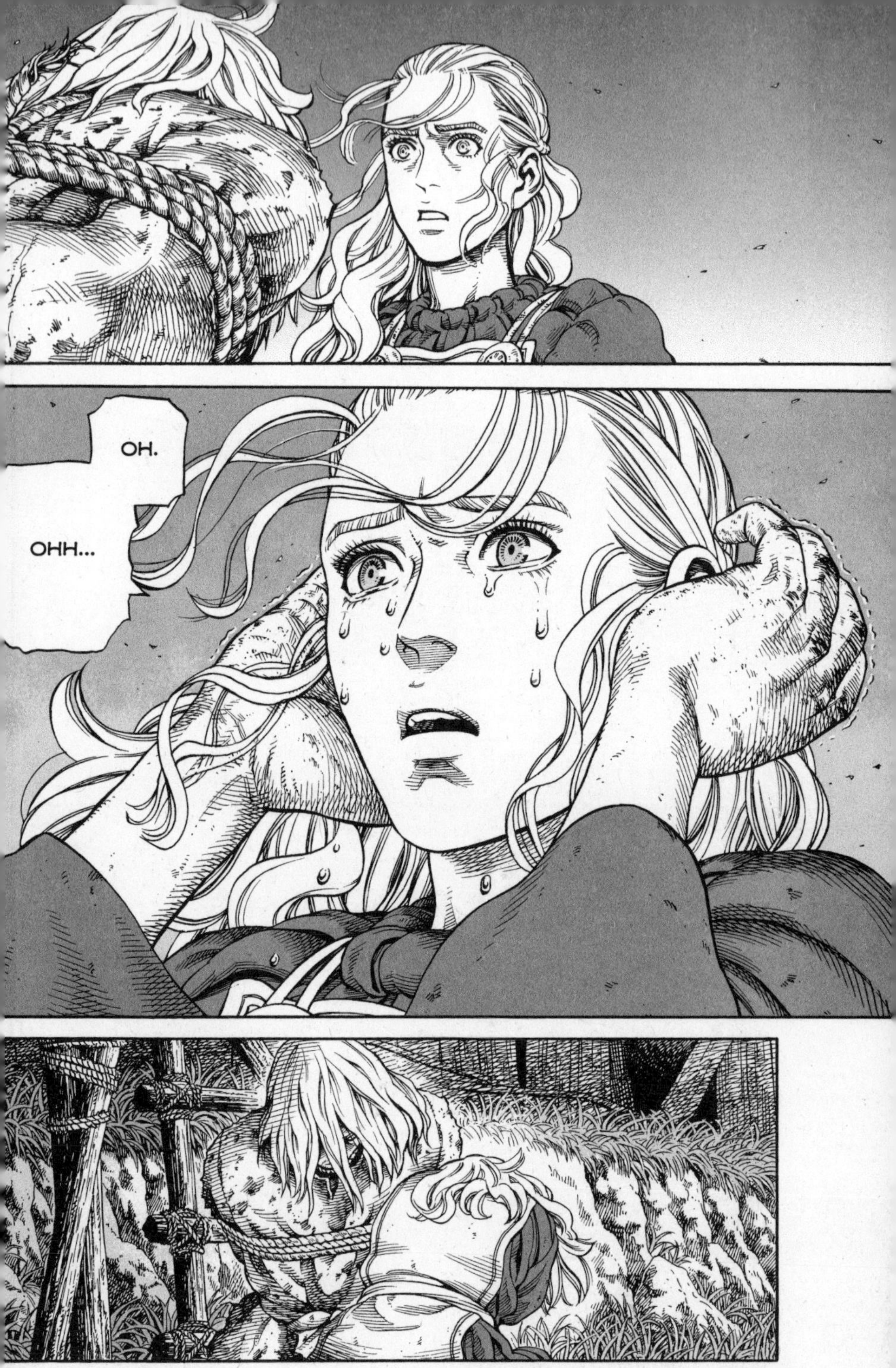
OH.
OHH...

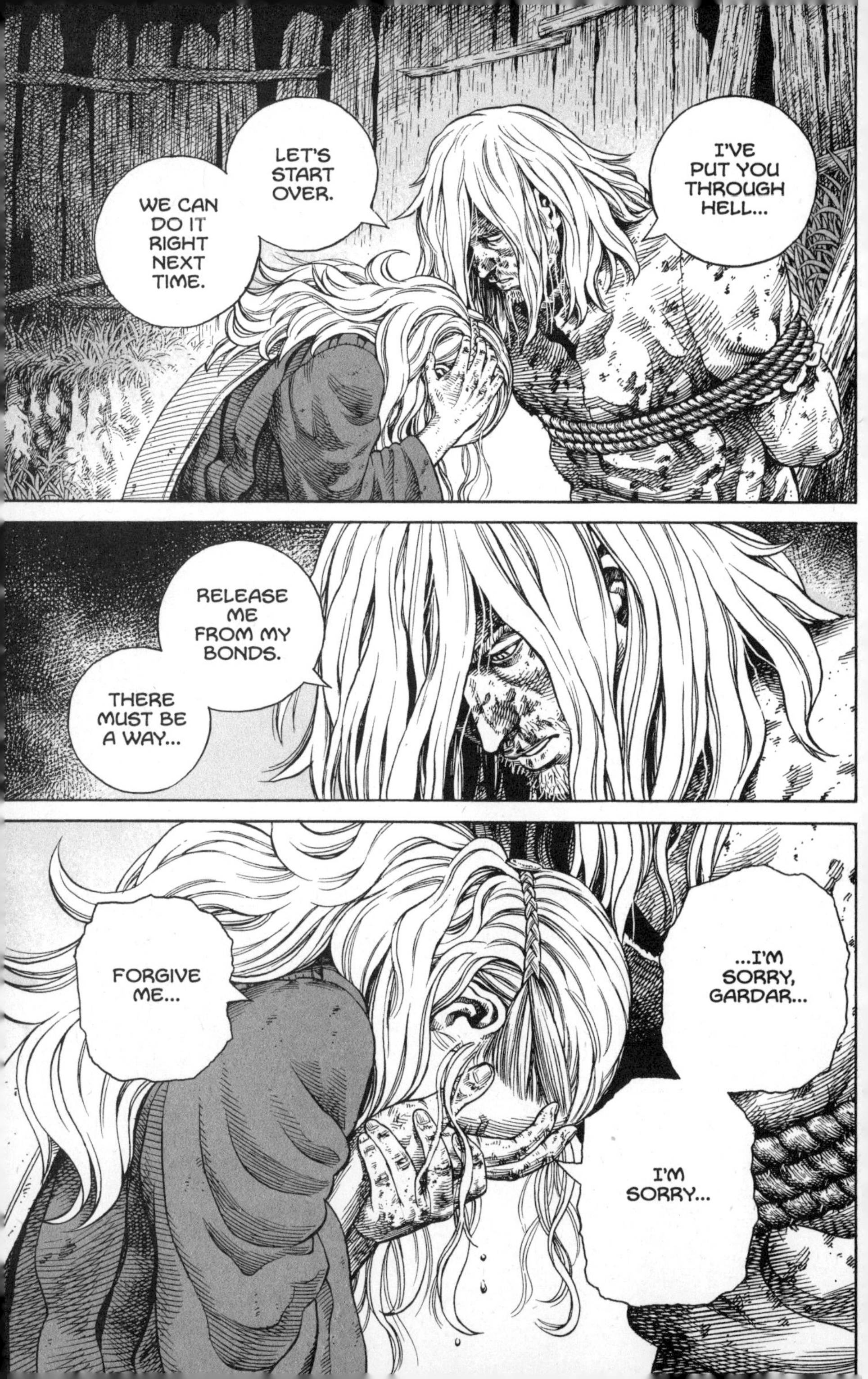
I'VE PUT YOU THROUGH HELL...
LET'S START OVER.
WE CAN DO IT RIGHT NEXT TIME.
RELEASE ME FROM MY BONDS.
THERE MUST BE A WAY...
...I'M SORRY, GARDAR...
I'M SORRY...
FORGIVE ME...

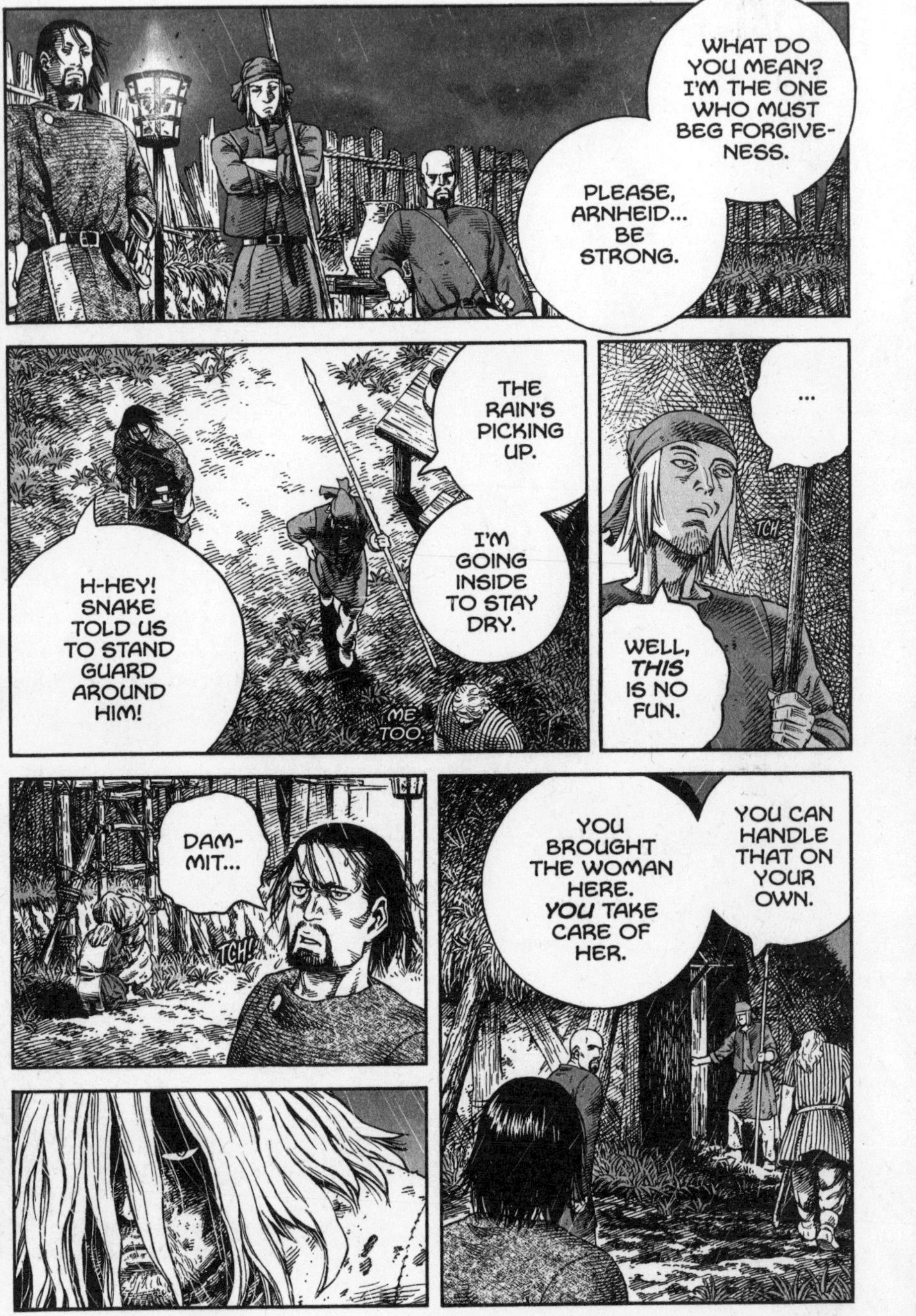
WHAT DO YOU MEAN? I'M THE ONE WHO MUST BEG FORGIVE-NESS.
PLEASE, ARNHEID... BE STRONG.
...
TCH
WELL, *THIS* IS NO FUN.
THE RAIN'S PICKING UP.
I'M GOING INSIDE TO STAY DRY.
ME TOO.
H-HEY! SNAKE TOLD US TO STAND GUARD AROUND HIM!
YOU CAN HANDLE THAT ON YOUR OWN.
YOU BROUGHT THE WOMAN HERE. *YOU* TAKE CARE OF HER.
DAM-MIT...
TCH!

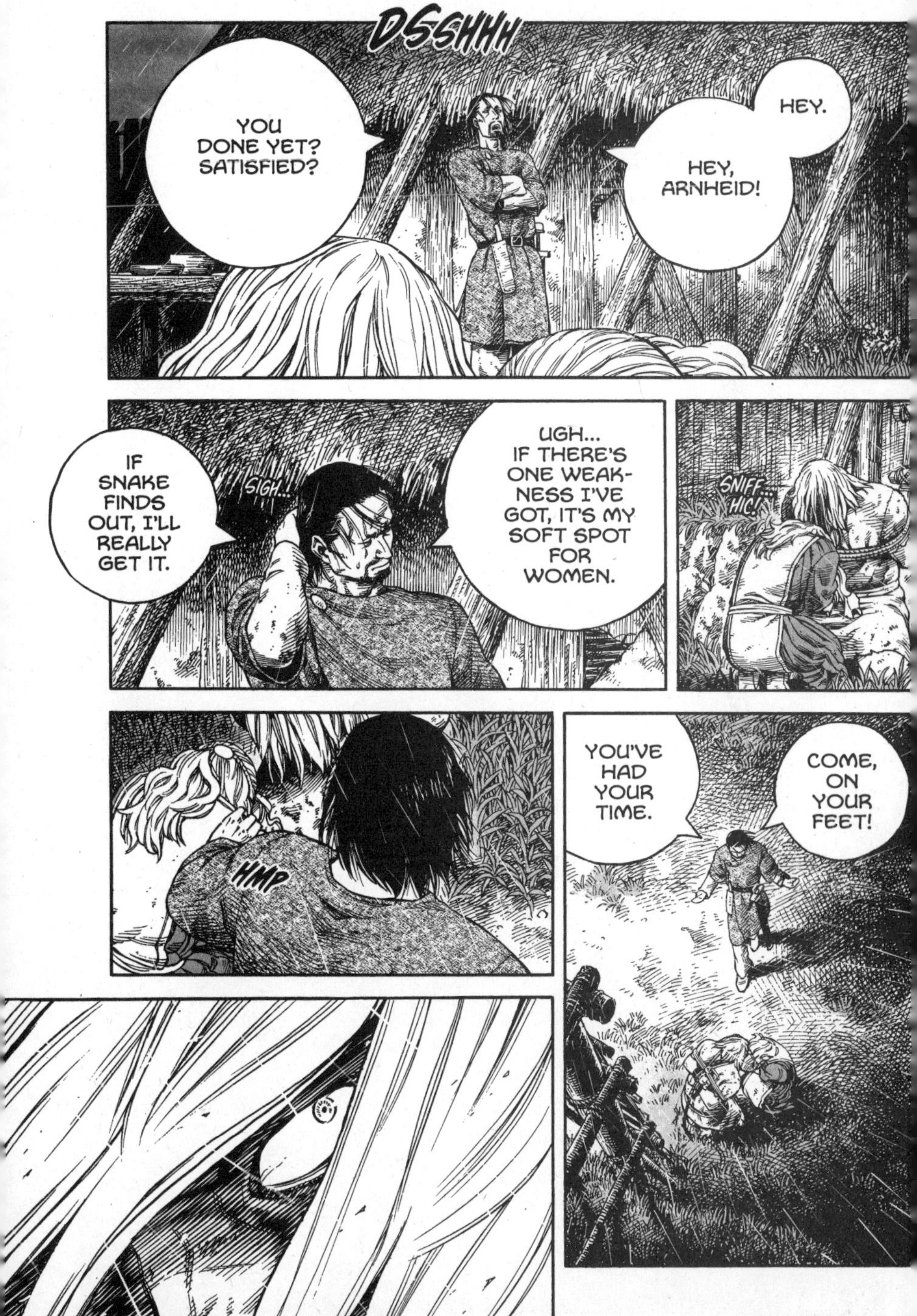
DSSHHH
HEY.
HEY, ARNHEID!
YOU DONE YET? SATISFIED?
SNIFF... HIC!
UGH... IF THERE'S ONE WEAK-NESS I'VE GOT, IT'S MY SOFT SPOT FOR WOMEN.
SIGH...
IF SNAKE FINDS OUT, I'LL REALLY GET IT.
COME, ON YOUR FEET!
YOU'VE HAD YOUR TIME.
HMP

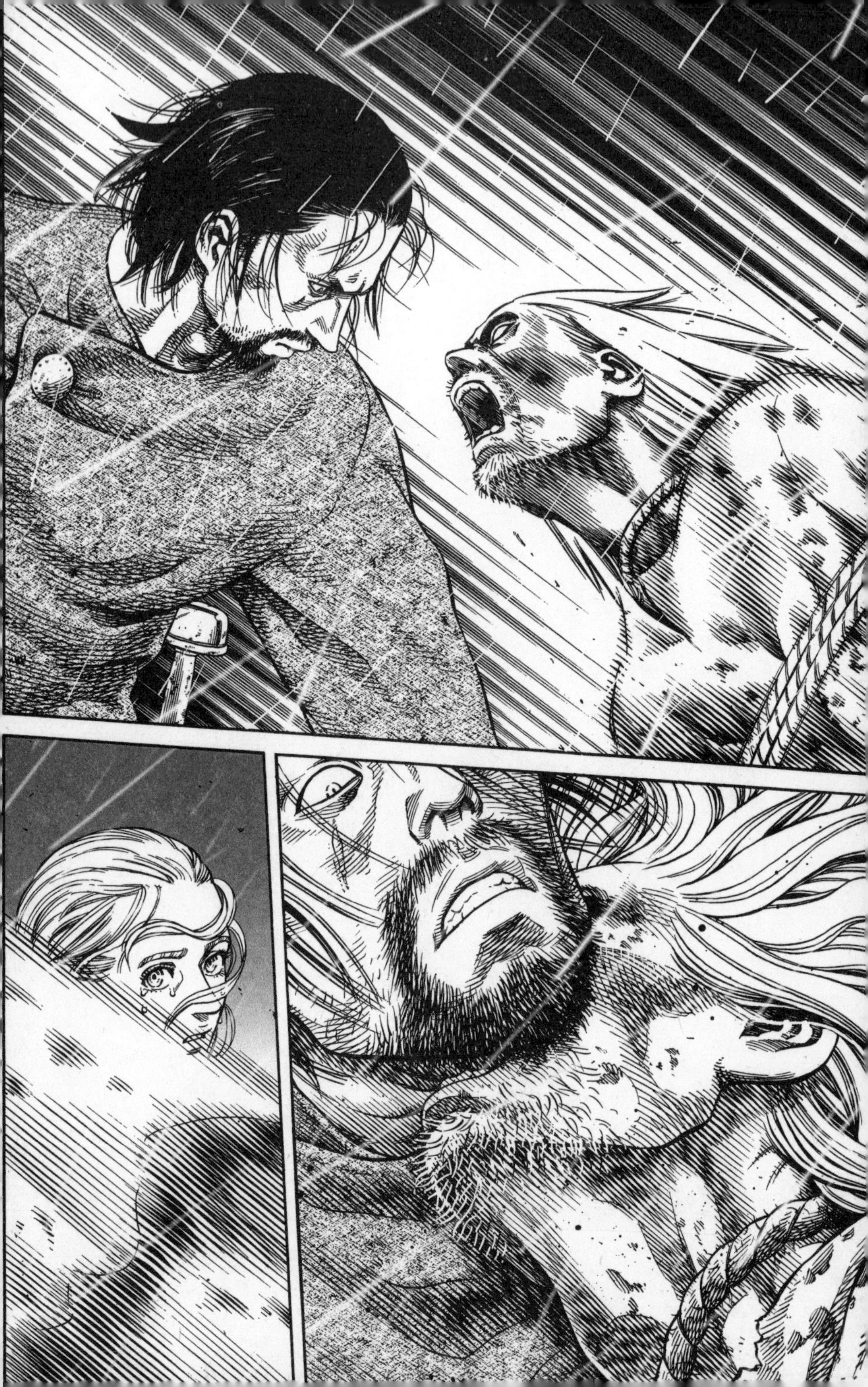

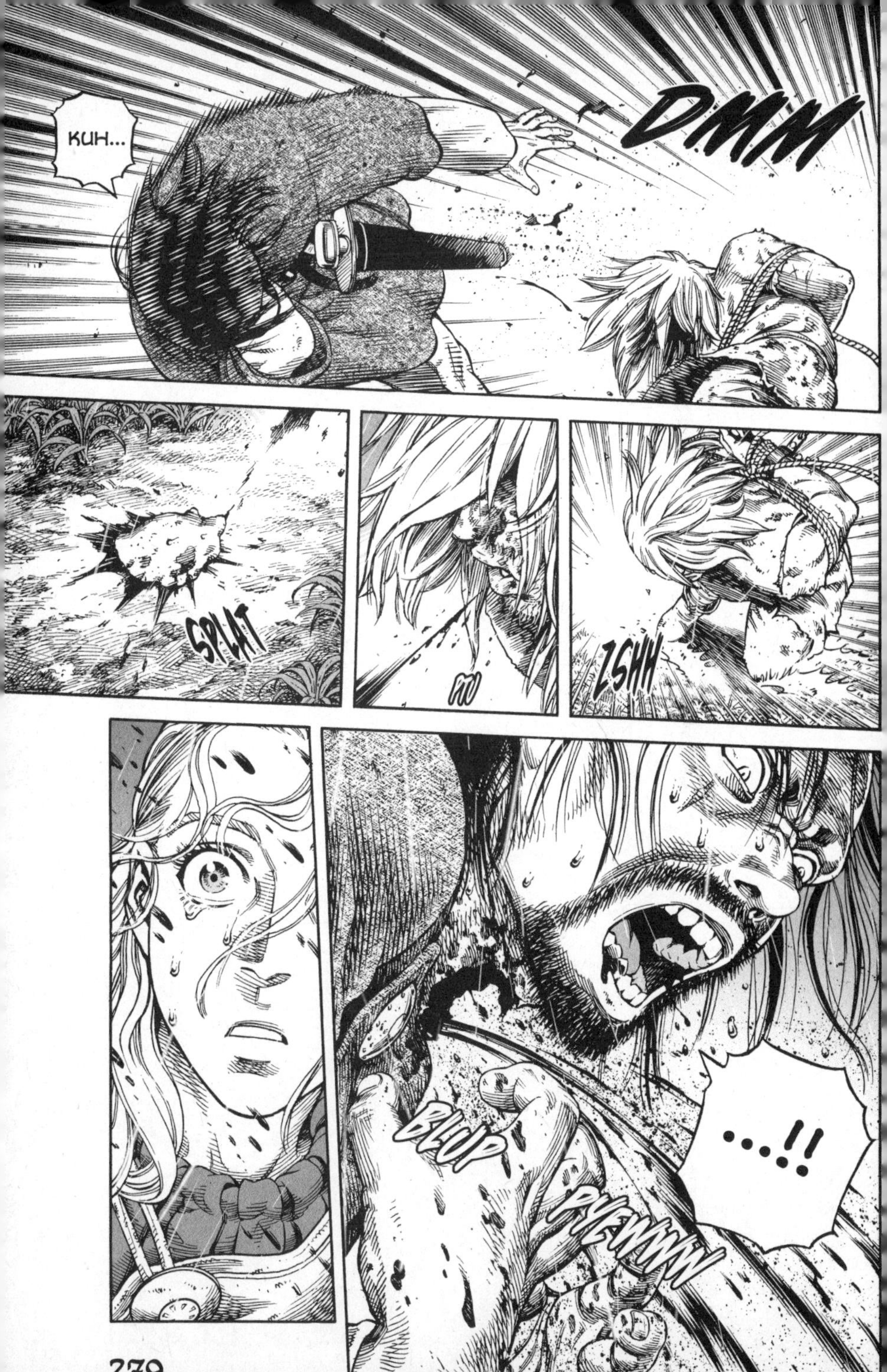
DMM
KUH...
ZSHH
SPLAT
...!!
BLUP

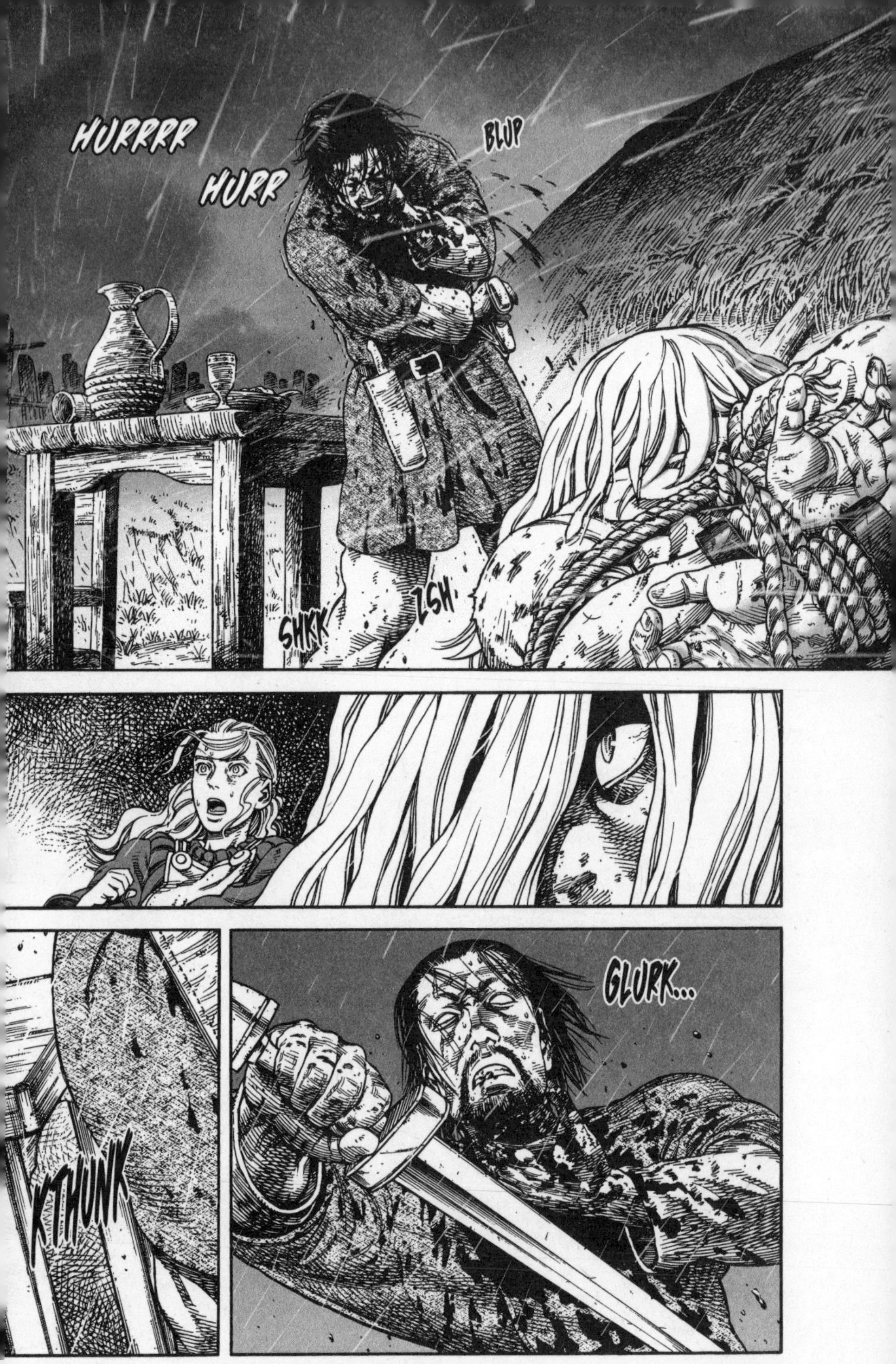
BLUP
HURRRR
HURR
ZSH
SHKK
GLURK...
KTHUNK

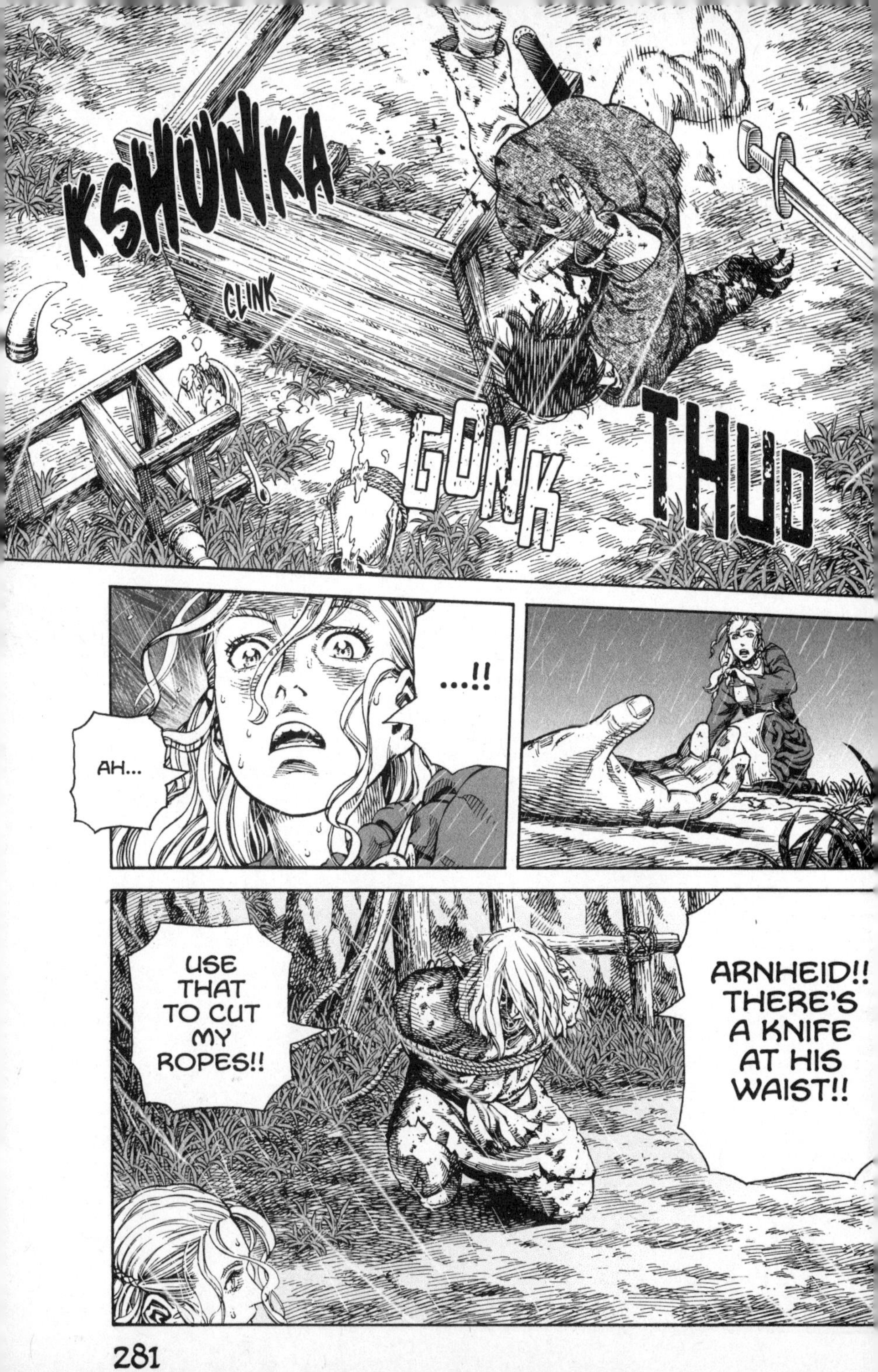
KSHUNKA
CLINK
THUD
GONK
...!!
AH...
ARNHEID!! THERE'S A KNIFE AT HIS WAIST!!
USE THAT TO CUT MY ROPES!!

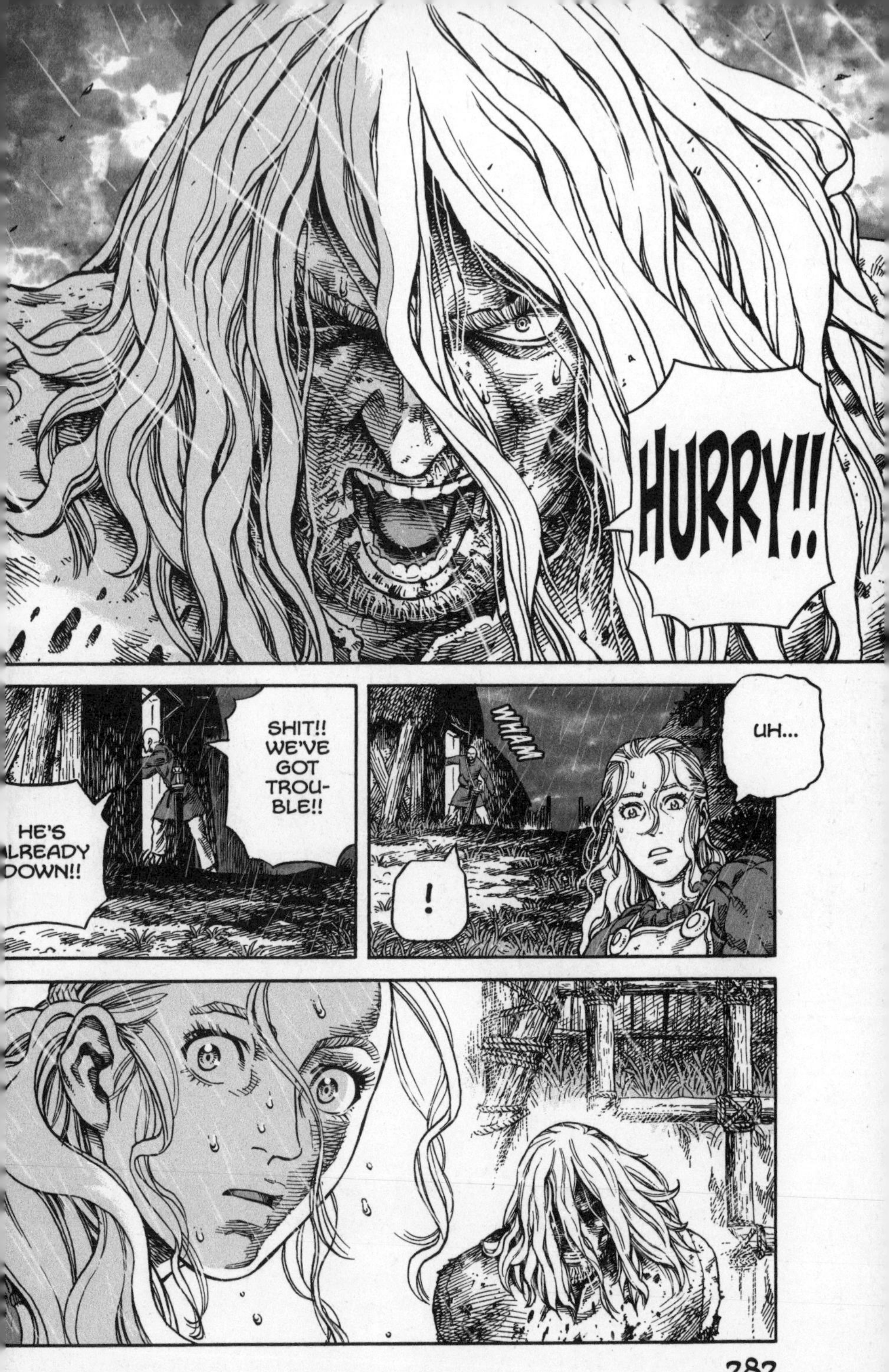
HURRY!!
UH...
WHAM
!
SHIT!! WE'VE GOT TROUBLE!!
HE'S ALREADY DOWN!!

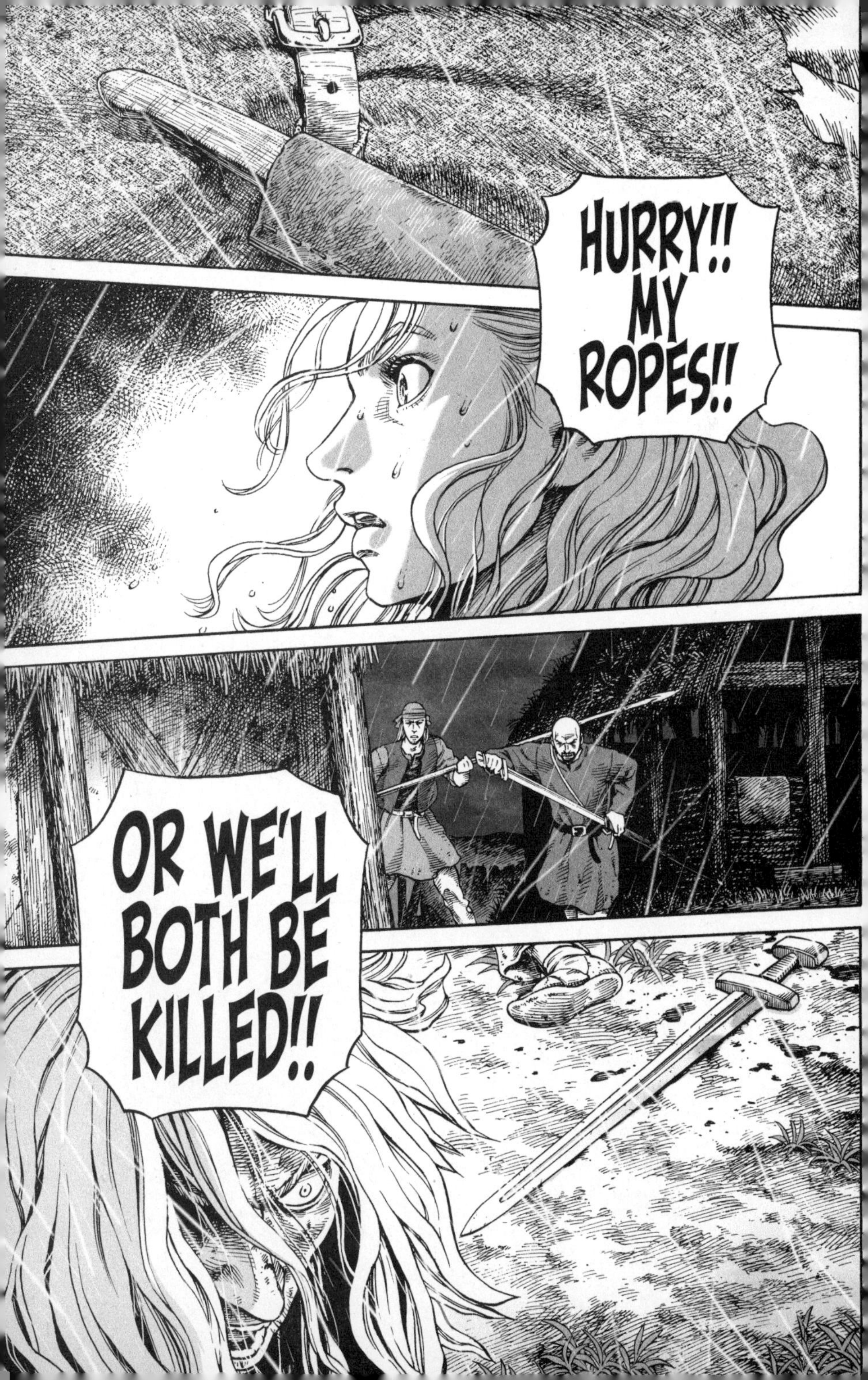
HURRY!! MY ROPES!!
OR WE'LL BOTH BE KILLED!!

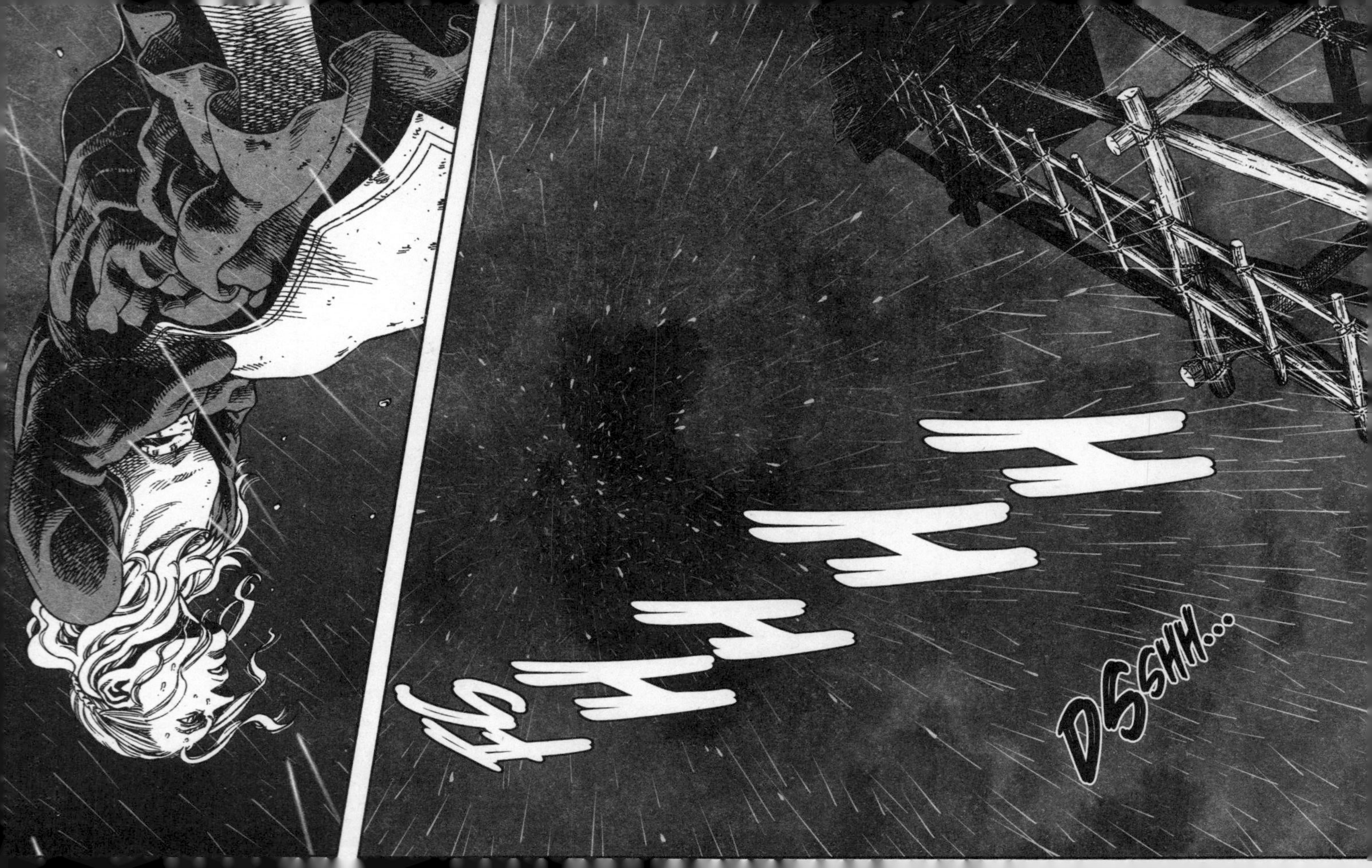
FSHHHH
DSSHH...

CHAPTER 83: ATONEMENT

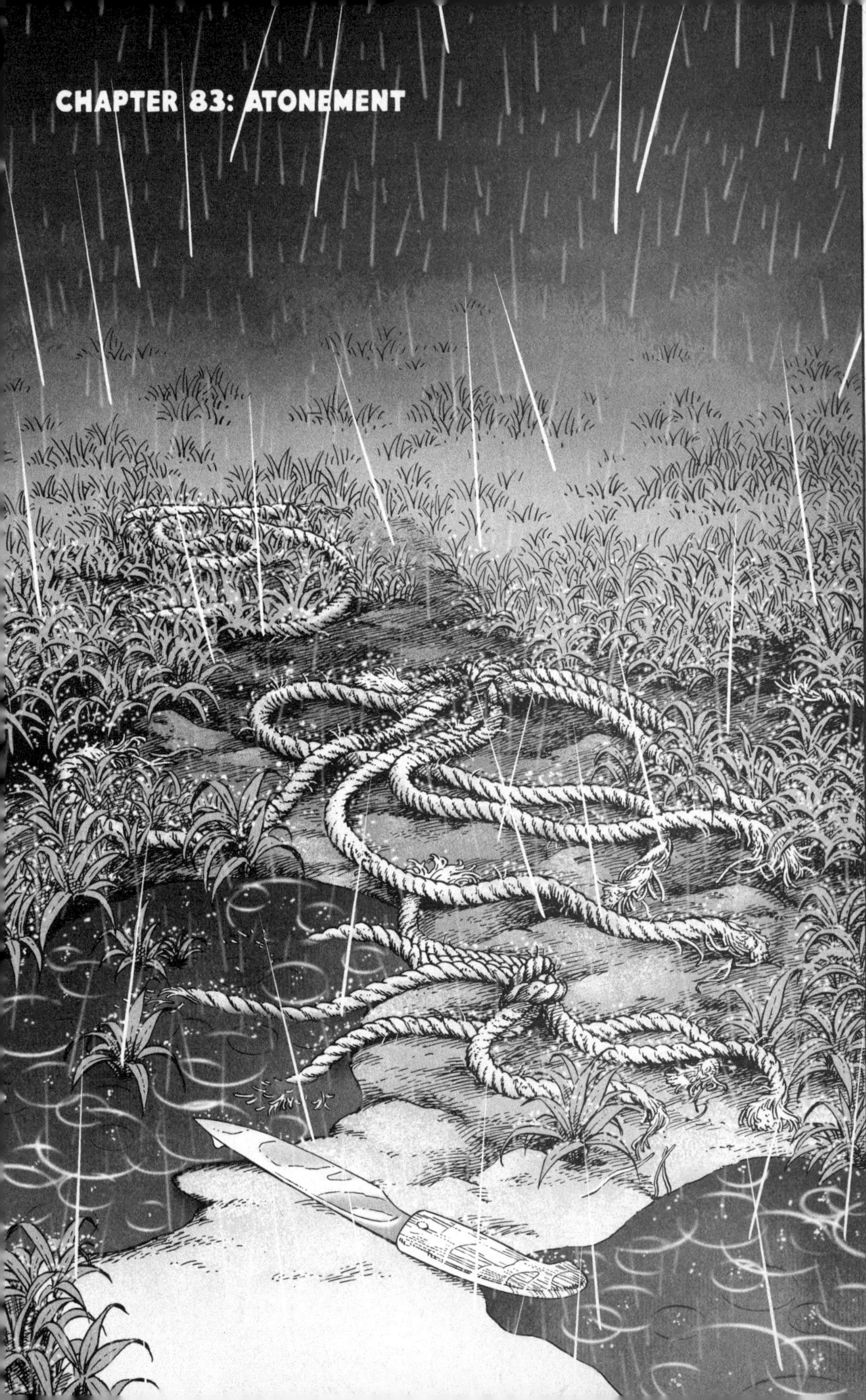

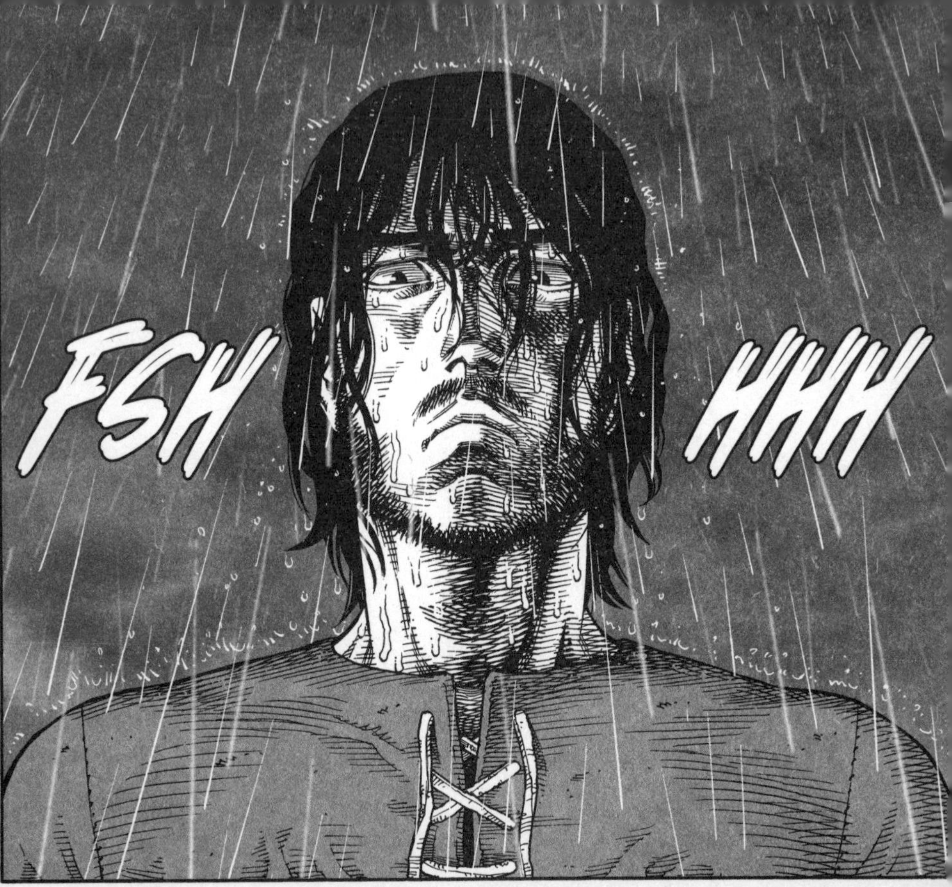
FSHHHH
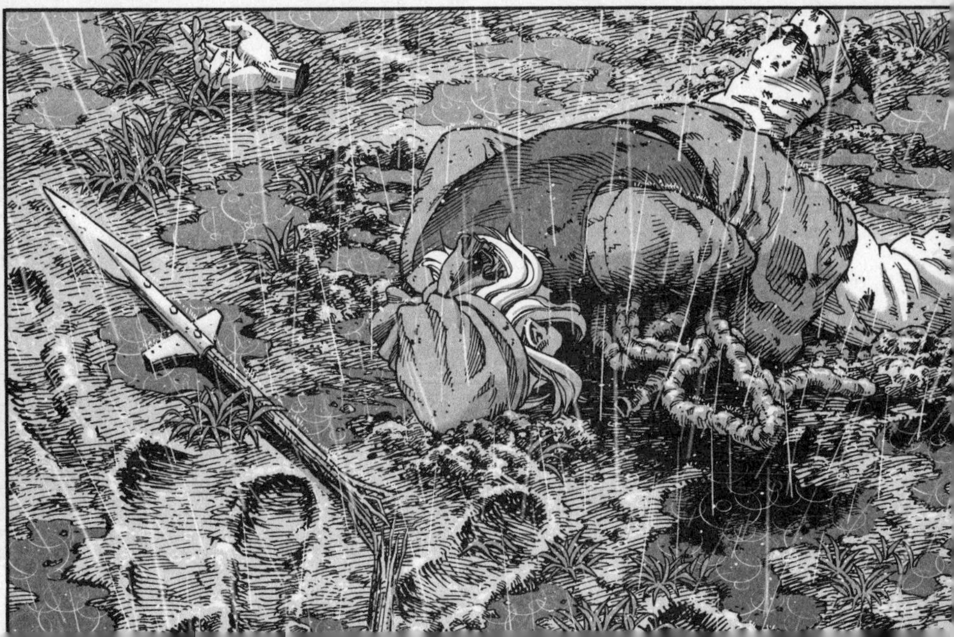

ALL FOUR ARE DEAD.

I'M SORRY, SNAKE...

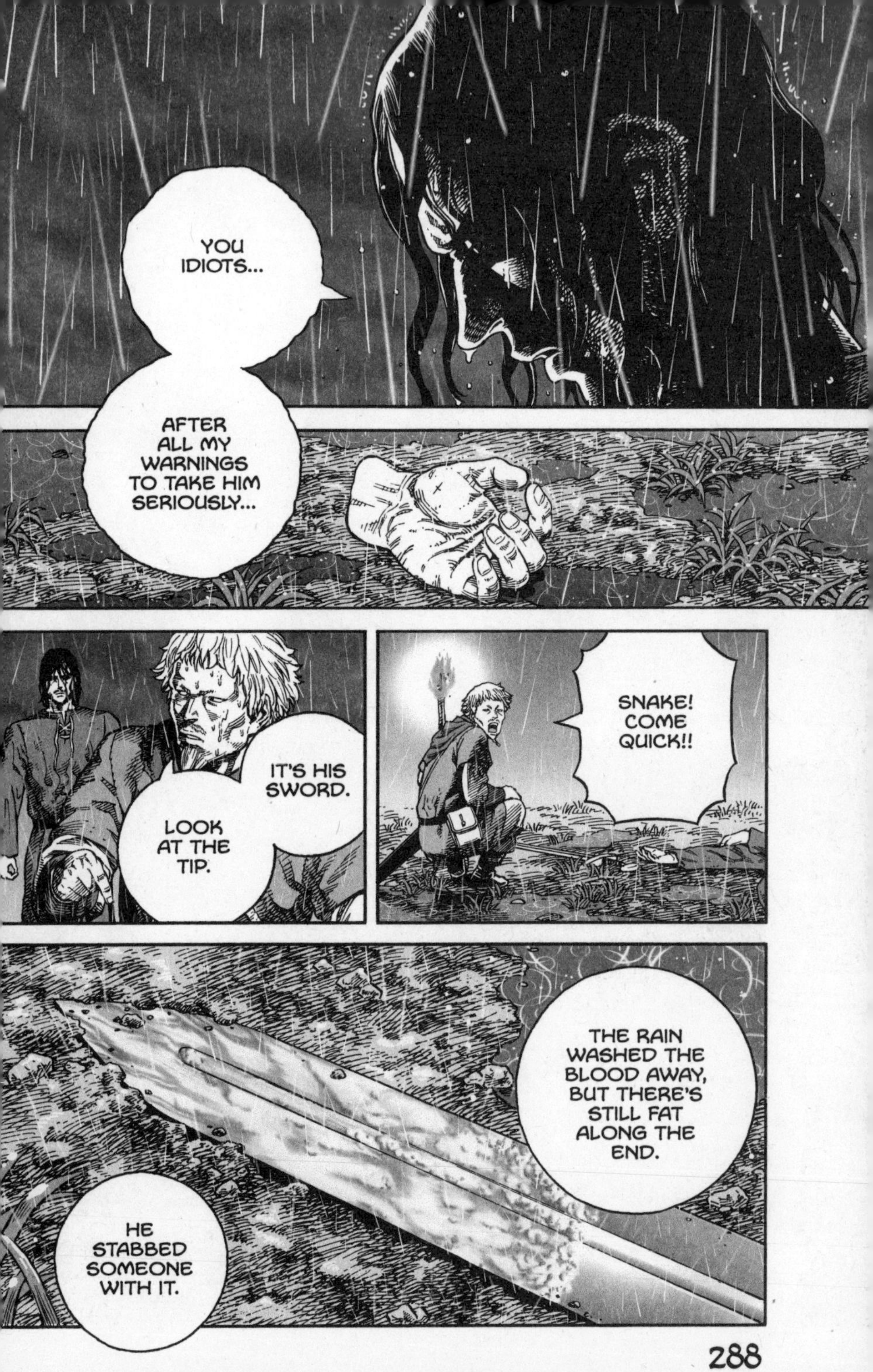
YOU IDIOTS...
AFTER ALL MY WARNINGS TO TAKE HIM SERIOUSLY...
SNAKE! COME QUICK!!
IT'S HIS SWORD.
LOOK AT THE TIP.
THE RAIN WASHED THE BLOOD AWAY, BUT THERE'S STILL FAT ALONG THE END.
HE STABBED SOMEONE WITH IT.

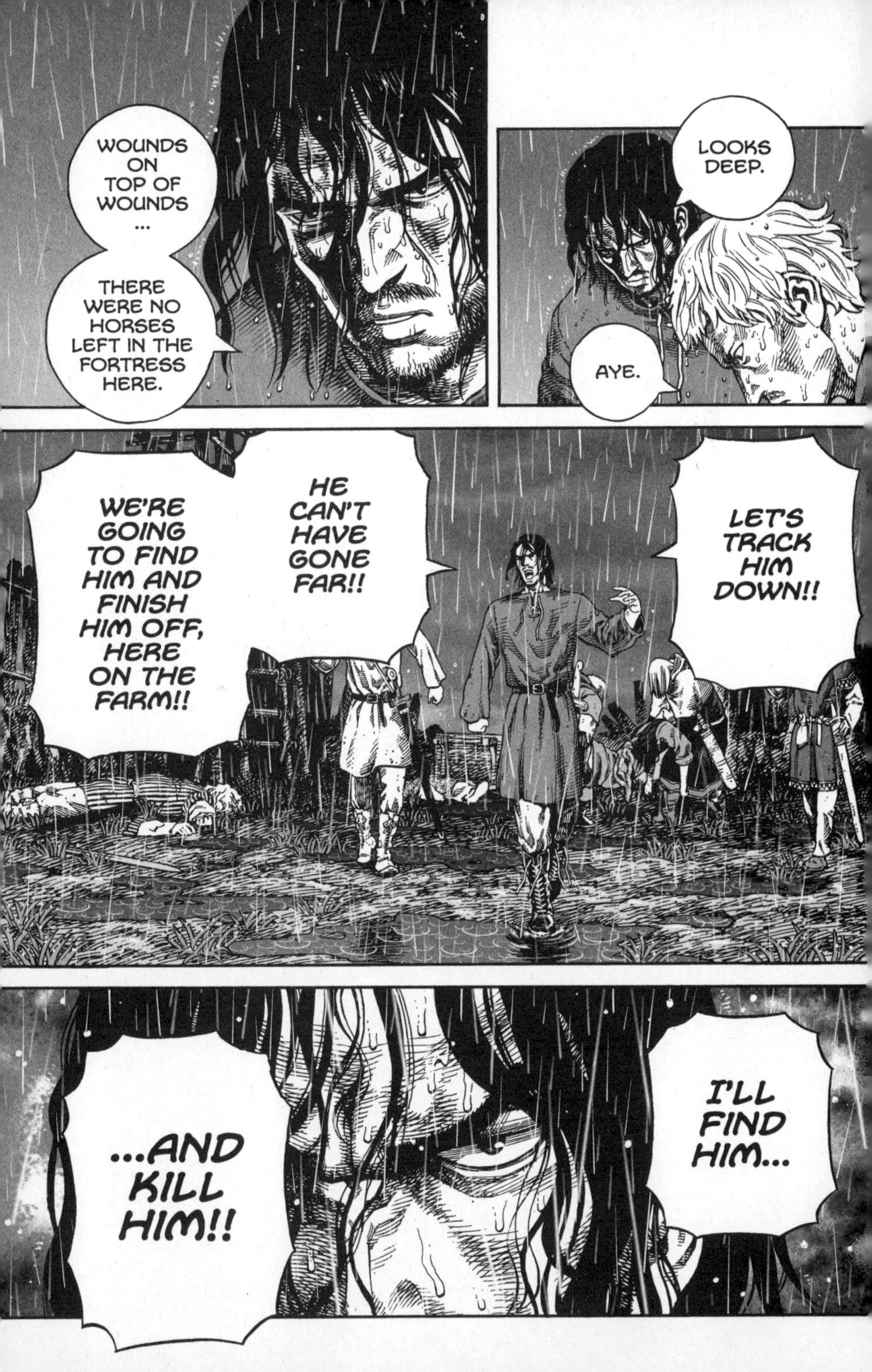
LOOKS DEEP.
AYE.
WOUNDS ON TOP OF WOUNDS ...
THERE WERE NO HORSES LEFT IN THE FORTRESS HERE.
LET'S TRACK HIM DOWN!!
HE CAN'T HAVE GONE FAR!!
WE'RE GOING TO FIND HIM AND FINISH HIM OFF, HERE ON THE FARM!!
I'LL FIND HIM...
...AND KILL HIM!!

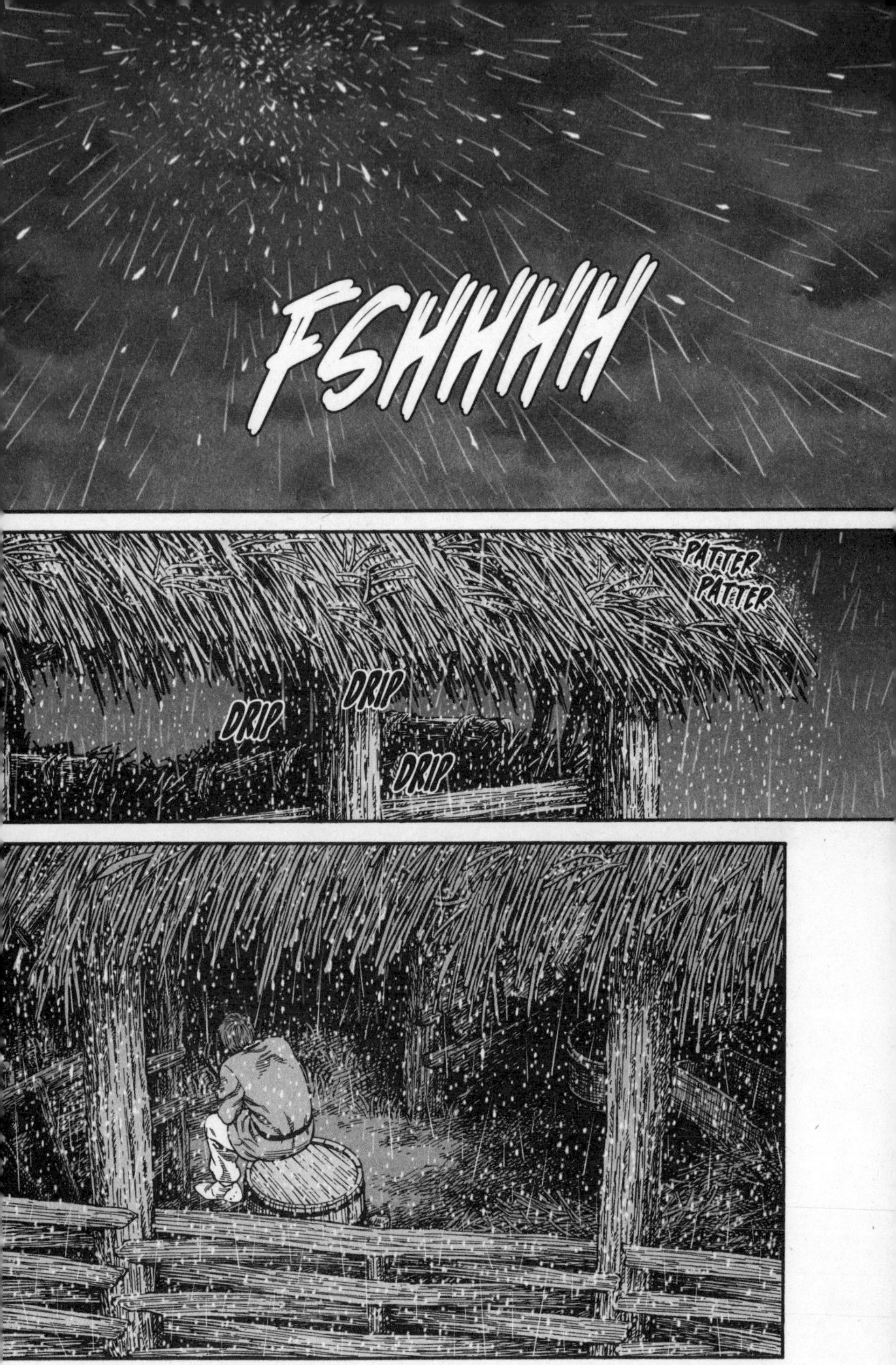
FSHHHH
PATTER PATTER
DRIP
DRIP
DRIP

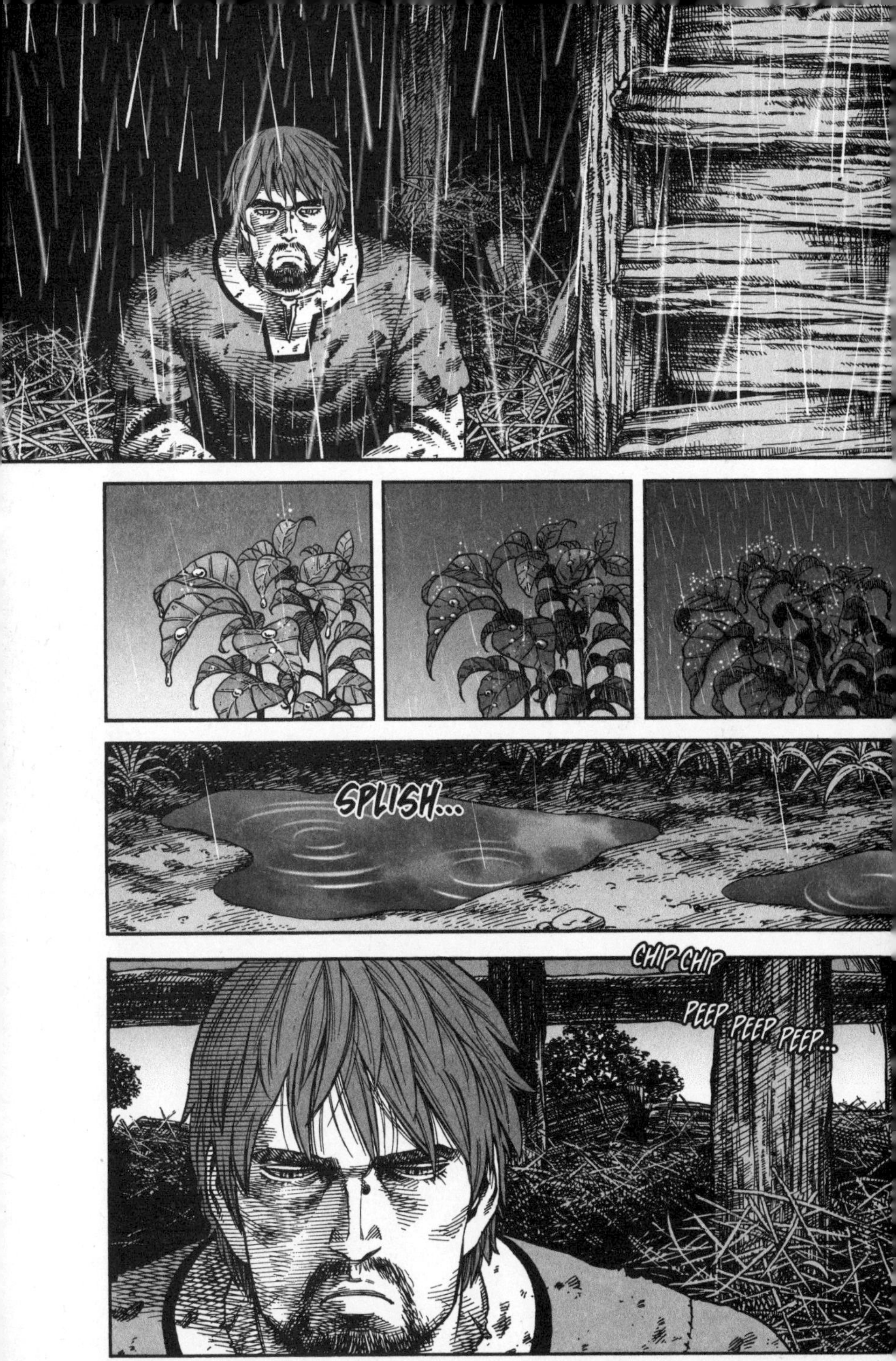
SPLISH...
CHIP CHIP
PEEP PEEP PEEP...

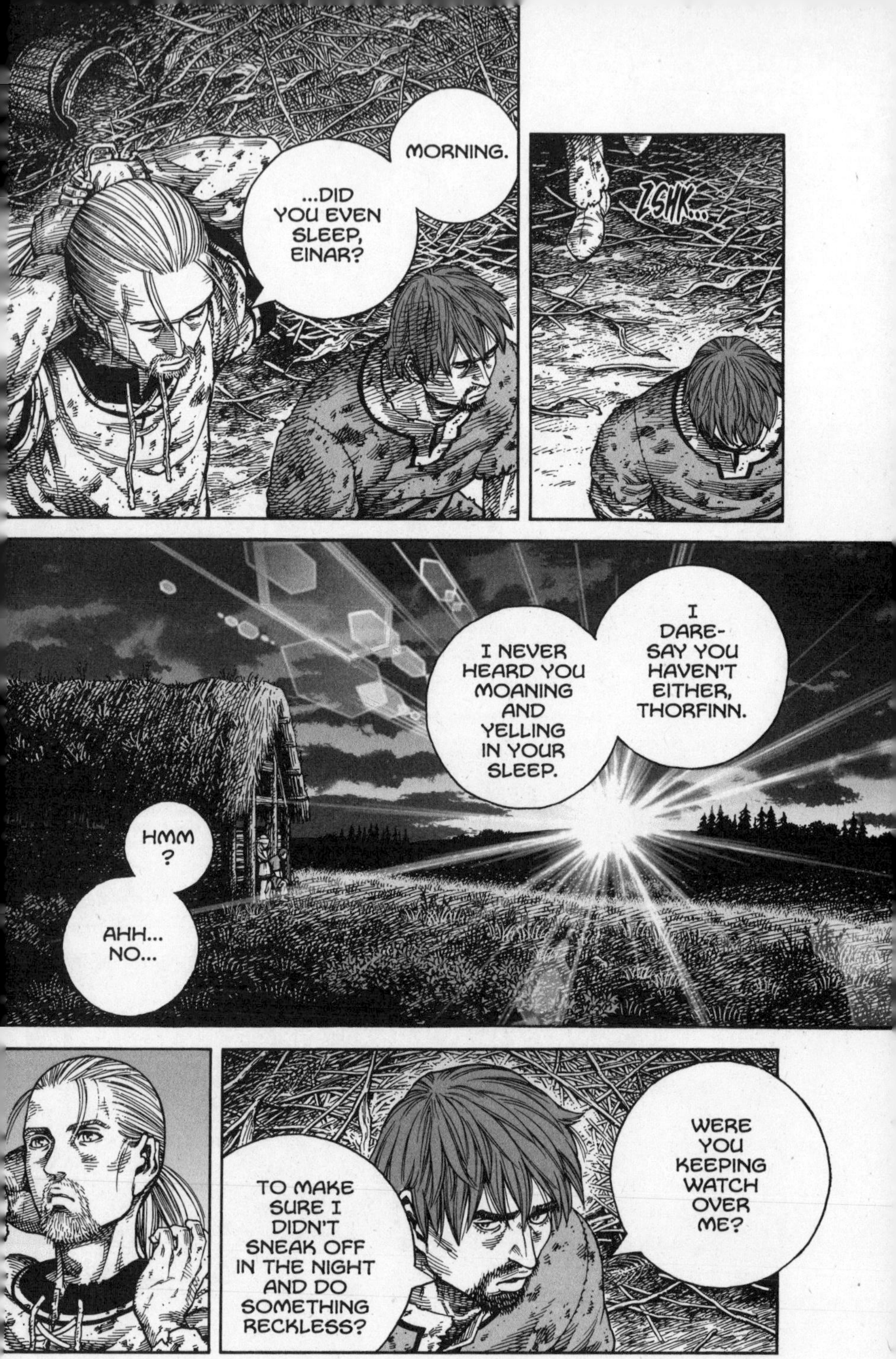
ZSHK...
MORNING.
...DID YOU EVEN SLEEP, EINAR?
I DARESAY YOU HAVEN'T EITHER, THORFINN.
I NEVER HEARD YOU MOANING AND YELLING IN YOUR SLEEP.
HMM?
AHH... NO...
WERE YOU KEEPING WATCH OVER ME?
TO MAKE SURE I DIDN'T SNEAK OFF IN THE NIGHT AND DO SOMETHING RECKLESS?

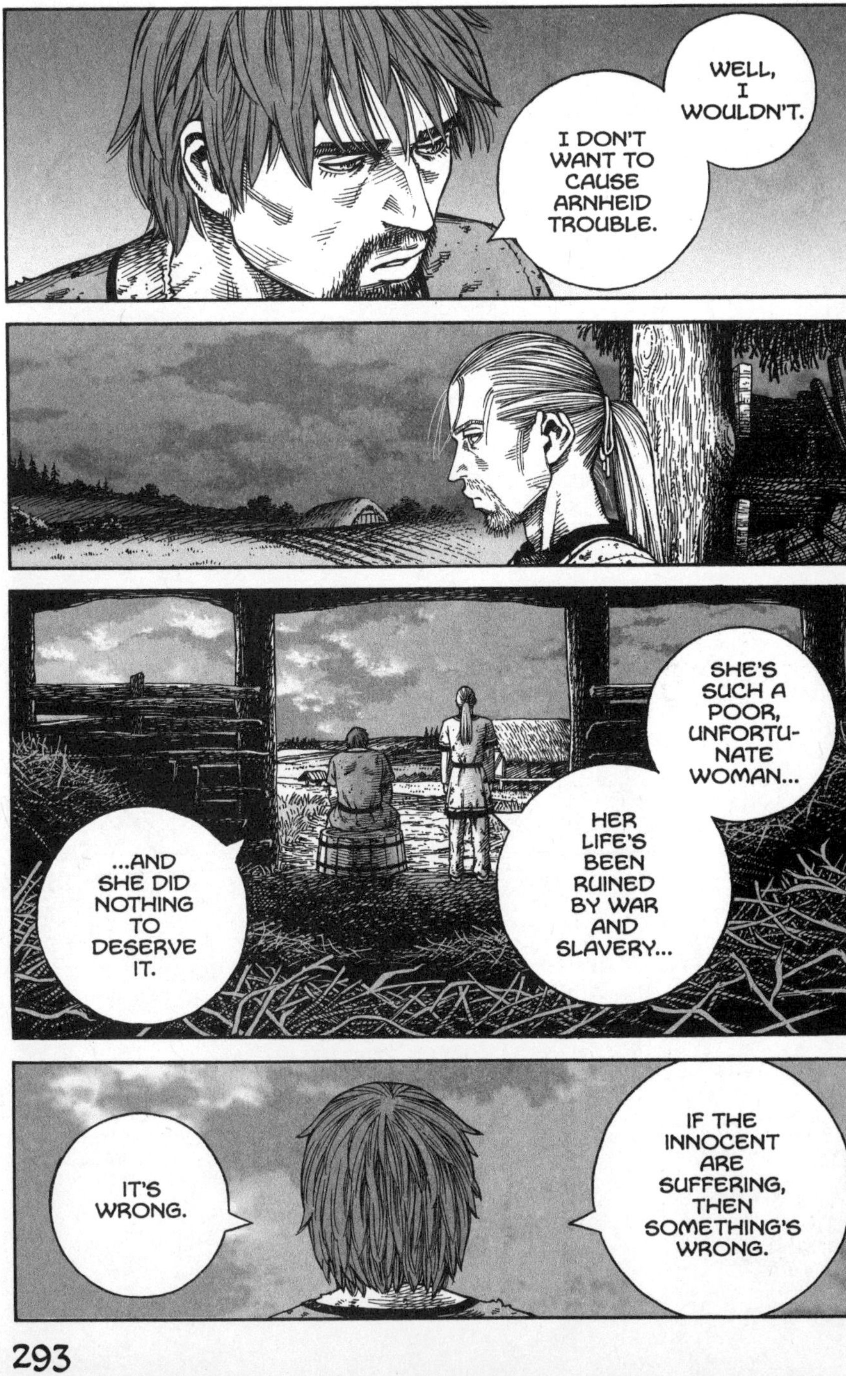
WELL, I WOULDN'T.
I DON'T WANT TO CAUSE ARNHEID TROUBLE.
SHE'S SUCH A POOR, UNFORTU-NATE WOMAN...
HER LIFE'S BEEN RUINED BY WAR AND SLAVERY...
...AND SHE DID NOTHING TO DESERVE IT.
IF THE INNOCENT ARE SUFFERING, THEN SOMETHING'S WRONG.
IT'S WRONG.

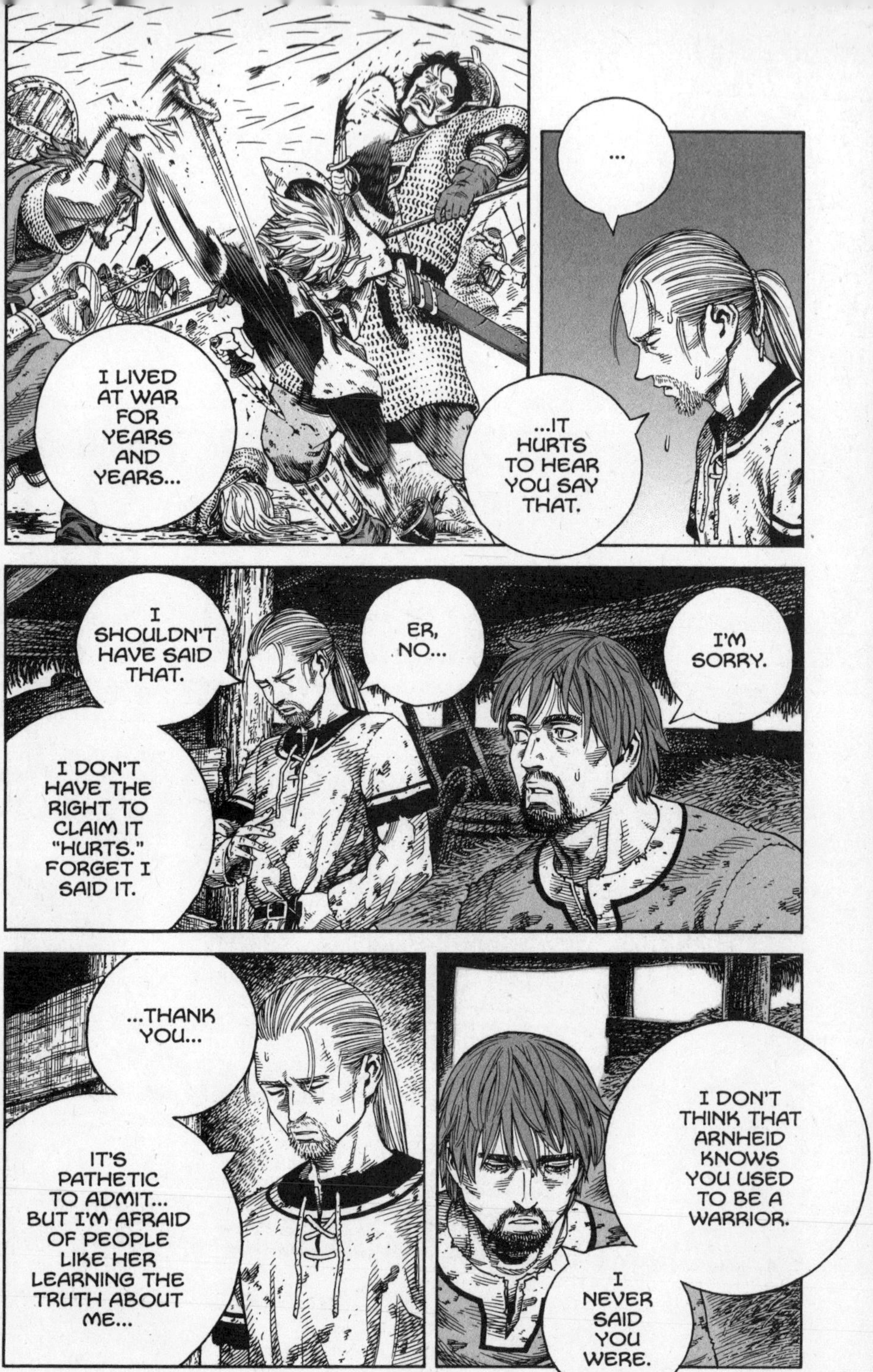
...
...IT HURTS TO HEAR YOU SAY THAT.
I LIVED AT WAR FOR YEARS AND YEARS...
I'M SORRY.
ER, NO...
I SHOULDN'T HAVE SAID THAT.
I DON'T HAVE THE RIGHT TO CLAIM IT "HURTS." FORGET I SAID IT.
I DON'T THINK THAT ARNHEID KNOWS YOU USED TO BE A WARRIOR.
I NEVER SAID YOU WERE.
...THANK YOU...
IT'S PATHETIC TO ADMIT... BUT I'M AFRAID OF PEOPLE LIKE HER LEARNING THE TRUTH ABOUT ME...

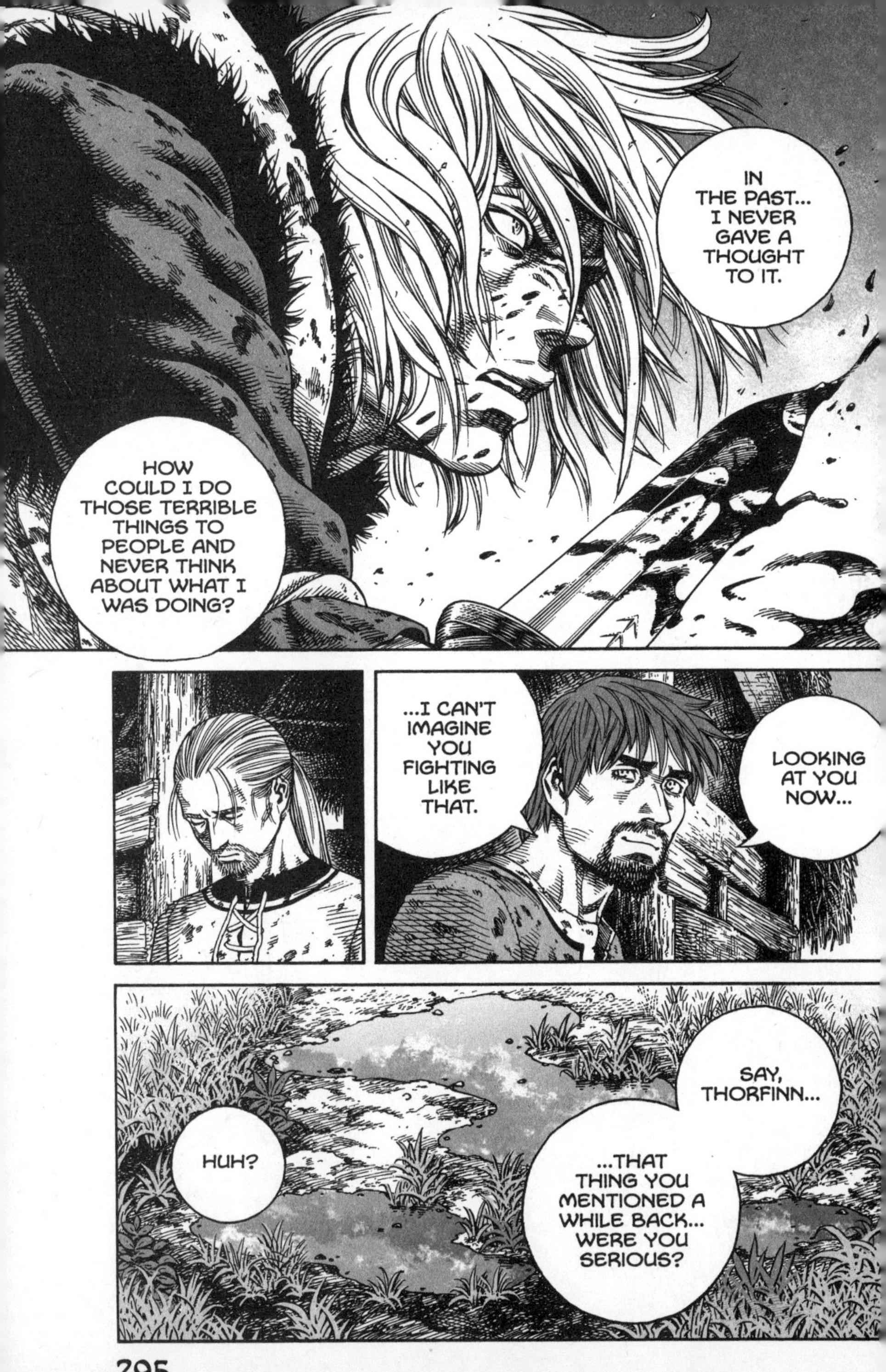
IN THE PAST... I NEVER GAVE A THOUGHT TO IT.
HOW COULD I DO THOSE TERRIBLE THINGS TO PEOPLE AND NEVER THINK ABOUT WHAT I WAS DOING?
LOOKING AT YOU NOW...
...I CAN'T IMAGINE YOU FIGHTING LIKE THAT.
SAY, THORFINN...
...THAT THING YOU MENTIONED A WHILE BACK... WERE YOU SERIOUS?
HUH?

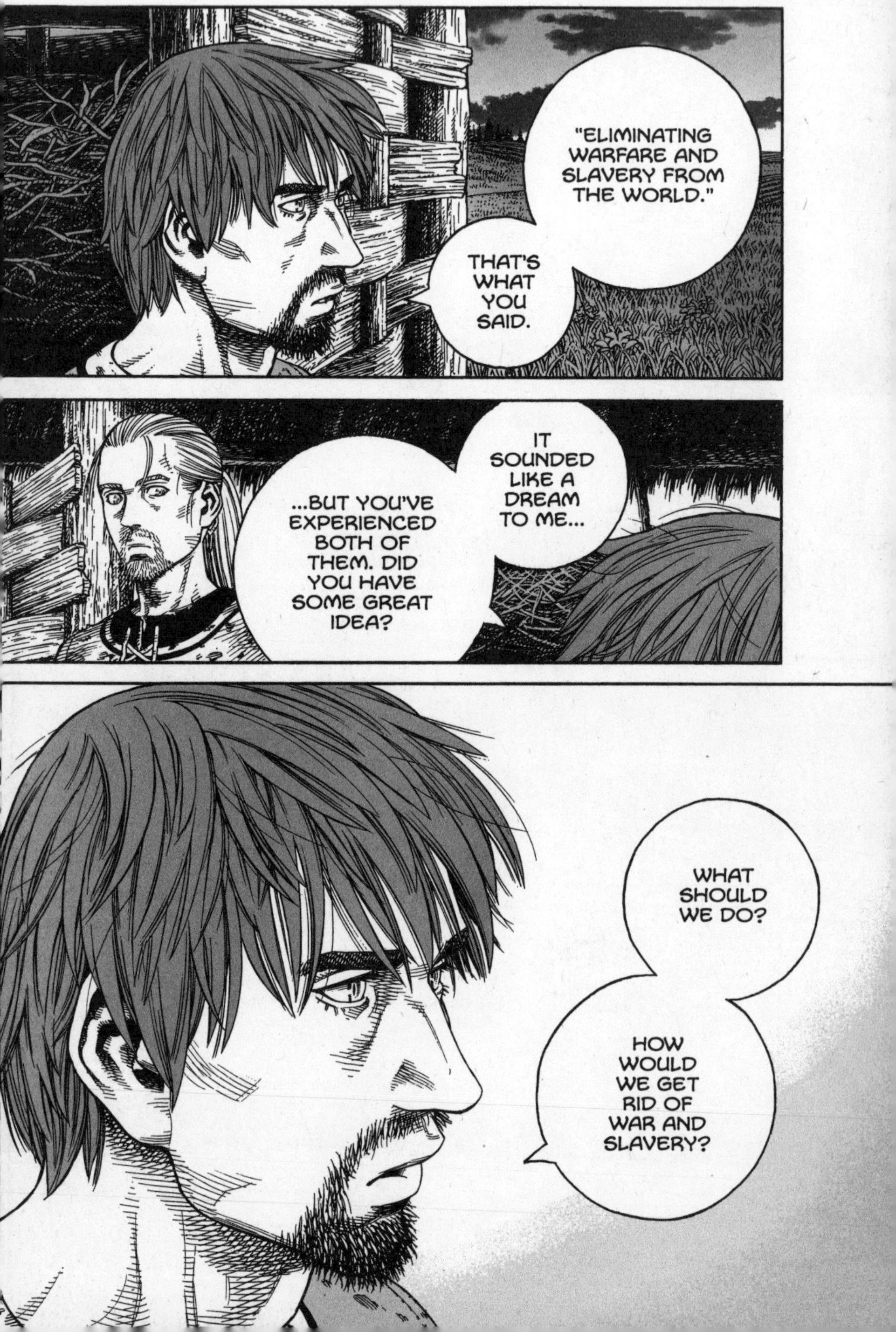
"ELIMINATING WARFARE AND SLAVERY FROM THE WORLD."
THAT'S WHAT YOU SAID.
IT SOUNDED LIKE A DREAM TO ME...
...BUT YOU'VE EXPERIENCED BOTH OF THEM. DID YOU HAVE SOME GREAT IDEA?
WHAT SHOULD WE DO?
HOW WOULD WE GET RID OF WAR AND SLAVERY?

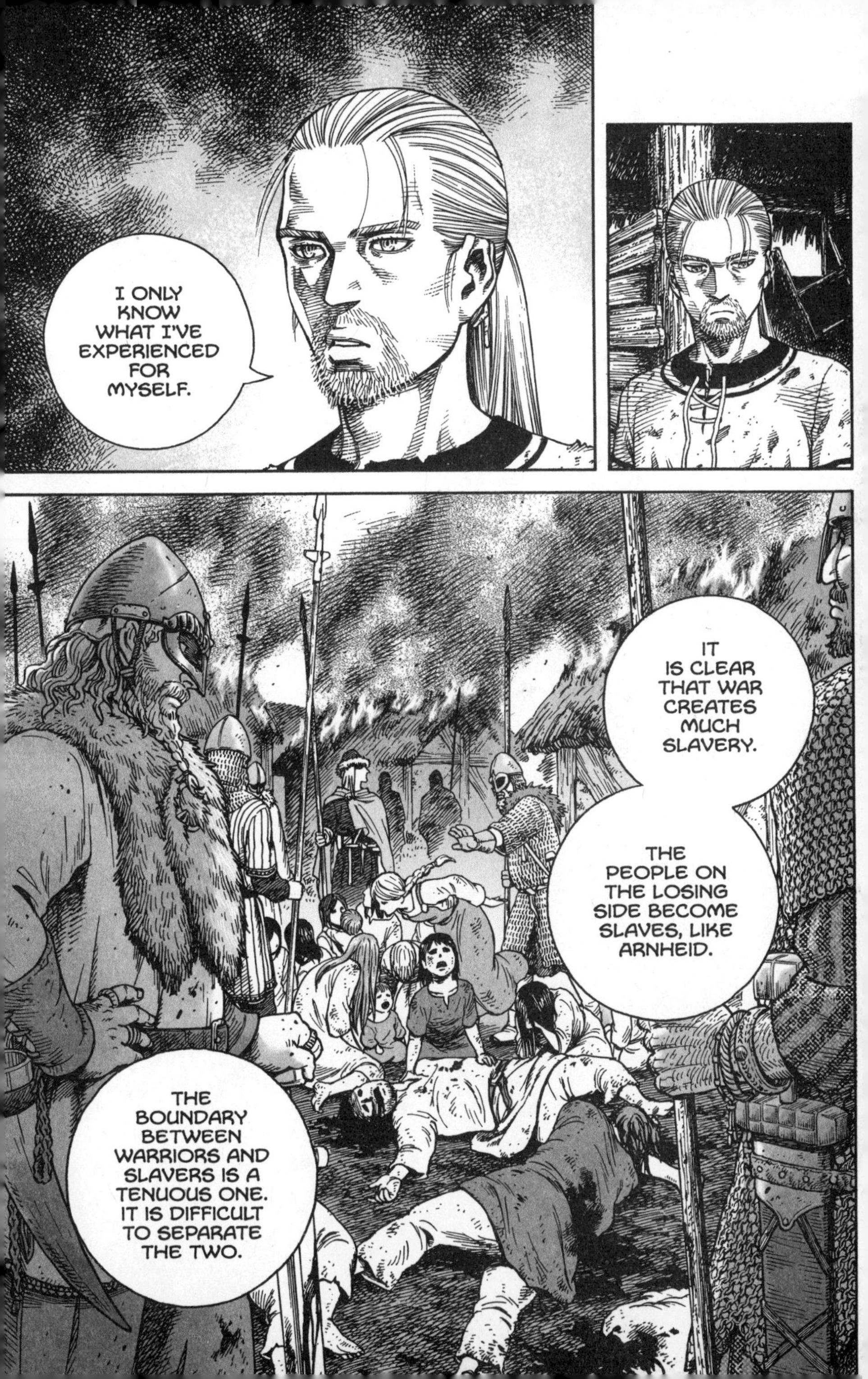
I ONLY KNOW WHAT I'VE EXPERIENCED FOR MYSELF.
IT IS CLEAR THAT WAR CREATES MUCH SLAVERY.
THE PEOPLE ON THE LOSING SIDE BECOME SLAVES, LIKE ARNHEID.
THE BOUNDARY BETWEEN WARRIORS AND SLAVERS IS A TENUOUS ONE. IT IS DIFFICULT TO SEPARATE THE TWO.

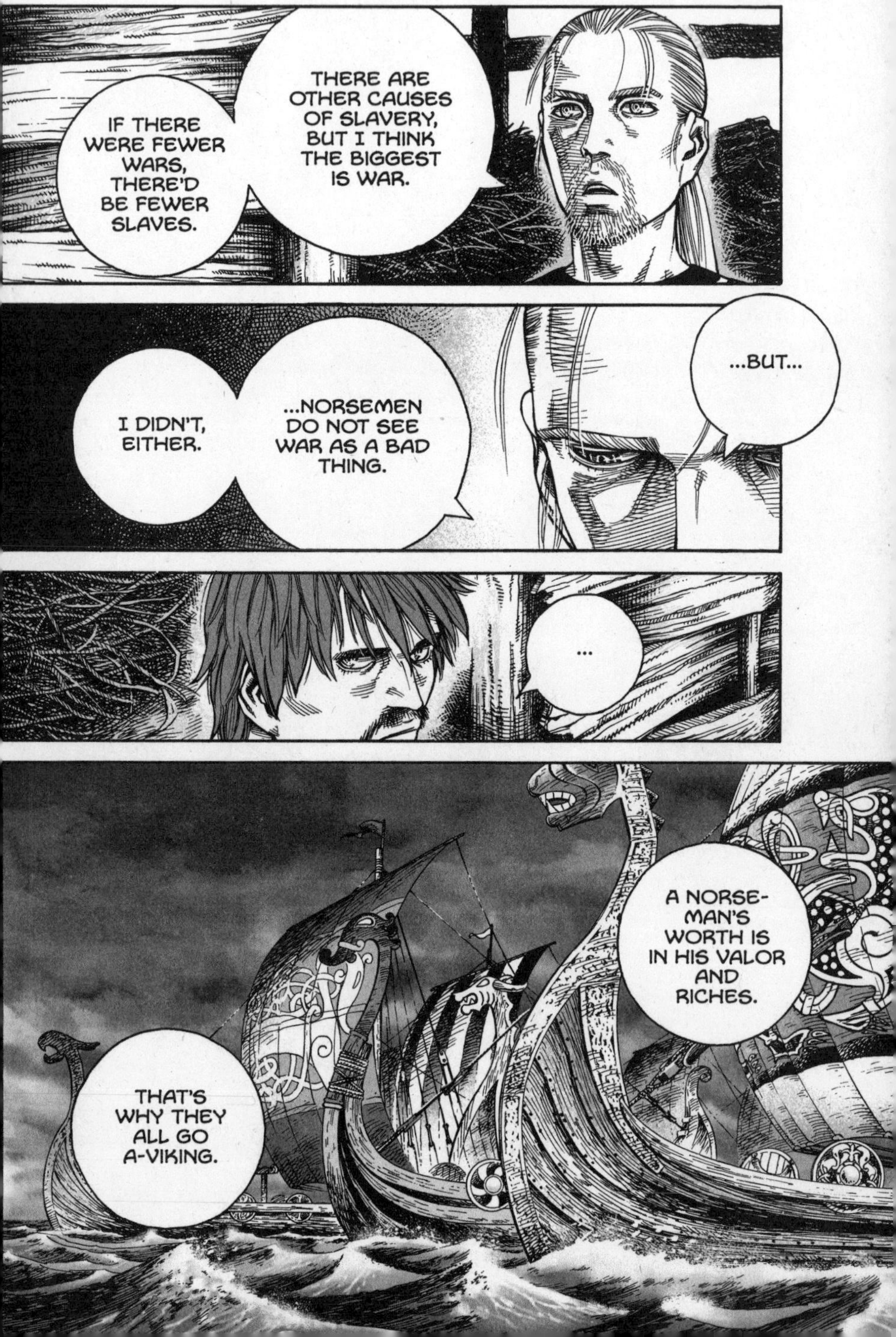
THERE ARE OTHER CAUSES OF SLAVERY, BUT I THINK THE BIGGEST IS WAR.
IF THERE WERE FEWER WARS, THERE'D BE FEWER SLAVES.
...BUT...
...NORSEMEN DO NOT SEE WAR AS A BAD THING.
I DIDN'T, EITHER.
...
A NORSE-MAN'S WORTH IS IN HIS VALOR AND RICHES.
THAT'S WHY THEY ALL GO A-VIKING.

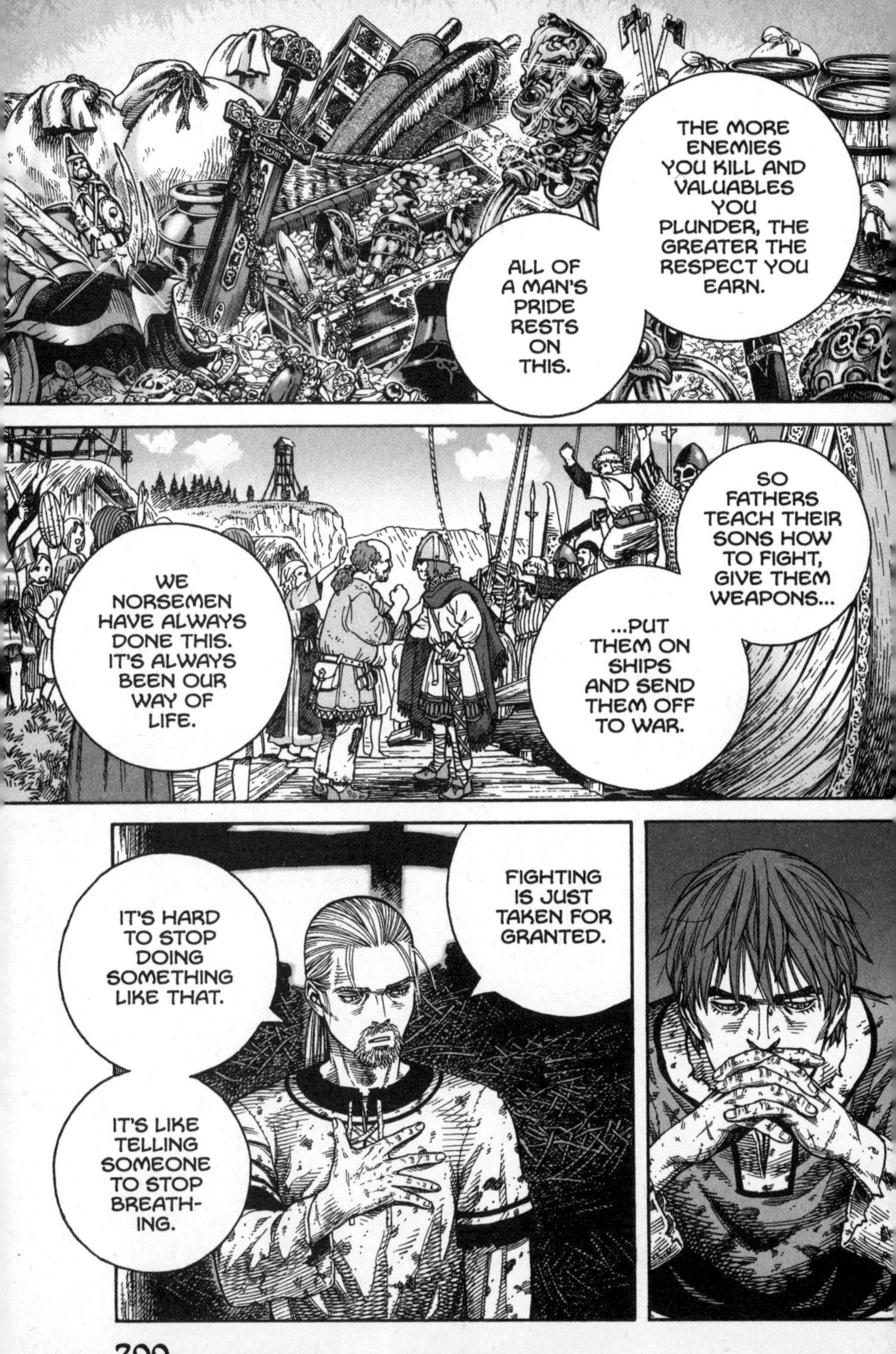
THE MORE ENEMIES YOU KILL AND VALUABLES YOU PLUNDER, THE GREATER THE RESPECT YOU EARN.
ALL OF A MAN'S PRIDE RESTS ON THIS.
SO FATHERS TEACH THEIR SONS HOW TO FIGHT, GIVE THEM WEAPONS...
...PUT THEM ON SHIPS AND SEND THEM OFF TO WAR.
WE NORSEMEN HAVE ALWAYS DONE THIS. IT'S ALWAYS BEEN OUR WAY OF LIFE.
FIGHTING IS JUST TAKEN FOR GRANTED.
IT'S HARD TO STOP DOING SOMETHING LIKE THAT.
IT'S LIKE TELLING SOMEONE TO STOP BREATH-ING.

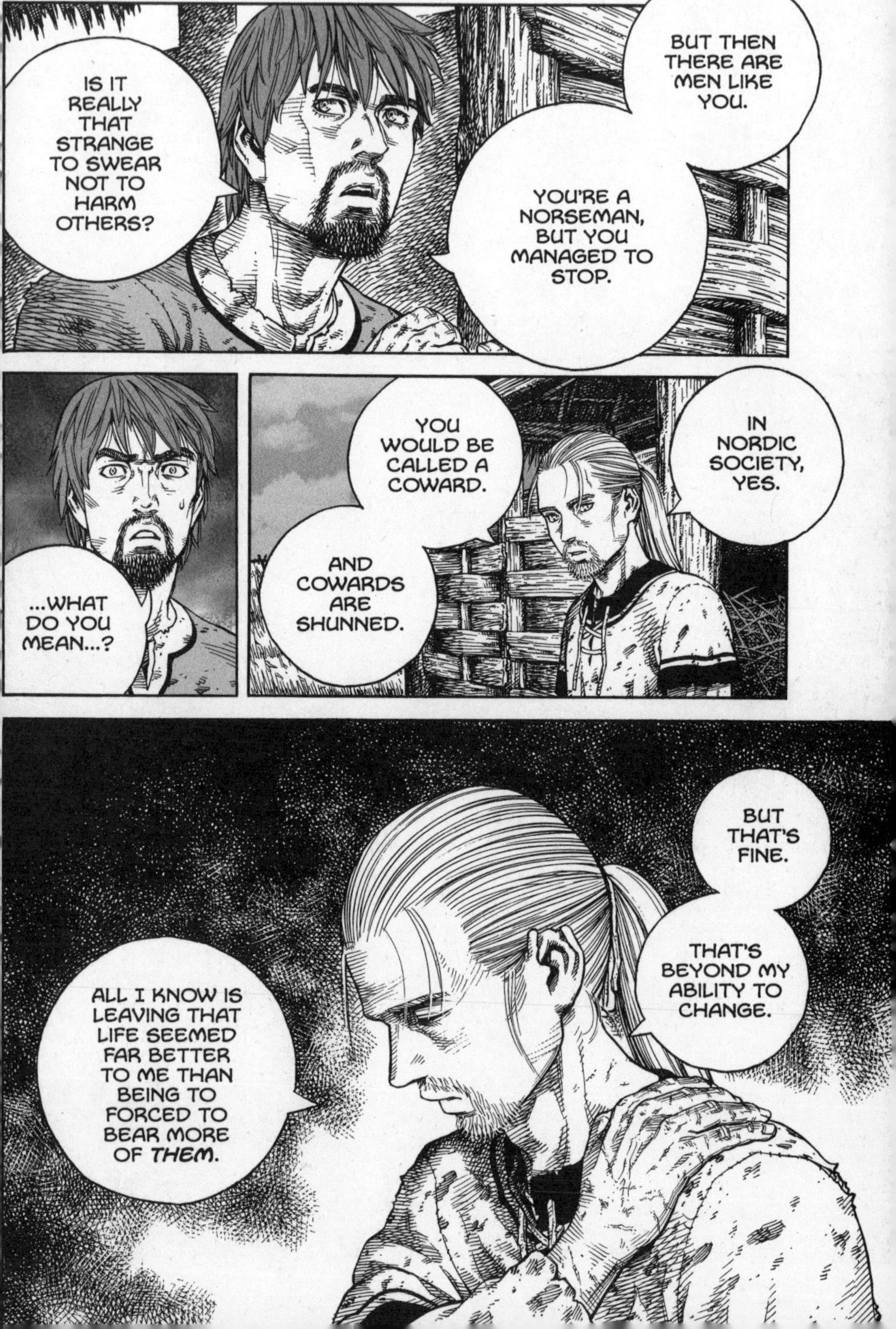
BUT THEN THERE ARE MEN LIKE YOU.
YOU'RE A NORSEMAN, BUT YOU MANAGED TO STOP.
IS IT REALLY THAT STRANGE TO SWEAR NOT TO HARM OTHERS?
IN NORDIC SOCIETY, YES.
YOU WOULD BE CALLED A COWARD.
AND COWARDS ARE SHUNNED.
...WHAT DO YOU MEAN...?
BUT THAT'S FINE.
THAT'S BEYOND MY ABILITY TO CHANGE.
ALL I KNOW IS LEAVING THAT LIFE SEEMED FAR BETTER TO ME THAN BEING TO FORCED TO BEAR MORE OF *THEM*.

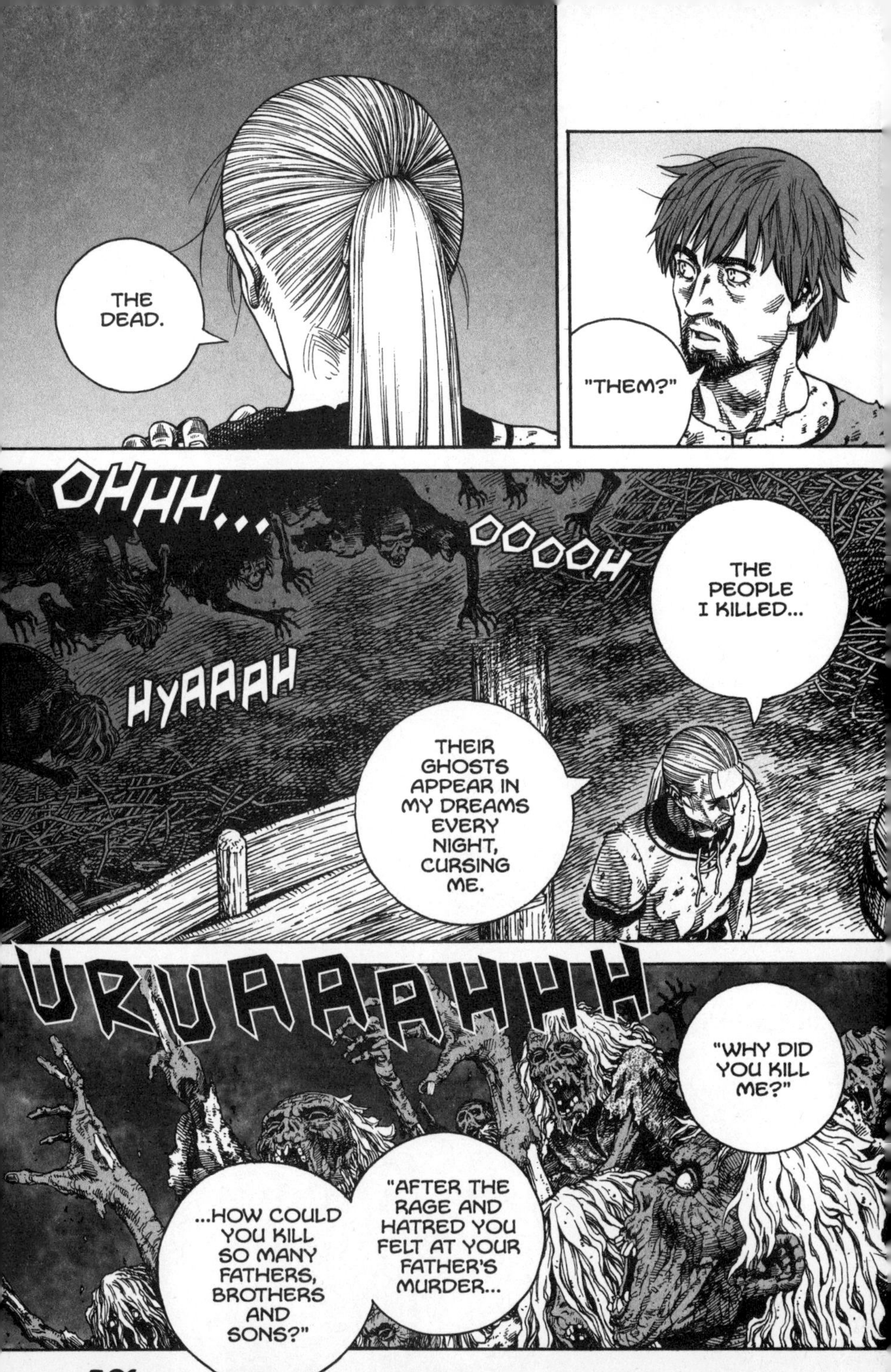
"THEM?"
THE DEAD.
THE PEOPLE I KILLED...
OHHH...
OOOOH
HYAAAH
THEIR GHOSTS APPEAR IN MY DREAMS EVERY NIGHT, CURSING ME.
URUAAAHHH
"WHY DID YOU KILL ME?"
"AFTER THE RAGE AND HATRED YOU FELT AT YOUR FATHER'S MURDER...
...HOW COULD YOU KILL SO MANY FATHERS, BROTHERS AND SONS?"

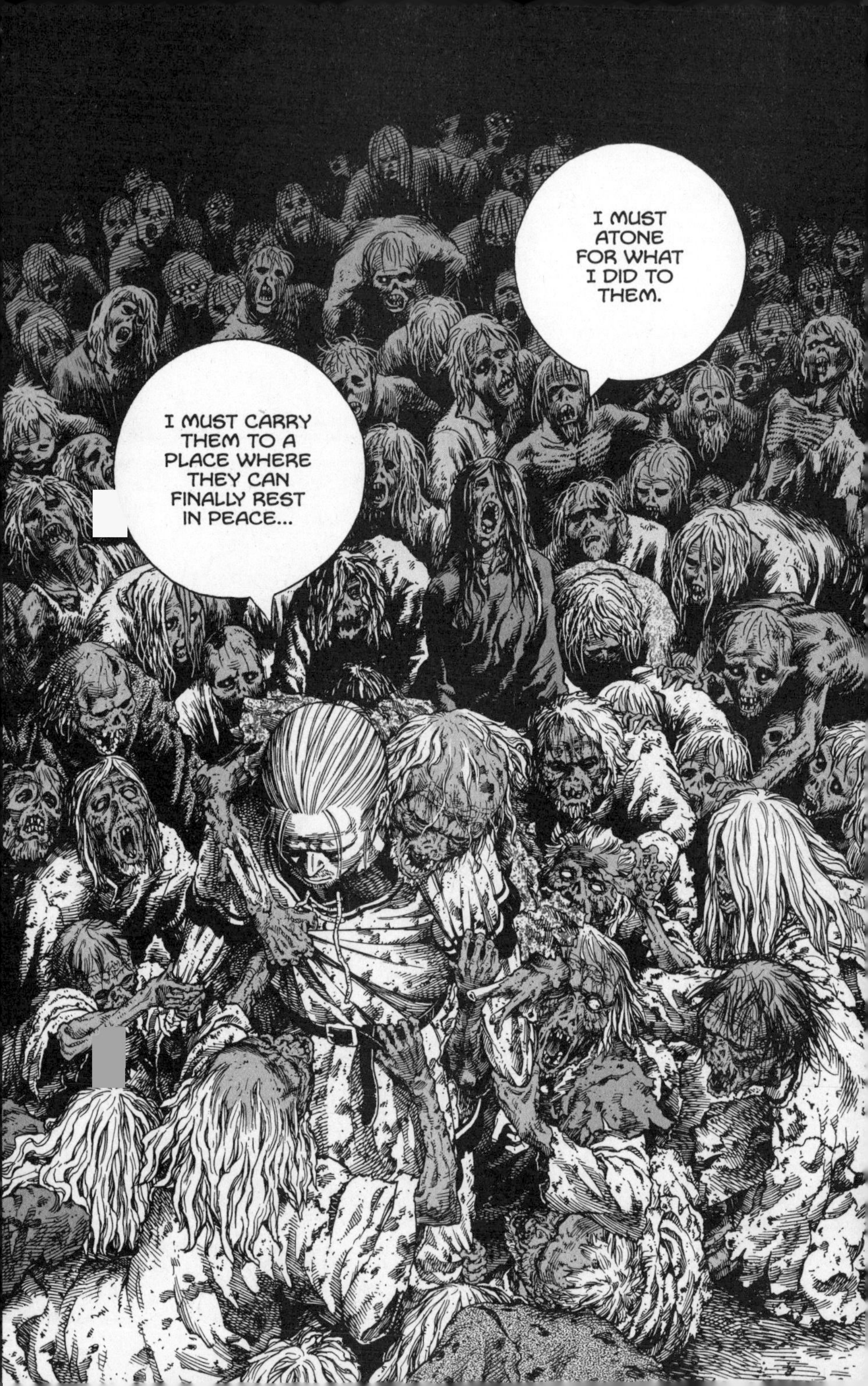
I MUST ATONE FOR WHAT I DID TO THEM.
I MUST CARRY THEM TO A PLACE WHERE THEY CAN FINALLY REST IN PEACE...

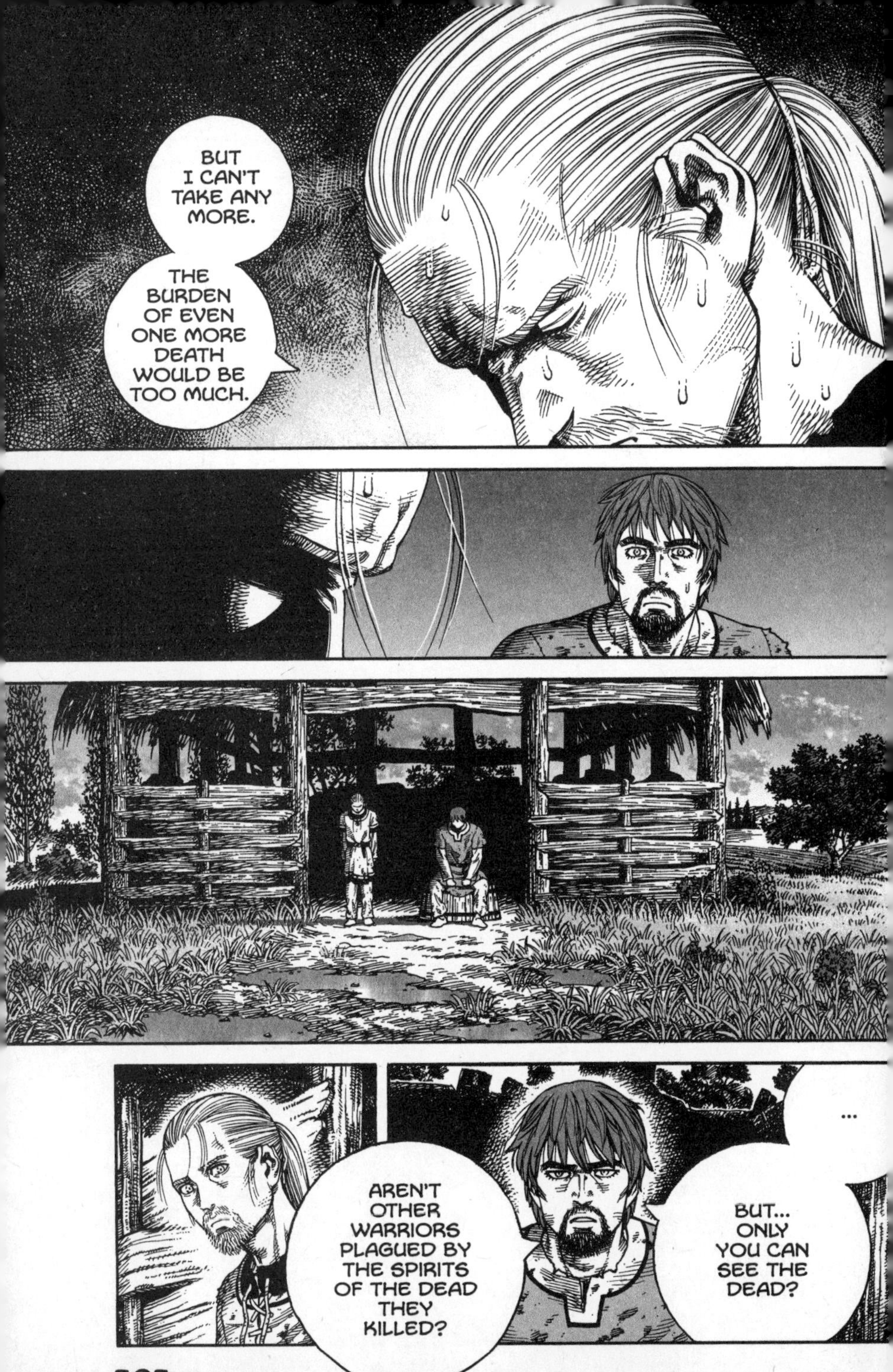
BUT I CAN'T TAKE ANY MORE.
THE BURDEN OF EVEN ONE MORE DEATH WOULD BE TOO MUCH.
...
BUT... ONLY YOU CAN SEE THE DEAD?
AREN'T OTHER WARRIORS PLAGUED BY THE SPIRITS OF THE DEAD THEY KILLED?

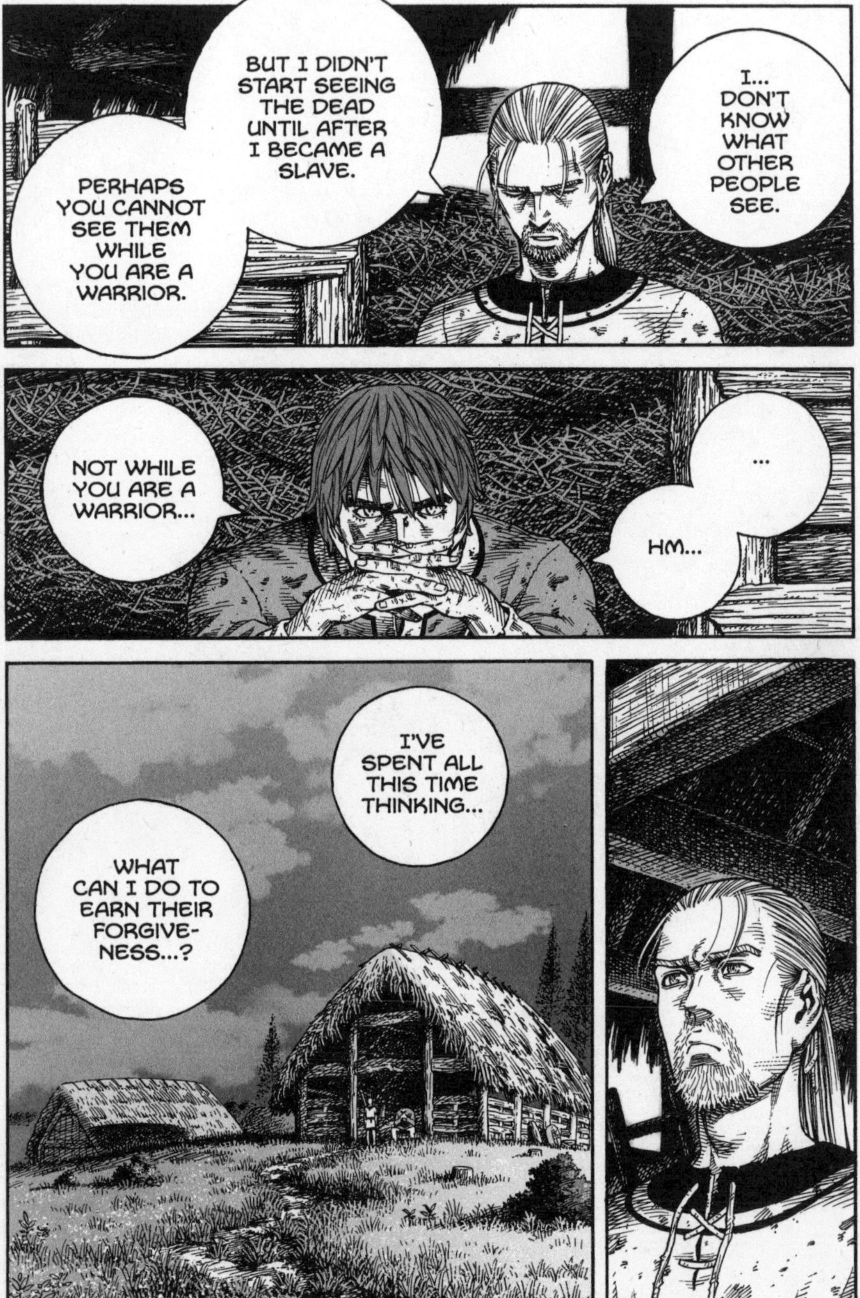
I... DON'T KNOW WHAT OTHER PEOPLE SEE.
BUT I DIDN'T START SEEING THE DEAD UNTIL AFTER I BECAME A SLAVE.
PERHAPS YOU CANNOT SEE THEM WHILE YOU ARE A WARRIOR.
...
HM...
NOT WHILE YOU ARE A WARRIOR...
I'VE SPENT ALL THIS TIME THINKING...
WHAT CAN I DO TO EARN THEIR FORGIVE-NESS...?

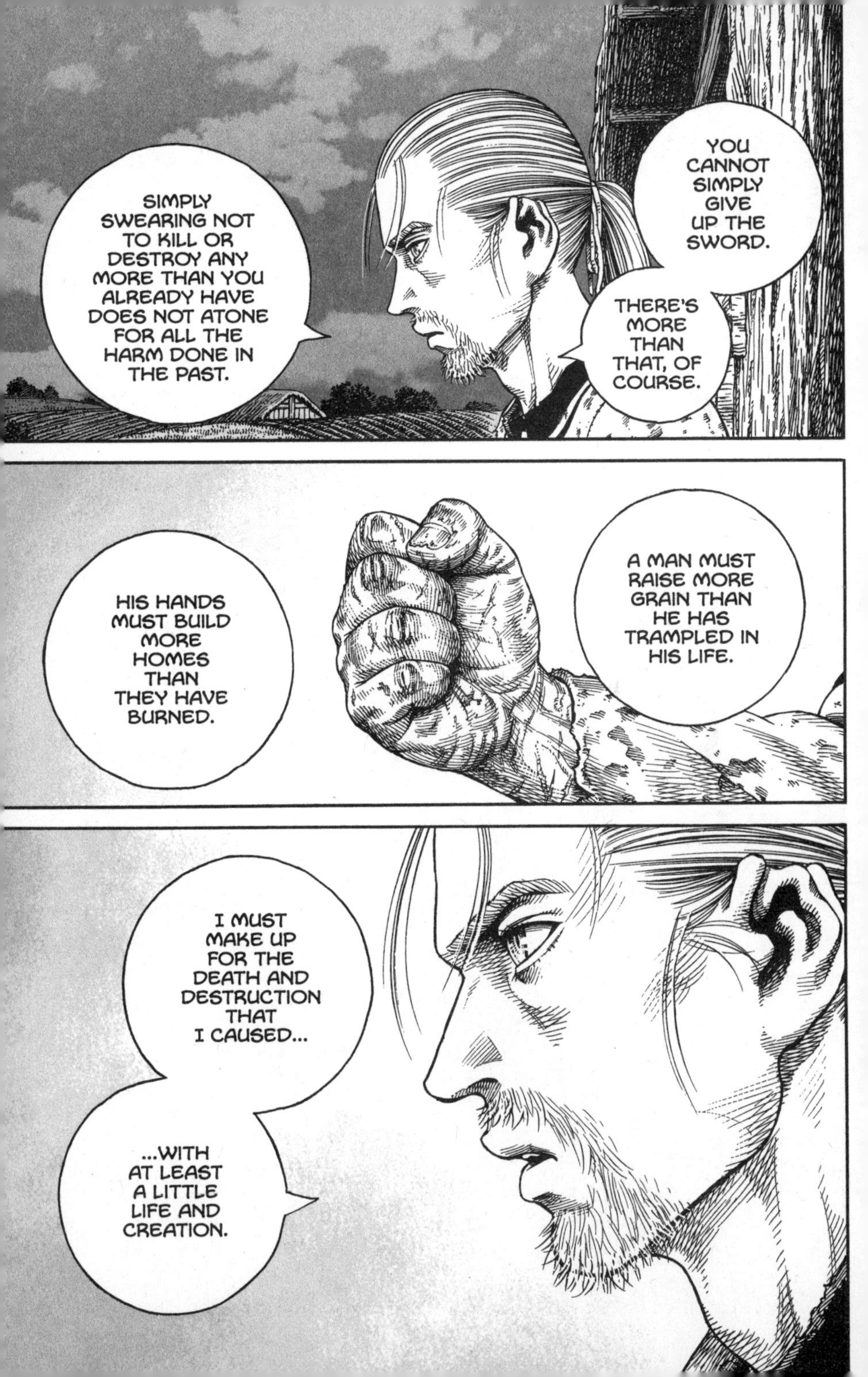
YOU CANNOT SIMPLY GIVE UP THE SWORD.
THERE'S MORE THAN THAT, OF COURSE.
SIMPLY SWEARING NOT TO KILL OR DESTROY ANY MORE THAN YOU ALREADY HAVE DOES NOT ATONE FOR ALL THE HARM DONE IN THE PAST.
A MAN MUST RAISE MORE GRAIN THAN HE HAS TRAMPLED IN HIS LIFE.
HIS HANDS MUST BUILD MORE HOMES THAN THEY HAVE BURNED.
I MUST MAKE UP FOR THE DEATH AND DESTRUCTION THAT I CAUSED...
...WITH AT LEAST A LITTLE LIFE AND CREATION.

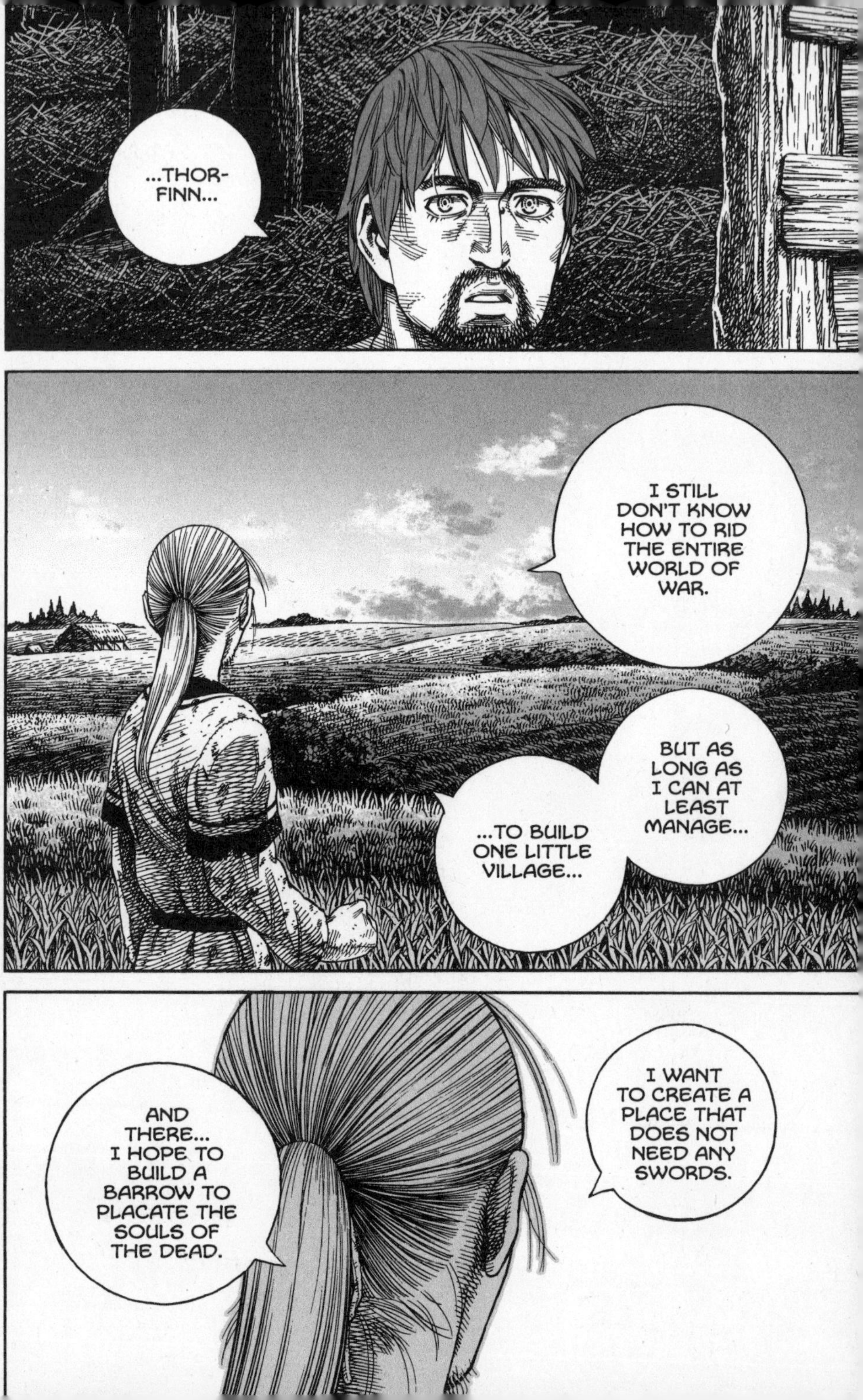
...THOR-FINN...
I STILL DON'T KNOW HOW TO RID THE ENTIRE WORLD OF WAR.
BUT AS LONG AS I CAN AT LEAST MANAGE...
...TO BUILD ONE LITTLE VILLAGE...
I WANT TO CREATE A PLACE THAT DOES NOT NEED ANY SWORDS.
AND THERE... I HOPE TO BUILD A BARROW TO PLACATE THE SOULS OF THE DEAD.

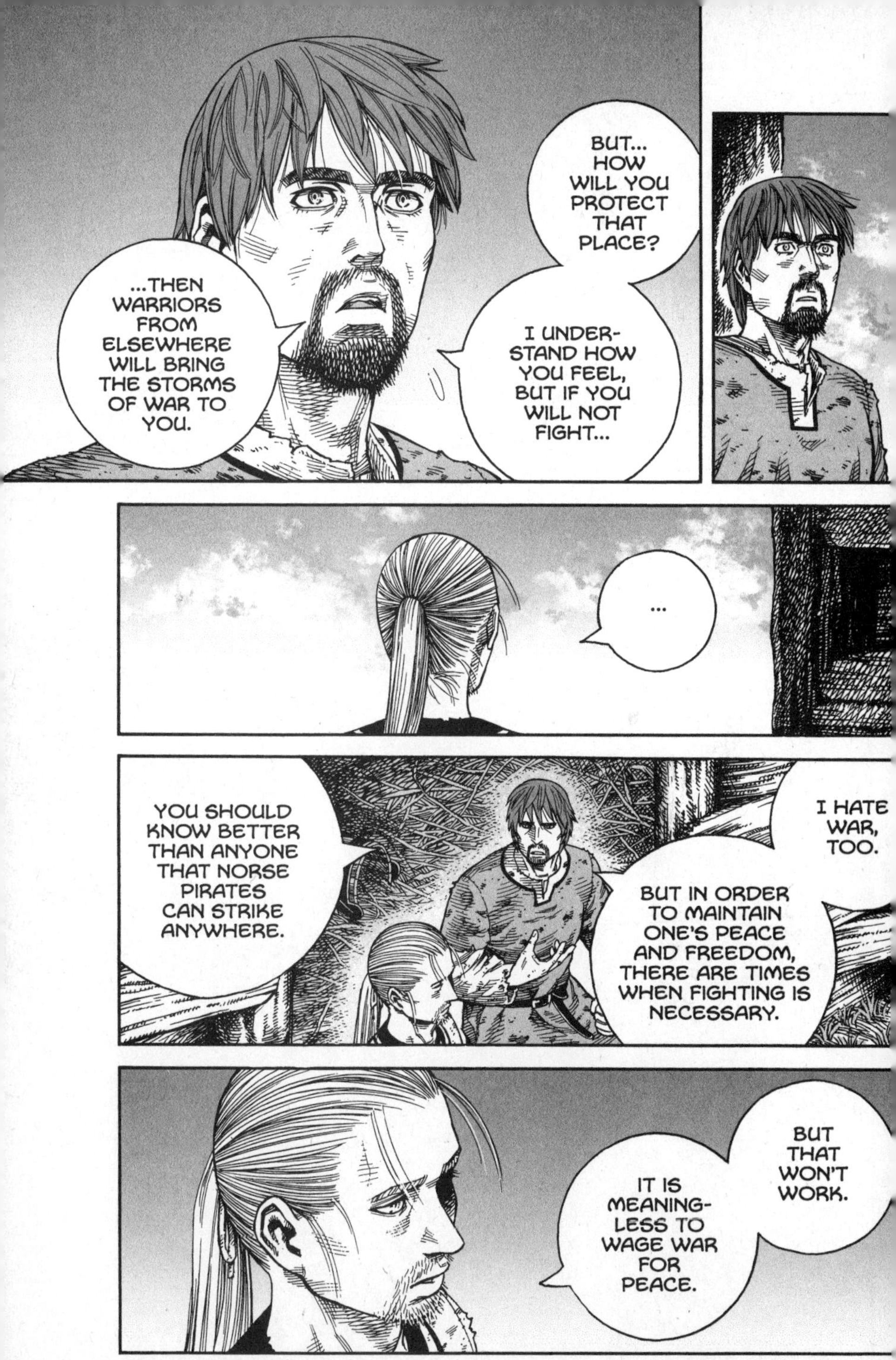
BUT... HOW WILL YOU PROTECT THAT PLACE?
I UNDER-STAND HOW YOU FEEL, BUT IF YOU WILL NOT FIGHT...
...THEN WARRIORS FROM ELSEWHERE WILL BRING THE STORMS OF WAR TO YOU.
...
I HATE WAR, TOO.
BUT IN ORDER TO MAINTAIN ONE'S PEACE AND FREEDOM, THERE ARE TIMES WHEN FIGHTING IS NECESSARY.
YOU SHOULD KNOW BETTER THAN ANYONE THAT NORSE PIRATES CAN STRIKE ANYWHERE.
BUT THAT WON'T WORK.
IT IS MEANING-LESS TO WAGE WAR FOR PEACE.

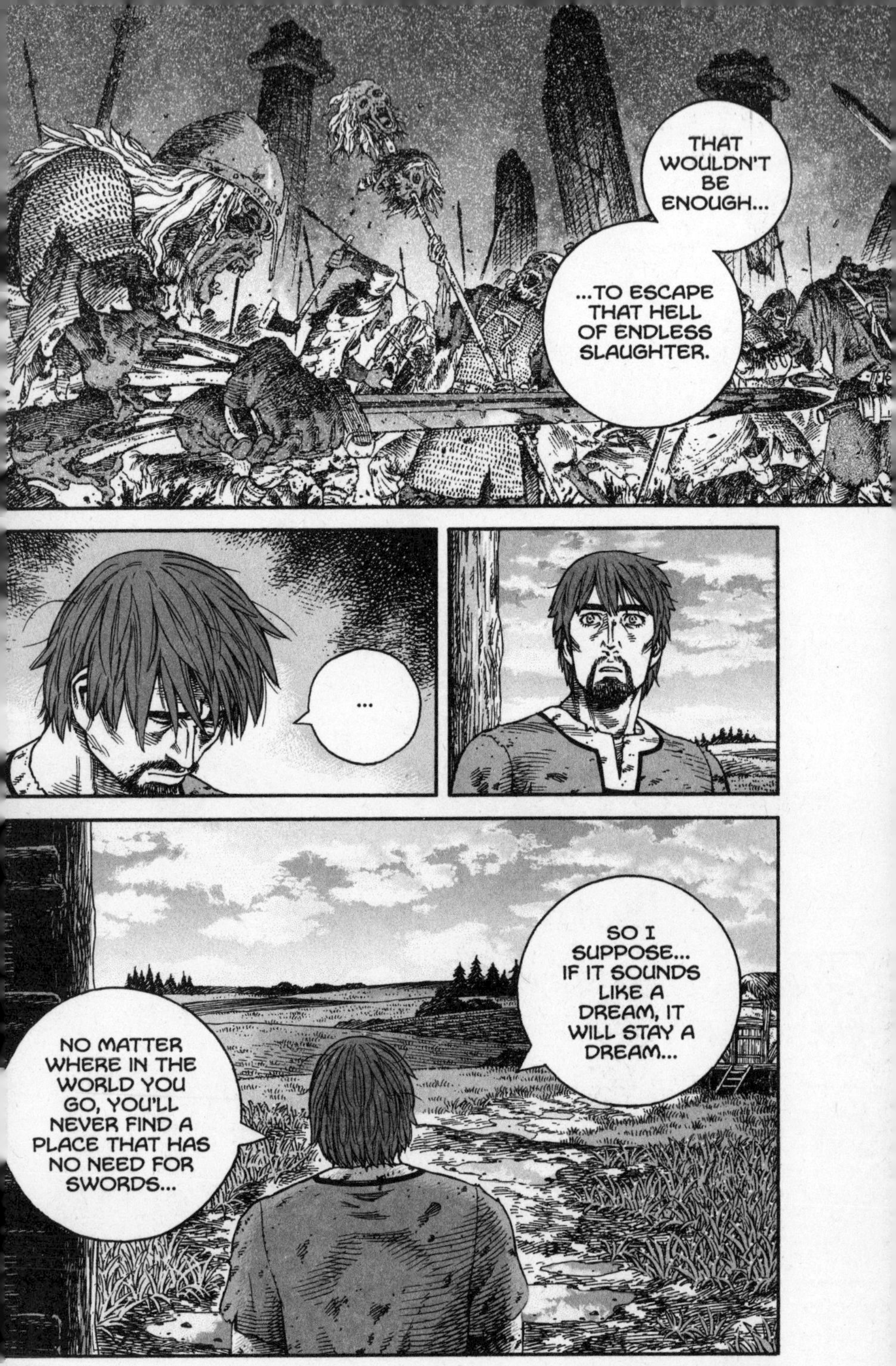
THAT WOULDN'T BE ENOUGH...
...TO ESCAPE THAT HELL OF ENDLESS SLAUGHTER.
...
SO I SUPPOSE... IF IT SOUNDS LIKE A DREAM, IT WILL STAY A DREAM...
NO MATTER WHERE IN THE WORLD YOU GO, YOU'LL NEVER FIND A PLACE THAT HAS NO NEED FOR SWORDS...

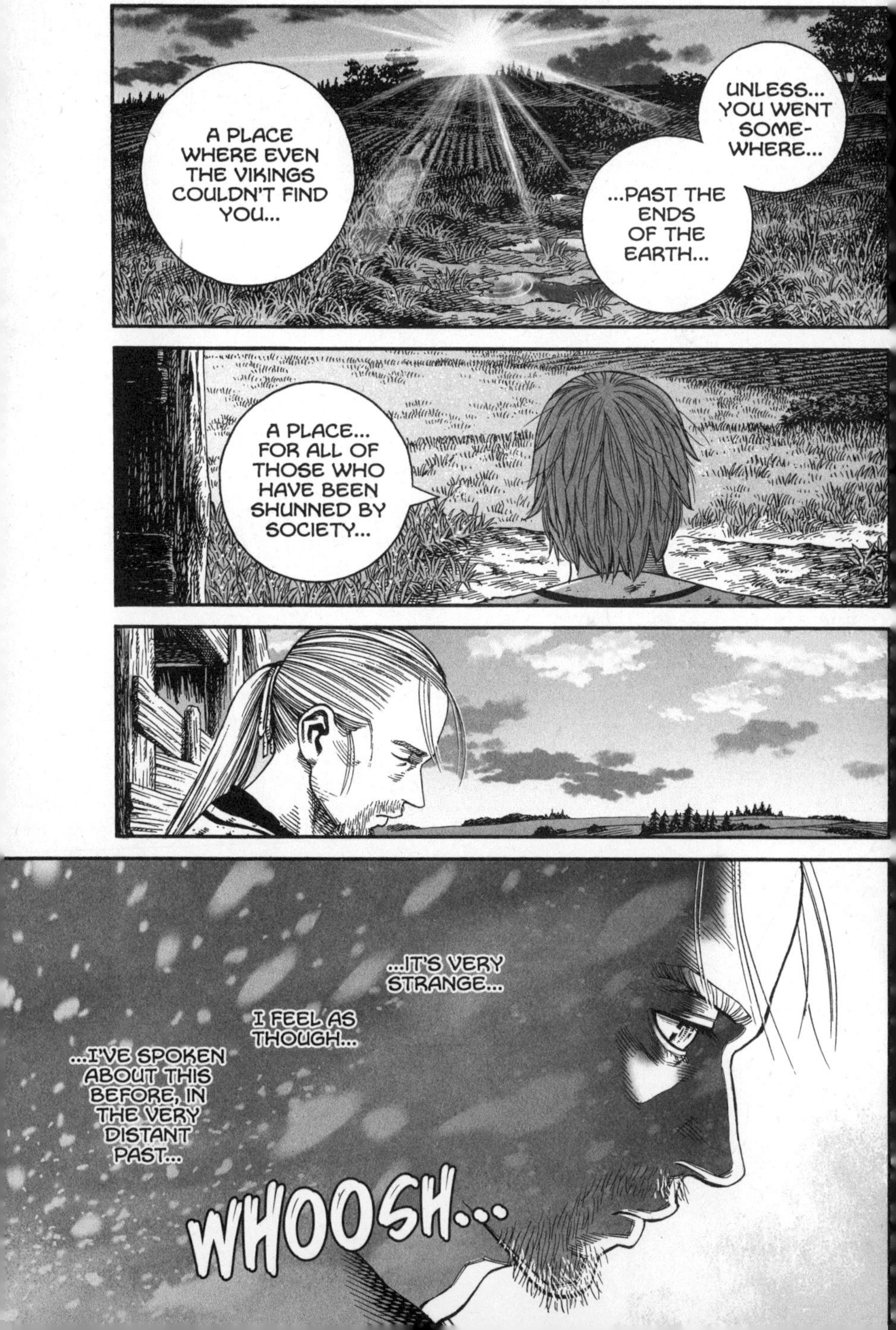
UNLESS... YOU WENT SOME-WHERE...
...PAST THE ENDS OF THE EARTH...
A PLACE WHERE EVEN THE VIKINGS COULDN'T FIND YOU...
A PLACE... FOR ALL OF THOSE WHO HAVE BEEN SHUNNED BY SOCIETY...
...IT'S VERY STRANGE...
I FEEL AS THOUGH...
...I'VE SPOKEN ABOUT THIS BEFORE, IN THE VERY DISTANT PAST...
WHOOSH...

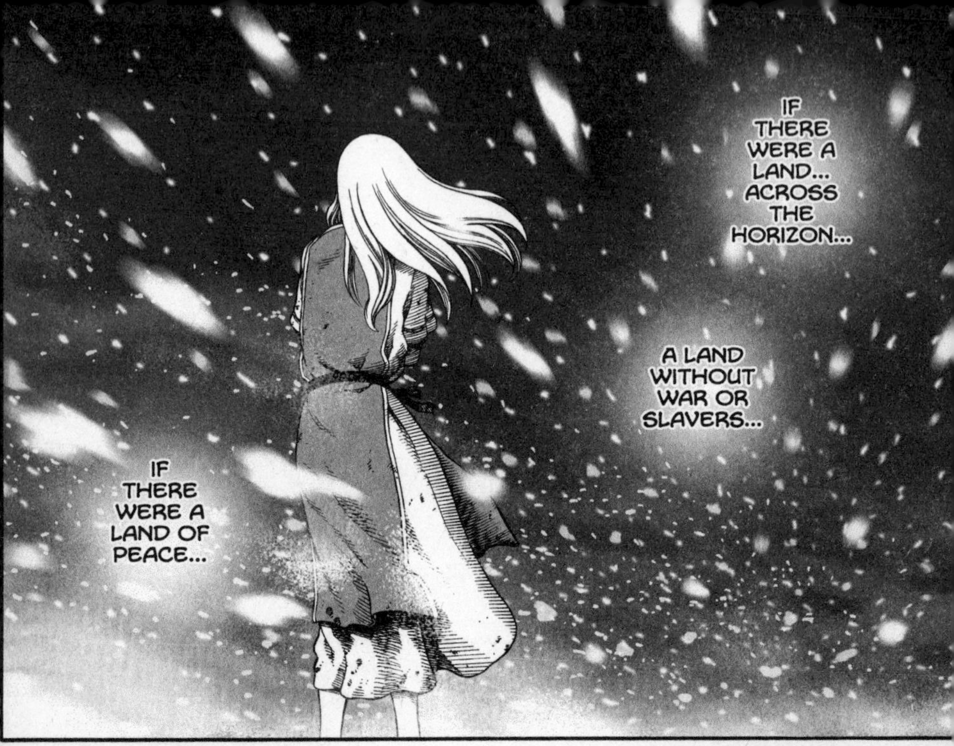
IF THERE WERE A LAND... ACROSS THE HORIZON...
A LAND WITHOUT WAR OR SLAVERS...
IF THERE WERE A LAND OF PEACE...

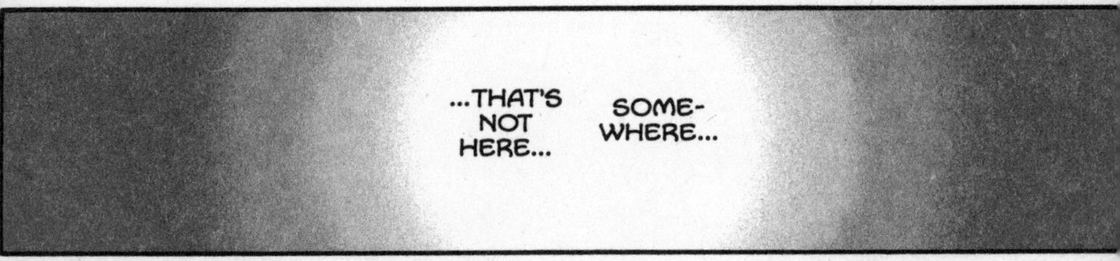
SOME-WHERE...
...THAT'S NOT HERE...

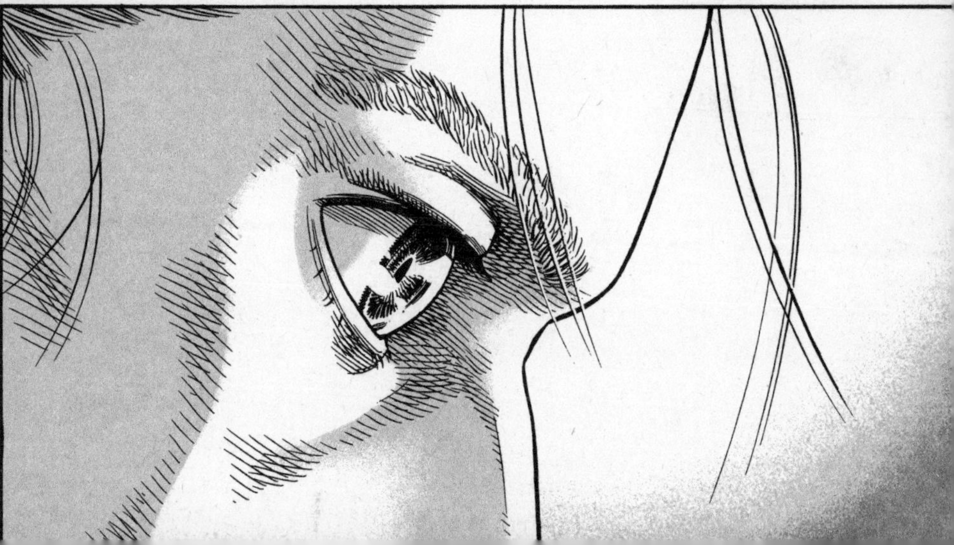

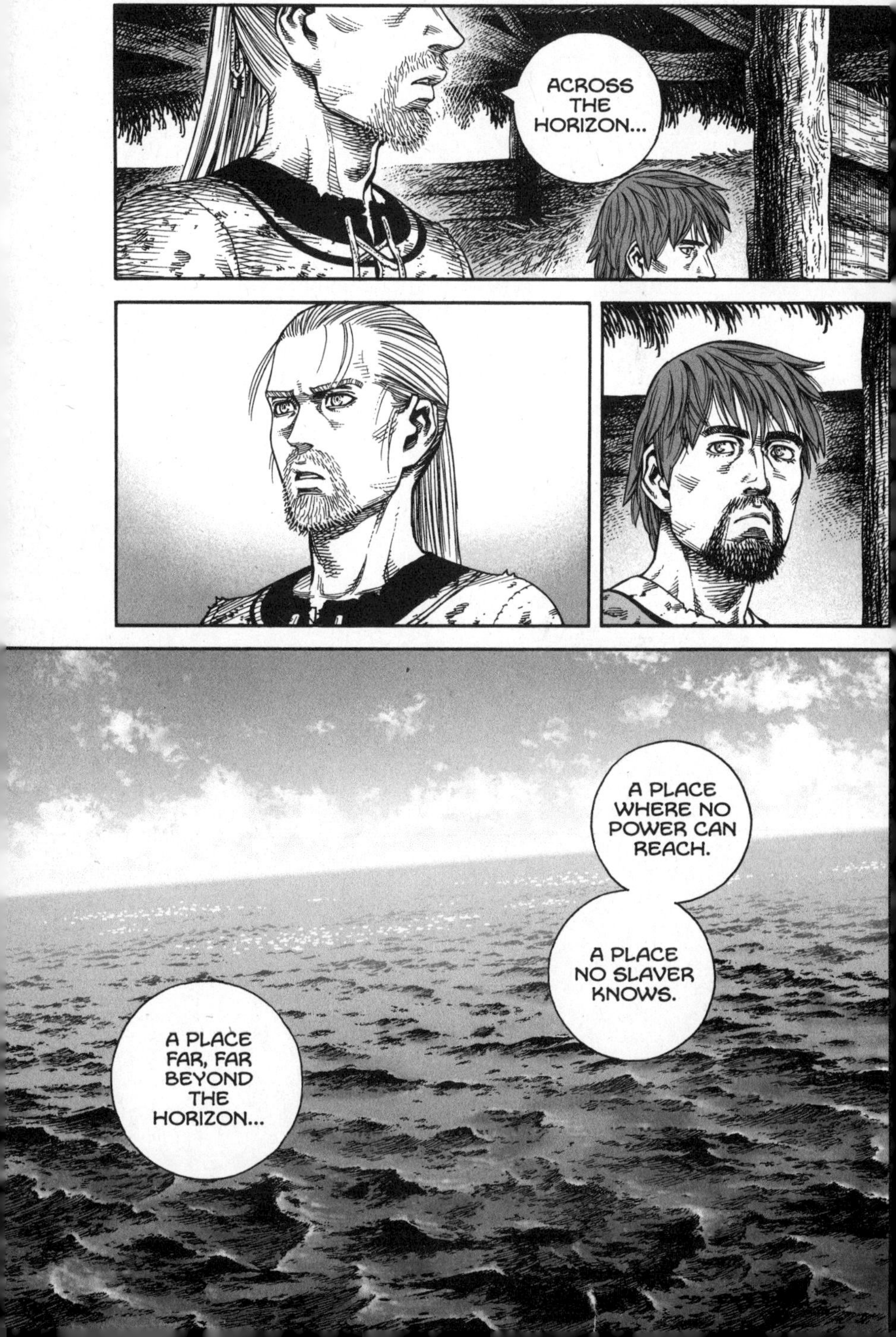
ACROSS THE HORIZON...
A PLACE WHERE NO POWER CAN REACH.
A PLACE NO SLAVER KNOWS.
A PLACE FAR, FAR BEYOND THE HORIZON...

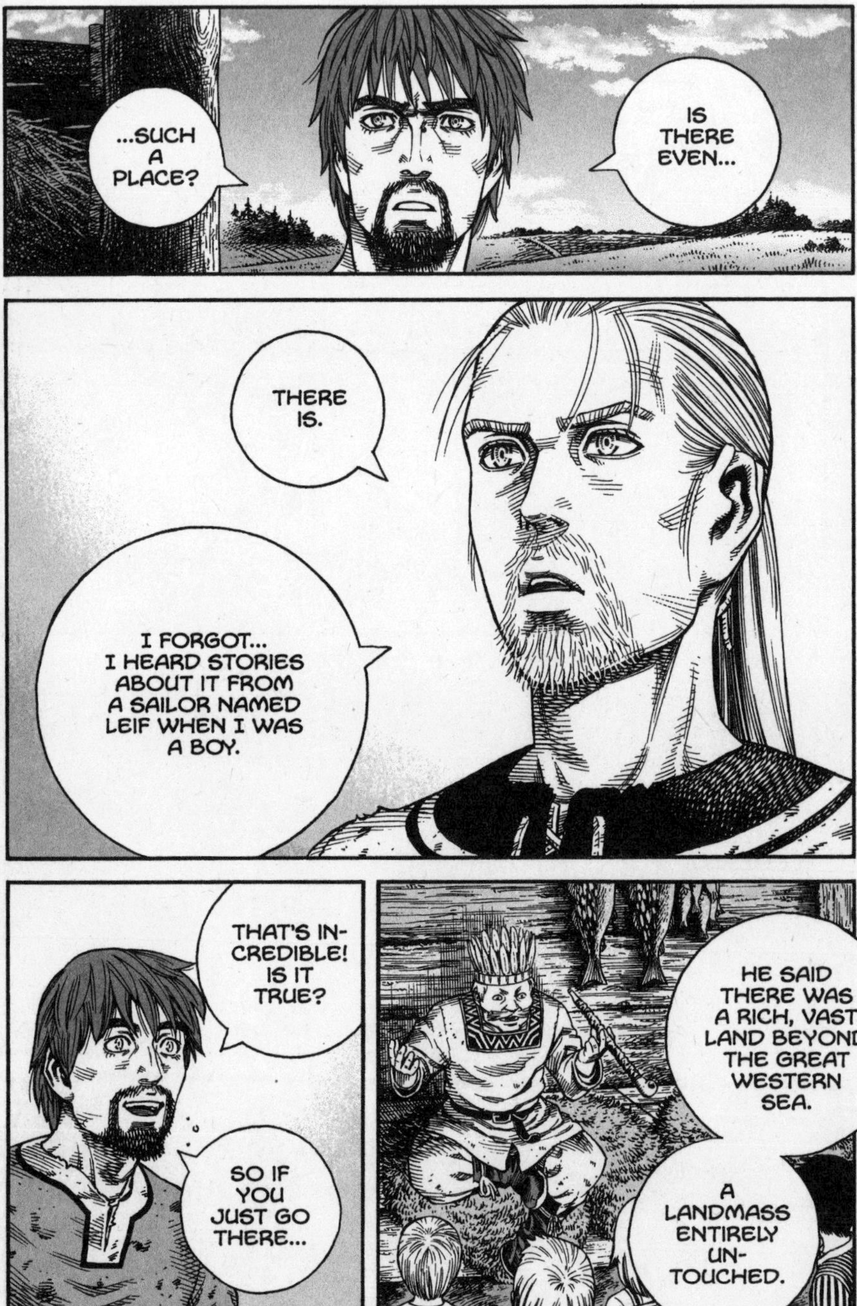
IS THERE EVEN...
...SUCH A PLACE?
THERE IS.
I FORGOT... I HEARD STORIES ABOUT IT FROM A SAILOR NAMED LEIF WHEN I WAS A BOY.
HE SAID THERE WAS A RICH, VAST LAND BEYOND THE GREAT WESTERN SEA.
A LANDMASS ENTIRELY UN-TOUCHED.
THAT'S IN-CREDIBLE! IS IT TRUE?
SO IF YOU JUST GO THERE...

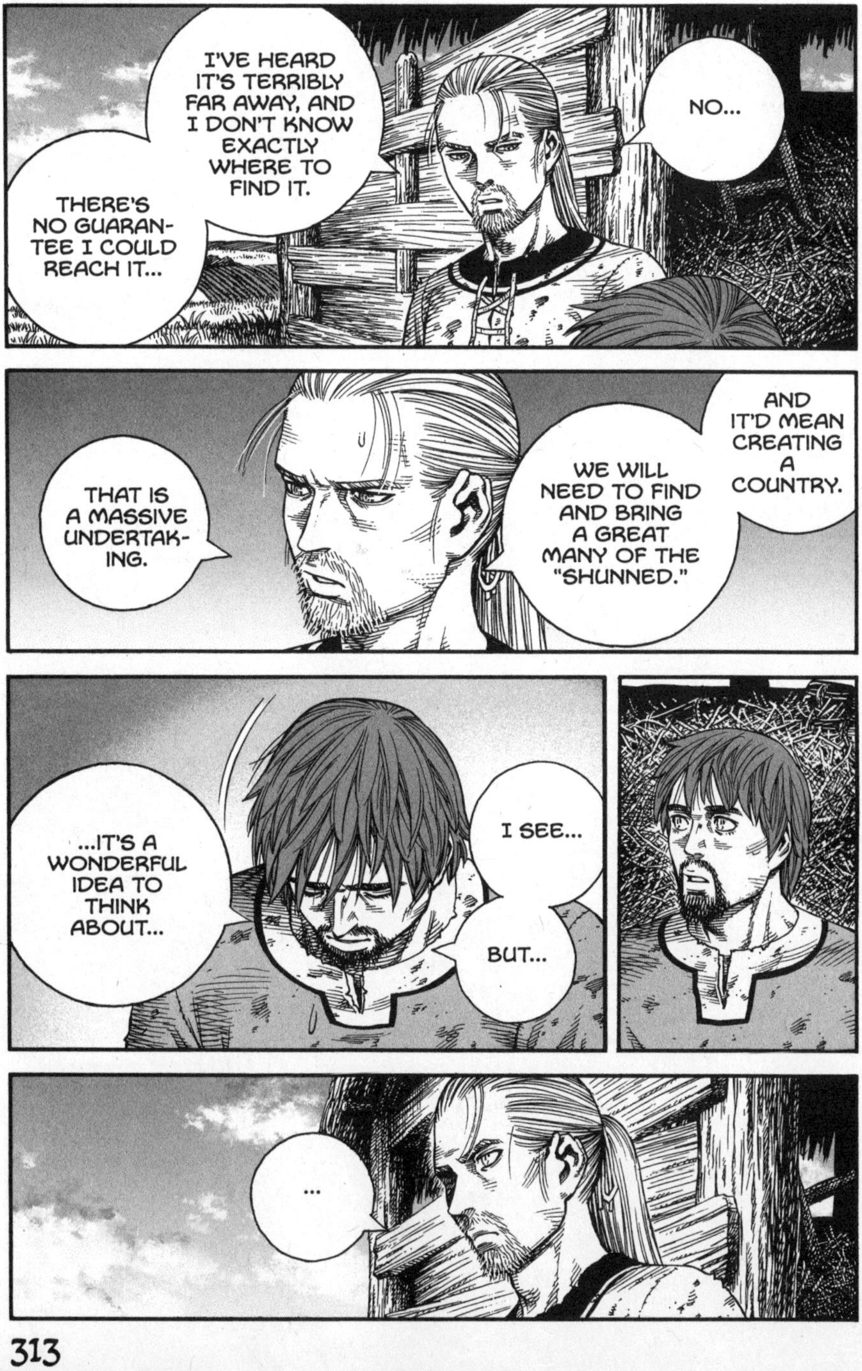
NO...
I'VE HEARD IT'S TERRIBLY FAR AWAY, AND I DON'T KNOW EXACTLY WHERE TO FIND IT.
THERE'S NO GUARAN-TEE I COULD REACH IT...
AND IT'D MEAN CREATING A COUNTRY.
WE WILL NEED TO FIND AND BRING A GREAT MANY OF THE "SHUNNED."
THAT IS A MASSIVE UNDERTAK-ING.
I SEE...
BUT...
...IT'S A WONDERFUL IDEA TO THINK ABOUT...
...

?

DADUM

DADUM DADUM DADUM

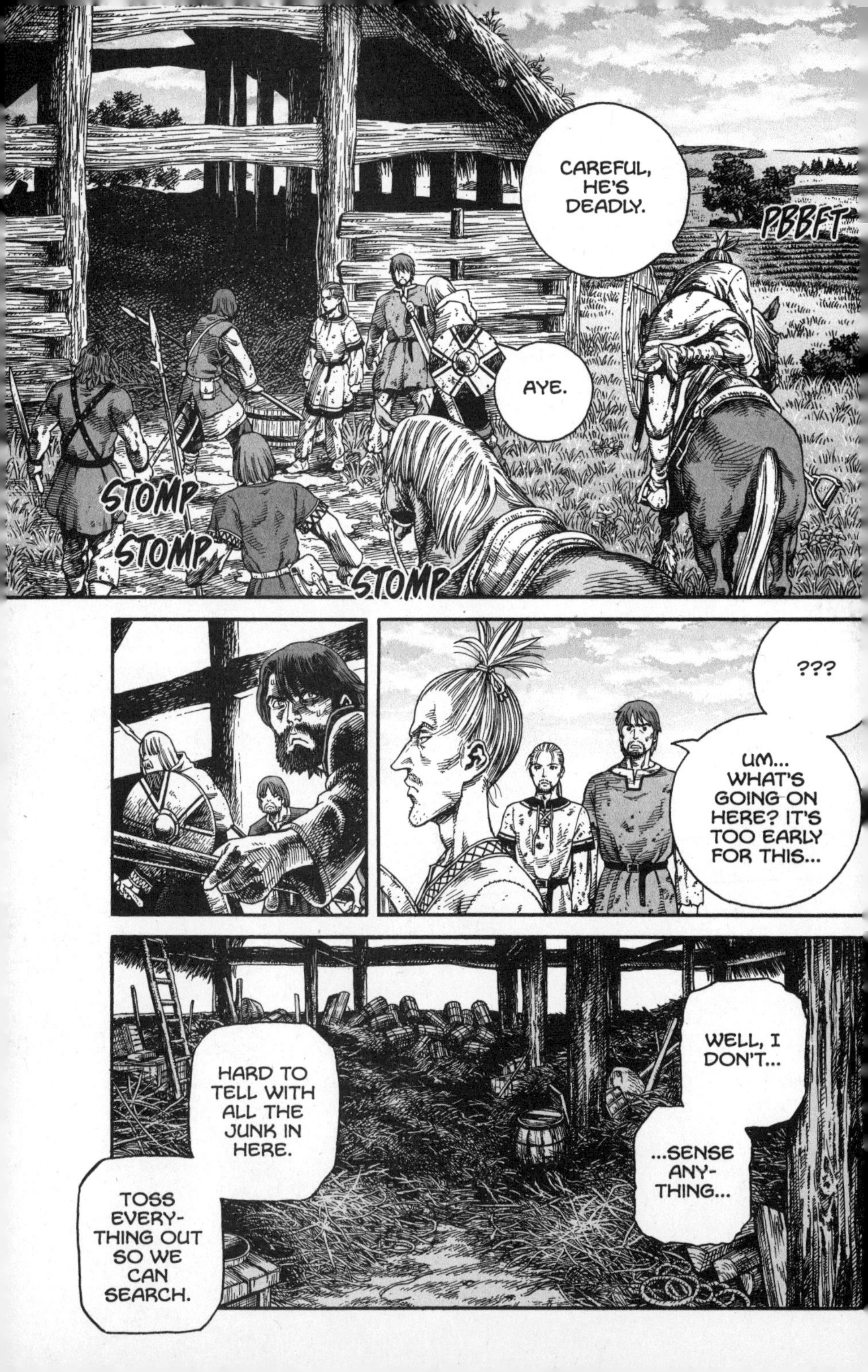
PBBFT
CAREFUL, HE'S DEADLY.
AYE.
STOMP
STOMP
STOMP
???
UM... WHAT'S GOING ON HERE? IT'S TOO EARLY FOR THIS...
WELL, I DON'T...
...SENSE ANY-THING...
HARD TO TELL WITH ALL THE JUNK IN HERE.
TOSS EVERY-THING OUT SO WE CAN SEARCH.

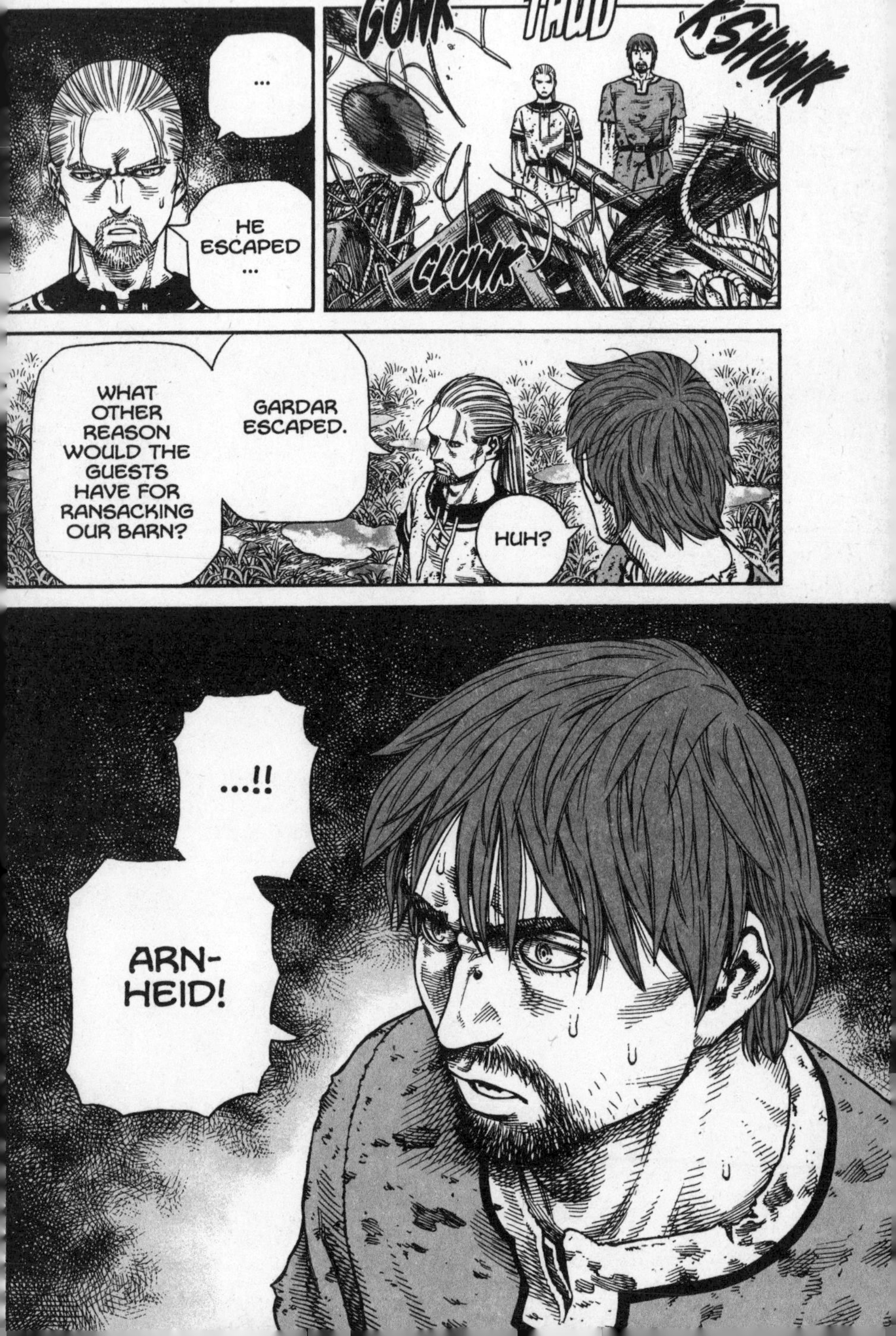
KSHUNK
THUD
GONK
CLUNK
...
HE ESCAPED ...
GARDAR ESCAPED.
HUH?
WHAT OTHER REASON WOULD THE GUESTS HAVE FOR RANSACKING OUR BARN?
...!!
ARN-HEID!

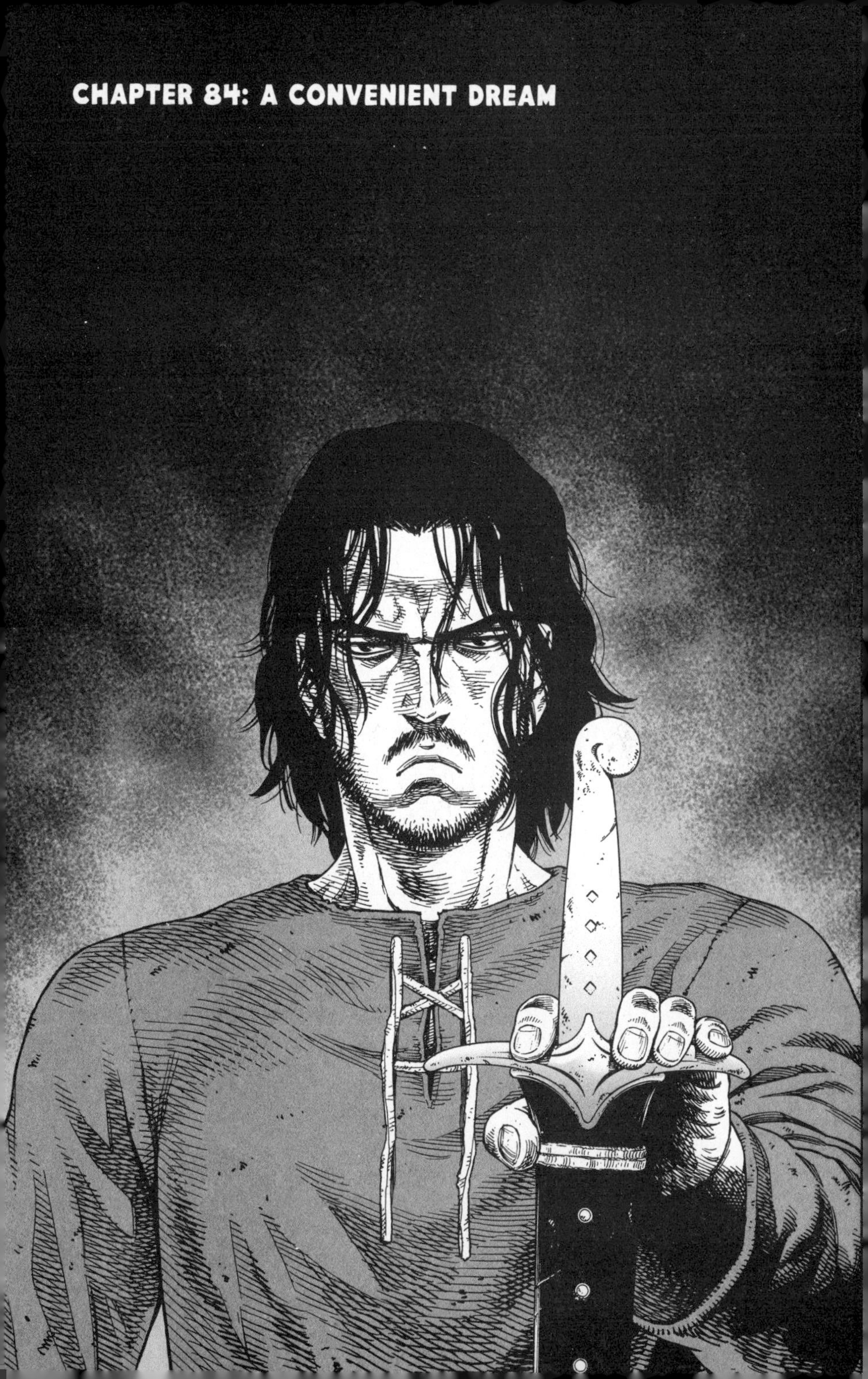
CHAPTER 84: A CONVENIENT DREAM

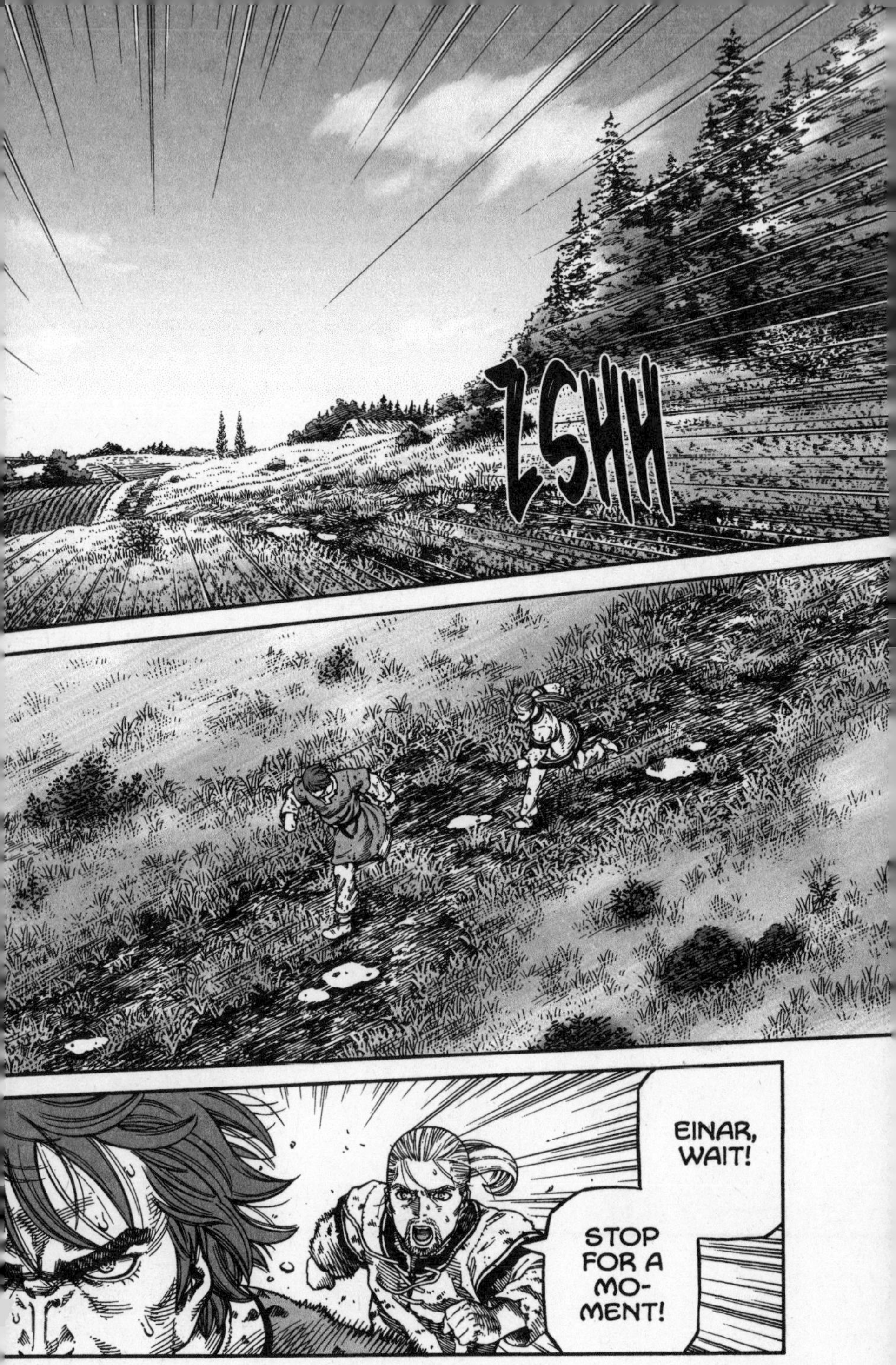
ZSHH
EINAR, WAIT!
STOP FOR A MO- MENT!

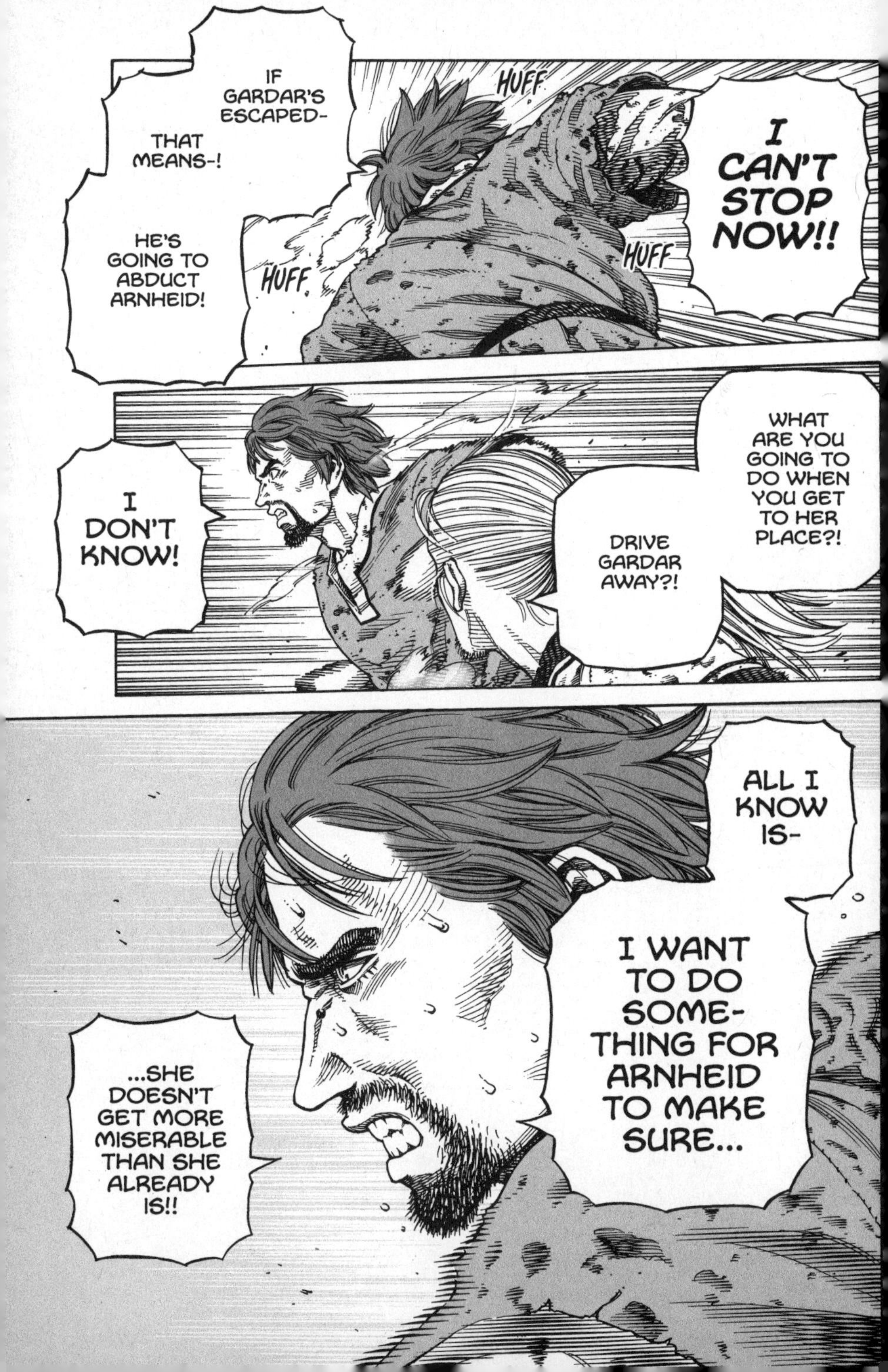
IF GARDAR'S ESCAPED-
THAT MEANS-!
HE'S GOING TO ABDUCT ARNHEID!
HUFF
I CAN'T STOP NOW!!
HUFF
HUFF
WHAT ARE YOU GOING TO DO WHEN YOU GET TO HER PLACE?!
DRIVE GARDAR AWAY?!
I DON'T KNOW!
ALL I KNOW IS-
I WANT TO DO SOME-THING FOR ARNHEID TO MAKE SURE...
...SHE DOESN'T GET MORE MISERABLE THAN SHE ALREADY IS!!

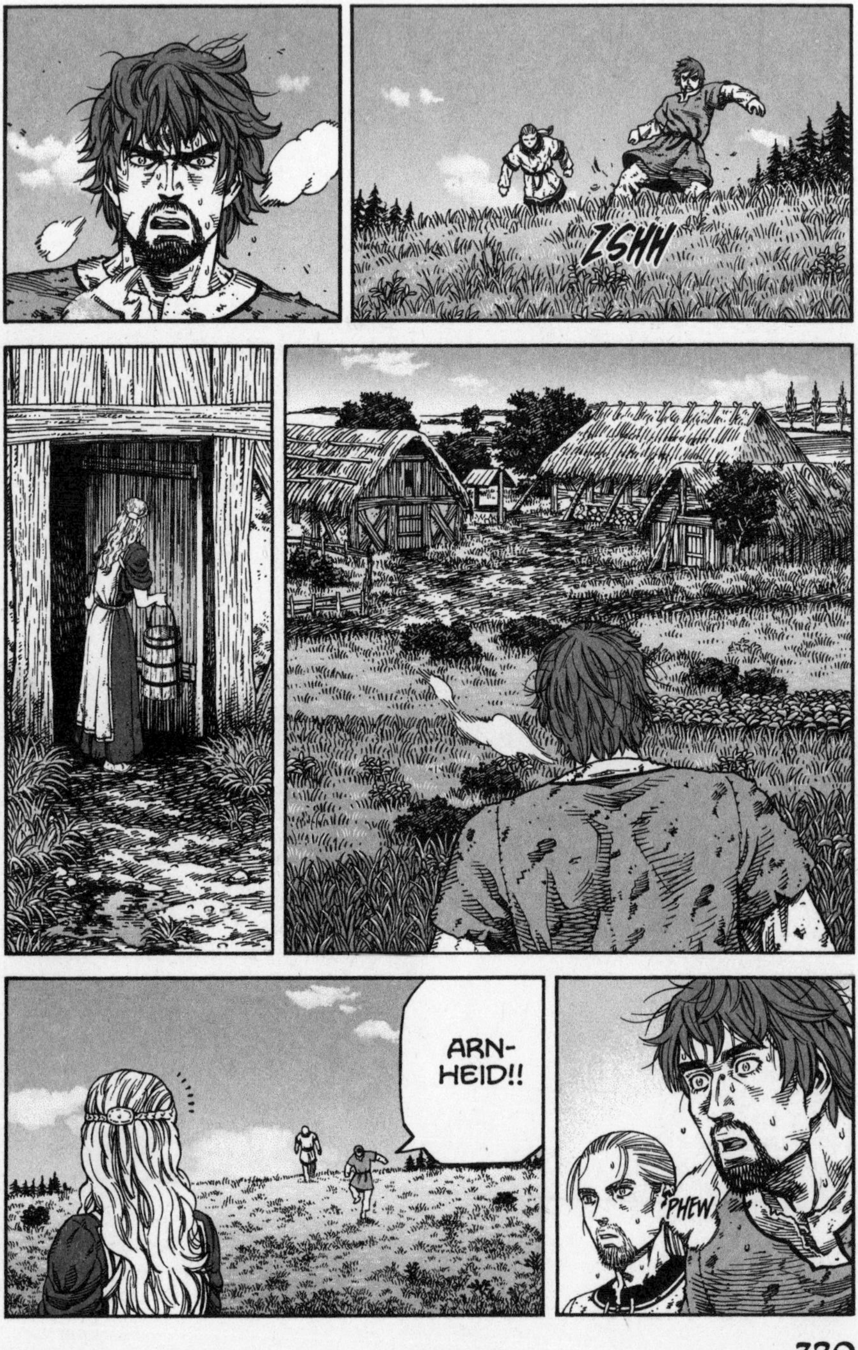
ZSHH
PHEW
ARN-HEID!!

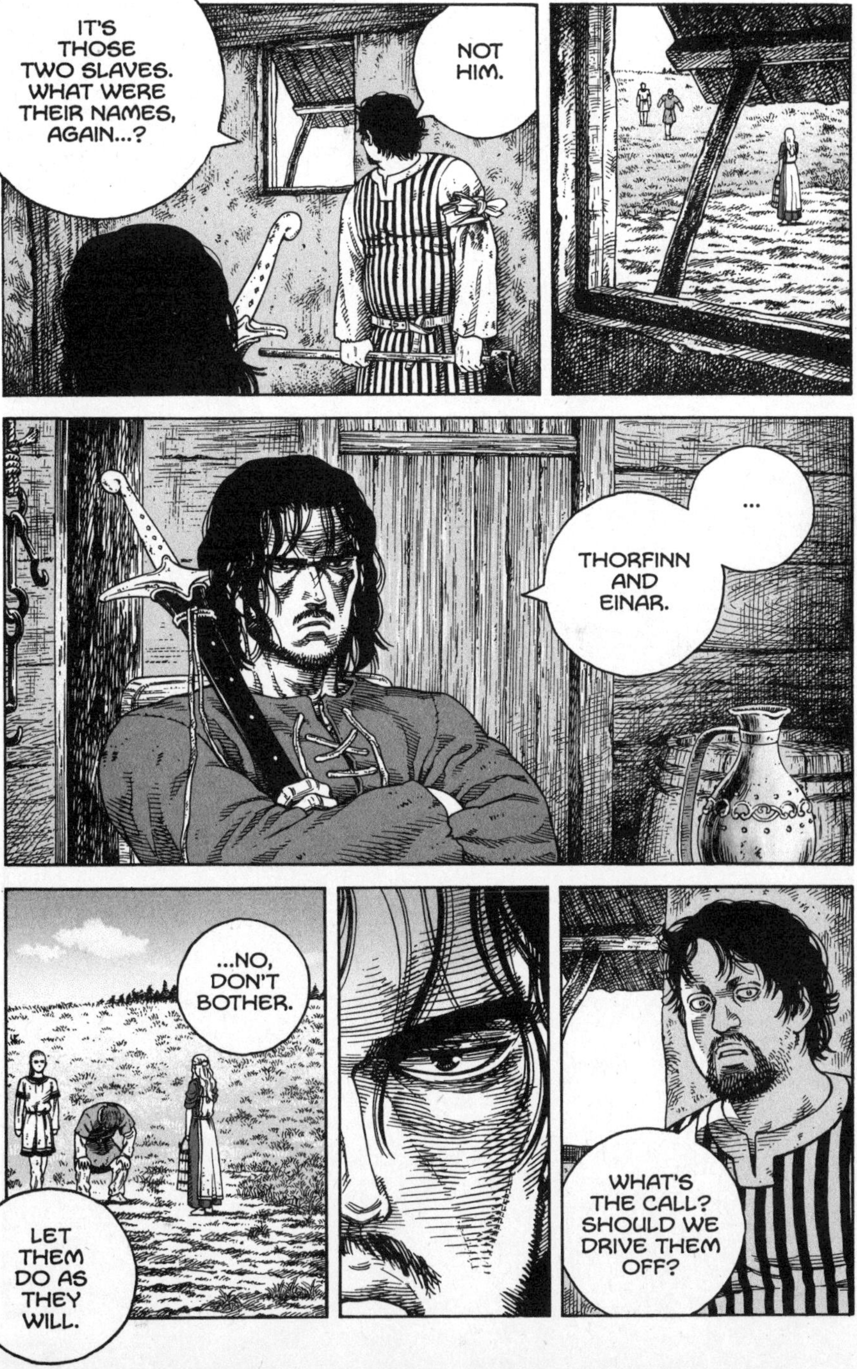
NOT HIM.
IT'S THOSE TWO SLAVES. WHAT WERE THEIR NAMES, AGAIN...?
...
THORFINN AND EINAR.
WHAT'S THE CALL? SHOULD WE DRIVE THEM OFF?
...NO, DON'T BOTHER.
LET THEM DO AS THEY WILL.

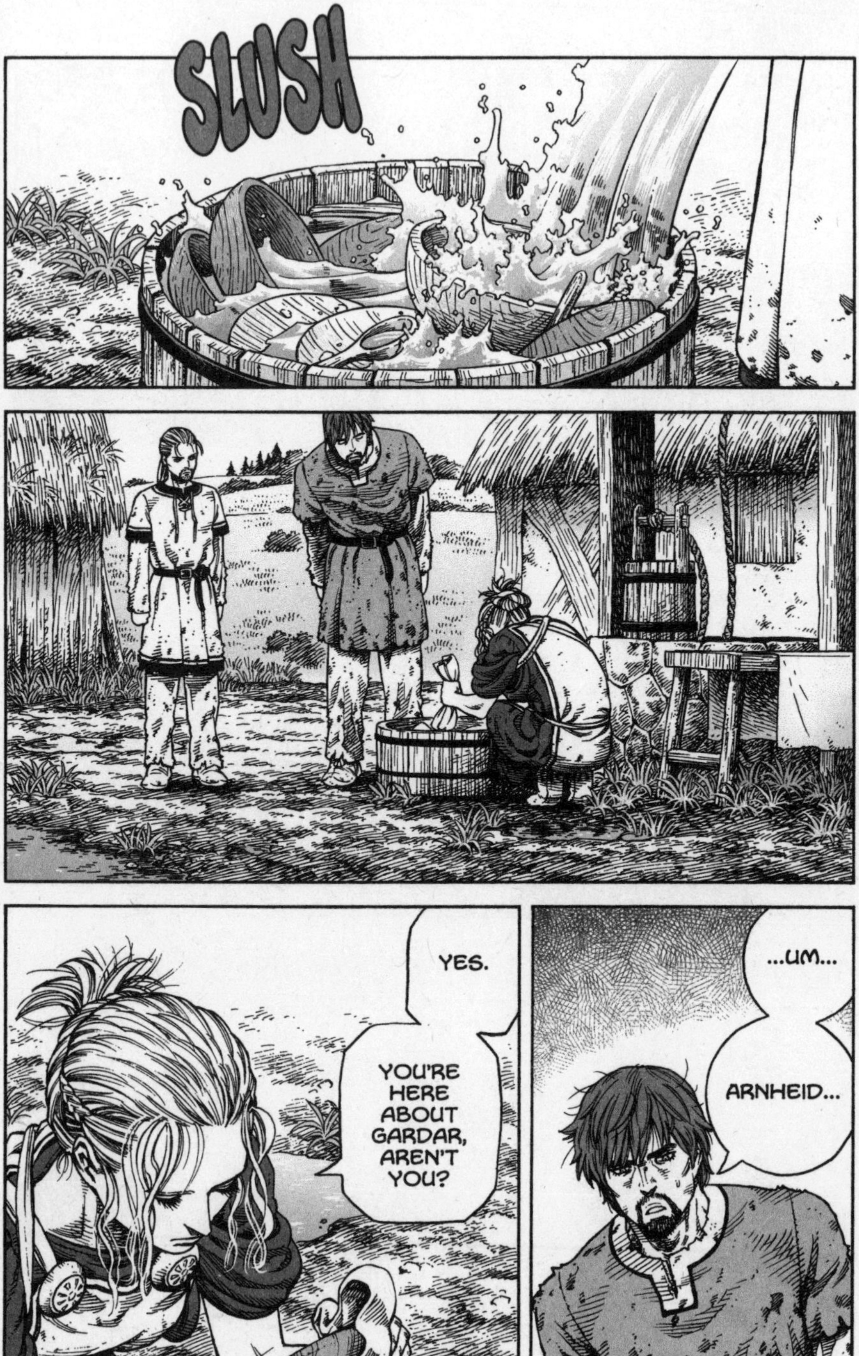
SLUSH
...UM...
ARNHEID...
YES.
YOU'RE HERE ABOUT GARDAR, AREN'T YOU?

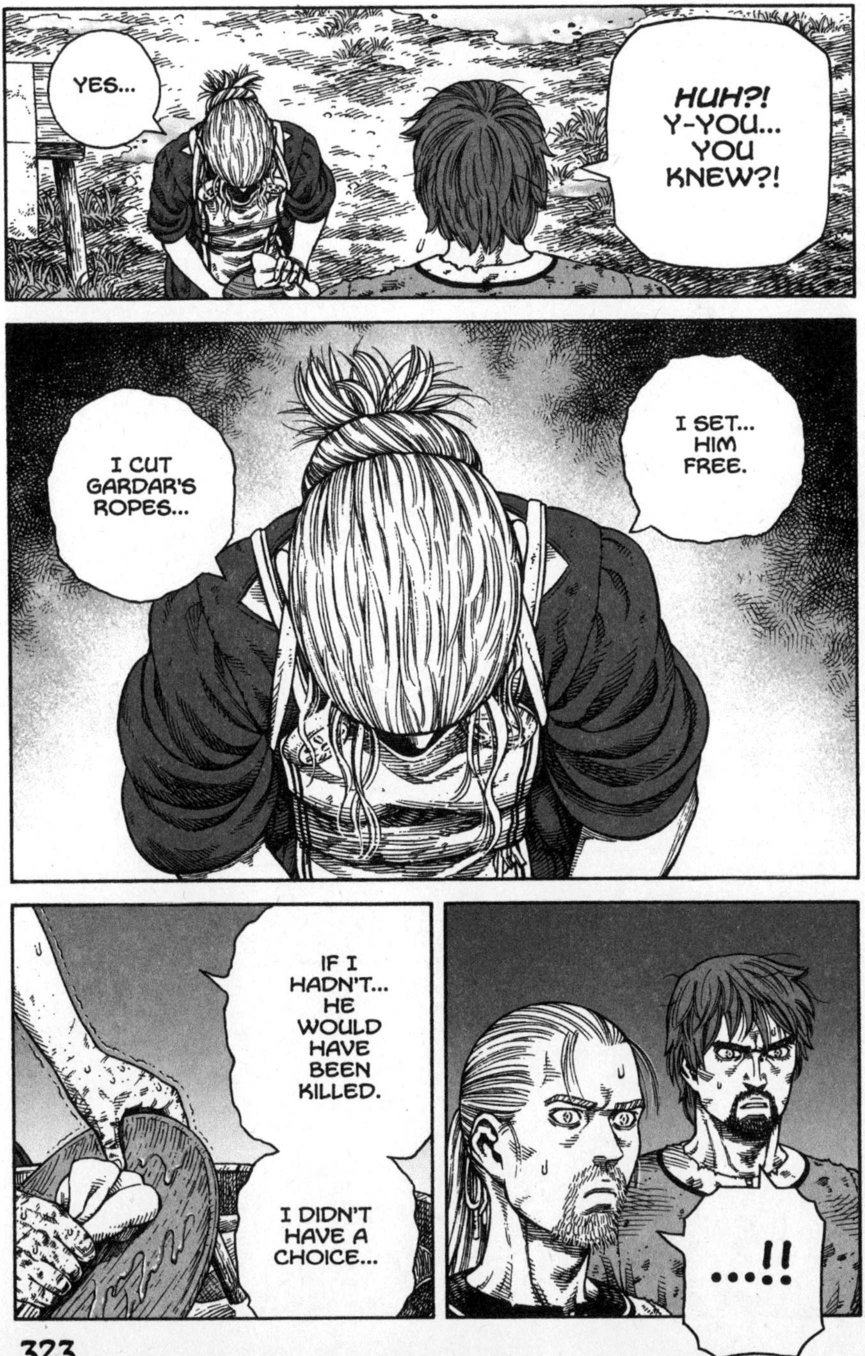
HUH?! Y-YOU... YOU KNEW?!
YES...
I SET... HIM FREE.
I CUT GARDAR'S ROPES...
...!!
IF I HADN'T... HE WOULD HAVE BEEN KILLED.
I DIDN'T HAVE A CHOICE...

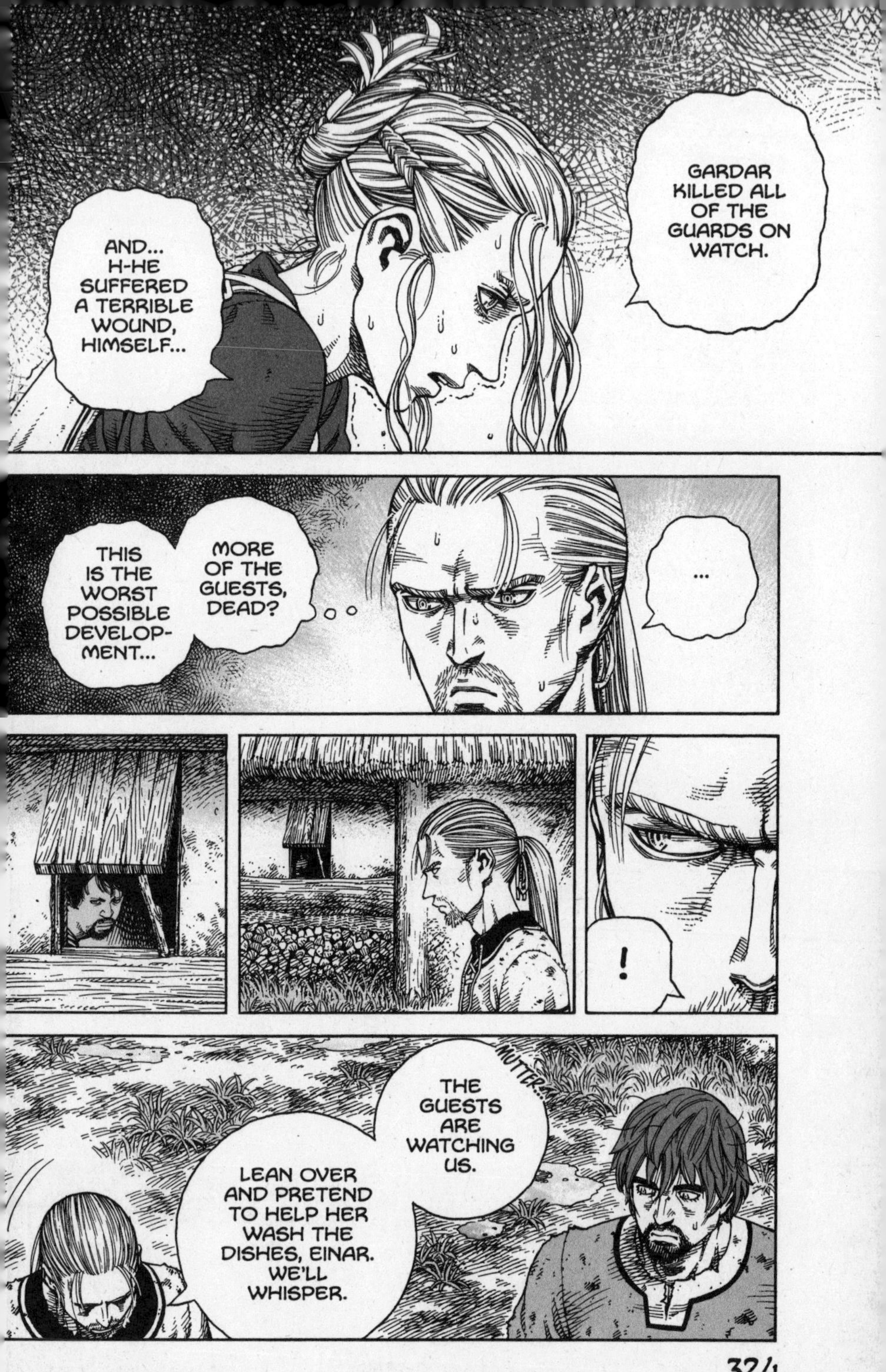
GARDAR KILLED ALL OF THE GUARDS ON WATCH.
AND... H-HE SUFFERED A TERRIBLE WOUND, HIMSELF...
...
MORE OF THE GUESTS, DEAD?
THIS IS THE WORST POSSIBLE DEVELOPMENT...
!
MUTTER...
THE GUESTS ARE WATCHING US.
LEAN OVER AND PRETEND TO HELP HER WASH THE DISHES, EINAR. WE'LL WHISPER.

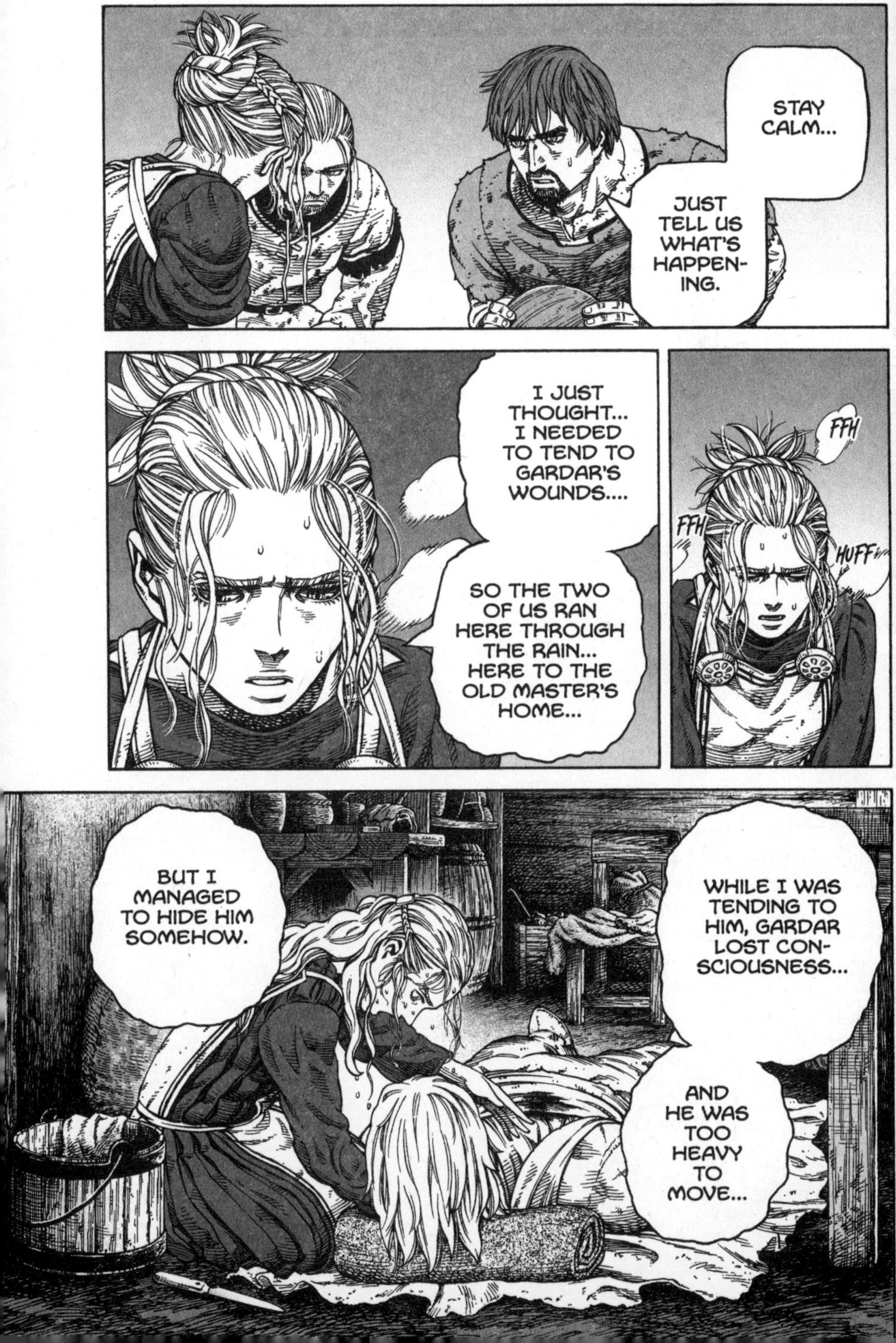
STAY CALM...
JUST TELL US WHAT'S HAPPEN-ING.
FFH
FFH
HUFF
I JUST THOUGHT... I NEEDED TO TEND TO GARDAR'S WOUNDS....
SO THE TWO OF US RAN HERE THROUGH THE RAIN... HERE TO THE OLD MASTER'S HOME...
WHILE I WAS TENDING TO HIM, GARDAR LOST CON-SCIOUSNESS...
AND HE WAS TOO HEAVY TO MOVE...
BUT I MANAGED TO HIDE HIM SOMEHOW.

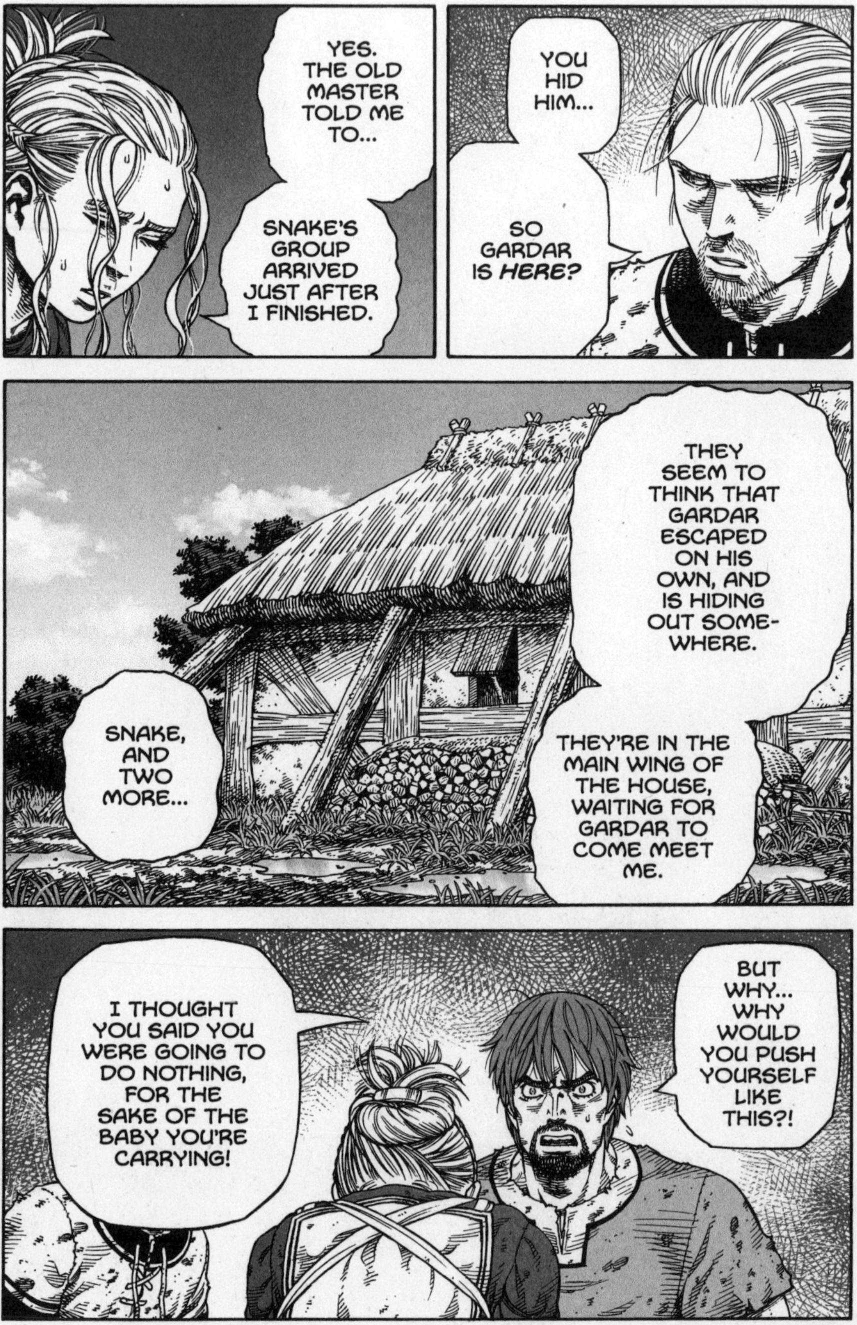
YOU HID HIM...
SO GARDAR IS *HERE?*
YES. THE OLD MASTER TOLD ME TO...
SNAKE'S GROUP ARRIVED JUST AFTER I FINISHED.
THEY SEEM TO THINK THAT GARDAR ESCAPED ON HIS OWN, AND IS HIDING OUT SOME-WHERE.
THEY'RE IN THE MAIN WING OF THE HOUSE, WAITING FOR GARDAR TO COME MEET ME.
SNAKE, AND TWO MORE...
BUT WHY... WHY WOULD YOU PUSH YOURSELF LIKE THIS?!
I THOUGHT YOU SAID YOU WERE GOING TO DO NOTHING, FOR THE SAKE OF THE BABY YOU'RE CARRYING!

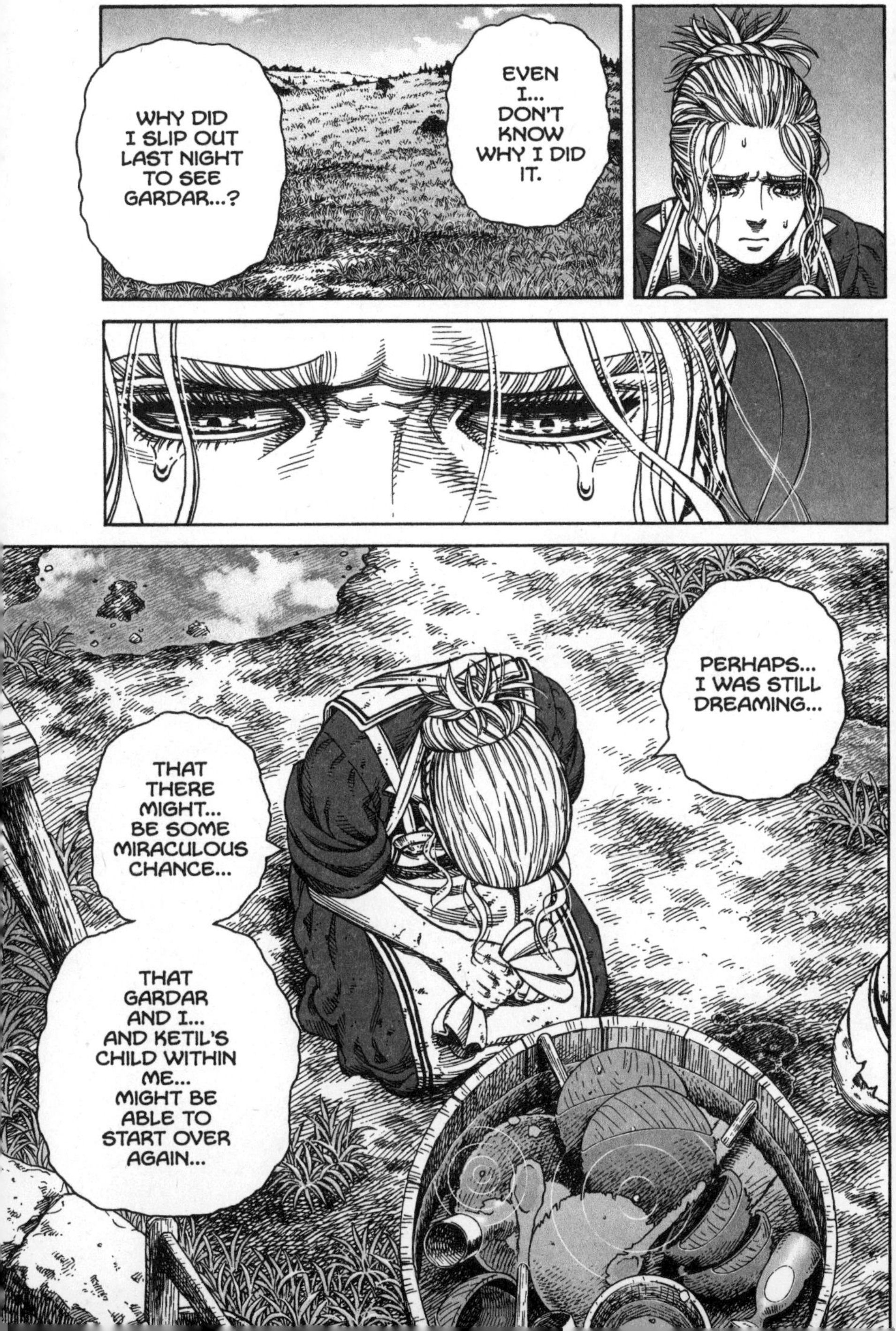
EVEN I... DON'T KNOW WHY I DID IT.
WHY DID I SLIP OUT LAST NIGHT TO SEE GARDAR...?
PERHAPS... I WAS STILL DREAMING...
THAT THERE MIGHT... BE SOME MIRACULOUS CHANCE...
THAT GARDAR AND I... AND KETIL'S CHILD WITHIN ME... MIGHT BE ABLE TO START OVER AGAIN...

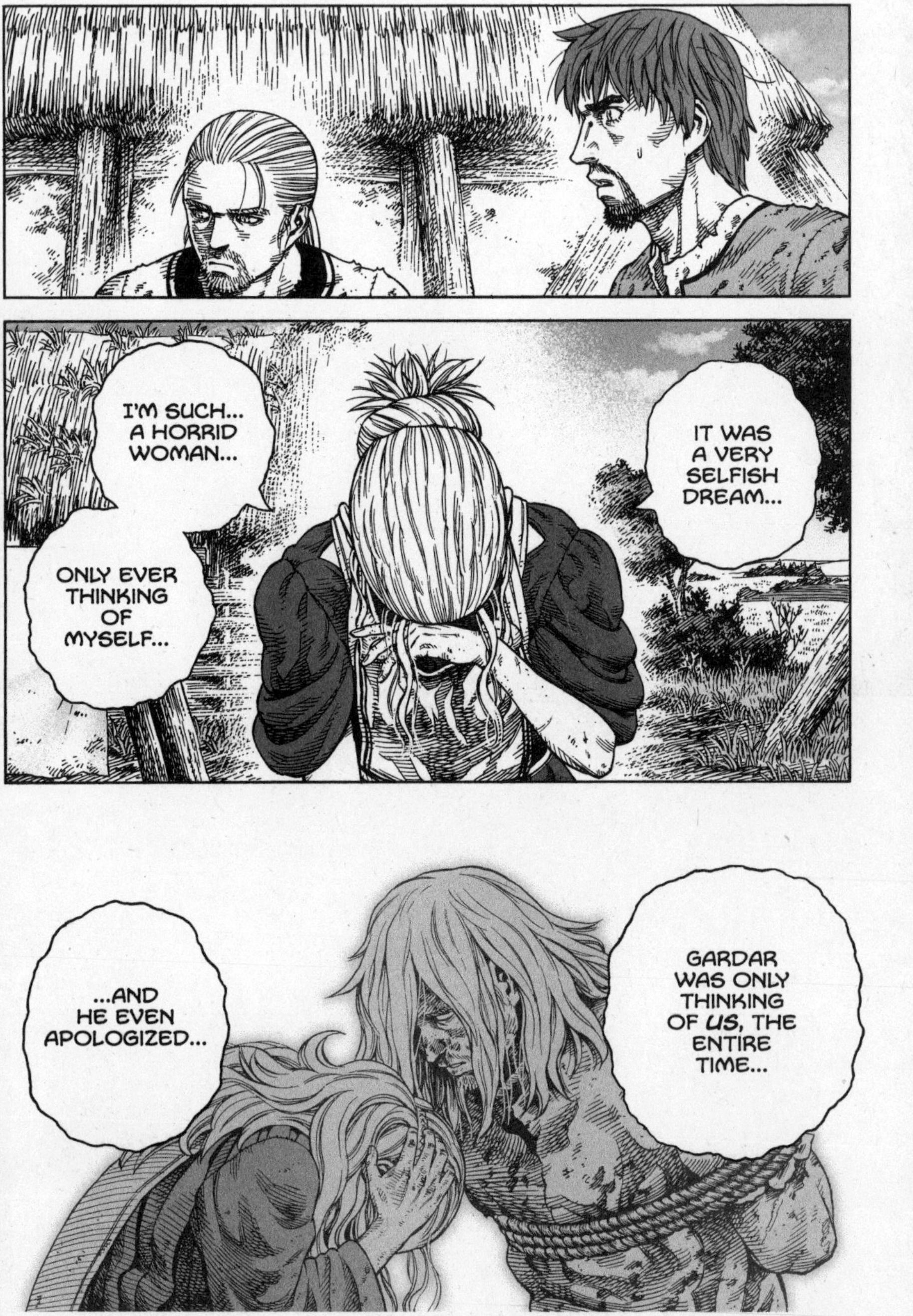
IT WAS A VERY SELFISH DREAM...
I'M SUCH... A HORRID WOMAN...
ONLY EVER THINKING OF MYSELF...
GARDAR WAS ONLY THINKING OF *US*, THE ENTIRE TIME...
...AND HE EVEN APOLOGIZED...

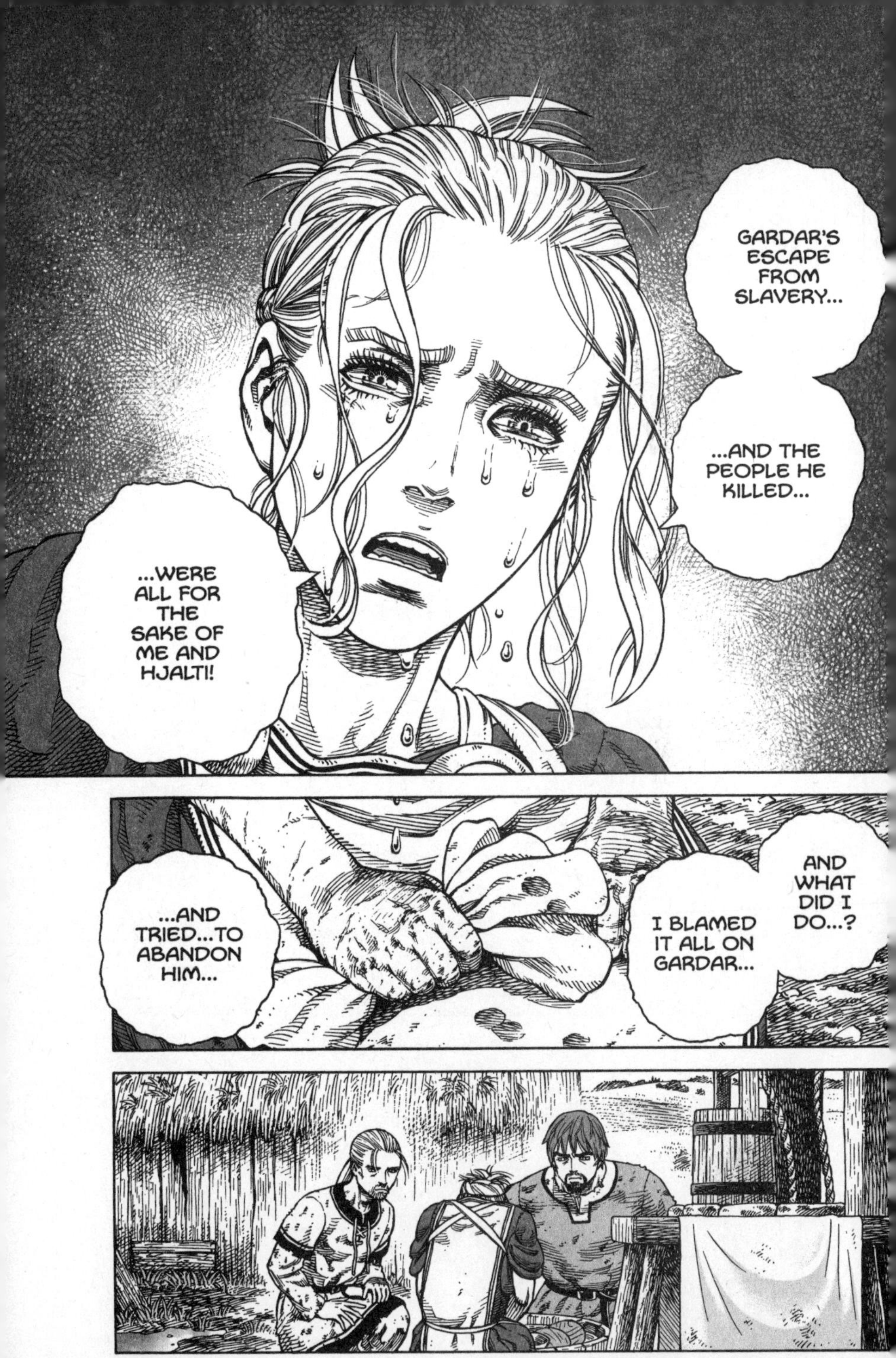
GARDAR'S ESCAPE FROM SLAVERY...
...AND THE PEOPLE HE KILLED...
...WERE ALL FOR THE SAKE OF ME AND HJALTI!
AND WHAT DID I DO...?
I BLAMED IT ALL ON GARDAR...
...AND TRIED...TO ABANDON HIM...

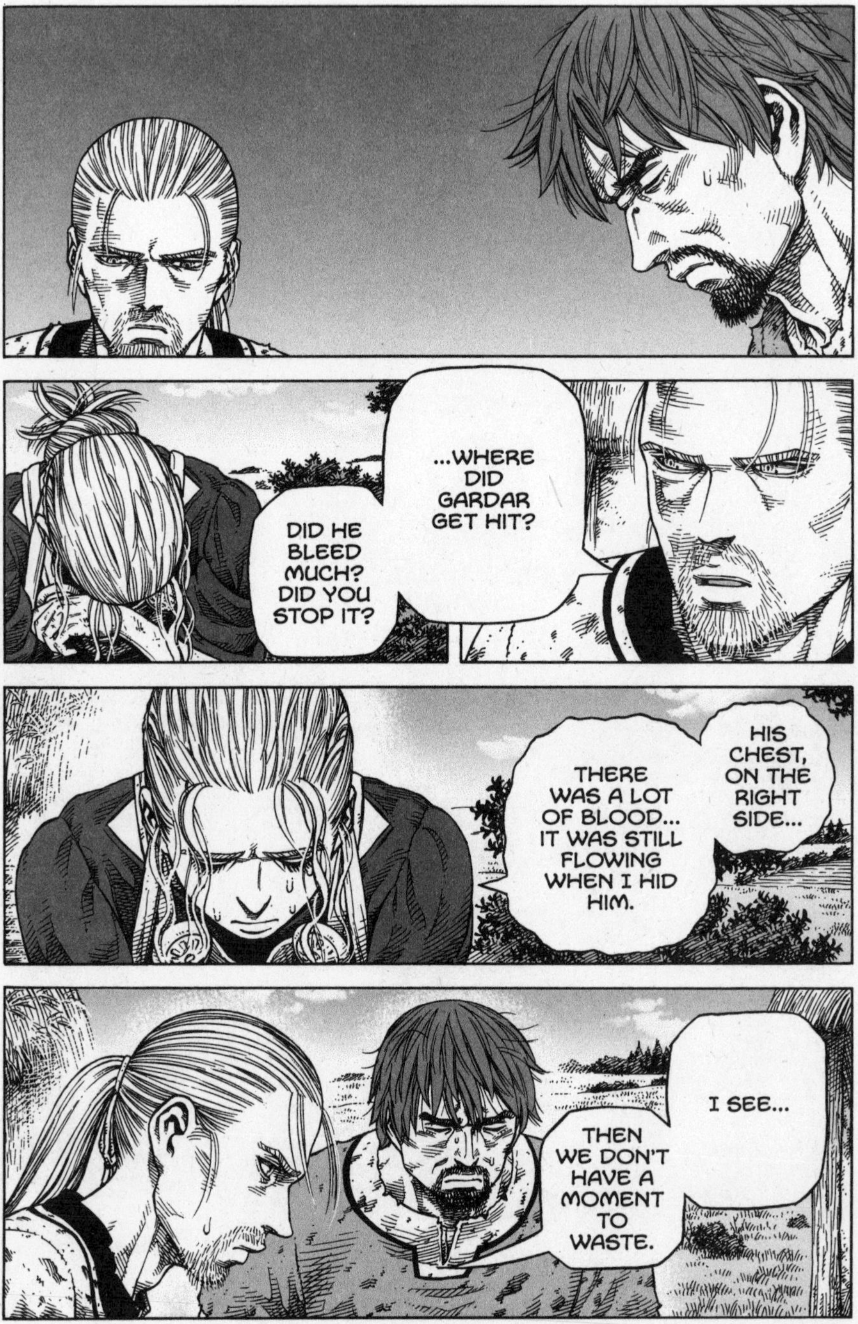
...WHERE DID GARDAR GET HIT?
DID HE BLEED MUCH? DID YOU STOP IT?
HIS CHEST, ON THE RIGHT SIDE...
THERE WAS A LOT OF BLOOD... IT WAS STILL FLOWING WHEN I HID HIM.
I SEE...
THEN WE DON'T HAVE A MOMENT TO WASTE.

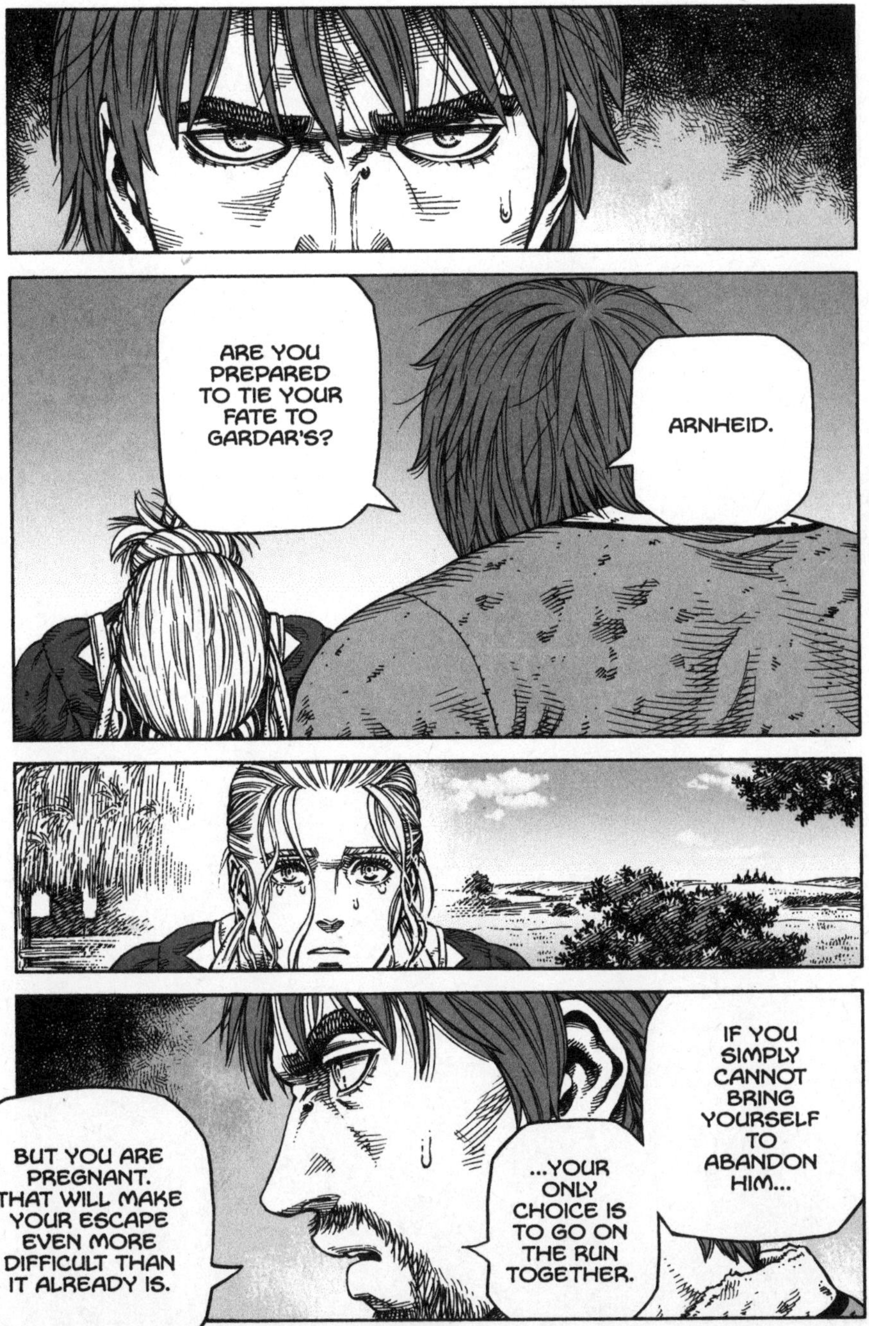
ARNHEID.
ARE YOU PREPARED TO TIE YOUR FATE TO GARDAR'S?
IF YOU SIMPLY CANNOT BRING YOURSELF TO ABANDON HIM...
...YOUR ONLY CHOICE IS TO GO ON THE RUN TOGETHER.
BUT YOU ARE PREGNANT. THAT WILL MAKE YOUR ESCAPE EVEN MORE DIFFICULT THAN IT ALREADY IS.

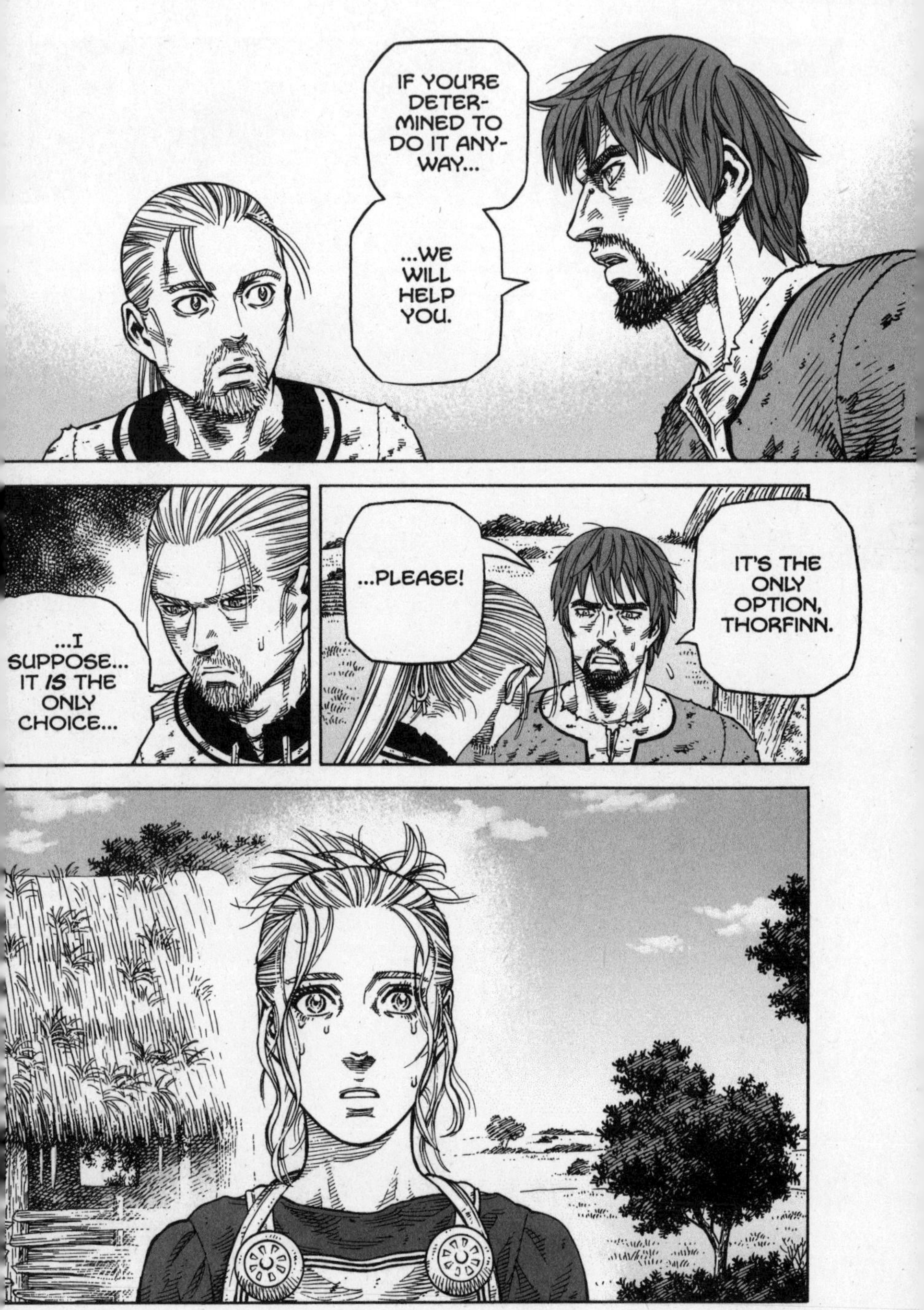
IF YOU'RE DETER-MINED TO DO IT ANY-WAY...
...WE WILL HELP YOU.
IT'S THE ONLY OPTION, THORFINN.
...PLEASE!
...I SUPPOSE... IT *IS* THE ONLY CHOICE...

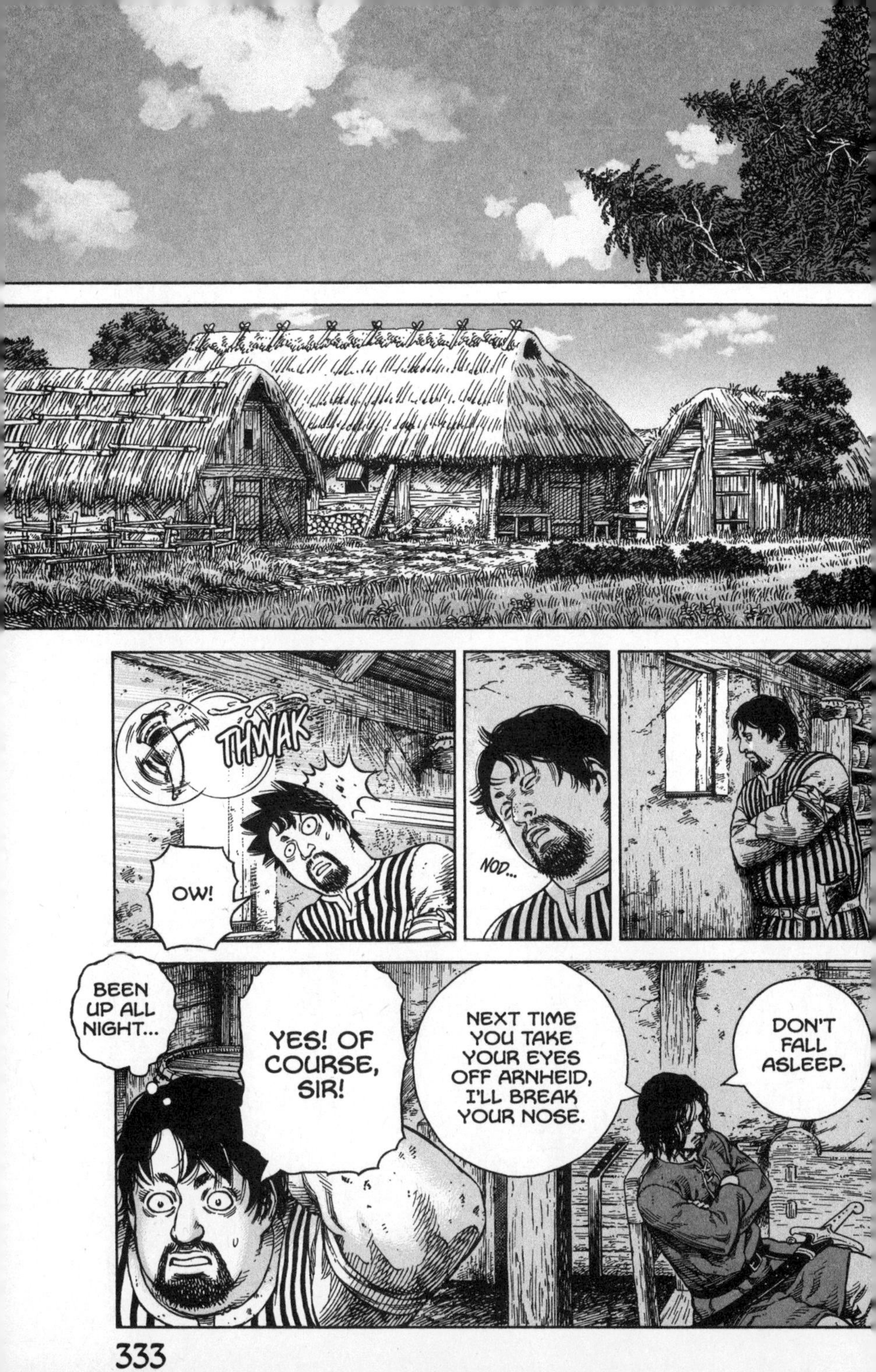
NOD...
THWAK
OW!
DON'T FALL ASLEEP.
NEXT TIME YOU TAKE YOUR EYES OFF ARNHEID, I'LL BREAK YOUR NOSE.
YES! OF COURSE, SIR!
BEEN UP ALL NIGHT...

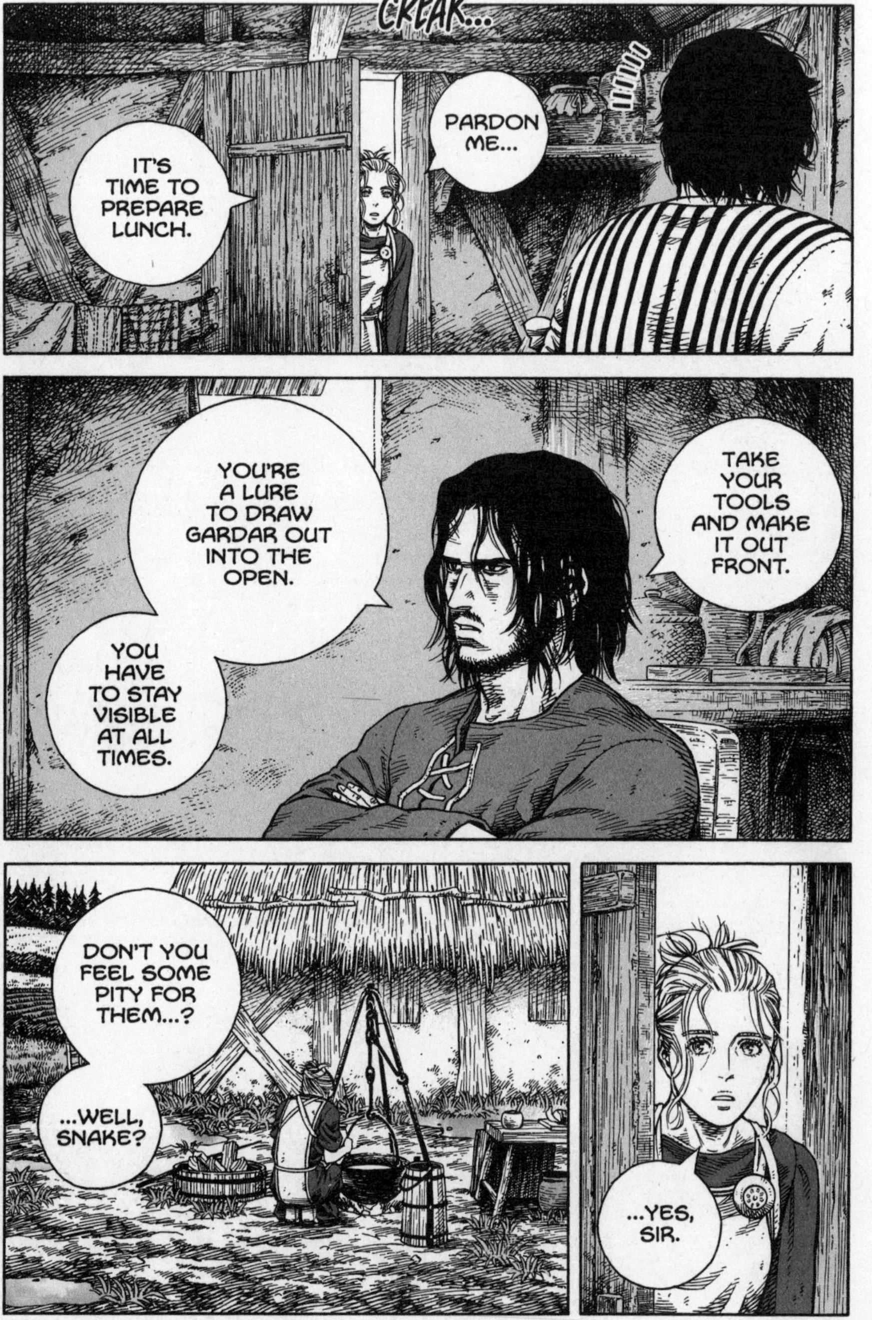
CREAK...
PARDON ME...
IT'S TIME TO PREPARE LUNCH.
TAKE YOUR TOOLS AND MAKE IT OUT FRONT.
YOU'RE A LURE TO DRAW GARDAR OUT INTO THE OPEN.
YOU HAVE TO STAY VISIBLE AT ALL TIMES.
...YES, SIR.
DON'T YOU FEEL SOME PITY FOR THEM...?
...WELL, SNAKE?

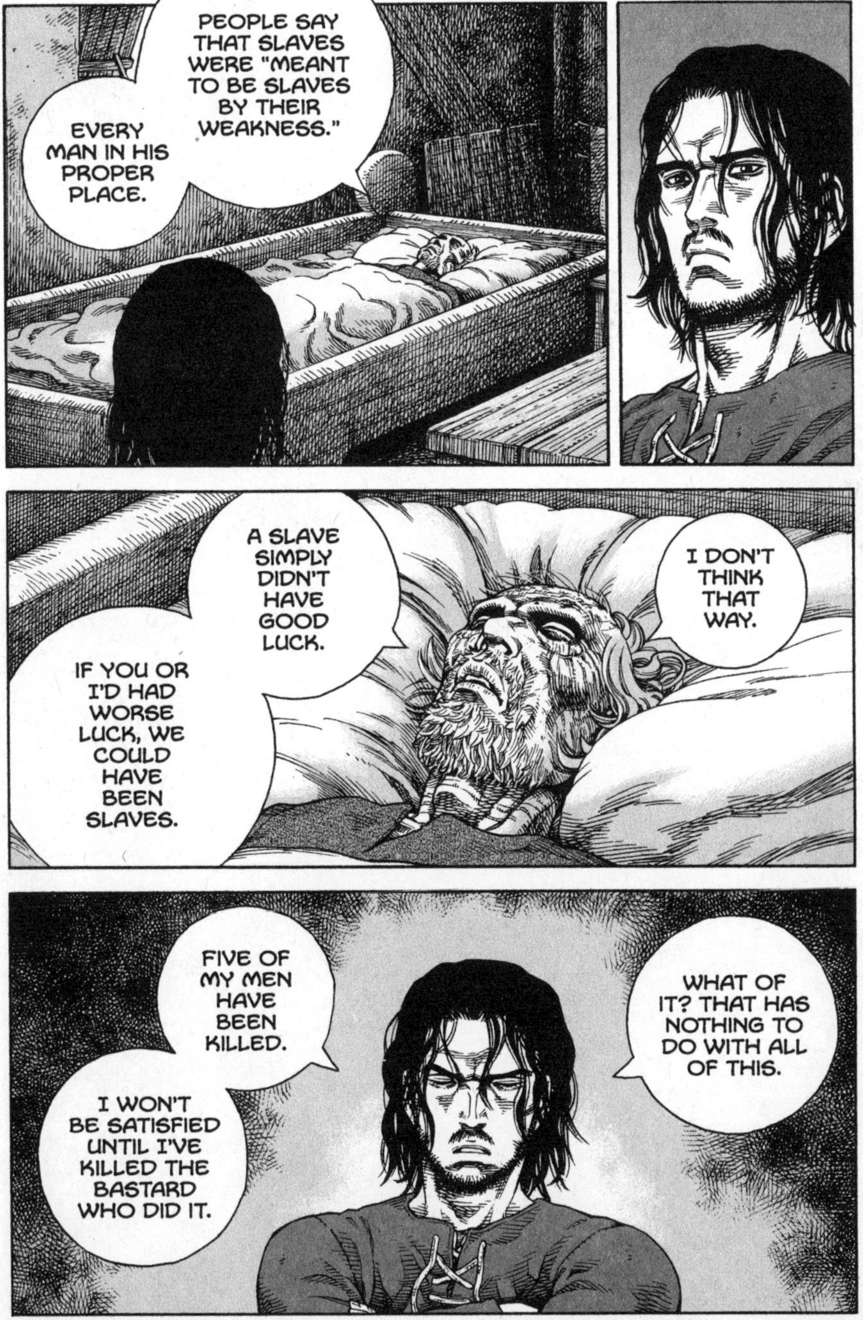
PEOPLE SAY THAT SLAVES WERE "MEANT TO BE SLAVES BY THEIR WEAKNESS."
EVERY MAN IN HIS PROPER PLACE.
I DON'T THINK THAT WAY.
A SLAVE SIMPLY DIDN'T HAVE GOOD LUCK.
IF YOU OR I'D HAD WORSE LUCK, WE COULD HAVE BEEN SLAVES.
WHAT OF IT? THAT HAS NOTHING TO DO WITH ALL OF THIS.
FIVE OF MY MEN HAVE BEEN KILLED.
I WON'T BE SATISFIED UNTIL I'VE KILLED THE BASTARD WHO DID IT.

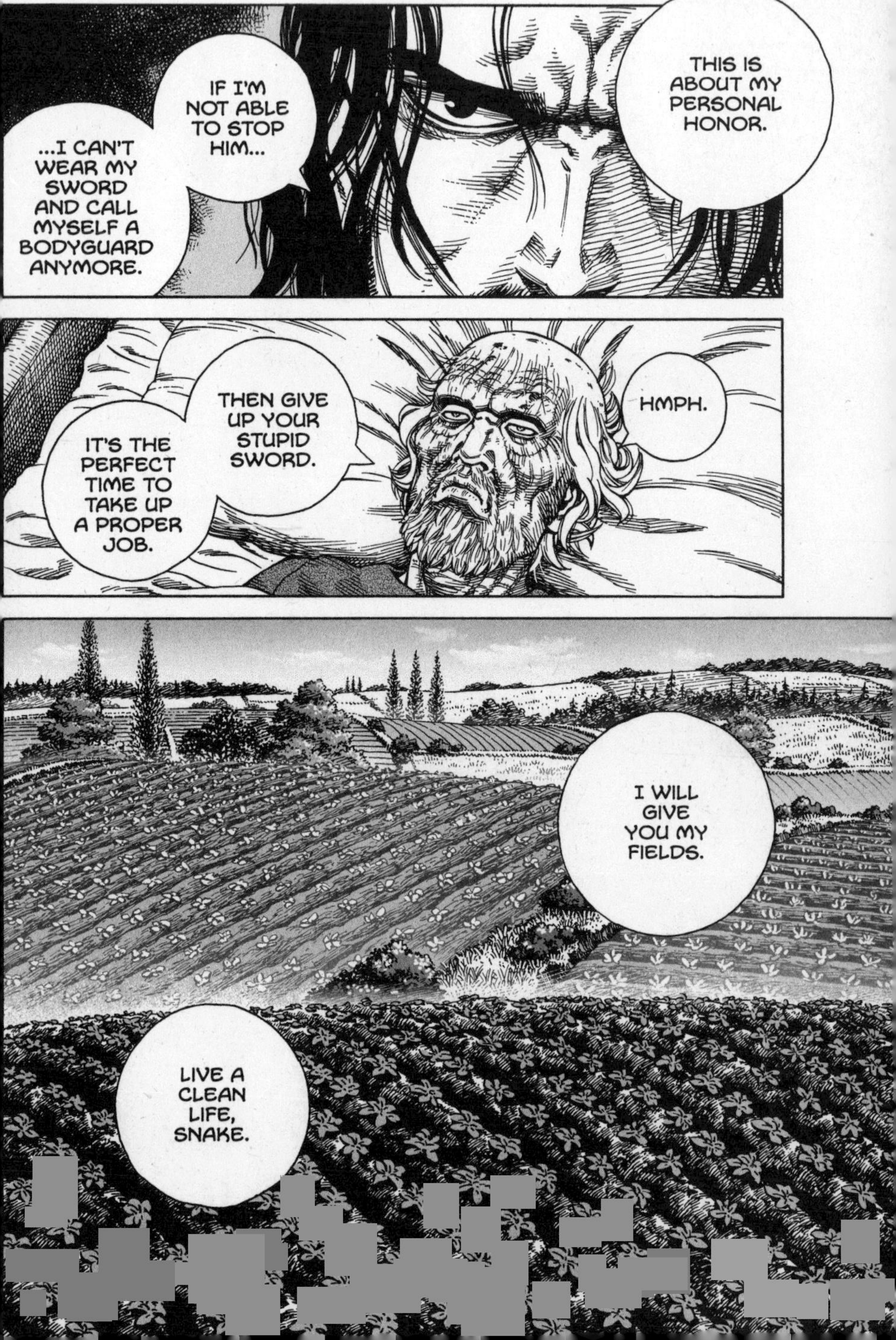
THIS IS ABOUT MY PERSONAL HONOR.
IF I'M NOT ABLE TO STOP HIM...
...I CAN'T WEAR MY SWORD AND CALL MYSELF A BODYGUARD ANYMORE.
HMPH.
THEN GIVE UP YOUR STUPID SWORD.
IT'S THE PERFECT TIME TO TAKE UP A PROPER JOB.
I WILL GIVE YOU MY FIELDS.
LIVE A CLEAN LIFE, SNAKE.

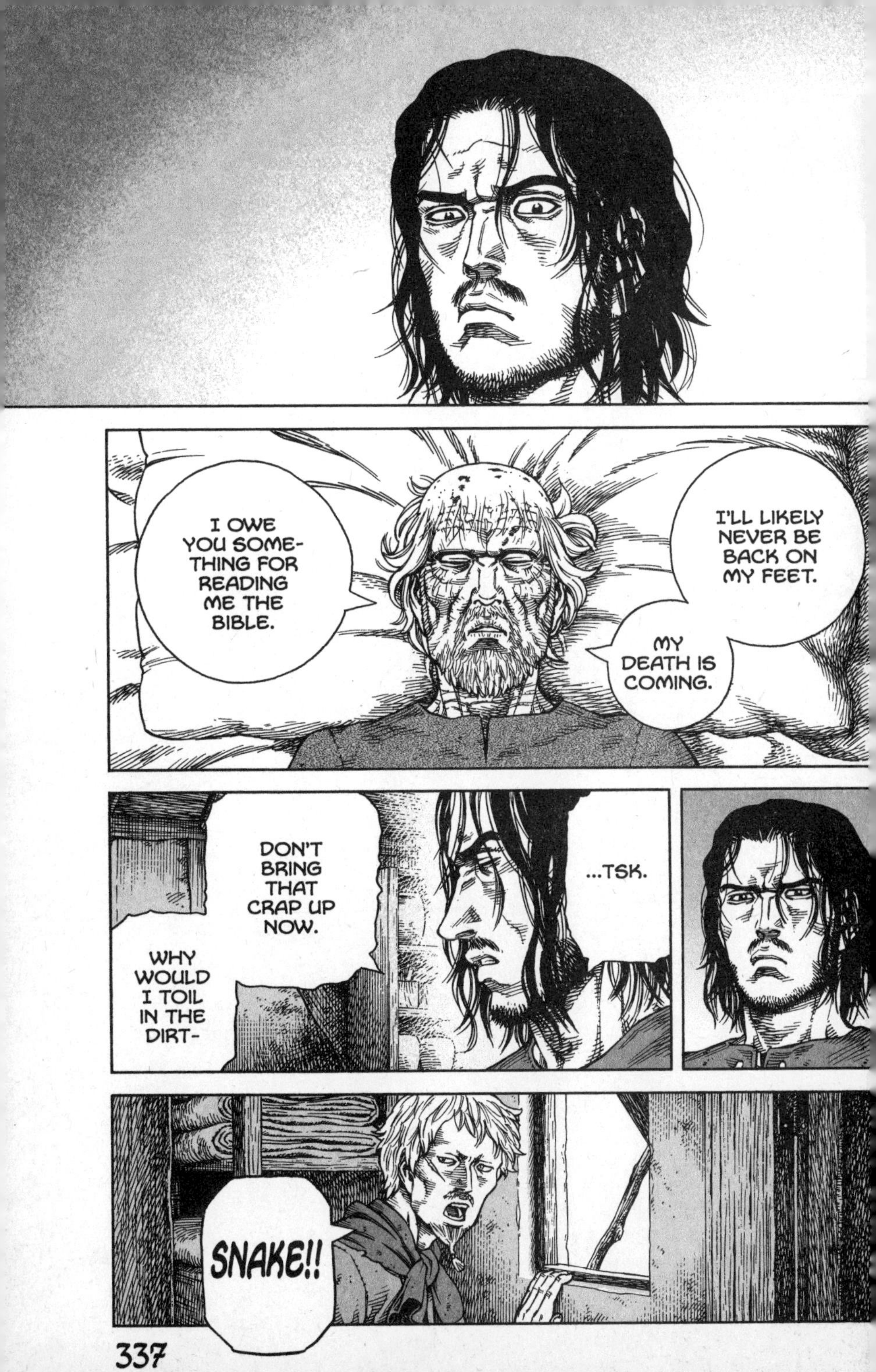
I'LL LIKELY NEVER BE BACK ON MY FEET.
MY DEATH IS COMING.
I OWE YOU SOMETHING FOR READING ME THE BIBLE.
...TSK.
DON'T BRING THAT CRAP UP NOW.
WHY WOULD I TOIL IN THE DIRT-
SNAKE!!

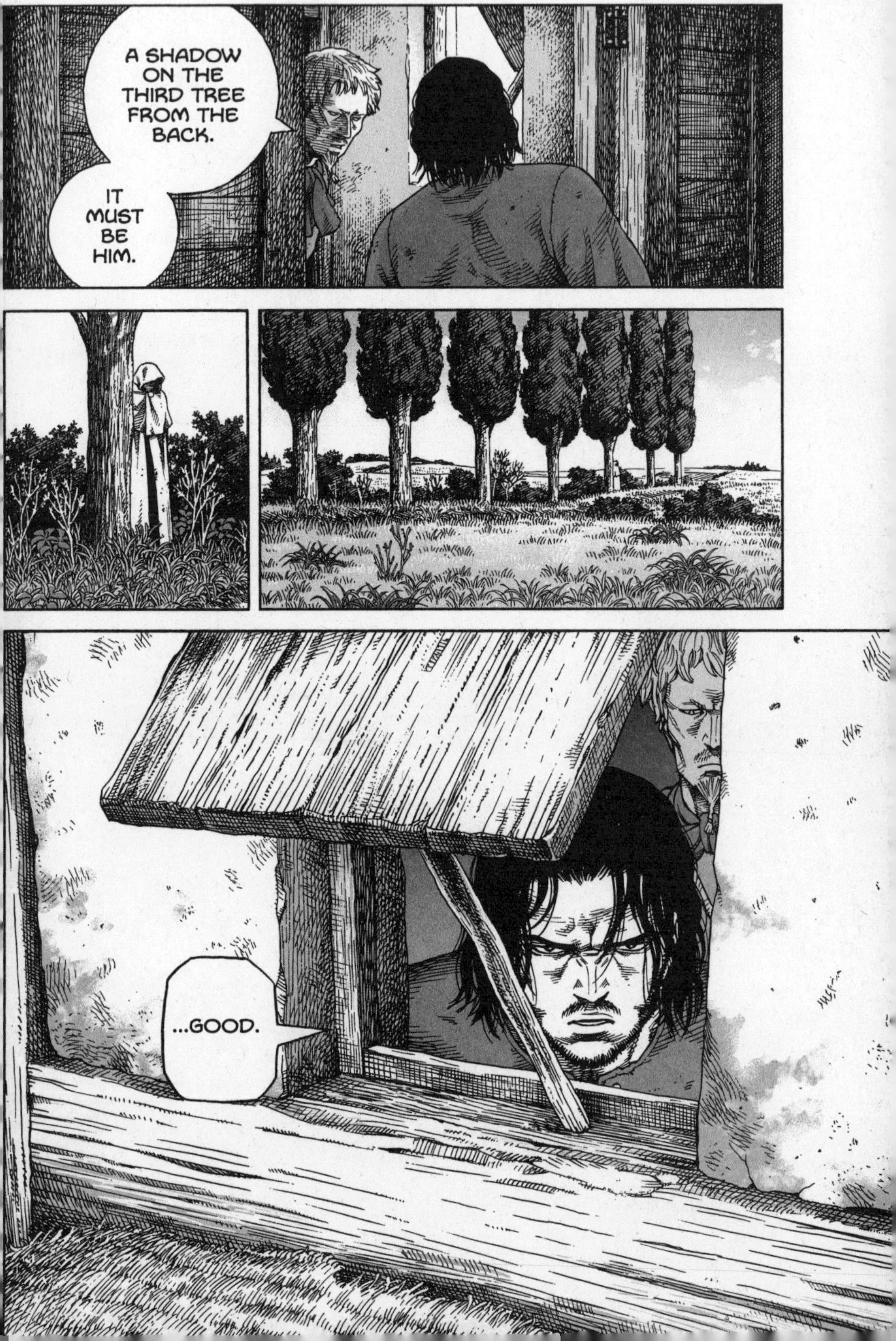
A SHADOW ON THE THIRD TREE FROM THE BACK.
IT MUST BE HIM.
...GOOD.

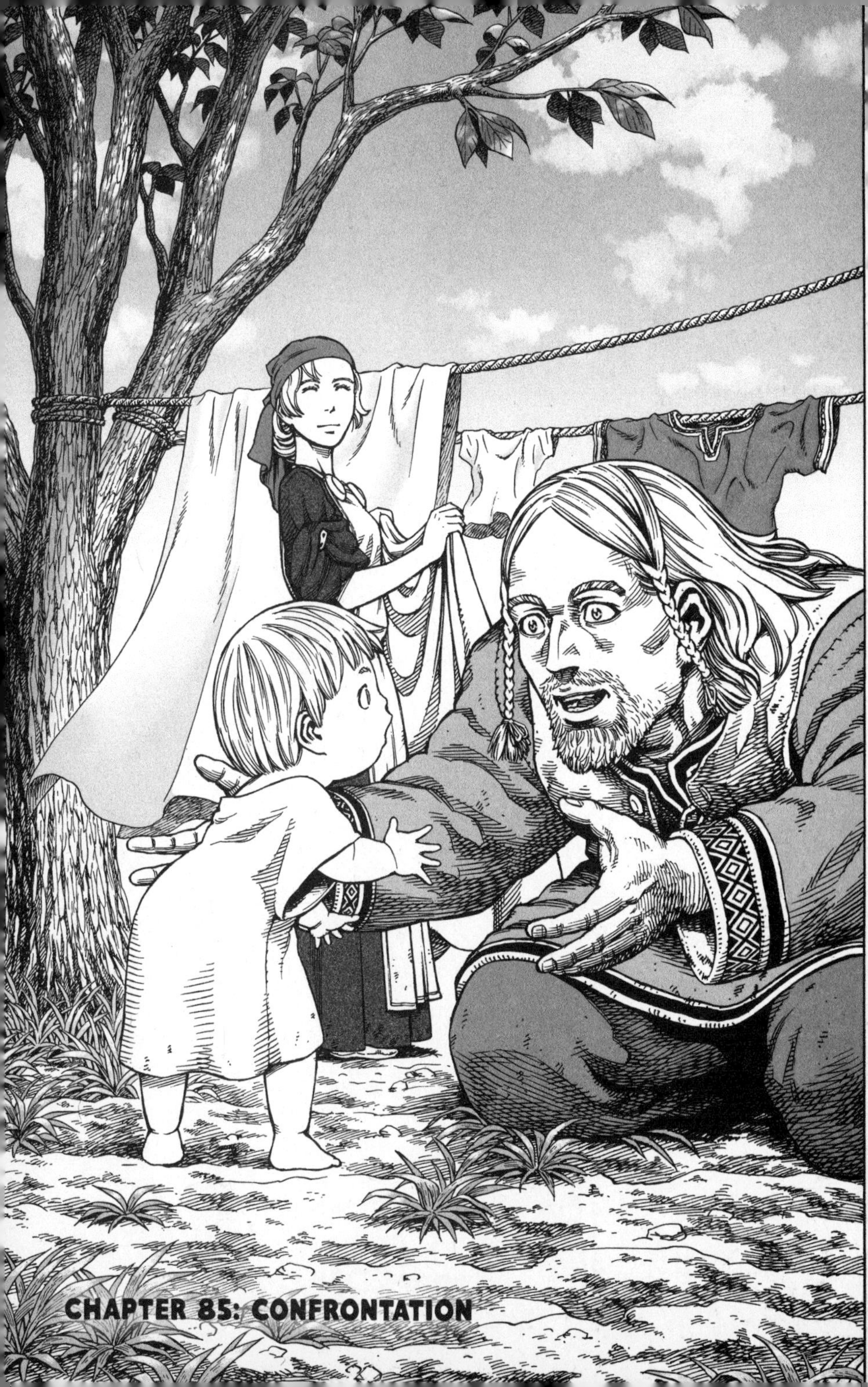

CHAPTER 85: CONFRONTATION

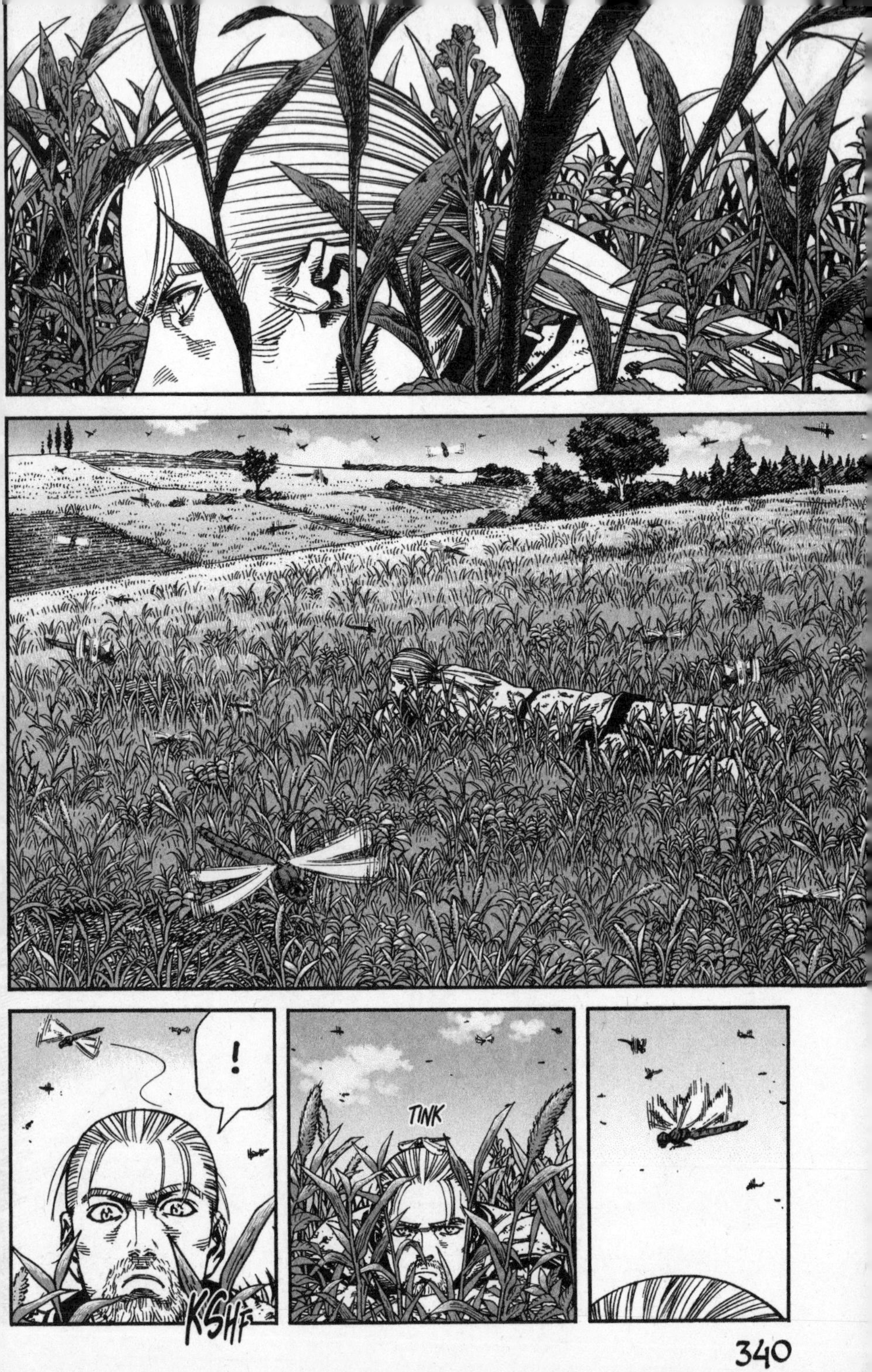
TINK
!
KSHF

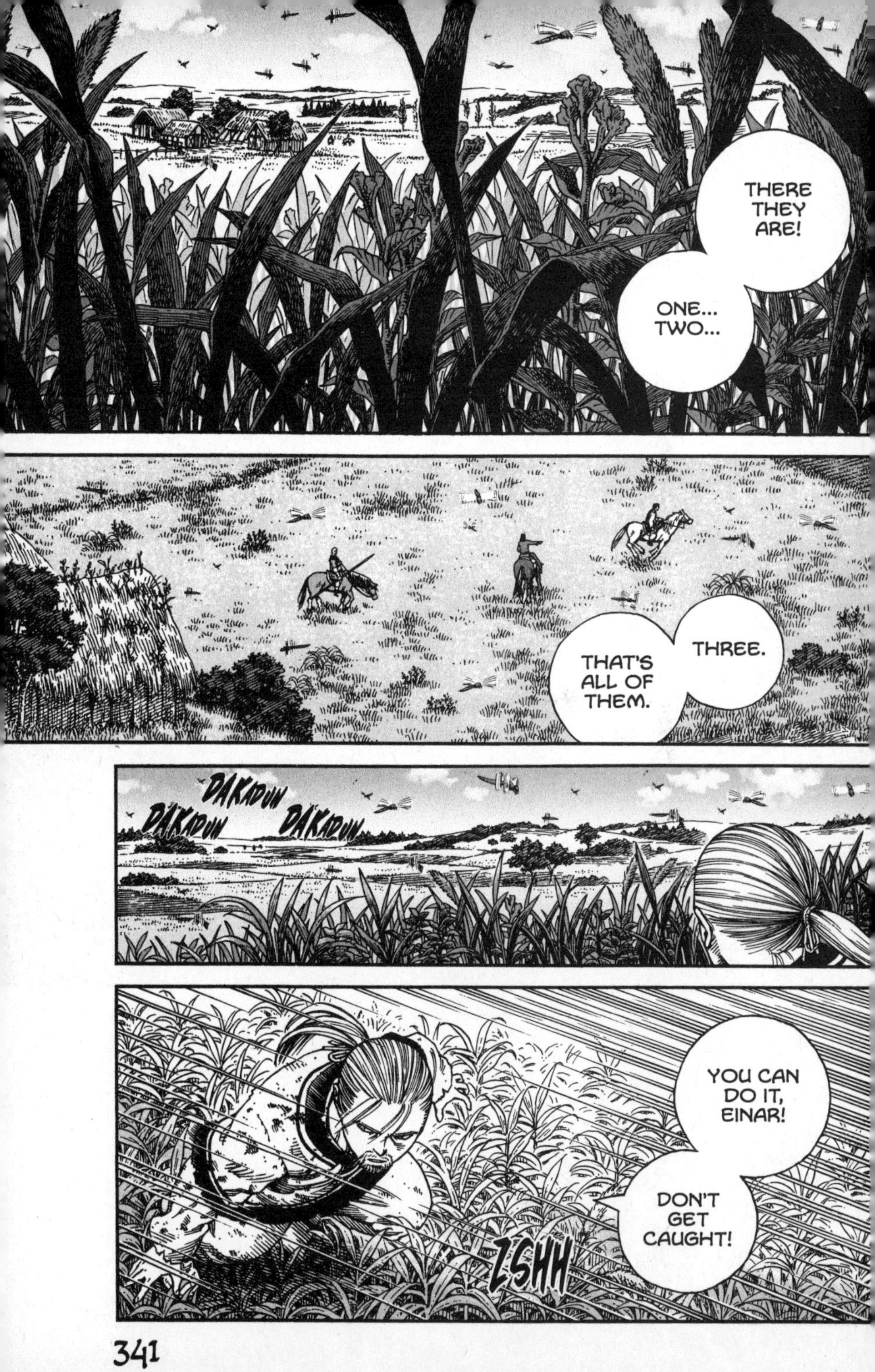
THERE THEY ARE!
ONE... TWO...
THREE.
THAT'S ALL OF THEM.
DAKADUN
DAKADUN
DAKADUN
YOU CAN DO IT, EINAR!
DON'T GET CAUGHT!
ZSHH

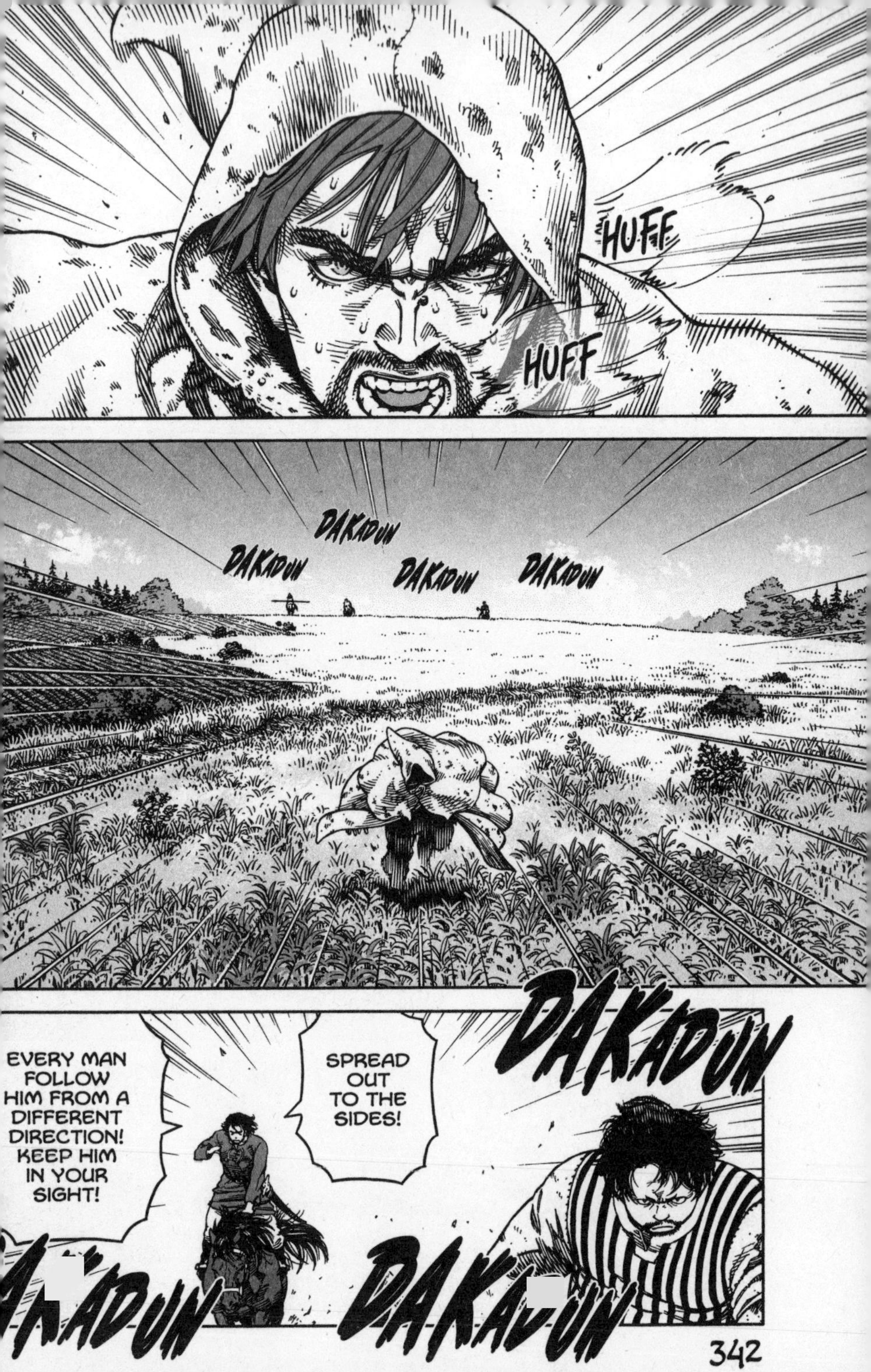
HUFF
HUFF
DAKADUN
DAKADUN
DAKADUN
DAKADUN
DAKADUN
DAKADUN
SPREAD OUT TO THE SIDES!
EVERY MAN FOLLOW HIM FROM A DIFFERENT DIRECTION! KEEP HIM IN YOUR SIGHT!
AKADUN

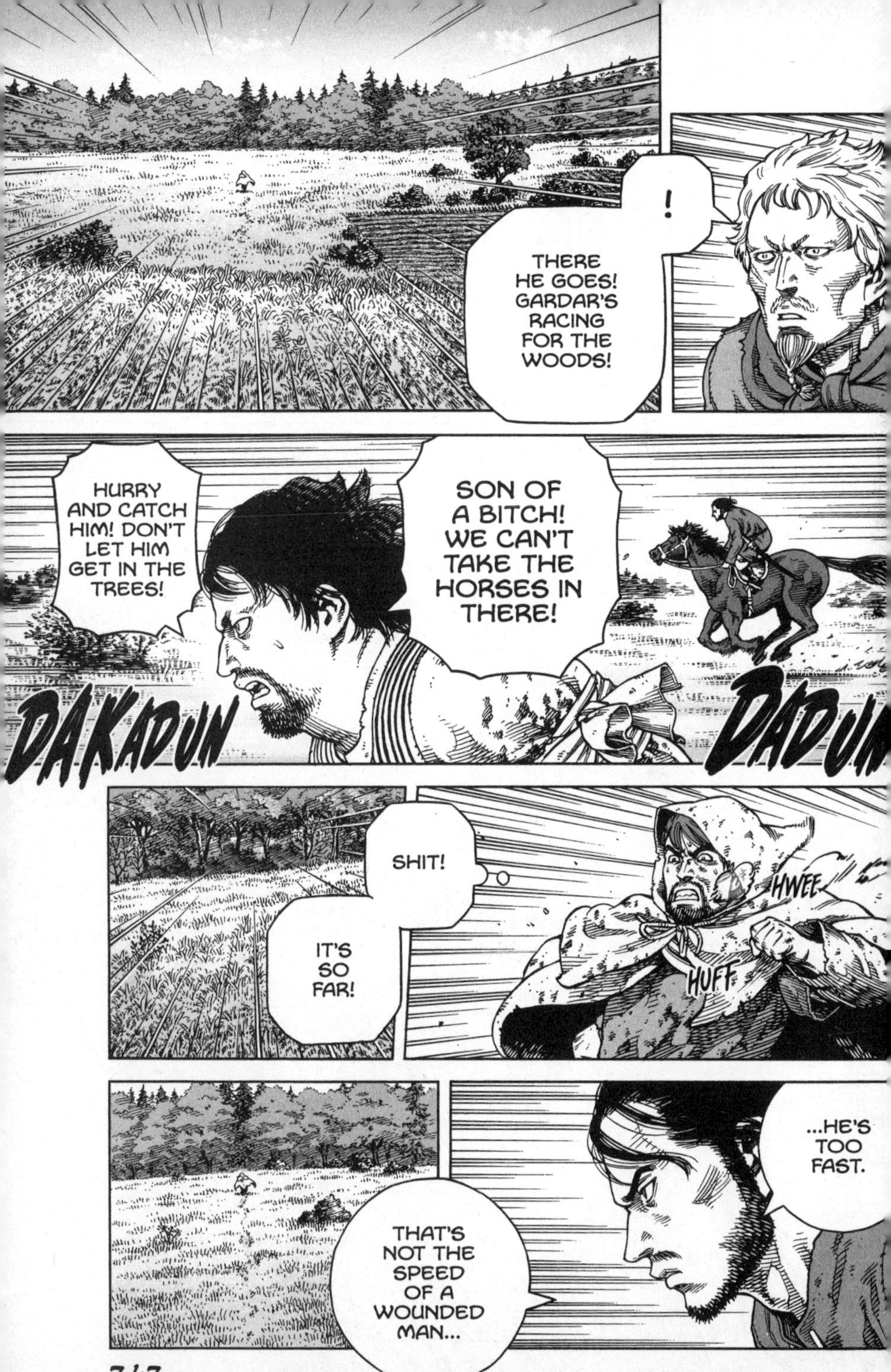
!
THERE HE GOES! GARDAR'S RACING FOR THE WOODS!
SON OF A BITCH! WE CAN'T TAKE THE HORSES IN THERE!
HURRY AND CATCH HIM! DON'T LET HIM GET IN THE TREES!
DADUN
DAKADUN
SHIT!
IT'S SO FAR!
HWEE
HUFF
...HE'S TOO FAST.
THAT'S NOT THE SPEED OF A WOUNDED MAN...

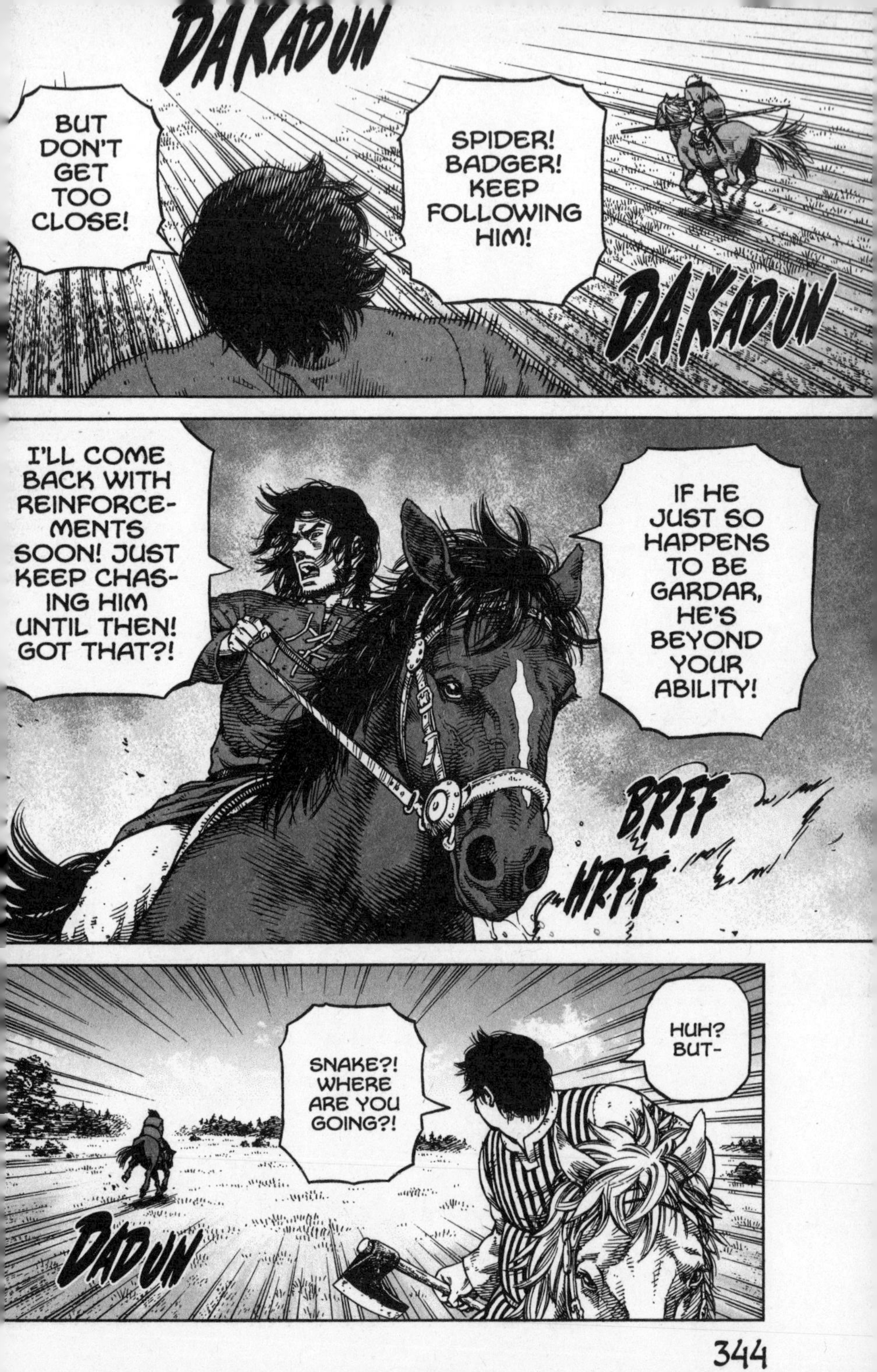
DAKADUN
SPIDER! BADGER! KEEP FOLLOWING HIM!
BUT DON'T GET TOO CLOSE!
DAKADUN
IF HE JUST SO HAPPENS TO BE GARDAR, HE'S BEYOND YOUR ABILITY!
I'LL COME BACK WITH REINFORCE-MENTS SOON! JUST KEEP CHAS-ING HIM UNTIL THEN! GOT THAT?!
BRFF
HRFF
HUH? BUT-
SNAKE?! WHERE ARE YOU GOING?!
DADUN

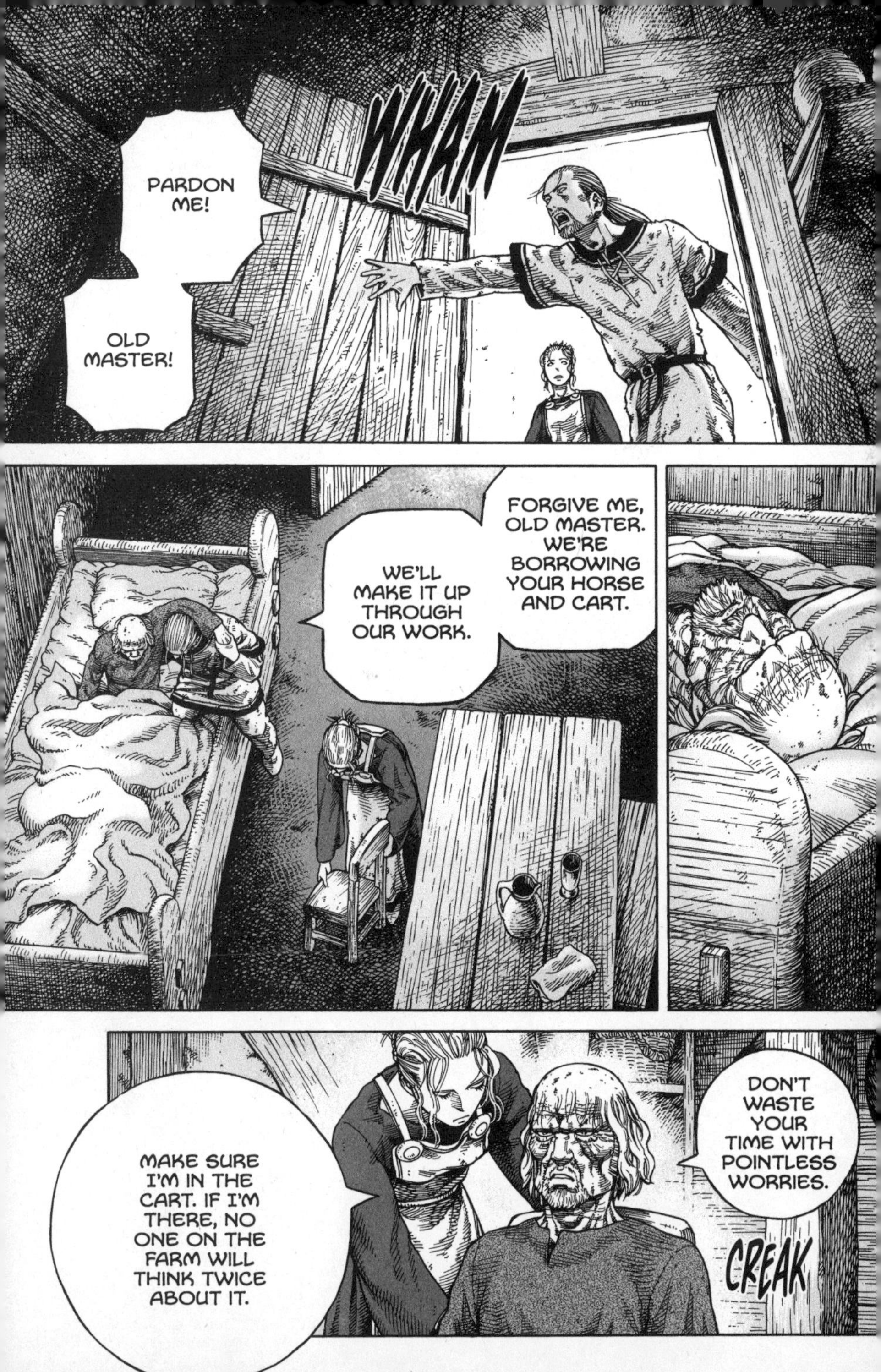
WHAM
PARDON ME!
OLD MASTER!
FORGIVE ME, OLD MASTER. WE'RE BORROWING YOUR HORSE AND CART.
WE'LL MAKE IT UP THROUGH OUR WORK.
DON'T WASTE YOUR TIME WITH POINTLESS WORRIES.
CREAK
MAKE SURE I'M IN THE CART. IF I'M THERE, NO ONE ON THE FARM WILL THINK TWICE ABOUT IT.

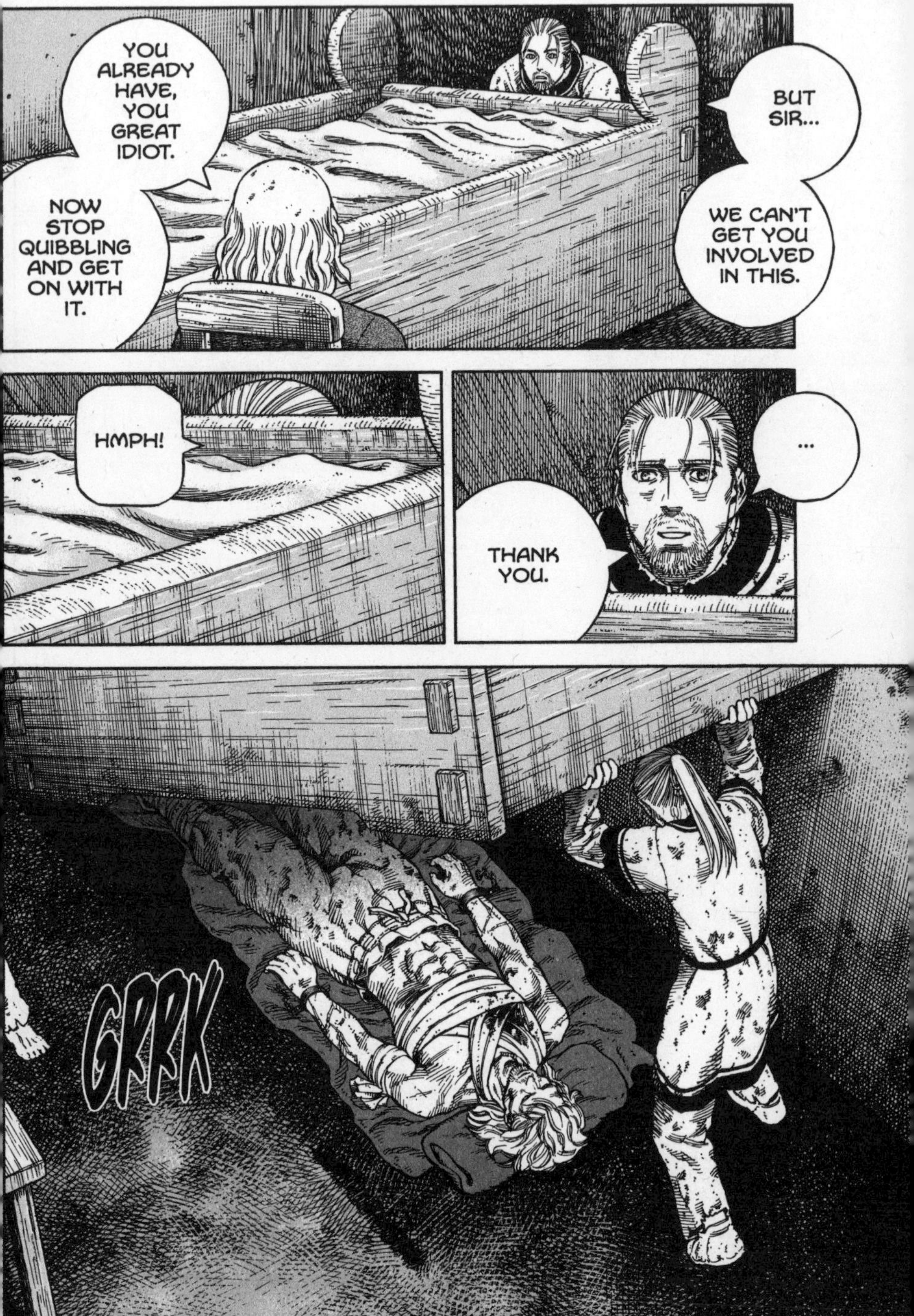
BUT SIR...
WE CAN'T GET YOU INVOLVED IN THIS.
YOU ALREADY HAVE, YOU GREAT IDIOT.
NOW STOP QUIBBLING AND GET ON WITH IT.
...
THANK YOU.
HMPH!
GRRK

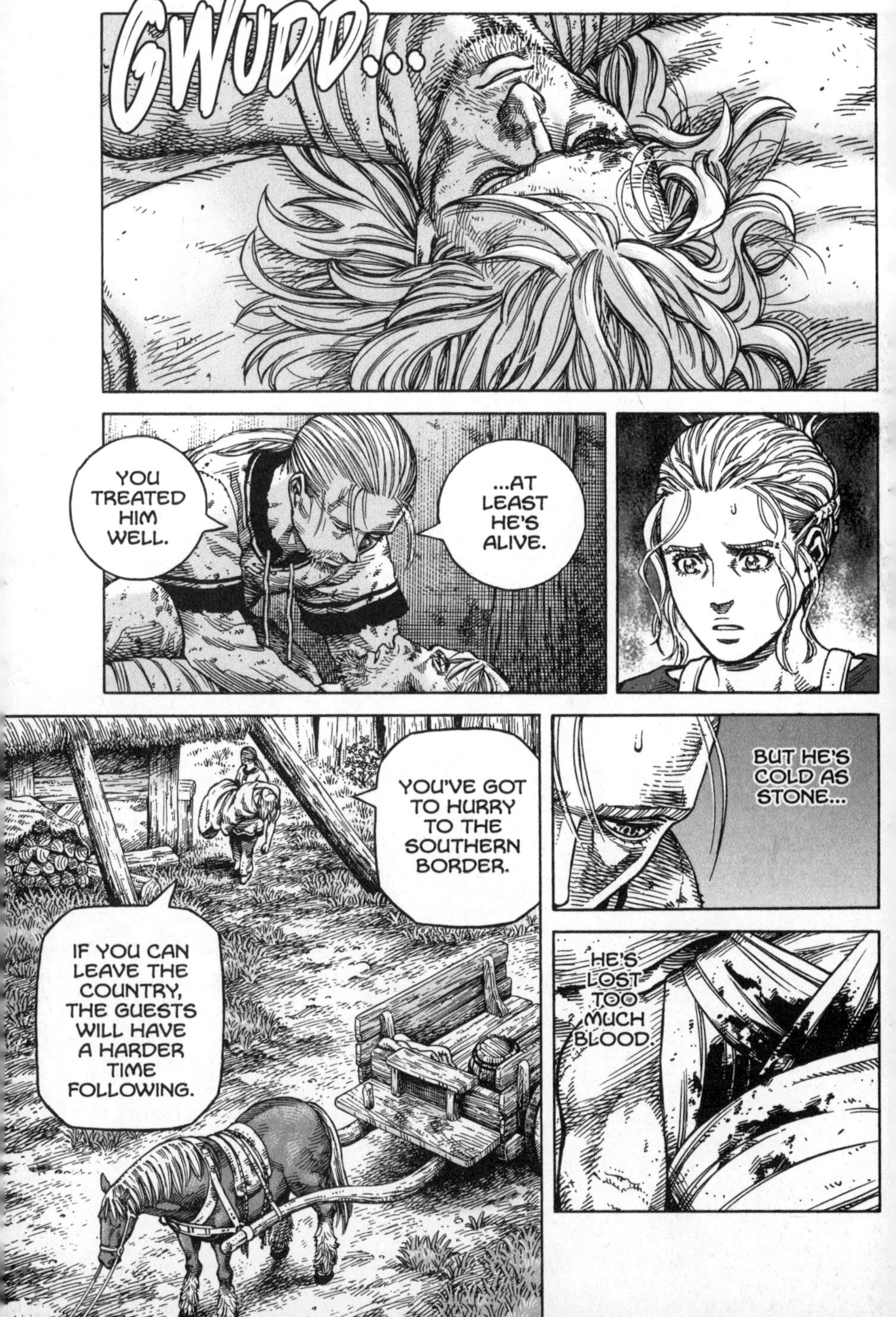
GWUDD...
...AT LEAST HE'S ALIVE.
YOU TREATED HIM WELL.
BUT HE'S COLD AS STONE...
HE'S LOST TOO MUCH BLOOD.
YOU'VE GOT TO HURRY TO THE SOUTHERN BORDER.
IF YOU CAN LEAVE THE COUNTRY, THE GUESTS WILL HAVE A HARDER TIME FOLLOWING.

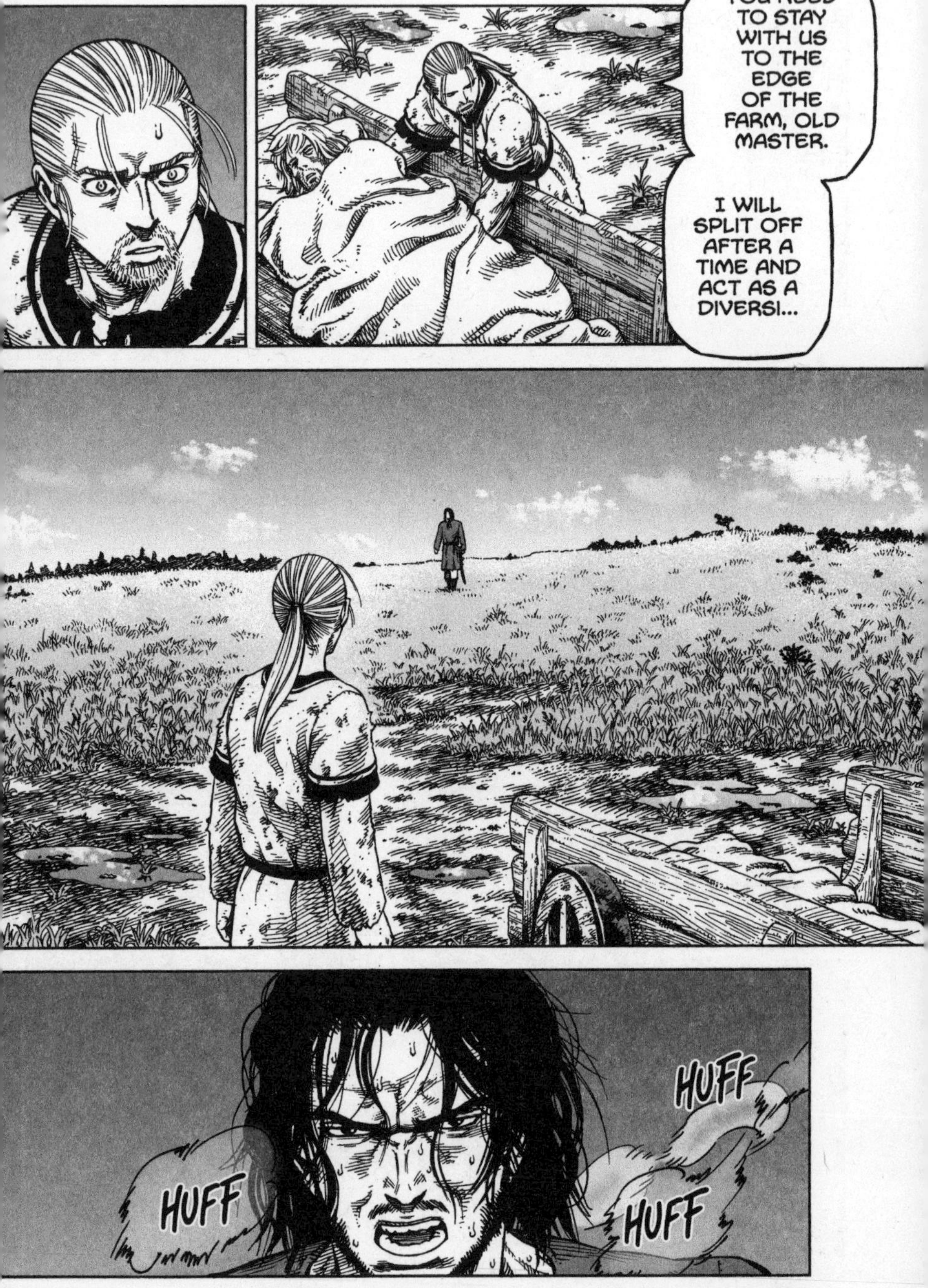
YOU NEED TO STAY WITH US TO THE EDGE OF THE FARM, OLD MASTER.
I WILL SPLIT OFF AFTER A TIME AND ACT AS A DIVERSI...
HUFF
HUFF
HUFF

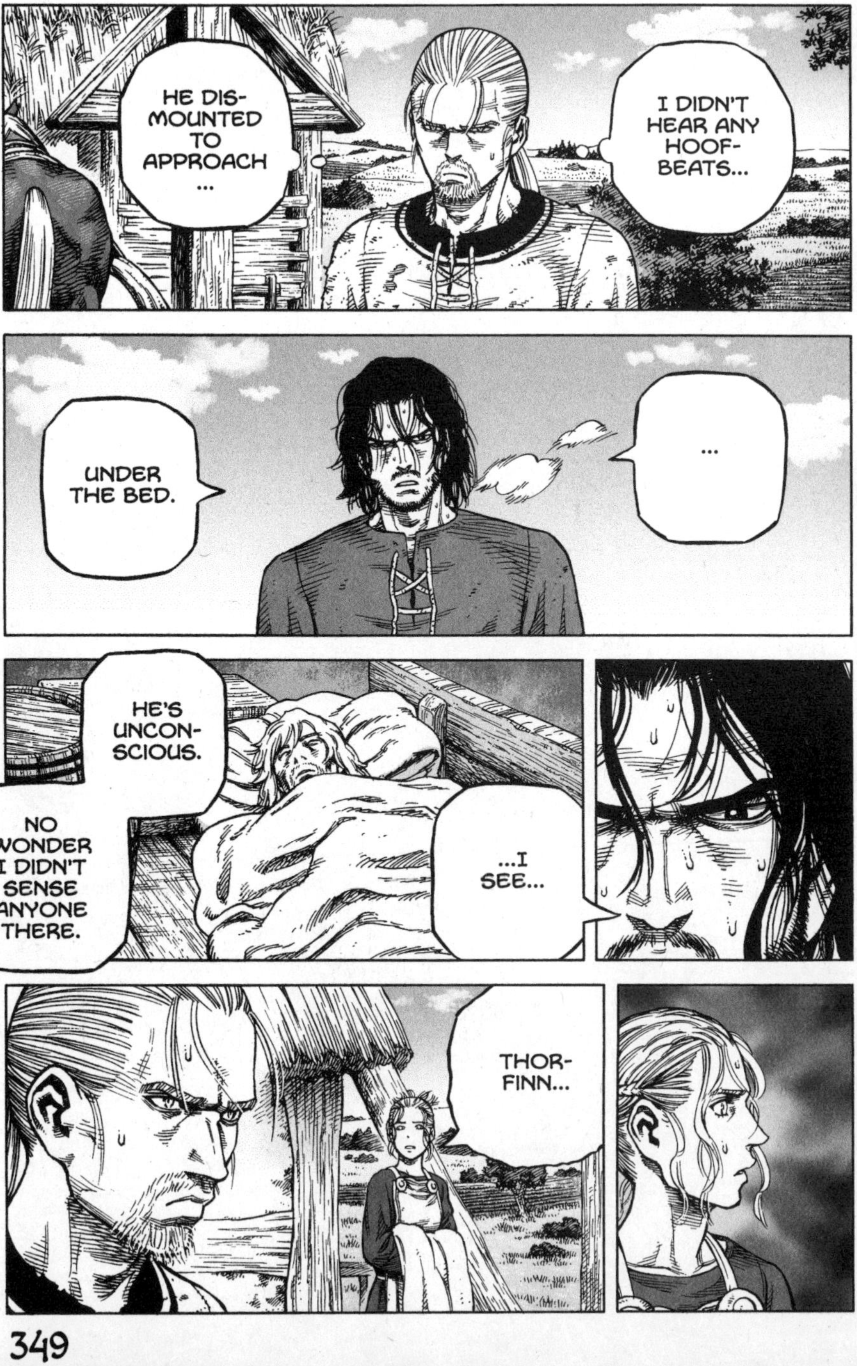
I DIDN'T HEAR ANY HOOF-BEATS...
HE DIS-MOUNTED TO APPROACH ...
...
UNDER THE BED.
HE'S UNCON-SCIOUS.
...I SEE...
NO WONDER I DIDN'T SENSE ANYONE THERE.
THOR-FINN...

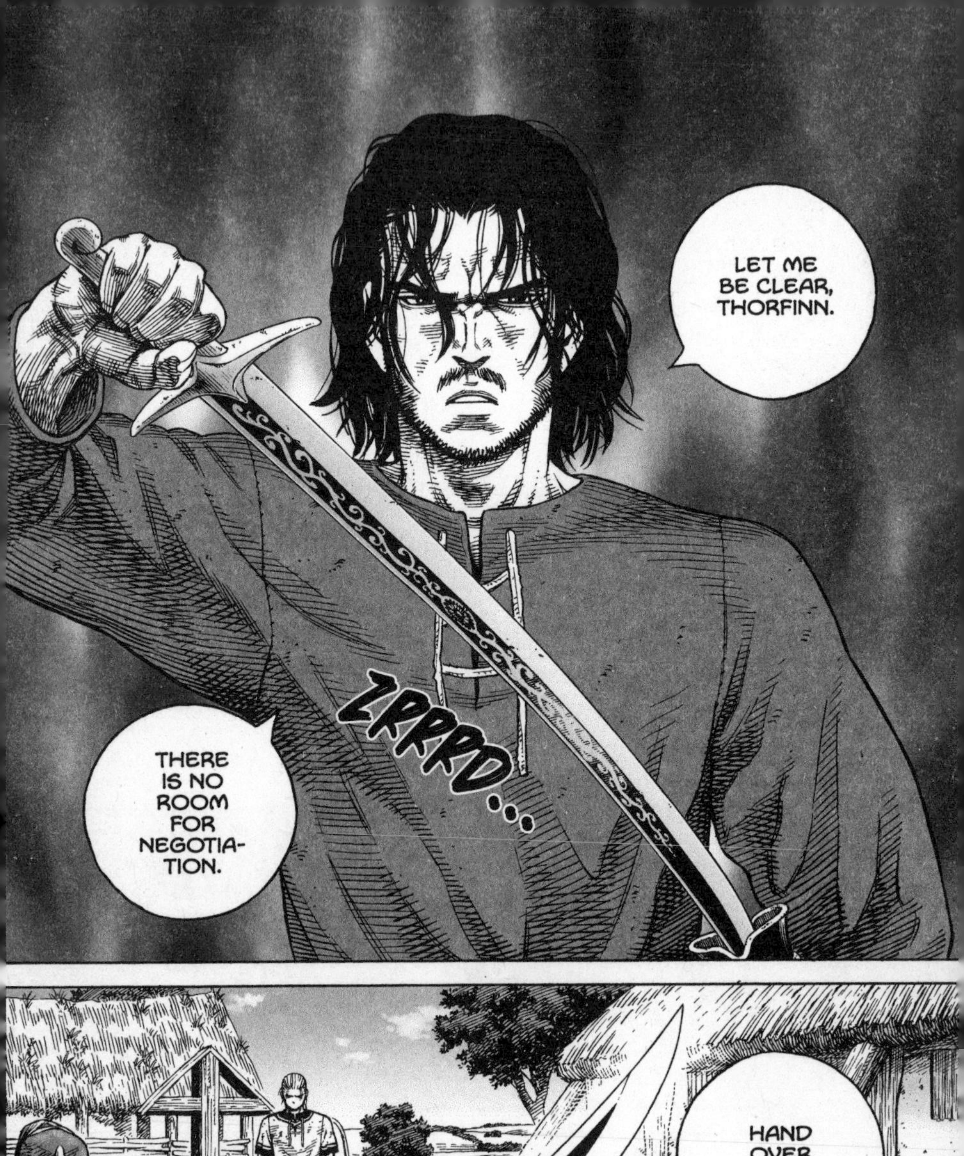
LET ME BE CLEAR, THORFINN.
ZRRRD...
THERE IS NO ROOM FOR NEGOTIA-TION.
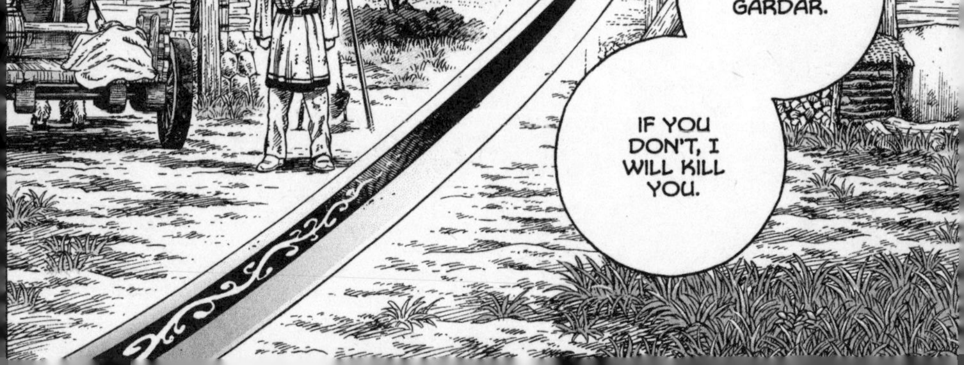
HAND OVER GARDAR.
IF YOU DON'T, I WILL KILL YOU.

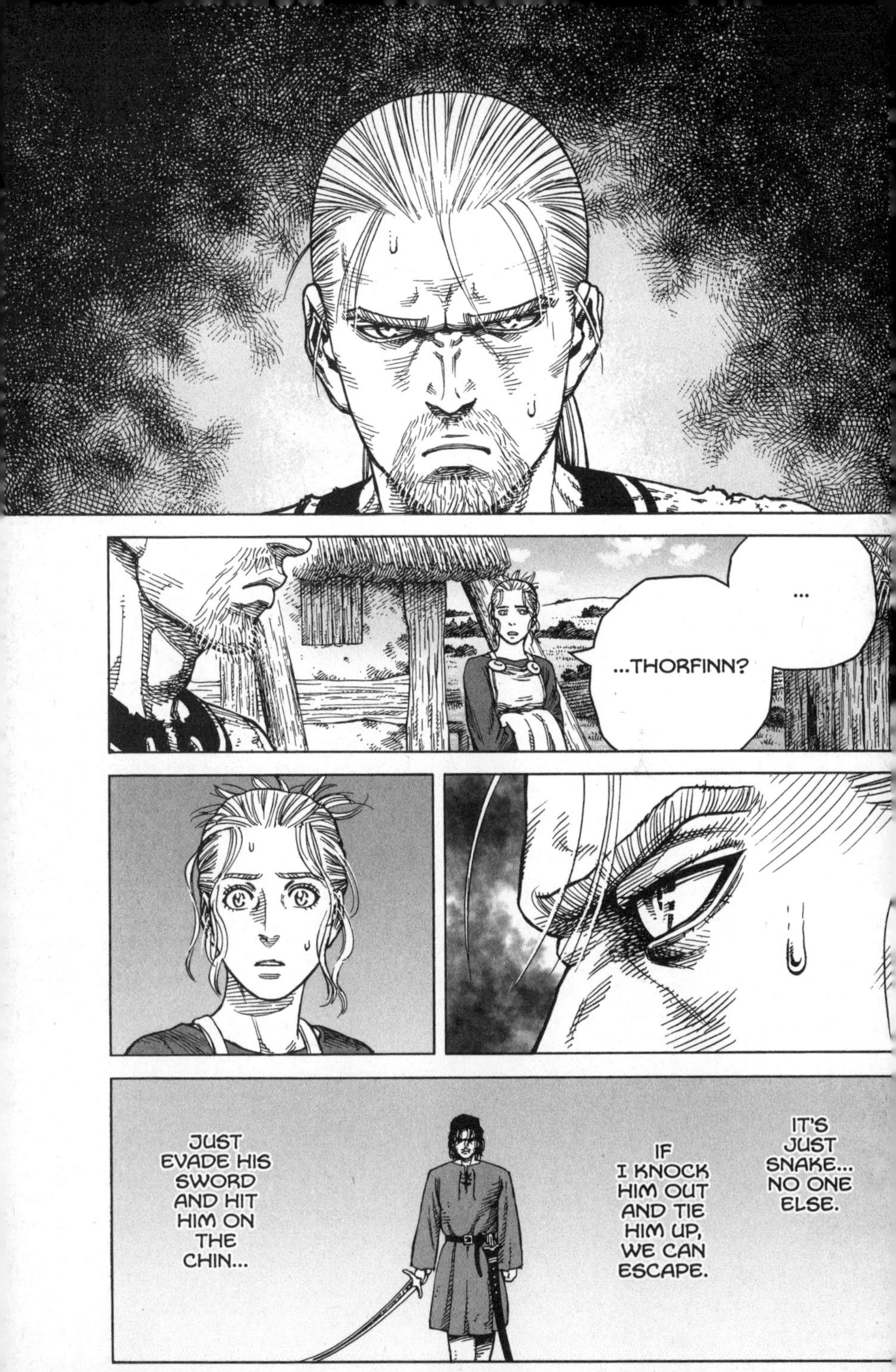
...
...THORFINN?
IT'S JUST SNAKE... NO ONE ELSE.
IF I KNOCK HIM OUT AND TIE HIM UP, WE CAN ESCAPE.
JUST EVADE HIS SWORD AND HIT HIM ON THE CHIN...

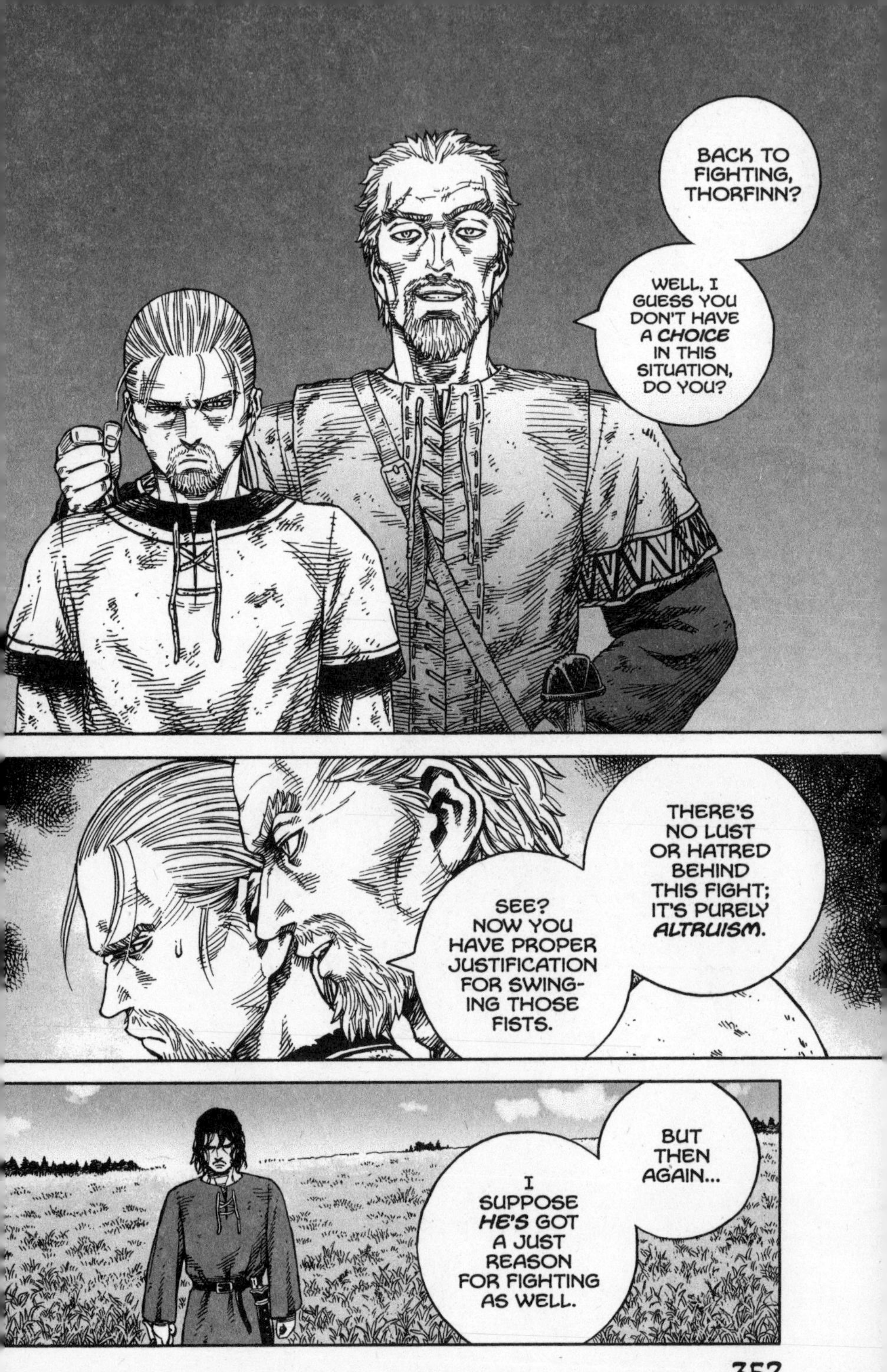
BACK TO FIGHTING, THORFINN?
WELL, I GUESS YOU DON'T HAVE A *CHOICE* IN THIS SITUATION, DO YOU?
THERE'S NO LUST OR HATRED BEHIND THIS FIGHT; IT'S PURELY ***ALTRUISM***.
SEE? NOW YOU HAVE PROPER JUSTIFICATION FOR SWING-ING THOSE FISTS.
BUT THEN AGAIN...
I SUPPOSE *HE'S* GOT A JUST REASON FOR FIGHTING AS WELL.

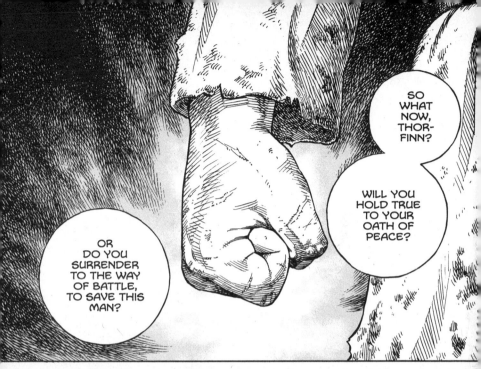

SO WHAT NOW, THORFINN?
WILL YOU HOLD TRUE TO YOUR OATH OF PEACE?
OR DO YOU SURRENDER TO THE WAY OF BATTLE, TO SAVE THIS MAN?
WHICH IS THE PATH TO BEING A "TRUE WARRIOR?"
NO TIME TO THINK.
YOU'VE GOT TO CHOOSE NOW.

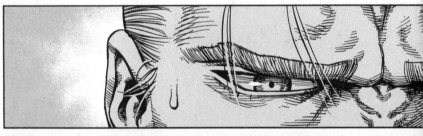

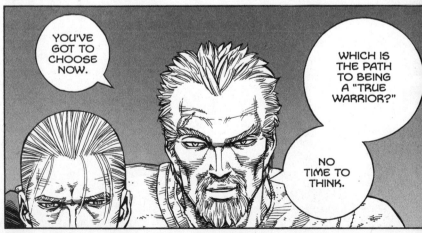

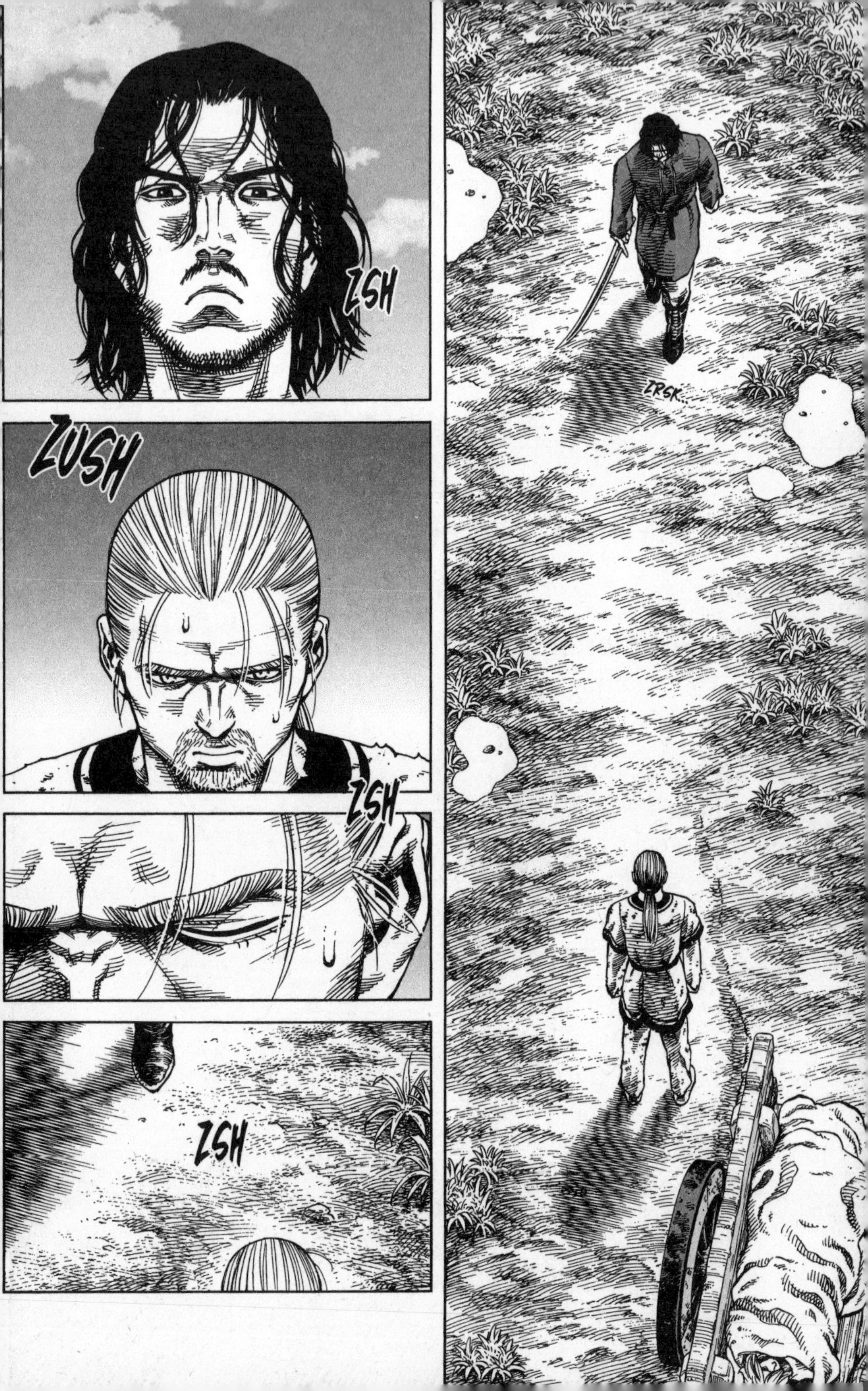
ZRSK...
ZSH
ZUSH
ZSH
ZSH

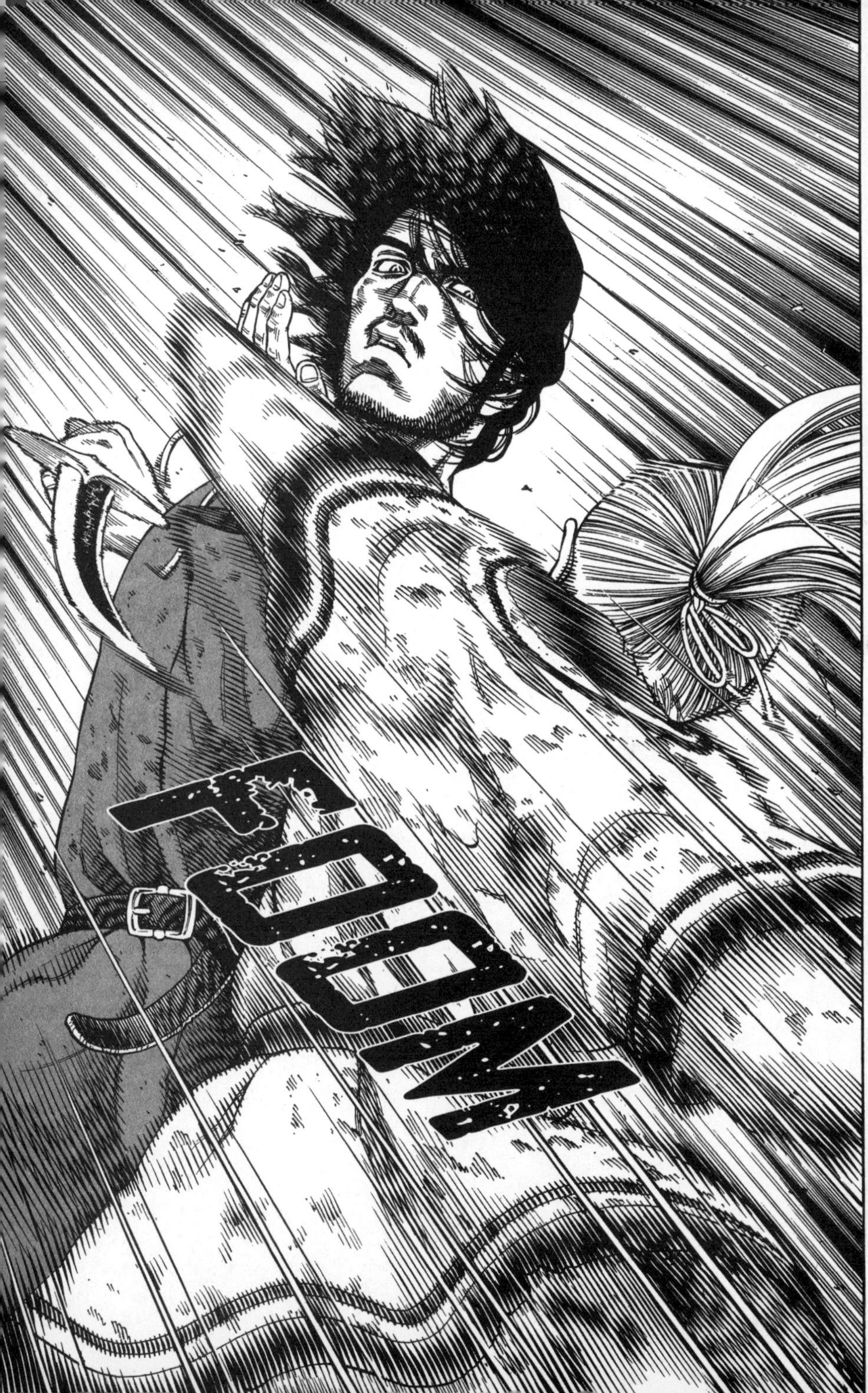
FOOM

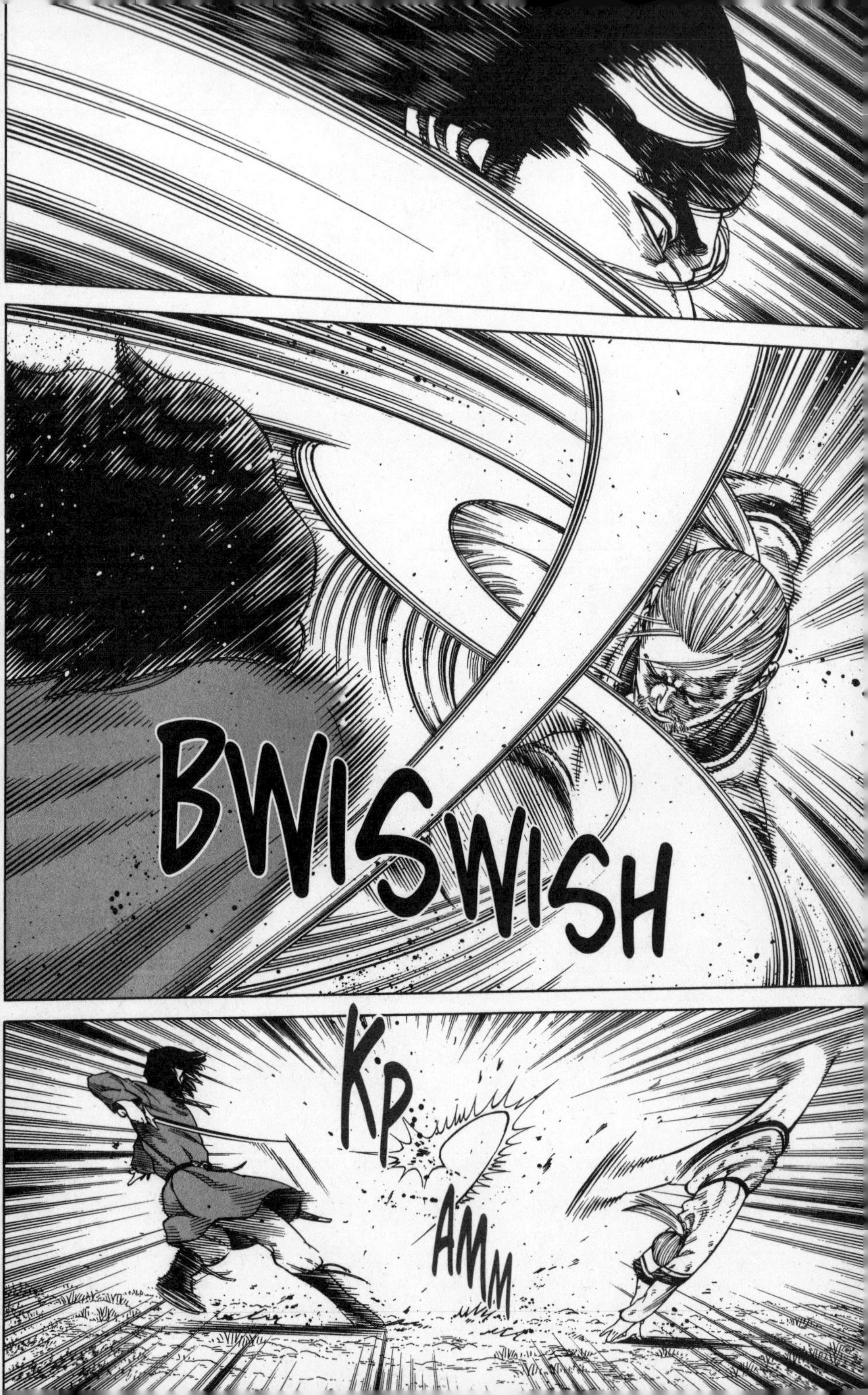
BWISWISH
KP
AMM

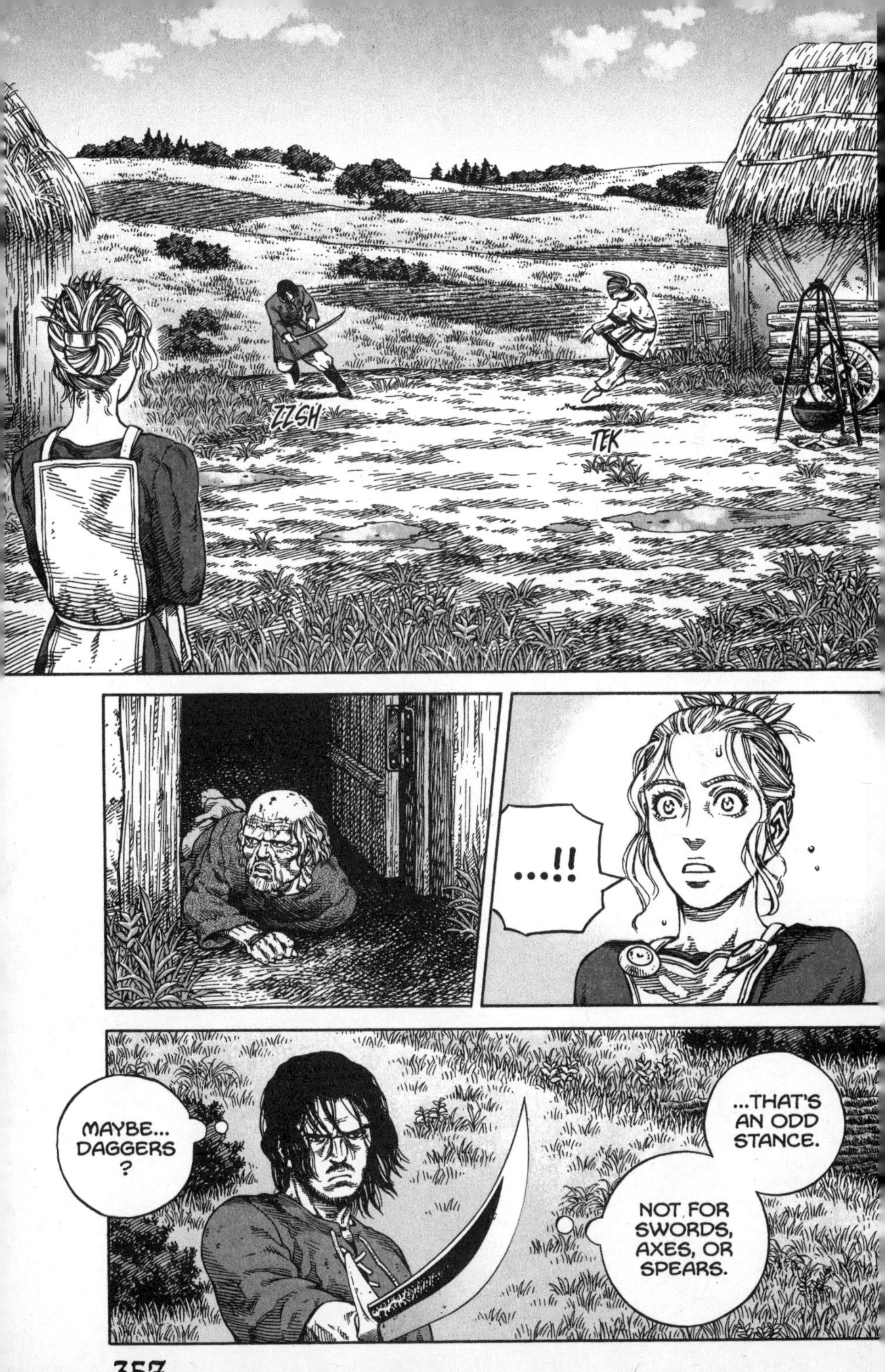
ZZSH
TEK
...!!
...THAT'S AN ODD STANCE.
NOT FOR SWORDS, AXES, OR SPEARS.
MAYBE... DAGGERS ?

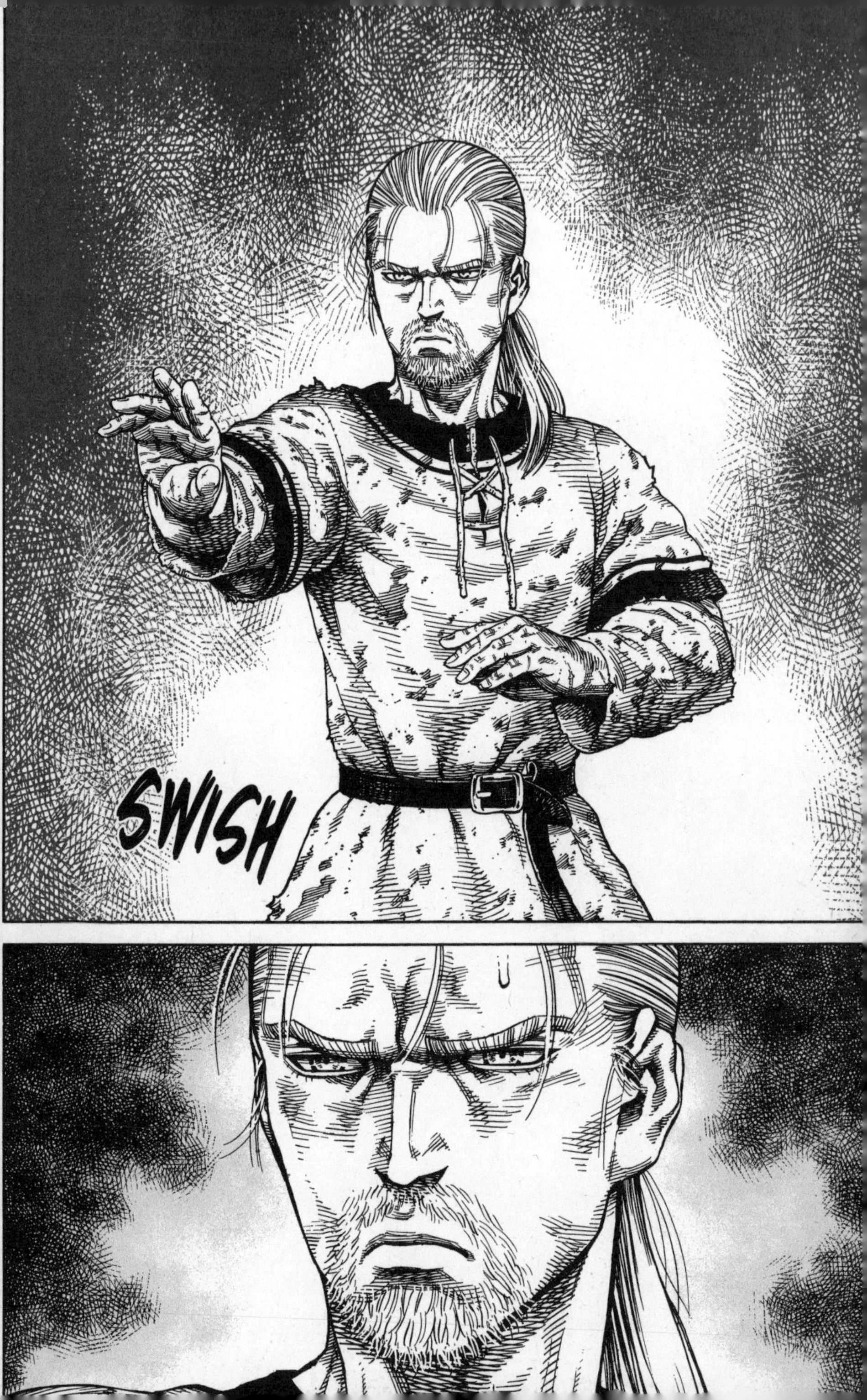
SWISH

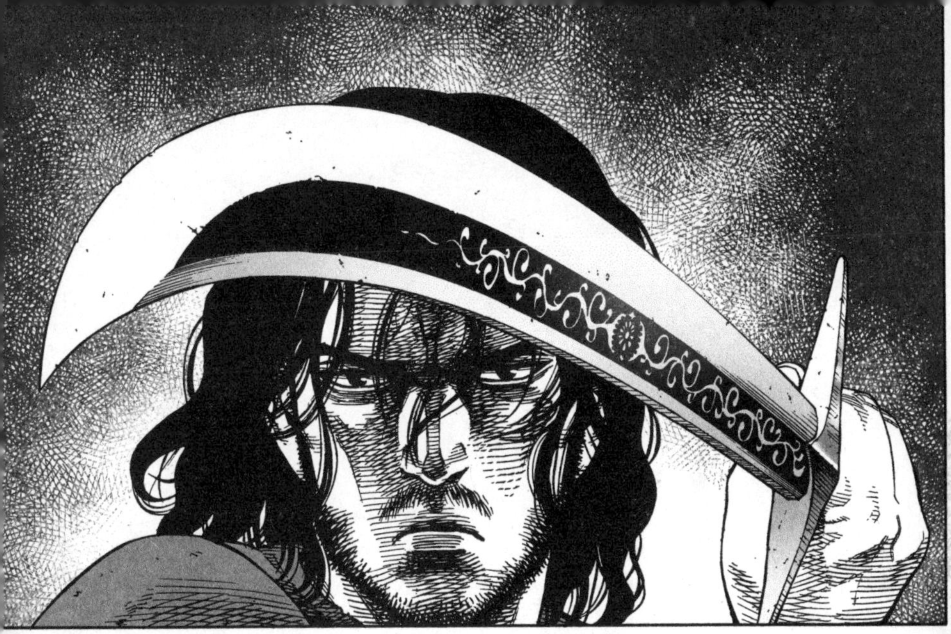

CHAPTER 86: NO GOING HOM

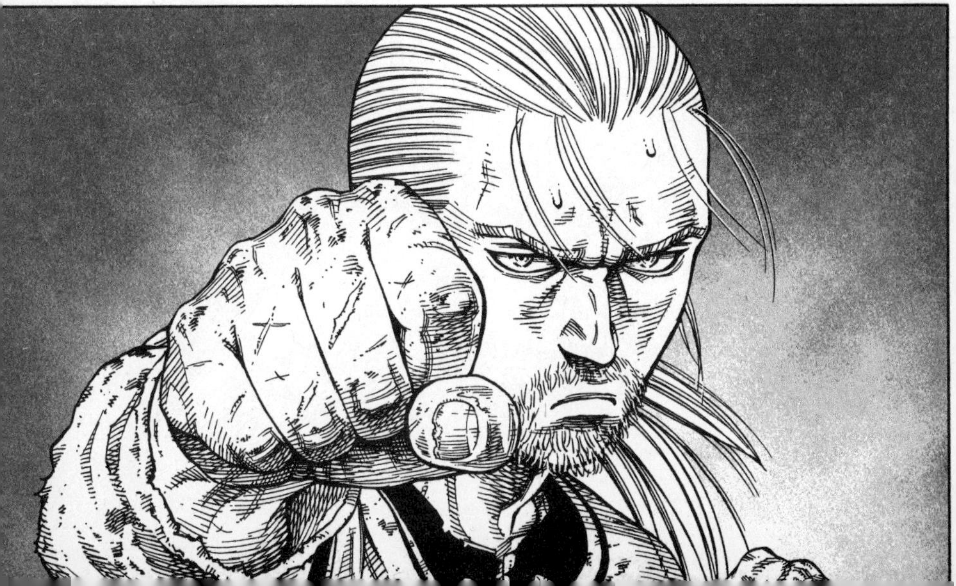

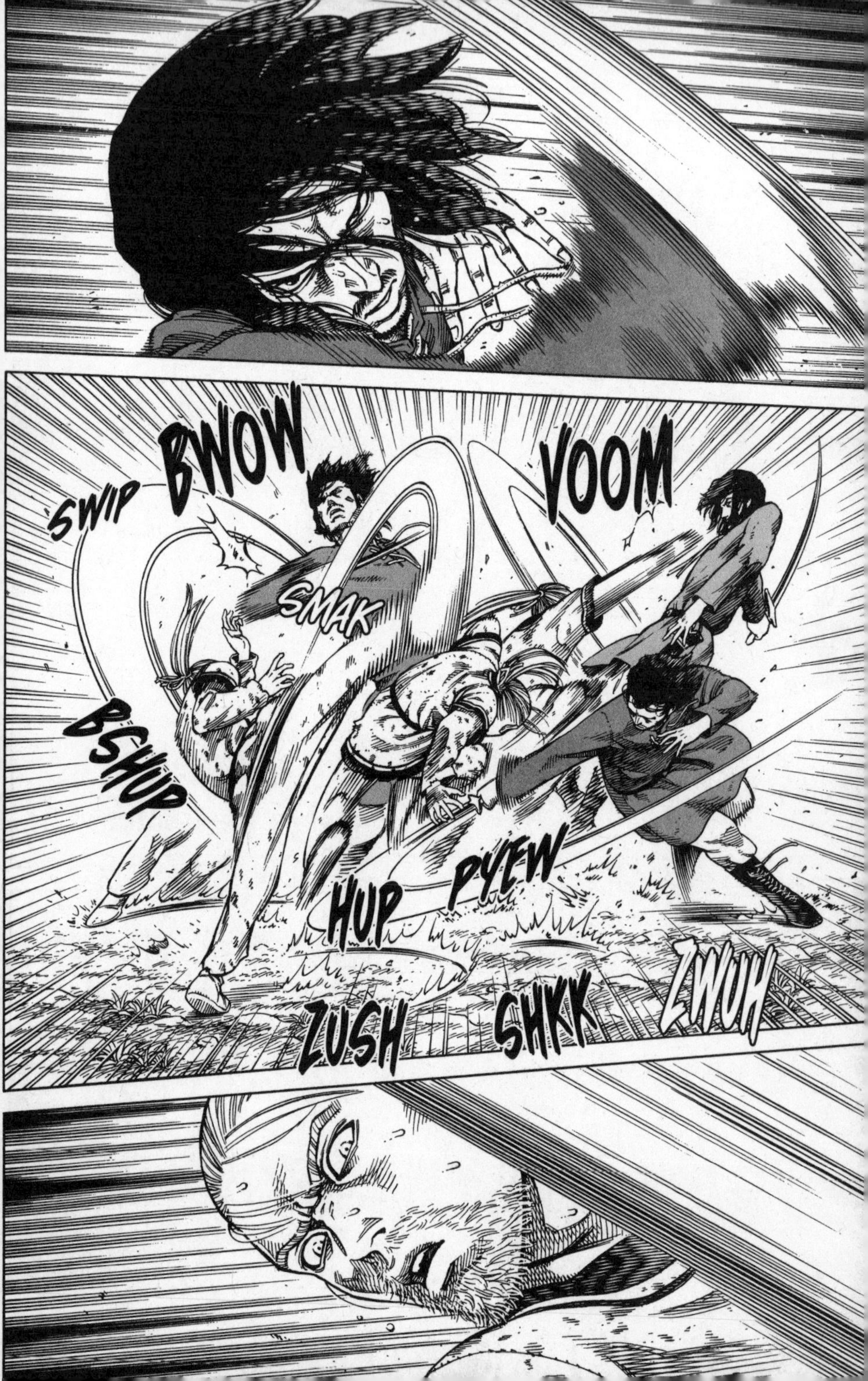
VOOM
BWOW
SWIP
SMAK
BSHUP
PYEW
HUP
ZWUH
SHKK
ZUSH

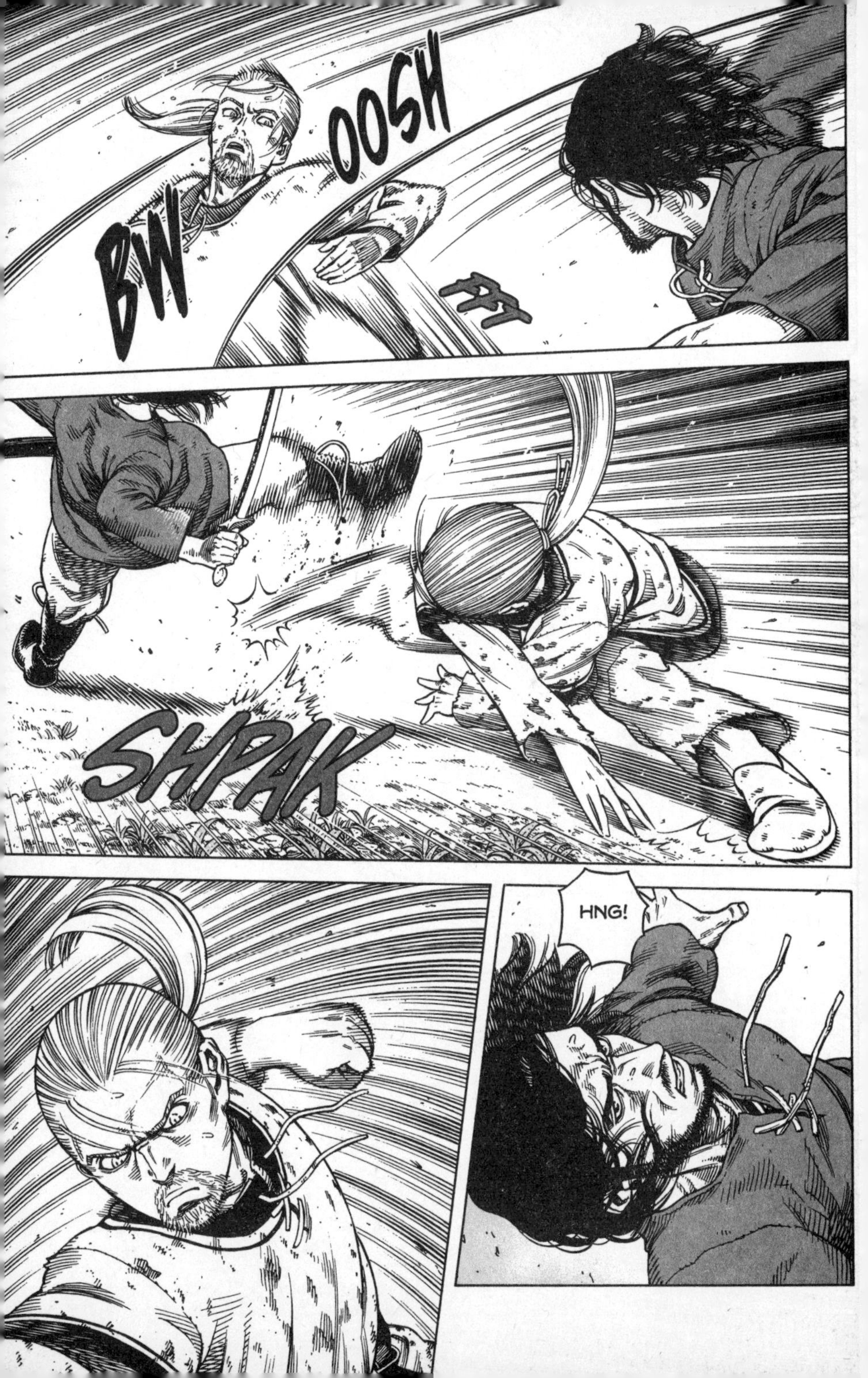
FFT
BW
OOSH
SHPAK
HNG!

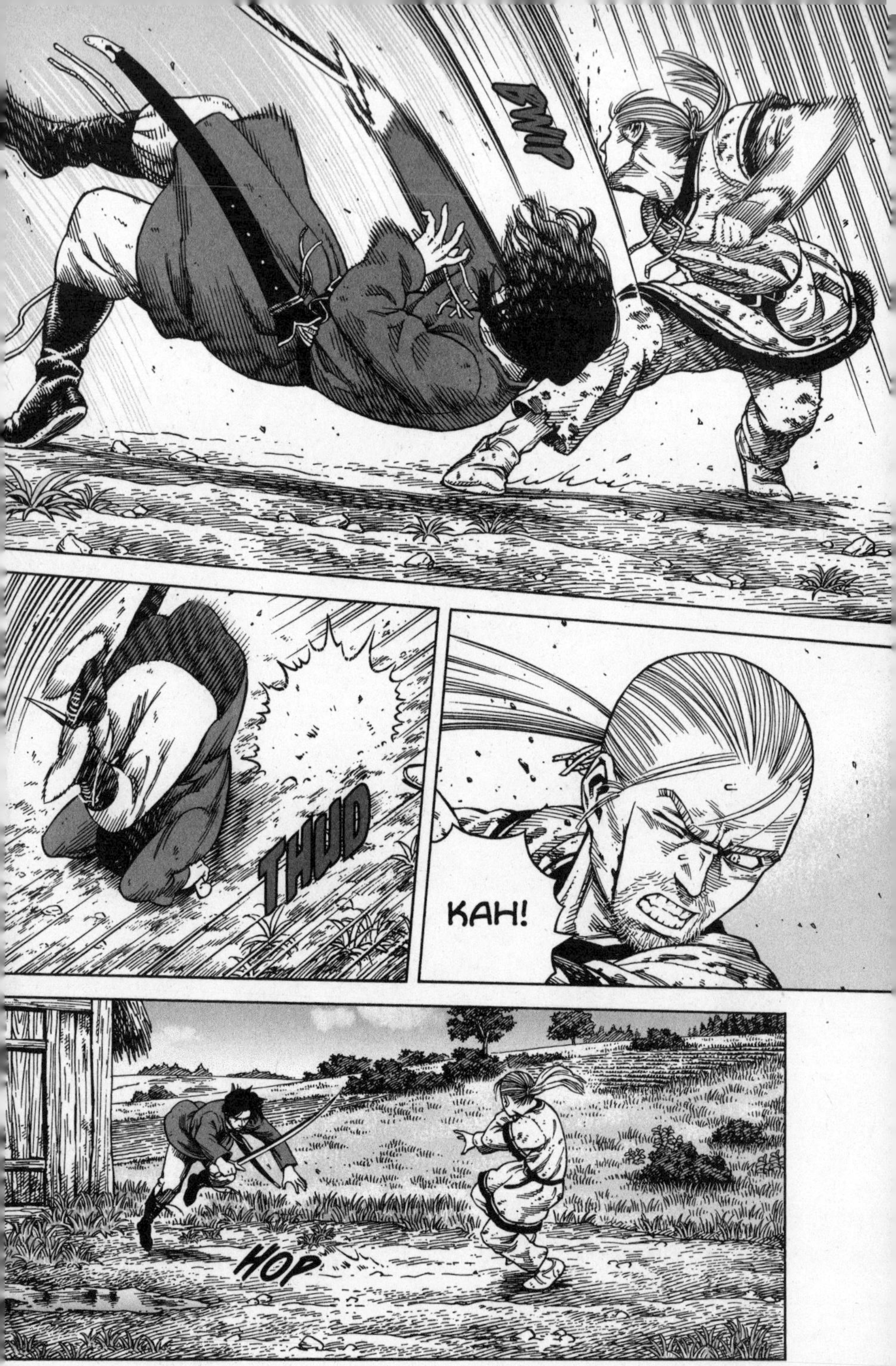
KAH!
THUD
HOP

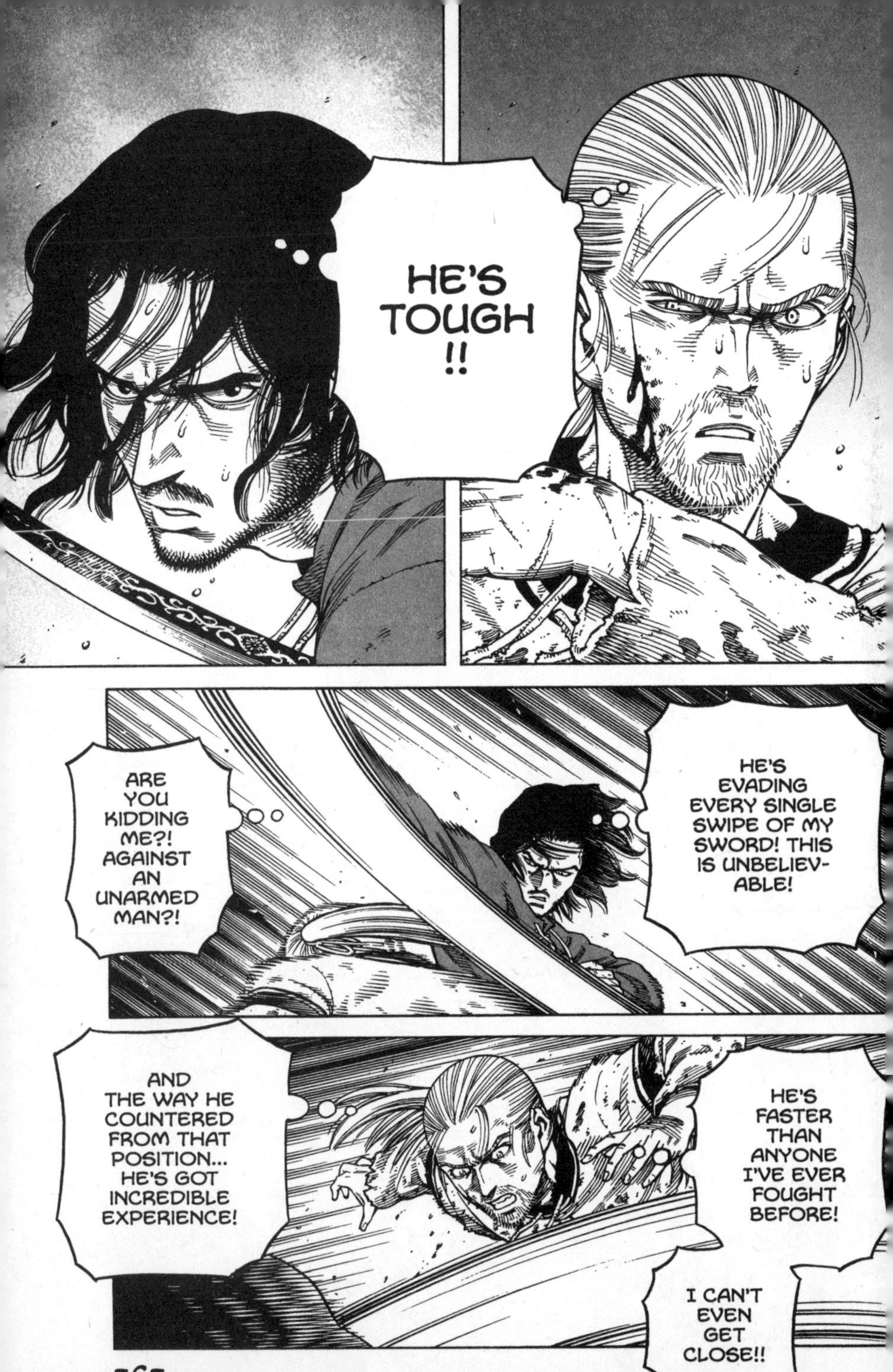
HE'S TOUGH !!
HE'S EVADING EVERY SINGLE SWIPE OF MY SWORD! THIS IS UNBELIEV-ABLE!
ARE YOU KIDDING ME?! AGAINST AN UNARMED MAN?!
HE'S FASTER THAN ANYONE I'VE EVER FOUGHT BEFORE!
AND THE WAY HE COUNTERED FROM THAT POSITION... HE'S GOT INCREDIBLE EXPERIENCE!
I CAN'T EVEN GET CLOSE!!

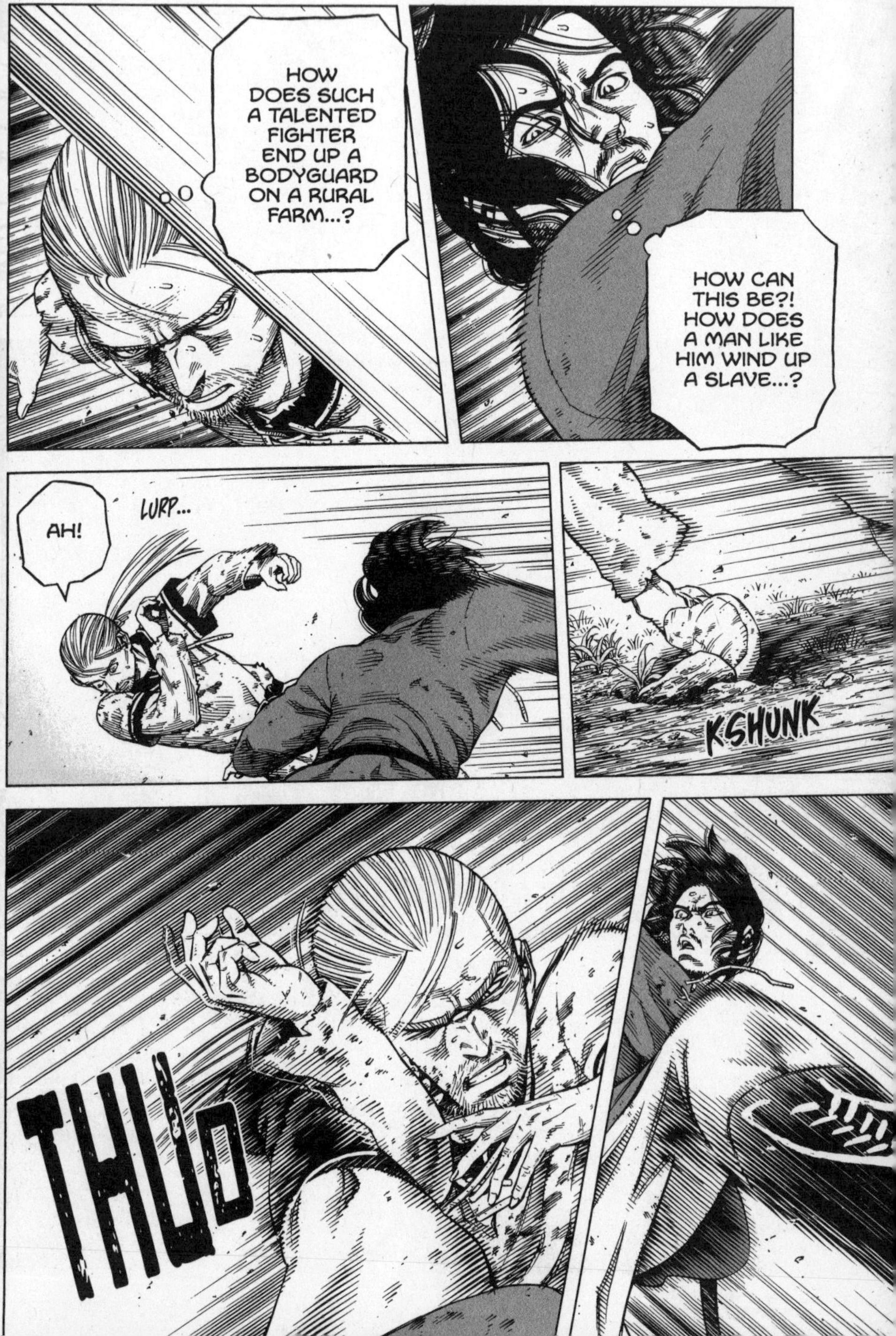
HOW CAN THIS BE?! HOW DOES A MAN LIKE HIM WIND UP A SLAVE...?
HOW DOES SUCH A TALENTED FIGHTER END UP A BODYGUARD ON A RURAL FARM...?
KSHUNK
LURP...
AH!
THUD

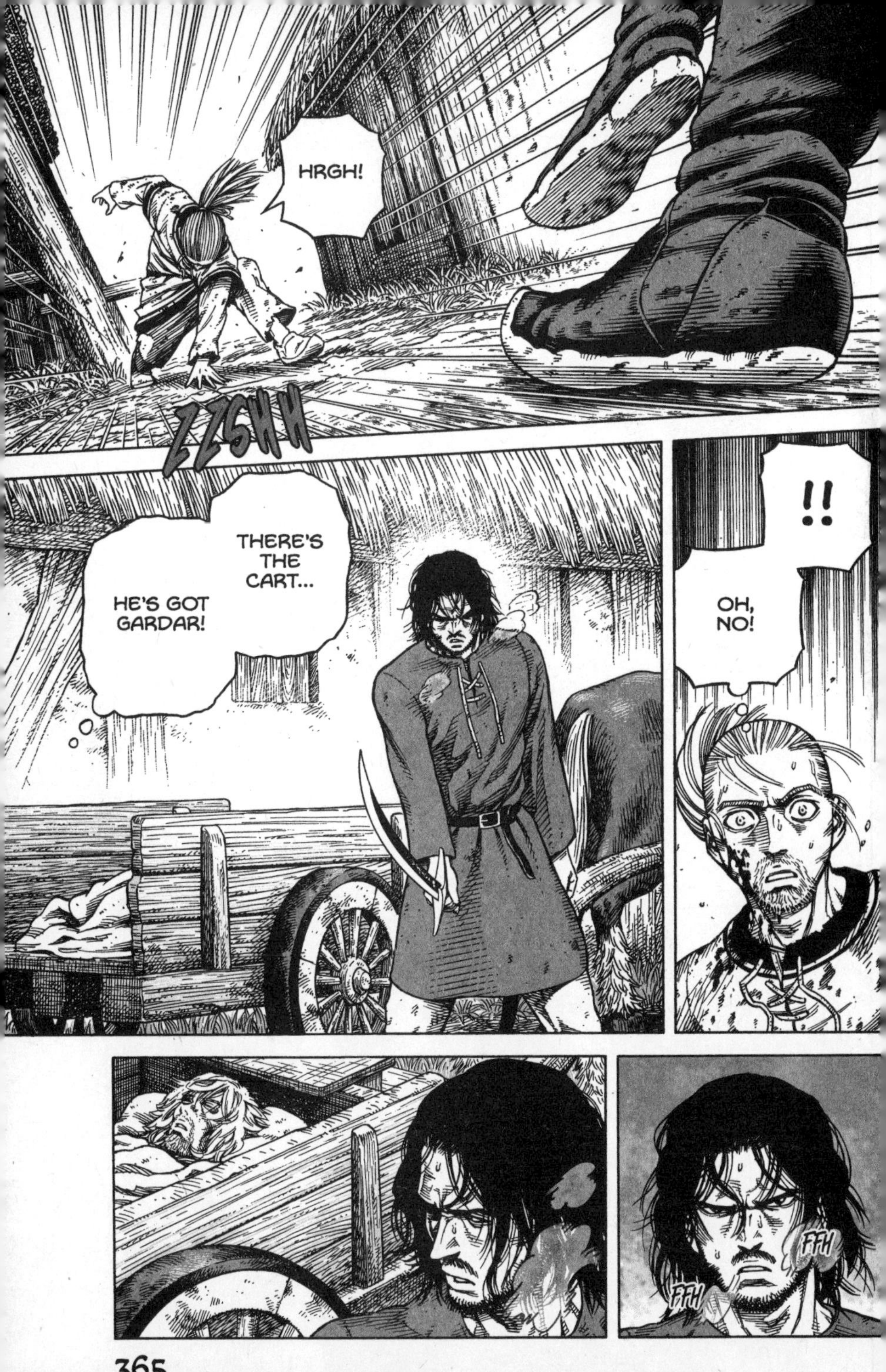
HRGH!
ZZSHH
!!
OH, NO!
THERE'S THE CART...
HE'S GOT GARDAR!
FFH
FFH

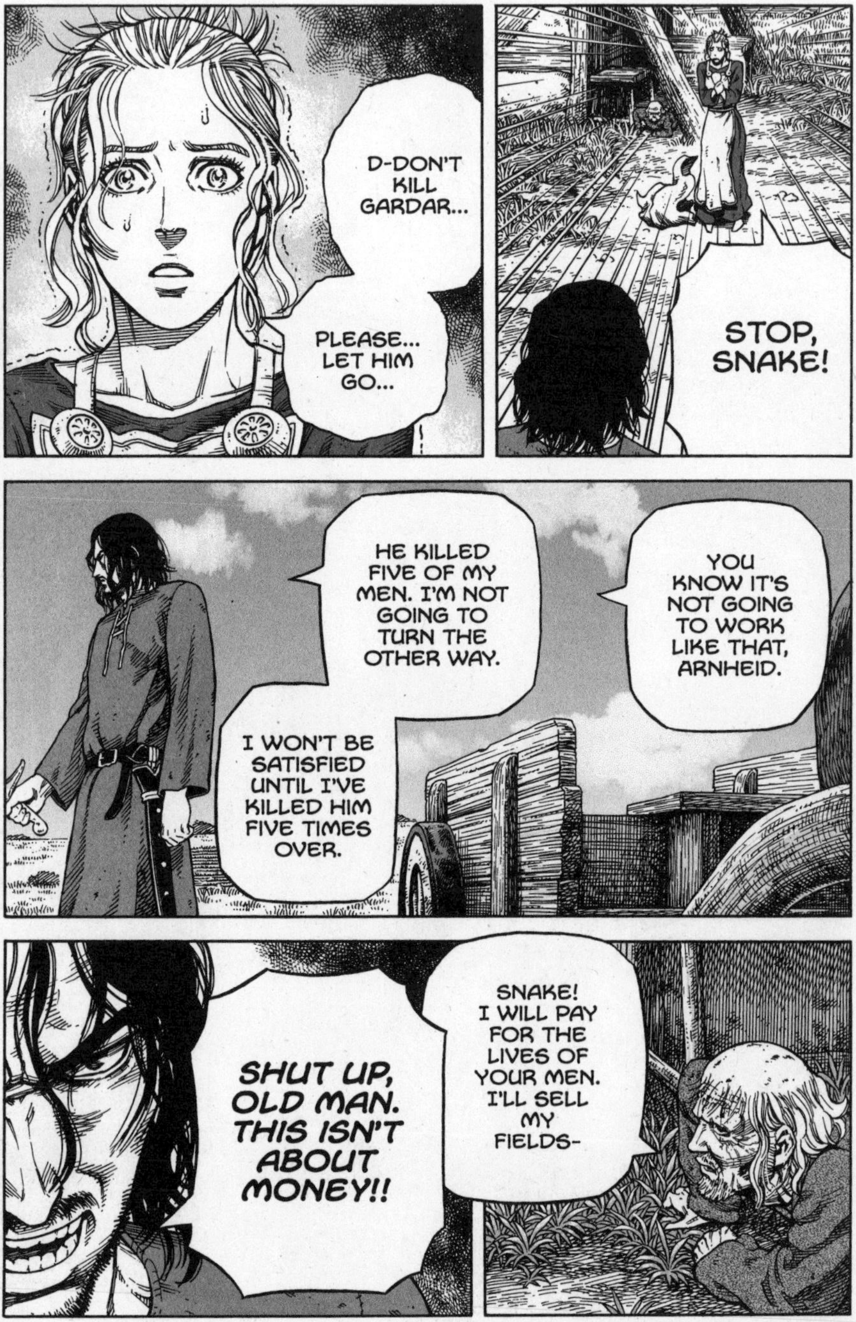
STOP, SNAKE!
D-DON'T KILL GARDAR...
PLEASE... LET HIM GO...
YOU KNOW IT'S NOT GOING TO WORK LIKE THAT, ARNHEID.
HE KILLED FIVE OF MY MEN. I'M NOT GOING TO TURN THE OTHER WAY.
I WON'T BE SATISFIED UNTIL I'VE KILLED HIM FIVE TIMES OVER.
SNAKE! I WILL PAY FOR THE LIVES OF YOUR MEN. I'LL SELL MY FIELDS-
SHUT UP, OLD MAN. THIS ISN'T ABOUT MONEY!!

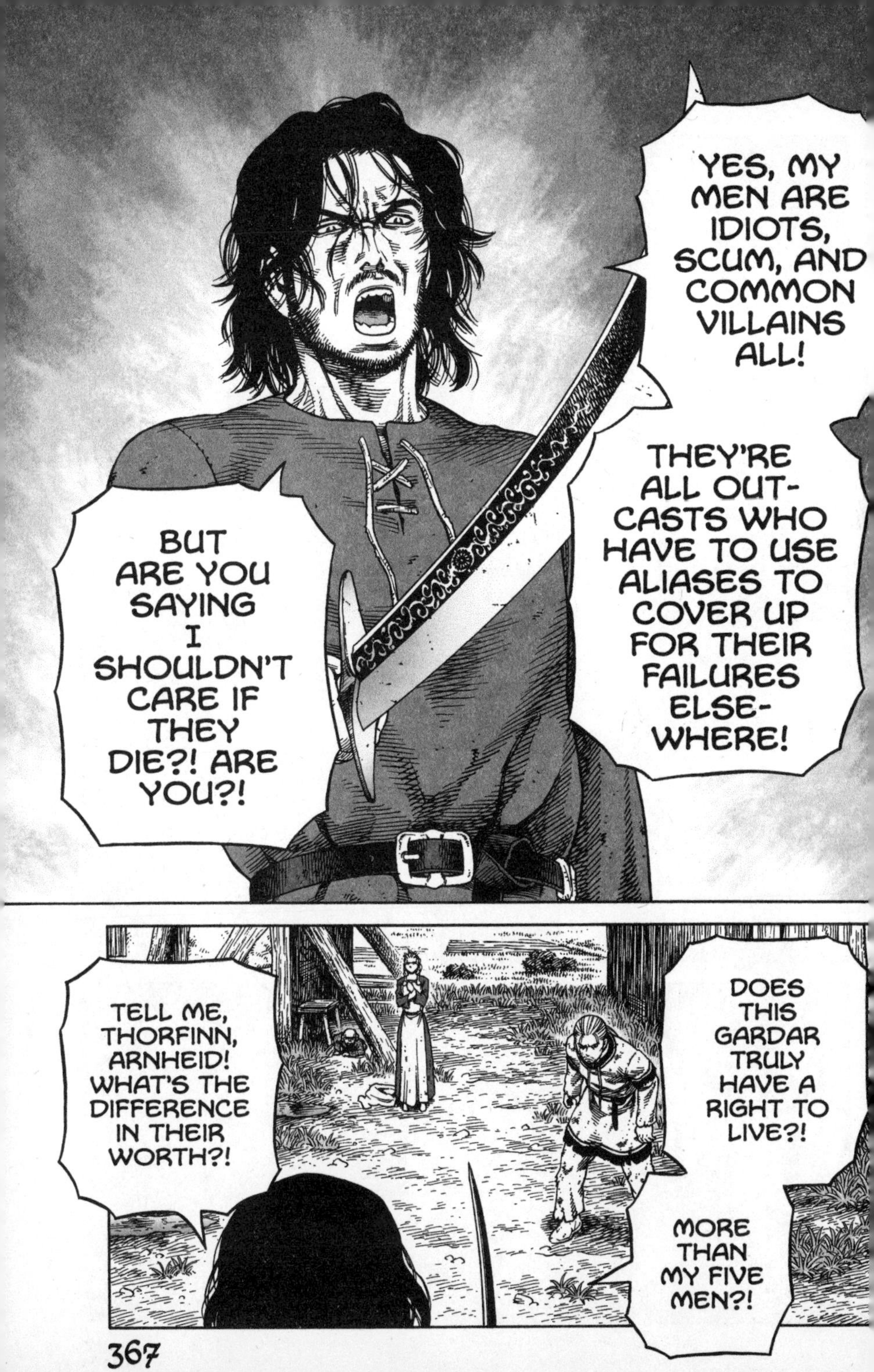
YES, MY MEN ARE IDIOTS, SCUM, AND COMMON VILLAINS ALL!
THEY'RE ALL OUT-CASTS WHO HAVE TO USE ALIASES TO COVER UP FOR THEIR FAILURES ELSE-WHERE!
BUT ARE YOU SAYING I SHOULDN'T CARE IF THEY DIE?! ARE YOU?!
DOES THIS GARDAR TRULY HAVE A RIGHT TO LIVE?!
MORE THAN MY FIVE MEN?!
TELL ME, THORFINN, ARNHEID! WHAT'S THE DIFFERENCE IN THEIR WORTH?!

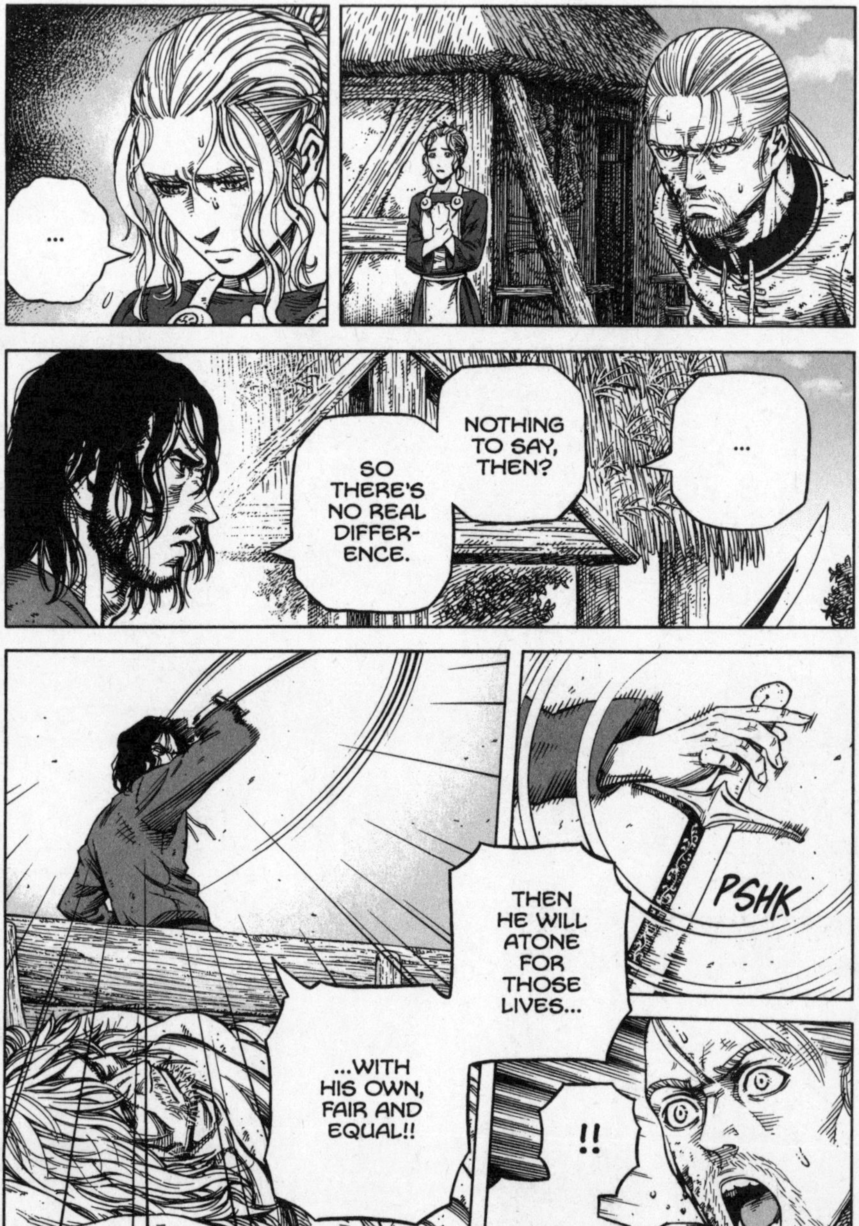
...
...
NOTHING TO SAY, THEN?
SO THERE'S NO REAL DIFFER-ENCE.
PSHK
!!
NO!
THEN HE WILL ATONE FOR THOSE LIVES...
...WITH HIS OWN, FAIR AND EQUAL!!

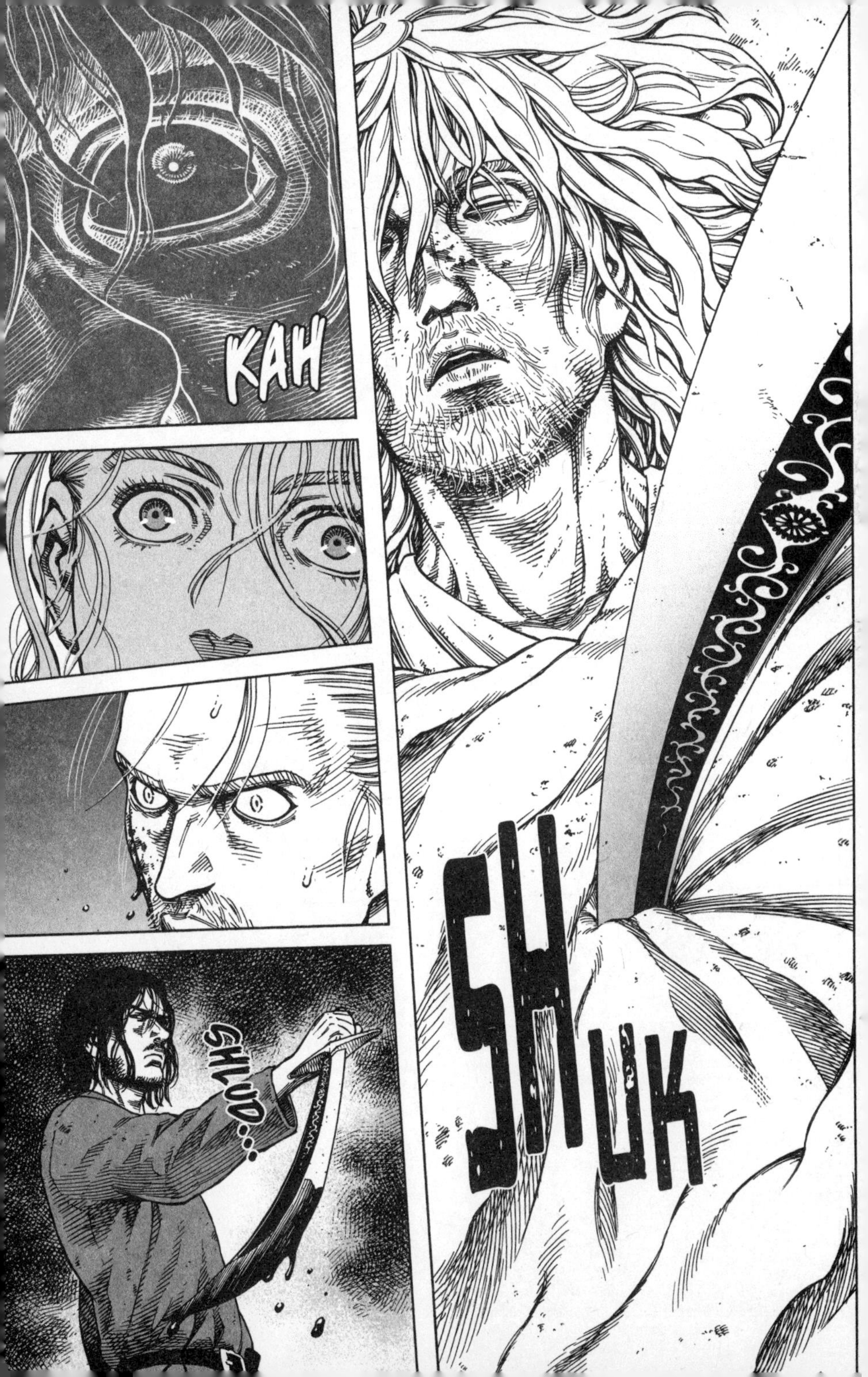
SHUK
KAH
SHLUD...

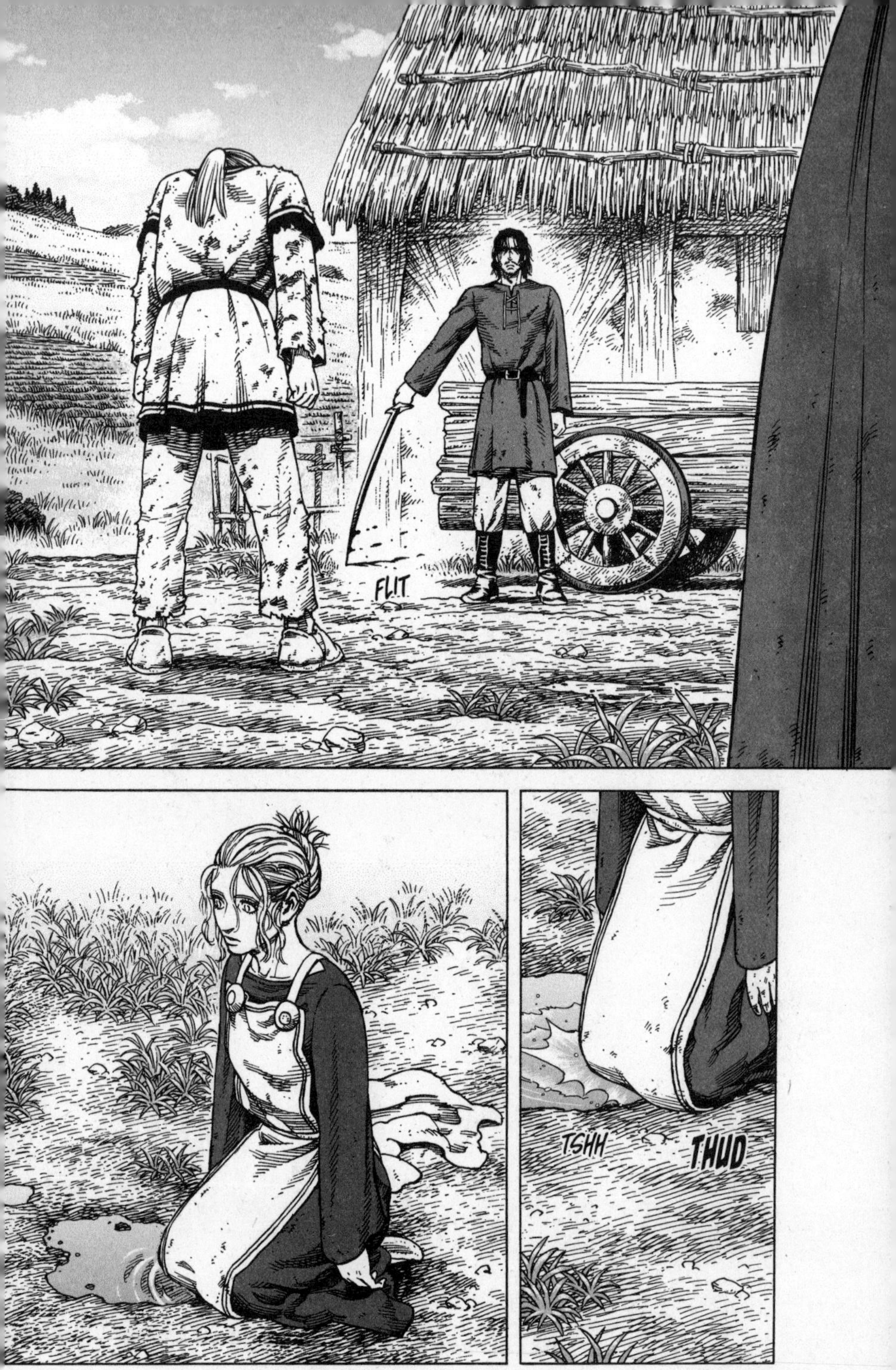
FLIT
TSHH
THUD

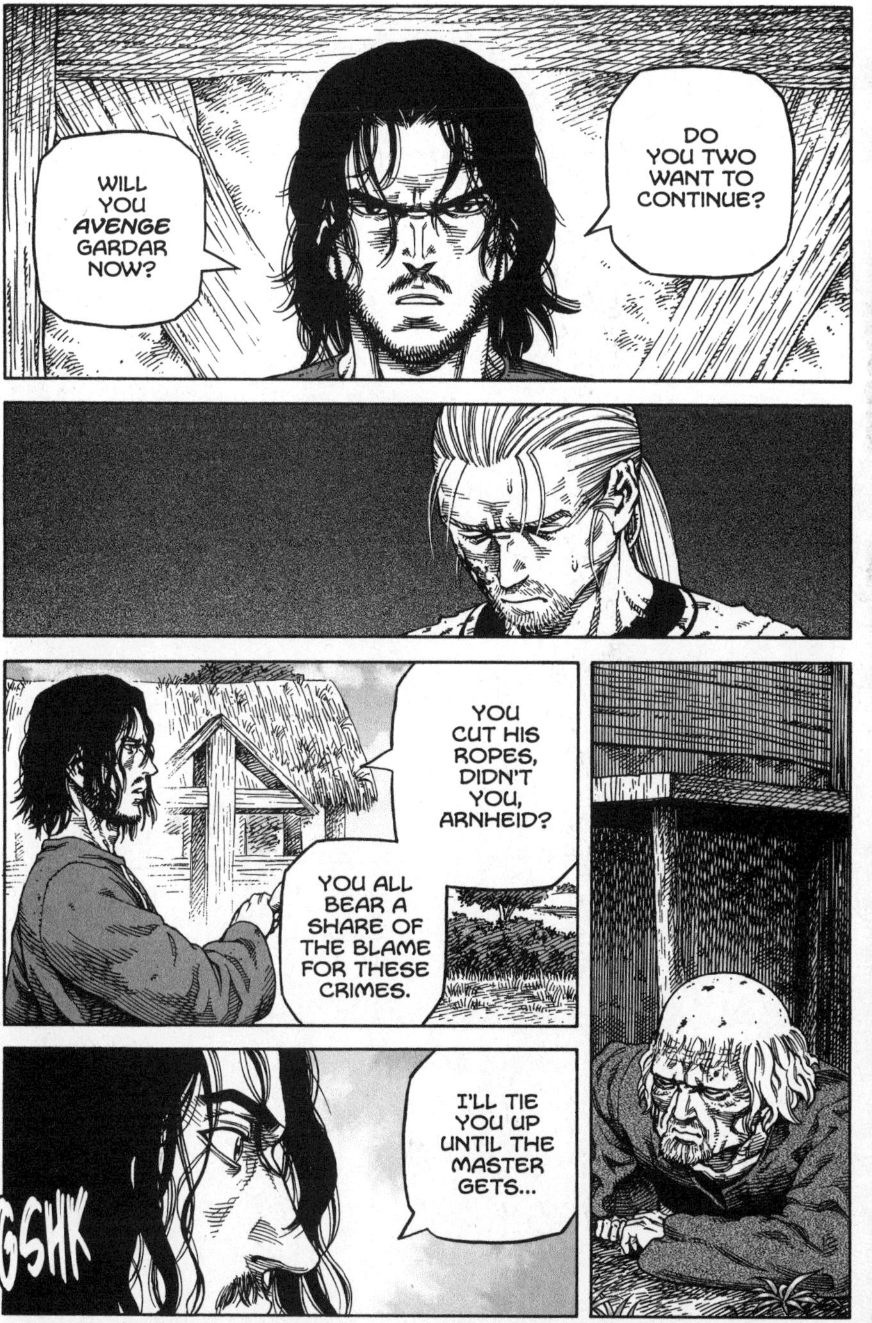
DO YOU TWO WANT TO CONTINUE?
WILL YOU *AVENGE* GARDAR NOW?
YOU CUT HIS ROPES, DIDN'T YOU, ARNHEID?
YOU ALL BEAR A SHARE OF THE BLAME FOR THESE CRIMES.
I'LL TIE YOU UP UNTIL THE MASTER GETS...
GSHK

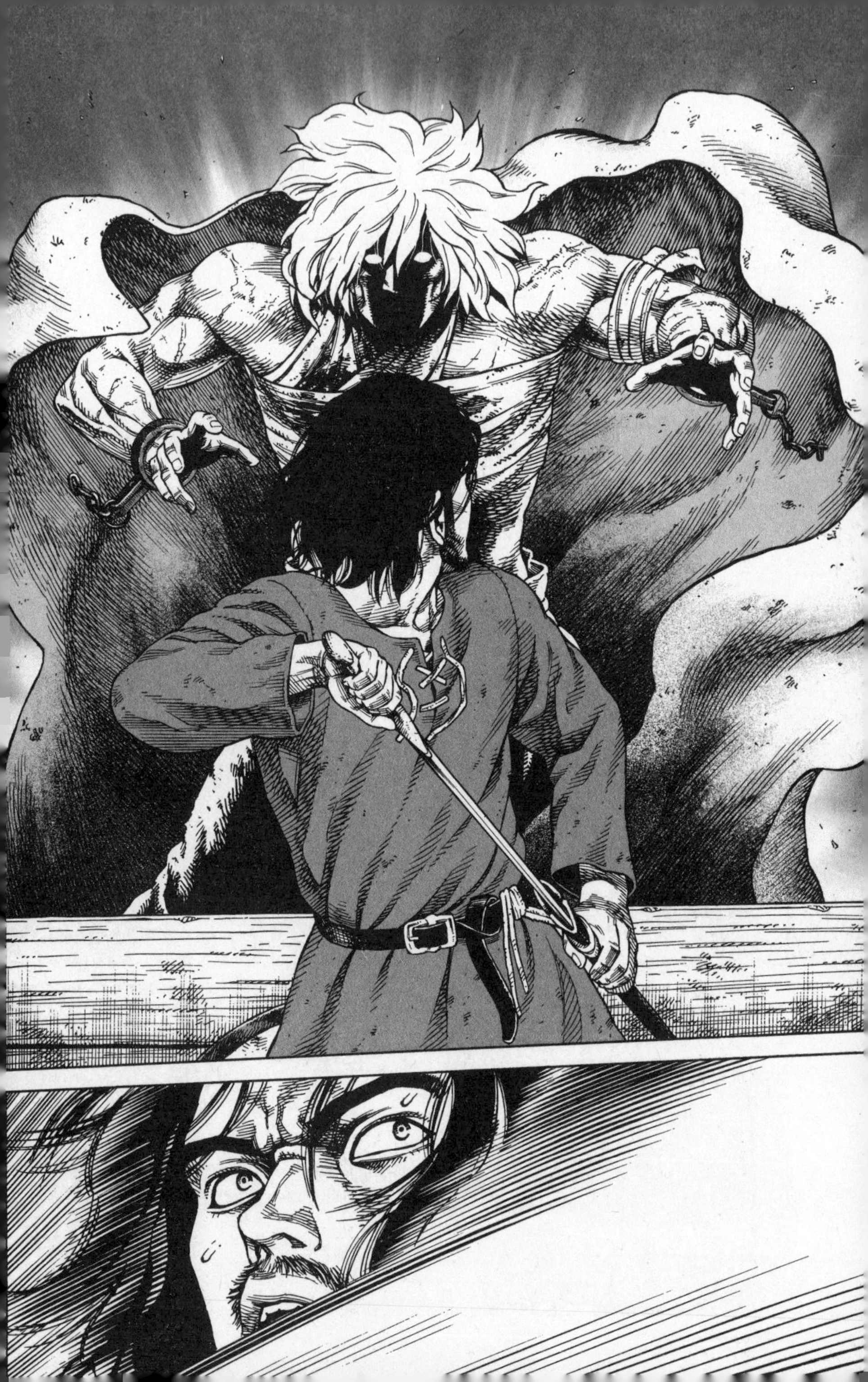

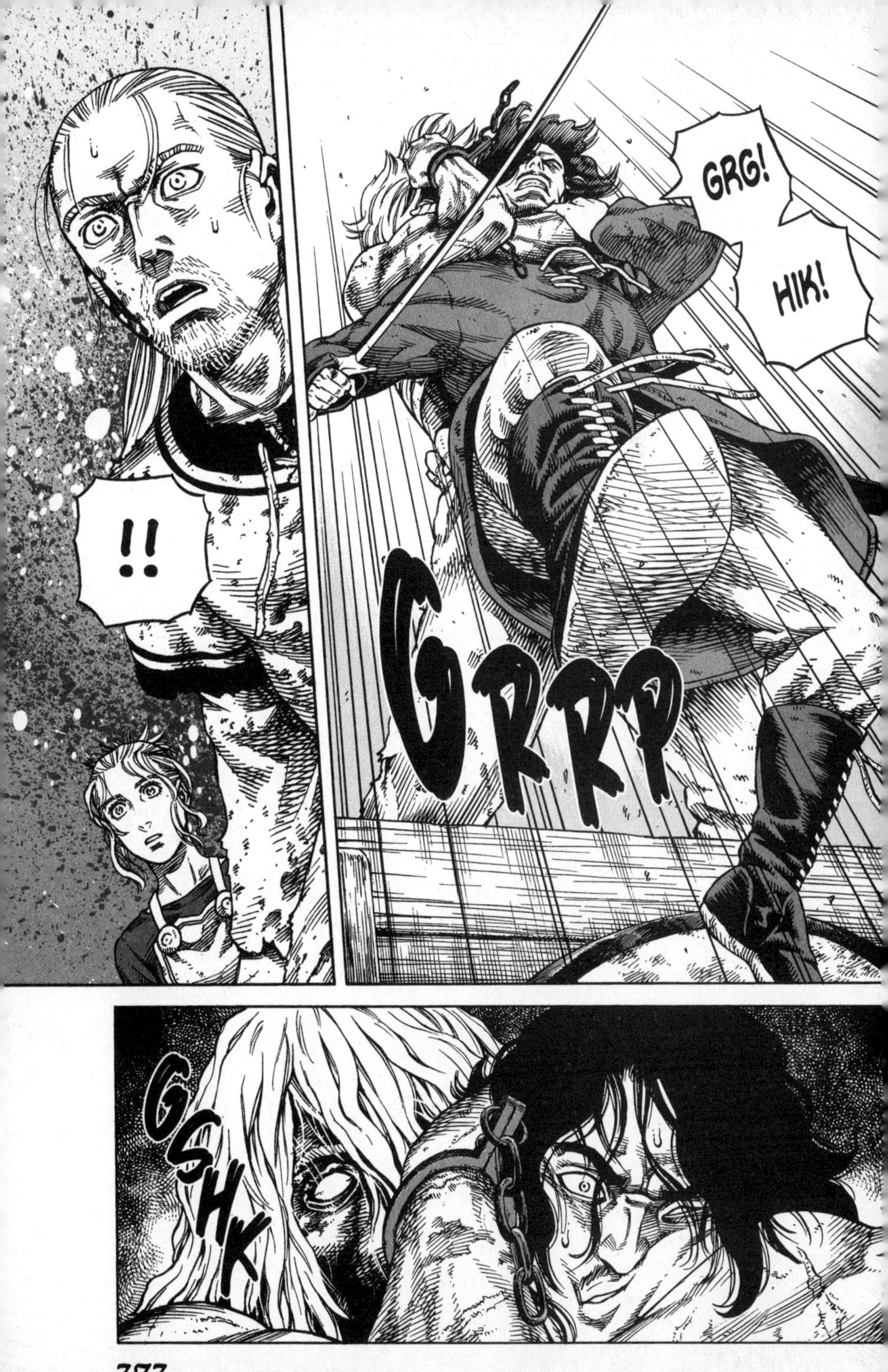
GRG!
HIK!
GRRP
!!
GSHK

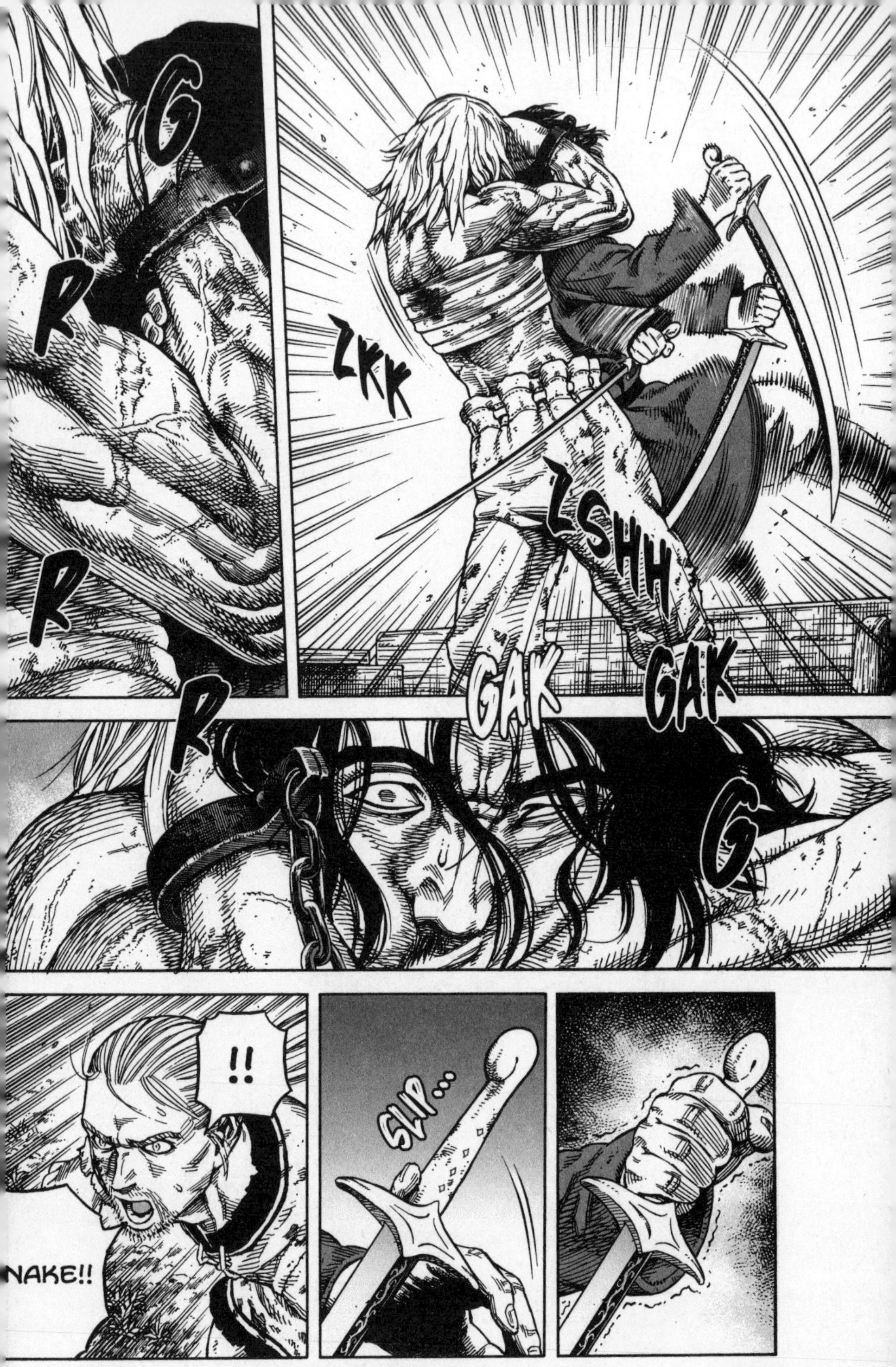
ZKK
ZSHH
GAK
GAK
G
R
R
R
G
SLIP...
!!
NAKE!!

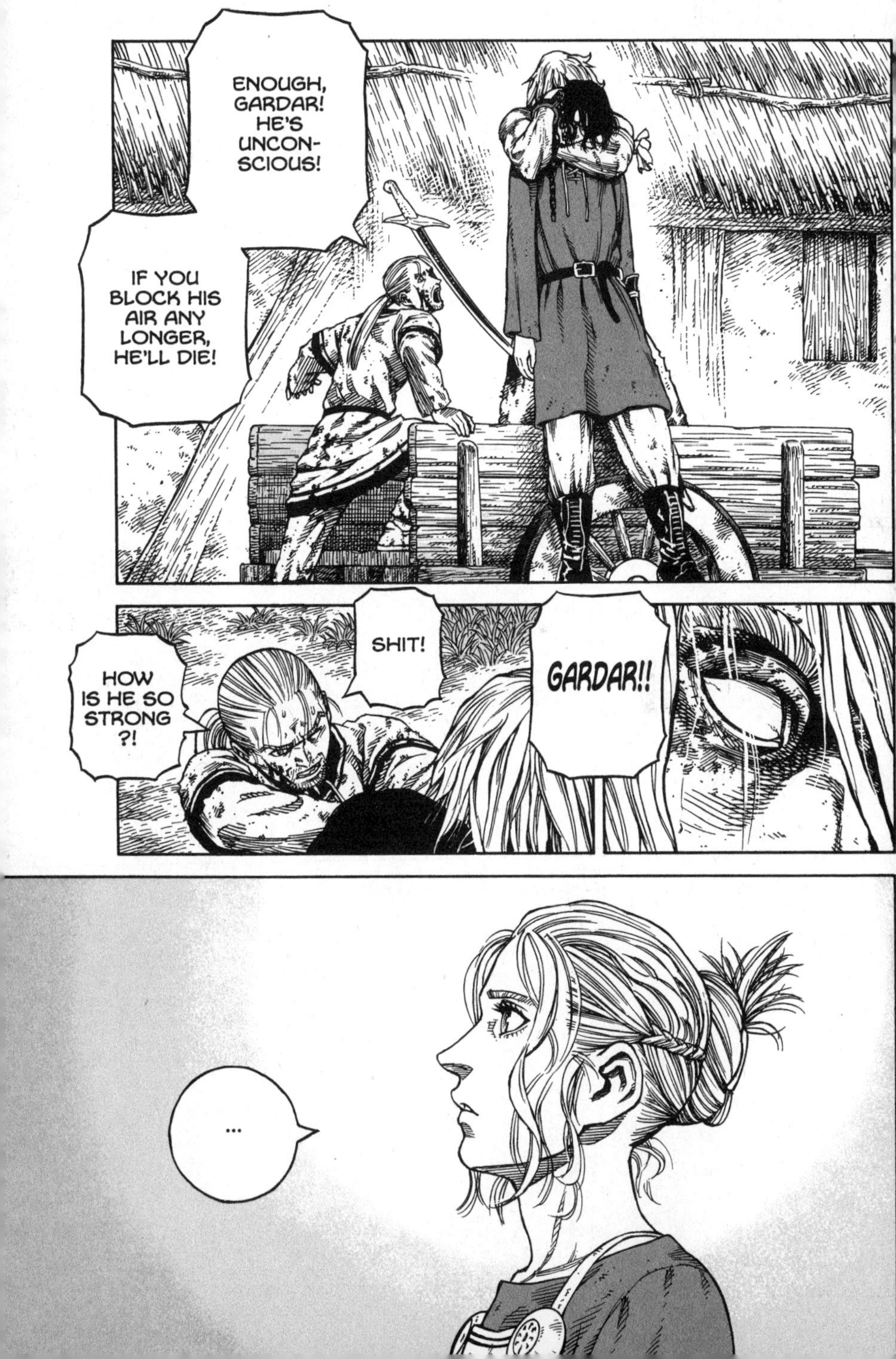
ENOUGH, GARDAR! HE'S UNCONSCIOUS!
IF YOU BLOCK HIS AIR ANY LONGER, HE'LL DIE!
GARDAR!!
SHIT!
HOW IS HE SO STRONG?!
...

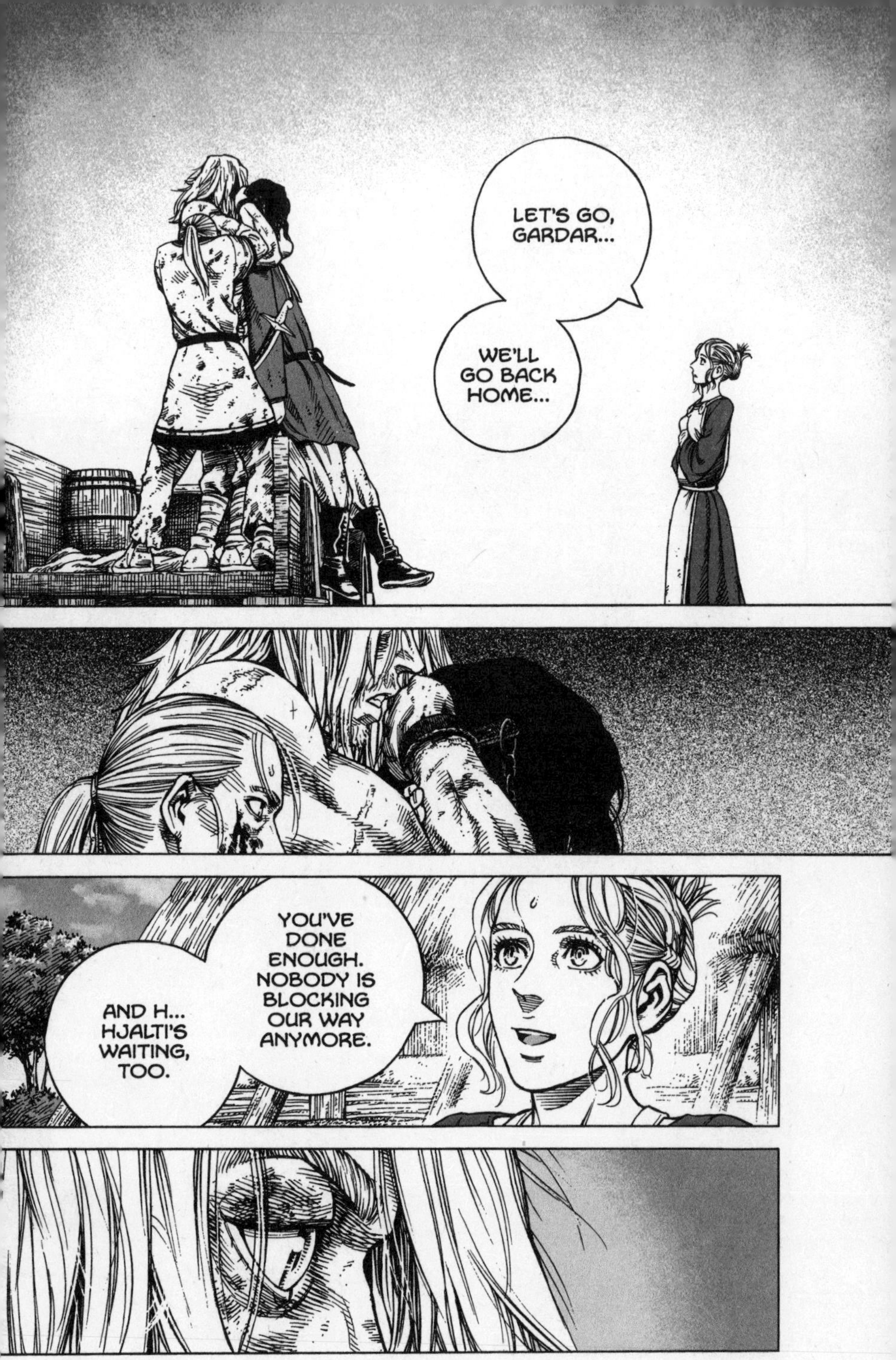
LET'S GO, GARDAR...
WE'LL GO BACK HOME...
YOU'VE DONE ENOUGH. NOBODY IS BLOCKING OUR WAY ANYMORE.
AND H... HJALTI'S WAITING, TOO.

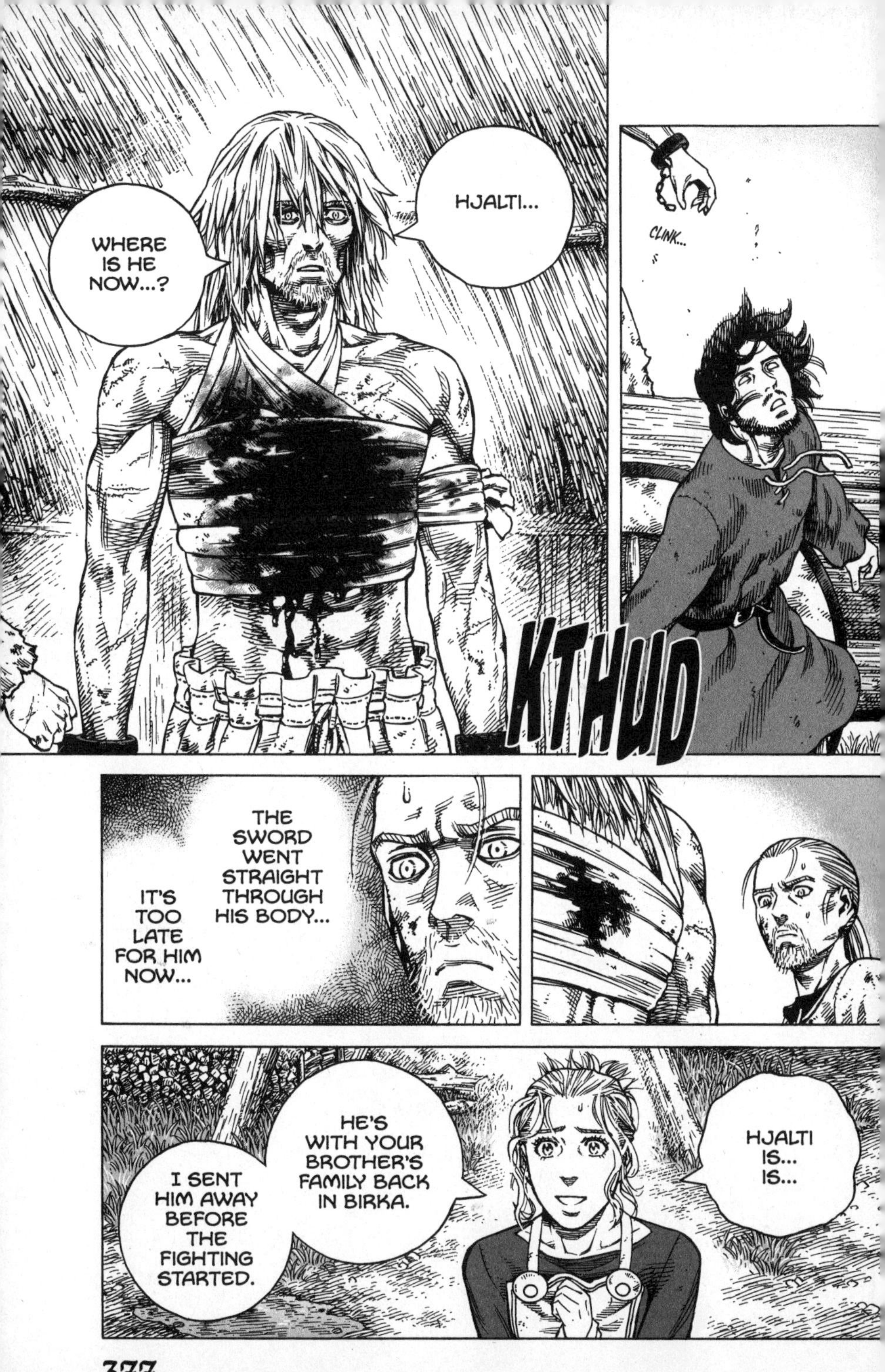
CLINK...
KTHUD
HJALTI...
WHERE IS HE NOW...?
THE SWORD WENT STRAIGHT THROUGH HIS BODY...
IT'S TOO LATE FOR HIM NOW...
HJALTI IS... IS...
HE'S WITH YOUR BROTHER'S FAMILY BACK IN BIRKA.
I SENT HIM AWAY BEFORE THE FIGHTING STARTED.

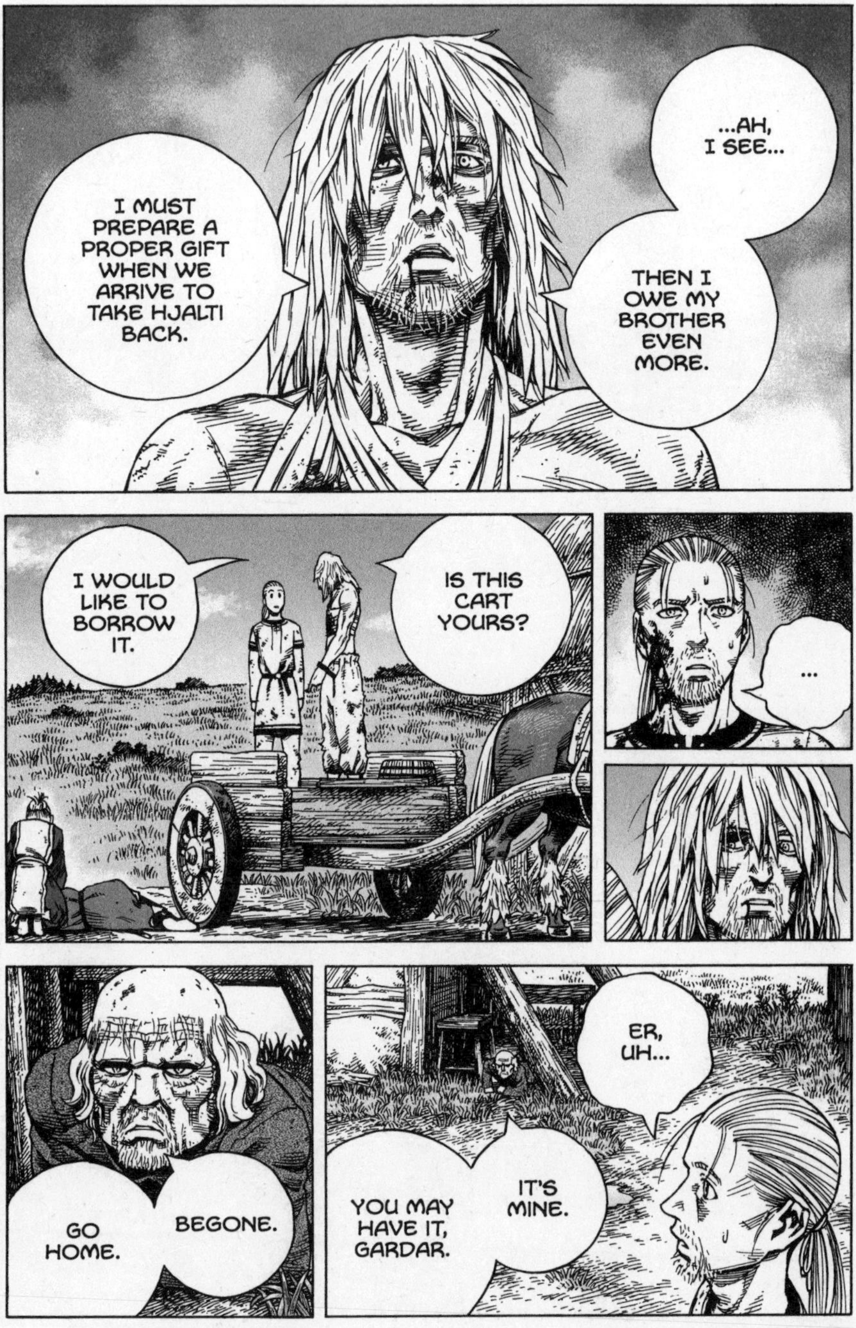
...AH, I SEE...
THEN I OWE MY BROTHER EVEN MORE.
I MUST PREPARE A PROPER GIFT WHEN WE ARRIVE TO TAKE HJALTI BACK.
...
IS THIS CART YOURS?
I WOULD LIKE TO BORROW IT.
ER, UH...
IT'S MINE.
YOU MAY HAVE IT, GARDAR.
BEGONE.
GO HOME.

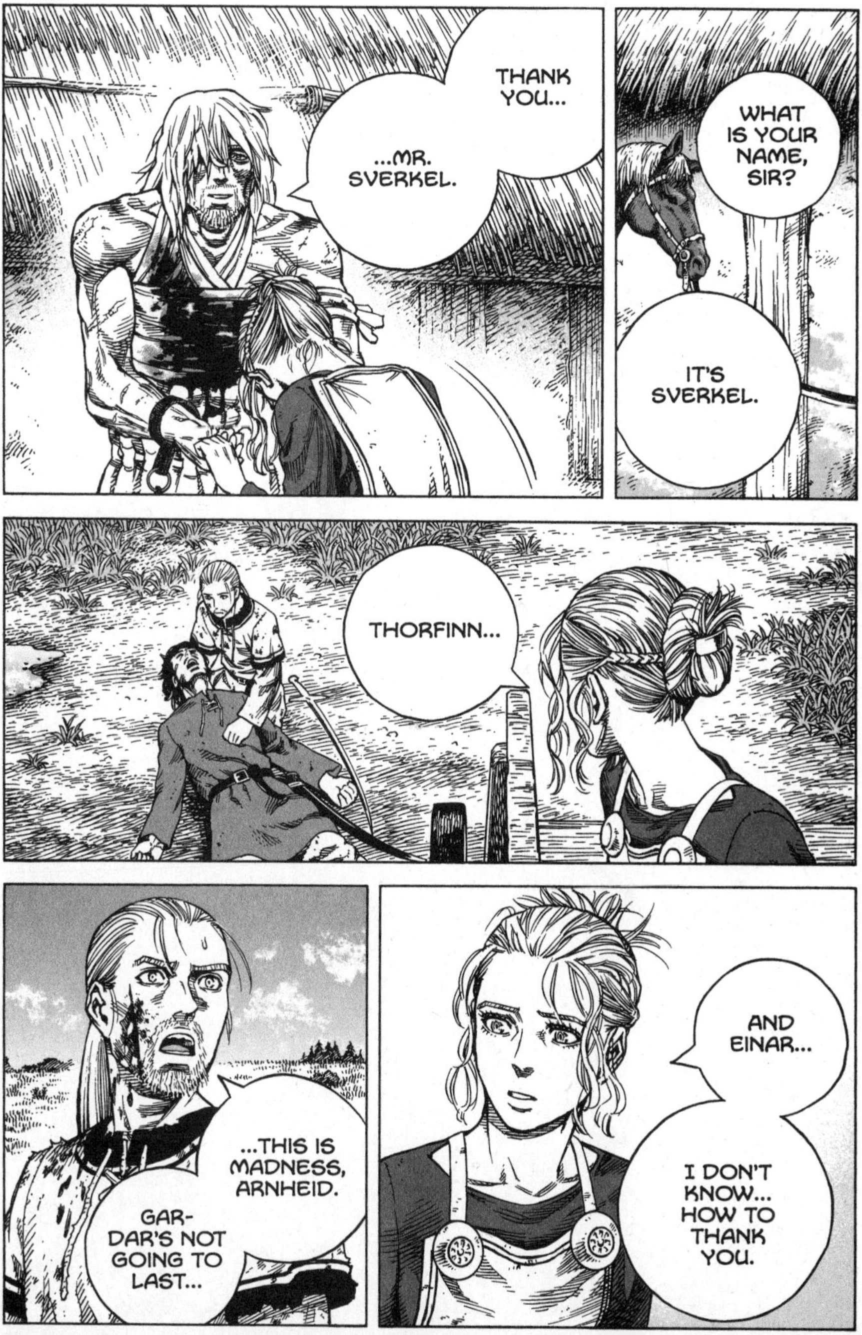
WHAT IS YOUR NAME, SIR?
IT'S SVERKEL.
THANK YOU...
...MR. SVERKEL.
THORFINN...
AND EINAR...
I DON'T KNOW... HOW TO THANK YOU.
...THIS IS MADNESS, ARNHEID.
GAR-DAR'S NOT GOING TO LAST...

IT'S FINE.

JUST LET US GO...

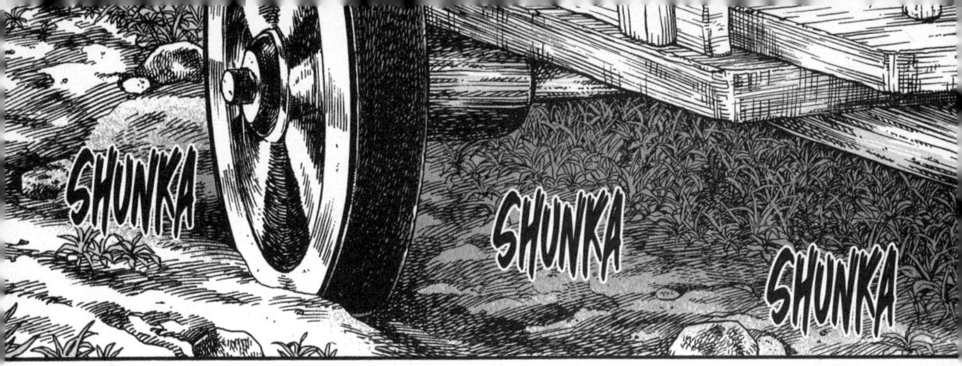
SHUNKA
SHUNKA
SHUNKA

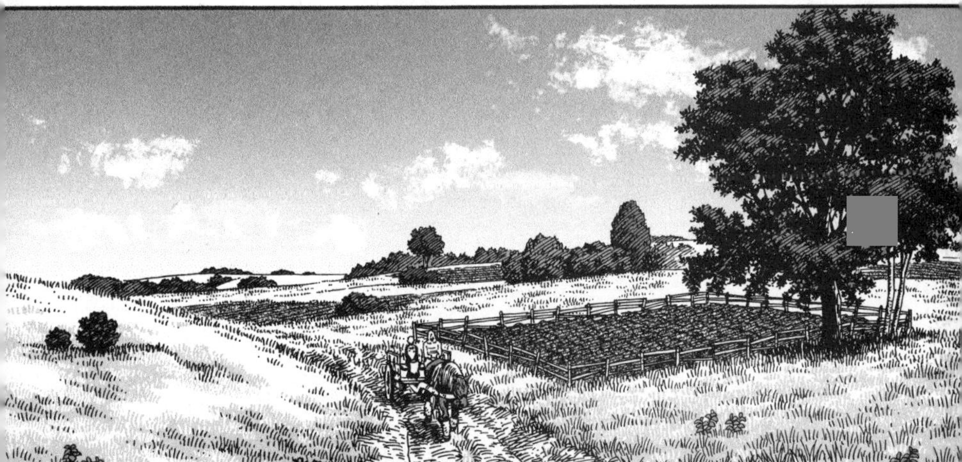

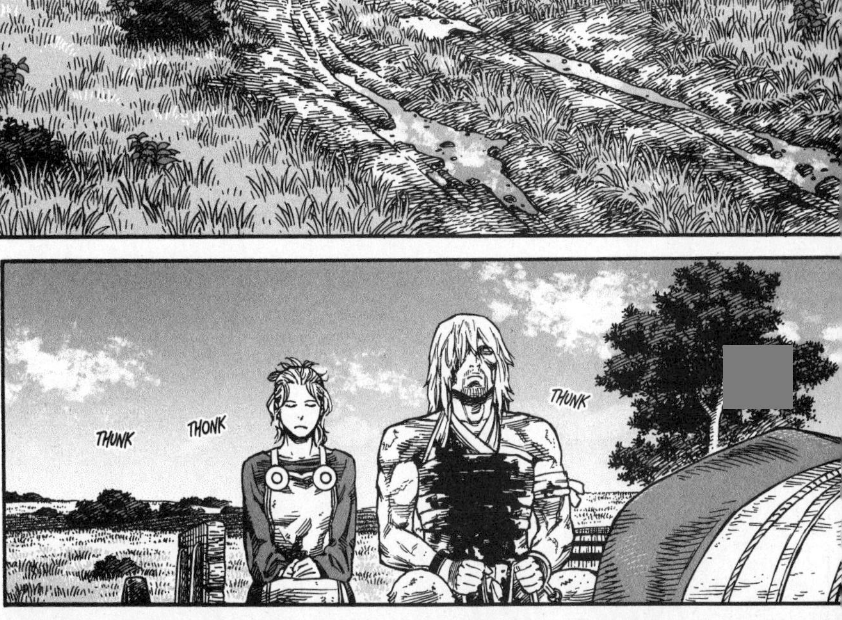
THUNK
THONK
THUNK

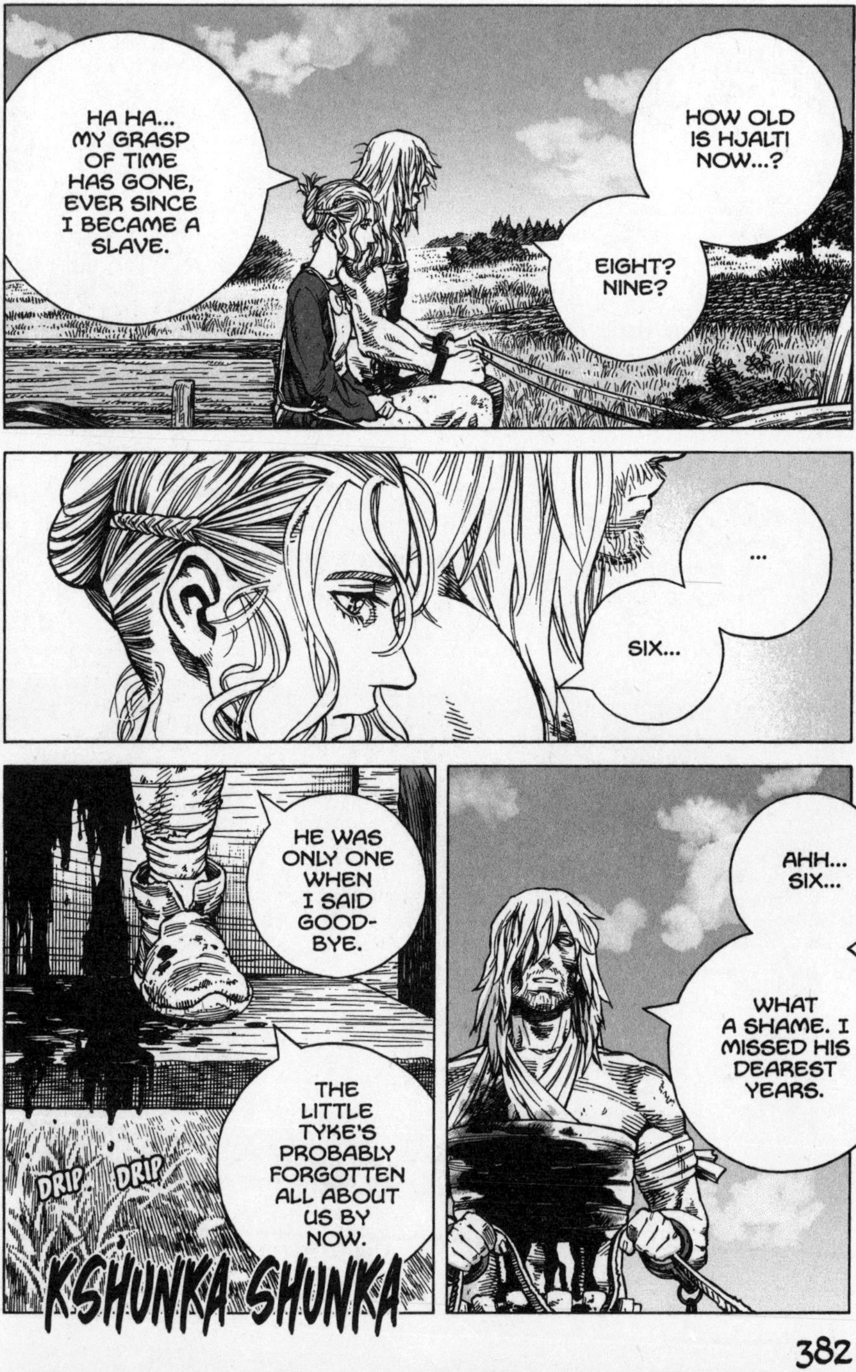
HOW OLD IS HJALTI NOW...?
EIGHT? NINE?
HA HA... MY GRASP OF TIME HAS GONE, EVER SINCE I BECAME A SLAVE.
...
SIX...
AHH... SIX...
WHAT A SHAME. I MISSED HIS DEAREST YEARS.
HE WAS ONLY ONE WHEN I SAID GOOD-BYE.
THE LITTLE TYKE'S PROBABLY FORGOTTEN ALL ABOUT US BY NOW.
DRIP DRIP
KSHUNKA SHUNKA

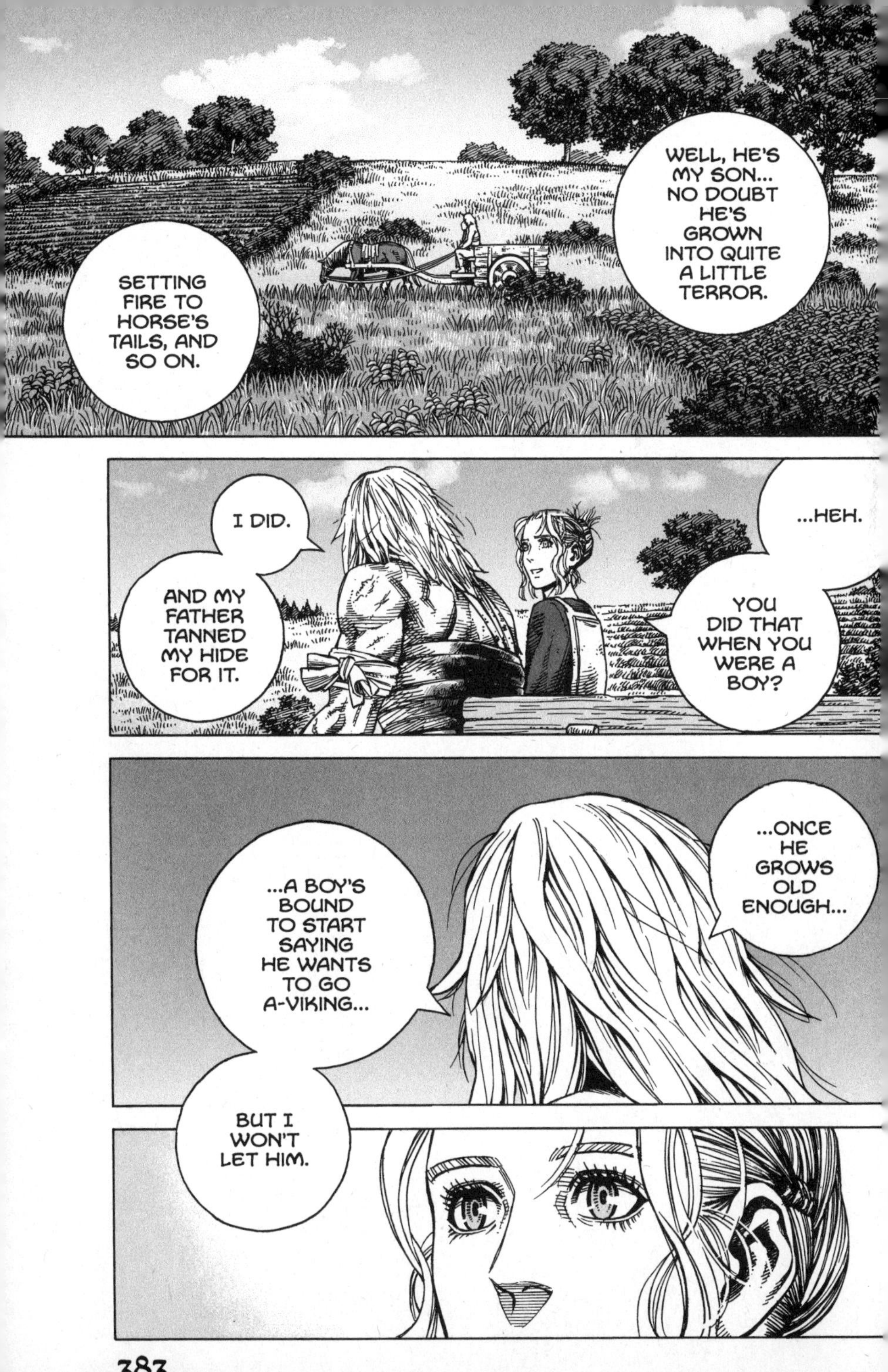
WELL, HE'S MY SON... NO DOUBT HE'S GROWN INTO QUITE A LITTLE TERROR.
SETTING FIRE TO HORSE'S TAILS, AND SO ON.
...HEH.
YOU DID THAT WHEN YOU WERE A BOY?
I DID.
AND MY FATHER TANNED MY HIDE FOR IT.
...ONCE HE GROWS OLD ENOUGH...
...A BOY'S BOUND TO START SAYING HE WANTS TO GO A-VIKING...
BUT I WON'T LET HIM.

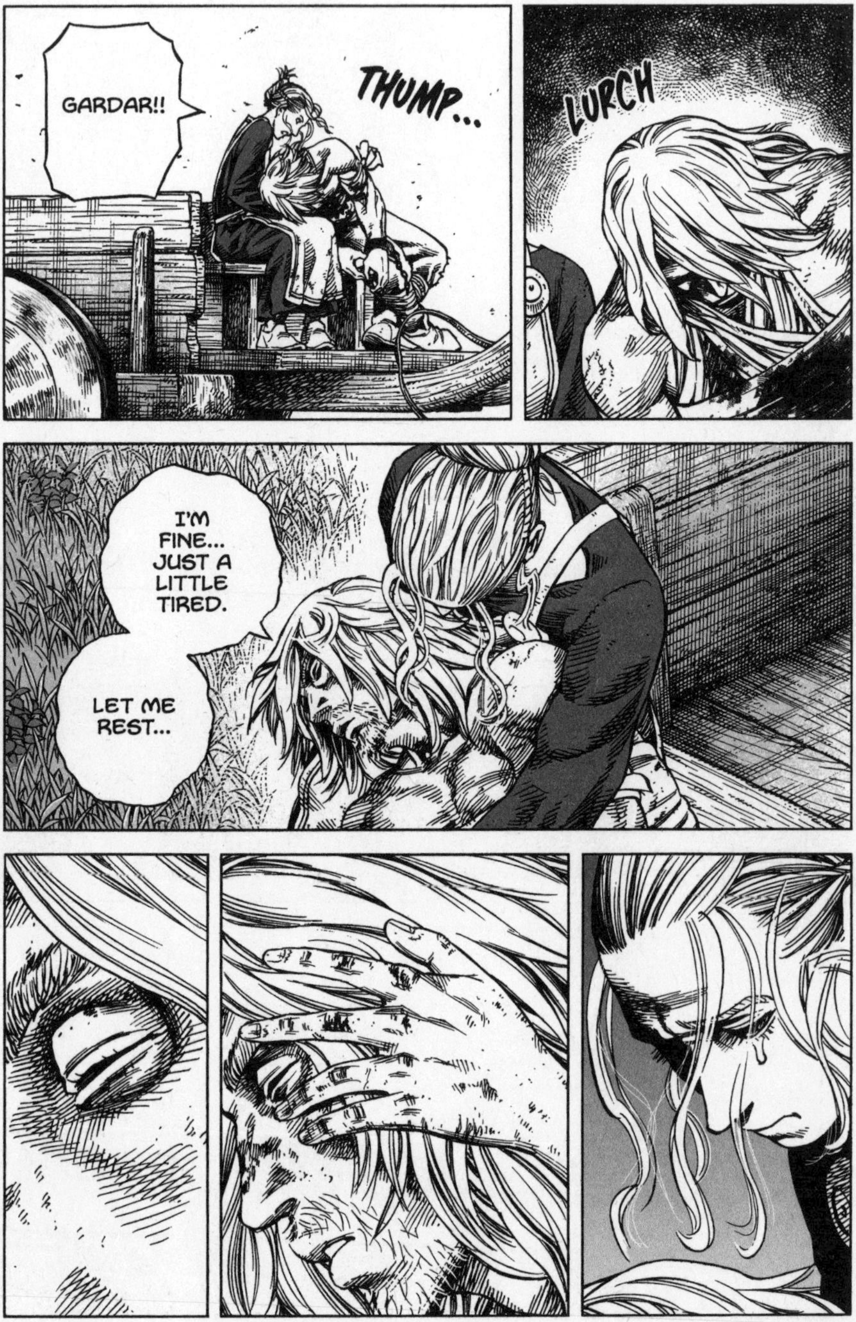
LURCH
THUMP...
GARDAR!!
I'M FINE... JUST A LITTLE TIRED.
LET ME REST...

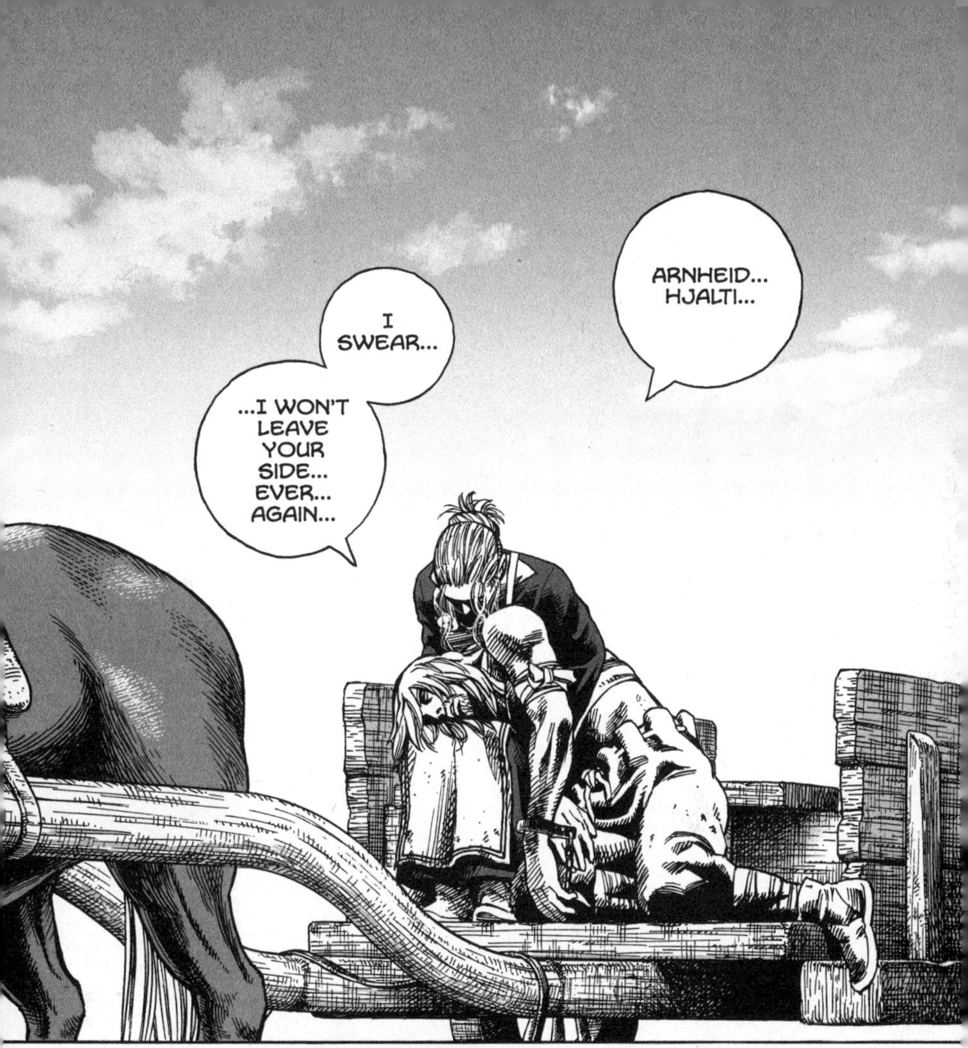
ARNHEID... HJALTI...
I SWEAR...
...I WON'T LEAVE YOUR SIDE... EVER... AGAIN...

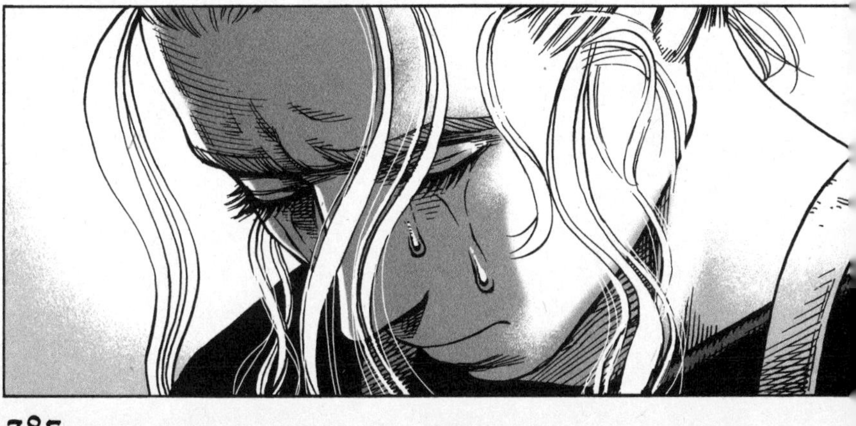

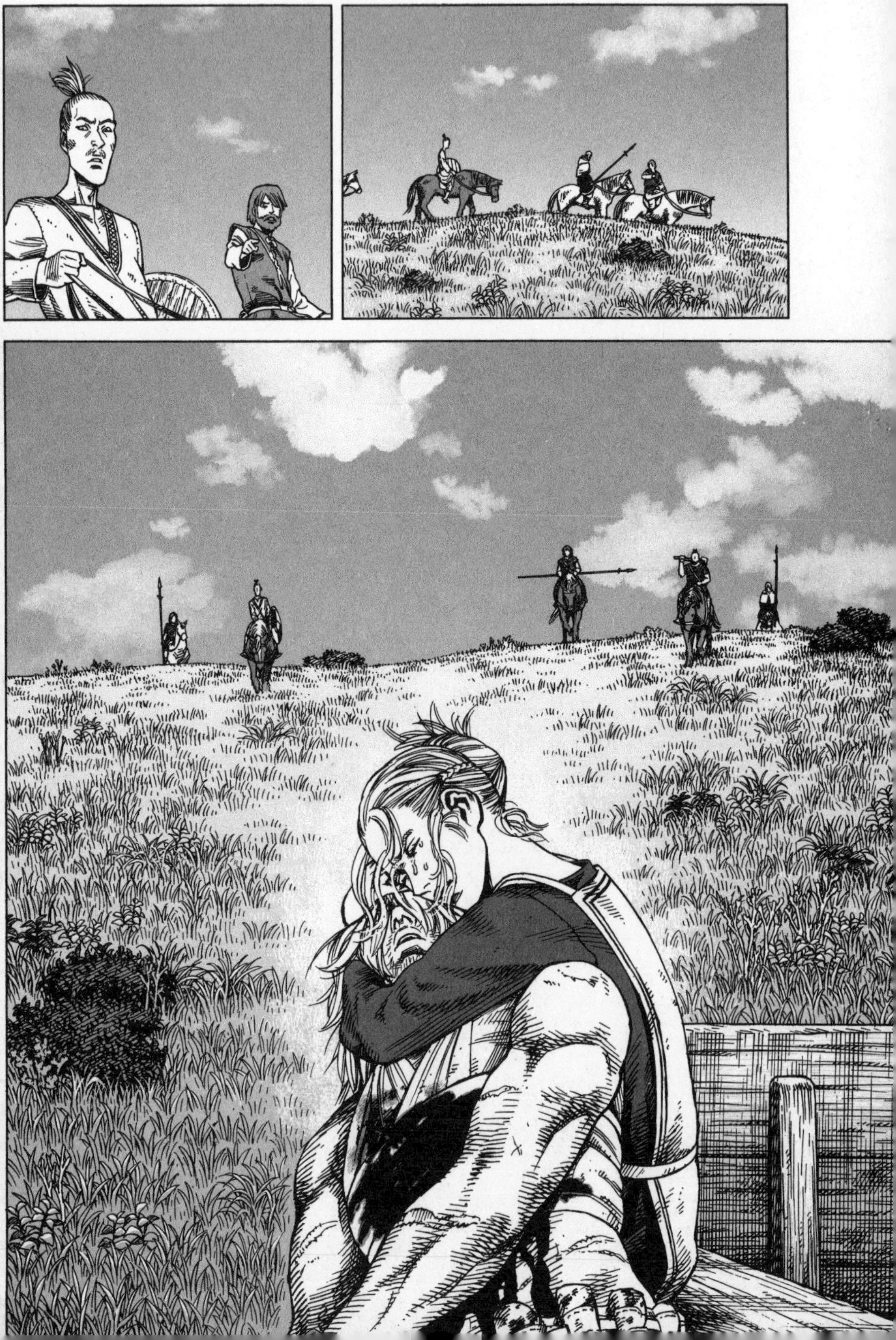

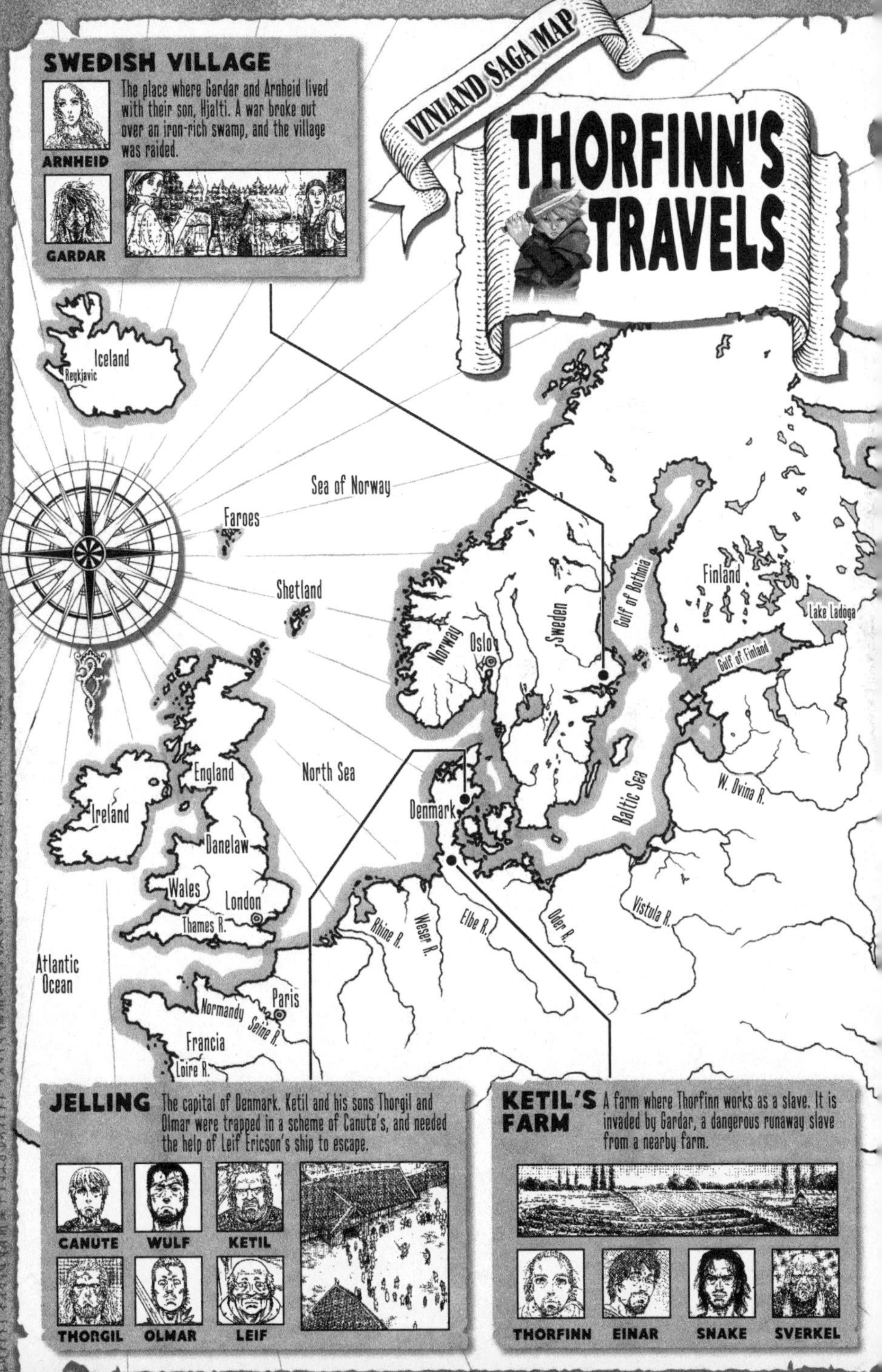

VINLAND SAGA MAP
THORFINN'S TRAVELS
SWEDISH VILLAGE
The place where Gardar and Arnheid lived with their son, Hjalti. A war broke out over an iron-rich swamp, and the village was raided.
ARNHEID
GARDAR
Iceland
Reykjavic
Sea of Norway
Faroes
Shetland
Finland
Lake Ladoga
Gulf of Bothnia
Sweden
Norway
Oslo
Gulf of Finland
England
North Sea
Ireland
Denmark
Baltic Sea
W. Dvina R.
Danelaw
Wales
London
Thames R.
Rhine R.
Weser R.
Elbe R.
Oder R.
Vistula R.
Atlantic Ocean
Paris
Normandy
Seine R.
Francia
Loire R.
JELLING
The capital of Denmark. Ketil and his sons Thorgil and Olmar were trapped in a scheme of Canute's, and needed the help of Leif Ericson's ship to escape.
CANUTE
WULF
KETIL
THORGIL
OLMAR
LEIF
KETIL'S FARM
A farm where Thorfinn works as a slave. It is invaded by Gardar, a dangerous runaway slave from a nearby farm.
THORFINN
EINAR
SNAKE
SVERKEL

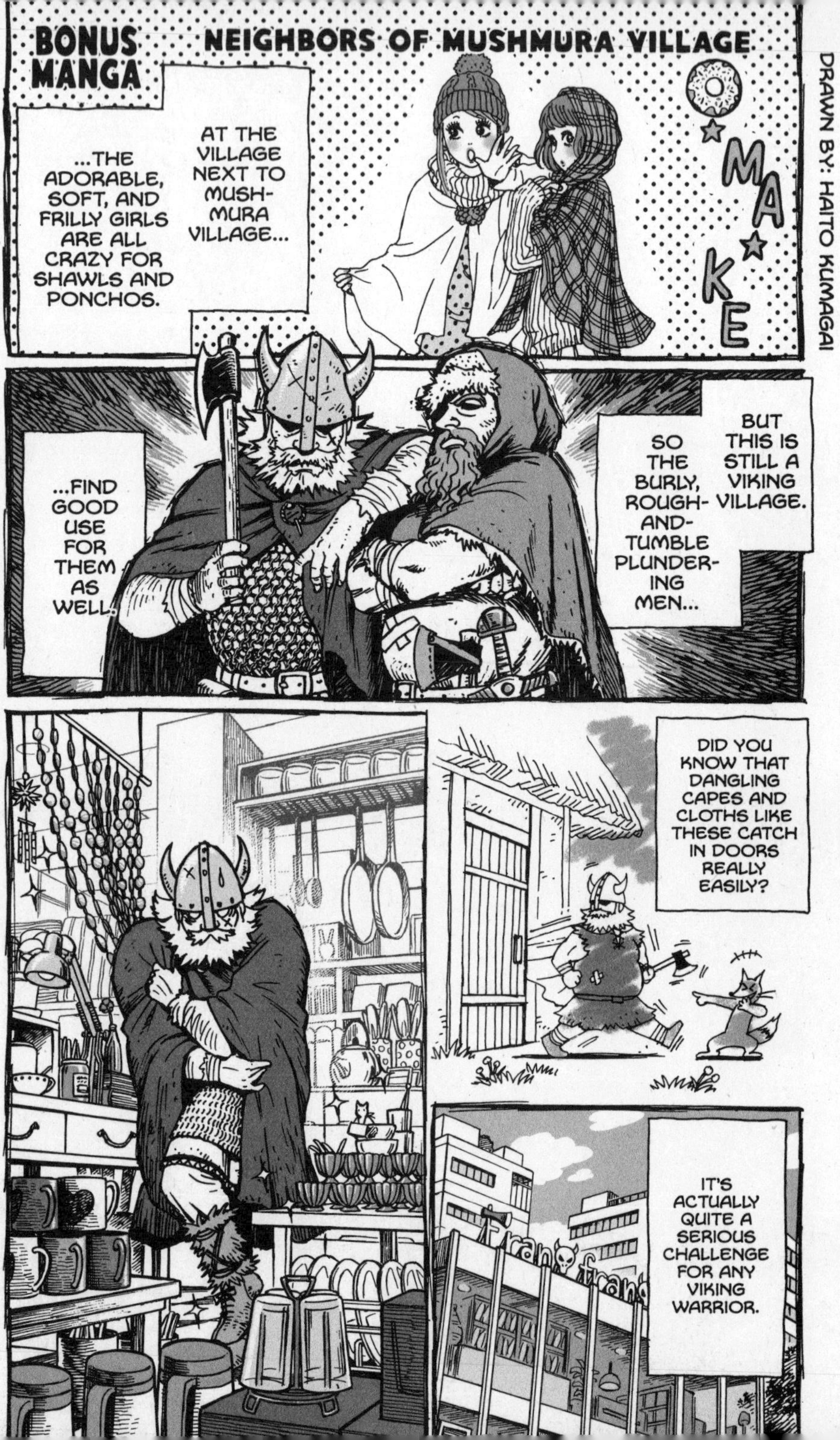
BONUS MANGA
NEIGHBORS OF MUSHMURA VILLAGE
DRAWN BY: HAITO KUMAGAI
OMAKE
AT THE VILLAGE NEXT TO MUSH-MURA VILLAGE...
...THE ADORABLE, SOFT, AND FRILLY GIRLS ARE ALL CRAZY FOR SHAWLS AND PONCHOS.
BUT THIS IS STILL A VIKING VILLAGE.
SO THE BURLY, ROUGH-AND-TUMBLE PLUNDER-ING MEN...
...FIND GOOD USE FOR THEM AS WELL.
DID YOU KNOW THAT DANGLING CAPES AND CLOTHS LIKE THESE CATCH IN DOORS REALLY EASILY?
IT'S ACTUALLY QUITE A SERIOUS CHALLENGE FOR ANY VIKING WARRIOR.

HAITO KUMAGAI ACCORDING TO MAKOTO YUKIMURA

IF, LIKE ME, YOU'VE GOT SOME LEFTOVER PAGES TO FILL AT THE END OF YOUR VOLUME, THIS TALENTED ASSISTANT IS YOUR MAN! KUMAGAI WHIPPED THIS UP FOR ME IN NO TIME AT ALL. HE REALLY DOES WORK FAST. WHAT WOULD I DO WITHOUT HIM?

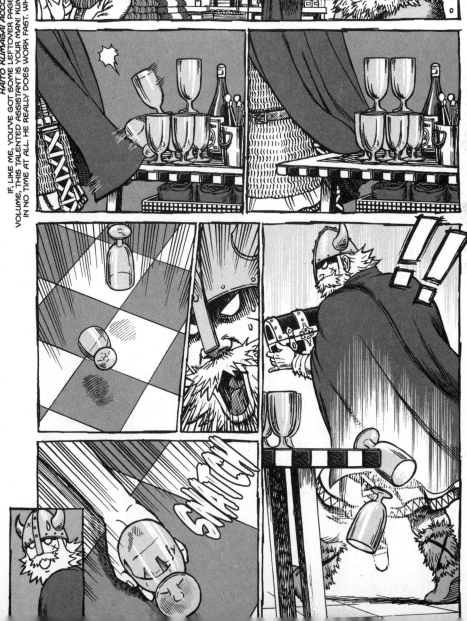

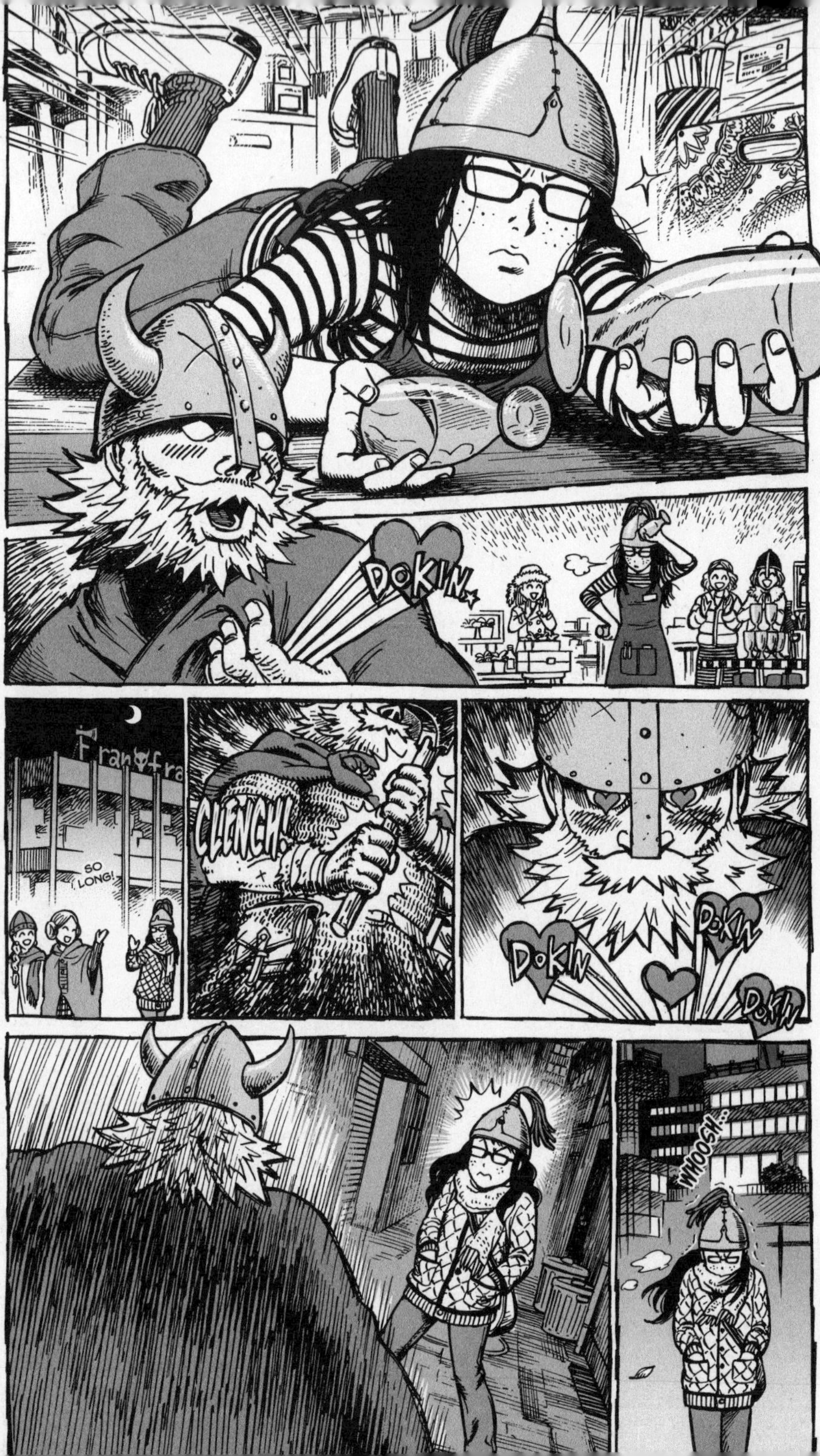
DOKIN
DOKIN
DOKIN
DOKIN
CLENCH!
SO LONG!
WHOOSH...

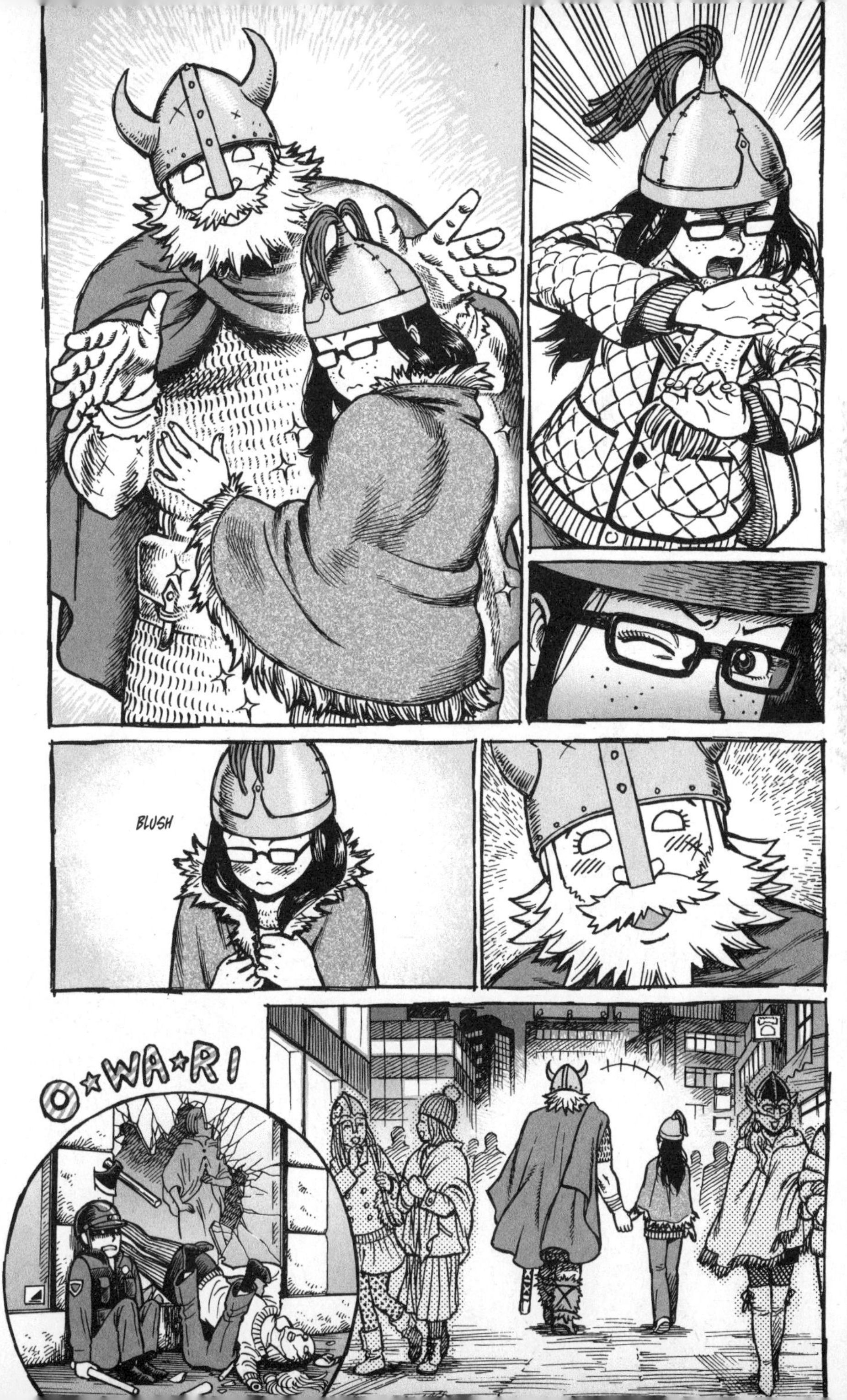
BLUSH
O☆WA☆RI

SUPPLEMENTAL DESIGNS

SNAKE'S SWORD

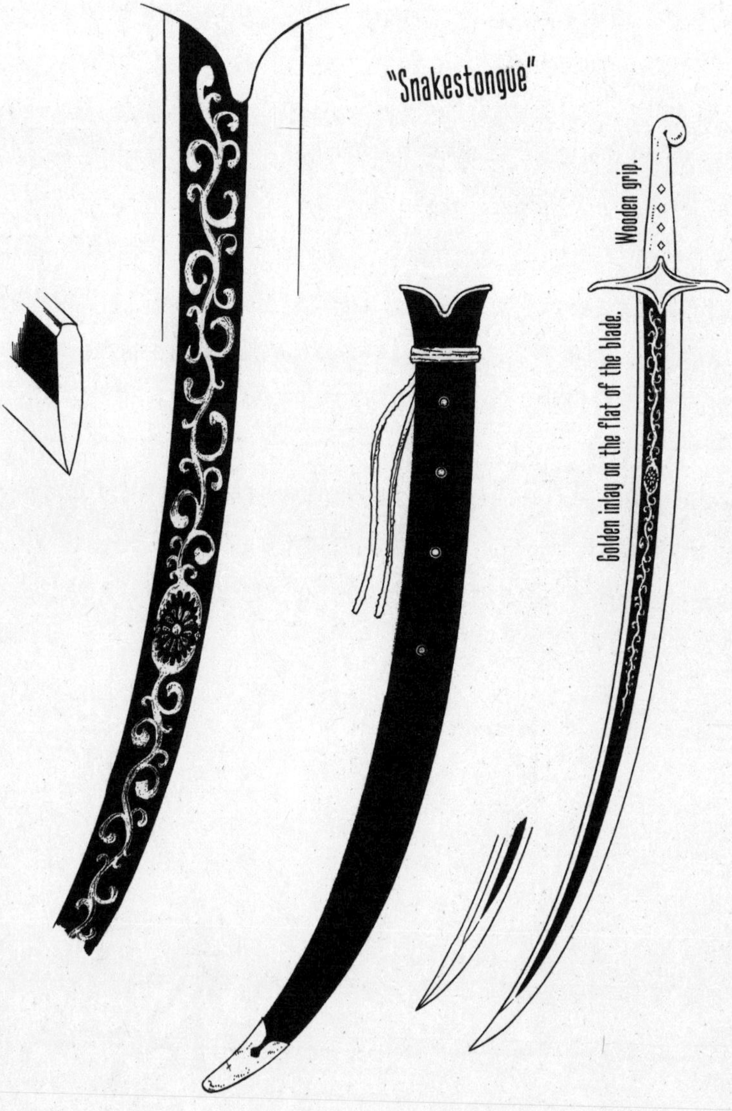
"Snakestongue"
Wooden grip.
Golden inlay on the flat of the blade.

In any text I consult, it always says that the Vikings loved freedom and hated control and restrictions. To them, freedom was something won and maintained by strength. There was no means to rule a Viking other than crushing him with military or economic force. "King" was just the title of the one who wielded the most power. On the flip side, this meant that those who were ruled over and lost their freedom suffered because they were too weak. In a society where power is everything, it is a matter of fact that the weakest will be slaves. It was a shared cultural understanding that those who were too weak to protect their own freedom were at fault for their plight. There was no guilt or doubt about the strong enslaving, subordinating, selling, or killing the weak. That was just the culture they lived in. So how did the kindhearted live in such a culture? There must have been some who hated the meritocracy and the punishment of the weak. It must have been very painful to have such a large gap between the customs of society and one's own sensibilities. Did they have to keep their ideas secret, and restrict themselves to silently lamenting the plight of mistreated slaves without taking action? Such a person adrift in the culture of the time must have been nameless and penniless. In fact, perhaps the only people who felt that way would've been slaves themselves. Only the strong leave their names in history; the stories of such ordinary minorities are not saved over the centuries. That's one of the more bothersome aspects of history. I just want to know.

MAKOTO YUKIMURA

Translation Notes

Thegn, page 102

A personal servant of a lord or king, in this case referring to official soldiers as opposed to militia men. The definition varies depending on the time and place; for example, the Scottish thanes as seen in Shakespeare's Macbeth were royal officials much like counts.

IF YOU'RE HERE TO WELCOME ME TO JELLING, THORGIL...
...DOES THAT MEAN KING CANUTE IS HERE AS WELL?
YEP.
I AM HIS LOYAL THEGN, BELIEVE IT OR NOT.

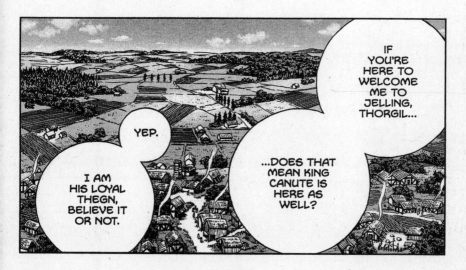

ASK YUKIMURA

his exclusive Q&A with series creator Makoto Yukimura appears only ı the U.S. edition of "Vinland Saga." Future volumes will include them, o, so if you have a question you'd like to ask Mr. Yukimura, please send to kodanshacomics@randomhouse.com, or to:

Kodansha Comics
451 Park Ave. South, 7th floor
New York, NY 10016

***odansha Comics:** Your impressive attention to detail in backgrounds always something Vinland Saga fans point out to us. How much time ɔ you typically spend on ɪckgrounds? What do ɔu think makes them so ɲportant to manga?*

lakoto Yukimura: The ɪckgrounds are a job done ʏ myself and my three staff ɪembers together. In other ords, they take four times ɪe work of the character awings, which I do myself. ne chapter of about 30 ɪges requires two weeks of orking 12 hours a day.

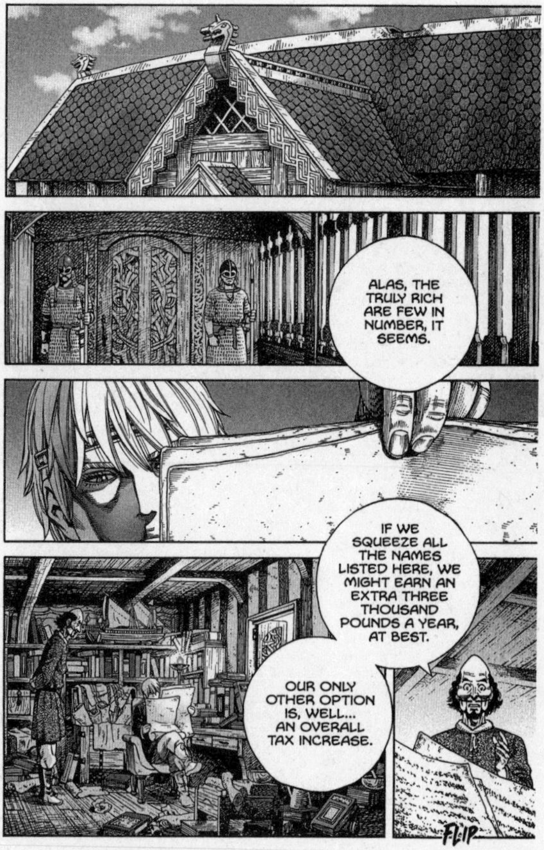
ALAS, THE TRULY RICH ARE FEW IN NUMBER, IT SEEMS.
IF WE SQUEEZE ALL THE NAMES LISTED HERE, WE MIGHT EARN AN EXTRA THREE THOUSAND POUNDS A YEAR, AT BEST.
OUR ONLY OTHER OPTION IS, WELL... AN OVERALL TAX INCREASE.
FLIP

ɔelieve background awings are quite essential. ne background is the orld. I don't think you ɪn tell a story with just the ɪaracters, divorced from ɪe world, and I don't think you should. But also, I simply find it a fun task to imagine and draw what food the characters eat, what kind of houses they sleep in, what kind of environment they live in.

Even saying that, of course, we are all human, so there are mistakes scattered here and there in the background images. I can't brag too much. In the future, it's all up to the extent of my diligence, too.

Kodansha Comics: *You said previously that one of the reasons you decided to draw Vinland Saga was because you wanted to address the theme of violence. Was there an event in your life or in the world that made you want to write about this theme?*

Makoto Yukimura: It's not that there was any specific experience or event that made me want to write about the theme of violence.

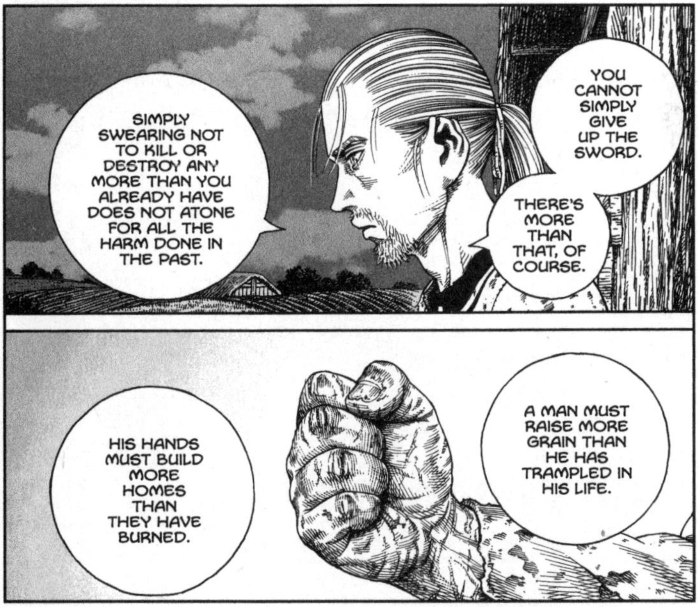
YOU CANNOT SIMPLY GIVE UP THE SWORD.
THERE'S MORE THAN THAT, OF COURSE.
SIMPLY SWEARING NOT TO KILL OR DESTROY ANY MORE THAN YOU ALREADY HAVE DOES NOT ATONE FOR ALL THE HARM DONE IN THE PAST.
A MAN MUST RAISE MORE GRAIN THAN HE HAS TRAMPLED IN HIS LIFE.
HIS HANDS MUST BUILD MORE HOMES THAN THEY HAVE BURNED.

It's just that, in the hero manga of my beloved Japan, no matter what the story is, most of the protagonists are the strongest in that they are the best at doing violence. Meanwhile, the characters who aren't skilled with violence are portrayed as weak. So the story unfolds with the hero repeatedly beating up the bad guys, one after another. Usually, no matter what happens, it's difficult for the hero to escape this destiny.

But what would happen to a hero manga if the protagonist really wished e could escape from this fate of violence? Could you still tell that story without it losing its entertainment value? I decided that I wanted to try hat out.

That's one of the many reasons I chose violence as a theme.

SO WHAT NOW, THOR-FINN?
WILL YOU HOLD TRUE TO YOUR OATH OF PEACE?
OR DO YOU SURRENDER TO THE WAY OF BATTLE, TO SAVE THIS MAN?

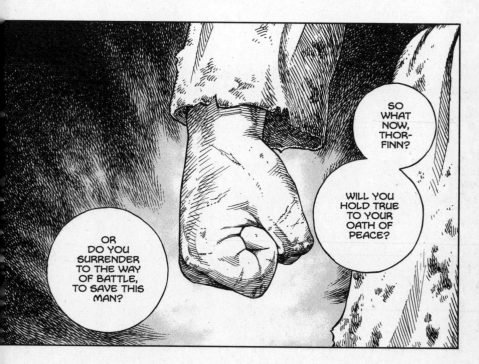

SEE YOU IN BOOK SEVEN, COMING DECEMBER 2015!

A Kodansha Comics Trade Paperback Original.

Vinland Saga volume 6 copyright © 2012 Makoto Yukimura
English translation copyright © 2015 Makoto Yukimura

Published in the United States by Kodansha Comics, an imprint of Kodansha USA Publishing, LLC, New York.

Publication rights for this English edition arranged through Kodansha Ltd., Tokyo.

First published in Japan in 2012 by Kodansha Ltd., Tokyo, as *Vinland Saga*, volumes 11 and 12.

ISBN 978-1-61262-803-5

Printed in the United States of America.

www.kodanshacomics.com

9 8 7 6 5 4 3 2 1

Translation: Stephen Paul
Lettering: Scott O. Brown
Editing: Ben Applegate
Kodansha Comics edition cover & endpaper design: Phil Balsman

Special thanks to Roderick Dale of the Centre for the Study of the Viking Age at the University of Nottingham for his assistance with the production of this book.